HONEST ANSWERS

About the Murder of President John F. Kennedy

A NEW LOOK at the JFK ASSASSINATION

Vince Palamara
Author of *Survivor's Guilt*

Honest Answers About The Murder Of President John F. Kennedy: A New Look at the JFK Assassination
Copyright © 2021 Vince Palamara. All Rights Reserved.

Published by:
Trine Day LLC
PO Box 577
Walterville, OR 97489
1-800-556-2012
www.TrineDay.com
trineday@icloud.com

Library of Congress Control Number: 2021902516

Palamara, Vince
Honest Answers About The Murder Of President John F. Kennedy—1st ed.
p. cm.

Epub (ISBN-13) 978-1-63424-335-3
Mobi (ISBN-13) 978-1-63424-336-0
Print (ISBN-13) 978-1-63424-334-6
1.Kennedy, John F. -- (John Fitzgerald), -- 1917-1963 -- Assassination. 2. United States. -- Warren Commission. -- Report of the President's Commission on the Assassination of President John F. Kennedy. 3. Oswald, Lee Harvey. 4. Conspiracies -- United States. 5. Kennedy, John F. -- (John Fitzgerald), -- 1917-1963. I. Palamara, Vince II. Title

FIRST EDITION
10 9 8 7 6 5 4 3 2 1

Distribution to the Trade by:
Independent Publishers Group (IPG)
814 North Franklin Street
Chicago, Illinois 60610
312.337.0747
www.ipgbook.com

"Facts do not cease to exist because they are ignored. That men do not learn very much from the lessons of history is the most important of all the lessons that history has to teach."

– English writer and philosopher Aldous Huxley,
the author of *Brave New World* and *The Doors of Perception*,
who also died on 11/22/63

"Thirst was made for water. Inquiry for Truth. For what you see and hear depends a great deal on where you are standing."

– English writer C.S. Lewis,
the author of *The Chronicles of Narnia*,
who also died on 11/22/63

Dedicated to my lovely wife Amanda, my mother, my father, my brother, my family, in general, and to the eternal memory of President John F. Kennedy.

This book is perhaps especially dedicated to my cousin Maryanne Palamara, who innocently asked me, "Vin, c'mon, now – I want to know: who killed Kennedy?"

While she was certainly not the first to ask me this question through the years, she was the most recent … and the main inspiration for this book.

TABLE OF CONTENTS:

INTRODUCTION

Well, after four books on the Secret Service and the assassination of President John F. Kennedy, I thought perhaps that was it. I would always be interested, of course, and I would continue to give conference lectures and the numerous radio/Skype interviews I do all the time, but I honestly figured that I had "said it all," so to speak. I recently gave filmed interviews that spanned over two years for a documentary produced by Meredith Mantik, the daughter of the renowned Dr. David Mantik (the same author who appeared with me on both *The Men Who Killed Kennedy* and *A Coup in Camelot*). With all that said and done, I really didn't think I had another book in me.

Then something occurred to me.

I am always asked "so, who killed Kennedy?" Honestly, a part of me cringes when I am asked this, often from well-meaning non-researchers who are curious. I cringe because, even after all these years (we are talking decades now, spanning most of my adult life), I myself am not sure and do not have all the answers. I am reminded of that old researcher joke: "The renowned author dies and goes to Heaven. He asks God "who killed Kennedy" and God responds "Well, I have a theory about that.""

I am also reminded of comedian Bill Maher in his epic movie *Religulous*. Maher says "I preach the gospel of I-Don't-Know"; meaning, he isn't sure *if* there is a God or not and he is quite skeptical of those who are so sure about everything espoused in the Bible and so forth. One cannot help also be reminded of another statement (one I believe which started with author Anthony Summers): "the more you learn about the assassination of JFK, the less you know."

This is my dilemma.

First the good news: I believe there was indeed a conspiracy. I will outline the reasons for this. However, I must state at the outset that I waffled on this back in 2007. You see, I was a big fan of renowned author Vincent Bugliosi (of *Helter Skelter*/Charles Manson fame) and I was seduced (some would argue fooled) by his massive tome *Reclaiming History*. I was also ripe for the picking, too: I had recently been through a divorce (happily married several years later and ever since) and I was burned out on the case. I was basically semi-retired from research (never thinking my first book would ever be published) and I just threw up my hands and attempted to move on. For the record, even at that time, I still believed there were multiple conspiracies to kill Kennedy. I just believed at the time that Oswald beat them all to the punch. This feeling lasted a few short months in 2007 but it was immortalized in a blurb I did for Bugliosi's *Four Days In November* (2008) which, unfortunately, also appeared in essentially the same book with a different title called *Parkland* (2013).

To back up a bit: I was born in 1966, three years after the assassination, and my interest in President Kennedy and his untimely death sprang to life in 1978 when I was a 12-year-old boy fascinated by the House Select Committee on Assassinations (HSCA) and their reinvestigation of the JFK assassination. My parents, avid Kennedy fans, had a beautiful color portrait of President Kennedy that they gave to me. In addition, I was actively collecting stamps and coins then and, whenever I ran across any with images of Kennedy on them, my parents would be prompted to regale me with stories both about his presidency and their despair upon learning of his death.

At the same time, I became hooked on reruns of the television classic *The Wild, Wild West*, the fictional program about the 19th-century Secret Service. The two interests became intertwined for me. I remember checking out the book *Four Days* from my middle school library and focusing in on a photo of both Secret Service agents Clint Hill and Sam Kinney at Dallas' Love Field (Ironically, I would go on to interview both men many years later). I remember watching the Martin Sheen docudrama *Kennedy* and the documentary *Being With John F. Kennedy*, both in 1983, as well as *Years of Lightning, Day of Drums* in high school during that same time period. I also remember catching some of the Showtime program *On Trial: Lee Harvey Oswald* in late 1986 to early 1987. However, when my interest in the assassination really took off, during the 25th anniversary of JFK's murder in 1988, I focused even more like a laser beam on the agents that guarded President Kennedy. Every time a newsreel of Kennedy would be shown during the numerous programs that aired on television, my eyes would immediately become transfixed on the faces of the Secret Service agents surrounding the president.

The first major book on the assassination I purchased was John Davis' *Mafia Kingfish*. However, the one that really did it for me was Harry Livingstone and Robert Groden's classic 1989 book *High Treason*. The small chapter on the Secret Service really got me going and there was no turning back. Ironically, I would go on to work with, present at conferences, and know all three of these authors. Still, at that point in time and for a couple years afterward, my intense interest was relegated to secondary sources: just reading other author's works.

I vividly remember writing a letter intended for Robert Groden (the more famous of the two authors of *High Treason*) in early 1991 and receiving a "somewhat rankled" response from Livingstone that included this line of advice: "Unless you have something original to offer, don't bother. You'll just run yourself into the ground." Sage and cutting advice, I thought at the time and still do. Then I remembered what author Penn Jones said: "Research the hell out of one area of the case." I scrapped my manuscript at the time entitled For National Security and began to write about the Secret Service and the assassination almost exclusively.

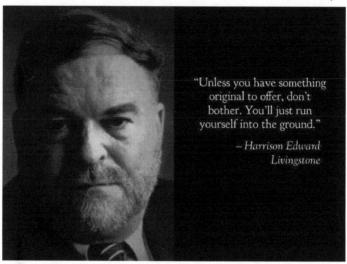

"Unless you have something original to offer, don't bother. You'll just run yourself into the ground."

– *Harrison Edward Livingstone*

It was also in 1991 (June, to be precise) that I ran into Livingstone and roughly 60 other authors and researchers at Professor Jerry Rose's first *Third Decade* research conference held in Fredonia, New York. Livingstone remembered me from my letter and we began an association that lasted through several more books he was to write and release (including filming an interview he did on 11/22/1991 at autopsy x-ray technician Jerrol Custer's home in Pittsburgh, Pennsylvania, as well as an interview he conducted with researcher Steve Barber in 1992 in Shelby, Ohio).

The June 1991 conference was where I gave my first presentation, preserved on video and You Tube. Although largely a skillful collection of secondary sources, it went over very well because the Secret Service was an area largely overlooked by the research community. The reception I received convinced me that I was onto something. This was further confirmed when Dr. Cyril Wecht (also from my hometown of Pittsburgh) phoned me and suggested that I do primary source research. In other words, I should contact former Secret Service agents.

In the largely pre-Internet age of the very early 1990's (excluding those primitive bulletin board functions largely unknown to me via Prodigy and Compuserve), one had to deal with "old-fashioned" avenues like directory assistance via the telephone and newspaper archives via microfiche in order to even attempt to find and interview these former agents (or anyone else, for that matter). Luckily for me, I was alone in the wilderness, so to speak: these former agents collecting their government pensions were, by and large, never contacted by any authors or researchers before (other than those interviewed by William Manchester for his Oswald-did-it book *The Death of a President*, Jim Bishop for his equally "official version" tome *The Day Kennedy Was Shot*, the Warren Commission, and the HSCA). My youth was a decided advantage, as well: I was only 25 when I started contacting these men old enough to be my grandfather. Since I didn't have a published book at the time and wouldn't for many years to come and was not a journalist, they felt comfortable talking to me.

As readers of my books *Survivor's Guilt, The Not-So-Secret Service* and *Who's Who in the Secret Service* well know, my many interviews and correspondence with the vast majority of the Kennedy detail (conducted largely between 1991 and 2007) yielded many answers and issues not addressed or adequately covered by official history. I learned that President Kennedy did not order the agents off his limousine; that he did not order the bubble top off his limousine; that JFK did not ask or order the motorcycles to get away from his car; that the Secret Service was the only boss the president of the United States truly had, not the other way around; and so forth. Luckily for myself and for history, I obtained these answers before a vast majority of these former agents shuffled off this mortal coil.

In addition, I also wrote a book about the medical evidence entitled *JFK: From Parkland to Bethesda*, focusing on all the medical witnesses from both Parkland Hospital in Dallas (where the mortally wounded president was given life-resuscitating measures) and Bethesda Naval Hospital in Maryland (where JFK was given an autopsy). Besides being a massive and detailed study of each and every witness and every statement they ever made on the medical evidence (in chronological order, to boot), I also ended up doing quite a bit of primary research, as well, interviewing and (mostly) corresponding with quite a few of the witnesses from both ends of the line and several points in between. In addition to the 11/22/91 videotaped interview of witness Jerrol Custer I was involved with for Harry Livingstone's book *High Treason 2*, I also was involved in the two-day videotaped interview of Custer conducted with author William Law in March 1998 for his book *In The Eye of History*. Finally, I personally videotaped an interview conducted on 11/22/1997 in Dallas with witness Aubrey Rike.

Still, after all this work and all these books, I am left with a lingering loose end:

"Who killed Kennedy?"

Here is my honest attempt at an answer. Be forewarned that I will not attempt to reinvent the wheel here and relitigate every conceivable aspect of the entire case: countless books and articles have preceded me on this key issue. I am only left with my learned opinion.

Vince Palamara
Pittsburgh, PA, February 2020

Special Author's Note:

The year is 2021, well over 57 years (and modestly into the 21rst century) since the assassination of President Kennedy. After a mountain of books, articles and Internet materials on the subject, I do not feel compelled in any way, shape or form to (as I stated in the Introduction) reinvent the wheel and go back over (for the umpteenth time) a biography of accused assassin Lee Harvey Oswald, the single bullet theory, and all the other very familiar aspects of the most famous murder mystery in American (indeed, in world) history. One assumes that, if you have come this far and have chosen to read this book, you are already well familiar with these sacred cows and well covered parts of the assassination story. I did not want to become bogged down with a massive volume that had me, out of necessity, covering well worn ground. I want to strip the bark away, so to speak, and offer a refreshing, easy to read alternative about the state of the case in 2021 and what I believe. I have already offered four massively researched and documented books on the assassination, the Secret Service and the medical evidence, as well as participation in many other author's books on these subjects. Please refer to them for the minutia, the split hairs, and so forth.

Thank you for your attention, patience, and understanding. As an author, I am forever humbled: I am nothing without you, the reader. With this firmly in mind, please read on.

The author and legendary White House reporter Sarah McLendon, a frequent sparring partner of JFK's, 10/21/1995 (a screen grab from my COPA conference presentation, Washington, D.C.)

CHAPTER ONE

WELL, WHAT IS THE VERDICT?

I firmly believe there was a conspiracy in the death of President John F. Kennedy. In fact, I *know* there was a conspiracy. I base this on 40-plus years of reading and researching the case, encompassing a mountain of both secondary and primary source research. As an author and researcher born after the assassination (in 1966) and one who is blessed with an open mind (not wedded to a certain theory or theories or even, for that matter, the notion that there *had* to be a conspiracy in the JFK case[1]), I feel that it is fortuitous that I missed or was too young to have experienced the post-Warren Commission days, the Jim Garrison trial and aftermath, and the pre-HSCA days. My mind was not weaned on or formed on pre-conceived notions. In fact, when I started truly being interested in an overt way on the case in 1988 (it was middling from 1978 onward), I actually first believed, somewhat incongruously, that Oswald probably fired at Kennedy *and* that there was some sort of conspiracy, most likely via a shot coming from the infamous grassy knoll to the front of JFK and most likely originating with the Mafia (in other words, a very conservative "Oswald, a friend on the knoll, and some mob boys" scenario). I also was very skeptical that Jack Ruby's shooting of Oswald was merely the act of yet "another" lone nut. I vividly remember viewing the 1988 PBS NOVA program *Who Shot President Kennedy?* and being compelled to believe there was a conspiracy, despite narrator Walter Cronkite and a host of other program participants attempting to dispel this notion.

Two things stood out from this program: the stunningly good quality Zapruder film they used which convinced me that there had to have been at least one shot from the front, as JFK's head goes violently backward and to the left (as a special note, I later obtained a copy of this same version of the "Z film" from author David Lifton in late 1990 on VHS which I then proceeded to add slow motions techniques and enlarge segments of the video, as well). The other thing that stood out was the use of several actual JFK autopsy photos (again provided by Lifton and used in the 1988

---

1   My Secret Service research does not necessarily absolutely depend on a conspiracy having taken place, as the failure of the Secret Service to protect Kennedy on 11/22/63 is obvious whether one believes Oswald acted alone or not.

paperback version of his seminal classic book *Best Evidence*). My mother, of all people, made a very telling statement in response to the depiction of the back-of-the-head autopsy photo, which is an interesting observation for a lay person: "Well … at least his head was in good condition." I could tell she was having difficulty squaring this image of the intact rear of the president's head with the Zapruder film, as well as with all the witness statements about the origin of the head shot(s) and the condition of the president's head, as well as in comparison to her own instincts and beliefs on the matter.

Quite frankly, so was I.

With this firmly in mind, here are the 12 reasons I believe there was a conspiracy in the death of JFK:

REASON #1: THE EVIDENCE OF THE ABRAHAM ZAPRUDER[2] FILM, AS WELL AS THE ORVILLE NIX,[3] MARIE MUCHMORE[4] AND CHARLES BRONSON[5] FILMS OF THE ACTUAL ASSASSINATION

As even those fortunate few at the Garrison trial in the late 1960's who saw the Zapruder film, as well as the millions who finally saw it when it was shown for the very first time to the general public on Geraldo Rivera's ABC program *Goodnight America* in March 1975 can attest to, it is quite clear that the president certainly appears to have been shot from the front, as his head goes violently backward and to the left, as if he was struck by an invisible baseball bat. In addition, the president and Governor John Connally of Texas definitely appear to have been hit by a separate shot (or shots) than one that can be accounted for by the so-called pristine bullet of single bullet theory infamy espoused by Warren Commission members Arlen Specter and future president Gerald Ford. The time span of the visible shots that one can see being depicted in the film, coupled with all the testimony from those associated intimately with it, such as the limousine occupants themselves (Jackie Kennedy, the Connallys, and even Secret Service agents Bill Greer

---

2   Abraham Zapruder himself, although a little ambiguous in some statements, said he had assumed the shots came from behind him because the President's head went backwards from the fatal shot, and also that the wound on the side of the President's head was facing that direction. He also said he believed it because police officers ran to the area behind him. That said, he did add: "I also thought it came from back of me": 7H 572. In addition, Secret Service agent Max Phillips, in a report dated 11/22/63, wrote: "According to Mr. Zapruder, the position of the assassin was behind Mr. Zapruder." Commission Document (CD) 87. See also *The Girl on the Stairs* by Barry Ernest (2013), page 83: witness Carolyn Walther said that Zapruder, moments after the assassination, told her: "They got him in the forehead, from the front."

3   Orville Nix himself believed the shots came from the grassy knoll: *Orville Nix: The Missing JFK Assassination Film* by Gayle Nix Jackson (2013), page 57; Mark Lane's *Rush to Judgment* film..

4   Marie Muchmore herself never indicated her impressions on the direction of the shots.

5   Charles L. Bronson himself did not indicate where the shots came from.

and Roy Kellerman), demonstrate (as Kellerman testified to the Warren Commission) that there have "got to be more than three shots," "a flurry of shells" had to have come into the limousine in rapid fashion, and "the films will perhaps" show something else than what official history – three shots all fired by Oswald from behind only – attempts to depict. Indeed.

The Orville Nix, Marie Muchmore and Charles Bronson[6] films confirm what we see in the Zapruder film: Kennedy's head going violently backward and to the left. Debris from the head shot went rapidly to the rear, as well: motorcycle officers Bobby Hargis, B.J. Martin, and James Chaney were all hit with blood, skull and brain matter,[7] as was Secret Service agent Sam Kinney, the driver of the follow-up car.[8] Mrs. Kennedy retrieved a piece of the president's skull that went rearward onto the trunk of the limousine.[9] Charles Brehm also saw a skull fragment fly to the left and backward in his direction.[10] If that wasn't enough, *two prominent witnesses – a top Secret Service agent and JFK's physician – confirm that skull particles and a misshapen bullet were found in the back seat area of the car!*[11]

In addition, author Sherry Fiester, a longtime student of forensic science, has demonstrated that the back spatter of blood as seen in the Zapruder film is genuine and proves that JFK was shot from the front.[12] Fiester also adds that the initial transfer of energy causes the target to move minutely into the force and against the line of fire (the minute forward movement one can see right before the fatal head shot at frame 313), before moving with the force of the bullet. The minute forward motion followed by the much more pronounced rearward movement is consistent with a shot from the front.[13] Fiester concludes: "Current forensic research supports a single gunshot originating in front of the President."[14] Based on his viewing of the Zapruder film in 1964 in the Dallas FBI office, FBI agent Don Adams, a Korean War veteran who saw serious action, firmly believed JFK was shot from the front.[15]

---

6   No relation to the famous actor with the same name.

7   6 H 292, 294; *Murder From Within*, pages 59-60.

8   Author's interview with Kinney.

9   Zapruder and Nix films; Clint Hill on *60 Minutes* December 1975.

10   Mark Lane's *Rush to Judgment* film. See also *The Girl on the Stairs* by Barry Ernest (2013), pages 89-90.

11   See Chapter Two.

12   *Enemy of the Truth* by Sherry Fiester (2012), pages 85-120.

13   *Enemy of the Truth* by Sherry Fiester (2012), pages 212, 264-265.

14   *Enemy of the Truth* by Sherry Fiester (2012), page 265.

15   *From an Office Building with a High-Powered Rifle: One FBI Agent's View of the JFK Assassination* by Don Adams (2012), pages 46-47.

As for the barely perceptible sudden two-inch forward movement of the president's head in the Zapruder film just before his head explodes (that some Oswald-did-it-alone authors claim is evidence that the lone shot came from the rear), this is revealed by legendary author and investigator Josiah Thompson to be a different interpretation than Fiester's, but no less satisfying: it is an optical illusion caused by the movement of Zapruder's camera. This leaves without further challenge clear evidence that this shot came from a specific location to the right front of the limousine.[16]

I am in good company:

THE TIMES-PICAYUNE,	STATES-ITEM
NEW ORLEANS, LA.,	NEW ORLEANS
FEBRUARY 18, 1969	FEBRUARY 19, 1969
Fired from Front, Says Pathology Expert	Dr. Nichols, a pathologist and expert on forensic medicine, testified Monday that he believes, on the basis of his study of color slides taken from the Abraham Zapruder film of the assassination of President John F. Kennedy, that the fatal bullet was fired from the front.
The expert, Dr. John Nichols, associate professor of pathology at the University of Kansas, said he was basing his opinion on numerous viewings of the Zapruder film of the assassination, slides made from the film and photographs.	

Finally, the Zapruder film is also grist for the mill for people like me with a special interest in the Secret Service:

1. First shot or shots ring out. The car slows with brake lights on;

2. Greer turns around the first time to stare at JFK;

3. Kellerman orders Greer to "Get out of line, we've been hit!";

4. Greer disobeys his superior's order and turns around to stare at JFK a second time, until after the fatal headshot finds its mark.

Reason #2: All the Witnesses Who Believed at Least One Shot Came From the Front

Whether one is a seasoned researcher who has read many books on the assassination or merely a concerned citizen who has seen the

---

16   *Last Second in Dallas* by Josiah Thompson (2020); Josiah Thompson 2013 Duquesne University conference presentation video

JFK movie, it is taken as an article of faith, and justifiably so, that at least one shot came somewhere from the front, as many people went on record stating that this was the case.[17] [18] [19] Valuable *first-day evidence* and words from *law enforcement officers in the motorcade* confirm a shot from the front. The Newman family appeared on WFAA/ABC TV on 11/22/63 and Bill Newman pointed to his temple as the location where the fatal shot made its mark and, perhaps more importantly, stated that the shot originated from behind them, "back up on the mall, I don't know what you call it [the grassy knoll]."[20]

Witness Jean Hill appeared via a telephone audio interview on WBAP/NBC TV on 11/22/63 and stated several times that the shots came from the hill in front of her.[21] Secret Service agent Paul Landis, riding in the Secret Service follow-up car behind Kennedy's car, stated in two reports that one of the shots came from the front. "My reaction at this time was that the shot came from somewhere towards the front" said Landis in his first report dated 11/27/63.[22] In his second report dated 11/30/63, Landis wrote: "...my reaction at this time was that the shot came from somewhere towards the front, right-hand side of the road."[23] If that wasn't enough, Landis also confirmed these perceptions in his statement to the HSCA in 1979.[24] Secret Service agent Forrest Sorrels, riding in the lead car in front of JFK's limousine, stated in his report dated 11/28/63: "I looked towards the top of the terrace to my right as the sound of the shots

---

17   Conspiracy author Richard Charnin has the tally at 84 (with 36 from the Texas School Book Depository/TSBD; 4 from elsewhere): *Reclaiming Science: The JFK Conspiracy* by Richard Charnin (2014), pages 53 and 55-61. Conspiracy author Harold Feldman has the tally at 51 (with 32 from the TSBD; 2 from both locations) in his classic article "51 Witnesses: The Grassy Knoll." Conspiracy author Stewart Galanor has the tally at 54 (with 44 from the TSBD; 9 from both locations; 4 from elsewhere) in his 1998 book *Cover Up*. Conspiracy author Josiah Thompson in his classic 1967 book *Six Seconds in Dallas* has the tally at 37 (with 27 from the TSBD). The HSCA has the tally at 20 (with 46 from the TSBD: see 2 HSCA122). Even anti-conspiracy author John McAdams concedes that at least 35 (with 61 from the TSBD; 5 from both locations; 2 from elsewhere) thought a shot came from the front: http://mcadams.posc.mu.edu/shots.htm.
18   See also *The Reckoning* by Marshal Evans (2018), pages 38-42: authors Josiah Thompson (55% of the 64 who responded said the knoll was the source of a shot or shots) and Stewart Galanor (50% of the 104 who responded said the knoll was the source of a shot or shots) also contributed valuable studies.
19   See chapter 9.
20   See also 19 H 490 / 24 H 219: Bill Newman's 11/22/63 Sheriff Dept. interview report; Complete Tom Alyea film from 11/22/63 (silent film) – Newman is shown pointing emphatically at his right temple; 1966 interview with Josiah Thompson for *Six Seconds in Dallas*, p. 126; see also *Reasonable Doubt* by Henry Hurt, p. 118.
21   *Treachery in Dallas* by Walt Brown (1995), pages 184-185.
22   18 H 758-759
23   18 H 751-757
24   HSCA Report, pp. 89, 606 (referencing Landis's interview, February 17, 1979 outside contact report, JFK Document 014571).

seemed to come from that direction."[25] Secret Service agent Lem Johns, riding a few cars behind Kennedy's in Vice President Lyndon Johnson's Secret Service follow-up car, stated to the HSCA in 1978: "The first two [shots] sounded like they were on the side of me towards the grassy knoll."[26] In addition, on the 2013 DVD about his life entitled *Lem Johns: Secret Service Man,* Johns stated that a shot came from the grassy knoll. I spoke to Johns in 2004 and he said the same thing.

Dallas Police motorcycle officer James Chaney stated on WFAA/ABC TV on 11/22/63 to reporter Bill Lord that he was "riding on the right rear fender" of JFK's limo during the shooting and that "the President was struck in the face" by the second shot. Lord ended the interview by telling the audience that "(Chaney) was so close his uniform was splattered with blood."[27] Fellow Dallas police motorcycle officer Bobby Hargis told the *New York Daily News* on 11/24/63 that he was struck so hard by a piece of skull bone that he said, "I thought at first I might have been hit." Hargis also stated in his Warren Commission testimony that "it sounded like the shots were right next to me ... they probably could have been coming from the railroad overpass, because I thought since I had got splattered, with blood – I was just a little back and left of – just a little bit back and left of Mrs. Kennedy ... it seemed like his head exploded, and I was splattered with blood and brain, and kind of bloody water."[28] (for his part, fellow Dallas police motorcycle officer B.J. Martin testified to the Warren Commission that "there was blood and other matter on my windshield and also on my motor."[29]) Dallas motorcycle officer Hollis B. "H.B." McClain, one of the two forward mid motorcade motorcycle officers, stated: "I feel like that there's somebody on that railroad track (that) shot him a second time."[30] Deputy Sheriff Jack W. Faulkner also conveyed in a report dated 11/22/63 that the shots came from the front.[31] (Interestingly, gunmen were spotted in Dealey Plaza on 11/20/63, two days before the assassination, as verified in a report that was buried for fifteen years and only released via a Freedom of Information Act lawsuit.[32] Two police officers on routine patrol saw several men aiming rifles over the fence on the grassy knoll in mock target practice. The police ran to the fence, but the men quickly departed in a car that was parked nearby. The

25   21 H 548
26   HSCA interview with Johns, 8/8/78: RIF# 180-10074-10079.
27   Lord himself commented on the video on my You Tube channel "Hey- that's me doing the interview!"
28   6 H 293-296 / testimony.
29   6 H 289-293 / testimony.
30   Mark Oakes' *Eyewitness Video Tape III* (1998).
31   Report dated 11/22/63 (19 H 511).
32   *Mafia Kingfish* by John Davis (1988), pages 175-176.

officers reported the incident after the assassination to the FBI. Needless to say, nothing came of this report).

Report mentioning the 11/20/63 Dealey Plaza target practice incident:

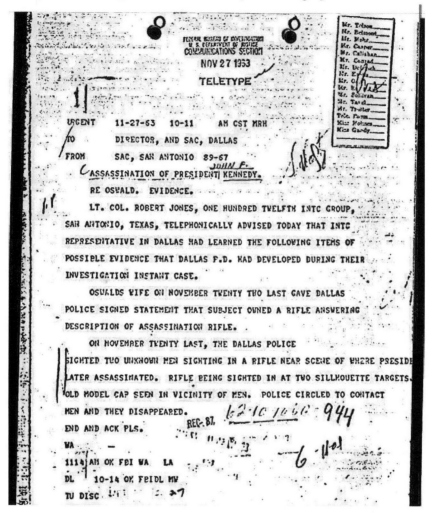

For their part, Deputy Sheriff Eugene Boone,[33] Deputy Constable Seymour Weitzman,[34] Deputy Sheriff Roger Craig,[35] Deputy Sheriff Harold Elkins,[36] Deputy Sheriff C.L. "Lummie" Lewis,[37] Deputy Sheriff A.D. McCurley,[38] Deputy Sheriff Luke Mooney,[39] Deputy Sheriff J.L.

33	19 H 507; 7 H 105-109
34	4 H 161
35	19 H 524
36	19 H 540
37	19 H 526
38	19 H 514
39	19 H 541

Oxford,[40] Deputy Sheriff L.C. Smith,[41] Deputy Sheriff I.C. Todd,[42] Deputy Sheriff Ralph Walters,[43] radio officer Jack Watson,[44] Deputy Sheriff Harry Weatherford,[45] Deputy Sheriff Buddy Walthers,[46] Dallas motorcycle officer Clyde Haygood,[47] and Officer Edgar Leon Smith, Jr.[48] all gave testimony or written statements that day or soon after that, at the very least, *indirectly* indicated that a shot came from the front (such as running to the knoll, as opposed to the Texas School Book Depository). For his part, Sheriff Bill Decker, the man who set up the ambush of the infamous Bonnie and Clyde,[49] said: "Have my office move all available men out of my office into the railroad yard to try to determine what happened in there and hold everything secure until Homicide and other investigators should get there."[50]

Dallas Police Chief Jesse Curry, riding with Sorrels, Decker, and Secret Service agent Winston Lawson in the lead car ahead of JFK's limousine, said that, from the direction of the blood and the brain matter, one shot had to have come from the front.[51] On 11/22/63, a press conference was held at Parkland Hospital that was headed by Assistant White House Press Secretary Mac Kilduff which was also filmed. Kilduff said: "Dr. Burkley told me, it is a simple matter, Tom, of a bullet right through the head": he then points to his right temple. Question: "Can you say where the bullet entered his head, Mac?" Kilduff then answers: "It is my understanding that it entered in the temple, the right temple. They [the shots] came from the right side."[52] This information was repeated by Chet Huntley on NBC that day for the whole world to hear: "President Kennedy, we are now informed, was shot in the right temple. 'It was a simple matter of a bullet right through the head,' said Dr. George Burkley, the White House medical officer."

40   19 H 530
41   19 H 516
42   19 H 543
43   19 H 505-506
44   19 H 522
45   19 H 502
46   19 H 502
47   6 H 297-299
48   7 H 565-569
49   *The Deputy Interviews: The True Story of J.F.K. Assassination Witness, and Former Dallas Deputy Sheriff, Roger Dean Craig* by Steve Cameron, 2019, pages 20-24.
50   23 H 913
51   *The Fifth Estate-Dallas and after 1977* CBC (interviewed by P.D. Scott) and *The Killing of President Kennedy* (1978/1983) [full length version of *Declassified: The Plot to Kill President Kennedy* (1978/1988)]
52   see Thomas Atkins' film clip as shown in *The Men Who Killed Kennedy, The Jim Garrison Tapes* video 1992, *JFK: The Case for Conspiracy* video 1993

Walter Cronkite of CBS reported to the entire world: "Some of the Secret Service agents thought the gunfire, however, came from an automatic weapon fired to the right rear of the Chief Executive's car, possibly from a grassy knoll, and that's that knoll to which motorcycle policemen were seen racing and where the huddled figures of a man and a woman were seen on the ground with a crowd surrounding, which suggests of course that perhaps this is where the shots came from. Governor Connally could very possibly have been shot in the back with the assassin's bullet still coming from the front of the car. He rode in a small jump seat in the center of the back of the specially-built presidential limousine."

WFAA ABC radio reported immediately after the shooting: "Some of the Secret Service agents thought the gunfire was from an automatic weapon fired from the right rear, probably from a grassy knoll where police rushed."

So, no kooks or conspiracy "buffs" here: first-day statements on film, video, television, or in writing by people who were there, including law enforcement officials.[53] If you think these people were all mistaken, I have a plot of land in Alaska to sell to you.

REASON #3: THE WITNESSES WHO SMELLED GUNPOWDER ON THE STREET OR BY THE KNOLL

Secret Service agent Rufus Youngblood, riding in LBJ's car, smelled gunpowder "after the last shot,"[54] as did fellow Secret Service agent Thomas "Lem" Johns, riding in the vehicle directly behind LBJ's car and who immediately sprang out onto the street.[55] *Dallas Morning News* photographer Tom

---

53   Honorable mention would have to go to the entire Willis family: Phil, Marilyn, Rosemary and Linda, who all believed a shot came from the front: *The Men Who Killed Kennedy* 1988; Re: Rosemary- *San Francisco Examiner*, 6/5/79. Also: Postal Inspector Harry D. Holmes- *No More Silence* by Larry Sneed (1998), pp. 351-371 + photo – [p. 352] "... there was just a cone of blood and corruption that went up right in the back of his head and neck. I thought it was red paper on a firecracker. It looked like a firecracker lit up which looks like little bits of red paper as it goes up. But in reality it was his skull and brains and everything else that went up perhaps as much as six or eight feet. Just like that!" Alan Smith: Chicago Tribune, 11/23/63, p. 9 [see also Murder From Within, p. 71]: "...The car was ten feet from me when a bullet hit the President in the forehead...the car went about five feet and stopped."

54   10/2/98 letter and photo from Howard Donahue to the author. Donahue served in the very same Air Force unit as Youngblood during WWII and appeared together – and were photographed – at a reunion conference in 1996.

55   Author's correspondence with Christopher Daniel Blain 3/10/20. Blain is a "distant cousin" of agent Gerald Blaine ('his [Gerald Blaine's] dad was my granddad's brother ... that side of the family doesn't even spell our name the same") and, while a member of the 101st Airborne Division of the U.S. Army, had worked with President George W. Bush's Secret Service, including the SAIC of PPD Carl Truscott. Blain confirmed that Lem Johns has a "son [Jeff] and grandson [Michael] who both were in the Secret Service" with John's grandson then being "the SAIC of Laura Bush." (Blain included photos of himself with President Bush and Lem John's grandson). Blain, a native of Birmingham, Alabama (Lem's hometown), "got to know Lem and [his wife] Anita very well. He [Lem] told me he could smell the cordite [gunpowder] and immediately knew what was happening ... being from Alabama he

15

Dillard, riding in the motorcade, also smelled gunpowder,[56] as did Dallas Police officer Earle Brown,[57] Mrs. Elizabeth "Dearie" Cabell and Congressman Ray Roberts,[58] Mrs. Donald Baker (nee Virgie Rackley),[59] Senator Ralph Yarborough,[60] Dallas motorcycle officer B.J. Martin,[61] reporter Robert H. Jackson,[62] and Dallas police officer Joe M. Smith (on the knoll itself),[63] at a location far from the so-called "Oswald" window in the Texas School Book Depository and way too soon after for it to have possibly drifted down from the window, as well. As the *Chicago Tribune* reported on 11/22/63: "…seconds later the cavalcade was gone. The area still reeked with the smell of gunpowder." Notice that no one said this was a cigar, cigarette, exhaust or steam smell; only the unique and pungent smell of gunpowder.

Dallas police officer Luke Mooney was on the sixth floor of the book depository shortly after the shooting and failed to smell any gunpowder.[64] No one else reported smelling any gunpowder there, either.

REASON #4: THE WITNESSES WHO SAW SMOKE ON THE KNOLL

James L. Simmons,[65] Richard Dodd, Sam Holland, and Lee Bowers all said they saw smoke on the knoll,[66] as did Nolan Potter,[67] Clemon Earl Johnson,[68] Austin Miller,[69] Thomas Murphy,[70] Walter Winborn,[71] Frank

[Lem] hunted as a kid and said there was no doubt what was happening. He responded immediately but he told me that LBJ's car was a rental and didn't have the running boards so he couldn't get on the car and jumped back off to keep from getting run over so for just a brief moment there was a Secret Service agent [Lem] on the ground in Dealey Plaza. I knew Lem personally. Anita made the best damn ice tea ever. Lem was a good humble man." I also spoke to Lem Johns in 2004 and he was interviewed extensively for a 2011 DVD about his life called Lem Johns: Secret Service Man. Johns was interviewed by the HSCA in 1978 and spoke to Newsday in 1999, as well.

56   6 H 165 + Pictures of the Pain by Richard Trask, p. 441.
57   6 H 233
58   7 H 487 + Capitol Records' The Controversy/ interview with Larry Schiller and Richard Lewis.
59   7 H 512 + CD5, pp. 66-67.
60   20 H 351 + The Death of a President, p. 156, Murder From Within page 65/ interview with Newcomb & Adams, The Truth About The Assassination by Charles Roberts, page 17, Crossfire by Jim Marrs, p. 16.
61   Early 1970's interview with Fred Newcomb and Perry Adams for Murder From Within (pages 33, 42, 58, 64-65, 71, 76, 89, 92, 96, 101 [see also Killing Kennedy by Harrison Livingstone, p. 152].
62   Murder From Within by Fred Newcomb and Perry Adams (1974/2011), page 59.
63   CD205, p. 310 + Texas Observer, 12/13/63 + Murder From Within, pages 65 and 92 + Conspiracy by Anthony Summers, p. 29.
64   3 H 289
65   22 H 833
66   Rush To Judgment film 1966; 19 H 480, 514, 530; 6 H 243; The Girl on the Stairs by Barry Ernest (2013), pages 77-80.
67   22 H 834
68   22 H 836 + No More Silence by Larry Sneed, pp.79-83.
69   19 H 485
70   5/6/66 interview (Best Evidence by David Lifton, pages 16 and 723 + Cover-Up by Stewart Galanor, page 59).
71   3/17/65 and 5/5/66 interviews (Best Evidence by David Lifton, pages 16 and 723 + Cover-Up by Stewart Galanor, pages 59-60).

Reilly,[72] Jean Hill,[73] Earle Brown,[74] Cheryl McKinnon,[75] Wilfred Daetz,[76] Rosemary Willis,[77] KBOX reporter Sam Pate,[78] Patsy Paschall,[79] and W.W. Mabra.[80] (Royce Skelton saw smoke but thought it was coming off the street from the shots[81]). Ed Johnson, a reporter riding in the motorcade press bus, wrote the day after the assassination: "Some of us saw little puffs of white smoke that seemed to hit the grassy area in the esplanade that divides Dallas' main downtown streets."[82] A.D. McCurley stated: "a railroad worker stated to me that he believed the smoke from the bullets came from the vicinity of a stockade fence which surrounds the park area."[83] J.L. Oxford likewise reported: "there was a man who told us that he had seen smoke up in the corner of the fence."[84]

---

72   6 H 230

73   1978 interview with Anthony Summers, as recounted in *Conspiracy*, 1980: "I heard four to six shots, and I'm pretty used to guns. They weren't echoes or anything like that. They were different guns that were being fired...The President was killed and then, of course, pandemonium reigned and I looked up, and at the time I looked up across the street I saw smoke like from a gun coming from the parapet, that built-up part on the knoll."; *Crossfire* by Jim Marrs (1989), p. 38; *Killing the Truth* by Harrison Livingstone (1993), page 92.

74   11-09-83 AP article found in the *Indiana Gazette*: "he heard shots and saw two or three puffs of white smoke wafting toward the bridge. The president, he said, was lying in his wife's lap as the car passed beneath him."

75   11/22/63 *San Diego Star News*.

76   12-7-66 letter from Dallas Police Chief Charles Batchelor to Dallas FBI agent-in-charge J. Gordon Shanklin: "The subject stated that on November 22, 1963, at the time of the assassination of President Kennedy, he was standing on the grass on the north side of Elm Street – on the slope approaching the triple underpass. He recalls only one shot and that immediately after the shot he ran up the slope toward the railroad tracks and was stopped by an unknown police officer who pointed a pistol at him and shouted 'Where are you going?' He then returned down the slope. The subject stated that he could hear very little out of his left ear and that he heard the shot with his right ear and in his opinion the shot came from his right which was in the direction of the railroad tracks. He also stated he saw a puff of smoke come from behind the fence near the railroad tracks. He stated that he was so excited he doesn't recall any additional shots." As researcher Pat Speer has written: "Daetz is a little-known witness, and is probably not worth mentioning, outside the intriguing possibility he was the other man on the steps with [Emmett] Hudson and [F. Lee] Mudd... He is reported to have called the Dallas Chief of Police in 1966 and to have said he'd been a witness. The Dallas Chief of Police told the FBI about him, and the FBI investigated. At that time, however, Daetz reportedly denied making the phone call to Dallas and denied being in Dallas in November 1963. When the FBI confronted him with the fact that the phone call had been billed to his phone, Daetz reportedly claimed the whole thing must have been a practical joke. It seems probable that Daetz lied to the FBI. Perhaps he'd called Dallas on a lark and was trying to cover up his behavior. On the other hand, it's possible he was afraid to tell the FBI what he'd seen or was intimidated into retracting his statements. It's unlikely we'll ever know." http://www.patspeer.com/chapter7%3Amorepiecesofthepuzzle.

77   11-19-93 article in *USA Today*: "She says she saw the gunsmoke of a second gunman - evidence of a conspiracy."

78   https://www.youtube.com/watch?v=ESXT-E2w9C4 : interview with researcher Al Chapman 1970.

79   November 1995 KDFW television interview.

80   *Crossfire* by Jim Marrs (1989), pp. 19-20, and *No More Silence* by Larry Sneed (1998), p.519.

81   6 H 236-238

82   11/23/63 *Fort Worth Star Telegram*; I do not include Mike Brownlow in my tally for those who said they saw smoke on the knoll because he only came forward over 40 years later.

83   19 H 514: 11/22/63 report

84   19 H 530: 11/23/63 report

Also, on page 204 of Robert Groden's *The Killing of a President* there is a still photo from the Dave Wiegman film which seems to show a puff of smoke lingering out from the trees on the knoll.[85] As researcher Pat Speer has observed: "There are frames in the Wiegman film and Zapruder film that convince me they [the witnesses] were [right]. In these frames, one can see what looks like a puff of smoke hovering in the trees. While one can easily see such things once one starts looking for them, and fool oneself, the fact is there are no other apparent puffs of smoke in the Zapruder film besides the one seen in the reddish tree by the stockade fence as the limousine heads for the underpass. Furthermore, that there appears to be smoke in the trees in the Wiegman film, at exactly this same time, seems too great a coincidence."[86] In addition, the Nix film, the John Martin film, and the Patsy Paschall film are all alleged to have evidence of smoke and/or flashes on them.

Screenshot from the Wiegman film showing the puff of smoke (in white circle), under the trees, and the Presidential limousine (in white circle), going underneath the triple underpass.

When coupled with those who *smelled* gunpowder, it is very hard if not impossible to give these sightings of smoke an innocent explanation, especially due to the timing and location. Lone-nut authors Jim Moore and Gerald Posner desperately (and lamely) attempted to show that the smoke came from either cigarettes or steam, but not only did several witnesses mentioned above smell gunpowder, even fellow lone-nut author H.R. Underwood conceded that Moore and Posner gave explanations that were

---

85   See also the Jim Marrs DVD edition of *Crossfire* and Robert Groden's *JFK: The Case for Conspiracy* DVD; see also *JFK: Absolute Proof* by Robert Groden (2013), page 305.

86   http://www.patspeer.com/chapter7%3Amorepiecesofthepuzzle.

"unlikely."[87] I strongly agree. 1978 news accounts of the HSCA acoustics tests mentioned seeing smoke from the rifle firing from the knoll.

Two of the men mentioned above, S.M. Holland and James L. Simmons, immediately ran from the overpass and into the railroad yard behind the picket fence. They found footprints behind the fence in the mud, as well as mud on the back bumper of a car from which a gunman, perhaps his spotter, could have stood on.[88] It is also imperative to realize that no one checked the closed trunks of the vehicles parked behind the fence. This would have been a fast and easy place to hide.[89]

REASON #5: THE WOUND IN THE BACK OF JFK WAS A WOUND IN THE BACK, NOT ON THE BACK OF THE NECK, AND THIS WOUND DID NOT EVEN PENETRATE THE CHEST

Secret Service agent Glen Bennett, riding in the follow-up car directly behind President Kennedy's car, wrote in his 11/22/63 report: "I heard a noise that immediately reminded me of a firecracker. Immediately, upon hearing the supposed firecracker, looked at the Boss's [JFK's] car. At this exact time I saw a shot that hit the Boss about four inches down from the right shoulder; a second shoot [sic] followed immediately and hit the right rear high [sic] of the Boss's head."[90] Proof that the wound was on JFK's back, not the back of the neck: The autopsy photo,[91] the death certificate signed by Dr. Burkley,[92] FBI Exhibit 60 (JFK's shirt),[93] FBI Exhibit 59 (JFK's jacket),[94] the autopsy face sheet,[95] the Sibert & O'Neill report,[96] the 1/13/64 FBI Supplemental Report,[97] Secret Service Agent Clint Hill's written report,[98] as well as the sworn testimonies of Secret Service agents' Hill,[99] Bill Greer,[100] and Roy Kellerman,[101] not to mention the

87   *Rendezvous With Death* by H.R. Underwood (2013), page 204.
88   *Who Shot JFK?* by Bob Callahan (1993), page 61; *Rush to Judgment* film; *JFK* movie.
89   13-year-old Victoria Wahlstrom Rodriguez she saw the Kennedy motorcade on Main Street and heard shots fired in Dealey Plaza. Several minutes later she observed three suspicious individuals in the area surrounding the grassy knoll and rail yards and felt that they may have been involved in the assassination: 1/7/2010 Sixth Floor Museum oral history.
90   24 H 541-542: includes Bennett's contemporaneous handwritten notes from 11/22/63
91   Numerous, including *Best Evidence*, autopsy photo 5.
92   Numerous, including *Cover-Up* by Stewart Galanor, p. 128.
93   *Best Evidence*, photo 18; 17 H 25-26.
94   *Best Evidence*, photo 17.
95   17 H 45; *Postmortem* by Harold Weisberg, p.310: "verified" by Dr. Burkley.
96   Numerous, including the DVD *JFK: The Case for Conspiracy* by Robert Groden. See also the HSCA and ARRB testimonies of both Sibert and O'Neill: HSCA rec. #002191, RIF# 180-10105-10164: interview with James Kelly and Andy Purdy, 8/25/77; RIF#180-10090-10044, HSCA rec. #006185: interview with Andy Purdy and Mark Flanagan, 1/10/78; ARRB depositions [see also *High Treason* (1998 edition), pp. 404-407]; see also *A Fox Among Wolves* by Francis X. O'Neill, Jr (2011), pages 14-15.
97   *Inside the ARRB* by Doug Horne (2009), page 1074.
98   18 H 744-745
99   2 H 143
100   2 H 127 and RIF#180-10099-10491: 2/28/78 HSCA interview
101   2 H 93

1/27/64 WC executive session transcript,[102] Dr. John Ebersole's statements,[103] Major General Godfrey McHugh's statements,[104] mortician Ed Stroble's recollections,[105] and Nurse Diana Bowron's early 1990's statements.[106] If all that wasn't enough, autopsy witnesses James Jenkins, Paul O'Connor, Ed Reed, Dr. James M. Young and Floyd Reibe also confirm that the wound was in the back and not the back of the neck.[107] It is a slam dunk: the official story is dead wrong. The alleged back-of-the-neck wound that supposedly went out the front of JFK's neck to go on to wound Governor Connally (the so-called single-bullet theory) was actually a *non-penetrating back wound*- it was too low to exit the front of the neck and several of these witnesses (Humes, as recorded by Sibert and O'Neill; Kellerman, Greer, Jenkins, O'Connor) said that there was no exit for this wound. Finally, autopsy witnesses Jerrol Custer and Paul O'Connor said that a bullet fragment fell from the back, while Tom Robinson told the HSCA that a bullet fragment originated from somewhere in the thorax.[108]

The following four images, which have *never before been published*, destroy the single bullet theory and prove conspiracy, all at the same time! The low back wound depicted in these photos conclusively demonstrate that there is no way on earth that the rearward bullet could have gone out the front of the throat, as the official fiction would have us believe. Whenever the front of the shirt was pictured before, the shirt was buttoned up and, thus, one could not make out the frontal perspective, while the jacket photo was also never shown from the front before!

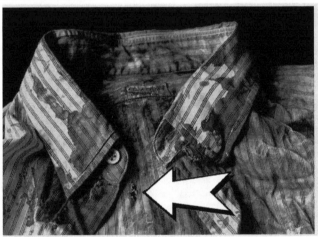

102   Groden's *The Killing of a President*, p. 118
103   Ebersole's 1992 interview with Dr. David Mantik (referenced in several books, an example of wish is 2004 book *The Radical Right and the Murder of John F. Kennedy* by Harrison Livingstone, page 218)
104   CFTR radio interview 1976: back wound was lower than neck wound.
105   The (Illinois) *Herald & Review*, 11/25/13. In a 1964 letter to a friend, Stroble said that JFK was hit "about the seventh vertebrae in his back."
106   *Killing the Truth* by Harrison Livingstone, p. 183
107   *Enemy of the Truth* by Sherry Fiester (2012), pages 272-273; Dr. Young: 2001 BUMED Office of Medical History oral history: https://www.dropbox.com/s/dk6dwvzn6yq2ukd/NM%20and%20the%20Kennedy%20Assassination.pdf?dl=0
108   *Inside the ARRB* by Doug Horne (2009), page 1016

This photo is from the official government re-enactment by the Warren Commission on 5/24/64. Even the government had to know that the wound was on the back, NOT the back of the neck above the shirt collar, thus invalidating both the single bullet theory and the no-conspiracy verdict.

Ford altered crucial JFK report

His revision raised the location of wound

By MIKE FEINSILBER
THE ASSOCIATED PRESS

WASHINGTON — Thirty-three years ago, Gerald Ford took pen in hand and changed — ever so slightly — the Warren Commission's key sentence on the place where a bullet entered John F. Kennedy's body when he was killed in Dallas.

The effect of Ford's change was to strengthen the commission's conclusion that a single bullet passed through Kennedy and severely wounded Texas Gov. John Connally — a crucial element in its finding that Lee Harvey Oswald was the sole gunman.

A small change, Ford said yesterday when it came to light, one intended to clarify meaning, not alter history. "My changes had nothing to do with a conspiracy theory," he said in a telephone interview from Beaver Creek, Colo. "My changes were only an attempt to be more precise."

At the time, Ford apparently did not have access to autopsy photographs and X-rays.

His editing was seized upon by students of the assassination, many of whom reject the conclusion that Oswald acted alone.

"This is the most significant lie in the whole Warren Commission report," said Robert Morningstar, a computer systems specialist in New York City who said he has studied the

assassination since it occurred and written an Internet book about it.

The effect of Ford's editing, Morningstar said, was to state that the bullet hit Kennedy in the neck, "raising the wound 2 or 3 inches. Without that alteration, they could never have hoodwinked the public as to the true number of assassins."

If the downward-angled shot hit Kennedy in the back, it could not have exited upward through his throat and struck Connally in the way the commission claimed, Morningstar said.

Ford's changes bolster the single-bullet theory by making a specific point that the bullet entered Kennedy's body "at the back of his neck" rather than in his upper back, as the commission staff originally wrote.

The Warren Commission concluded in 1964 that a single bullet — fired by a "discontented" Oswald — passed through Kennedy's body and wounded his fellow motorcade passenger, Connally, and that a second, fatal bullet, fired from the same place, tore through Kennedy's head.

The commission had to concede that another shot missed, nicking a bystander. It found that Oswald could have fired only three times.

Many researchers of the event thus argue that two or more gunmen must have been involved.

The assassination of the president occurred Nov. 22, 1963, in Dallas; Oswald was arrested that day but was shot and killed in the city jail two days later.

Ford's handwritten notes were contained in 40,000 pages of records kept by J. Lee Rankin, chief counsel of

the Warren Commission. They were made public yesterday by the Assassination Record Review Board, an agency created by Congress to amass all relevant evidence in the case. The documents will be available to the public in the National Archives.

The staff of the commission had written: "A bullet had entered his back at a point slightly above the shoulder and to the right of the spine."

Ford suggested changing that to read: "A bullet had entered the back of his neck at a point slightly to the right of the spine."

The final report said: "A bullet had entered the base of the back of his neck slightly to the right of the spine."

Ford, then House Republican leader and later elevated to the presidency with the 1974 resignation of Richard Nixon, is the sole surviving member of the seven-member commission chaired by Chief Justice Earl Warren.

In the interview, he recalled making the change, but said that clarity, not conspiracy, was the purpose.

He said he supposed the commission's overriding conclusion — that Oswald acted alone — would always be challenged, but, "I think our judgments have stood the test of time."

James Lesar, a lawyer who operates the Assassination Archive Research Center, the largest non-governmental collection of materials on the assassination, said that both Ford's description and the commission staff's were in conflict with the Kennedy death certificate, "which said the bullet entered in the upper back region, well below the neck."

Former President and Warren Commission member Gerald Ford altered the Warren Report to move the back wound to the back of the neck.

REASON #6: THE HEAD WOUND WAS OVERWHELMINGLY DESCRIBED AS ONE THAT APPEARED TO HAVE ORIGINATED VIA A SHOT FROM THE FRONT: AN EXIT WOUND IN THE OCCIPITAL-PARIETAL (RIGHT REAR) LOCATION OF THE SKULL[109]

An entrance wound is almost always smaller than an exit wound. Keeping in mind what we see in the Zapruder film, as demonstrated via tremendous detail and documentation in my second book *JFK: From Parkland to Bethesda*, the massive and overwhelming majority of witnesses in Dealey Plaza, Parkland Hospital and Bethesda Naval Hospital described a head wound that appeared to originate via a shot from the front (a large wound in the right occipital-parietal region of the skull and/or cerebellum was present and/or they explicitly stated that the head wound was an exit wound caused by a frontal shot). The witnesses in question from Dealey Plaza and/or especially from Parkland Hospital:[110] Dr. William Kemp Clark – Chief Neurosurgeon; Dr. Malcolm Oliver "Mac" Perry, Attending Surgeon; Dr. Robert Nelson McClelland, Attending Surgeon; Dr. Marion Thomas "Pepper" Jenkins, Chief Anesthesiologist; Dr. Charles James "Jim" Carrico, Resident Surgeon; Dr. Ronald Coy Jones, Chief Resident Surgeon; Dr. Gene Coleman Akin, Resident Anesthesiologist; Dr. Paul Conrad Peters, Urologist; Dr. Charles A. Crenshaw, Resident Surgeon; Dr. Charles Rufus Baxter, Attending Surgeon; Dr. Richard Brooks Dulany, Resident Surgeon; Dr. Adolph Hartung "Buddy" Giesecke, Jr., Anesthesiologist; Dr. Fouad A. Bashour, Chief Cardiologist; Nurse Patricia B. "Trish" Hutton (Gustafson); Chief Supervising Nurse Doris Mae Nelson; Nurse Audrey N. Bell; Nurse Diana Hamilton Bowron; Dr. Robert Grossman, Resident Neurosurgeon,[111] Dr. Don Teel Curtis, Resi-

---

109   This is not meant to imply, however, that every single medical evidence related witness saw and described the head wound exactly the same way. Some saw a lower right rear wound; some saw a higher right rear wound; some saw a wound that encompassed both the rear and the side. The Parkland witnesses seem to have seen a smaller wound than the ones at Bethesda. The jury is out as to whether this is due to body tampering, body alteration or merely seeing the head wound after the scalp was peeled back and what remained of the brain was removed. In any event, I believe these witnesses saw a head wound that indicated a shot from the front side of the president, although, as researcher Pat Speer has demonstrated on his brilliant and meticulously detailed website, it is a fallacy to act like every medical witness saw the head wound the exact same way: same location and same dimensions: http://www.patspeer.com/chapter18b%3Areasontobelieve.

110   Please see the author's second book *JFK: From Parkland to Bethesda* for all the documentation on these witnesses; see also *The JFK Assassination Debates: Lone Gunman versus Conspiracy* by Michael L. Kurtz (2006), pages 107-110.

111   6 H 81 (Salyer) – confirms Grossman's presence in Trauma Room One; He said he saw a hole near the external occipital protuberance in the back of the skull. And through it he observed what he thought was cerebellum. He was then shown the famous Ida Dox drawing prepared for the HSCA which depicts an intact rear of the skull. He replied quite simply with "That's completely incorrect." Grossman insisted without qualification that "there had been a hole devoid of bone and scalp about 2 centimeters in diameter near the center of the occipital bone." ARRB interview

dent Oral Surgeon; Dr. Philip Earle Williams; Nurse Margaret M. Hinchliffe (Hood); Dr. Jackie Hansen Hunt, Anesthesiologist; Dr. Donald W. Seldin, Chief Internist; Dr. William H. Zedlitz, Resident Surgeon; Surgeon David Stewart; Dr. William Kenneth Horsley,[112] Nurse Sharon Tuohy,[113] Nurse Phylis Hall,[114] JFK's physician Dr./Admiral George Burkley,[115] White House physician Dr. James Young,[116] Justice of the Peace Theran Ward; First Lady Jackie Bouvier Kennedy (Onassis); eyewitness Mary Woodward, *Dallas Morning News* reporter[117] Photographer James Altgens[118] Asst. Undertaker Aubrey "Al" L. Rike; Texas State Highway Patrolman Hurchel D. Jacks; Secret Service agent Samuel A. Kinney; Milton T. Wright, Jr. :Texas Highway Patrolman; Presidential aide David F. Powers; Fort Worth Newsman Roy Stamps; Drs. Jack C. Harper, A.B. Cairns, and Gerard Noteboom, Methodist Hospital (re: the Harper fragment, found 11/23/63 by Dr. Harper's nephew William Allen "Billy" Harper, a medical student)[119]; Dr. Lito Porto; Robert E. Schorlemer, M.D. ; Dr. James "Red" Duke (operated on Connally)[120]; Secret Service Agent William R. Greer; Secret Service Roy H. Kellerman;[121] Secret Service Agent Clinton J. Hill; Secret Service Agent Winston G. "Win" Lawson; Dallas Police Officer James W. ("J.W.") Courson, one of two mid motorcade motorcycle officers; and JFK's Air Force Aid, Major General Godfrey "God" T. McHugh.

Dr. Kemp Clark, the Chief Neurosurgeon, perhaps summed up this grouping best when he wrote on 11/22/63: "There was a large wound beginning in the right occiput extending into the parietal region ..."[122] At

---

3/21/97; *Inside The ARRB* by Doug Horne (2009), page 656.

112   Courtesy researcher Matt Douthit.

113   HSCA interview of Tuohy: https://www.youtube.com/watch?v=OcArjV84Tkl&feature=emb_logo.

114   *JFK: Absolute Proof* by Robert Groden (2013), page 153.

115   *The JFK Assassination Debates: Lone Gunman versus Conspiracy* by Michael L. Kurtz (2006), pages 39-40.

116   See chapters 2 and 9 for more.

117   11/7/15 conversation with researcher Matt Douthit at the Sixth Floor Museum.

118   11-21-93 Reporters Remember conference, as shown on C-Span: "John Kennedy was hit by this bullet that obliterated the back of his head ... there was a tremendous amount of blood on the left hand side, and at the back of the head..."; 11-22-63 eyewitness account, presented as an AP dispatch presumably around 1:30 PM. This more detailed account was also published in the 11-25-63 issue of *Stars and Stripes*: "At first I thought the shots came from the opposite side of the street. I ran over there to see if I could get some pictures."; 11-21-85 interview with Richard Trask in Dealey Plaza as quoted in *Pictures of the Pain*, 1994. On the rush of witnesses to the grassy knoll: "Well, I thought they were onto something.."

119   *John F. Kennedy's Head Wounds: A Final Synthesis – and a New Analysis of the Harper Fragment* by Dr. David Mantik (2015).

120   *JFK Absolute Proof* by Robert Groden (2013), page 153.

121   See also *The JFK Assassination Debates: Lone Gunman versus Conspiracy* by Michael L. Kurtz (2006), page 128.

122   WR 524-525/ 17 H 9-10 /CE 392: handwritten report 11/22/63.

a press conference at Parkland Hospital on the same day and broadcast to the entire world, Clark said: "The head wound could have been either the exit wound from the neck or it could have been a tangential wound, as it was simply a large, gaping loss of tissue."[123]

The witnesses in question from the official site of the autopsy at Bethesda Naval Hospital[124]: Autopsy photographer John Thomas Stringer, Jr; FBI Agents James W. Sibert and Francis X. O'Neill, Jr.; Mortician Thomas Evan Robinson; Pathologist Dr. Robert Frederick Karnei, Jr.; Joseph E. Hagan, Chief Asst. to Joseph H. Gawler, undertaker; Paul Kelly O'Connor, Bethesda laboratory technologist; James Curtis Jenkins, Bethesda laboratory technologist; Edward F. Reed, Jr., Bethesda X-ray technician; Jerrol F. Custer, Bethesda X-ray technician; Jan Gail "Nick" Rudnicki, Dr. Boswell's lab assistant; James E. Metzler, Bethesda Hospital corpsman; Dr. Robert Canada, commanding officer of the medical hospital at Bethesda;[125] Dr. John H. "Jack" Ebersole, Assistant Chief of radiology; Maj. Gen. Philip C. Wehle, Commanding Officer of the Military District of Washington, D.C.; Floyd Albert Riebe, a medical photographer at Bethesda; Lt. Cmdr. Gregory H. Cross, resident in surgery; Richard A. Lipsey, Aide to General Wehle;[126] John Van Hoesen, Gawler's Funeral Home; White House Photographer (Chief Petty Officer) Robert L. Knudsen, USN; Saundra Kay "Sandy" Spencer, a lab technician at the Naval Photographic Center; and Joe O'Donnell, a government photographer employed by USIA in 1963.

FBI agent Francis O'Neill, present at the Bethesda autopsy, perhaps summed up this grouping best when he stated on video: "There was a massive wound in the right rear of the head [demonstrates this on his head at least four times] … a massive defect in the head … pretty large hole in the back of his head-bigger than an orange. [There was only a] portion of the brain in the cranium … not a total brain. It was a pretty mish-mash of total pulp. I saw them take out what remained in the area there … no cutting [needed]."

---

123   Parkland Press conference, 11/22/63, 3:16 PM CST [*Assassination Science* by Prof. James Fetzer (1998), pp. 427].

124   Please see the author's second book *JFK: From Parkland to Bethesda* for all the documentation on these witnesses.

125   *The JFK Assassination Debates: Lone Gunman versus Conspiracy* by Michael L. Kurtz (2006), page 39.

126   1/18/78 HSCA interview: "Lipsey says he feels he knows "for a fact" that someone shot JFK three times and that these bullets came from behind" and said that the autopsy doctors "were 'absolutely, unequivocally' convinced that he (JFK) had been shot three times…there were three separate wounds and three separate bullets." Lipsey's drawing is interesting: the diagram he drew depicts an area of the right lateral skull missing, both anterior and posterior to the ear. In an 8/27/98 letter to the author, Lipsey wrote: "Because of the location (entrance) of the head wound, just above the earline [sic? Hairline?] and center right, in the back of the head, it was impossible for me to see the size of the entrance wound. The explosion did remove quite a bit of his scalp from the right ear forward in the hair line to the far right side of his forehead. I'm sorry I cannot offer you more information."[?]

Secret Service agent Clint Hill demonstrating the rear head wound on television in 2013:

Secret Service agent Winston Lawson demonstrating the head wound location on television in 2003 (left) and 2013 (right).[127]

Aubrey Rike demonstrating the head wound location to the author on 11/22/97 in Dallas.

Assistant White House Press Secretary Malcolm Kilduff and eyewitness Bill Newman on 11/22/63.

---

127   Lawson stated that he "saw a huge hole in the back of the president's head," as reported in *The Virginian-Pilot* on June 17, 2010.

Dr. David Mantik, one of the very rare handful of people who has been granted permission to view the actual JFK autopsy photos at the National Archives (multiple times, as well), has stated that the below photo is the back of Kennedy's head and it depicts an exit wound caused by a shot from the front. People who view the bootleg photos (like the below photo) are

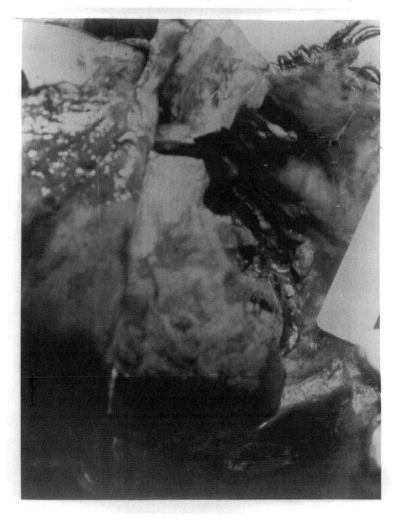

handicapped by the cropping of the photo, the build-up of contrast, and resolution issues. Mantik stated that one can see, when viewing the original color photos (photos no. 44 and 45) as stereo pairs inside the National Archives, and above the top (upper left) of the frame of the original version of the below bootleg photograph (which is known as Fox Photo 8), he could see in the color positive transparencies a tangential view of President

Kennedy's chest and abdomen (with fat pads folded back from the open abdominal incision, indicating that this photo was taken after the Y-incision was made). Additionally, Mantik stated that he could see a nipple in profile in that tangential view, confirming beyond all doubt that he was viewing the chest and the abdomen at the top frame, and that we are therefore definitely looking at <u>the posterior skull</u> while the body of JFK is lying supine on the autopsy table! People like Dr. Baden to the HSCA, lone-nut fanatic John McAdams, lone-nut advocate Dr. Robert Artwohl and others who have only seen the bootleg photos are dead wrong when they try to falsely claim that this is actually the anterior view ... *it is definitely the rear of the head.*

In addition, the autopsy photographer (John Stringer), the autopsy radiologist (Dr. John Ebersole) and the original pathologists (Dr. James J. Humes and Dr. J. Thornton Boswell) all originally reported that this was indeed a posterior view of the head back in 1966, when the four were classifying the photos for the *Military Review* – they actually labeled it as depicting the <u>posterior view of Kennedy's skull</u>. In addition, autopsy technician Paul O'Connor and the ARRB's Doug Horne believe the photo depicts the rear of the head, as does the author and researcher Pat Speer.[128]Dr. Ebersole told the HSCA that a large skull fragment was brought to the morgue late in the autopsy and he called it occipital bone: the rear of the skull.[129]Finally, Dr. Humes, when testifying under oath to the Warren Commission's Allen Dulles in 1964, gave the following statement: "Scientifically, sir, it is impossible for it to have been fired from other than behind. *Or to have exited from other than behind* [emphasis added]."[130]

12/18/63 *Washington Post*-article by Nate Haseltine entitled "Kennedy Autopsy Report": "President Kennedy was shot twice, both times from the rear, and would readily have survived the first bullet which was found deep in his shoulder. The second bullet to hit the President, however, tore off the right rear portion of his head so destructively as to be "completely incompatible with life." A fragment was deflected and passed out the front of the throat, creating an erroneous belief he may have been shot from two angles. These are the findings of the as yet unofficial report of the pathologist who performed the autopsy.... The disclosure that a bullet hit the President in the back shoulder, 5 to 7 inches <u>below the collar</u> line ... "

128   *John F. Kennedy's Head Wounds: A Final Synthesis – and a New Analysis of the Harper Fragment* by Dr. David Mantik, 2015. During televised HSCA hearings, Dr. Michael Baden displayed this photo incorrectly. *Inside The ARRB* by Doug Horne (2009), pages 898-900, 918; *The Mysterious Death of Number Thirty-Five* DVD (2009) by Pat Speer.
129   *Inside The ARRB* by Doug Horne (2009), page 921.
130   *Inside the ARRB* by Doug Horne (2009), page 922.

1/26/64 *New York Times*: "The third bullet, according to an autopsy in Bethesda Naval Hospital in Maryland, ripped away a portion of the back of the President's head on the right side. Fragments from the bullets cut a wound in the President's throat and damaged the windshield of the Presidential limousine."

In this overlooked article I came across recently, a very valid explanation for the head wound is given – Dum Dum bullets:

Herald-Journal - Nov 27, 1963   Browse this newspaper »   Browse all newspapers »

Kennedy Assassin May Have Used Dum Dums

WASHINGTON (AP) — The assassin who murdered John F. Kennedy may have purposely fashioned outlawed "Dum Dum" bullets to produce maximum wounds, an expert on ballistics said today.

A Dallas doctor's report on the character of at least one of two wounds suggests this possibility, said Dr. James Beyer of Arlington Hospital in Virginia. He is a civilian pathologist, formerly with the Armed Forces Institute of Pathology, who wrote the section on wound ballistics in the Army's official history of World War II.

Dum Dum bullets are conventional bullets purposely deformed so as to flatten the tips and thus cause the target to be struck by a larger surface. This makes for a larger and more destructive wound.

Such bullets flatten out even after striking tissue and may turn sideways after entering the body. That presents still more surface and transfers still more of the bullet's energy to the target tissue.

Dum Dum bullets are now barred from warfare by the Geneva Convention.

REASON #7: WITNESSES WHO SAW A FRONT TEMPLE WOUND

Interestingly, the Dallas death certificate states: "The cause of death was due to massive head and brain injury from a gunshot wound of the left temple."[131] In addition to Dr. Robert McClelland, Dr. Marion Jenkins, Dr. Adolph Giesecke, Dr. Lito Porto, Dr. Charles Crenshaw, Dr. Ronald Jones, Dr. Gene Akin, Dr. David Stewart, Father Oscar Huber and Thomas Robinson all stated that there was a wound in either the right or left temple (keeping in mind that some of the witnesses may have merely reversed left for right – they may have meant

---

131   Dr. Robert McClelland's report, CE 392, Warren Report page 527.

from their anatomical right or left perspective and not necessarily JFK's anatomical position).[132] Reporter Seth Kantor, present at Parkland Hospital, wrote the following in his notes: "intered (sic) right temple."[133] Hugh Huggins claimed he saw a wound in the left temple.[134] Texas State Trooper Hurchel Jacks wrote in his report the bullet struck JFK "above the right ear or near the temple."[135] Three other eyewitnesses who stated that President Kennedy was struck in the temple were Marilyn Sitzman,[136] Norman Similas,[137] and Bill Newman (who pointed to his temple in two different film/video clips).[138] As noted earlier, White House Press Secretary Malcolm Kilduff, attributing his remarks to White House Physician George Burkley, said: "It is my understanding that it entered in the temple, the right temple. They [the shots] came from the right side." (Kilduff also pointed to his temple)[139]

In addition, two witnesses, Dennis David and Joe O'Donnell, claim to have seen autopsy photos (in the possession of William Bruce Pitzer and Robert Knudsen, respectively) with both the right rear of Kennedy's head missing and, to the point, a small hole in the right temple area that they believed was an entrance wound.[140] Finally, Bethesda autopsy x-ray technician Jerrol Custer told author David Lifton on 10/7/79 that he remembered a possible entry wound above the right eye,[141] while Bethesda technician James Curtis Jenkins told author Harry Livingstone on 10/8/90 and 5/24/91 that he saw a possible right temple wound.[142]

---

132   *High Treason* by Harrison Livingstone and Robert Groden (1998 edition), pages 197 and 398; 9/8/98 call from Dr. Boris Porto to Vince Palamara (relaying info. from his father Lito); *John F. Kennedy's Head Wounds: A Final Synthesis – and a New Analysis of the Harper Fragment* by Dr. David Mantik (2015); *Inside The ARRB* by Doug Horne (2009), pages 599, 765-768; 6/28/84 FBI Memorandum, SA Udo H. Specht to SAC, Dallas, re: interviews with Akin (RIF#124-10158-10449).

133   20 H 353: Kantor's notepad for 11/22/63: *Inside the ARRB* by Doug Horne (2009), page 71..

134   March 1993 interview with Bill Sloan for *JFK: Breaking the Silence*, p. 185.

135   18 H 801: 11/28/63 report re: 11/22/63; *Inside the ARRB* by Doug Horne (2009), page 70..

136   11-22-63 notes on an interview of Sitzman by a *Dallas Times-Herald* reporter, presumably Darwin Payne, as presented in *The Zapruder Film* by David Wrone, 2003: "Shot hit pres. Right in the temple."

137   *New York Times*, 11/23/63: "I could see a hole in the President's left temple and his head and hair were bathed in blood."

138   11/22/63 WFAA/ABV interview: "a gunshot apparently from behind us hit the President in the side of the temple." (As he says this last line he points to his left temple).

139   see Thomas Atkins' film clip as shown in *The Men Who Killed Kennedy, The Jim Garrison Tapes* video 1992, *JFK: The Case for Conspiracy* video 1993.

140   Dennis David: *The Men Who Killed Kennedy* 1995; Joe O'Donnell: *Inside the ARRB* by Doug Horne (2009), pages 285-286.

141   *Inside the ARRB* by Doug Horne (2009), page 456; *John F. Kennedy's Head Wounds: A Final Synthesis – and a New Analysis of the Harper Fragment* by Dr. David Mantik (2015).

142   *Killing the Truth* by Harrison Livingstone (1993), pages 691-692.

REASON #8: THE OVERWHELMING MAJORITY OF MEDICAL WIT-NESSES AT PARKLAND STATED THAT THE THROAT WOUND WAS ONE OF ENTRANCE, NOT EXIT, THUS ORIGINATING FROM THE FRONT[143]

The witnesses in question from Parkland Hospital[144]: Dr. William Kemp Clark, Chief Neurosurgeon; Dr. Malcolm Oliver "Mac" Perry, Attending Surgeon; Dr. Robert Nelson McClelland, Attending Surgeon; Dr. Charles James "Jim" Carrico, Resident Surgeon; Dr. Ronald Coy Jones, Chief Resident Surgeon; Dr. Gene Coleman Akin, Resident Anesthesiologist; Dr. Paul Conrad Peters, Urologist; Dr. Charles A. Crenshaw, Resident Surgeon; Dr. Charles Rufus Baxter, Attending Surgeon; Nurse Audrey N. Bell; Nurse Diana Hamilton Bowron; Donna Willie; Nurse Margaret M. Hinchliffe (Hood); Dr. Joe D. "Jody" Goldstrich; and Dr. Robert Roeder Shaw.[145]

At a press conference at Parkland Hospital broadcast to the entire world on 11/22/63, Dr. Malcolm Perry said: "There was an entrance wound in the neck.... It appeared to be coming at him.... The wound appeared to be an entrance wound in the front of the throat; yes, that is correct. The exit wound, I don't know. It could have been the head or there could have been a second wound of the head."[146] NBC's Robert MacNeil reported on 11/22/63: "Dr. Malcolm Perry reported that a bullet struck him [JFK] as he faced the assailant." Reporter Richard Dudman reported on 12/7/63 that Dr. Robert McClelland, who assisted Perry, said that the neck wound "had the appearance of the usual entrance wound of a bullet."[147]

NBC anchorman Frank McGee, after showing his viewers a photo of a sniper rifle being removed from the book depository, reported "The best

---

143   Nurse Patricia B. "Trish" Hutton (Gustafson) denounced the trach wound as seen in the autopsy photos: 1/8/83 interview by David Lifton (*Best Evidence*, p. 706) – "The large throat wound shown in the photographs was not the tracheotomy incision that she saw in the emergency room on November 22,1963 ("It doesn't look like any that I've taken part in, let me put it that way."). Likewise, Chief Supervising Nurse Doris Mae Nelson said much the same thing: 12/82 interview with David Lifton (*Best Evidence*, p. 704) – "Doris Nelson told me the tracheotomy was not the one she remembered: "Looks a little large to me ... [it] shouldn't be that big ... It wasn't any 7-8 cm. [It was] just wide enough to get the trach tube in." Nurse Audrey N. Bell: autopsy photo depicting the frontal neck wound: "Looks like somebody has enlarged it.... You don't make trachs that big. Not if you've got as much experience as Perry has." (12/82 interview by David Lifton- *Best Evidence*, p. 704.).

144   Please see the author's second book *JFK: From Parkland to Bethesda* for all the documentation on these witnesses.

145   Shaw: 11/27/63 *New York Herald-Tribune*: article by Martin Steadman: a bullet had entered the front of JFK's throat and "coursed downward into his lung [and] was removed in the Bethesda Naval Hospital where the autopsy was performed."; 11/29/63 *Houston Post:* "The assassin was behind him [JFK], yet the bullet entered at the front of his neck. Mr. Kennedy must have turned to his left to talk to Mrs. Kennedy or to wave to someone."

146   Parkland press conference, 11/22/63 [see Assassination Science by Prof. James Fetzer (1998), pp. 419-427; silent film clip used in *Reasonable Doubt* video (1988), *20/20* (4/92), etc.].

147   *Accessories after the Fact* by Sylvia Meagher (1967), page 153.

we can make out now [is] the President's motorcade had really traveled perhaps a few yards beyond this point and that the fatal shots that were fired were fired from behind and struck him in the back of the head." He then added, with a pained look on his face, "and then incongruously, some way or another, a bullet struck him in the front of the neck."

Typical made-up lies to try to explain the entrance wound on the throat – the 12/6/63 *Life* magazine article by Paul Mandel: *"the 8 mm. film shows the President turning his body far around to the right as he waves to someone in the crowd. His throat is exposed – towards the sniper's nest – just before he clutches it."* The *New York Times* from both 11/27/63 and 12/5/63 reported: "...[Oswald] started shooting as the President's car started coming toward him [while still on Houston Street]..."

If a proper autopsy would have been performed as was demanded by Judge Theran Ward and state law (incredibly, the murder of a president in 1963 was a state crime, not a federal crime), many of these questions and more would have been thoroughly resolved, as Dallas County Medical Examiner Dr. Earl Rose was a highly competent doctor with a long history of performing autopsies. Also, we must realize that all these medical conundrums would also have been revealed, as well, so a conspiracy would have been impossible to contain if this autopsy would have been allowed to go ahead. However, as author Anthony Summers wrote: "The Secret Service agents put the doctor and the judge up against the wall at gunpoint and swept out of the hospital with the President's body."[148]

On or around 12/11/63, Moore and another agent, Roger C. Warner, interviewed the Dallas physicians who treated JFK.[149] As the 12/18/63 *St. Louis Post-Dispatch* reported: "Secret Service gets revision of Kennedy wound – after visit by agents, doctors say shot was from rear. [The Secret Service] obtained a reversal of their original view that the bullet in his neck entered from the front. The investigators did so by showing the surgeons a document described as an autopsy report from the United States Naval Hospital at Bethesda. The surgeons changed their original view to conform with the report they were shown."[150] Secret Service agent Elmer Moore told graduate student James Gochenaur that he "felt remorse for the way he (Moore) had badgered Dr. Perry into changing his testimony to the effect that there was not, after all, an entrance wound in the front of the president's neck." Furthermore, Gochenaur quoted Moore as saying that

148   *Conspiracy* by Anthony Summers (1980), page 42.
149   See *Murder in Dealey Plaza* by James Fetzer (2000), pages 115, 165, 256, and especially 272.
150   See also 2 H 39, 41; *Best Evidence* by David Lifton (1981/1988), pages 156, 166-167, 196, and 286.

Kennedy was a traitor for giving things away to the Russians; that it was a shame people had to die, but maybe it was a good thing; that the Secret Service personnel had to go along with the way the assassination was being investigated: "I did everything I was told, we all did everything we were told, or we'd get our heads cut off." According to Gouchenaur, Moore was the "liaison between the staff of the Warren Commission and the Secret Service."[151] As Chief Justice Earl Warren himself said to Jack Ruby, "You know that Mr. Moore is a member of the Secret Service, and he has been a liaison officer with our staff since the Commission was formed."[152]

Dr. Robert Livingston told autopsy Doctor James Humes about the news reports of the neck wound to the president being one of entrance before the start of the autopsy![153]

The newspapers reported the truth, but people were too grief stricken to notice – JFK was shot from the front.

REASON #9: WITNESSES SAW A MISSED SHOT HIT THE STREET, LEAVING ONLY TWO OFFICIAL SHOTS TO INFLICT ALL THE DAMAGE TO BOTH JFK AND CONNALLY, AS WELL AS THE LIMOUSINE

Dallas Police motorcycle officer Stavis Ellis,[154] Virgie Baker,[155] Royce Skelton,[156] Austin Miller,[157] Jack Franzen,[158] Mrs. Franzen,[159] Marvin Faye Chism,[160] Harry Holmes,[161] Secret Service agent Warren Taylor,[162]

---

151   HSCA 6/1/77 interview transcript RIF#180-10109-10310; see also CD 379; 3 H 363, 364, 387; 6 H 6,7, 17, 27, 44, 50-51, 57,63, and 75.
152   5 H 210
153   5/2/92 letter/ fax to Harry Livingstone in *Killing the Truth* (1993), pages 114-115 and *Killing Kennedy* (1995), pages 7, 193, 207, 208, 216, 276, 316, 354; see also *Bloody Treason* by Noel Twyman (1997/1998), pages 201-202; for the actual letter, in the form of a letter to Lifton, see *Assassination Science* by Prof. James Fetzer (1998), pages 168-171.
154   12 HSCA 23; *No More Silence* by Larry Sneed, page 145.
155   7 H 507, 515
156   6 H 236-238 + 19 H 496
157   19 H 485
158   17 H 840
159   24 H 525
160   Call Report on 2-27-96 phone call with ARRB investigator Dave Montague; 11-20-13 appearance by Ricky Chism at the Sixth Floor Museum, in which he presented his mom›s recollections.
161   7 H 290-292
162   18 H 782

and James Tague, himself injured on the cheek by a missed shot,[163] all testified to a missed shot, thus doing great damage to the official story.

REASON #10: TOO MANY (MISSED) SHOTS – WITNESSES ALSO SAW A MANHOLE COVER, THE NEARBY TURF, OR THE STEMMONS FREEWAY SIGN HIT BY A MISSED SHOT

The statements of Dallas Police officer J.W. Foster,[164] Hugh Betzner,[165] Wayne and Edna Hartman,[166] Clemon Earl Johnson,[167] Newsman Harry Cabluck,[168] Dallas Police officer D.V. Harkness,[169] Dallas Police officer Carl Day,[170] Jean Hill,[171] Deputy Sheriff Roger Craig,[172] (who said that is was a .45 caliber slug),[173] Deputy Sheriff Buddy Walthers,[174] as well as news stories in the 11/24/63 *Dallas Times-Herald* and the 12/21/63 *New Republic*,[175] all act as evidence of these missed shots.

In the *Dallas Times-Herald* article, Dallas Police Lt. Carl Day stated that he "estimated the distance from the sixth floor window the slayer used, to the spot where one of the bullets was recovered, at 100 yards."[176] In the *New Republic* story by Richard Dudman, he reported: "A group of police officers were examining the area at the side of the street where the President was hit, and a police inspector told me they had just found another bullet in the grass."[177] A series of photos by photographers Jim Murray and William Allen document Deputy Sheriff Buddy Walthers, patrolman J.W. Foster, and an unidentified man who Chief Jesse Curry stated was an FBI agent (and who researcher Mark Oakes specifically identified as agent Bob Barrett). The FBI

163   7 H 552-558
164   6 H 252 + *No More Silence* by Larry Sneed, pp. 212-213 + Mark Oakes' videotaped interview 1991.
165   24 H 200, 24 H 540
166   FBI report dated 7/10/64 + *Crossfire*, pp. 315-316 + videotaped interview with Mark Oakes 1991 + *Who's Who in the JFK Assassination*, p. 175.
167   *No More Silence* by Larry Sneed, p. 82.
168   *Crossfire*, p. 315.
169   *No More Silence* by Larry Sneed, p. 207.
170   *No More Silence* by Larry Sneed, p. 235.
171   6 H 221
172   19 H 524 + *Two Men In Dallas* video 1976.
173   *Inside the ARRB* by Doug Horne (2009), pages 1106-1107.
174   7 H 546 + 19 H 518 + *High Treason*, p. 131 + Mark Oakes' letter from Walthers' widow Dorothy + *No More Silence*, p.509 + Al Maddox' 7/12/96 interview with Mark Oakes; Mark Oakes *Eyewitness Video 3* (1998).
175   *The Deputy Interviews: The True Story of J.F.K. Assassination Witness, and Former Dallas Deputy Sheriff, Roger Dean Craig* by Steve Cameron, 2019, pages 154-165.
176   *Trauma Room One* (2001) by Charles Crenshaw, page 99.
177   see also *Crossfire*, p. 315 + *JFK Assassination File* by Curry, p. 57 + *Pictures of the Pain* by Richard Trask, pp. 496-498; *Rendezvous with Death* by H.R. Underwood (2013), page 333 .

agent reaches down with his left hand toward an object that could be the .45 slug Roger Craig spoke of, walks away with something cupped in his left hand, then finally puts whatever it was in his left pants pocket. The three men, as Allen told author Richard Trask, were examining a mark in the cement around the manhole cover and a discussion about a search for either a bullet or bullet fragments in the grass surrounding the storm drain.[178] The 11/23/63 edition of the *Fort Worth Star-Telegram* printed a photograph of a bullet lying in the grass and described it as a rifle bullet lying "in the grass across from Elm Street."[179] Also, a bullet mark on the sidewalk north of Elm Street was noted by several authors.[180]

Finally, witness James Hicks said that the Stemmons Freeway sign was hit and that it was "removed almost immediately after the assassination."[181] Witness Mrs. Donald Baker stated: "I saw the bullet hit on down this way, I guess, right at the sign, angling out."[182] Witness Emmett Hudson, also the Dealey Plaza groundskeeper, said: "the Stemmons sign had been shifted from its place after the assassination."[183] Both the sign being hit by a bullet, and its subsequent removal, was also noted by Dallas County Surveyor Bob West and fellow surveyor Chester Breneman. Both men were part of both Warren Commission re-enactments of the assassination. Breneman stated: "...right after the assassination, they were mentioning a [highway] sign which had a stress mark from a bullet on it. It's my understanding that this particular sign was taken down and no one has been able to locate it."[184] Breneman concluded that, as a result of these re-enactments, "I wish to state that both investigations led us to believe beyond any doubt there were two assassins." Bob West totally agreed with Breneman.[185]

Again, inconvenient evidence of more shots than the official story would account for.

---

178   *Pictures of the Pain* by Richard Trask (1994), pages 471, 497-499, 543; *Inside the ARRB* by Doug Horne (2009), pages 1107-1108; *The Killing of a President* by Robert Groden (1993), pages 68 and 70.
179   *Crossfire* by Jim Marrs (1989), page 315; *The Deputy Interviews: The True Story of J.F.K. Assassination Witness, and Former Dallas Deputy Sheriff, Roger Dean Craig* by Steve Cameron, 2019, page 165.
180   *Rendezvous With Death* by H.R. Underwood (2013), pages 335-338; *The Girl on the Stairs* by Barry Ernest (2013), pages 63-64, 75; *Inside the ARRB* by Doug Horne (2009), page 1108.
181   *New Orleans Times-Picayune*, 1/12/68.
182   7 H 508-509
183   7 H 562-563
184   *Crossfire* by Jim Marrs (1989), page 456.
185   *Crossfire* by Jim Marrs (1989), pages 454-456.

REASON #11: WITNESSES SAW A HOLE IN THE LIMOUSINE'S WINDSHIELD WHERE, OFFICIALLY, THERE WASN'T ONE, BRINGING UP THE ISSUES OF "TOO MANY BULLETS" AND POSSIBLY ORIGINATING FROM THE FRONT, AS WELL

The witnesses who saw this hole in the windshield of Kennedy's limousine: Dallas Police officer Harold R. ("H.R.," "Harry") Freeman, one of the lead motorcycle officers in the motorcade,[186] Dallas Police officer Stavis "Steve" Ellis, one of the five lead motorcycle officers in the motorcade,[187] Nurse Evalea Glanges,[188] head of security for Ford Motor Company (Dearborn Division) Carl Renas,[189] newsmen Richard Dudman and Frank Cormier,[190] Secret Service agent Abraham Bolden,[191] Secret Service agent Charles Taylor,[192] Secret Service agent Joseph Paolella,[193] and a witness from the Ford Motor Company, George Whitaker, Sr.,[194] who believed the specific evidence of how the hole looked, based on his 40 years in the industry, indicated that the shot came from the front.[195]

Interestingly, Michael Paine, the estranged husband of Ruth Paine (who took in Marina Oswald and her children, as well as obtaining the book depository job for Lee Oswald), testified to the Warren Commission: "Somebody else said there was a shot through the windshield of the car. We went

---

186   4/21/71 interview with Gil Toff for *Murder From Within* [see also *Best Evidence*, pp.370-371n].
187   4/21/71 interview with Gil Toff for *Murder From Within* [see also *Best Evidence*, pp.370-371n]; CFTR radio Canada interview 1976; 9/8/98 letter to Vince Palamara: "Yes, I did see a hole in the limousine windshield at Parkland Hospital."
188   1998 correspondence with Vince Palamara + *The Men Who Killed Kennedy* (2003) DVD.
189   *JFK: Conspiracy of Silence*, pages 105-107, 110.
190   *St. Louis Post-Dispatch*, 12/1/63; for Cormier, see *Seeds of Doubt: Some Questions About The Assassination* by Jack Minnis and Staughton Lynd, 12/63, p. 4; *Killing the Truth*, p. 64, and 17 H 614; Dr. Robert Livingston stated: "I learned from a former classmate of mine from Stanford who was then a reporter for the *St. Louis Post-Dispatch*, Richard Dudman, that he was one of the White House press group that accompanied the President to Dallas. Not getting much information from the Parkland Hospital, Dick went out to inspect the Lincoln limousine in which the President and Connally and their wives had been riding. He thought he saw, for certain, that there was a through-and-through hole in the upper left margin of the windshield. He described the spraying-splintering of glass at the margins as though the missile had entered from front of the vehicle. When he reached over to pass his pencil or pen through the hole to test its patency, an FBI or Secret Service man roughly drew him away and shooed him off, instructing him that he wasn't allowed to come so close to that vehicle." 5/2/92 letter/ fax to Harry Livingstone in *Killing the Truth* (1993), pages 114-115 and *Killing Kennedy* (1995), pages 7, 193, 207, 208, 216, 276, 316, 354; see also *Bloody Treason* by Noel Twyman (1997/1998), pages 201-202; for the actual letter, in the form of a letter to Lifton, see *Assassination Science* by Prof. James Fetzer (1998), pages 168-171.
191   9/16/93 interview with Vince Palamara; see also *Murder in Dealey Plaza* (2000), page 140.
192   CD 80
193   https://www.youtube.com/watch?time_continue=4&v=Wg_x4sx_m-w&feature=emb_logo.
194   *The Reckoning* by Marshal Evans (2018), pages 35-36.
195   *Murder in Dealey Plaza* edited by Professor James Fetzer (2000), pages 142-146 (article by Attorney Doug Weldon [identity of source protected]) and episode 7 of *The Men Who Killed Kennedy* (2003), also with Doug Weldon (includes photo and audio of the source).

down to the place [Dealey Plaza] and looked around, and he thought that
– he had a theory that the man [JFK] had been shot from a manhole in the
street, so I recognized that my views could change with evidence."[196] U.S.
Park Policeman Nick Prencipe claims that Secret Service agent Bill Greer,
the driver of JFK's limousine, told him a bullet came through the windshield.[197] Needless to say, a hole in the windshield, whether from the back
but especially from the front, does great damage to the official story.

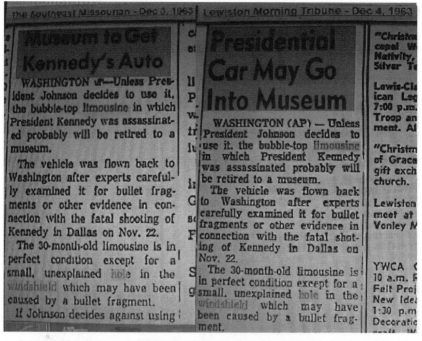

Contemporary news articles (12/3-12/4/63) mentioning bullet hole in windshield:

There was a bullet hole in the windshield.

I believe that the entire story has never been told.

Sincerely,

Evalea Glanges, M.D.

Evalea Glanges letter to the author-bullet hole in windshield:

Stavis Ellis letter to the author-bullet hole in windshield:

---

196   2 H 423
197   *The JFK Assassination: A Researcher's Guide* by Don Becker (2010), page 211.

TP 44-187
JPO:jw

ADMINISTRATIVE

Re speech by OREN FENTON POTITO, St. Petersburg, Florida,
January 16, 1964.

On January 17, 1964 TP 100 PCI (RAC) furnished to SAs JAMES
P. O'NEIL and JAMES E. WALLACE the following information:

On the evening of January 16, 1964 a dinner sponsored by
OREN FENTON POTITO was held at Donat's Restaurant, 6001 Haines Road,
North St. Petersburg, Florida. The dinner meeting was informal pub-
lic in nature and approximately 41 persons were in attendance.

The source has identified POTITO as a member of the National
States Rights Party (NSRP) in the Spring of 1963 at which time POTITO
resigned while holding the office of National Organizer. Since that
time POTITO has held meetings of a public nature under various titles
all of which are non-existent organizations. He is not known to have
any national affiliation at the present time although he is in contact with various leaders of right-wing groups in the United States.

In the course of his speech of some 3 hours following the
dinner POTITO touched on the association between LEE HARVEY OSWALD
and RUBY.

POTITO identified RUBY, real name RUBENSTEIN, as a Communist Party Member since 1929 and through this connection linked him
to OSWALD. He identified OSWALD as a Communist through his association
with the Fair Play for Cuba Committee (FPCC).

According to POTITO only two organizations knew the route
of the parade in Dallas on November 22, 1963 for any period of time
prior to the parade and these two were the United States Secret Service and the Dallas Police Department. RUBY had insinuated himself
into the Police Department circle, obtained the route and arranged
with OSWALD to take the job at the state school building along the
route to carry out the assassination.

POTITO said the "Surgeon General's report" on the assassination stated the first bullet entered the President's throat below
the adams apple clearly showing that two persons were involved with
the first shot being fired from the bridge across the park way in
front of the car. To further substantiate this, POTITO said there
was a bullet hole in the wind shield of the President's car.

Cover Page
H

From the 2017 document releases-bullet hole in windshield:

was removed. A meticulous examination was made of the back
seat of the car and the floor rug, and no evidence was found.
In addition, of particular note was the small hole just left of
center in the windshield from which what appeared to be bullet
fragments were removed. The team of agents also noted that the
chrome molding strip above the windshield, inside the car, just

11/27/63 Secret Service report from Charles Taylor-bullet hole in windshield:

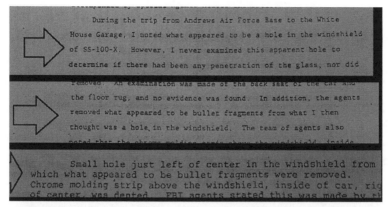

Three excerpts from Secret Service agent Charles Taylor's March 1976 Church Committee testimony-bullet hole in windshield:

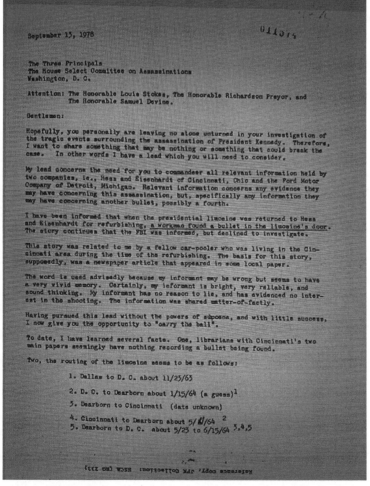

Then there is this HSCA-era document concerning yet another bullet, this one being found in the limousine door:

Reason #12: Witnesses Who Saw Two Men on the Sixth Floor of the Texas School Book Depository on 11/22/63 When, Officially, There Should Only Have Been One Man (Presumably, Oswald)

Here are the witnesses in question: L.R. Terry,[198] Arnold Rowland,[199] John Powell, a prisoner on the sixth floor of the Dallas County Jail,[200] and Carolyn Walther.[201] Richard Randolph Carr saw a man who definitely was not Oswald on the sixth floor. The man was heavy-set wearing a hat, horn-rimmed glasses, and wearing a tan sportscoat.[202] James Worrell saw a man run from the rear of the Book Depository building moments after the assassination.[203] In addition, as HSCA photographic consultant and esteemed author Robert Groden has stated at a recent JFK assassination conference, not only does the Robert Hughes and Charles Bronson films show evidence of movement in the sixth floor windows by at least two figures, the Tom Dillard photo shows a distinct figure of a man in the western-most window of the book depository (whom he dubs The Western-End Man).[204] Two men equals a conspiracy, just all by itself.

So there you have it. Without even having to get into theories of "who did it" and "why," when looking just at the hard evidence and the eyewitness evidence (some would argue that they are one and the same), the case evidence is, in my opinion, overwhelming that there was a conspiracy to kill President Kennedy on 11/22/63. Regardless of whether or not one man (Oswald or anyone else) fired on the limousine from behind, a conspiracy, out of necessity, involves at least one other person. Without having to trudge through "who planned it and why" or "who helped the rear shooter" (Oswald or whoever it was), just the fact that there is evidence of at least one shot from the front is the end of the ballgame.

---

198   *Encyclopedia of the JFK Assassination* by Michael Benson (2002), pages 250-251.

199   *Encyclopedia of the JFK Assassination* by Michael Benson (2002), page 224; *JFK: Absolute Proof* by Robert Groden (2013), pages 309-310; *The Girl on the Stairs* by Barry Ernest (2013), page 83.

200   Earl Golz , *Dallas Morning News*, 12/19/78; *JFK: The Book of the Film* by Oliver Stone and Zachary Sklar (1992), page 163.

201   24 H 522-523; *Encyclopedia of the JFK Assassination* by Michael Benson (2002), page 277; *The Girl on the Stairs* by Barry Ernest (2013), pages 82-83; I do not include Ruby Henderson in my tally because it sounds like she may be describing the two African-American men below the sniper's nest window..

202   *Encyclopedia of the JFK Assassination* by Michael Benson (2002), page 38.

203   *The Girl on the Stairs* by Barry Ernest (2013), page 64.

204   *JFK: Absolute Proof* by Robert Groden (2013), page 294. See also Groden's DVD *JFK: The Case for Conspiracy*. However, I do not believe the Geraldine Reid story: https://kennedysandking. com/john-f-kennedy-reviews/groden-robert-absolute-proof.

To summarize the 12 reasons that lead me to believe that a conspiracy took place in the death of JFK:

1. The evidence of the Abraham Zapruder film, as well as the Orville Nix, Marie Muchmore and Charles Bronson films of the actual assassination;

2. All the witnesses who believed at least one shot came from the front;

3. The witnesses who smelled gunpowder on the street or by the knoll;

4. The witnesses who saw smoke on the knoll;

5. The wound in the back of JFK was a wound in the BACK, not on the back of the neck, and this wound did not even penetrate the chest;

6. The head wound was overwhelmingly described as one that appeared to have originated via a shot from the front: an exit wound in the occipital-parietal (right rear) location of the skull;

7. Witnesses who saw a front temple wound;

8. The overwhelming majority of medical witnesses at Parkland stated that the throat wound was one of entrance, not exit, thus originating from the front;

9. Witnesses saw a missed shot hit the street, leaving only two official shots to inflict all the damage to both JFK and Connally, as well as the limousine;

10. Too many (missed) shots: witnesses also saw a manhole cover, the nearby turf, or the Stemmons Freeway sign hit by a missed shot;

11. Witnesses saw a hole in the limousine's windshield where, officially, there wasn't one, bringing up the issues of "too many bullets" and possibly originating from the front, as well;

12. Witnesses who saw two men on the sixth floor of the Texas School Book Depository on 11/22/63 when, officially, there should only have been one man (presumably, Oswald).

A conspiracy in the death of President Kennedy has already been demonstrated ... and we are just into chapter one of this book!

Now, having said that, let me just say from the outset that I am not naïve: I know full well that a dyed-in-the-wool, ardent and rabid lone-nut true believer will not be swayed by any of this. Just as with religion and politics, people who fervently (want to) believe that Oswald acted alone and that there was no conspiracy will appeal to a higher authority, a personal loyalty (or belief) or a pre-conceived bias; perhaps all of these traits and more. I can see it all now: "Vince, the autopsy report proves" such and such; "several official panels concluded" so on and so forth; "You just want to believe that a mighty man must have been felled by an equally mighty conspiracy and that no puny runt like Oswald could have done it all by himself"; "Posner and Bugliosi demonstrate" and so on. You get the picture.

You see, I hold a unique position in this case: I once drifted to the dark side (briefly in 2007), so I see and feel both sides of the matter. I have weighed and considered the case evidence with an open mind. I could have written a 1,000 page, 2,000 page or 3,000-plus page gargantuan encyclopedia-like volume of a book seeking to relitigate each and every aspect of this case (Oswald's biography, Ruby's biography, the shooting of J.D. Tippit, the single bullet theory, the history of the prior investigations, etc.), but it is over 57 years later and no one has the time or patience for that; there are countless books written before mine and no need to reinvent the wheel, so to speak. In fact, that is why I wrote my second book on the medical evidence called *JFK: From Parkland to Bethesda*: this was a roadmap or GPS thru literally thousands of pages of books, documents, testimony, etc. In that respect, this current book in your hands achieves the same purpose and goal, except it focuses on the assassination, in general.

Jefferson Morley said these epic words in 2015: "Suspicions of conspiracy did not originate with conspiracy theorists, they did not begin with Oliver Stone. Suspicions of a conspiracy originated in the circumstances of the crime.... Some people say, 'the President was shot and everyone knew what had happened, and then conspiracy theorists came along later and drummed up these theories.' In fact, what happened was when people saw and learned about what occurred in the assassination, they immediately came to the conclusion that one person couldn't have done this. So, it wasn't that someone later on wrote an article or a book or published a movie that put forth a conspiracy theory and the only motive was that these people were trying to sell something. Instead, it was the facts themselves. It was the facts of the events that made people question what happened. So, I'm trying to draw a distinction between when people say that Oliver Stone just conned people into believing a conspiracy theory. No, it doesn't work that way. It was the facts of the crime that made people think it happened in a different way than the way the Warren Report set forth. That's what I'm trying to say." Agreed.

This is my final verdict after decades of deliberation: a conspiracy killed President Kennedy.

Some of the amazing people I have met in Dallas 1997-2019 (clockwise, left to right) – Mary Ann Moorman (a Facebook friend for years) and Hubert Clark; Buell Wesley Frazier; James Gochenaur; Oliver Stone; Shari Angel; Dennis David:

CE 399

FBI C1

National Archives

NATIONAL ARCHIVES AND RECORDS ADMINISTRATION 1985

CHAPTER TWO

Smoking Guns and New Evidence

In conjunction with all the evidence of conspiracy demonstrated in chapter one, in this chapter, I will explore some of the new and exciting evidence that further leads me to believe that a conspiracy took the life of President Kennedy. Keep in mind, in some cases, when I say "new" I really mean "newer," as some of these discoveries of mine took place in the early 1990's. While still roughly 30 years or so after the assassination, they are now, in some cases, 20-30 years old. That said, they are certainly not known to 99.9 percent of the public and are rarely, if ever, mentioned in mainstream conspiracy books (other than, in a few cases, my previous books). So here goes:

Item #1: Video Evidence that the So-Called Magic (or Pristine) Bullet of the Single Bullet Theory Scenario was Still in Governor Connally's Leg Well After it Was Allegedly Discovered on a Stretcher at Parkland Hospital

Secret Service agent Roy Kellerman testified to the Warren Commission: "There was in the early – this was on the day [11/22/63] in Parkland Memorial Hospital, and this information comes from Dr. George Burkley ... I asked him the condition of Governor Connally, and have they removed the bullet from him.... Dr. Burkley said that to his knowledge he still has the bullet in him.... This was after we got into the hospital after the shooting, sir, between then and 2 o'clock."[1]

Pretty amazing testimony, correct? Well, believe it or not, this snippet of sworn testimony was basically totally ignored by the research community. Why? I believe because there was nothing to back it up. Tantalizing? Yes. Proof? Maybe; maybe not.

Fast forward to 1991.

I obtained roughly 15 hours of unedited WFAA/ABC footage from 11/22-11/24/63 that was aired once again, uncut, in 1983 for the 20th anniversary. WFAA ran this only one time, some guy from the Dallas area recorded it on VHS tapes and, luckily, it landed in the hands of a collector from Canada. It was from this gentleman that I obtained the tapes.

---

1   2 H 91.

In the midst of all this lengthy and daunting video footage was this gem: Dr. Robert R. Shaw's Press Conference (Connally's chief surgeon), 7:00 CST 11/22/63.2 Dr. Shaw tells millions of people around the world the following: "The bullet is in the leg … it hasn't been removed … it will be removed before he goes to the recovery room."

Wow.

What about CE399 (the stretcher bullet) that entered the record around *five* hours earlier?

AP dispatch/*Atlanta Constitution*, 11/23/63, a day after the press conference, quotes Dr. Shaw: "[The Governor] seems to have been struck by just one bullet.… We know the wound of entrance was along the right shoulder. He was shot from above … [the bullet] entered the back of his chest and moved outward.… It emerged from his chest and struck his wrist and thigh.… The bullet is still in his leg."

Needless to say, Dr. Shaw doubted that CE399 caused the Connally wrist wound.[3] Shaw also remarked: a bullet had entered the front of JFK's throat and "coursed downward into his lung [and] was removed in the Bethesda Naval Hospital where the autopsy was performed."[4] In addition, Shaw was also on record as saying: "The assassin was behind him [JFK], yet the bullet entered at the front of his neck. Mr. Kennedy must have turned to his left to talk to Mrs. Kennedy or to wave to someone."[5] Shaw further told author Anthony Summers: "Dr. Robert Shaw … has never been satisfied that the "magic bullet" caused all his patient's injuries."[6] For his part, Dr.

Dr. Robert Shaw

George Thomas Shires, who also operated on Governor Connally and, later, on Oswald, also testified that did not think JFK and Connally were struck by the same bullet.[7]

But back to Shaw's videotaped statement:

"The bullet is in the leg … it hasn't been removed … it will be removed before he goes to the recovery room."[8]

2   *Treachery In Dallas by Walt Brown* (1995), p. 158: video snippet provided to author.

3   4 H 101-117 and 6 H 83-95 / testimony; 4 H 113-114; see also pages 73 and 90 of *Best Evidence* and numerous references in Post Mortem.

4   11/27/63 *New York Herald -Tribune*: article by Martin Steadman.

5   11/29/63 *Houston Post*.

6   1978 interview with Anthony Summers (see *Conspiracy*, pages 36 and 540). See also Shaw's powerful anti-single bullet theory statements on JFK: The Case for Conspiracy DVD.

7   6 H 104-113 / testimony.

8   See the video here: https://www.youtube.com/watch?v=aQ8NJwq58Fg.

Additional note: in an FBI report dated 11/22/63 from Alan Belmont to Clyde Tolson, it is duly noted that a bullet "was lodged behind the President's ear" when, officially, this bullet should obviously not exist.[9] What's more, there are photos of the alleged bullet in question.[10]

ITEM #2: VIDEO EVIDENCE OF A SECRET SERVICE AGENT BEING REMOVED FROM THE AREA OF THE REAR OF THE LIMOUSINE

Unbelievably, also back in 1991 from this very same large video source, the aforementioned WFAA/ABC videos from 11/22/63, I made yet another amazing discovery: video evidence of a Secret Service agent being ordered away from the rear of the limousine. This particular clip I later showed during major conference presentations in 1995, 1996 and 1997, as well as on The History Channel in 2003 for *The Men Who Killed Kennedy* (later also shown on Newsmax TV in 2019-2020) and in the DVD/Blu Ray, *A Coup in Camelot*. In the video, one can see agent Donald J. Lawton[11] jogging at the rear of the limousine on JFK's side only to be recalled by none other than Emory P. Roberts, who rises in his seat in the follow-up car and, using his voice and several hand-gestures, orders Lawton to cease and desist.

As the ARRB's Doug Horne wrote in a memo dated 4/16/96, based on viewing the aforementioned video shown during the author's presentation at a 1995 research conference: "The bafflement of the agent who is twice waved off of the limousine is clearly evident. This unambiguous and clearly observed behavior would seem to be corroboration that the change in security procedure which was passed to SA Clint Hill earlier in the week by ASAIC Floyd Boring of the Secret Service White House Detail was very recent, ran contrary to standing procedure, and that not everyone on the White House Detail involved in Presidential protection had been informed of this change." In regard to the Love Field video, former agent Larry Newman told me he "never saw that before." This clip has become a You Tube sensation and was later shown in the 2009 Discovery Channel documentary *Secrets of the Secret Service* (I was an uncredited researcher). Most everyone who sees the clip is astounded by what they see – Emory Roberts rises in his seat, uses hand gestures, and obviously says something to Lawton before Lawton speaks. Only then does Lawton stop, turn, and raise his arms three times high in the air in response to

---

9   *High Treason* by Harrison Livingstone and Robert Groden (1998 edition), pages 560-561.
10   *High Treason* by Harrison Livingstone and Robert Groden (1998 edition), pages 562 and photo on next page.
11   25 H 787.

what Roberts said and did. Agent Landis even makes room for Lawton on the running board and none of the people in the car can be seen reacting positively to what Lawton is expressing. Agent Don Lawton told me on 11/15/95: "JFK was very personable ... very warm. Everyone felt bad. It was our job to protect the President. You still have regrets, remorse. Who knows, if they had left guys on the back of the car ... you can hindsight yourself to death." A friend of Lawton's said he felt guilty and kept saying 'I should have been there [on the back of the car].'[12]

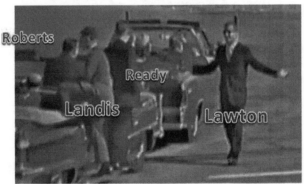

Secret Service agent Don Lawton being recalled by Shift Leader Emory Roberts at Love Field.

In fact, TWO agents were jogging with the limousine at Love Field, Henry Rybka (left) and Don Lawton. Rybka is literally out of the picture by the time Lawton, by himself, appears in the WFAA/ABC black and white video footage (Rybka only appears in newsreel film out of the WFAA camera angle).

Postscript: in a recent discovery, it turns out that Lawton also worked the Secret Service follow-up vehicle and jogged briefly beside the presidential limousine that very same morning in Fort Worth:

---

12   *Idaho State Journal* 11/24/13.

Item #3: CIA presence at Parkland Hospital

Secret Service agent Andy Berger[13] (who would go on to drive the hearse containing JFK's body out of Parkland) reported meeting the following person at Parkland Hospital shortly after the assassination: an "unidentified CIA agent" who had credentials. This report was pretty much overlooked by everyone until I pointed it out to researchers back in 1991. Interestingly, there are not one but two specific candidates for the CIA agent in question.

Hugh Huggins (aka Hugh Howell), Marine and undercover CIA agent, 4/55 to 10/65. Huggins claims, among other things, to have been at both Parkland and Bethesda on 11/22/63: "I distinctly saw an entry wound in the left temple. To my knowledge, only two other people beside myself have admitted to seeing this wound. It was assumed to be a blood clot by the doctors at Parkland, but it was an entry wound, and it could not have been fired from the rear. The bullet from this wound exited the right side of the president's head, blowing out a section of skull and obscuring the entry wound of a second bullet that struck him from the right front almost simultaneously. There were two large, separate holes in the upper right side of the head, separated by about three-quarters of an inch of bone matter and skin tissue. The wound in the throat, although greatly enlarged by a tracheostomy, was also an entry wound. All the wounds had a puffy, torn appearance as though they had been probed prior to the autopsy. There was also an entry wound high in the back, between the neck and the shoulder. It had penetrated approximately the depth of one finger joint – I actually put my small finger into the hole – then made a forty-five degree turn to the left. To my knowledge, this bullet never left the body."[14]

Phyllis Bartlett, the chief telephone operator at the hospital, recalled conversing at the time of the assassination with a man fitting Hugh Howell's description. "My little office was overflowing with as many as fifty people at once back then," she said, "but I do remember talking to a short man with a crewcut who identified himself in that capacity [CIA], and I do believe he said his name was Howell."[15]

The other candidate for being the unidentified CIA agent, or perhaps another one altogether, is Colonel William C. Bishop, CIA contract agent: "Over at Dallas' Parkland Hospital ... another military man was standing

---

13   Report: 18 H 795.

14   1993 interview (s) with Bill Sloan for *JFK: Breaking the Silence* (1993), Chapter 9, pp. 175-189 [Includes photo of Huggins circa 1962].

15   March 1993 interview with Bill Sloan for *JFK: Breaking the Silence*, p. 185.

OPTIONAL FORM NO. 10
5010-106

UNITED STATES GOVERNMENT

PAGE # 1

Memorandum

TO : Chief James J. Rowley

DATE: November 30, 1963

Confidential

FROM : SA Berger, 1-16 - White House Detail

SUBJECT: Activities of this Special Agent in Dallas, Texas, on Friday, November 22, 1963.

On Friday, November 22, 1963, this Special Agent was a member of the 4:00PM - 12:00MN shift under ATSAIC Stout which departed Fort Worth, Texas via USAF # 6970 at 11:20 A.M. arriving at Dallas, Texas, Love Field, at 11:40 A.M. Upon deplaning we were met by SA Lawson, the White House Detail Advance Agent, who instructed us to depart for the Dallas Trade Mart in waiting unmarked Dallas Police cars. Upon arriving at the Trade Mart, I reported to SA Grant, another White House Detail Advance Agent, who assigned me my designated post which was the press area in the second balcony.

When I received word from a newspaper man that the President had been shot I immediately went downstairs to tell ATSAIC Stout, who at this time was confirming the incident. At this time I saw Doctor Hurkley and Chief Hendricks and asked them to accompany me to Parkland Hospital in a Police car which they did. Upon arriving at the hospital I assumed a post in the entrance of the emergency room. The remainder of the 4:00PM - 12:00MN shift then arrived with SA Johnsen being posted with me. Soon after Mr. Dave Powers asked where the priest was. With SA Johnsen holding our post the reporting agent went to the outside of the hospital where I saw two Catholic priests who I asked to accompany me to the emergency room.

Shortly thereafter FBI agent Vincent E. Drain, commission book # 5067, Dallas office arrived at the room entrance. He showed me his credentials & said he had received a telephone call from Director Hoover telling him to make himself available to us. This information was conveyed to ASAIC Kellerman. When I inquired of Agent Drain who the unidentified male was who accompanied him, he replied that he was a doctor friend of his. The agent & unidentified male then proceeded to the end of the hall. Approximately 5 minutes subsequent to the visit of agent Drain a unidentified CIA agent, after showing his credentials said that he would be available.

At approximately 1:30 PM, the Chief Supervising nurse, a Mrs Nelson started to enter the emergency room with an unidentified male(WM, 45yrs, 6'2", 185-190lbs, grey hair) As the reporting agent and SA Johnsen started to ask his identity he shouted that he was a FBI. Just as we began to ask for his credentials he abruptly attempted to enter the emergency room and had to be forcibly restrained by us. ASAIC Kellerman then appeared and asked this individual to go to the end of the hall.

Confidential

Continued on PAGE #2

Secret Service agent Andy Berger's largely ignored report.
COMMISSION EXHIBIT 1024—Continued

in the doorway to Trauma Room 1. This was Colonel William Bishop, who had been working for months with the anti-Castro Cuban exiles on behalf of the CIA. "I had been in Palm Beach at the Berkeley Hotel," Bishop told me [author Dick Russell] in 1990, "when I received a phone call telling me to be in Dallas on the morning of November 21. I wasn't the only Army officer called, that's all I can say about that. I was flown to Dallas by military aircraft and checked into a Holiday Inn, at which time I received instructions that I was to make sure the press had proper credentials at the Trade Mart when Kennedy came to speak the next afternoon. I was in position and waiting for his arrival, when I heard over a squad car parked at the curb that shots had been fired in Dealey Plaza. I commandeered a police car and ordered the driver to take me directly to Parkland Hospital. With the ID I had, that was not a problem. There the Secret Service instructed me to secure the area outside the Trauma Room and make myself available to the First Lady or medical staff."[16]

Incredibly, former Secret Service agent Gerald Blaine writes on page 233 of his book *The Kennedy Detail*, with regard to Parkland Hospital: "A representative of the CIA appeared a while later."

ITEM #4: THE DEATH OF A SECRET SERVICE AGENT WHO WOULD HAVE DRIVEN KENNEDY IN DALLAS A MONTH BEFORE THE ASSASSINATION

Secret Service agent Thomas B. Shipman, one of three agents who drove President Kennedy or his Secret Service follow-up vehicle on many trips between Election Night 1960 and the Fall of 1963, died 10/14/63[17] of an alleged heart attack at (of all places) Camp David, the month before the Kennedy assassination.[18] Where is Shipman's death certificate? At present, it is unavailable and, without an exhumation and toxicology tests, at this late juncture, a verdict of "heart attack" is a country doctor "catch-all" that is unsatisfactory and inconclusive, given the subject at hand (a presumably fit Secret Service agent who had to pass annual physicals and perform the rare honor of driving several presidents).

It was not until 2013, thanks to the help of researcher Deb Galentine, that an obscure news article was found that mentioned the death of Shipman (*The News*, Frederick, Maryland, 10/16/63). After a coroner's report furnished the day after his death, Shipman was quickly buried only two days later. Obviously, no toxicology tests were performed, as these can take quite a while, often weeks and sometimes months to process. In the last couple of years, I have discovered similar newspaper articles, more data, and new information from surviving members of Shipman's family. Former agent Winston Lawson wrote to me in a letter dated 1/20/04: "Tom Shipman, also a driver, died of a heart attack while up at Camp Da-

---

16   5/8/90 interview of Colonel William C. Bishop by Dick Russell for *The Man Who Knew Too Much*, numerous – see esp. pages 570-571 [see also *Who's Who in the JFK Assassination* by Michael Benson (1993), pp. 40-41 and *Murder in Dealey Plaza* by James Fetzer (2000), pages 68, 259, 404.
17   Interestingly, on the very same day that Ruth Paine phoned the Texas School Book Depository about a job opening for Oswald: *JFK and the Unspeakable* by James Douglass (2010), page 171.
18   See the author's books *The Not-So-Secret Service* (2017) and *Who's Who in the Secret Service* (2018).

vid, prior to retirement. I don't know the year and couldn't find out. I believe Sam Kinney found his body. They would have roomed together in one of the cabins up there."

Researcher Tyler Newcomb, the son of author Fred Newcomb of *Murder From Within* fame, wrote to me on 2/5/14: "I got a private eye to try and look into any information on him (Shipman). He apparently died of a heart attack and his widow Jacqueline just plain disappeared from what I found. No trace whatsoever after the funeral. Shipman had 2 brothers I believe and both are deceased." While I found several similar contemporary news articles mentioning Shipman's death (all only available after paying a fee and searching the archives), Tyler was kind enough to forward this information on to me, as well:

From the Associated Press, "White House Chauffeur Dies at Camp David," *Washington Post*, October 16, 1963, p.C9: "Thomas Shipman, 51, one of President Kennedy's Secret Service drivers, died Monday at the presidential retreat at nearby Camp David. The cause of death was not immediately determined pending a coroner's report. Mr. Shipman, a native of Washington, was a District policeman from 1936 until 1950 when he transferred to the White House police force. He became a Secret Service agent in 1954. Mr. Shipman occasionally drove the President's limousine, but, more normally, drove the carload of Secret Service agents who follow directly behind the President. He is survived by his wife, Jacqueline, of the home address, 3817 Van Ness St. NW."

New information was gleaned from unsolicited contacts from Shipman's family in 2015. Christine Jones, Shipman's niece, wrote to me on 10/3/15: "Jacqueline was my mother's older sister and went by 'Jackie.' She grew up in Pittsburgh, and her maiden name was Maglaughlin. Her parents lived at 7004 Meade Place in Pittsburgh until her mother, Marion E. Maglaughlin died in July of 1975. Uncle Tom and Aunt Jackie had a daughter named Laura, who was approximately five years old when her dad died. Jackie and Laura later moved to Colorado where Laura still lives and works under the name Laura Shipman-Hamblin. Jackie was Tom's second wife. Laura knew Tom's children from his first marriage, and I guess that they are in their 60's or 70's. Tom and my mother were going to meet for dinner the day that JFK came to Dallas. (My mom and dad moved to Texas in 1950 and Dallas was our home.) Prior to the scheduled dinner with my mom, Tom expressed concern to her that JFK refused to use the protective bubble for the car to ensure his safety. During their phone conversation, Tom said that he was prepared to pull quickly out of the motorcade and do whatever was necessary to protect JFK if anything was to happen. When my mom received the call that Tom had died, she was shocked. According to Aunt Jackie, Tom had received a clean bill of health for his annual physical the month before his death. Aunt Jackie told my mom that after Tom had eaten lunch at Camp David, he told others that he did not feel well and went to take a nap. Sometime during the nap, he suffered a heart attack. The fact that no autopsy was ordered, and that Aunt Jackie was encouraged to bury Tom quickly, seemed strange."

In a follow-up message the next day, Christine Jones wrote: "The following information is what I remember from conversations with my mother, Josephine Maglaughlin-Leonard: Tom Shipman called his sister-in-law, Josephine Maglaughlin-Leonard (Jackie Shipman's younger sister and only sibling) when he found out that he would be in Dallas with JFK. The exact date of that phone call is not known but it was before Tom went to Camp David. It was during this same call that Tom expressed his concern to Josephine about JFK refusing to use the protective bubble and that he was prepared to quickly pull out of the motorcade if anything was to happen. Josephine was looking forward to meeting Tom for dinner when he was in Dallas since she had not seen him in 10 years. Jackie called her sister, Josephine to tell her that Tom died at Camp David. During that conversation, Jackie told Josephine that there would not be an autopsy and that she was encouraged to bury Tom quickly. My mother (Josephine) said that Tom had received his annual physical a month earlier and received a clean bill of health. (I can't verify the timing of Tom's annual physical.) Josephine stated that Tom's death came as a shock to her and her sister, Jackie. The details that I outlined in the e-mail was information that Josephine (my mother) shared with me when I was an adult. I did not ask my mother for specific dates or timing regarding the circumstances she described to me. Also, I never met my uncle and only learned about him through my mother, Josephine. She held Tom Shipman in high regard and said that JFK would have survived if Tom had been the driver that day in Dallas."

On 10/6/15, I had a nice conversation with Laura Shipman, Tom Shipman's youngest daughter. She corroborated and did not dispute anything her cousin Christine Jones (her father's niece) had to say; no wet blankets. She also said her older sister always criticized Greer. Their father has a box of items that she was going to look through and scan for me, as well. In addition, her brother said her dad thought that JFK would be killed one day! It is true that Tom Shipman knew of JFK's upcoming Dallas trip, had planned to be part of it, and arranged a dinner meeting with his sister in law Josephine who lived in Dallas since 1950. Josephine was Christine Jones' mother. One more thing – she also views it as suspicious that her father was quickly buried and corroborates Christine that her mother was urged to bury him quickly! She also said that, when her father passed away, Kennedy's personal physician, Dr. George Burkley, took care of everything.

Agents didn't always travel in the presidential helicopter. Left to right: Crew chief, SA Paul Burns, Driver Tom Shipman, Dr. George Burkley, SA Jack Ready, and SA Jerry Blaine. (PERSONAL COLLECTION OF GERALD BLAINE)

(From Gerald Blaine's book) He includes a photo of Tom Shipman (appears to be the Conservation Tour, shortly before Tom's death), yet nothing is written about Shipman or his untimely passing in his book, nor in any of Clint Hill's three books:

Interestingly, Shipman's final motorcade had him driving at the Mary Pinchot Meyer estate on 9/24/63. Shipman then dies 10/14/63. Mary Pinchot Meyer, Kennedy's lover and the ex-wife of CIA officer Cord Meyer, dies 10/12/64. 10/16/63, two days after Shipman's death and the date of his burial – *Cord Meyer of the CIA* and others have lunch with JFK.[19] In addition, Camp David, formerly known as Shangri-La by FDR, also served as a training ground for the OSS, the forerunner of the CIA.[20]

---

19   Secret Service log via JFK Library.
20   From *Reilly of the White House*, page 67: "With the coming of war Shangri-La served him well. We had a good deal of trouble finding this vacation spot which met with his demands that it be within a reasonable driving distance of Washington and our insistence that it provide him a secure home. Shangri-La was in a state park on Catoctin Mountain, near Thurmont, Maryland. Originally there had been three separate camps there. They had been built for underprivileged children for use in the summer. Colonel Wild Bill Donovan's "cloak and dagger" boys had taken over one camp for training. The Marines had another for the same purpose, and the Boss had the third. The OSS men were training in sabotage and other weird and unpleasant phases of underground

Shipman's grandson, John Thomas, wrote to me on 10/27/17: "My grandfather, Thomas Shipman was a good and honorable man. I was always told how proud he was that he protected the President of the United States and that he would have sacrificed his life to save the President. If John Kennedy's assassination was planned by anyone within the Secret Service I cannot imagine that he would have ignored it, I believe that he would have taken active steps to prevent it. However, I am probably not an objective commentator on this matter."

Author Christopher Fulton obtained a statement from an agent that Shipman was indeed murdered.[21]

Secret Service agent (driver) Thomas B. Shipman driving the Kennedys:

ITEM #5: SECRET SERVICE AGENTS AND OTHER PROMINENT PRINCIPAL WITNESSES DID NOT BELIEVE THE WARREN COMMISSION'S SINGLE BULLET THEORY!

Secret Service agent Clint Hill waited until his third book *Five Presidents*, published in 2016, to reveal that he does not believe the single bullet theory, the keystone to believing that Oswald acted alone[22]:

> I was satisfied with the commission's conclusion that Oswald acted alone, and to this day, I believe that to be the case—there has never been any factual evidence to prove otherwise. The one conclusion with which I disagree is the "Magic Bullet Theory"—the notion that the first shot which passed through President Kennedy's neck then entered Governor Connally's body. Governor and Mrs. Connally and I were all of the same opinion—having been up-close witnesses—that the governor's wounds were caused by the second shot, the one that did not hit President Kennedy.

warfare, and their camp was necessarily rather overloaded with dark and mysterious foreigners. However, we didn't worry too much, because we had plenty of Marines around."

21   *The Inheritance* by Christopher Fulton (2018), page 292.
22   *Five Presidents* by Clint Hill (2016), page 178.

From his Secret Service report and Warren Commission testimony, Hill was already on record stating that the right rear of JFK's head was missing and that the wound on the back was indeed a back wound, not a back-of-the-neck wound.[23] In fact, Hill is still stating these very same things to this day in his books co-authored by Lisa McCubbin: *The Kennedy Detail* (2010), *Mrs. Kennedy and Me* (2012), *Five Days in November* (2013), and *Five Presidents* (2016), as well as numerous media appearances 2010-present. However, this is the first time he came out publicly against the single bullet theory, the keystone to believing the Warren Commission's central conclusion that Oswald acted alone.

Likewise, Secret Service agent Paul Landis, who stated in his original reports that a shot came from the front[24], also waited until 2016 to reveal that he does not believe the single bullet theory[25]:

> He sounds almost proud of not having read the Warren Report, and said they got it right about no conspiracy and that Oswald as the lone actor, but blew it with the single-bullet theory. That theory holds that a single shot struck the President and also wounded Governor John Connally.
>
> And "I was never interviewed by the Warren Commission and still don't understand why," he said Saturday.

Secret Service agent Bill Greer testified to the Warren Commission: "...they [the autopsy doctors] saw this hole in the right shoulder or back of the head, and in the back ... this wound was in the back ... they took a lot of X-rays, we looked at them and couldn't find any trace of any bullet anywhere in the X-rays at all, nothing showed on the X-rays where this bullet or lead could have gone ... in the soft part of the shoulder.... I believe the doctors probed to see if they could find that there was a bullet there.... I questioned one of the doctors in there about that, and when we found out that they had found a bullet in Dallas, I questioned the doctor about it and he said if they were using pressure on the chest that it could very well have been, come back out, where it went in at, that is what they said at the time.... I hadn't heard anything like that, any traces of it going on through."[26]

---

23   18 H 740-745: 11/30/63 report of activities on 11/22/63; 2 H 138-144 /testimony (3/9/64).
24   18 H 758-759: report dated 11/27/63 – "My reaction at this time was that the shot came from somewhere towards the front."; 18 H 751-757: detailed report dated 11/30/63 – "my reaction at this time was that the shot came from somewhere towards the front, right-hand side of the road."
25   https://www.cleveland.com/metro/2016/11/shaker_heights_man_guarding_jfk_witnes.html.
26   2 H 124 and 127/ testimony (3/9/64).

During a rare taped interview Greer did with researcher Gary Murr on 12/6/70,[27] Greer revealed the following information: When told that Connally has always insisted that he was hit with a different bullet from JFK, Greer said, "I feel that way, too. They [the Warren Commission] had lawyers working on it ... these lawyers had already made up their mind." Greer also believed that the back wound, which he referred to as being in the "back of the shoulder," did not go through, and said that was also the first thought of the autopsy doctors in attendance.

During Greer's 2/28/78 HSCA interview, the former agent said: "He was puzzled about the single bullet (399) theory. He could not see how one bullet could have caused both Kennedy and Connally such extensive wounds." The interview report continues: "Greer recalls Kellerman going to a telephone and talking to someone about a bullet found in Dallas. The doctors turned Kennedy over and found the bullet hole in his shoulder. He indicated a point on his right shoulder, which approximated the spot. He said one of the doctors inserted a metal probe in Kennedy's back, which only went in a short way. Greer says he asked the doctor if the bullet in [the] back could have worked itself out during heart message. The doctors continued to take x-rays, looking for lead, but they couldn't find where the bullet went."[28]

Once the autopsy at Bethesda Naval Hospital was underway, Greer "said that a bullet had been found on a stretcher – or rather as it fell from a stretcher – in Parkland Hospital ... could this be the bullet that went into the neck and, in the jostling of the President on the stretcher, fell out?" As author Jim Bishop reported (thru his interviews with Greer and Kellerman)," Greer's thesis had a supporter. Roy Kellerman ... said he remembered a Parkland doctor astride the chest of the dead President, applying artificial respiration. Kellerman... thought the bullet in the back ... might have been squeezed out by manual pressure..."[29]

For his part, Secret Service agent Roy Kellerman testified to the Warren Commission[30]: "A Colonel Finck – during the examination of the President, from the hole that was in the shoulder, and with a probe, and we were standing right alongside of him, he is probing inside the shoulder with his instrument and I said, 'Colonel, where did it go?' He said, 'There are no lanes for an outlet of this entry in this man's shoulder' ... I said,

27   See my book *Survivor's Guilt*, page 205.
28   See also *A Fox Among Wolves* by Francis X. O'Neill, Jr (2011), pages 14-15.
29   *The Day Kennedy was Shot*, page 498,530; see also Tomlinson-2 H 412; Greer-2 H 127; Kellerman-2 H 93.
30   2 H 73-74, 78-82, 85, 90-91, 93/testimony (3/9/64).

'Colonel, would it have been possible that while he was on the stretcher in Dallas that it works itself out?' And he said, 'Yes.'"[31]

Dr. James J. Humes, Chief autopsy doctor at Bethesda, testified to the Warren Commission: [CE399 involved in Connally's right wrist wound?] "I think that that is most unlikely.... The reason I believe it most unlikely that this missile could have inflicted either of these wounds is that this missile is basically intact; its jacket appears to me to be intact, and I do not understand how it could possibly have left fragments in either of these locations." [CE399-Connally's thigh wound?] "I think that extremely unlikely.... I can't conceive of where they [bullet fragments] came from this missile."[32] Furthermore, "According to Commander Humes, the autopsy surgeons hypothesized that the bullet might have been forced out of the back of the President on the application of external heart message after they were advised that a bullet had been found on a stretcher at Parkland Hospital."[33] According to the FBI agents present at the autopsy: "During the latter stages of this autopsy, Dr. Humes located an opening which appeared to be a bullet hole which was below the shoulders and two inches to the right of the middle line of the spinal column. This opening was probed by Dr. Humes with the finger, at which time it was determined that the trajectory of the missile entering at this point had entered at a downward position of 45 to 60 degrees. Further probing determined that the distance travelled by this missile was a short distance inasmuch as the end of the opening could be felt with the finger." Continuing further: "... since cardiac massage had been performed at Parkland Hospital, it was entirely possible that through such movement the bullet had worked its way back out of the point of entry and had fallen on the stretcher."[34]

Needless to say, both FBI agents (James Sibert and Francis X. O'Neill) who attended the autopsy never believed the single bullet theory,[35] nor did FBI Director J. Edgar Hoover.[36] James Sibert told author William Law: "I told them before they asked me to come up for the [ARRB] deposition, I said: 'Well, before I come up, I want to tell you one thing: I don't buy the single bullet theory.... In the first place, they moved the bullet wound, the one in the back ... here's the pathetic part – they found the wound in the

31   See also *A Fox Among Wolves* by Francis X. O'Neill, Jr (2011), pages 14-15.
32   2 H 347-376 / testimony (3/16/64, with Boswell and Finck present).
33   3/11/64 interview with the WC's Arlen Specter and Joseph A. Ball, Esq. (memo dated 3/12/64 on the matter, Specter to Rankin) [see *Post Mortem* by Harold Weisberg, pp. 539-540].
34   11/26/63 FBI (Sibert & O'Neill) report [see *Post Mortem* by Harold Weisberg, pp. 533-536]; see also *A Fox Among Wolves* by Francis X. O'Neill, Jr (2011), pages 14-15.
35   Numerous, including *In The Eye of History* by William Matson Law (2005/2013) and *The JFK Assassination* by James DiEugenio (2018), page 141.
36   *Into The Nightmare* by Joseph McBride (2013), pages 114 and 119.

back, of course, they took the wound in the neck as a straight tracheotomy and they didn't find out that it was a bullet wound until the next morning when they called Parkland. ... See, the way they got the single-bullet theory, was by moving that back wound up to the base of the neck. ... There is no way I will swallow that. They can't put enough sugar on it for me to bite it. That bullet was too low in the back.'"[37] O'Neill stated in his book: "As God as my witness, at no time during the autopsy or at its completion did any of the doctors offer any explanation other than the back wound was the result of a bullet that worked its way out of the president's back, and dropped on the Dallas stretcher."[38] Fellow FBI agent Don Adams, based in the Dallas office in 1964, also did not believe the single bullet theory.[39]

Secret Service agent Thomas "Lem" Johns said "If you get the tie [JFK was wearing] nicked by a different bullet, you've got a second gunman – simple as that. I've never thought that was out of the question."[40] Regarding the shooting, Johns stated, "The first two [shots] sounded like they were on the side of me towards the grassy knoll."[41] Johns also told me in 2004 that he thought a shot came from the grassy knoll, as he also later stated on the 2011 DVD *Lem Johns: Secret Service Man.*

For his part, fellow autopsy doctor J. Thornton Boswell said "that all three autopsy doctors probed the back wound with their fingers but could not penetrate past an inch or so. A thin metal probe was also used but no bullet track could be located."[42]

The third autopsy doctor, Pierre Finck, told the Warren Commission that he agreed with the testimony of Humes. Finck also agreed with him that all of Connally's wounds were not made by CE399: "...there are too many fragments described in that wrist."[43]

Dr. Joseph Dolce, chief consultant in wound ballistics for the U. S. Army, who supervised the ballistics test for the Warren Commission, stated on video: "So they gave us the original rifle – the Mannlicher Carcano, plus 100 bullets, 6.5 millimeters, and in every instance [of firing into cadaver wrists] the front of the bullet was smashed. It's impossible for a bullet to strike a bone, even at low velocity and still come out with a perfectly

37   *In The Eye of History: Disclosures in the JFK Assassination Medical Evidence* by William Law (2005/2015).

38   *A Fox Among Wolves* by Francis X. O'Neill, Jr (2011), page 15.

39   *From an Office Building with a High-Powered Rifle: One FBI Agent's View of the JFK Assassination* by Don Adams (2012), pages 119-132 .

40   February 1999 *Newsday* article written by Michael Dorman.

41   HSCA interview with Johns, 8/8/78: RIF# 180-10074-10079.

42   interview with Josiah Thompson (*Six Seconds in Dallas*; see also *Crossfire*, p. 371, and *Who's Who in the JFK Assassination*, pp. 46-47).

43   2 H 377-384 / testimony.

normal tip ... under no circumstances do I believe that this bullet could hit the wrist and still not be deformed. We proved it by our experiments."[44]

Secret Service agent Sam Kinney told me that he saw all three shots hit and there was no missed shot.[45] He told the HSCA on 2/26/78 that "he immediately recognized the first sound as that of gunfire, realizing that it was a "shot from over our right shoulder" which hit the President in the throat ... the second shot (hit Connally and) left Connally's back open. The third shot hit the president."

On the NBC program the *Today* show on 11/22/93, Kinney gave his first and last television interview. He stated: "[after the first shot] I saw the President grab his neck [indicating]. Then there were two following shots: pow, pow." Kinney told me in lengthy interviews between 1992-1994 that he saw all three shots hit and there was no missed shot (first shot hit JFK, second hit Connally, third hit JFK).

Presidential aide Dave Powers, riding in the same car as Kinney, stated that the same bullet that hit JFK did not hit Connally.[46] Like Kinney, he also stated that all three shots hit the two men in the car (first shot hit JFK, second hit Connally, third hit JFK).[47]

Assistant Press Secretary Malcolm Kilduff stated in a 11/22/66 AP article found in the *Cedar Rapids Gazette*: "Kilduff says he does disagree with the Commission's finding that the first bullet that struck Kennedy and passed through his neck was the one that wounded Texas Gov. Connally. A second shot in the head killed Kennedy. 'In my mind,' Kilduff said, 'there were three shots fired. I have verified that with other people who were riding in the same car. I have verified it with Secret Service Agents' ... Kilduff said he had talked to Connally who agrees he was hit by a separate bullet, that the governor said he heard the first shot and was turning to look back when he was hit." Kilduff also told author Harrison Livingstone: "I do not accept the so-called 'Magic' Bullet Theory... No, I can't buy that one... I have [sic] been swimming with Connally in the pool at the White House, and I saw a clean scar in his back... I talked to Connally about it several times, and his feeling on that and mine are precisely the same."[48]

Secret Service agent Gerald O'Rourke told the *Rocky Mountain News* on 11/20/03 that "The trajectory of one of the shots could not have been made from a gunman on the sixth floor of the Texas Book Depository.

---

44   *Reasonable Doubt: The Single Bullet Theory*, A & E Network 1988 (also a VHS release).
45   10/19/92, 3/5/94, and 4/15/94 interviews with Vince Palamara.
46   *Legacy of Secrecy* by Lamar Waldron (2008), page 214.
47   *JFK: The Day The Nation Cried* video/DVD 1988.
48   *High Treason 2*, pp. 443-450: 4/17/91 interview with Harry Livingstone.

The shot entered Kennedy's body at his lower back and [allegedly] traveled up, to exit near his throat."

Eyewitness S.M. Holland stated: "[The] Warren Commission is in error on that because I was a eyewitness to that the same bullet that hit President Kennedy did not hit Governor Connally. At the first bullet, the President slumped over and Governor Connally made his turn to the right and then back to the left, and that's when the second shot was fired and knocked him down on the floorboard."[49]

Dr. William Osborne, one of the doctors who operated on Governor Connally, wrote to me on 9/3/98: "As far as any theory about a single bullet, I guess theoretically it could have evolved from a single bullet, however it is also quite possible, maybe even probable that there was more than one bullet fired, and maybe even one from the grassy knoll."

Dr. Robert Shaw, Connally's chief surgeon, was an ardent critic of the single bullet theory.[50] As mentioned previously, Dr. Tom Shires also did not think JFK and Connally were struck by the same bullet.[51] And, as most people know, the Connallys themselves always disputed the Warren Commission's single bullet theory.[52]

Dr. Donald E. Jackson[53] wrote to me on 9/8/98: "I continue to be dissatisfied with the explanation of the Warren Commission. The reason for my skepticism is linked to discrepancies in descriptions of the Kennedy wounds between the Parkland Emergency Room and the autopsy findings. Drs. McClelland, Perry, and Jenkins gave accurate descriptions of the wounds as they saw them in the Emergency Room. The descriptions in Washington were radically different. In addition, Dr. McClelland and several other colleagues went to Washington and reviewed the findings with the medical authorities. It seemed at that time, that they then reversed themselves on the findings that they had described in Dallas. I do not question their veracity but I am confused by this discrepancy."

Dr. William Risk[54] wrote to me on 9/8/98: "as a physician, I have the feeling there was more than one 'shooter' and more than one bullet in-

---

49   *Rush to Judgment* film.
50   4 H 101-117 and 6 H 83-95 / testimony; 1978 interview with Anthony Summers (see *Conspiracy*, pages 36 and 540; Interviewed for *Reasonable Doubt* video 1988; Interviewed for *JFK: The Case for Conspiracy* video 1993; *The JFK Assassination* by James DiEugenio (2018), page 134; *Who Really Killed Kennedy?: 50 Years Later: Stunning New Revelations About the JFK Assassination* by Jerome Corsi (2016)- kindle edition.
51   6 H 104-113 / testimony.
52   Many sources- see, for example, the filmed interview of Governor Connally in the Mark Lane film *Rush to Judgment*.
53   21 H 171, 205, 215.
54   3 H 384; January 1964 *Texas State Journal of Medicine* article "Three Patients at Parkland," pages 72 and 73 re: involvement in treatment of LHO

volved because of the nature of the wounds. I would suggest that, if you have not already done so, you get a copy of an article from the *Journal of the Texas Medical Association*, January 1964, entitled "Three Patients at Parkland." This article is a *medical* version of those days. The wounds described there, to me, suggest entrance and exit wounds which differ from the "one bullet theory."[55]

The 1/27/64 Warren Commission Executive Session is quite illuminating with regard to their thoughts on the matter relatively early on:

> **Mr. J. Lee Rankin**: Then there is the great range of material in regard to the wounds, and the autopsy and this point of exit or entrance of the bullet in the front of neck and that all has to be developed much more than we have at the present time.
>
> We have an explanation there in the autopsy that probably a fragment came out the front of the neck, but with the elevation the shot must have come from, and the angle, it seems quite appare[nt] now, since we have the picture of where the bullet entered in the back, that the bullet entered below the shoulder blade to the right of the backbone, which is below the place where the picture shows the bullet came out in the neckband of the shirt in front, and the bullet, according to the autopsy didn't strike any bone at all, that particular bullet, and go through.
>
> So that how it could turn and–
>
> **Rep. Hale Boggs**: I thought I read that bullet just went in a finger's length.
>
> **Mr. Rankin**: That is what they first said. They reached in and they could feel where it came, it didn't go any further than that, about part of the finger or something, part of the autopsy, and then they proceeded to reconstruct where they thought the bullet went, the path of it, and which is, we have to go into considerable items and try to find out how they could reconstruct that when they first said that they couldn't even feel the path beyond part of a finger."

President Lyndon Johnson and Warren Commission member Richard Russell also did not believe the single bullet theory, as a recorded phone conversation proves.[56] On 9/18/64, in a phone conversation with LBJ, Russell said: "They were trying to prove that the same bullet that hit Kennedy first was the one that hit Connally, went through him and through his hand, his bone, into his leg and everything else.... The commission

---

55   See also *The JFK Assassination Debates: Lone Gunman versus Conspiracy* by Michael L. Kurtz (2006), pages 112-114.
56   *The Kennedy Half-Century* by Larry Sabato (2013), page 137.

believes that the same bullet that hit Kennedy hit Connally. Well, I don't believe it." Fellow Commissioners John Sherman Cooper and Hale Boggs also did not accept the single bullet theory.[57] Cooper said: "it seems to me that Governor Connally's statement negates such a conclusion." He later confirmed his stance in an interview for the BBC documentary *The Killing of President Kennedy*.

A member of the HSCA, Congressman Steward B. McKinney of Connecticut, received detailed briefing materials demonstrating that the magic bullet, CE399, could not have caused all the damage it had been alleged to have done[58]

David P. Osborne, a military physician present at the autopsy at Bethesda, told the HSCA that he "thought he recalled seeing an intact slug roll out from the clothing of President Kennedy and onto the autopsy table."[59] Osborne told author David Lifton that a "reasonably clean" and "unmarred" bullet fell from the clothing that was around JFK's body. "The bullet was not deformed in any way … I had that bullet in my hand, and looked at it … I know the Secret Service had it … the Secret Service took it."[60]

Finally, one must keep in mind the official FBI and Secret Service conclusions: All three shots hit within the limousine – without acknowledging the known missed shot that injured bystander James Tague.[61]

Author Sherry Fiester has demonstrated in exhaustive detail that the single bullet theory is a myth.[62]

ITEM #6: SEVERAL PROMINENT PRINCIPALS IN THE CASE BELIEVED THERE WAS A CONSPIRACY

Dr. Gene Coleman Akin, Resident Anesthesiologist, testified to the Warren Commission: "The back of the right occipital-parietal portion of his head was shattered, with brain substance extruding … I assume the right occipital-parietal region was the exit, so to speak, that he had probably been hit on the other side of the head, or at least tangentially in the back of the head … this [the neck wound] must have been an entrance wound…"[63] Akin came forward in 1984 and stated that "when he

---

57   *Into The Nightmare* by Joseph McBride (2013), pages 162-163; *Enemy of the Truth* by Sherry Fiester (2012), page 267.

58   From the newly-released files (in the midst of other interesting material): https://www.archives.gov/files/research/jfk/releases/2018/180-10128-10002.pdf.

59   6/20/78 Outside contact report with the HSCA's Mark Flanagan (RIF#18010102-10415 [see also 7 HSCA 15-16]).

60   11/4/79 interview with David Lifton (*Best Evidence*, Chapter 29: pp. 645-647, in particular).

61   CD1, p. 1; CD87, SS235, p. 1; *Six Seconds in Dallas* by Josiah Thompson (1967), page 64.

62   *Enemy of the Truth* by Sherry Fiester (2012), pages 266-332.

63   6 H 65 and 67 / testimony.

saw President Kennedy in the emergency room on 11/22/63, he thought he saw a bullet entrance wound on the President's forehead. The President was covered with blood in the head area and the back of his head was blown wide open. Akin feels that his observation as to the possible entrance wound on the President's forehead is significant and that he did not mention this item when he was interviewed in 1963-1964 because he did not want to be killed by any conspirators. Akin stated that if this entrance wound was not documented in the Presidential autopsy, then plastic surgery was probably conducted to cover this up."[64]

JAMA reported in 1992: "Robert McClelland, MD, is a respected surgeon who assisted in the last steps of the tracheostomy on President Kennedy. Interviewed in Dallas, he told this reporter that he maintains a "strong opinion" that the fatal head wound came from the front. Pressed on his reasons, he says, 'After I saw the Zapruder film in 1969, I became convinced that the backward lurch of the head had to have come from a shot from the front. Unlike Crenshaw, I do not believe that one can tell the direction from which the bullet came simply by looking at the head wound, as I did, but the wound I observed did appear consistent with a shot from the front. That observation is secondary to my viewing of the Zapruder film, which convinced me that the shots were from the front.'"

McClelland wrote to me in September 1998: "The Zapruder film causes me to believe the wound I drew below is an exit wound in the back of the head, not because of what can be seen about the wound per se on the film (I saw this much better on my direct inspection), but because the shot from the front propelled the President's head and body violently backward and to his left – a bullet from behind could not do this in defiance of the laws of physics and motion ("jet effect" of brain is untenable)."

Dr. Ronald Jones told author David Lifton: "If you brought him in here today, I'd still say he was shot from the front."[65] In a 10/13/98 letter to the author, Jones wrote: "President Kennedy had very thick dark hair that covered the injured area. In my opinion it was in the occipital area in the back of the head. Because the scalp partially covered the wound. I cannot give an exact size of the defect in the skull. There was no obvious injury to the face. The wound in the neck was very small, perhaps no larger than 1/4 of an inch and the wound in the back of the head was much larger. It was for this reason that I initially thought that the injury to the neck was an entrance wound." Jones told the ARRB that during his Warren

64   6/28/84 FBI Memorandum, SA Udo H. Specht to SAC, Dallas, re: interviews with Akin (RIF#124-10158-10449).

65   *Best Evidence* by David Lifton (1988 edition), page 705.

Commission interview with Arlen Specter, he alluded more than once to the throat wound being a wound of entry. Specter seemed to question his expertise with projectiles. When Jones stepped down, Specter followed him out into the hallway. He then said, "I want to tell you something that I don't want you to say anything about. We have people who will testify that they saw the President shot from the front. You can always get people to testify about something. But we are pretty convinced he was shot from the back." Jones said that the message was that although he may have thought the neck wound was an entrance, it wasn't. And that was that. Jones replied that he was only 31 at the time, so he didn't say anything about this exchange. But he did think it was unusual.[66]

Dr. Charles A. Crenshaw,[67] Resident Surgeon, stated: "His entire right cerebral hemisphere appeared to be gone. It looked like a crater – an empty cavity.... From the damage I saw, there was no doubt in my mind that the bullet had entered his head through the front, and as it surgically passed through his cranium, the missile obliterated part of the temporal and all the parietal and occipital lobes before it lacerated the cerebellum…I also identified a small opening about the diameter of a pencil at the midline of his throat to be an entry bullet hole. There was no doubt in my mind about that wound."[68] Crenshaw wrote to me on 8/26/98: "Wound in right rear of head – behind ear – occipital-parietal portion of head."

From the HSCA's Richard Sprague to a file memorandum March 18, 1977: "William F. Illig, an attorney from Erie, Pa., contacted me in Philadelphia this date, advising me that he represents Dr. George G. Burkley, Vice Admiral, U.S. Navy retired, who had been the personal physician for presidents Kennedy and Johnson. Mr. Illig stated that he had a luncheon meeting with his client, Dr. Burkley, this date to take up some tax matters. Dr. Burkley advised him that although he, Burkley, had signed the death certificate of President Kennedy in Dallas, he had never been interviewed and that he has information in the Kennedy assassination indicating that others besides Oswald must have participated. Illig advised me that his client is a very quiet, unassuming person, not wanting any publicity whatsoever, but he, Illig, was calling me with his client's consent and that his client would talk to me in Washington."[69] Dr. Burkley told author Henry

---

66   *Inside The ARRB* by Doug Horne (2009), pages 769-770.
67   WC references to his presence on 11/22/63: 6 H 40 (Baxter), 6 H 31-32 (Mc Clelland), 6 H 80-81 (Salyer), 6 H 141 (Henchcliffe), 6 H 60 (Curtis) +15 H 761: index + 21 H 265; see also January 1964 *Texas State Journal of Medicine* article entitled "Three Patients at Parkland," p. 72.
68   *Conspiracy of Silence* (1992), pages 79 and 86 (and throughout [Includes photos of himself]) [later renamed *Trauma Room One* (2001) and *JFK Has Been Shot* (2013).
69   RIF#180-10086-10295.

Hurt that he believed that President Kennedy's assassination was the result of a conspiracy.[70] Burkley said the very same thing to Professor Michael Kurtz.[71]

Secret Service agent Sam Kinney, the driver of the follow-up car in Dallas, told me that he believed a conspiracy took the life of President Kennedy. "I believe there was a conspiracy," Kinney told me: "This thing was so well set up – whoever did the shooting – he picked that area where he knew there wouldn't be any men by the car." [72] Kinney had also conveyed to the HSCA that he found the notion of conspiracy plausible.[73]

Interestingly, Vincent J. Gullo, a member of the C-130 crew from the 76th Air Transport Squadron from Charleston, South Carolina who were in charge of shipping the presidential limousine and Secret Service follow-up car to and from Washington, D.C., corroborated Kinney on some important details. In a letter to Gullo dated 8/27/98, I wrote "Sam [Kinney] told me that a) he found the piece of the right rear of President Kennedy's skull on the C-130 while en route back to AAFB after the tragedy and b) that one of you guys got sick from seeing the rear of the limousine with all the blood and gore ... do you remember any of these specific events?"

Gullo responded: "... I am totally familiar with the facts as you outline them.... This was a bench mark in my life and I have shared my thoughts on this incident with few individuals – mostly federal agents. I am sure you can understand my reluctance to entertain your questions given the sensitivity of the matter even to this date." Gullo did not respond to my follow-up letter.[74]

With regard to what Kinney told the HSCA (in documents that only became available in the late 1990's): he found "the view of conspiracy plausible for two reasons." First, the view of the Presidential limousine that presented itself from the vantage point of the alleged sniper's nest is consistent with careful planning. From that vantage point, tracking the target through a scope did not require a side-to-side movement but required the use of vertical movement in order to track for distance. SA Kin-

---

70   *Reasonable Doubt*, p. 49 (1982 interview by Henry Hurt + letters of 10/6/82 and 10/14/82).

71   *The JFK Assassination Debates: Lone Gunman versus Conspiracy* by Michael L. Kurtz (2006), pages 39-40.

72   10/19/92, 3/5/94, and 4/15/94 interviews with Vince Palamara.

73   RIF # 180-10078-10493: HSCA summary of an interview with Sam Kinney conducted on 2/26/78 only released in the 1990's, after my interviews.

74   For the record, the members of the 76th Air Transport Squadron from the Charleston, S.C. Air Force Base: Capt. Roland Thomason, Wayne Schake, Vincent Gullo, Hershal Woosley, David Conn, Stephen Bening, and Frank Roberson [these names are revealed via Sam Kinney's copy of the flight manifest].

ney stated that tracking for distance is much easier than tracking from side to side. He also indicated that the sequencing of the shots – one before the sign, once after – suggested that the sniper was familiar with the scene.

Second, SA Kinney reported that on the day of the assassination, SA Stuart Stout of the four-to-twelve shift was driving into Dallas to man a post at the Trade Mart in time for the President's arrival at the Mart. Stout was passed by a car leaving Dallas at a speed of 110 m.p.h. Stout remarked that "that car must have robbed a bank." SA William Duncan, who was on the same shift had given notice that it was five minutes away from the Mart. Duncan's story places the appearance of the speeding car at approximately 12:30 P.M.[75]

Interestingly, during Secret Service agent Roger Warner's 5/25/78 HSCA interview, it was written: "Warner observed the hearse arrive and the casket being loaded on the aircraft. Agent Mike Howard came over and told Warner that a subject had been arrested driving at a very high rate of speed from Dallas towards Fort Worth. The Fort Worth police thought this may be a suspect in the President's shooting. Mike Howard and Warner were to go to Fort Worth and talk to the subject. While they were in the process of speaking to the subject, a report came in that Oswald had been arrested."

Secret Service agent Robert Bouck told the ARRB on 5/2/96 "that his personal opinion was that although Lee Harvey Oswald was the assassin, he did feel that there was a conspiracy." He also conveyed the same thing to the author on 9/27/92. That said, he posited a more wide-ranging conspiracy to author Christopher Fulton in 1997.[76] In addition, Bouck told the ARRB that Inspector Thomas Kelley told him immediately following the assassination that he believed there may very well have been a conspiracy but that he just couldn't get his arms around it, or words to that effect.[77]

Secret Service agent Bill Greer said that the Warren Commission closed up shop too soon and that "there might have been a conspiracy in another part of the country."[78]

According to his widow June, former Secret Service agent Roy Kellerman "accepted that there was a conspiracy." This was based on June overhearing Roy's telephone conversation with someone from the HSCA in approximately 1977 or 1978. "I'll accept that" was Roy's telephone reply

75   HSCA Document # 180-10078-10493.
76   *The Inheritance*, pages 96-103; see also *The JFK Assassination Debates: Lone Gunman versus Conspiracy* by Michael L. Kurtz (2006), page 128.
77   *Inside The ARRB* by Doug Horne (2009), page 1506.
78   December 6, 1970 and June 26, 1971 taped interviews of Greer for Newcomb & Adams's project, courtesy of researcher Gary Murr.

to the Committee.[79] One of Kellerman's two daughters told Harold Weisberg in the 1970's: "I hope the day will come when these men [Kellerman and Greer] will be able to say what they've told their families."[80]

Another widow, Marina Oswald, *now* believes (since at least around 1988 onward) that there was a conspiracy in the death of JFK and her husband was innocent although, to be fair, she thought he was guilty during the Warren Commission and HSCA days.[81] Speaking of Marina, Secret Service agent Bill Carter wrote in his book: "not only did I know about the supposed brainwashing [of Oswald's family, whom he guarded after the assassination], but I was one of the people responsible for it. You hear about alleged conspiracy theories, and it's odd to realize you were a part of the conspiracy."[82]

Secret Service agent John Marshall, the head of the Miami field office during the JFK years, told the HSCA in 1978: "Twice during the [HSCA] interview, Mr. Marshall mentioned that, for all he knew, someone in the Secret Service could possibly have been involved in the assassination. This is not the first time an agent has mentioned the possibility that a conspiracy existed, but it is the first time that an agent has acknowledged the possibility that the Secret Service could have been involved."[83]

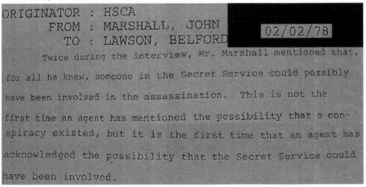

Secret Service agent John Marshall to the HSCA 2/2/78

Secret Service agent Gerald O'Rourke, on Kennedy's Texas trip, told the *Rocky Mountain News* on 11/20/03:

> Lee Harvey Oswald didn't act alone when he killed President John
> F. Kennedy, a retired agent said Wednesday, and the president

79   Author's interview with June Kellerman 3/2/92; *Vanity Fair*, Dec. 1994, p. 88 – information provided to authors; *Brothers* by David Talbot (2007), page 14.
80   Letter from Harold Weisberg to the author March 1992.
81   *American Expose: Who Murdered JFK?* with Jack Anderson (1988); *High Treason 2* by Harry Livingstone (1992)-chapter on Marina; *Case Closed* by Gerald Posner (1993), page 345; *The Men Who Killed Kennedy* (1995); *Oprah* 11/22/96; etc..
82   *Get Carter* by Bill Carter (2005), page 54.
83   HSCA interview with Marshall, 2/22/78: RIF#1801007410393.

died because Secret Service agents failed at their jobs. 'Officially, the answer to Oswald when somebody asks – because we were ordered to say it – is that the Warren Commission found that he acted alone,' retired agent Jerry O'Rourke said. "But was there more than one gunman? Yes, personally I believe so. And my personal opinion about Jack Ruby is that he was paid to kill Oswald." O'Rourke grew up in Telluride and attended Western State and Regis colleges, then spent 22 years in the Secret Service.

Now retired and back home, he spoke Wednesday to the downtown Grand Junction Rotary Club. O'Rourke said his group of agents, about 10 of them, had protected Kennedy the morning of Nov. 22, 1963, at a breakfast speech in Fort Worth. Then the group left by air for Austin, the next stop planned for the president's Texas tour. "We got the word (of the assassination) in the air, and we didn't believe it at first," he said. "We were joking. But later, most of the agents had tears in their eyes. Agents believed in Kennedy, and we knew we failed our job in Dallas."

After his White House tour ended during Johnson's presidency, O'Rourke spent a year in the Secret Service intelligence division, which offered him glimpses into the investigation of Kennedy's death. Those glimpses, and the accounts of other agents, have convinced O'Rourke that Oswald didn't act alone. He cited several reasons: Kennedy had a number of enemies, any of whom could have plotted against him. They included Southerners angered by his insistence on civil rights; organized crime; labor unions unhappy with investigations of them by Attorney General Robert F. Kennedy; Cuban dissidents angry over the failed Bay of Pigs invasion; and FBI Director J. Edgar Hoover.

The shots were impossible to make. O'Rourke learned to shoot as a boy and trained as a marksman in the military. He said his visits to Oswald's perch at the Texas Book Depository convince him that no one could have fired a rifle three times so quickly, hitting the president and Texas Gov. John Connally. The trajectory of one of the shots could not have been made from a gunman on the sixth floor of the Texas Book Depository. The shot entered Kennedy's body at his lower back and [allegedly] traveled up, to exit near his throat.

The circumstances of the autopsy were irregular. Texas law requires autopsies to be done in state, but agents, acting on the orders of White House, took Kennedy's body back to Washington, D.C. The autopsy was performed at Bethesda Naval Medical Center under secrecy that prevails to this day. Evidence was destroyed.

O'Rourke said that on the day of the assassination, one agent was ordered to clean out the cars used in the motorcade, getting rid of blood and other evidence. The agent told O'Rourke that he found a piece of skull, asked the White House doctor what to do with it, and was told to destroy it. Instructions were given to lie.

The agent in charge of motorcade protection [presumably Kellerman] told O'Rourke that he was told by the Warren Commission during his testimony that he did not hear a fourth shot and he did not see someone running across the grassy knoll. But the agent insisted that his account was accurate. Evidence about the shots is in conflict. An open microphone on a motorcycle in the motorcade picked up four shots, not three. "In my opinion, Hoover wanted the commission to find that Oswald acted alone," O'Rourke said. "The complete file won't be released until 2027, and the reason for that is most of us will be dead by then.'"

The author spoke to and corresponded with O'Rourke in 2004 and 2005 and he reiterated what he said above, adding:

> Keep in mind, some of the former agents you interview are not going to be receptive to you. Most don't mind talking about the assassination but they still are very protective. Also, many continue to have some problems (mental?) dealing with what they feel as a failure on their part.... Some of the retired agents have contested my beliefs on the assassination but most of those agents were still in diapers when 11/22/63 came about. I always answer them by stating, "I was there, were you?" Some of those guys you interviewed are great guys while the others are ... [O'Rourke broke off here].

O'Rourke added:

> As I told you a couple agents have problems with the assassination, Clint [Hill] being one. He is a good friend of mine but I have not seen him in 25 years.... Yes, Clint still has problems with 11/22/63.... Again, there are a lot of "people" (and agents) that disagree with my findings [regarding] Nov. 22nd but they have not done any research.... I have visited with several of the agents that were right with JFK, at the time, and plied them with drink [!] When all of the records are completely released we will know [what happened], if [we are] still alive.

Another ardent believer in a conspiracy was Democratic National Committee (DNC) advance man Martin E. "Marty" Underwood who worked on the planning of JFK's Texas tour; specifically, his stop at Houston and his proposed stop at Austin. In an exclusive interview conducted on 10/9/92, the author obtained the following new information: Marty was dispatched to Mexico by President Johnson to learn more about the assassination. As Underwood tells it, "Johnson said, 'Marty, there are two cancers killing my presidency. One is Vietnam. The other is, invariably, every six months or so, one of the newspapers would come out and say 'Johnson was behind the assassination.' Johnson said, 'I wonder if your friends south of the border would help clear this up.'"

Once in Mexico, Underwood said, "I was met by a little Mexican, tapped me on the shoulder, and got me in a CIA safe house, probably, ya know, totally insulated, and that's probably where I learned more about the assassination." Underwood stated that the CIA, the FBI, and the mafia "knew (JFK) was going to be hit" on 11/22/63. This information came from his direct contacts with CIA officer Win Scott, the Mexico City Station Chief during Oswald's visit to that region. Underwood said, "His [JFK's] number was on the board. I found out later, if they missed him in Dallas, they were thinking of getting him at the [LBJ] ranch."

However, Marty said that he also asked Scott if LBJ was involved in the assassination. Scott told him "not in any way, none whatsoever." Underwood "had a good speaking acquaintance with [Chicago Mafia boss Sam] Giancana, he liked me. I said to him, 'The President [LBJ] is disturbed about all of these reports.' Giancana got mad – he's very hot headed. He says, 'You go back and tell the President his number was on the board, too.' I said, 'C'mon.' He said, 'No, we don't want any more investigations.' When Johnson put in the Warren Commission, Hoover was tickled to death and so was Johnson because they knew it was a whitewash."

Underwood also stated that, eighteen hours before Kennedy's murder, "we were getting all sorts of rumors that the President was going to be assassinated in Dallas; there were no if's, and's, or but's about it." When Underwood told JFK about these disturbing reports, the President merely said, "'Marty, you worry about me too much.' Eighteen hours later, he was dead."

Indeed, JFK told San Antonio Congressman Henry Gonzalez on 11/21/63, "The Secret Service told me that they have taken care of everything. There's nothing to worry about."[84] The reason Underwood opened up to the author is best expressed by himself: "Everyone who had anything to do with Dallas in any way – Kenny O'Donnell, the Secret Service – they're practically all dead now. I just think people should know the truth."

84   *High Treason* by Robert Groden and Harrison Livingstone (1989), page 127.

Ironically, LBJ believed there was a conspiracy in the death of his predecessor.[85]

FBI Director J. Edgar Hoover told Billy Byars, Jr. in 1964 the following: "If I told you what I really know, it would be very dangerous to this country. Our whole political system could be disrupted."[86]

Ted Sorenson, JFK's speechwriter, came out shortly before his death to confirm his belief in a conspiracy.[87]

Dick Goodwin, Kennedy's Deputy Assistant Secretary of State for Inter-American Affairs said:

"We know the CIA was involved, and the Mafia. We all know that."[88]

The president's own brother, Attorney General Robert Kennedy, harbored much suspicion that there was a conspiracy and believed the Warren Commission to be "a shoddy piece of craftsmanship," to quote his son RFK Jr. on the 50th anniversary of the assassination[89]

Former President and Warren Commission member Gerald Ford privately believed that Oswald had help in the assassination, although he believed Oswald to be the lone shooter. This is still a conspiracy.[90] Valérie Giscard D'Estaing, ex-president of France, said: "Once I was making a car trip with him, he was then President as I was myself. I said to him: 'Let me ask you an indiscreet question: you were on the Warren Commission, what conclusions did you arrive at?' He told me: 'It's not a satisfactory one. We arrived at an initial conclusion: it was not the work of one person, it was something set up. We were sure that it was set up. But we were not able to discover by whom.'"[91]

Former Senator and Warren Commission member Richard Russell also shared Ford's private view on the assassination, believing "someone else worked with him [Oswald] on the planning."[92]

According to Bernard Fensterwald: "Almost from the beginning, Congressman Boggs had been suspicious over the FBI and CIA's reluctance

85   *The Kennedy Half-Century* by Larry Sabato (2013), pages 193-194; *Not In Your Lifetime* by Anthony Summers (2013), page 115.
86   *Official and Confidential* by Anthony Summers (1993), page 383.
87   *JFK Assassination from the Oval Office to Dealey Plaza* by Brent Holland (2013), page 29.
88   *Brothers* by David Talbot (2007), page 303.
89   *Brothers* by David Talbot (2007); https://www.usatoday.com/story/news/nation/2013/01/12/rfk-kennedy-assassination-warren/1828405/.
90   PR News Channel, "Book Publisher: President Ford Knew of CIA Coverup in Kennedy Assassination" (November 27, 2007); *The Man Who Killed Kennedy* by Roger Stone (2014 edition), pages 329 and 346- re: Tim Miller, the publisher of Ford's 2007 memoir.
91   https://www.rtl.fr/actu/international/kennedy-le-reve-a-ete-assassine-avec-l-homme-dit-giscard-7767111282.
92   *Brothers* by David Talbot (2007), page 282; *Who Really Killed Kennedy?: 50 Years Later: Stunning New Revelations About the JFK Assassination* by Jerome Corsi (2016)- kindle edition; *Not In Your Lifetime* by Anthony Summers (2013), page 138.

to provide hard information when the Commission's probe turned to certain areas, such as allegations that Oswald may have been an undercover operative of some sort. When the Commission sought to disprove the growing suspicion that Oswald had once worked for the FBI, Boggs was outraged that the only proof of denial that the FBI offered was a brief statement of disclaimer by J. Edgar Hoover. It was Hale Boggs who drew an admission from Allen Dulles that the CIA's record of employing someone like Oswald might be so heavily coded that the verification of his service would be almost impossible for outside investigators to establish." According to one of Boggs friends: "Hale felt very, very torn during his work (on the Commission) … he wished he had never been on it and wished he'd never signed it (the Warren Report)." Another former aide argued that, "Hale always returned to one thing: Hoover lied his eyes out to the Commission – on Oswald, on Ruby, on their friends, the bullets, the gun, you name it."[93]

For his part, W. David Slawson of the Warren Commission came clean later in life: "Slawson's silence has ended once and for all. Half a century after the commission issued an 888-page final report that was supposed to convince the American people that the investigation had uncovered the truth about the president's murder, Slawson has come to believe that the full truth is still not known. Now 83, he says he has been shocked by the recent, belated discovery of how much evidence was withheld from the commission – from him, specifically – by the CIA and other government agencies, and how that rewrites the history of the Kennedy assassination."[94]

H.R. "Bob" Haldeman, former Nixon chief of staff, wrote in his book: "After Kennedy was killed, the CIA launched a fantastic cover-up. Many of the facts about Oswald unavoidably pointed to a Cuban connection… In a chilling parallel to their cover-up at Watergate, the CIA literally erased any connection between Kennedy's assassination and the CIA."[95]

Future Vice President Al Gore stated his belief in a conspiracy in McKeesport, PA in 1992. I was a stunned witness to this event.[96]

CIA officers David Atlee Phillips and E. Howard Hunt stated before their deaths that a conspiracy took the life of JFK. Phillips said: "My final take on the assassination is there was a conspiracy, likely including Ameri-

93   *Coincidence or Conspiracy* by Bernard Fensterwald (1977), page 96; https://kennedysandking.com/john-f-kennedy-articles/jfk-and-the-unforgivable-how-the-historians-version-of-the-jfk-assassination-dishonors-the-historical-record-part-1.
94   https://www.politico.com/magazine/story/2015/02/warren-commission-jfk-investigators-114812.
95   *The Ends of Power* by H.R. Haldeman with Joseph DiMona (1978), p. 39..
96   *Los Angeles Times,* 7/20/92.

can intelligence officers."[97] A book by Hunt's son espouses the notion that the former Watergate burglar came clean about the assassination on his death bed.[98]

Secret Service officer John Norris, during an exclusive interview with the author on 3/4/94, conveyed his conviction that there was indeed a conspiracy in the death of JFK. Furthermore, Norris discovered a carefully concealed lookout post in the Executive Office Building's (EOB) attic in the early summer of 1963 (the EOB was the home of the Secret Service's Protective Research Section (PRS). This vantage point provided an observer with a view directly into the private living quarters of the White House, obviously for the express purpose of spying on the First Family. As Norris told author Bill Sloan: "There were cigarette butts all over the floor and all of them looked fairly fresh.... There were even some mattresses up there, so it was pretty apparent that someone had been spending a lot of time up there ... a crack marksman with a telescopic sight could conceivably even have killed Kennedy from there."[99] Norris added, "It was obvious to me that somebody had been keeping Kennedy under regular covert surveillance.... Maybe it was for his own protection, but frankly I doubted it, and it struck me as very peculiar, very suspicious. That was one main reason that I tried to relay a warning to Kennedy. Another was that everybody was tense and edgy, and there was a lot of talk going around about threats and plots."[100]

Perhaps to be taken with a little grain of salt, but the following was reported back in 1968: "Ten hours after the assassination, Secret Service Chief James Rowley knew that there had been three gunmen, and perhaps four, firing in Dallas that day. Robert Kennedy, who had already interrogated [Roy] Kellerman, learned that evening from Rowley that the Secret Service believed the President had been the victim of a powerful organization."[101] The year before, in 1967, this time based on actual documented 1964-era interviews, author William Manchester wrote: "Forrest Sorrels was on the telephone with Jerry Behn, discussing how the Ruby-Oswald connection could be quickly uncovered. Behn said, "It's a plot." Sorrels said, "Of course."[102]

---

97   *Someone Would Have Talked* by Larry Hancock (2006).

98   *Bond of Secrecy* by Saint John Hunt (2012).

99   *JFK: Breaking the Silence,* pp. 115-116. Norris also said, "There's strong evidence that the KGB had successfully infiltrated the Secret Service by late 1961 or early 1962." [p. 115] .

100   *Ibid.* p. 116.

101   *Farewell America* by James Hepburn (pseud.), 1968, page 301; see also *High Treason* by Livingstone and Groden, 1998 edition, page 128.

102   *The Death of a President* by William Manchester, 1967 [1988 edition], page 528. Manchester interviewed Behn once (12/18/64) and Sorrels twice (8/26/64 & 9/24/64)]. A variation on a theme-another book reported: "later on the telephone Jerry Behn remarked to Forrest Sorrels (head of the Dallas Secret Service) 'It's a plot.' 'Of course,' was Sorrel's reply." [*Farewell America* by James Hepburn (pseud.), 1968, page 301; see also *High Treason* by Livingstone and Groden, 1998 edition, page 128.

DNC advance man Jacob L. "Jack" Puterbaugh, who rode in the pilot car in the motorcade, said in 1970: "he has some doubts about the validity of the Warren Commission's findings, since "the ballistics stuff doesn't add up."[103]

The second major government investigation of the assassination conducted by the House Select Committee on Assassinations (HSCA) from 1976-1979 found a "probable conspiracy." As Congressman Louis Stokes, the Chair of the HSCA, told *Face The Nation* in early 1979, upon the release of the official report, the finding of a probably conspiracy was based on factors other than just the acoustics evidence. For his part, HSCA Chief Counsel G. Robert Blakey told author Anthony Summers: "I think our conclusion [of a probable conspiracy] was correct. On balance, I say there were two shooters in the Plaza, and not just because of the acoustics ... (but because of) all the other evidence and testimony ... I find on balance that the earwitness and eyewitness testimony is credible."[104] Still, many people erroneously believe that the acoustics evidence was the sole basis for their bottom line finding, but this is obviously false. What this means is we are stuck with two official government verdicts: no conspiracy (the Warren Commission) and a probable conspiracy (the HSCA). Although the HSCA was another flawed investigation, they were an improvement over the Warren Commission and came up with some good work. In any event, always remind people that there is a second government verdict, not just the debunked first verdict of the Warren Commission.

William Walton, a friend of the Kennedys, speaking on behalf of RFK and Jacqueline Kennedy: "Perhaps there was only one assassin, but he did not act alone .... Dallas was the ideal location for such a crime."[105]

Evelyn Lincoln was JFK's secretary and rode in the motorcade. She wrote: "As for the assassination is concerned [sic] it is my belief that there was a conspiracy because there were those that disliked him and felt the only way to get rid of him was to assassinate him. These five conspirators, in my opinion, were Lyndon B. Johnson, J. Edgar Hoover, the Mafia, the CIA, and the Cubans in Florida. The House Intelligence Committee investigation, also, came to the conclusion that there was a conspiracy."[106] Evelyn also conveyed to author Harry Livingstone: "It was a conspiracy. There was no doubt about that ... J. Edgar Hoover was involved in it."[107]

---

103   Larry Haapanen's interview with Puterbaugh, 9/5/70 (transcript provided to the author)
104   *Not In Your Lifetime* by Anthony Summers (2013), pages 29-30.
105   *Brothers* by David Talbot (2007), page 32.
106   10/7/94 letter to Richard Duncan. See also *Bloody Treason* by Noel Twyman, p. 831, and *Assassination Science*, by James Fetzer, p. 372.
107   4/21/91 interview with Harry Livingstone for *High Treason 2*, pp. 435-437; Lincoln conveyed the same thoughts to Anthony Summers: see *The Fourth Decade journal*, May 1998 issue, p. 14

There is no doubt in my mind that there was a conspiracy. The participants were Lyndon B. Johnson (he had the most to gain), J. Edgar Hoover, the Mafia, the CIA and the FBI. Oliver Stone's movie is on the right track.

With every good wish.

Sincerely,

Evelyn Lincoln

One of Evelyn Lincoln's 1994 letters.

October 7, 1994

Dear

It was a pleasure to receive your kind letter concerning your desire to obtain my assessment of President Kennedy's administration and assassination to pass along to your students.

I am sending along to you an article which was written by Muriel Pressman for the "Lady's Circle" October 1964, and was recently reprinted in a current issue of that magazine, which will give you an insight into my impression of the man.

As for the assassination is concerned it is my belief that there was a conspiracy because there were those that disliked him and felt the only way to get rid of him was to assassinate him. These five conspirators, in my opinion, were Lyndon B. Johnson, J. Edgar Hoover, the Mafia, the CIA and the Cubans in Florida. The House Intelligence Committee investigation, also, came to the conclusion that there was a conspiracy.

My very best wishes to you and your students.

Sincerely,

Evelyn Lincoln

The more famous 1994 Evelyn Lincoln letter.

August 26, 1994

Dear Karl:

Once again it was a pleasure to hear from you and I have been pleased to sign the picture of our late President Kennedy according to your wishes.

You also wanted me to tell you what I believe about the assassination of President Kennedy. It is my belief that there was a conspiracy. In the Kennedy administration there were people who loved him - and people who hated him. And the people who hated him wanted him out of office. One was Lyndon B. Johnson. Others were the Mafia, J. Edgar Hoover, the CIA and the Cubans in Florida. The House Intelligence Committee, after holding hearings, came to the conclusion that there was a conspiracy.

Many thanks for the pen.

Sincerely,

Evelyn Lincoln

Karl Poretta
The Brandeis School
25 Frost Lane
Lawrence, N.Y. 11559

Another 1994 Evelyn Lincoln letter.

JFK aide's unusual suspects

New York Post, Sunday, December 12, 2010   nypost.com   8

By SUSANNAH CAHALAN

John F. Kennedy's closest aide was the queen of conspiracy theorists.

Evelyn Lincoln, his personal secretary, wrote down a list of suspects in her beloved boss' assassination — and it included both Lyndon Johnson and Richard Nixon.

The never-before-seen personal note, scribbled by Lincoln as she sat aboard Air Force One returning to Washington on the day of JFK's death, lists those she thought might be behind the president's murder.

The note, estimated to be worth $30,000, is now on the auction block.

Lincoln was Kennedy's personal secretary from 1953 until his death on Nov. 22, 1963, and was riding in the Dallas motorcade that fateful day. She died in 1995 at age 85.

Her note listed "Lyndon, KKK, Dixiecrats, [Teamsters boss Jimmy] Hoffa, [the] John Birch Society, Nixon, [South Vietnam President Ngo Dinh] Diem,

Rightist, CIA in Cuban fiasco, Dictators [and] Communists."

On the back of the list is another note, written more than 20 years later when she passed on her letters to Kennedy collector Robert White.

"There is no end to the list of suspected conspirators to Pres. Kennedy murder. Many factions had their reasons for wanting the young president dead. That fact alone illustrates how the world suffers from a congenital proclivity to violence," it reads.

The 10-month Warren Commission investigation concluded that Lee Harvey Oswald acted alone in assassinating the president.

The note, consigned by the Gettysburg Museum of History, will be auctioned by Alexander Autographs in Stamford, Conn., on Thursday.

THEORIES: This list of suspects – jotted down by JFK secretary Evelyn Lincoln (here with him and JFK Jr.) after the assassination – is up for sale.

New York Post article showing yet another Evelyn Lincoln letter/note, this one from 11/22/63.

Secret Service agent Abraham Bolden[108] conveyed to myself many times between 1993 and the present time that he believed JFK was killed by a conspiracy.[109]

---

108   Document # 180-10104-10324: 3-page interview summary with Secret Service agent Conrad Cross. An excerpt: "We began discussing Abraham Bolden and Conrad Cross stated that he knew Bolden well, although they did not socialize too often. He stated that when Bolden was arrested, he (Cross) couldn't understand some of the allegations against Bolden regarding time and place, because he was with Bolden on some of those dates. Cross stated that he believes Bolden was set up, but he has no idea who would have done it. Cross stated that Bolden had a big mouth and did not think before he said things. He believes this was a contributing factor to Bolden's troubles. Bolden had a personality clash with ASAIC Maurice Martineau and they were always at each other. Cross stated that the Bolden incident was the main cause of his resignation. Cross became very disillusioned with the Secret Service because he felt Bolden had been "shafted." He stated that he began to feel useless and lost faith in the Secret Service and felt it was time to get out. Cross stated his supervisors tried to dissuade him but he resigned."
109   See my first book *Survivor's Guilt*, Chapter 17.

Secret Service agent Maurice Martineau, head of the Chicago field office and Bolden's boss, told me that he believed there was a conspiracy to murder JFK.[110] Interestingly, Mr. Martineau revealed that he "was subpoenaed to testify before" the HSCA,[111] which he declared "a lot more valid than the Warren Commission." He believed "there was more than one assassin" on 11/22/63, stemming from the HSCA's report, his own role in the investigation, his extensive experience with firearms, and his own gut feelings on 11/22/63, "As soon as I learned some of the details…" When the author conveyed to him Agent Kinney's own beliefs (see above), including Agent Kinney's qualification that his own "outfit was clean," Mr. Martineau stated: "Well … ah … (long pause) … I've got some theories, too, but, ah … without any actual data to back them up, I think I'll keep them to myself."

Col. George J. McNally, WH Signal Corps and former Secret Service agent, wrote the following in his obscure self-published book *A Million Miles of Presidents*: "But during the Chicago visit [3/23/63], the motorcade was slowed to the pace of a mounted Black Horse Troop, and the police got a warning of Puerto Rican snipers. Helicopters searched the roofs along the way, and no incidents occurred."[112] Indeed, "A postcard was received in the Saturday morning mail of the Chicago office threatening the life of the President during the [3/23/63] motorcade from O'Hare Field to the Conrad Hilton Hotel."[113]

Hubert Clark, one of the members of the Military District of Washington casket team (one of the pallbearers for JFK), believes a conspiracy murdered President Kennedy in Dallas.[114]

Paul Kelly O'Connor, Bethesda laboratory technologist, James Curtis Jenkins, Bethesda laboratory technologist, James E. Metzler, Bethesda Hospital corpsman, Edward F. Reed, Jr., Bethesda X-ray technician and Jerrol F. Custer, Bethesda X-ray technician all believed there was a conspiracy in the death of JFK.[115] The basis of their beliefs was largely based on the wounds they saw on the body of the president.

110   Author's interviews with Martineau, 9/21/93 and 6/7/96.
111   Executive Session testimony of Martineau, HSCA, 3/15/78 [RIF# 180-10116-10084]; 2/1/78 HSCA interview with Martineau; see also 3 HSCA 339.
112   *A Million Miles of Presidents*, page 204.
113   RIF #154-10003-10012: Chicago, IL trip 3/23/63 Secret Service survey report. 6 motorcycles surrounding limo, Lawton riding on (JFK's side of) rear of limo, Mayor's follow-up car with four detectives in addition to SS follow-up car, police facing crowd (not JFK) on the route, no-one permitted on overpasses except four policemen guarding them, press/photographers close to JFK, Hatcher with Kilduff. PRS: one threat (the postcard).
114   12/19/67 interview with David Lifton (*Best Evidence*, pages 408-413 [see photo 26 B]; 398, 578, 586, 695, 696; see also *A Complete Book of Facts* by Duffy and Ricci, pages 125-126, *Who's Who in the JFK Assassination* by Michael Benson, page 80, *Conspiracy* by Anthony Summers, page 483, *Bloody Treason* by Noel Twyman, pages 174 and 211, and *Between The Signal and the Noise* by Roger Bruce Feinman, page 59; *Betrayal: A JFK Honor Guard Speaks* by Hugh Clark and William Law (2016).
115   See my second book *JFK: From Parkland to Bethesda*.

To both add to and sum up the prominent people who believed there was a conspiracy in the death of JFK, *Washington Post* journalist Jefferson Morley, one-time BBC correspondent Anthony Summers, author Norman Mailer, and author David Talbot all wrote in an article they collaborated on: "The following people to one degree or another suspected that President Kennedy was killed as a result of a conspiracy, and said so either publicly or privately: Presidents Lyndon Johnson and Richard Nixon; Attorney General Robert Kennedy; John Kennedy's widow, Jackie; his special advisor dealing with Cuba at the United Nations, William Attwood; FBI director J. Edgar Hoover; Senators Richard Russell (a Warren Commission member), and Richard Schweiker and Gary Hart (both of the Senate Intelligence Committee), seven of the eight congressmen on the House Assassinations Committee and its chief counsel, G. Robert Blakey; the Kennedy associates Joe Dolan, Fred Dutton, Richard Goodwin, Pete Hamill, Frank Mankiewicz, Larry O'Brien, Kenneth O'Donnell and Walter Sheridan; the Secret Service agent Roy Kellerman, who rode with the president in the limousine; the presidential physician, Dr. George Burkley; Mayor Richard Daley of Chicago; Frank Sinatra; and *60 Minutes* producer Don Hewitt."[116]

(Left) My 11/22/1991 video of Jerrol Custer (along with author Harry Livingstone and Tom Wilson) used for *High Treason 2*. (Right) My March 1998 video used for author William Law's book *In The Eye of History*.

Item #7: Commission Exhibit (CE) 399, The So-Called Magic Bullet of Single Bullet Theory (SBT) Infamy, Had No Proper Chain of Possession

O.P. Wright, Darrell C. "D.C." Tomlinson, Chief James J. Rowley, and SA Richard E. Johnsen could NOT identify CE399 as the bul-

---

let they all allegedly handled on 11/22/63.[117] Although two FBI agents (Todd and Frazier) initialed the bullet they received from the Secret Service, Johnsen and Rowley did not, breaking the legal chain of custody.[118] Although the bullet was "officially" found on a stretcher in a corridor of Parkland Hospital, FBI agents James Sibert and Francis O'Neill reported that it was found in the emergency room![119] FBI Director J. Edgar Hoover told President Johnson in a recorded phone conversation 11/23/63 that the bullet was found "on the stretcher that the President was on. It apparently had fallen out when they massaged his heart, and we have that one." The same FBI agents, Sibert and O'Neill, bypassed Agent Johnsen and spoke instead to Behn (not even in Dallas) about "the location of a bullet which had been found on a stretcher at Parkland."[120]

Incredibly, Behn "stated that he was in the chain of custody of CE 399 ... Behn received the bullet from Johnsen, then turned it over to the FBI [what about Chief Rowley?]."[121] O.P. Wright, the man who allegedly gave the bullet to Johnsen at Parkland, does not even mention this very important find at all in his report.[122] Darrel Tomlinson, O.P. Wright, and Nathan Pool all described a different bullet than CE399, stating that it was a pointed hunting-type bullet.[123] According to research done by Josiah Thompson, the bullet was found on a stretcher used by a young boy named Ronny Fuller.[124]

According to Chief James J. Rowley, CE399 "was found amongst the clothes on one of the stretchers."[125] If that wasn't enough, Governor Connally stated in his autobiography called *In History's Shadow*: "But the most curious discovery of all took place when they rolled me off the stretcher, and onto the examining table. A metal object fell onto the floor, with a click no louder than a wedding band. The nurse picked it up and slipped it into her pocket. It was the bullet from my body, the one that passed through my back, chest, and wrist, and worked itself loose from

---

117   "Over-the-counter" references: *JFK-Conspiracy of Silence*, p. 133; *Crossfire*, p. 365; *Reasonable Doubt*, p. 70; *The People Vs. Lee Harvey Oswald* by Walt Brown, p. 623 [for Tomlinson: 6 H 128-134 / testimony; on video, see Part 2 of "CBS News Inquiry: The Warren Report," 6/26/67, and *Nova*, 11/15/88; *Triangle of Fire* by Bob Goodman (1993), page 111; *The JFK Assassination* by James DiEugenio (2018), pages 88-92.

118   24 H 412.

119   CD 7.

120   Sibert and O'Neill interview of SAIC Jerry Behn, 11/27/63.

121   RIF#180-10104-10481: HSCA interview of SAIC Behn.

122   Price Exhibits, Warren Commission Volume 21.

123   *Six Seconds in Dallas; High Treason*, p. 102; HSCA document-interview with Nathan Pool, 1/10/77.

124   See also 21 H 156 and *The JFK Assassination* by James DiEugenio (2018), pages 247-250.

125   LBJ Library document-Memorandum to File.

my thigh."[126] Corroborating Connally's memory, from the 11/21/93 *Dallas Morning News* interview with Henry Wade: "I also went out to see Connally, but he was in the operating room [note the time frame]. Some nurse had a bullet in her hand and said this was on the gurney that Connally was on ... I told her to give it to the police, which she said she would. I assume that's the pristine bullet."[127]

Finally, Gary Shaw (in the 11/22/93 *Dateline: Dallas* issue) came across this passage from the Warren Commission testimony of Parkland nurse Jeanette Standridge:

> **Specter**: Did you notice any object in Governor Connally's clothing?
>
> **Standridge**: Not unusual.
>
> **Specter**: Did you notice a bullet, specifically?
>
> **Standridge**: No.
>
> **Specter**: Did you hear the sound of anything fall?"
>
> **Standridge**: I didn't.

Is this "CE399"? What's going on here?

Although it is an "official" fact that Agent Richard Johnsen gained possession of CE399 (a.k.a. "the magic bullet," linked to Oswald's rifle) via O.P. Wright (who obtained it thru Darrel Tomlinson and Nathan Pool, who obtained it in the presence of Secret Service agents) at Parkland Hospital, what has never been widely reported is the fact that Agent Greer maintained very close proximity to Johnsen and the bullet in question:[128]

- Both agents guarded the emergency room (Trauma Room 1) Greer inside, Johnsen outside.[129]

- If the FBI's report is accurate,[130] Greer was the only agent stationed inside the emergency room with JFK.

- Johnsen rode with Greer in a car on the way to Air Force One (along with fellow agents David B. Grant, Samuel E. Sulliman, Ernest E. Olsson, Jr., and Paul Landis)-and we're supposed to believe that *all* these agents remained silent about the bullet.[131]

---

126   p. 18; see also the journal *The Investigator* Feb-May 1994.
127   *The Investigator* Feb-May 1994.
128   18 H 799-800.
129   2 H 126; 18 H 798.
130   CD 7.
131   18 H 799; 18 H 723.

- Greer rode with Johnsen near the casket in the rear of Air Force One (from the point of time starting with the swearing in of LBJ, when the majority of agents and people were up front.[132]

When we consider that both Greer and Kellerman remained silent about this bullet until it was announced by Chief Rowley that night during the autopsy (via a phone call to Kellerman), we have to wonder about the implications of this "silence": in a recently uncovered HSCA document, Roy Kellerman stated that SA Johnsen told him about the bullet while they were still at Parkland.[133] This early knowledge is troubling because of the following: Once the autopsy at Bethesda Naval Hospital was underway, Greer "said that a bullet had been found on a stretcher-or rather as it fell from a stretcher- in Parkland Hospital … could this be the bullet that went into the neck and, in the jostling of the President on the stretcher, fell out?" As author Jim Bishop reported (thru his interview with Greer and Kellerman)," Greer's thesis had a supporter. Roy Kellerman … said he remembered a Parkland doctor astride the chest of the dead President, applying artificial respiration. Kellerman … thought the bullet in the back...might have been squeezed out by manual pressure…"[134] Why would they even need Rowley's call to "alert" them to the bullet found at Parkland and given to the FBI (two agents-Sibert and O'Neill-were in attendance with Greer and Kellerman at the autopsy)? Why would Rowley "order" Kellerman to tell the autopsy doctors about something he already knew about?

During an interview conducted on 9/29/92, the author learned that Agent Richard Johnsen *did not seem to remember* having possession of CE399! Furthermore, Johnsen mentions in his first report that the bullet, quote, "may" have originated from Governor Connally's stretcher – obviously, one of the components of the "single bullet theory" is having the bullet on Connally's stretcher; if the bullet was found on JFK's stretcher (or Ronny Fuller's, or elsewhere), the theory is in big trouble. Interestingly, Johnsen retired in 1979, having never been questioned by the FBI, the Warren Commission, or the HSCA, and when I tried, I received very cantankerous responses. As for Johnsen's "second" report, a sort of mini report enclosed with his first report having to do with the acquisition of CE399, it is unsigned.[135] There may be more to Johnsen's seeming "amnesia" over this evidence than meets the eye.

132   18 H 799; 2 H 126.
133   HSCA document, interviews with Kellerman, outside contact report, 8/24-8/25/77.
134   *The Day Kennedy was Shot*, page 498,530; see also Tomlinson-2 H 412; Greer-2 H 127; Kellerman- 2 H 93.
135   18 H 799-800; this report actually exists separately, as new documents uncovered from

O.P. Wright told CBS newsman Eddie Barker[136]: "I got hold of a Secret Service man, and they didn't seem to be interested in coming and looking at the bullet in the position it was in then. So I went back to the area where Mr. Tomlinson was and picked up the bullet and put it in my pocket, and I carried it some 30 or 40 minutes. And I gave it to a Secret Service man that was guarding the main door into the emergency room." Who was the first agent Wright spoke to? And was his use of the word "they" a mistake? No:

HSCA attorney Belford V. Lawson, in charge of the Secret Service area of the investigation, is the author of a recently uncovered memo concerning an interview with Nathan Pool conducted on 1/10/77 and headlined "POOL'S CO-DISCOVERY OF THE 'TOMLINSON' BULLET." In the memo, Pool mentions the fact that two Secret Service agents were by the elevator, one of which "remained there throughout most or all of Pool's stay." Before we can catch our breath, a third Secret Service agent enters the picture. Although all these men were in the immediate vicinity of the discovery of the bullet, one particular agent "was within 10 feet when Pool recognized the bullet." According to Pool, the bullet was pointed, and he added that it "didn't look like it had hit anything and didn't look like it had been in anything." Belford Lawson felt that further development of Pool's testimony may reveal the following: "*A Secret Service agent was for a significant period of time close enough to the elevator to plant a bullet; may lead to an identification of that agent...*"[137]

Nathan Pool provided more details during his 1977 HSCA testimony:

> **Pool:** We [Pool and Tomlinson] were just standing there talking and one of us leaned up against the thing and kind of pushed it up against the wall, you know, and this bullet fell out ... when it hit the wall the projectile fell of there, or the bullet..."
>
> **Question:** "And was the Secret Service agent present at all times?"
>
> **Pool:** "He was right there by the door.... Between those swinging doors ... right in that area." [Regarding the bullet] "It looked like any G.I. issue bullet to me. It was a fairly long projectile ... in pretty good condition. It wasn't beat up or anything.... Didn't look like it had hit bone or anything like that.... It was jacketed."

---

the LBJ Library reveal, although the same report as reproduced in the Warren Commission Volumes gives the impression it is part of the same [first] report, due to its juxtaposition on TOP of the first report).

136   *Postmortem* by Harold Weisberg, p. 46.

137   Nathan Burgess Pool-RIF#180-10097-10261; 7/12/78 (audio-taped) testimony before the HSCA.

Question: "After the bullet was found and Tomlinson obtained possession of it, what did he do with it that you observed? What did you observe?"

Answer: "He took it over and gave it to the guy over by the door ... [the Secret Service agent] took it through the door and gave it to someone else, I assume. I don't know ... I don't think there was ever a time that there wasn't a Secret Service man by that door." [Regarding JFK] "But that's the first time I had any idea he was dead was when they rolled him out of there because they had him covered with a ..." (interrupting).

Question: "With a sheet?"

Answer: "No; with a purple cover."

Question: "Did the Secret Service agents stay there after Kennedy left?"

Answer: "Yes."

Question: "Was the Secret Service agent there when you left?"

Answer: "I'm not sure the same one stayed there, though, but there was a Secret Service agent there."[138]

Mrs. Wright-Good is the widow of O.P. Wright, Parkland Hospital security chief. Wallace Milam interviewed her on 6/23/93 and Mark Oakes did the same on video on 10/11/94. Besides her belief, shared by her husband, that the shots had to have come from more than one direction, she showed Oakes on camera an unfired .38 special Western Cartridge Company revolver bullet which she said was the bullet that her husband had attempted in vain to give to "an FBI agent." She showed the bullet to Henry Wade, which is backed up by Oakes videotaped interview with Wade in May 1992 [although, as Oakes and Good acknowledge, Wade got her name wrong] and, to a lesser extent, Wright's mention of Wade.[139]

Interestingly, three witnesses – Seth Kantor, Roy Stamps and Wilma Tice – saw none other than Jack Ruby at Parkland Hospital. Some researchers suspect Ruby of planting the bullet.[140]

If all of this were not enough, FBI agent Bardwell Odum, the agent who officially showed CE 399 to Tomlinson and Wright, was interviewed by Josiah Thompson and Dr. Gary Aguilar. Odum denied that he had ever handled the CE 399 bullet![141] Aguilar deserves to be quoted at length on

138   Nathan Pool- 7/12/78 (audio-taped) testimony before the HSCA.
139   21 H 196.
140   *Rendezvous With Death* by H.R. Underwood (2013), pages 365-366.
141   https://history-matters.com/essays/frameup/EvenMoreMagical/EvenMoreMagical.htm.

this historic and important matter[142]: "With Josiah Thompson's help, I tracked Odum down in 2002 and sent him the original July 7th FBI report and the June 20, 1964 FBI Airtel from Dallas. In a recorded call we had the following exchange:

> **Aguilar**: "[F]rom what I could gather from the records after the assassination, you went into Parkland and showed (#399 to) a couple of employees there."
>
> **Odum**: "Oh, I never went into Parkland Hospital at all. I don't know where you got that.... I didn't show it to anybody at Parkland. I didn't have any bullet. I don't know where you got that but it is wrong."
>
> **Aguilar**: "Oh, so you never took a bullet. You were never given a bullet..."
>
> **Odum**: "You are talking about the bullet they found at Parkland?"
>
> **Aguilar**: "Right."
>
> **Odum**: "I don't think I ever saw it even."

My first inclination was to wonder if Odum might have forgotten his trip to the hospital. But if so, that meant that Odum's memory was good enough to recall that a bullet had been found at Parkland but not good enough to remember that he had carried it around Parkland himself. I re-reviewed the entire file on #399 and confirmed that Odum's name was nowhere in it. Unwilling to leave it at that, on November 21, 2002 Josiah Thompson and I both visited Bardwell Odum in his home in a suburb of Dallas. Concerned as to what his age and the passage of 38 years might have done to the 78-year old's recall, we were both struck by how very bright and alert Odum was. To ensure that there was no misunderstanding, we laid out on a coffee table before Odum copies of all the relevant documents. We then read aloud from them.

Again, Odum said that he had never taken a bullet – any bullet – to Parkland to show to witnesses. Nor had he ever had any bullet related to the Kennedy assassination in his possession during the FBI's investigation in 1964 or at any other time. Because a record from the Washington FBI office seems to prove that #399 had indeed been sent back and forth to Dallas in the appropriate time frame, we gently asked Odum whether he might have forgotten the episode. Answering somewhat stiffly, he said that he doubted he would have ever forgotten investigating so important a piece of evidence in the Kennedy case. But even if he had forgotten, he said he would certainly have turned in the customary 302 field report

---

142   https://kennedysandking.com/john-f-kennedy-reviews/395.

covering something that important and he dared us to find it. The files support Odum; as noted above, there are no 302s in what the National Archives states is the complete file on #399.

To recap, the FBI's Washington office advised the Warren Commission on July 7, 1964 that two Parkland Hospital eyewitnesses, Darrell Tomlinson and O. P. Wright, had told Agent Bardwell Odum that #399 looked like the bullet that they had found on a hospital stretcher. No internal FBI records corroborate that, including the two documents (the June 20th Airtel and the June 24th memo) that touch on #399 and that predate the July 7th report. To the contrary: the two June documents contradict the July 7th report in that they say, simply, that neither witness could identify #399.

Then, in 1966, Wright, who was experienced in firearms, flatly denied that there was a resemblance, and, in 2002, a suppressed FBI file from the Dallas office turned up – the only Dallas file that mentioned Wright – saying only that Wright could not identify #399. Also in 2002, Odum, the FBI agent who was supposed to have originally heard Wright say that there was a resemblance, insisted that Wright had never told him that, that he had never interviewed Wright, and that he had never even seen #399."

So, as you can plainly see, there are very grave doubts about the provenance of CE399, to put it mildly.[143]

Excerpt from Nathan Pool HSCA interview:

exited from the elevator. ~~~ ~~~ ~~~~ ~~~
in front of the elevator, they noticed that the same
stretcher which Pool had noticed when he first arrived
was still in the same disorderly position. They then
decided to push the stretcher so that it slong side
would stand flush with the wall next to this elevator.
Pool cannot recall a specific reason for moving the
stretcher other than to get it out of the way, nor can
he remember who pushed the stretcher first. He definitely
recalls that the bullet was not visible on the surface
of the stretcher.

    Pool heard an object fall from the stretcher as the
stretcher was pushed. Pool bent over to pick it up and
discovered a bullet which, based on his familiarity with
guns, he judged to beaa 6mm, i.e. less than a 30-30 caliber. He described the bullet as bronze, long, pointed,
and smooth and gave this interviewer the opinion that
the bullet didn't look like it had hit anything and didn't
look like it had been in anything. A Secret Service
agent was within ten feet when Pool recognized the bullet.

    Pool gave the bullet to Tomlinson who in turn gave
it to either a Secret Service agent or to the security
officer, Wright. Pool does not remember to whom Tomlinson
delivered the bullet because Tomlinson went around a
corner to deliver it.

---

143   http://22november1963.org.uk/ce-399-magic-bullet-planted-or-genuine

ITEM #8: SUSPICIOUS IMAGES ON THE OVERPASS AND ON THE KNOLL

I usually hate "photo analysis"! It feels like one big, subjective Rorschach Test: you see what you want to see; wishful thinking. With that caveat in mind, and proving that there are exceptions to every rule of thought, here are two photos from 11/22/63 I do feel compelled to believe something is amiss. This one seems to show a man on the overpass with a walkie-talkie (ostensibly, the overpass was supposed to be cleared of spectators. Agent Lawson was distressed by this) [Harry Cabluck photo- motorcade cars still going under the underpass at this time]:

The Mary Moorman photo: blowup of arrowed area – man behind the fence or, rather, his fedora cap, a la Jack Ruby's? Even Mary Moorman herself (a Facebook friend I finally met in person in 2019) said that this was "very interesting." Indeed. See for yourself:

Item #9: The Assassination Predictions of Joseph Milteer, Eugene Dinkin, David Christensen, Rose Cherami, Thomas Mosley, an Anonymous Caller, John Martino, and Richard Case Nagell[144]

Nov. 9, 1963 – Miami Police tape-record a conversation in which extreme right-wing political organizer Joseph Milteer[145] accurately predicts the assassination of President John F. Kennedy, just as it was to happen 13 days later, to informant William Somersett. The man said the President would be killed by shots fired "from an office building with a high-powered rifle." Then he dropped his tape-recorded bombshell.

> **Somersett**: …I think Kennedy is coming here on the 18th … to make some kind of speech.… I imagine it will be on TV.
>
> **Milteer**: You can bet your bottom dollar he is going to have a lot to say about the Cubans. There are so many of them here.
>
> **Somersett**: Yeah, well, he will have a thousand bodyguards. Don't worry about that.
>
> **Milteer**: The more bodyguards he has the easier it is to get him.
>
> **Somersett**: What?
>
> **Milteer**: The more bodyguards he has the easier it is to get him.
>
> **Somersett**: Well, how in the hell do you figure would be the best way to get him?
>
> **Milteer**: From an office building with a high-powered rifle. How many people does he have going around who look just like him? Do you know about that?
>
> **Somersett**: No, I never heard he had anybody.
>
> **Milteer**: He has about fifteen. Whenever he goes anyplace, he knows he is a marked man.
>
> **Somersett**: You think he knows he is a marked man?
>
> Milteer: Sure he does.
>
> **Somersett**: They are really going to try to kill him?

---

144   I have a tough time believing the allegations of Garrett Trapnell, as he had a history of mental illness, lying, criminal behavior, and of being a conman: *The Man Who Knew Too Much*, pages 414-418; FBI report dated 12/20/63 in CD 196. I am also on the fence about the allegations of former FBI agent M. Wesley Swearingen, who claimed that a Cuban exile informant told him of a conspiracy to kill JFK (Swearingen, *To Kill A President*). While I wouldn't necessarily rule out the allegations of Trapnell or Swearingen, the ones I do credit appear more solid and credible.

145   *From an Office Building with a High-Powered Rifle: One FBI Agent's View of the JFK Assassination* by Don Adams (2012).

Milteer: Oh, yeah, it is in the working. Brown himself, Brown is just as likely to get him as anybody in the world. He hasn't said so, but he tried to get Martin Luther King.

After a few more minutes of conversation, Somersett again spoke of assassination.

Somersett: ... Hitting this Kennedy is going to be a hard proposition, I tell you. I believe you may have figured out a way to get him, the office building and all that. I don't know how the Secret Service agents cover all them office buildings everywhere he is going. Do you know whether they do that or not?

Milteer: Well, if they have any suspicion they do that, of course. But without suspicion, chances are that they wouldn't. You take there in Washington. This is the wrong time of the year, but in pleasant weather, he comes out on the veranda and somebody could be in a hotel room across the way and pick him off just like that.

Somersett: Is that right?

Milteer: Sure, disassemble a gun. You don't have to take a gun up there, you can take it up in pieces. All those guns come knock down. You can take them apart.

Before the end of the tape, the conversation returns to Kennedy.

Milteer: Well, we are going to have to get nasty...

Somersett: Yeah, get nasty.

Milteer: We have got to be ready, we have got to be sitting on go, too.

Somersett: Yeah, that is right.

Milteer: There ain't any countdown to it, we have just got to be sitting on go. Countdown, they can move in on you, and go they can't. Countdown is all right for a slow prepared operation. But in an emergency operation, you have got to be sitting on go.

Somersett: Boy, if that Kennedy gets shot, we have go to know where we are at. Because you know that will be a real shake. . .

Milteer: They wouldn't leave any stone unturned there. No way. They will pick up somebody within hours afterwards, if anything like that would happen, just to throw the public off.

Somersett: Oh, somebody is going to have to go to jail, if he gets killed.

Milteer: Just like Bruno Hauptmann in the Lindbergh case, you know.[146]

---

146   *From an Office Building with a High-Powered Rifle: One FBI Agent's View of the JFK Assassination* by Don Adams, 2012.

The Secret Service knew about this Milteer prophecy before Dallas, yet did not properly act on it.[147] Former FBI agent Don Adams 2012 book *From an Office Building with a High-Powered Rifle: One FBI Agent's View of the JFK Assassination* is highly recommended on this subject. The Florida trip of 11/16-11/18/63 was cause for worry for the members of the Secret Service. In an article by the *Tampa Tribune* dated November 23, 1963 entitled "Threats On Kennedy Made Here":

> Tampa police and Secret Service agents scanned crowds for a man who had vowed to assassinate the President here last Monday, Chief of Police J. P. Mullins said yesterday. In issuing notice to all participating security police prior to the President's motorcade tour in Tampa, Mullins had said: "I would like to advise all officers that threats against the President have been made from this area in the last few days."
>
> A memo from the White House Secret Service dated Nov. 8 reported: "Subject made statement of a plan to assassinate the President in October 1963: Subject stated he will use a gun, and if he couldn't get closer he would find another way. Subject is described as: White, male, 20, slender in build, etc."
>
> Mullins said the Secret Service had been advised of three persons in the area who reportedly had made threats on the President's life. One of the three was – and still is – in jail here under heavy bond. Mullins said he did not know if the other two men have followed the Presidential caravan to Dallas. Sarasota County Sheriff Ross E. Boyer also said yesterday that officers who protected Kennedy in Tampa Monday were warned about "a young man" who had threatened to kill the President during that trip.

A CO2 PRS file, released to the HSCA on 5/3/78 and available only recently, reveals this probable threat subject by name: John Warrington.[148] As Secret Service agent Dale Wunderlich confirmed to me: "CO-2 cases were individuals who were of record with the Protective Research Division of the United States Secret Service."[149] WHD advance agent Lubert "Bert" DeFreese admitted to the HSCA that "a threat did surface in connection with the Miami trip ... there was an active threat against the President which the Secret Service was aware

147   See chapter two of my first book *Survivor's Guilt* (2013); *From an Office Building with a High-Powered Rifle: One FBI Agent's View of the JFK Assassination* by Don Adams (2012), pages 81-85.
148   RIF#'s 180-10118-10041 and 10033.
149   E-mail to author dated 10/9/99.

in November 1963 in the period immediately prior to JFK's trip to Miami made by a group of people."[150]

Kinney told the author, "we had a scare" down there, an unspecified "organized crime" threat related to this same trip.[151] In fact, there were six pages of threat subjects and information, including the subjects Orlando Bosch, Pedro Diaz Lanz, Enrique Llaca, Jr., and others.[152]

An HSCA interview with Secret Service agent Robert J. Jamison states: "the threat of November 18, 1963 was posed by a mobile, unidentified rifleman with a high-powered rifle fitted with a scope."[153] The author interviewed Special Agent in Charge of PRS, Robert Bouck, on September 27, 1992. Bouck was responsible for monitoring all threats to the life of the President, as well as informing his agents of those threats. Bouck knew about the 11/9/63 Joseph Milteer threats that were monitored by the Miami Secret Service field office before the assassination.[154] It is easy to see, then, why JFK said to Dave Powers, upon his return from the Florida trip, "Thank God nobody wanted to kill me today!"[155]

Eugene Dinkin[156] [157]was an Army Cryptographer (an NSA code-breaker) stationed in France who intercepted two secret military codes (one in mid-October 1963 and the other on 11/2/63) about a specific plot to kill Kennedy which was to occur on 11/28/63 and was to be blamed on a Communist or a Negro who would be designated as the assassin. Based on this alarming information, Dinkin wrote a letter to RFK before the assassination but heard nothing back in response. Alarmingly, a declassified CIA document places intelligence operative/assassin Jean Souetre "in Fort Worth on the morning of November 22 and in Dallas in the afternoon," exactly where JFK was at those times. This mortal threat to French President Charles DeGaulle was "expelled from the U. S. at Fort Worth or Dallas eighteen hours after the assassination," according to this document.[158]

---

150   HSCA document 180-10083-10419.

151   Author's interview with Sam Kinney 3/4/94.

152   RIF#154-10002-10422: Miami, FL 11/18/63.

153   HSCA document 180 – 10074-10394.

154   HSCA Report, page 233. See also *The Killing of a President* by Robert Groden (1993), pages 153-155 and *The Men Who Killed Kennedy*.

155   *A Hero for Our Time* by Ralph Martin (1988), page 503.

156   *They Killed Our President: 63 Reasons to Believe There Was A Conspiracy to Assassinate JFK* by Jesse Ventura (2013), pages 297-300; *Bloody Treason* by Noel Twyman (1997), pages 522-531.

157   https://www.maryferrell.org/pages/Allegations_of_PFC_Eugene_Dinkin.html.

158   See also: https://www.archives.gov/files/research/jfk/releases/2018/104-10185-10009.pdf.

CIA HISTORICAL REVIEW PROGRAM
RELEASE IN FULL 1995

-2-

1964

8. Jean SOUETRE aka Michel ROUX aka Michel MERTZ - On 5 March, Mr. Papich advised that the French had hit the Legal Attache in Paris and also the SDECE man had queried the Bureau in New York City concerning subject stating that he had been expelled from the U.S. at Fort Worth or Dallas 48 hours after the assassination.* He was in Fort Worth on the morning of 22 November and in Dallas in the afternoon. The French believe that he was expelled to either Mexico or Canada. In January he received mail from a dentist named Alderson living at 5803 Birmingham, Houston, Texas. Subject is believed to be identical with a Captain who is a deserter from the French Army and an activist in the OAS. The French are concerned because of De Gaulle's planned visit to Mexico. They would like to know the reason for his expulsion from the U.S. and his destination. Bureau files are negative and they are checking in Texas and with INS. They would like a check of our files with indications of what may be passed to the French. Mr. Papich was given a copy of CSCI-3/776,742 previously furnished the Bureau and CSDB-3/655,207 together with a photograph of Captain SOUETRE. WE/3/Public; CI/SIG; CI/OPS/Evans

* of President Kennedy

Air Force Sergeant David Frederick Christensen,[159] like Dinkin, also intercepted cable traffic of an impending assassination. This information only became public in 2017 thanks to the file releases.[160] [161] Christensen claimed that in the run up to Kennedy's death, he had intercepted an encrypted communication between certain individuals in the Cuban Government and an individual well known in the organized crime world, plotting the assassination. His attempts to get the intercept to NSA were thwarted, causing him (he claimed) to have a mental breakdown, a divorce, etc.

An excerpt from Christensen's letter:

Christ, you remember the position I worked at, in Sgt Praters section, don't you? You remember about a month or 6 weeks before I left Scotland, when I picked up a link mentioning the assassination of President Kennedy. How hard I tried to get it sent out, and because of that fuckin Forney and Delaughter they wouldn't send it to NSA. Since I have learned that the man's name, most mentioned was number 4 in a certain branch of organized crime at the time. Was number 2 last year. I will send you a form for proof of claim. This guy here "the 203" says I should be getting a service connected disability for my nerves. The "link was" Lisbon to Tangiers you remember. How I got my ass chewed for not dropping the link. Have learned that this branch of crime often will put out a feeler of forthcoming things. By sending it as a practice message.

Nick it really broke me up after Nov. 22, 63. Especially when I had it all before hand. It was first like the 202's said, Ha. I was nuts when the Russians

159   https://www.findagrave.com/memorial/115870312/david-frederick-christensen.
160   https://wikispooks.com/wiki/David_Christensen.
161   https://www.archives.gov/files/research/jfk/releases/docid-32270296.pdf.

Rose Cherami,[162] real name Melba Christine Marcades, was hospital-ized on 11/20/63, two days before the assassination, at Moosa Memorial Hospital in Eunice, Louisiana. Cherami had been en route from Florida to Dallas with two men who looked either Italian or Cuban. All three were part of a drug-smuggling ring but the two men told her that they were go-ing to assassinate the president in Dallas in just a few days. Cherami had been thrown out of the car and, soon after, was hit by another car while hitchhiking. The driver took her to the hospital.

After the assassination, Cherami told Dr. Victor Weiss that she knew both Ruby and Oswald and had seen them sitting together on several oc-casions at Ruby's club. She also said she was acting as a drug courier for Ruby (she was a stripper for Ruby, as well) and that Ruby was involved in the assassination plot.

On November 21, 1963, a government informant named Thomas Mosley was negotiating the sale of machine guns to a Cuban exile named Homer Echevarria. In the course of the transaction, Echevarria said that "we now have plenty of money – our new backers are Jews" and would close the arms deal "as soon as we [or they] take care of Kennedy." The next day, Kennedy was assassinated in Dallas. Mosley, an ATF informant, reported his conversation to the Secret Service, and that agency quickly began investigating what it termed "a group in the Chicago area who may have a connection with the JFK assassination." Echevarria was a member of the 30th November group, associated with the DRE with whom Os-wald had dealings the previous summer. Mosley said the arms deal was being financed through Paulino Sierra Martinez and his J.G.C.E. – Sierra interestingly was connected to Bobby Kennedy's effort to unite various exile groups, through Harry Ruiz Williams.[163]

During the HSCA's interview of former Secret Service agent Joseph Noonan,[164] who served on both Kennedy's White House Detail and in the Chicago office, stated that he "participated directly in surveillance in-volving Tom Mosely and Homer Echevarria ... he and [the] other agents were uneasy that the Cubans might have some ties to the Central Intelli-gence Agency and they called Assistant Chief Paul Paterni [himself a for-mer OSS man] and asked him to check on this possibility. Paterni assured

---

162   *Rose Cherami-Gathering Fallen Pedals* by Michael Marcades (2016/2020); *A Rose By Many Other Names: Rose Cherami and the JFK Assassination* by Todd C. Elliott (2013); the *JFK* movie (1991); *The Assassinations: Probe Magazine on JFK, MLK, RFK and Malcolm X* by James DiEugenio and Lisa Pease, Editors (2003), pages 225-237; from the new file releases: https://www.archives.gov/files/research/jfk/releases/2018/docid-32261445.pdf.

163   Secret Service report- Commission Document (CD) 87.

164   4/13/78 HSCA interview with Joseph Noonan.

them shortly thereafter that it was all right to proceed with their investigation. A little later they received a call from Headquarters [where Paterni was located] to drop everything on Mosely and Echevarria and send all memos, files, and their notebooks to Washington and not to discuss the case with anyone."

Twenty-five minutes before John F. Kennedy was assassinated, a British newspaper received an anonymous tip about "some big news" in the United States. The mystery call was made to a senior reporter at the *Cambridge News*, a paper that serves the East Anglia area of eastern England, on Nov. 22, 1963, at 6:05 p.m. local time. Kennedy was shot shortly afterward, as he rode in a presidential motorcade in Dallas, Texas, at 12:30 p.m. CST. Dallas is six hours behind Britain.

"The caller said only that the Cambridge News reporter should call the American Embassy in London for some big news and then hung up," the memo from the CIA's James Angleton to FBI director J. Edgar Hoover said. The memo, dated Nov. 26, 1963, says: "After the word of the President's death was received the reporter informed the Cambridge police of the anonymous call, and the police informed MI5. The important point is that the call was made, according to MI5 calculations, about 25 minutes before the President was shot. The Cambridge reporter had never received a call of this kind before, and MI5 state that he is known to them as a sound and loyal person with no security record."

MI5 is Britain's domestic security agency.

An excerpt from the memo:

2 3 NOV 1963

MEMORANDUM FOR: Director
Federal Bureau of Investigation

SUBJECT: Assassination of President Kennedy—Reported
Anonymous Telephone Message

1. The following cable from the CIA Station in London was reported orally to Mr. Samuel Papich at 0930 on 23 November:

2. The British Security Service (MI-5) has reported that at 1805 GMT on 22 November an anonymous telephone call was made in Cambridge, England, to the senior reporter of the Cambridge News. The caller said only that the Cambridge News reporter should call the American Embassy in London for some big news and then hung up.

Former Cuban prisoner and anti-Castro activist John Martino[165] accurately predicted that the president would be assassinated in Dallas on

165   *Someone Would Have Talked* by Larry Hancock (2006), numerous.

94

11/22/63. Martino was directly connected not just to the anti-Castro movement (Felipe Vidal Santiago, Gerry Patrick Hemming, Eddie Bayo, Frank Fiorini/Sturgis, David Morales, Rip Robertson, etc.) but to two of Jack Ruby's close associates, R.D. Matthews and Louis McWillie.

Martino was also much aware of Amador Odio and his daughters Sarita, Annie and Sylvia.

Richard Case Nagell was one of the most important witnesses there was in the JFK case. The only two rivals he has in regard to a conspiracy before the fact are Sylvia Odio (more on her in a moment) and the aforementioned Rose Cherami.

The following is merely a detailed summary from Dick Russell's book *The Man Who Knew Too Much* (1992/updated in 2003)[166]:

On 9/20/63, Nagell first went to a nearby post office before entering State National Bank in El Paso, Texas. He mailed five hundred-dollar bills to an address in Mexico. He then mailed two letters to the CIA. From the post office, Nagell walked over to the bank. There was a young police officer in plain sight. Nagell walked over to a teller and asked for a hundred dollars in American Express traveler's checks. But before Nagell could retrieve the checks, he turned and fired two shots into a wall right under the ceiling. He calmly returned the revolver to his belt and walked out the front door into the street. He stepped into his car and waited. When no one came out, he pulled his car halfway into the street. He saw the policeman from inside and stopped his car. When the policeman came over to his car with his gun pulled, Nagell put his hands up and surrendered.

The arresting officer was Jim Bundren. When Bundren searched Nagell one of the odd things he found on him was a mimeographed newsletter from the Fair Play for Cuba Committee. When Bundren searched the trunk of Nagell's car, there was a suitcase, two briefcases filled with documents, a 45-rpm record box, two tourist cards for entry into Mexico (one in the name of Aleksei Hidel, amazingly similar to Oswald's alias of Alex Hidell), a tiny Minolta camera, and a miniature film development lab. The personal effects Nagell had bore an uncanny resemblance to Oswald's.

A most compelling piece of evidence that Nagell had at the time of his arrest in September of 1963 was this near duplicate of Oswald's Uniformed Services Identification and Privileges Card. In the card seized by the Dallas Police, there is an overstamp that appears which says "October 1963." In the version that Nagell had, the imprint does not appear. Why?

---

166   Thanks also to renowned author James DiEugenio for his insights on the newer (2003) edition of this important book.

Because Nagell was in jail after September 20, 1963. Also, the photo of Oswald in the Nagell version is different. That photo is from a different ID card. And on that card, Oswald used his Alex J. Hidell alias. As Russell notes, this second card is believed to have been fabricated by Oswald himself, including the added picture. In other words, Nagell had to have been very close to Oswald prior to his September 1963 arrest. For he actually had access to Oswald's identification cards. Some versed in espionage would say that this indicates Nagell might have been either a "control agent" or a "surveillance operative" for Oswald. (The cards are pictured in the photo section of his book.) Nagell had other things in his possession similar to what Oswald had in November: names in their notebooks, Cuba-related leaflets, and miniature spy cameras.

After his arrest, on the way to the El Paso Federal Building, Nagell issued a statement to the FBI: "I would rather be arrested than commit murder and treason." At a preliminary hearing for Nagell, the defendant related to the officer the obvious: that he wanted to be caught. To which Bundren replied that he knew Nagell was not out to rob the bank. The following exchange then occurred:

> **Nagell**: Well, I'm glad you caught me. I really don't want to be in Dallas.
>
> **Bundren**: What do you mean by that?
>
> **Nagell**: You'll see soon enough.

After the assassination and the murder of Oswald by Jack Ruby, Officer Bundren was hit with the ramifications of Nagell's prediction. Bundred stated: "How the hell would he have previous knowledge of it? How would he know what was coming down in Dallas? Nagell knew a lot more about the assassination than he let on, or that the government let on. It's bothered me ever since."

Nagell had been monitoring Oswald in both 1962 and 1963. This surveillance, plus information gathered from others, led him to conclude that:

1. Oswald had no real relations with the FPCC;

2. He also had no real relations with pro-Castro elements, but he was gulled into believing he did;

3. He had no real relations with any Leftist or Marxist group;

4. He was not an agent or informant, in the generally accepted sense of the word;

5. He was involved in a conspiracy to murder President Kennedy which was not communist inspired or instigated by a foreign government.

One can see why New Orleans District Attorney Jim Garrison called Nagell the most important witness there is.

From the new file releases- yet another prediction:

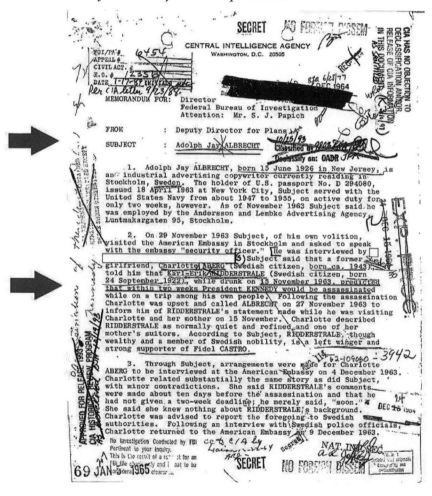

ITEM #10: THE SYLVIA ODIO INCIDENT

Numerous books,[167] as well as the *JFK* movie, cover this provocative incident well. Anti-Castro Cuban activist Sylvia Odio was visited by three men, two Cubans and a man named Leon Oswald, sometime in September 1963 (Sylvia's sister Annie was present while the other sister

---

167   See, for example, *The JFK Assassination* by James DiEugenio (2018), pages 50, 263-266, and 314.

who was not present, Sarita, told a friend named Lucille Connell about the incident early on). The men said they had come from New Orleans and were about to depart on a trip. One of the Cubans named Leopoldo called Sylvia back a day or two later and said the American, Leon Oswald, was an ex-Marine who was "loco" and a fine marksman. Leopoldo added that Oswald said that the Cubans should have killed Kennedy because of the Bay of Pigs and that the Cubans should have done it since he was the one holding the freedom of Cuba hostage.

While the incident is shocking, in and of itself, what is even more disturbing is the fact that the FBI knew about it in November 1963![168]

ITEM #11: 1996-ERA EVIDENCE LARGELY IGNORED

A prominent Secret Service agent, ASAIC Floyd Boring, and (brand new evidence) a White House Physician to the president, James Young,[169] spoke about skull fragments and, in Young's case, a misshapen bullet being found in the back seat area of the car, *more evidence of a frontal shot!*

In about the middle of the interview, Mr. Boring remembered that he and Mr. Paterni had inspected the President's limousine and the Secret Service follow-up car, but was unsure whether they had inspected them the night President Johnson returned to Washington (11/22/63), or the next morning (11/23/63). After independently recalling that they had searched the cars, Mr. Boring said that he (Boring) had discovered a piece of skull bone with brain attached in the rear of the follow-up car (the black Cadillac convertible called the "Queen Mary"), in the footwell just in front of the back seat bench. He said during follow-up questioning that the dimensions of this skull bone-brain fragment were approximately 1" X 2". He said he never picked it up or touched it himself, but that he simply pointed it out to Mr. Paterni. (Mr. Paterni was Deputy Chief of the Secret Service.) He said he did not write a report about this, and he did not know whether Mr. Paterni had written a report or not. He said he did not know what the disposition was of this debris/medical evidence. Mr. Boring made very clear during the interview that this fragment was in the rear of the follow-up car, not in the rear seat of the Presidential limousine. Initially, ARRB staff members Zimmerman and Horne had misunderstood Mr. Boring to mean that the bone-brain fragment was in the rear seat of the President's limousine, and Mr. Boring took specific pains to correct our misunderstanding during follow-on discussion of this matter.

Following his independent and spontaneous recollection of the car searches and his discovery of a skull bone-brain fragment in the rear of the follow-up car, ARRB questions moved into various documents related to the examination of the automobiles in the White House garage. Mr. Boring was shown the HSCA interview of SA Hickey, and was asked to read the portion wherein Mr. Hickey stated that Mr. Boring came down to the garage and told him statements were being collected in the White House, and directed (or suggested) that he go and write down his written statement. His response to this was that he did not remember even seeing SA Hickey in the White House garage, nor did he remember seeing SA Kinney, or any other Secret Service agents, or FBI agents, during the automobile searches. He did have some vague recollection of White House police being in the area.

When asked who directed he and Paterni to search the automobiles, he said that no one had; he said he thought it might be a good idea and had suggested it himself to Paterni, and that they undertook this search as independent action on their own initiative.

Next, Mr. Boring was asked what he remembered about bullet fragments which had been found in the Presidential limousine, and he said he did not remember anything about this.

In December of 2001 and January of 2002 during an interview with U.S. Navy Bureau of Medicine and Surgery historians,[170] Dr. James Young,

168   *The JFK Assassination* by James DiEugenio (2018), page 263; HSCA Volume 10, page 34
169   https://en.wikipedia.org/wiki/James_Young_(physician)
170   https://www.dropbox.com/s/dk6dwvzn6yq2ukd/NM%20and%20the%20Kennedy%20Assassination.pdf?dl=0

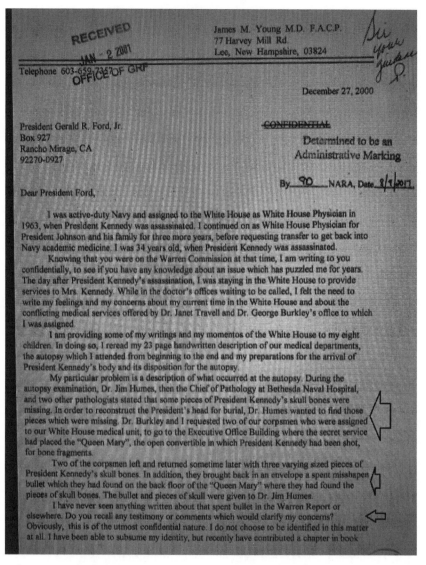

Telephone 603-659-7362

James M. Young M.D. F.A.C.P.
77 Harvey Mill Rd.
Lee, New Hampshire, 03824

December 27, 2000

President Gerald R. Ford, Jr.
Box 927
Rancho Mirage, CA
92270-0927

~~CONFIDENTIAL~~

Determined to be an
Administrative Marking

By 90 NARA, Date 8/1/2011

Dear President Ford,

I was active-duty Navy and assigned to the White House as White House Physician in 1963, when President Kennedy was assassinated. I continued on as White House Physician for President Johnson and his family for three more years, before requesting transfer to get back into Navy academic medicine. I was 34 years old, when President Kennedy was assassinated.

Knowing that you were on the Warren Commission at that time, I am writing to you confidentially, to see if you have any knowledge about an issue which has puzzled me for years. The day after President Kennedy's assassination, I was staying in the White House to provide services to Mrs. Kennedy. While in the doctor's offices waiting to be called, I felt the need to write my feelings and my concerns about my current time in the White House and about the conflicting medical services offered by Dr. Janet Travell and Dr. George Burkley's office to which I was assigned.

I am providing some of my writings and my momentos of the White House to my eight children. In doing so, I reread my 23 page handwritten description of our medical departments, the autopsy which I attended from beginning to the end and my preparations for the arrival of President Kennedy's body and its disposition for the autopsy.

My particular problem is a description of what occurred at the autopsy. During the autopsy examination, Dr. Jim Humes, then the Chief of Pathology at Bethesda Naval Hospital, and two other pathologists stated that some pieces of President Kennedy's skull bones were missing. In order to reconstruct the President's head for burial, Dr. Humes wanted to find those pieces which were missing. Dr. Burkley and I requested two of our corpsmen who were assigned to our White House medical unit, to go to the Executive Office Building where the secret service had placed the "Queen Mary", the open convertible in which President Kennedy had been shot, for bone fragments.

Two of the corpsmen left and returned sometime later with three varying sized pieces of President Kennedy's skull bones. In addition, they brought back in an envelope a spent misshapen bullet which they had found on the back floor of the "Queen Mary" where they had found the pieces of skull bones. The bullet and pieces of skull were given to Dr. Jim Humes.

I have never seen anything written about that spent bullet in the Warren Report or elsewhere. Do you recall any testimony or comments which would clarify my concerns? Obviously, this is of the utmost confidential nature. I do not choose to be identified in this matter at all. I have been able to subsume my identity, but recently have contributed a chapter in book

a physician who had worked with White House Physician Admiral George Burkley during the Kennedy administration, related that during the autopsy he had been given a bullet in an envelope by White House Medical Corpsman Chief Petty Officer Thomas Mills after his return from the White House garage to retrieve skull fragments from the rear of the limousine. Young described this bullet as jacketed, straight but with a bent tip and visually close in diameter to CE399, which he estimated to be ½ centimeter. Dr. Young voiced his concerns to the interviewers that he had never seen any reference to it in the Warren Commission investigation. The last thing he remembers is that he gave the envelope containing the bullet with the bent tip to Dr. Humes, the head autopsy pathologist, and that the bullet was never seen or documented after that.

Some of the major revelations:

- "Within five minutes Doctor Burkley and his group were at the [Parkland] hospital. When Doctor Burkley arrived, the President was already in the emergency room. He had a cut-down in place and a tracheotomy was being performed. Meanwhile, external cardiac massage was being applied. Solu-cortef was given IV [intravenously] and an external cardiac pacemaker was obtained. Doctor Burkley immediately evaluated the situation as hopeless as soon as he saw the gaping, bloody macerated huge wound and defect in the right posterior occipital area. ";

- "[W]hat happened was the body coming back from Texas landed at the Air Force Base there in D.C., Andrews I think it was ... [as]they were offloading the casket to put it into a Navy ambulance it slipped and actually one of the handles broke off the coffin. So there's been a lot of furor about Kennedy leaving Texas in no body bag. And, lo and behold, when he got to Bethesda they had a different coffin and they had him in a body bag. Well that's what happened. They had to change coffins before they took him out to Bethesda. So they changed the coffin to get one that did not have a broken handle on it, and apparently put him in a body bag.";

- "The autopsy began around five or five-thirty in the afternoon and actually went until four-thirty the following morning ... I stayed at the autopsy all night long ... it's terribly unfortunate that Dr. [George] Burkley actually gave an order to [autopsy doctor] Jim Humes ... that all of the autopsy notes that he had taken and done during the autopsy should be destroyed...";

- "When seeing him, I walked to the head of the table and looked at the gaping defect in the right posterior and middle cerebral areas, which had no obvious skull covering lying anywhere in sight. ";

- "[W]e had asked the two corpsmen to go down to the White House and pick up what was in the back of the car. They picked up the bullet off of the floor in the back of the car. Well, I decided that this is something, you know, the third bullet has never been decided about ever, apparently. So what I did was I decided there was only person still alive from the original Warren Commission [Gerald Ford]. I went through the entire Warren Commission book. I've got the whole report of the Warren Commission as a matter of fact. I went through the whole thing and there was nothing in it. Now, at that particular time nobody said anything about this. And I know what we did. We brought that in, I mean Chief [William] Martinell and Chief [Thomas] Mills went to the White House, went to the Queen Mary, got the stuff off of the floor in the back seat, brought it back to us and we gave that to Commander Humes at the time.";

• "I was in contact with the hospital notifying Captain [Robert] Canada [commander of Naval Hospital at Bethesda] of the projected arrival time, the probability of transport by helicopter of the body ... changes then indicated that the body would be brought to Bethesda by Navy ambulance.";

• "[W]e were joined by Chief Hendrix who had just happened to go to the hospital as well. We shortly were joined by Chiefs Mills and Martinell who had brought an envelope to Bethesda which contained material removed from the convertible which they had been requested to obtain."

This I'm going to put in parenthetically. This is not written. Doctor Burkley and I had requested them, at the request of Doctor Humes, to go down to the White House after three or four hours in the autopsy room. And Doctor Humes had said that he was missing some bones from the President's skull. And he wondered whether there might be some pieces left in the back of the "Queen Mary" and that he would like to get those pieces and bring them back to Bethesda so he could reconstruct the head. That was the car in which President Kennedy was riding in Texas. And they did. They went down, both Chiefs Mills and Martinell went down to the White House.... The envelope contained three pieces of skull bone, one about three inches in diameter, another two inches in diameter and the third about one to one and a half inches in diameter. It also contained a brass slug about half a centimeter in diameter and distorted. These were found on the floor of the blood-spattered convertible. The convertible was splattered with considerable brain tissue. ";

Pretty powerful new information. Even if one concedes that Young may be referring to the presidential limousine as the "Queen Mary"[171],

---

171   Curiously, Boring phoned the ARRB the next day and said he meant the president's limousine, despite being adamant the day before. It could very well be that Boring realized the implications of the bone fragment being found in the follow-up car and the implications of this finding going against official history that made him change his mind and, with concern, take the extra step of actually phoning the ARRB to issue a retraction of sorts. Doug Horne of the ARRB is highly alarmed and suspicious of this retraction as to what vehicle the fragment was found in, as am I: *Inside The ARRB* by Doug Horne (2009), pages 1098-1099, 1145-1146

the additional bullet he speaks of, the description of the head wound (also shared by Burkley), the body bag, the helicopter information and the destruction of Humes notes are of prime importance, to say the least. Coupled with Boring's information, this is more evidence of data going against official history. It is important to keep in mind that, according to official history, only bullet *fragments*, not a whole bullet, were found in the *front* of the car, not the back.[172]

ITEM #12: UNAUTHORIZED "SECRET SERVICE" AGENTS IN DEALEY PLAZA

Finally, perhaps the greatest smoking gun in the entire JFK assassination case: the presence of unauthorized "Secret Service" agents in Dealey Plaza, as verified by the accounts of five police officers and at least six spectators, not including Lee Harvey Oswald himself.[173] Was it a case of mistaken identity? Was he a fake agent? Was he a real agent?[174] These were the questions the author felt he had to answer or try to the best of his ability to do so. What does the "official" record reveal about these alleged 'sightings'? We think we know ... but do we? Reading the original official statement, or party line, was quite an eye-opening experience: "All the Secret Service agents assigned to the motorcade stayed with the motorcade all the way to the hospital. None remained at the scene of the shooting, and none entered the School Book Depository at or immediately after the time of the shooting."[175] In actual fact, this statement, drafted by Secretary of the Treasury C. Douglas Dillon and General Counsel G. d'Andelot Belin, only accounts for the sixteen agents traveling in the motorcade – two in the lead car (Lawson and Sorrels), two in the limousine (Greer

---

172   3 H 497.
173   Officers – Joe M. Smith: 7 H 535 & 2/8/78 HSCA interview (JFK Document 005886); D. V. Harkness: 6 H 312, *Reasonable Doubt* by Henry Hurt (New York: Henry Holt & Co., 1985), pp. 110-111 & *No More Silence*, pp. 206 and 209; Seymour Weitzman: 7 H 107; Roger Craig: *Crossfire*, p. 330; Edgar L. Smith: *No More Silence*, p. 199. Spectators – Malcolm Summers: "Nova" PBS documentary 11/88 and 1988 Jack Anderson documentary *Who Murdered JFK?* ; Gordon Arnold: *Dallas Morning News*, 8/27/78; Ron Fischer: 6 H 196; Ed Hoffman: *Eyewitness* by Ed Hoffman and Ron Friedrich (Texas: JFK Lancer Publications, 1998); Sam Holland: 6 H 247-254; John Martin, Jr.: *Encyclopedia of the JFK Assassination*, p. 149; Lee Harvey Oswald 24 H 479..
174   DPD Officer Joe Marshall Smith had drawn his revolver on an individual he had confronted on the grassy knoll: "Just as I did, he showed me that he was Secret Service." The "agent" produced credentials and said he was a Secret Service Agent. However, the man had dirty hands and untidy clothes. In fact, Smith later told author Fred Newcomb in the early 1970's that he believed that (real) Secret Service men had positioned themselves among bystanders, presumably a standard security measure ... but it was not and, officially, no one was there." (*Murder From Within*, pp. 75 & 101).
175   Commission Document 3, p. 44 – emphasis added. Former agent Bill Livingood even told researcher Gary Rowell in 1991: "There were no Secret Service agents on the grassy knoll." [Author's article in the Dec. 1994 "Investigator" research journal; author's interview with Bill Livingood, 11/92; author's phone conversations with Gary Rowell].

and Kellerman), eight in the follow up (Kinney, Roberts, Hill, McIntyre, Ready, Landis, Bennett, Hickey), one in LBJ's car (Youngblood), and the three in the VP follow-up car (Johns, Taylor and Kivett). We can discard the notion that "Lem" Johns was the agent: Johns told the author on 2/11/04 that he "ran right to the first convertible" and was only on the street very briefly: "Time enough to catch a ride."[176] In fact, in the 2013 DVD *Lem Johns: Secret Service Man*, Johns is equally adamant in his refutation of the notion that he was the "agent" on the knoll. "Absolutely not," Johns stated, adding that he stood in the street to hitch a ride for a minute or less and did not go to the knoll. If we stipulate from the record that the other WHD agents assigned to the Trade Mart, Love Field, Austin, and other places, were really there the whole time,[177] what does that leave us?

For one thing, there were, officially speaking, six agents in the Dallas field office of the Secret Service: SAIC Sorrels, as noted, in the lead car; Robert Steuart and John Joe Howlett, at the Trade Mart; Roger C. Warner (of the Washington Field Office on his first presidential assignment) and William H. Patterson, both stationed at Love Field. But that is only four of the six agents. And there's the rub. The Secret Service reports in the Warren Commission Volumes confirm what all the aforementioned agents were doing on November 22, but what about the other two: Charles E. Kunkel and James F. "Mike" Howard? There are no reports from these two men in the volumes (quite a strange departure), and no testimony was taken from them (although, with no testimony taken from seven of the eight SS agents in the follow up, that should not surprise us).

Coincidentally (?), both of these agents would go on to guard the Oswald family after the assassination and subsequent death of Lee Oswald; in fact, his mother Marguerite Oswald felt that these agents were involved in the actual conspiracy itself![178] Howard, who would go on to join the WHD on March 29, 1964, was interviewed in an AP story covered in the *Fresno Bee* on 11/22/93, the 30th anniversary of JFK's murder, as well as a *Houston Post* story of a similar nature. Despite the obvious need to focus on the assassination, there was no mention in that interview of where

---

176   See also Michael T. Griffith's important article titled, "The Man Who Wasn't There, Was There." In addition to what he told the author, Johns told the HSCA: "…I was running towards LBJ's car, which was now some distance away from us and picking up speed. I was left on the street with no way to get back in our car. A passing car with White House photographers in it came by and one of them recognized me. He said 'Hey, there's Lem Johns. Let's give him a ride.' They stopped and picked me up and we drove to the Trade Mart…" This further debunks the notion that Johns was the agent of unknown repute in Dealey Plaza [HSCA interview with Johns, 8/8/78: RIF# 180-10074-10079].
177   This, of course, does not rule them out.
178   1H 169-170.

either Howard or Kunkel were during the critical time of the shooting.[179] However, in 1999, during a lecture in Dallas, Howard made the claim that he was cleaning the room JFK had used at the Hotel Texas, and that Kunkel was in Washington, D.C on an unspecified investigation at the time. Still, Howard and Kunkel's whereabouts remain unverified.[180] Likewise, WHD Agent Ronald M. Pontius has a murky record of his exact whereabouts between 11/21 and 11/22/63.[181]

Another clue to the mystery of the "unknown agent" in Dealey Plaza on November 22 may come from the statements of former Dallas agent Robert A. Steuart, as revealed in Bill Sloan's 1993 work, *JFK: Breaking the Silence*.[182] Although the agent who spoke to Sloan was unnamed in the book, Sloan confirmed to this author the agent's identity based on the firm conviction that this agent had to have been Steuart. Why? Because, as the author told Sloan, the agent used identical phrases during two interviews with Steuart conducted in 1992 and 1993. In any event, Sloan did indeed confirm the author's suspicions. So, just what did Steuart say to Sloan? Sworn to absolute secrecy about the "Kennedy thing," Steuart went on to say, "I can't talk about it.... There are so many things I could tell you, but I just can't ... I can't tell you anything ... I'd like to, but I can't.... It was a very heavy deal, and they would know. Someone would know. It's ... too dangerous, even now." This from a local agent, stationed at the Trade Mart on November 22, 1963.

Secret Service agent Abraham Bolden stated that it was "a matter widely known in the Service" that some unauthorized person had used Secret Service credentials in Dallas on 11/22/63 (again, perhaps the greatest smoking gun in the entire case). Accordingly, all Special Agents were required to surrender their identification documents for "an unprecedented

179   FROM 18 H 675:"On December 4, 1963, Special Agent James M. Howard, assigned to the Dallas, Texas, office, and who assisted in the advance arrangements at Fort Worth, Texas, advised that he was on duty at the Texas hotel from the time the president arrived until 4:00 a.m. On November 22, 1963; that he was representing the Dallas Office and had occasion to meet and to talk to many of the Special Agents accompanying the President from Washington in the lobby, at the President's suite and in the Agents' rooms. He stated that at no time did he ever see any Special Agent of this Service in an intoxicated condition; that he himself was not at the Press Club [how about the Cellar?]. This Special Agent's remarks are worthy of comment, as it is known that he does not drink intoxicants of any kind, and it is believed that any remarks by him would be unbiased [!]." [emphasis added] Thus, by the written record, Howard is unaccounted for after 4 a.m. on 11/22/63 until approximately 2 p.m. or so, when he shows up at Love Field in a car driven by SA Bill Duncan [report of Agent Roger Warner, CD 3].

180   Re: Kunkel – *Austin American-Statesman*, 6/29/92; See Gus Russo's book, *Live By The Sword*, p. 473, for more revisionist statements from Secret Service agent Mike Howard, Robert Gemberling, and Frank Ellsworth, a Dallas ATF agent, on the likely agent on the knoll.

181   Agent Pontius himself mentioned this, based on my first book, during his appearance on *The Kennedy Detail* documentary from 2010.

182   pp. 1-5.

Service-wide check."[183] Bolden further added, "Do you know what happened to Harvey Henderson? I heard that he had been relieved of his Detail by President Kennedy himself … Harvey had made some threats like, 'We'll get you' … I understand that he told the President 'I'll get you', or something to that effect … (it was) no secret that Kennedy wanted him removed from the detail … Harvey was a quick-tempered guy who couldn't take the heat.… Where is Harvey Henderson at? I think that you would do well if you could find out where Harvey Henderson was on November 22. Can you track him down?"

In reference to the illicit Secret Service credentials present in Dealey Plaza on 11/22/63,[184] Mr. Bolden said, in reference to Harvey Henderson, "that's the first thing that crossed my mind – he would have the nerve, the guts, the anger, the craziness, the instability … I'm not saying he was in Dallas, but I'm saying that … it would be something to look at."

Dallas Police Chief Jesse Curry stated in 1977: "I think he must have been bogus – certainly the suspicion would point to the man as being involved, some way or another, in the shooting, since he was in an area immediately adjacent to where the shots were – and the fact that he had a badge that purported him to be Secret Service would make it seem all the more suspicious."[185]

So, to summarize the 12 additional items (in addition to the 12 reasons for conspiracy in chapter one) I consider smoking guns, including new evidence:

1. Video evidence that the so-called magic (or pristine) bullet of the single bullet theory scenario was still in Governor Connally's leg well after it was allegedly discovered on a stretcher at Parkland Hospital;

2. Video evidence of a Secret Service agent being removed from the area of the rear of the limousine;

3. CIA presence at Parkland Hospital;

4. The death of a Secret Service agent who would have driven Kennedy in Dallas a month *before* the assassination;

5. Secret Service agents and other prominent principal witnesses did *not* believe the Warren Commission's single bullet theory!

183   *A Citizen's Dissent*, Mark Lane (New York: Holt, Rhinehart & Winston, 1968), p. 193; AARC files on Bolden provided by researcher Bill Adams; Author's interview/correspondence with Bolden, 9/15 & 9/16/93.
184   Agent Marty Venker later said, " … they'd [the Secret Service] given him phony ID's so he could work undercover at demonstrations." (*Confessions of an Ex-Secret Service Agent*, p. 246).
185   *Conspiracy* by Anthony Summers (1980), page 51

6. Several prominent principals in the case believed there was a conspiracy;

7. Commission Exhibit (CE) 399, the so-called magic bullet of single bullet theory (SBT) infamy, had no proper chain of possession;

8. Suspicious images on the overpass and on the knoll;

9. The assassination predictions of Joseph Milteer, Eugene Dinkin, David Christensen, Rose Cherami, Thomas Mosley, an anonymous caller, John Martino and Richard Case Nagell;

10. The Sylvia Odio incident;

11. 1996-era evidence largely ignored: A prominent Secret Service agent, ASAIC Floyd Boring, and *(brand new evidence)* a White House Physician to the president, James Young, spoke about skull fragments and, in Young's case, a misshapen bullet being found in the back seat area of the car, more evidence of a frontal shot!;

12. Unauthorized "Secret Service" agents in Dealey Plaza.

Two chapters, 24 factors pointing to conspiracy. I believe the case is overwhelming for conspiracy and it is very hard to dismiss these all as mere coincidences, confusion, mistakes and so forth. To put it another way: if the official story (well, at least the first one from the Warren Commission) would have stated that Oswald fired from the *front*, you can bet your bottom dollar that much of this evidence would suddenly appear very credible in the eyes of lone-nutters, albeit with a spin to explain some of the still-apparent discrepancies, while the remaining factors that aren't seemingly explained by a frontal shooter would be dismissed or denied.

In this fictional scenario (Oswald allegedly firing from the front), the arguments would seem comical to a lot of us, because they would mirror what we believe about conspiracy in the real non-fictional world: "The majority of the witnesses said the shots came from the front where Oswald was"; "they smelled gunpowder and saw the smoke from Oswald's frontal assault on the president"; "the Zapruder film and the other films show Kennedy's head rocketing backwards and to the left from the shot fired from Oswald in his front perch"; "the neck wound was of course an entrance wound-what else can it be?"; "the head wound was obviously caused by Oswald's shot from the front"; and so on.

Furthermore, if the government would have admitted to a "limited" conspiracy like in the Lincoln assassination (one obvious shooter who never denied his deed with several like-minded conspirators) or the Truman assassination attempt (two obvious shooters in a conspiracy that began and ended just with them), even more of this evidence would be explained away by them: "Ok, so Oswald had help from a few like-minded 'lone nuts' like himself-so what?"; "Odio did see the real Oswald – and your point is what?"; "perhaps those agents encountered in Dealey Plaza were afraid to come forward because they failed to stop Oswald"; and so on.

In any event, can you now see how impossible it is to explain the Kennedy assassination as the act of one person, Oswald or anyone else?

More of the amazing people I have met in Dallas 1997-2019 (clockwise, left to right) – Dr. David Mantik, Robert Groden and his lovely wife Janet, Beverly Oliver, Judyth Baker, Gary Shaw, Ed Tatro, Matt Douthit and (center) Pat Speer:

CHAPTER THREE

MANDATORY READING AND VIEWING

This may feel like an intermission, but it is not intended to be. I just feel that, after fifty-plus years and hundreds (if not thousands) of works on the assassination, it is very important to exercise some judgement and select what I consider to be the very best books on the subject. In my opinion, many books, even the so-called classics, are dated now, as much new research has eclipsed those seminal works. We were once in a guessing game and theorizing ruled the day. However, after the many releases of the Assassination Records Review Board (ARRB) in the late 1990's, the days of guessing, theorizing and speculating are over.

It is important to go with the most up to date and scholarly works. We must think like scholars and historians and not as the "buffs" some choose to denigrate us by. While there are a few notable exceptions (*Best Evidence* by David Lifton, *High Treason 2* by Harrison Livingstone, *The Warren Omission* by Walt Brown, perhaps *Bloody Treason* by Noel Twyman and *Conspiracy* by Anthony Summers, as well), I feel the very best titles are those which have come out in the 21st century. Not that quite a few older books are not (still) good, per se. It is just that the newer works offer all that and much more.

So, without further ado, here is my list of the best works on the assassination.

Reclaiming Parkland: Tom Hanks, Vincent Bugliosi, and the JFK Assassination by James DiEugenio (2013) and updated as *The JFK Assassination: The Evidence Today* (2018): This is a highly entertaining and well written work. This is my favorite book on the subject. I truly admire Jim DiEugenio's work and he is at all times witty and knowledgeable. This is the ultimate rebuttal to Vincent Bugliosi's massive tome *Reclaiming History*, as well as the movie loosely based off it called *Parkland*. That said, it is so much more. DiEugenio demonstrates the case for conspiracy while debunking Bugliosi, yet he does it in a respectful way, demonstrating what is valuable about his work at the same time. This is one of those books that is hard to put down that you just want to reread again and again (get the 2018 edition).

The Lee Harvey Oswald Files: Why the CIA Killed Kennedy by Flip de Mey (2016): This book is truly amazing for its detailed demolition of so many sacred cows of the lone nut/Warren Commission camp. Items that we take as an act of faith (the rifle being dismantled in a bag, then put together), the paper bag, the bullets, the casings, and more are expertly shown to not be anywhere near as conclusive as the official story would have us believe, to put it mildly. Quite frankly, I was blown away by this book. The first part of the work is worth the price of admission alone and, like DiEugenio's book above, it is one you will find yourself rereading again and again. There was much lone nut evidence that even I used to grudgingly take as compelling. No longer. You will see the impossibility of the basic evidence used to convict Oswald in the minds of most people being legitimate and persuasive. I am amazed it took this long for someone to dissect the case evidence in such a scholarly way without speculation, rationalizing, grasping at straws and way-out theories. I would also recommend his first book *Cold Case Kennedy: A New Investigation Into the Assassination of JFK* (2013). But read the second book first.

Destiny Betrayed: JFK, Cuba, and the Garrison Case by James DiEugenio (2012/ the Second Edition, not the original 1992 version): This is a massively updated and revised version of DiEugenio's seminal first book. Essentially, it is a brand new book, as little remains from that slimmer (and now dated) first edition. DiEugenio takes advantage of the many document releases from the ARRB to pepper his book with many new and intriguing facts about the Jim Garrison case and more. This is truly a scholarly, well written book. You will never look at the Garrison case the same way again. DiEugenio does much to vindicate the former New Orleans District Attorney and his controversial case. This book is also the title of the new Oliver Stone documentary. Highly recommended.

The Girl on the Stairs: The Search for a Missing Witness to the JFK Assassination by Barry Ernest (2013 Pelican edition): This book is extremely valuable for it proves that Oswald could not have been firing a rifle up on the sixth floor during the assassination because he wasn't even on the floor at the time. Very well written and documented, Ernest researched this topic thoroughly and it shows. This one is a game changer.

Inside the Assassination Records Review Board: The U.S. Government's Final Attempt to Reconcile the Conflicting Medical Evidence in the Assassination of JFK – Volumes 1-5 by Douglas Horne (2009): Warts and all, this is a very important series of books, as much of the ARRB medical testimony is revealed with salient commentary by Horne. Vital medical evidence witnesses like the three autopsy doctors (James Humes, J. Thornton Boswell, and Pierre Finck), as well as Dr. Robert Karnei, Ed Reed, Jerrol Custer, Floyd Reibe, Dr. Robert McClelland, and a host of others were interviewed, often with amazing results that went against official history.

In the Eye of History: Disclosures in the JFK Assassination Medical Evidence by William Matson Law (new 2015 edition updated and expanded with DVD): Law has written a seminal book on the medical evidence. His interviews of FBI agents Sibert and O'Neill, Bethesda autopsy witnesses Jerrol Custer (which I was a part of) and James Jenkins, and others are essential. Law lets the witnesses speak at length and asks cogent questions. This is a book that is very hard to put down.

Enemy of the Truth: Myths, Forensics, and the Kennedy Assassination by Sherry Fiester (2012): Another "warts and all" volume. While it has some specious arguments and some flawed logic, what is good about it is worth the price of admission alone. Fiester proves conspiracy and a frontal head shot, so it is hard to get too down on some of the problems in the book. Despite a few misgivings, still highly recommended.

From an Office Building with a High-Powered Rifle: One FBI Agent's View of the JFK Assassination by Don Adams (2012): This slim volume is quite important for two reasons: it is the perspective of an honorable FBI agent in the case and it demonstrates how important Joseph Milteer's foreknowledge of the assassination truly was. Yes, this story has been told before, but not in this detail and from this unique vantage point.

John F. Kennedy's Head Wounds: A Final Synthesis – and a New Analysis of the Harper Fragment by Dr. David Mantik (2015): Dr. Mantik is a highly qualified physician who has studied the autopsy x-rays and photos at the National Archives many times in detail. He proves conspiracy and cover-up in the medical evidence by the government. A thorough analysis that is hard to put down. On a personal note, I am a big fan of Dr. Mantik, having met him at several conferences and having participated in two documentaries with him (*The Men Who Killed Kennedy* and *A Coup in Camelot*). I even participated in a documentary his daughter Meredith was making.

First On the Scene: Interviews With Parkland Hospital Doctors on the Assassination of President John F. Kennedy by Brad Parker (2014): Brad Parker does a masterful job both compiling the essential medical evidence from Parkland and conducting valuable new interviews. In other words, primary source evidence is his guide. Brad provides a very useful compilation of the Parkland doctors and nurses testimony before the Warren Commission, the HSCA and the ARRB. He also skillfully juxtaposes his original interviews and correspondence against both the medical personnel's prior statements and their (alleged) comments to author Gerald Posner of *Case Closed* infamy. I met Brad in Dallas on 11/22/97 and he even participated in a part of my on-camera interview with eyewitness Aubrey Rike. Parker is one of the good guys.

Someone Would Have Talked by Larry Hancock (2006): Hancock's roughly 600-page tome is a masterwork of research. Hancock is one of the true scholars in the field and is also an excellent writer. This book is a masterful synthesis of the surprisingly large number of people in the know who predicted the assassination to some extent or another. The connections and backgrounds of these people are deeply disturbing, fascinating and intriguing. An important work.

The Deputy Interviews: The True Story of J.F.K. Assassination Witness, and Former Dallas Deputy Sheriff, Roger Dean Craig by Steve Cameron (2019): This is a really good, straightforward book about one of the true heroes of this case, Roger Craig. Craig ran to the knoll right after the shots were fired and gained valuable first-hand knowledge. His plight after the assassination was a tragic one. Cameron does a masterful job culling all the known information about Craig and, more importantly, conducts some important new interviews with friends and relatives of Craig.

Into The Nightmare by Joseph McBride (2013): This is a large book with a lot of new information and several new twists on a well-worn subject. In particular, McBride's lengthy work on the Tippit case is very well done, indeed. In fact, this part of the book is worth the price of admission alone.

JFK & The Unspeakable by James Douglass (2010): Douglass book is universally acclaimed and justifiably so. While other books tackle the nuts and bolts of the case, his work tackles more the forest from the trees; the who and why are front and center. This is a very well written book that contains just enough specific details to keep one with an analytical bent interested. Essential.

Crossfire DVD by Jim Marrs (2014): While Marrs seminal book with the same title is truly a classic book from the late 1980's (and one of the major books the *JFK* movie was based on), this DVD, being an audio/visual presentation, is in many respects even more valuable and current. Told in a folksy, laidback conversational style, Marrs demonstrates in plain English all the tenets of conspiracy and cover-up. Its charm is that it is not high tech: just Marrs talking to the camera from a comfortable chair with a desk and computer. The visuals he inserts into the presentation add to the narrative. Highly recommended for the novice and even for the jaded expert.

A Coup in Camelot DVD/Blu Ray (2016): I am honored to have participated in this program- they did a very good job editing the major points I made about Secret Service malfeasance and worse into a user-friendly presentation. In addition, the other authors/researchers on the program (Sherry Fiester, Doug Horne, Jerry Dealey, Barry Ernest, Dr. David Mantik, and Dick Russell) do a masterful job espousing their ideas and work on the case. This program has a high-budget feel and is also highly recommended.

JFK by Oliver Stone (1991): Despite some flaws, this is an epic masterpiece that did more than hundreds of books on the case ever could. It presented the case for conspiracy in a very palatable and entertaining fashion with a veritable who's who of actors. In addition, the movie spawned actual legislation in the form of the JFK Records Act, which led directly to the formation of the ARRB. This is must-see viewing. Stone's movie will never be equaled, surpassed or even attempted again. In fact, it is amazing that it was made and became such a success, given the opposition to it by critics and even some in the government.

JFK: The Case for Conspiracy DVD by Robert Groden (1993/2003): Groden, an HSCA photographic expert, author, and major advisor to Stone's *JFK* movie, has created a terrific audio/visual presentation involving all the known films and photos of the assassination. Touching on the medical evidence, as well, Groden makes a powerful case for conspiracy, indeed. This is another must for your personal library. His other DVD, the 1995/2003 *The JFK Assassination Files* (Films), is also a must-have, although I would get this one first.

The Men Who Killed Kennedy (1988/1991/1995/2003): Flawed but indispensable. Yes, there are a few questionable ideas and witnesses, but, once you get passed them, there is a lot of value in this 9-part series (I was honored to be a part of number 7). Controversial and riveting, this Nigel Turner production was a popular A & E Network and History Channel presentation that has now recently been revived (parts 7-8) on Newsmax TV (and is still available on You Tube and on DVD-well, at least parts 1-6).

CHAPTER FOUR

Secret Service Findings—
A New Discovery and Much More

As many of you are no doubt aware, I am the author of four previous books, three of which centered on the Secret Service, in general, and the agents who were assigned to President Kennedy, in particular. In this regard, rather than try to reinvent the wheel and merely repeat much from my prior books, in this chapter, I am going to present new evidence not revealed in my prior books. Out of necessity, a fair amount of my previous research will appear in some shape or form, but it will be framed by new evidence and new perspectives. This will enable the new reader to not have to refer back to my previous books, while the experienced reader who may have read one or all of my prior books will not feel this section is overly repetitive due to this new information. I believe you will find this chapter quite informative, to say the least. It will be very difficult to view the agents who guarded JFK the same way ever again.

THE CURIOUS CASE OF BILL GREER AND HIS WIFE:

While doing my routine Internet searches of former Secret Service agents and family members, I also check to see who has recently passed away (for the record, from the Dallas motorcade, only agents Clint Hill and Paul Landis are left). I clicked on William Greer's Find-A-Grave site: https://www.find-agrave.com/memorial/17844947.

Then I clicked on his second wife's site: https://www.findagrave.com/memorial/200944121/mary-elizabeth-greer.

It was here that I found out that Mary Elizabeth (Finger [her maiden name]) Greer, Bill Greer's second wife, passed away recently: 7/6/2019, age 96.

But here is the real startling information:

"…in 1944, at the age of 21, Mary was recruited by the Department of the Navy to work in Washington, D.C. where she lived in a women's dormitory. In 1958, she began working for the National Security Agency (the NSA) in Fort Meade, Maryland, until she retired in 1973."

In the NSA from 1958-1973! (the NSA had a top secret file on Lee Harvey Oswald, as the newly-released files confirm[1]). Mary's first husband, a WWII veteran buried in Arlington National Cemetery, died at the young age of 40 in 1966, just as Bill Greer was retiring from the Secret Service: https://www.findagrave.com/memorial/49337589/joseph-c-wolfe

---

1   NSA doc dated 10/8/76 released via FOIA request. It appears that this file was destroyed. *JFK Beyond A Question Of Conspiracy: An Investigation And Revision Of History - Including New 2018 Material!* By Ralph Thomas (2018).

Interestingly, Greer was in the Navy at this time, then he was assigned to FDR's yacht before entering the Secret Service ... did Greer know his SECOND wife before marrying his FIRST wife?

GREER

Greer's first wife Ethel died in 1969. His only child–his son Richard (named after Bill's father) – had some very interesting things to say to me when I spoke to him in 1991 (more on this in a moment).

What is very telling is what Greer's widow told author Christopher Fulton: "he really disliked the president."[2] (Fulton was also able to speak to former agent Robert Bouck, who told him, as he told me, that there was a conspiracy. Fulton also spoke to former agent *and CIA officer* Roger Warner, even getting Warner to commit to writing some important information).[3]

A recent article from Ireland noted the following[4]:

"In a new book – *Survivor's Guilt: The Secret Service and the Failure to Protect President Kennedy* – author Vince Palamara dedicates a whole chapter to Greer, who he calls "the most important agent."

After emigrating to the US in 1929 aged 19 [note: Greer said it was in February 1930[5]], farm laborer's son William Robert Greer worked as a chauffeur in the Boston and New York areas before participating in the Second World War with the US Navy in November 1942.

His final wartime posting was as a crew member on board the presidential yacht.

Drumbonaway lodge secretary Edgar Kirkpatrick said he was shocked to see Greer's name on the records when asked to check by the *News Letter*.

"I have it all here in the lodge books. We have the records right the way to when the lodge was formed. We don't have any Greers nowadays but I always remember my father talking about Richard Greer (Bill's father) who was a servant man around here working for the farmers.

"But I didn't know about his son at all until I read up in the books. There were a lot of people emigrating around that time and I notice from the lodge records that they were bought presents by the lodge – the man got a walking stick and the lady got an umbrel-

---

2 *The Inheritance* by Christopher Fulton (2018), page 31.

3 *The Inheritance* by Christopher Fulton (2018), pages 28-29, 32, 398.

4 https://www.newsletter.co.uk/news/crime/tyrone-born-jfk-driver-mired-in-conspiracy-was-in-orange-order-1-5699969.

5 2 H 113.

la," Mr. Kirkpatrick said.

Within two weeks of discharge from the Navy in October 1945 Greer was sworn into the Secret Service.

He had been a favorite driver and bodyguard of both presidents Truman and Eisenhower before joining the Kennedy protection detail.

The lodge secretary said the membership has been told about the JFK connection but won't believe it until they see it in print.

"They're not taking it seriously, but I took an evening and read through all the books and it was interesting. I couldn't believe he'd come from here and went on to drive for Kennedy," Mr. Kirkpatrick added.

The discovery of Greer's Orange affiliations could breathe new life into the countless conspiracy theories that have sprung up around the assassination.

The Tyrone man's Protestant upbringing was known to many commentators in the US, but the revelation about his Orange Order past could well add renewed vigor to the anti-Catholic conspiracy school of thought."

Greer died in 1985. When I asked his son Richard in 1991, "What did you father think about JFK," he did not respond the first time I asked. When I asked him a second time, Richard responded: "Well, we're Methodists and JFK was Catholic." Bill Greer was born and raised in County Tyrone, Ireland. Greer worked as a chauffeur for a wealthy family in Brookline, Massachusetts, where JFK was born and raised. He also lived in Boston "for a little while."[6] Greer "worked one summer on the estate of Henry Cabot Lodge,"[7] a staunch Republican defeated twice by Kennedy in both his Senate campaign and when Lodge was Nixon's Vice Presidential candidate in 1960. Lodge was Ambassador to South Vietnam in 1963, and principally involved in the CIA/U.S. government-sponsored assassination of President Diem of Vietnam on 11/2/63. Obviously, Greer, from his association with Lodge, as well as his work in and around Boston, had to have known about Kennedy and his wealthy family, Ambassador father Joe, and their controversial heritage of alleged bootlegging, Nazi sympathizing, and political history in Boston.

Another recent article from Ireland reported[8]:

What the records do show is that a William Greer[9] sailed from Belfast to Quebec on the Cunard ship, 'Andania' as a third class pas-

6 See my first book *Survivor's Guilt*, chapter 8.
7 2 H 113.
8 https://www.tyronetimes.co.uk/news/did-stewartstown-native-kill-jfk-1-1747006.
9 The prior article had his age at 19 [I had his age around 18-19], while Greer testified to the Warren Commission that he came to America in February 1930: 2 H 113. However, perhaps that is the time period he came from Quebec, Canada to America.

senger on 25th May 1929. His address was listed as Drumbanaway, Stewartstown, Co. Tyrone. A further record exists of a William Greer crossing into America at Vanceboro, Maine not long after that date.

The Stewartstown Greers feature heavily in the history of the Unionist Party, the Orange Order, and the UVF between 1912 and 1917. In 1916, a Thomas MacGregor Greer was commended in a letter from Sir Edward Carson for his help in recruiting battle casualty replacements for the 36th Ulster Division.

At the time of his retirement through ill health in 1966, William Greer had a sister, Ella Torrens, living in Dunmurry and several cousins living in Lisburn.

Before continuing on, author Christopher Fulton received a 6/5/1992 letter from JFK's secretary Evelyn Lincoln to Robert White with some highly disturbing information, to put it mildly: "On November 20, 1963, my husband, Harold Lincoln, overheard a conversation at a bar in Washington, D.C. Secret Service agents in Vice President Johnson's detail were discussing President Kennedy being shot at in Dallas, Texas. I was shaken, and pleaded with the president not to go, but he was fearless."[10]

Further revelations from author Christopher Fulton:

Fulton interviewed Robert Bouck on the phone and in person in August 1997. Bouck shockingly told Fulton: "Dallas's Mayor, Earle Cabell, and Sheriff Bill Decker were both CIA assets. They told the police to stand down from their protection of President Kennedy by order of the Secret Service. At the same time, several key men in the president's Secret Service detail were told that there would be a test of the president's security in Dallas, and that there would be a staged event that would lead to the door of the pro-Castro Cubans, and to stand down. The men following that order thought they were doing the right thing for the country. It's how the loyal Secret Service men were made part of the plan and played a role in the assassination. I remember debriefing a CIA man who had been sent to Dallas to abort the false flag assassination attempt; he was shocked and horrified when he saw the president shot in the head … agents of the Secret Service betrayed me, they betrayed their president, and they betrayed their country."[11]

On 3/22/98, Fulton had a face to face meeting with none other than John F. Kennedy, Jr himself, who told him: "Uncle Bobby opened a clandestine investigation into the Secret Service and their role in my father's assassination; not one shot was fired to protect my father. They knew what <u>was about to happen</u>, and they not only allowed it, they participated. …

10   *The Inheritance* by Christopher Fulton (2018), page 81.
11   *The Inheritance* by Christopher Fulton (2018), pages 102-103, 105.

When my father was president, key members of the detail were corrupted, they subverted his protection, and the rest followed orders to stand down. I always believed that certain Secret Service agents had to be complicit in his murder, so did my mother; now I know for sure."[12]

Secret Service agent Ernest Aragon told the HSCA on 3/25/78: "Aragon said that he became aware of the deficiencies of the Secret Service in Presidential protection very early in his career... Aragon was more than mildly critical of the performance of the Secret Service in the area of Presidential Protection. He said that most agents including some of the White House Detail were less than proficient in their approach to this subject... former SA Aragon seemed to feel that the Secret Service was not always doing its best to protect the President."

JFK's Secret Service Hierarchy – strange
CONNECTIONS AND SENTIMENTS

First JFK Secret Service Chief U.E. Baughman: made the Chief via a call on 11/22/48 (excerpt from Baughman's 1962 book *Secret Service Chief*).

Baughman was "retired"/fired by RFK and JFK around the very same time the CIA agents responsible for the Bay of Pigs debacle were "retired"/fired, including Director Allen Dulles (later of Warren Commission infamy), Charles Cabell (whose brother, who we now know had CIA connections of his own, was the mayor of Dallas who rode a mere few cars behind President Kennedy on 11/22/63) and Richard Bissell.

Interestingly, Deputy Director and former OSS man Paul Paterni, who worked with future CIA men James Jesus Angleton and future Warren Commission liaison man Ray Rocca during WWII,[13] was up for being his replacement. Here is Paterni as he looked during his OSS days.

CHAPTER 3
The Reluctant Chief

I remember with absolute clarity the details of that call which was to change my life, give it its final shape.
    The date was November 22, 1948. When the phone rang I glanced toward the door of my small office, which looked out on my secretary's even smaller one. As New York Supervision Agent I rated a secretary, or rather a clerk, who could take shorthand and typewrite. The clerk's desk was empty. I

---

12   *The Inheritance* by Christopher Fulton (2018), page 178-181.
13   Julius Mader, *Who's Who in the CIA* (Berlin: Julius Mader, 1968); *Cloak and Gown*, page 363; Burton Hersh, *The Old Boys: The American Elite and the Origins of the CIA* (New York: Scribner's, 1992), page 182.

Paterni would go on to perform the critical limousine inspection on the night of 11/22/63 with ASAIC Floyd Boring (more on him in a moment). Paterni had replaced Russell "Buck" Daniels as Deputy Director in early 1961.

The man who replaced Baughman: Former SAIC of the White House Detail (1946-1961), James J. Rowley, was a former FBI agent and friend of Hoover.

WHY was Baughman let go? Because he was in direct conflict with the Kennedy brothers and their war on Organized Crime – he proclaimed (like FBI Director J. Edgar Hoover) that the Mafia did not exist!

There must have been some form of animus at Secret Service headquarters during the JFK administration, as well – it is common procedure and protocol to have the current president's portrait on the wall, yet a photo of headquarters from the 1962 book *What Does A Secret Service Agent Do* by Wayne Hyde (written with the general help of the Secret Service and with the specific cooperation of Chief Inspector Michael Torina and Chief James Rowley) shows not only a photo of Ike but a derogatory "I Miss Ike" sticker on the bottom of Ike's portrait!

Rowley was apparently more in line with the Kennedy brother's beliefs.

Secret Service chief resigns

WASHINGTON (UPI) — U. E. Baughman, chief of the U.S. Secret Service since 1948, submitted his resignation today effective Aug. 31.

Treasury Secretary Douglas Dillon accepted "with genuine regret" Baughman's decision to retire after 33 years service.

The Secret Service is responsible for guarding the life of the President and his family. Its major assignment is to stamp out counterfeiting of U.S. currency and coins.

There was no announcement of Baughman's successor. But Treasury sources said the job may go to Paul J. Paterni, deputy chief who was transferred to Washington less than a year ago. He previously headed the agency's Chicago office.

"No Mafia Here," He Says.

Baughman said he is convinced there is no such thing as a national crime syndicate or a Mafia (black hand society) in this country.

He said there has been no Mafia in the United States for at least 40 years and that there is no such thing as a national crime syndicate.

Rowley's replacement as SAIC was veteran Gerald Behn.

Unfortunately, Behn took his *first* vacation during the JFK administration during the week involving both the Florida and Texas trips! In Florida, he was replaced by #2 man, ASAIC Floyd Boring (one of the heroes of the 11/1/50 assassination attempt on President Truman).

Boring was the planner of the Texas trip from the Secret Service's point of view (although he himself was not physically present) and he also took it upon himself to tell the agents between 11/19-11/21/63 that JFK did not want agents riding on the rear of his limo in Dallas, a blatant lie that has been debunked by many fellow agents and White House aides ... including Boring himself! Boring also gave lead advance agent Winston Lawson the Dallas assignment. Boring is one of my three suspects.

ASAIC Roy Kellerman, a third stringer who proved totally ineffective during and after the assassination, was making one of his first major trips on his own without either Behn or Boring!

There were three Shift Leaders (designated ATSAIC: Assistant To the Special Agent In Charge) on the Texas trip. Sadly, the two best ones, decorated WWII veterans Stu Stout and Art Godfrey were not on the specific leg of the Dallas part of the Texas trip (interestingly, like Boring, Stout was one of the heroes of the 11/1/50 assas-

"Our conference with Chief Rowley dealt with general subjects and subjects to which we are giving particular attention." Mr. Weisheit said. "Mr. Rowley reiterated the importance of continuing the tested policies and objectives passed along to him by his distinguished predecessor, former Chief U. E. Baughman.

"He stressed that the Secret Service Agency is to be closely connected with the campaign that Attorney General Kennedy is conducting against organized crime in every form, and especially in the fields in which we operate against counterfeiting, theft and forgery of Government checks, and theft and peddling of Federal securities, especially Savings Bonds."

sination attempt on President Truman. Godfrey was also a Truman-era veteran).

The shift leader in Dallas and commander of the other seven agents in the follow-up car, Emory Roberts, conveyed Boring's "wish" and at Love Field ordered away agents Henry Rybka and Don Lawton from the limousine, ordered the agents not to move during the shooting itself, and usurped Kellerman's authority at Parkland Hospital, telling his boss to stay with Kennedy while he went to Johnson. Roberts also was responsible for LBJ taking over Air Force One. Roberts is one of my three suspects (see Boring above)– he became too close to Johnson after the assassination and died young in 1973 without speaking to anyone except William Manchester. Interestingly, Roberts shift of agents were the worst offenders by far in the drinking incident of early 11/22/63 in which 9 agents drank alcohol.

Don Lawton with LBJ and at Love Field on 11/22.

The day after the infamous umbrella man appeared during the assassination, Roberts became an umbrella man of his own as he shields LBJ. What appears to be a look of disgust on fellow Dallas motorcade agent Jerry Kivett can be seen in the photo.

The lead advance agent for the Dallas trip was the aforementioned Winston Lawson.

However, I harbor no real suspicion towards him, as I feel he was merely following orders from above (Boring). While not necessarily one of my three suspects (two of whom you know about from above – Boring and Roberts – and the other I will get to in a moment), I feel that Lawson's assistant in the Dallas advance, David Grant (interestingly, Clint Hill's brother-in-law!), should be viewed a little more critically, although he may have also been a victim of following orders from above, as well (with regard to motorcycle formations, agents on the limousine, and other security matters).

DAVE GRANT

From the Warren Report itself- Grant joined Sorrels after completing advance work on the president's trip to Tampa:

> men available to permit two agents to be assigned to all the advance work. Consequently, Agent Lawson did the advance work alone from November 13 to November 18, when he was joined by Agent David B. Grant, who had just completed advance work on the President's trip to Tampa.

Winston Lawson wrote to me and confirmed that Grant came to Dallas "quite late in the advance" to assist him after doing advance work in Florida:

TX. In fact Dave Grant who quite late in the advance, came to help me— had been on advance in FL I believe. He was senior to me + would have been in charge in Dallas if he had gone there before me. I believe Walt had been on an advance before he went to his stop in TX.

Sincerely,
Win Lawson

The two advance agents for Tampa, officially speaking, were (also, in addition to David Grant) Gerald Blaine (the author of *The Kennedy Detail*) and Frank Yeager.

Interestingly, Yeager did not think JFK was difficult to protect and seems

JERRY BLAINE   FRANK YEAGER

to imply (like O'Rourke and Pontius) that O'Donnell had something to do with the agents not being on the car in Dallas, yet the agents who testified and wrote reports to the Warren Commission (and Blaine and Hill in their books) never blamed O'Donnell for this, while Powers denied there was any truth to JFK ordering the agents off his limo.

As most readers know from my books and my blogs, I don't find Blaine credible.

Agent Walt Coughlin is a dear friend of Blaine (and many of the other agents), and was on the Florida and Texas trips, as well as many other trips from election day 1960-11/22/63 ... and he wrote to me that he "had no idea if JFK ordered the agents off his limo"?

Blaine remarked on C-SPAN in 2010 and in his book that in the month prior to the 28-mile Tampa motorcade the White House detail had lost eleven agents and he had only one experienced agent available to rely on in Tampa.

WALT COUGHLIN

There was one *other* agent who "left," but he had no choice: he *died*! Driver agent Thomas B. Shipman died on 10/14/63 of an alleged heart attack at Camp David.

Fellow driver agent Sam Kinney (image on right), who believed there was a conspiracy and that the back of JFK's head was blown out on 11/22/63 (and had possession of the piece of the back of the head on the

C-130 plane heading back to D.C.), was one of the good guys. Sam was adamant to me – on three occasions – that he (Sam) was solely responsible for the bubble top's removal, but I hold no suspicion towards him just the same. This was merely an option not explored, not a sinister removal, per se. Interestingly, according to Lawson's letter to me (excerpt below), it was Kinney who found Shipman's body at Camp David, as "they would have roomed together in one of the cabins up there."

SAIC of the driver detail Morgan Gies[14] (right photo, arrow, and middle photo) was in Washington and likewise garners no suspicion (fellow new driver agents Andrew Hutch [no photo available] and Henry Rybka also are not suspicious):

This leaves my third suspect (with Boring and Roberts), driver agent William R. "Bill" Greer, who drove President Kennedy quite ineptly and negligently during the assassination (see chapter 8 of my first book *Survivor's Guilt* for much more). As Greer told the HSCA: "He recalls embracing Mrs. Kennedy and saying something about wishing he could have been more evasive or avoided the tragedy."

14   https://military.wikia.org/wiki/Morgan_L._Gies

PRS agent Glen Bennett (arrow) was made a temporary White House Detail agent on 11/10/63, while fellow PRS agent Howard K. Norton [no photo available] was on both the Florida and Texas trips.

SAIC of the VP LBJ detail Stu Knight (later the Director of the Secret Service from 1973-1981, replacing Rowley) was not on the Texas trip.

Knight's transfer was to have taken place 11/25/63. Knight's deputy, ASAIC of VP LBJ detail Rufus Youngblood took his place on the Texas trip (Youngblood, later the author of a 1973 book just recently re-released by his daughter, *Twenty Years in the Secret Service*, became the SAIC of the WHD and Assistant Director shortly after the assassination).

Treasury Secretary (and former OSS man) C. Douglas Dillon was on a crowded cabinet plane heading to Hawaii (then onto Japan) along with Press Secretary Pierre Salinger, a man agent Bob Lilley stated was extremely knowledgeable about motorcade security and planning, as they had worked with Pierre on many advances. In fact, Salinger stated in his 1997 book *John F. Kennedy: Commander in Chief* that he missed only "one or two trips" with JFK ... Texas was one of them!

Salinger's deputy, Andy Hatcher, also was not on the Texas trip.

As with Kellerman, another third stringer, Mac Kilduff, was on the trip, making his first major trip on his own!

In Dillon's place: Acting Secretary Gaspard d'Andelot Belin (General Counsel of the Treasury Department and married to one of the Bundy sisters).

Making his very first presidential trip (from the Washington D.C. field office, presumably): future CIA agent[15] Roger Warner.

Two agents along on the trip because Jackie Kennedy was there: Clint Hill (who has said from day one in testimony, reports, and his books that the back of JFK's head was gone and that the wound in the back was a back wound, not a neck wound) and Paul Landis (who stated in two reports that one of the shots came from the front).

Before he wrote books, Hill was more contrite.

Houston / *Chronicle* / *'It's My Fault'* ⟸

Ex-Agent Says He Willingly Would Have Taken JFK Shot

New York (AP)—A former Secret Service agent guarding President John F. Kennedy when Kennedy was assassinated in 1963 says if he'd reacted faster when he heard gunfire, he would have willingly taken the shot that killed the President.

"That would have been fine with me," said Clinton J. Hill, who retired from the Secret Service last July after 17 years of duty at the White House, eight of them as head of the presidential security detail.

Hill, 43, spoke in an interview to be broadcast Sunday night on CBS' "60 Minutes" program.

The former agent, who was riding on the back of Kennedy's limousine when Kennedy was killed in Dallas, said he "wouldn't be here today" had he reacted "about five-tenths of a second faster, maybe a second faster" when Kennedy came under fire.

Hill said: "I have a great deal of guilt about it. Had I turned in a different direction I'd have made it. It's my fault." ⟸

Hill was cited for bravery in trying to protect Kennedy.

Hill, who said he's convinced Lee Harvey Oswald acted alone in killing Kennedy, said he took early retirement from the Secret Service because of emotional problems stemming from the assassination.

He said his doctors say he has a "severe neurological problem caused by what happened in the past. And they've recommended psychiatric help. They trace it all back to 1963."

Hill said the late President Lyndon B. Johnson expressed concern for his safety in 1968, shortly after the assassination of the Rev. Martin Luther King Jr. in Memphis, Tenn.

He said Johnson, scheduled to attend a memorial service for the slain civil rights leader, called him at home at least twice before dawn of the day before the service.

Johnson "requested that I be as close to him as possible the next day, preferably not a foot and a half away from him," Hill said.

He said Johnson "had the feeling, a premonition, that something was going to happen to him."

CLINTON HILL

A racist agent from Mississippi (confirmed by Abraham Bolden, Walt Coughlin and Clint Hill in the book *Out From The Shadow*) gone from the detail by 1961 or 1962 but still an active agent (most likely in the Birmingham, Alabama office) and a definite candidate for the mysterious agent on the knoll – Harvey Henderson.

San Francisco agent Elmer Moore (sometimes confusingly named a Dallas office agent) harassed the Parkland doctors (especially Dr. Perry) and got them to change their tune regarding the wounds. He harbored hatred toward JFK and would definitely be a possible additional suspect.[16]

---

15   Warner himself revealed this startling information on his own personal Facebook page!.
16   *The JFK Assassination* by James DiEugenio (2018), pages 168-169. Interestingly, Arlen Specter claimed at the 2003 Duquesne University conference that Secret Service Agent Elmer Moore showed him an autopsy photo of Kennedy's back before the May, 1964 re-enactment.

Two agents who appear to have left the detail in 1962 to head toward field offices, Mike Mastrovito and Jack Warner, have colorful backgrounds. Mastrovito, like Warner above, became a CIA agent and also controlled the JFK assassination file for the Secret Service for years, destroyed part of Kennedy's brain, and was interviewed by the ARRB. For his part, Warner became a decades-long spokesman and consultant for the Secret Service on everything from assassination attempt damage control (Ford, Reagan) to *In The Line of Fire* movie technical assistance.

Interestingly, Hillary Rodham Clinton's older first cousin (and "kinda uncle," as several people viewed him and actually referred to him as her uncle), Wade Rodham, was the SAIC of the Kennedy residence in Middleberg, VA (he was famous for being one of the agents who was decorated for protecting VP Nixon in Caracas. He was at Middleberg when the assassination happened. One wonders where he was when Bill Clinton met JFK at the White House).

MOTIVE FOR INACTION ON THE PART OF SOME OF THE AGENTS ON 11/22/63

As for a possible motive for some of the agents to stand down that fatal day in Dallas, grist for the mill was provided via the revelations follow-up car agent Tim McIntyre and three of his Secret Service colleagues (and, second-hand, Emory Roberts) shared with author Seymour Hersh in 1997,[17] and, soon after, on ABC television,[18] concerning JFK's private life … but not for the reason the reader might think: a disturbing and alarming mindset was demonstrated by these men concerning the president they were sworn to protect. As McIntyre put it,

> "His shift supervisor, the highly respected Emory Roberts, took him aside and warned … that 'you're going to see a lot of shit around here. Stuff with the President. Just forget about it. Keep it to yourself. Don't even talk to your wife' … Roberts was nervous about it. Emory would say, McIntyre recalled with a laugh, 'How in

17   For Hersh's book *The Dark Side of Camelot*.
18   *Dangerous World: The Kennedy Years*, 12/4/97, ABC, hosted by Peter Jennings (also a home video).

the hell do you know what's going on? He could be hurt in there. What if one bites him' in a sensitive area? Roberts 'talked about it a lot', McIntyre said. 'Bites' ... In McIntyre's view, a public scandal about Kennedy's incessant womanizing was inevitable. 'It would have had to come out in the next year or so. In the campaign, maybe'. McIntyre said he and some of his colleagues ... felt abused by their service on behalf of President Kennedy ... McIntyre said he eventually realized that he had compromised his law enforcement beliefs to the point where he wondered whether it was 'time to get out of there. I was disappointed by what I saw.'"

McIntyre repeated the Roberts story on ABC (without naming Emory), with this comment included: "Prostitution-that's illegal. A procurement is illegal. And if you have a procurer with prostitutes paraded in front of you, then, as a sworn law enforcement officer, you're asking yourself, 'well, what do they think of us'?" McIntyre felt this way after having only spent a brief time with JFK before the assassination: he joined the WHD in the fall of 1963.[19]

Tony Sherman, who spent two years at the White House with JFK:

"I wanted out ... I didn't want a part of it ... I got mad ... I got angry at any president who doesn't treat the White House like I think he should ... "[20]

Sherman added,

"Seventy to eighty percent of the agents thought it was nuts.... Some of us were brought up the right way. Our mothers and fathers didn't do it. We lived in another world. Suddenly, I'm Joe Agent here. I'm looking at the president of the United States and telling myself, 'This is the White House and we protect the White House.'"[21] On the ABC special, Sherman related a tale of JFK and prostitutes that occurred during the President's trip to Honolulu, Hawaii, in June of 1963 (incidentally, two clips are shown of this trip, depicting agents running with the limousine on all four corners during the motorcade, motorcycles beside JFK, and SAIC Behn on the trip, among other things). Sherman said, "The Honolulu episode made me angry. It did make me angry ... I'm not a holier-than-thou guy ... but he shouldn't be doing this in public."

19   Hersh, pp. 240-241.
20   Wire service story picked up by many newspapers and media outlets, an example of which was the *Chattanooga Times* in an article written by Sandra Sobieraj on 12/18/97.
21   *The Atlantic Online*, January 1998.

The agent also added that this debauchery "continued constantly" and was "a regular thing."

Former agent Larry Newman:

> "It [JFK's behavior] caused a lot of morale problems with the Secret Service ... you felt impotent and you couldn't do your job. It was frustrating ... "[22]

On the ABC special, Newman mentioned JFK's sexual trysts with White House secretaries who were known by the nicknames of "Fiddle" and "Faddle." The agent also said that this facet of JFK made them not want to associate with the man in any way.

Former agent Joseph Paolella:

> "[He] acknowledged that the Secret Service's socializing intensified each year of the Kennedy administration, to a point where, by late 1963, a few members of the presidential detail were regularly remaining in bars until the early morning hours."[23]

This is corroborated by what Abraham Bolden told the author, and it also is best exemplified by the drinking incident of 11/21-11/22/63. Agent Tony Sherman also told author Edward Klein,

> "His womanizing was so routine and common ... that we slipped into the nefarious duty of protecting Kennedy from his wife by alerting him is she was returning to the White House unexpectedly ... Some agents felt that if the President could get away with this kind of stuff, so could they.... Drinking, partying, and sex became part of traveling with the President."[24]

Agent Larry Newman wasn't finished. He spoke at even greater length to author Barbara Leaming about JFK's womanizing several years later.[25] The author did contact Newman, Sherman, Paolella, and McIntyre, but did not discuss JFK's womanizing at any length.

Lastly, we cannot rule out that several of these agents had further intelligence connections and/or were angry at JFK for his views on Cuba, his perceived views on Vietnam, Civil Rights, etc. (see Elmer Moore,

---

22   Hersh, p. 230.
23   Hersh, p. 244.
24   *The Kennedy Curse*, pp. 171 & 173.
25   *Mrs. Kennedy: The Missing History of the Kennedy Years* by Barbara Leaming (Free Press, 2002). See especially pp. 61-63, 142, 167, 204, & 252-253 Newman also spoke to author Edward Klein [*Just Jackie: Her Private Years*, p. 374], and is acknowledged for his help in *The Fourth Perimeter* by Tim Green (Warner Books, 2003).

above). An unnamed agent told Author William Matson Law: "You know, I thought the Kennedys were a bunch of users, and I didn't want anything to do with them."[26] In addition, Law adds: "I've talked to half a dozen agents over the years that were connected to Kennedy's detail in one way or another, and I definitely got the feeling that Kennedy's womanizing lowered the agents respect to almost nothing for JFK."[27]

Published for the first time ever, these disturbing comments about the Special Agent in Charge of the Dallas Secret Service office, Forrest Sorrels, who rode in the lead car, the vehicle directly in front of Kennedy's limousine on 11/22/63 and who helped plan the motorcade route. The FBI got a call on 11/27/1963 from a woman who had heard a recent speech by Forrest Sorrels at her Lady's Club. She told the FBI that Sorrels was "anti-government, against the Kennedy administration, and she felt his position was against the security of not only the President but the United States."

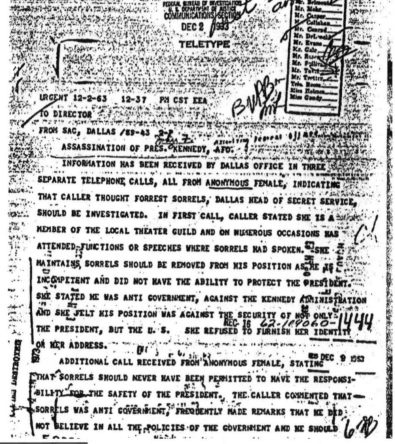

```
PAGE TWO
BE INTESTIGATED.
     THE THIRD ANONYMOUS CALL STATED THAT SORRELS SHOULD
BE CHECKED ON.  THE CALLER STATED SHE WAS A MEMBER AT ONE TIME
OF THE LEAGUE FOR WOMEN VOTERS, AS WAS THE WIFE OF SORRELS.  SHE
CALIMED MRS. SORRELS, WHEN TAKING HER TURN TO MAKE A BOOK REVIEW,
DID NOT MAKE A BOOK REVIEW AS MOST OF THE MEMBERS DID, BUT INSTEAD
GAVE A REPORT ON OVERTHROWING THE GOVERNMENT.  THE CALLER STATED
ON THIS BASIS, SHE THOUGHT MR. SORRELS ACTIVITIES SHOULD BE
CHECKED INTO.
     THE LAST TWO CALLS WERE RECEIVED IN THE DALLAS OFFICE BY
THE SAME AGENT AND THE AGENT IS OF THE OPINION THE SAME WOMAN
WAS CALLING ON BOTH OCCASIONS.  IN ALL THREE INSTANCES, THE CALLER
APPEARED TO BE AN INTELLIGENT PERSON AND WAS WELL SPOKEN AT THE
TIME SHE CALLED.
     INFORMATION CONCERNING THE THREE ANONYMOUS TELEPHONE
CALLS RELATIVE TO SORRELS HAS BEEN FURNISHED TO INSPECTOR TOM
KELLEY, SECRET SERVICE OF WASH., WHO IS PRESENTLY IN DALLAS.
END ACK FOR TWO MESSAGES PLS

ACK YOUR TWO MSG  1-44 PM OK FBI  WA   LA
TU CLEAR
```

In light of this disturbing report about Sorrels, the following report, also published for the first time ever, is also troubling- Sorrels told the FBI on 11/20/63 that he did not anticipate any trouble for the upcoming trip to Dallas and did not take up the FBI's offer of assistance:

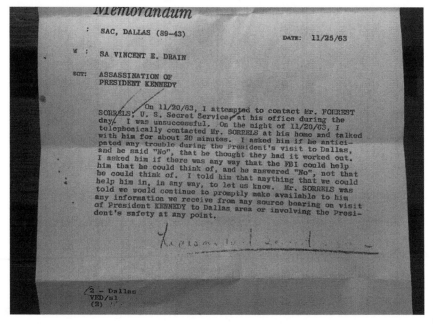

MY THREE MAIN SECRET SERVICE SUSPECTS:[28]

1. FLOYD BORING: Boring was *the planner of the Texas trip from the Secret Service's point of view* (although he himself was not present) and he also took it upon himself to tell the agents between 11/19-11/21/63 that JFK did not want agents riding on the rear of his limo in Dallas, a blatant lie that has been debunked by many fellow agents and White House aides...including Boring himself! Boring also gave lead advance agent Winston Lawson the Dallas assignment and was involved in the critical limousine inspection.

2. EMORY ROBERTS: The shift leader in Dallas and *commander of the other 7 agents in the follow-up car*, Emory Roberts, conveyed Boring's "wish" and ordered away two agents at Love Field, Henry Rybka and Don Lawton, from the limousine, ordered the agents not to move during the shooting itself, and usurped Kellerman's authority at Parkland Hospital, telling his boss to stay with Kennedy while he went to Johnson. Roberts also was responsible for LBJ taking over Air Force One. Roberts became very close to Johnson after the assassination and died young in 1973 without speaking to anyone except William Manchester. Interestingly, Roberts shift of agents were the worst offenders by far in the drinking incident of early 11/22/63 in which 9 agents drank alcohol.

First discovered by the author, Emory Roberts was the first and only active Secret Service agent to also act as a member of the president's staff! Agents are supposed to be apolitical:

---

28   Please see my books *Survivor's Guilt, The Not-So-Secret Service* and *Who's Who in the Secret Service*

3. BILL GREER:

- slowed the limousine down;
- looked back at JFK, which he denied doing;
- disobeyed a direct order from his superior, Roy Kellerman, to get the limo out of line;
- looked back at JFK a second time, an action he denied doing, and stares at Kennedy until the fatal shot arrives;
- stays with the body from Parkland thru/ including Bethesda;
- withholds JFK's clothing from the autopsy doctors;
- I asked Richard Greer, his son, what his father thought of Kennedy. He said "Well, we're Methodists … and JFK was Catholic." Greer was born and raised in County Tyrone, Ireland, coming to America around the age of 19. He later worked for Henry Cabot Lodge and had to have been aware of Joe Kennedy Senior's alleged bootlegging and other Kennedy controversies.

My second-tier Secret Service suspects would be Roy Kellerman (if any agent is a suspect for tampering and/or hijacking JFK's body, it is him), Elmer Moore (for badgering Dr. Perry to change his tune on the neck wound and calling Kennedy a traitor) and Forrest Sorrels (for the previously-mentioned reports and for some issues addressed in chapter 5).

BUILDINGS – ROOFTOPS AND WINDOWS – WERE INDEED NORMALLY GUARDED BEFORE THE ASSASSINATION

```
File - CD 1141 and other documents

1.  Handbook - Principles of Protection of the President
                 and Other Dignitaries
                 The Secret School
                 January 4, 1954
    -Pg. 56-7 "If great danger is suspected, the occupants
    of buildings facing parade routes should be checked
    and a person of known reliability should be given the
    responsibility in each location of assuring that no
    suspicious persons are allowed at windows or on roof
    tops in the danger area."  Note "at windows or on
    roof tops" is specifically stated.  This is contrary
    to testimony given by several secret service agents.

    CD 1550:  S.S. White House Manual in Effect 11/22/63
    note to Goldberg to Rankin attached: "This contradicts
    Lawson's statement in hearings"  Copy requested.  Rest
    of Com. No. 1550 in White House Detail manual.

    Q.  Is there formal or informal instructions in protecting the
        President in an emergency?
    A.  Cover the President as close as possible--shield
        him--remove him as quickly as possible.
```

Excerpt from HSCA summary of Warren Commission CDs re: Secret Service (from Harold Weisberg files)

JFK IN NASHVILLE

Other officers were assigned to stations atop the Municipal terminal and other buildings along the route.

These men took their posts at 8 a.m. and remained at their roof-top stations until the President and his party had passed.

The same was true at Vanderbilt stadium where Metropolitan officers and state patrolmen were assisted by members of the Metropolitan fire department and members of the armed forces.

---

2   CORPUS CHRISTI TIMES, Friday, June 21, 1963

President Will Have Plenty Of Protection While Abroad

By DOUGLAS B. CORNELL.

WASHINGTON. (P)—When President Kennedy visits Europe, he's going to be just about as safe as if he stayed home.

In fact, he would stay home if there were any question about his safety—the U.S. Secret Service would see to that.

The Secret Service, by law, is charged with protecting the President anywhere. And it does so in shifts around the clock, at a palace or embassy abroad as it does at the White House in Washington.

In this country, the Secret Service has the sole responsibility for safeguarding the Chief Executive, although it also calls on local and state police and occasionally the military for assistance. On trips to other countries, the foreign counterpart of the Secret Service is responsible technically for the security of the President. But actually it is the Secret Service that sets forth the security requirements, working in close cooperation with its opposite number abroad.

WHEN A president travels in other lands, the sharp-eyed, well-built young men constantly by his side draw exclamations from the crowds. Foreigners always figure they are FBI men or G-men. But the FBI has no specific authority for guarding the president.

Congress put this power in the hands of the Secret Service years ago. The Secret Service is an agency of the U.S. Treasury Department, and one of its other major duties is running down counterfeiters.

A Special Secret Service detail is assigned to the White House

under Gerald A. Behn, a young-looking, gum-chewing veteran who goes back to the days of the late President Franklin D. Roosevelt.

As on all presidential trips, the one to Europe which begins tomorrow night is being checked out carefully by an advance party which includes Secret Service agents. These agents and plenty of others—the White House doesn't wish to advertise the exact number—will accompany Kennedy when he starts his 10-day travels to West Germany, Ireland, Britain and Italy.

PROBABLY A flying though specially built and equipped car for the Secret Service, as well as Kennedy's limousine with a removable metal or plastic top.

The Secret Service car has running boards and hand grips. In a motorcade, agents are hopping on and off constantly and racing ahead to run alongside Ken-

San Francisco To Be Site of U. S. World Trade Fair

SAN FRANCISCO. (P) — San Francisco will host the seventh United States World Trade Fair Sept. 10-20 — the first time the event has been held outside New York City — Mayor George Christopher announced yesterday.

More than 60 nations in Europe, Asia, Africa, the Middle East, and Central and South America have exhibited at the international trade event in the past.

nedy's car. The two cars travel almost bumper to bumper.

Usually each is driven by an agent. Now and then there are exceptions, as when a turbaned, red-coated Indian was at the wheel of the president's car when former President Dwight D. Eisenhower visited New Delhi.

At the airports, along the roads and streets, at public buildings, and at all other places the President will visit. Secret Service and local security agents will have combed over the entire route in advance.

They ask local authorities to put police on top of buildings and along the streets. Bridges get special attention. Servants, waiters and other employes in places the President visits will be checked. So will kitchens.

ALL THIS doesn't mean that crowds won't get a good look at the President or the photographers and reporters won't be able to cover his activities.

At ceremonies, representatives of the press probably will be no more than 30 feet away. And at times even closer. The general public may not be much farther away. In fact, some people are likely to see Kennedy close up. He is a gregarious kind of person who seldom passes up the chance to wander over to a crowd behind a fence or other barricade and walk along with a smile and outstretched hand, offering handclasps and sometimes yielding to requests for autographs.

Or he might get right into the crowd and mingle. This rather worries the Secret Service, because it never knows for sure what the President is going to do about joining the crowd. That's the kind of man he is.

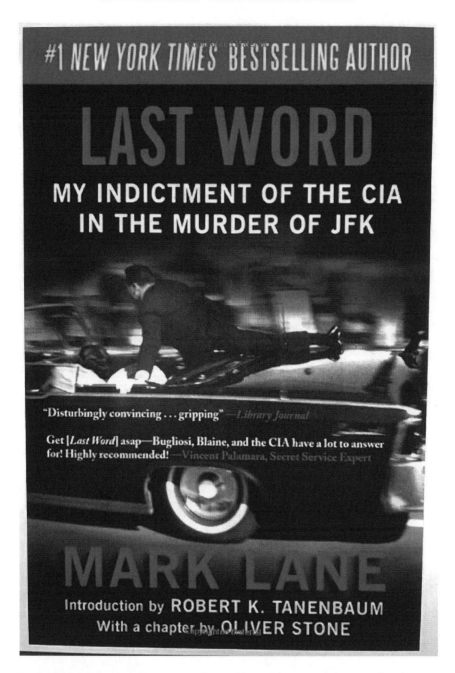

It was indeed an honor to have my work noted favorably on several pages of Mark Lane's final JFK book. The paperback edition even had my review on the cover:

CHAPTER FIVE

WHO DID IT AND WHY

Writing about the JFK assassination requires that one make judgements when evaluating a mass of conflicting evidence. Making judgments requires having the courage to do so, knowing that you could be wrong in your interpretation of the evidence. Attempting to explain the JFK assassination is not for the fainthearted, for it is an activity bound up with risk; each researcher must have the curiosity and courage to engage in intelligent speculation while respecting the facts, and the humility to know that subsequent evidence or interpretations may prove him wrong on occasion.

– Doug Horne of the ARRB[1]

S o, who killed Kennedy?

If you mean the specific shooters, we will never know for sure. Way too much time has gone by and it is impossible to be definitive. It is literally a parlor game to merely guess potential suspects at this juncture. Some posit James "I am not in any" Files as one suspect, but there is no evidence to back up his claim. Members of the mafia, Corsican gunmen, anti-Castro Cubans, CIA agents, mercenaries, other "lone nuts" coincidentally working in tandem... beats me.[2] [3] [4]

Now, if you mean "who was behind the assassination," while we also will never know for sure, at least in this instance we have a general idea or deep suspicion. In other words, at least we have a somewhat firm foundation for an educated guess to "satisfy" a curious person. Since this question is almost always asked by a well-meaning lay person, it is easier to get by with generalities like a rogue element of the CIA or (although not true) "the mob."

Now, having said that, the ironic thing is this: I do believe a rogue element of the CIA was indeed behind the assassination.[5] No, not the CIA

1   *Inside the ARRB* by Doug Horne (2009), pages 961-962
2   Watergate burglar Frank Sturgis was a suspect, as well, according to this newly-released file: https://www.archives.gov/files/research/jfk/releases/2018/docid-32191601.pdf
3   Bernardo de Torres might have been in Dealey Plaza, according to this newly-released HSCA memo: https://www.archives.gov/files/research/jfk/releases/2018/104-10067-10357.pdf
4   Charles Harrelson was a suspect, according to this newly-released file: https://www.ar-chives.gov/files/research/jfk/releases/2018/docid-32174310.pdf
5   A female CIA staff member in France overheard agents talk about taking care of Kennedy: https://www.archives.gov/files/research/jfk/releases/124-10020-10285.pdf

as an agency; not Director John McCone and company; not a gaggle of then-current agents and officers. We are talking former Director Allen Dulles, fired by JFK over the Bay of Pigs debacle[6] and in Dallas in November 1963 about three weeks before the assassination[7]; David Atlee Phillips (a.k.a. Maurice Bishop[8]) from Fort Worth[9]; Cord Meyer, who hated JFK[10]; James Angleton; David Sanchez Morales; William Harvey[11], who was in Dallas in November 1963[12]; E. Howard Hunt[13], accused of being in Dallas on 11/22/63, leading the CIA to construct an alibi for him[14] (later of Watergate fame); and former Deputy Director Charles Cabell, brother of the Mayor of Dallas, Earle Cabell. Cabell, who also hated JFK and even called him a traitor,[15] was also, like Dulles, fired by Kennedy over the Bay of Pigs fiasco.[16] [17] Cord Meyer may have had an extra incentive: his wife Mary Pinchot Meyer was having a torrid affair with President Kennedy.[18] Also, one cannot underestimate the importance of the connections between the CIA and the Secret Service, as demonstrated in my last book, where I depict friendly correspondence between JFK Secret Service Chiefs U.E. Baughman and James Rowley with Allen Dulles and Charles

6   *The Devil's Chessboard* by David Talbot (2015)
7   *Reclaiming Parkland* by James DiEugenio (2013), page 273
8   *Trained to Kill: The Inside Story of CIA Plots against Castro, Kennedy, and Che* by Antonio Veciana (2017), pages 187-192
9   https://en.wikipedia.org/wiki/David_Atlee_Phillips
10   *A Very Private Woman: The Life and Unsolved Murder of Presidential Mistress Mary Meyer* by Nina Burleigh (1998), page 48
11   CIA document regarding authorization of payment to QJWIN as part of ZRRIFLE program run by William Harvey, according to this newly-released file: https://www.archives.gov/files/research/jfk/releases/2018/104-10214-10003.pdf
12   *The Devil's Chessboard* by David Talbot (2015), page 477
13   *Last Word* by Mark Lane (2011), pages 44-63
14   *Destiny Betrayed* by James DiEugenio (2012), page 363
15   https://spartacus-educational.com/JFKcabelC.htm
16   John Newman has authored what associate Alan Dale refers to as a "new paradigm." This theory postulates that "a campaign of misdirection [was] launched by Antonio Veciana the day he walked out of the Atlanta Federal Penitentiary in February 1976." The purpose of this misdirection campaign, achieved through the "sudden early release of Veciana," was to "control the narrative of the unfolding congressional investigations" and to "place blame on the CIA and direct attention away from the Pentagon." However, others, including Jim DiEugenio, debunk this notion: "This is BS. Tanenbaum told me that they had affirmation through the CIA that Bishop was Phillips. His chief investigator Cliff Fenton got this through his working contacts inside the Agency that he had in New York."
17   In a recent discovery, it turns out Dallas Mayor Earle Cabell was a CIA asset! Best-selling author David Talbot wrote: "What a cozy setup the CIA had in Dallas in 1963. Mayor Earle Cabell was not only the brother of Charles Cabell, the former CIA deputy chief who, along with his boss Allen Dulles, was fired by JFK. Now we learn that the Dallas mayor was also a CIA asset! This is part of a pattern: the Texas School Book Depository where Oswald supposedly fired from his sniper's nest was owned by right-wing oilman D.H. Byrd, who also had deep national security connections; the press corps covering the Kennedy motorcade was riddled with CIA assets." https://whowhatwhy.org/2017/08/02/dallas-mayor-jfk-assassination-cia-asset/
18   *Mary's Mosaic: The CIA Conspiracy to Murder John F. Kennedy, Mary Pinchot Meyer, and Their Vision for World Peace* by Peter Janney, 2012

Cabell.[19] Cabell, Deputy Director of CIA under Allen Dulles, was forced by President Kennedy to resign, on January 31, 1962, following the failure of the Bay of Pigs Invasion. At the very least, I believe some of these men, if not actual participants, had (fore)knowledge of the

Mary Pinchot Meyer and Cord Meyer

event. For his part, Cord Meyer was asked who was behind the murder of his ex-wife. He responded: "The same sons of bitches who killed John F. Kennedy."[20] As mentioned earlier, CIA officers David Atlee Phillips and E. Howard Hunt stated before their deaths that a conspiracy took the life of JFK. Phillips said: "My final take on the assassination is there was a conspiracy, likely including American intelligence officers."[21] A book by Hunt's son espouses the notion that the former Watergate burglar came clean about the assassination on his death bed.[22] In 1978, the HSCA asked Hunt: "Do you have any knowledge about the CIA's surveillance of Lee Harvey Oswald when he made his trip to Mexico City in the fall of 1963?" Hunt gives a very interesting answer: "Only what I have read in such books, for example, as "Night Watch" by David Phillips."[23] According to a recent book by RFK, Jr., his father initially believed that the CIA was responsible for his brother's murder.[24]

> The C.I.A.'s growth was "likened to a malignancy" which the "very high official was not sure even the White House could control . . . any longer." "If the United States ever experiences [an attempt at a coup to overthrow the Government] it will come from the C.I.A. and not the Pentagon." The agency "represents a tremendous power and total unaccountability to anyone."

The *New York Times*, 10/3/63- article by Arthur Krock:

19   *Who's Who in the Secret Service* by Vince Palamara (2018), Appendix 1
20   *A Very Private Woman: The Life and Unsolved Murder of Presidential Mistress Mary Meyer* by Nina Burleigh (1998), page 48
21   *Someone Would Have Talked* by Larry Hancock (2006)
22   *Bond of Secrecy* by Saint John Hunt (2012)
23   Document # 180-10131-10342: 87-page deposition from E. Howard Hunt taken November 3, 1978. Present were Robert W. Genzman and Mike Ewing, HSCA counsels and Hunt and his counsel Ellis S. Rubin. Hunt was placed under oath by reporter Shirley B. Dempsey.
24   *American Values: Lessons I Learned from My Family* by Robert Kennedy, Jr. (2018)

November 22. 2013

Dear Marie Fonzi:

You may publish the following statement from me:

"Maurice Bishop, my CIA contact agent was David Atlee Phillips. Phillips or Bishop was the man I saw with Lee Harvey Oswald in Dallas on September 1963."

Best Regards,

Antonio Veciana

CIA's David Atlee Phillips=Maurice Bishop, as verified by Antonio Veciana, after years of hedging, in 2013. Phillips/Bishop met with Oswald in Dallas in September 1963:

CUBA, YES. VIETNAM? MAYBE, MAYBE NOT

People quite often believe the motive for the assassination was to eliminate Kennedy due to his supposed desire to nip in the bud the notion of a full-scale ground war in Vietnam. However, there is current debate about this, as RFK appears to make clear during his JFK Library oral history that his brother was not withdrawing from Vietnam after all. Author Larry Hancock and respected researcher Deb Galentine both believe this to be the case, as well.

No, it appears the catalyst may have been Cuba, not Vietnam. The Cuban community despised President Kennedy for the Bay of Pigs, the rotting and dying of their brother Cubans in Fidel Castro's prisons, and their return home where they only received a few dollars and a change of clothes while Castro received millions in medical aid as a ransom for all of them. To say they were livid at JFK (and Castro) would be putting it mildly.

Think about it: you had the Bay of Pigs debacle of 4/15-4/19/61, with the CIA-trained Cuban exile brigade angered at President Kennedy for the supposed lack of air support and combat troops. One thousand of the Cubans were taken prisoner. Then you had Kennedy's 11/30/61 approval of "Operation Mongoose," a covert-action program to help the Cubans overthrow the Communist Castro regime. Less than a year later, you had the Cuban Missile Crisis of October 1962, which led to JFK's refusal to bomb Cuba into the stone age (to paraphrase General Curtis LeMay), followed by the president's promise not to invade the island of Cuba.

The men of Brigade 2506, the survivors of the Bay of Pigs and Castro's prisoners, were unaware of this promise not to invade Cuba when President Kennedy essentially sealed his fate on 12/29/62 at the Orange Bowl in Miami, Florida when, going off script, he unwisely said "I can assure you that this flag will be returned to this Brigade in a free Havana." As Ken O'Donnell later wrote: "Diplomatically, it was the worst possible gesture that a President of the United States could have made at the time."[25]

As author James Douglass states, on March 19, 1963,

> ...the CIA-sponsored Cuban exile group Alpha 66 announces its having raided a Soviet "fortress" and ship in Cuba, causing a dozen casualties. The secret purpose of the attack in Cuban waters, according to Alpha 66's incognito CIA adviser, David Atlee Phillips, is "to publicly embarrass Kennedy and force him to move against Castro." Then, "on March 31, 1963, President Kennedy orders a crackdown on Cuban refugee gunboats being run by the CIA out of Miami."[26]

JFK also started having the FBI close down the anti-Castro training camps in Louisiana and elsewhere. In addition, one must factor into the equation Kennedy's attempt at rapprochement with Castro through a backchannel communication shortly before his assassination. One must also view Kennedy's American University "Peace Speech" on 6/10/63, basically a call to end the entire Cold War, as a major contributing factor, as well. A newly-released file, an FBI memo dated 9/27/63, shows that anti-Castro Cubans were planning another covert invasion of Cuba two months before the assassination that JFK disapproved of.[27] All these moves were viewed as treasonous in the eyes of both the anti-Castro Cubans and the hardline CIA people, including several "ex" members.

Speaking of Deb Galentine, I owe her a big debt of thanks for opening my eyes to this new way of thinking about Vietnam. As Deb conveyed to me, based on her intense research and reading on this subject:

> Vietnam President Diem was notoriously difficult to work with and this showed in the negative results within the North Vietnamese Army (NVA). They were difficult to train and didn't want to fight. They wanted the Americans to fight this civil war for them. That was not JFK's foreign policy though. So they needed something to convince Diem that he could either become more cooperative or the United States would leave. THAT was a bargaining chip but at no time was JFK serious about doing that – and this is KEY.
> This is what McNamara and Taylor advised JFK and this is

---

25   *Brothers* by David Talbot (2007), pages 175-176.
26   *JFK and the Unspeakable* by James Douglas (2010), page xxv.
27   https://www.archives.gov/files/research/jfk/releases/2018/124-10201-10416.pdf.

what they stated in their report. Diem needed to be "convinced." The hawks in the cabinet wanted Diem removed. JFK was more into detente. Negotiating. He thought problems could be resolved by talking, which he found out didn't always work. He had some confidence in Lodge, but was fast losing it.

So he signed NSAM 263 which was to be filed and *not* released, which is a sure message to get it leaked – and I think that is exactly what JFK wanted to happen to a small degree. In other words, to Diem.

NSAM 263 cannot be taken out of context of the Taylor-McNamara report in that this was an advisory proposal in the report meant to convince Diem to cooperate with the US Generals in Vietnam.

U.S. POLICY ON VIETNAM: WHITE HOUSE STATEMENT, OCTOBER 2, 1963

Secretary [of Defense Robert S.] McNamara and General [Maxwell D.] Taylor reported to the President this morning and to the National Security Council this afternoon. Their report included a number of classified findings and recommendations which will be the subject of further review and action. Their basic presentation was endorsed by all members of the Security Council and the following statement of United States policy was approved by the President on the basis of recommendations received from them and from Ambassador [Henry Cabot] Lodge.

1. The security of South Viet-Nam is a major interest of the United States as other free nations. We will adhere to our policy of working with the people and Government of South Viet-Nam to deny this country to communism and to suppress the externally stimulated and supported insurgency of the Viet Cong as promptly as possible. Effective performance in this undertaking is the central objective of our policy in South Viet-Nam.

2. The military program in South Viet-Nam has made progress and is sound in principle, though improvements are being energetically sought.

3. Major U.S. assistance in support of this military effort is needed only until the insurgency has been suppressed or until the national security forces of the Government of South Viet-Nam are capable of suppressing it.

Secretary McNamara and General Taylor reported their judgment that the major part of the U.S. military task can be completed by the end of 1965, although there may be a continuing requirement for a limited number of U.S. training personnel. They reported that by the end of this year, the U.S. program for training Vietnamese should have progressed to the point where 1,000 U.S. military personnel assigned to South Viet-Nam can be withdrawn.

4. The political situation in South Viet-Nam remains deeply serious. The United States has made clear its continuing opposition to any repressive actions in South Viet-Nam. While such actions have not yet significantly affected the military effort, they could do so in the future.

5. It remains the policy of the United States, in South Viet-Nam as in other parts of the world, to support the efforts of the people of that country to defeat aggression and to build a peaceful and free society.

Now read this draft from a 10/5/63 meeting. They are specific instructions for dealing with Diem:

NATIONAL SECURITY ACTION MEMORANDUM NO. 263
TO: Secretary of State
 Secretary of Defense
Chairman of the Joint Chiefs of Staff

SUBJECT: South Vietnam
At a meeting on October 5, 1963, the President considered the recommendations contained in the report of Secretary McNamara and General Taylor on their mission to South Vietnam.

The President approved the military recommendations contained in Section I B (1 -3) of the report but directed that no formal announcement be made of the implementation of plans to withdraw 1,000 U.S. military personnel by the end of 1963.

After discussion of the remaining recommendations of the report, the President approved the instruction to Ambassador Lodge which is set forth in State Department telegram No. 534 to Saigon. McGeorge Bundy

Copy furnished: Director of Central Intelligence
Administrator, Agency for International Development 11/21/63

DRAFT
TOP SECRET
NATIONAL SECURITY ACTION MEMORANDUM NO

The President has reviewed the discussions of South Vietnam which occurred in Honolulu and has discussed the matter further with Ambassador Lodge. He directs that the following guidance be issued to all concerned:

1. It remains the central object of the United States in South Vietnam to assist the people and Government of that country to win their contest against the externally directed and supported Communist conspiracy. The test of all decisions and U.S. actions in this area should be the effectiveness of their contributions to this purpose.

2. The objectives of the United States with respect to the withdrawal of U.S. military personnel remain as stated in the White House statement of October 2, 1963.

3. It is a major interest of the United States Government that the present provisional government of South Vietnam should be assisted in consolidating itself in holding and developing increased public support. All U.S. officers should conduct themselves with this objective in view.

4. It is of the highest importance that the United States Government avoid either the appearance or the reality of public recrimination from one part of it against another, and the President expects that all senior officers of the Government will take energetic steps to insure that they and their subordinate go out of their way to maintain and to defend the unity of the United States Government both here and in the field. More specifically, the President approves the following lines of action developed in the discussions of the Honolulu meeting of November 20. The office or offices of the Government to which central responsibility is assigned is indicated in each case.

5. We should concentrate our own efforts, and insofar as possible we should persuade the government of South Vietnam to concentrate its efforts, on the critical situation in the Mekong Delta. This concentration should include not only military but political, economic, social, educational and informational efforts. We should seek to turn the tide not only of battle but of belief, and we should seek to increase not only our control of land but the productivity of this area whenever the proceeds can be held for the advantage of anti-Communist forces. (Action: The whole country team under the direct supervision of the Ambassador.)

6. Programs of military and economic assistance should be maintained at such levels that their magnitude and effectiveness in the eyes of the Vietnamese Government do not fall below the levels sustained by the United States in the time of the Diem Government. This does not exclude arrangements for economy on the MAP accounting for ammunition and any other readjustments which are possible as between MAP and other U.S. defense sources. Special attention should be given to the expansion of the import

distribution and effective use of fertilizer for the Delta. (Action: AID and DOD as appropriate.)

7. With respect to action against North Vietnam, there should be a detailed plan for the development of additional Government of Vietnam resources, especially for sea-going activity, and such planning should indicate the time and investment necessary to achieve a wholly new level of effectiveness in this field of action. (Action: DOD and CIA)

8. With respect to Laos, a plan should be developed for military operations up to a line up to 50 kilometers inside Laos, together with political plans for minimizing the international hazards of such an enterprise. Since it is agreed that operational responsibility for such undertakings should pass from CAS to MACV, this plan should provide an alternative method of political liaison for such operations, since their timing and character can have an intimate relation to the fluctuating situation in Laos. (Action: State, DOD and CIA.)

9. It was agreed in Honolulu that the situation in Cambodia is of the first importance for South Vietnam, and it is therefore urgent that we should lose no opportunity to exercise a favorable influence upon that country. In particular, measures should be undertaken to satisfy ourselves completely that recent charges from Cambodia are groundless, and we should put ourselves in a position to offer to the Cambodians a full opportunity to satisfy themselves on this same point. (Action: State.)

10. In connection with paragraphs 7 and 8 above, it is desired that we should develop as strong and persuasive a case as possible to demonstrate to the world the degree to which the Viet Cong is controlled, sustained and supplied from Hanoi, through Laos and other channels. In short, we need a more contemporary version of the Jordan Report, as powerful and complete as possible. (Action: Department of State with other agencies as necessary.)

McGeorge Bundy"

Deb Galentine added:

Notice this sentence: 'The President approved the military recommendations contained in Section I B (1-3) of the report, but directed that no formal announcement be made of the implementation of plans to withdraw 1,000 U.S. military personnel by the end of 1963.' This is important because JFK had NO intention of withdrawing troops. He was threatening Diem with a withdrawal he had no intention of making."

See also the Telegram from the Department of State to the Embassy in Vietnam.[28]

Deb Galentine stated further:

These are the instructions cabled to Lodge: "Actions are designed to indicate to Diem Government our displeasure at its political policies and activities and to create significant uncertainty in that government and in key Vietnamese groups as to future intentions of United States. At same time, actions are designed to have at most slight impact on military or counterinsurgency effort against Viet Cong, at least in short term.

There you have it. The "actions are designed to indicate to Diem Government our displeasure..."

This is how JFK worked. He negotiated. He pulled rank. He finagled. He did all the things a good negotiator does, but at heart, JFK was a hard-core Cold War warrior. He had zero intention of allowing South Vietnam to topple into Communism. The domino principle was alive and well in the JFK White House.

From the speech Kennedy was to deliver at the Trade Mart on 11/22/63, JFK was going to say that Vietnam was going to be "painful, risky and costly ... but we dare not weary of the task," adding that "reducing our efforts to train, equip and assist [the allied] armies can only encourage Communist penetration and require in time the increased overseas development of American combat forces."

The motive behind the assassination was Cuba, not Vietnam. After all, Oswald was part of a (phony) Fair Play for Cuba organization, attempted to join an anti-Castro group while also portraying a pro-Castro role. He attempted to go to Cuba and Russia, as well as actually living in Russia for a time. Diem and Vietnam were never issues with Oswald. It was as if that did not matter one bit to him; only Cuba, for better or for worse. Castro's Cuba would be vulnerable in the wake of the assassination, not Vietnam. Cuba was the only patsy at play here. Twice in 1962, the Pentagon proposed another invasion of Cuba. The first was Operation Northwoods, which called for attacks to be carried out on Guatemala, Guantanamo Bay, American cities, and military bases, then blamed on Cuba. Basically, the military wanted to conduct a false flag operation on Caribbean, and American soil.[29]

---

28   https://history.state.gov/historicaldocuments/frus1961-63v04/d181?fbclid=IwAR0fN-scHijAJBHd-izFzvafshcaPUUCA2cBJZsLtpiEMZnXHenxRnVtcuQY.
29   *Death of Democracy* by Willy O'Halloran (2020), Chapter 1, page 15.

While I highly doubt that JFK would have escalated the Vietnam situation into a full-scale ground war like LBJ did with Marine boots on the ground (along with the deception of a Gulf of Tonkin incident), I believe that Castro's Cuba was the bigger and more overarching factor here, although I do concede it may have been viewed as a lesser factor; perception can be reality. It may have been *perceived* that Kennedy would be less aggressive in Vietnam, true. However, once again, it was his betrayals (plural) with regard to Cuba that had several factions (renegade members of the CIA, past and present, Anti-Castro Cubans, and, yes, even, to a certain extent, the Mafia, who desperately wanted their lucrative casinos back) wanting blood. Ultimately, it was the recent past and present situation in Cuba, not the possible future in Vietnam, that may have lit the spark for the conspirators.

A CENTRAL ISSUE: THE SHOOTING ITSELF

Keeping in mind that we will never know for sure, here is my take on the shots in Dealey Plaza on 11/22/63:

I believe someone using Oswald's rifle (but *not* Oswald, safely down on the second floor[30]) fired at least two if not three shots at the limousine, one of which struck JFK in the back that was intended for his head. This shot travelled down into the chest and did not exit. Another shot from the sixth floor window of the Texas School Book Depository using this rifle missed the limousine in entirety. I also do not rule out that a third shot from this rifle and location was one of two near-simultaneous head shots (the other originating from the front). It is also possible that the Oswald rifle bullets were actually fired with a technically better weapon through the use of sabots,[31] while the Carcano rifle itself lay stuffed between boxes to be later discovered by the police.

Although the Sherry Fiester/south knoll theory (as she espouses in her book *Enemy of the Truth* and on the documentary *A Coup in Camelot*) is compelling and one not to be ruled out, I still am an ardent believer in a shot from the traditional north knoll location, possibly even from the junction of the overpass and the fence itself (due to eye and ear witness accounts, including those who saw smoke and smelled gunpowder). A shot from this location caused JFK's throat wound, possibly the same shot that penetrated the windshield. The head shot (again, possibly one of the two near-simultaneous head shots[32]) originated from this location.

---

30   See chapter seven for much more.

31   A sabot is a metal shell that fits around a bullet so it can be fired by a different caliber rifle. *Cold Case Kennedy* by Flip de Mey (2013), pages 146-147, 365; *The Lee Harvey Oswald Files* by Flip de Mey (2016), page 74; *Bloody Treason* by Noel Twyman (1997), page 101.

32   *John F. Kennedy's Head Wounds: A Final Synthesis – and a New Analysis of the Harper Fragment* by Dr. David Mantik (2015); *Not In Your Lifetime* by Anthony Summers (2013), page 53.

I believe that Connally was shot from the rear at least once if not twice. While I do not rule out an Oswald-rifle shot, I believe either he was struck via a shot from the Dal-Tex Building next to the book depository or from one of the more westward sixth floor depository windows (in 1975, a .30-06 shell casing was found on the roof of the Dal-Tex Building[33]). I believe CE399, the so-called magic bullet of single-bullet theory infamy, was planted to frame Oswald. Another bullet (or bullets) was recovered: the actual projectile that struck Connally. The other bullet or bullets were made to disappear and CE399 took their place. I obviously do not believe the single bullet theory.

Finally, we must factor in the possible (but unprovable) usage of silencers when trying to determine the number of shots that were fired. In addition, a 21-gun salute can and quite often does sound like "just" one shot,[34] so a witness hearing "just" one report/shot certainly does not rule out there having been more gunmen shooting at (almost) the exact same time. One must also keep in mind that, even for the majority of witnesses who heard "only" three shots, the vast majority of them – a whopping 102 by one detailed count[35] – heard a "bang" [pause] "bang-bang": the last two shots in very rapid succession, suggesting more than one gunman in and of itself.[36]

A rare view from the Dal-Tex Building

ANOTHER CENTRAL ISSUE: BODY ALTERATION– THE WORK OF DAVID LIFTON AND DOUG HORNE

"It strikes me that perhaps we should keep an agent with President Kennedy's body – out of respect for both President and Mrs. Ken-

33   *Rendezvous With Death* by H.R. Underwood (2013), page 197.

34   As one can hear on the David Wolper special *Four Days In November* (1964), as well as on *Best Evidence: The Research Video* (1990) by David Lifton.

35   http://www.patspeer.com/chapter9%3Apiecingittogether.

36   *Killing JFK: 50 Years, 50 Lies* by Dr. Lance Moore (2013), page 46 (as best exemplified by the testimony of Lee Bowers in the film *Rush to Judgment*); *They Killed Our President: 63 Reasons To Believe There Was A Conspiracy To Assassinate JFK* by Jesse Ventura (2013), pages 49-50; *Assassination Science* Edited by Prof. James Fetzer (1998), page 296; see also http://www.patspeer.com/chapter7%3Amorepiecesofthepuzzle.

nedy, and in light of the questions that were raised at Parkland Hospital about taking the body back to Washington for the autopsy. This way, if there is ever any doubt about whether Dr. Burkley stayed with the body until the autopsy, *or suspicions about tampering, there will be a Secret Service agent who also remained with the casket and can vouch for the integrity of the body. Agent Dick Johnsen is selected for the post because he is an agent who was with President Kennedy from the beginning and is familiar to Mrs. Kennedy, O'Donnell, and Powers."*–Secret Service agent Clint Hill, *Five Days in November*, page 124 (emphasis added)

What? Beyond the absurdity of picking an agent as somehow relieving any person's suspicion that something could possibly be amiss ("oh, an agent was there? Alright, no suspicion there"), the agent chosen was none other than the official keeper of CE399, aka the magic bullet. What's more, Lifton's best-selling book did not appear until the early 1980's and the issue of body tampering/alteration was not on anyone's minds until the early-mid 1970's at the earliest … why would Hill write these comments?

As for body alteration, I believe the president's body was tampered with haphazardly in an ad hoc fashion (possibly on Air Force One itself, possibly at Bethesda before the formal autopsy began) in order to covertly obtain bullets and fragments and to obscure the wounds (or this tampering had the unintended effect of doing so). The seminal work of David Lifton in *Best Evidence*, augmented by Doug Horne in his five-part series *Inside The ARRB*, makes this notion compelling, although I do not agree that this was planned in advance. While the important work of Harry Livingstone (especially in *High Treason 2*) pokes holes in the Lifton/Horne theory, it ironically adds to it, as well, by demonstrating tampering of some sort. The Secret Service (Roy Kellerman jumps high on the list) had to have been involved, as they maintained control of the body and were close by at all times between Parkland and Bethesda.

There are fourteen "smoking guns" when it comes to alteration. The first is the famous FBI FD-302 Report prepared by agents James Sibert and Francis O'Neill. Based on an "oral utterance" by Dr. James J. Humes, the chief autopsy doctor, the agents recorded that there had been "… surgery of the head area, namely, in the top of the skull."[37] In O'Neill's 2011 autobiography *A Fox Among Wolves* that was released by his family two

---

37   As made famous by David Lifton in *Best Evidence*, this was also carried further in Doug Horne's *Inside The ARRB*, page xxii.

years after his passing, the former agent wrote (page 13): "Humes ... indicated that he believed that some type of surgical procedure had been performed in the head region, possibly cutting of hair or removal of some slight tissue to view the massive wound in the right rear of the president's head ... parts of the brain were still there, but not much." It is important to keep in mind a crucial point that no one disputes: there was no surgery on the head of any kind even attempted at Parkland Hospital in Dallas; only the tracheostomy on the front neck region. Another very important factor to keep in sharp focus: O'Neill was a Hoover loyalist who believed Oswald acted alone; same with his partner Jim Sibert. These were no "conspiracy buffs"; far from it, in actual fact, thus making their observations even more strong, as they had no axe to grind or pre-conceived bias favoring a conspiracy.[38]

The second one comes from the second of three autopsy doctors, J. Thornton Boswell, during his testimony before the ARRB. *He testified under oath "there was an incised wound up there* that extended into the right eye socket and then back across his temporal and frontal bone [emphasis added]." Amazingly, Boswell also drew on a model of a skull that a significant portion of the right rear of the head was missing!

The third one comes from fellow autopsy doctor Pierre Finck who testified to the ARRB on 5/24/96 that one of the color autopsy photos (color transparency no. 38 titled "posterior view of wound of entrance of missile high in shoulder") depicted "an incision" – as Doug Horne wrote, "Was this incision ... evidence of post mortem surgery to gain access to the skull and remove evidence from the brain?"[39]

The fourth one comes from the ARRB testimony of X-ray technologist Ed Reed on 10/21/97. Reed testified that he was present for the first incision at the autopsy. When asked what the first incision was, Reed responded: "The cranium. The scalp, right here [the frontal bone behind the hairline] ... Humes made an incision – that I could see from my vantage point – an incision in the forehead, and brought back the scalp ... with a scalpel." Furthermore, Reed said: "Humes took out a saw and began to cut the forehead ... with the saw. Circular, small, mechanical – almost like a cast saw."[40]

The fifth one comes from the ARRB testimony of mortician Tom Robinson on 6/21/96. On the diagram he executed for the ARRB, Robinson drew horizontal lines representing "saw cuts," both above and

38   *Inside the ARRB* by Doug Horne (2009), pages 816-817.
39   *Inside the ARRB* by Doug Horne (2009), pages 379-380.
40   *Inside the ARRB* by Doug Horne (2009), pages 436-437; 628-629.

below the circular posterior skull defect. This was done, Robinson said, by the autopsy doctors so they could remove what was left of the brain: a hurried, modified craniotomy, something Humes denied was even necessary. Combined with Reed's testimony above, this is evidence of autopsy chicanery on the part of Humes. During Robinson's HSCA testimony, he made an ominous statement in response to Andy Purdy's questions: "You said that later, when you read some things about the assassination or autopsy, you heard or read some things which struck you as incorrect. What would those things be?" Robinson responded [statement exactly as recorded]: "The time the people moved (autopsy). The body was taken ... and the body never came ... lots of little things like that." This alarming statement was made years before publication of David Lifton's *Best Evidence* with its body alteration and body theft theories.[41]

The area Dr. Peters describes next:

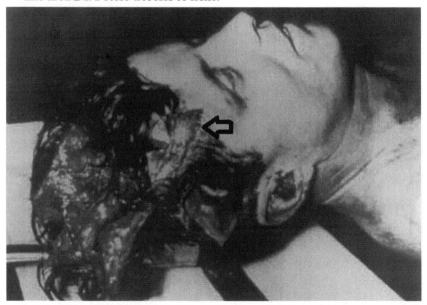

The sixth one comes from Dr. Paul Peters from Parkland Hospital. On the Nova PBS program *Who Shot President Kennedy?* from 11/15/88, "I would have to say, honestly, in looking at these photos, they're pretty much as I remember President Kennedy at the time, except for that little incision that seems to be coming down in the parietal area [outlining it on his right temple]. In looking at the photographs, I could envision that an incision might have been made in order to pull the scalp back to expose this bone

41   *Inside the ARRB* by Doug Horne (2009), pages 603, 629-630.

to make a photograph of that area." As narrator Walter Cronkite then says: "Perhaps this explains the surgery of the head area that Lifton describes." Wrong! Again, no surgery *was performed at Parkland.* Referring to his *Nova* commentary cited above, Peters told researcher Joanne Braun "It appeared to me, in reviewing the photos, that the incision was very sharp, as if cut by a knife, and I thought at the time that the prosector might have made it to enhance the removal of the brain and contents. I suppose it could have been an extension of the tear from the wound, but I did not notice it at the time we operated on President Kennedy."[42] In addition, Dr. Malcolm Perry stated that "there was no incision or indentation [in the right forehead]."[43] Dr. Ronald Jones did not see the V-shaped feature at Parkland.[44] Dr. Adolph Giesecke also did not see the V-shaped feature at Parkland.[45] Dr. Kenneth Salyer said he also did not see the V-shaped feature at Parkland.[46] Dr. Martin White also did not see this V-shaped feature at Parkland.[47] Finally, Dr. Donald Curtis agreed with all of his colleagues and stated that he did not see the V-shaped feature at Parkland.[48]

The seventh one comes from the 3/11/78 HSCA testimony of the acting chief of the radiology department at Bethesda Naval Hospital, Dr. John Ebersole. Ebersole testified that he saw "a neatly sutured transverse surgical wound across the low neck." Ebersole stated later in the deposition that this wound in the lower neck "had been surgically repaired," as well as repeating that "there was a sutured wound, a transverse wound at the base of the neck."[49]

The eighth one comes from a news story from 2014 from *Radar Online*: "Betrayed! Secret Service Photographer Secretly Tried To Sell JFK Autopsy Pics."[50] The article states: "The agent, Jim Fox, was desperate for money when he enlisted self-proclaimed JFK expert, Mark Crouch, to broker the black-and-white photos on his behalf, an audiotape has revealed. "They are quite gross and definitely of Kennedy. There's a bullet in his head," according to the audio recording of a reporter who was approached about buying the photos. The recording indicated that the pictures raised questions in the newsman's mind – deepening the mysteries

---

42   8/25/89 letter to Joanne Braun (*The Third Decade,* March 1991).

43   8/29/89 letter to Joanne Braun (*The Third Decade,* March 1991).

44   1989 letter to Joanne Braun (*The Third Decade,* March 1991).

45   1989 letter to Joanne Braun (*The Third Decade,* March 1991).

46   1989 letter to Joanne Braun (*The Third Decade,* March 1991).

47   1989 letter to Joanne Braun (*The Third Decade,* March 1991).

48   9/8/89 letter to Joanne Braun (*The Third Decade,* March 1991).

49   *Inside the ARRB* by Doug Horne (2009), pages 397-399.

50   https://radaronline.com/exclusives/2014/11/secret-service-agent-sells-jfk-autopsy-pictures/.

surrounding the murder. The wound in the back of JFK's head was the size of an egg, according to accounts. But after seeing the pictures, the reporter noted, "It's more like the size of four eggs. *Plus, there is an incision over the eye that raises questions* [emphasis added]."

The ninth is the statement by autopsy doctor Pierre Finck that President Kennedy's spinal cord was already severed when his body arrived at Bethesda Naval Hospital and that the autopsy report described this! Since the autopsy report officially submitted does not mention this, this is also further evidence that the autopsy report we have today is not the original one and significant changes were made.[51] There are two points of corroboration for Finck's statement: Bethesda technician James Curtis Jenkins also said that the brain stem was severed before the body arrived,[52] while FBI agent Francis O'Neill stated on video in 1992 that "there was no cutting" of the brain stem as would normally be the case after the autopsy began: "I saw them take out what remained [of the brain] in the area there … no cutting of the main thing (indicates with his hand the upper back of the neck) which I understand is normally done."[53]

The tenth comes from an oral history White House physician Dr. James Young gave in 2001,[54] "what happened was the body coming back from Texas landed at the Air Force Base there in D.C., Andrews I think it was...[as] they were offloading the casket to put it into a Navy ambulance it slipped and actually one of the handles broke off the coffin. So there's been a lot of furor about Kennedy leaving Texas in no body bag. And, lo and behold, when he got to Bethesda they had a different coffin and they had him in a body bag. Well that's what happened. They had to change coffins before they took him out to Bethesda. So they changed the coffin to get one that did not have a broken handle on it, and apparently put him in a body bag." Coupled with the HSCA, Lifton and Horne/ARRB witnesses to a body bag,[55] a plain shipping casket (as opposed to the bronze

51   *Inside the ARRB* by Doug Horne (2009), pages 836-837.

52   *Killing the Truth* by Harrison Livingstone (1993), page 714: interview of 5/20/91; Jenkins noted that, "Dr. (James) Humes, who removed the brain, made an exclamatory statement. 'The damn thing fell out in my hand.'" Jenkins said that, "The brain stem had already been severed."- Videotaped interview with researcher Bill Law, 1998, as reflected in this 10/5/98 LancerLINE news story: see also *JFK: From Parkland to Bethesda* by Vince Palamara (2015), page 124.

53   *Killing the Truth* by Harrison Livingstone (1993), page 714: 1992 video *Research v. Witness: Questioning the Facts*.

54   https://www.dropbox.com/s/dk6dwvzn6yq2ukd/NM%20and%20the%20Kennedy%20 Assassination.pdf?dl=0.

55   Body bag: 7 witnesses – Paul O'Connor (7 HSCA 15; *Best Evidence* by David Lifton, page 599; *Best Evidence: The Research Video*; *The Men Who Killed Kennedy*), Jerrol Custer (*Killing the Truth* by Harrison Livingstone, page 675: referencing interviews dated 9/23/91 and also one from 11/22/91 that the author filmed/participated in), Floyd Reibe (*Killing the Truth* by Harrison Livingstone, page 675: referencing interviews dated 4/1/91 and 4/5/91; *The JFK Assassination Revisited: A Synthesis* by

ceremonial ornate casket),[56] a black Cadillac hearse (as opposed to the grey Navy ambulance)[57] and a decoy ambulance,[58] this is powerful new information.

The eleventh one comes from an unnamed "Bethesda Nurse," an Ensign in the Navy working in the OB-GYN. From a March 1992 *Network Publications* article entitled "Bethesda Nurse" by Woody Woodland: "Network Publications has spoken with a woman, now living in New Hampshire, who was working as a Navy nurse on the evening of November 22, 1963, at Bethesda Naval Hospital. She says that she saw a simple casket arrive by helicopter accompanied by men in trench coats, and she is convinced it contained the president's body. At her request, her identity is being protected." Bethesda Nurse:

> There was the discussion that, in fact, there had been – and this was the exact word used – that there were alterations. And the word alterations was [used] relative to the autopsy itself.... It was announced that this helicopter would be landing and that [it] would be [carrying] the president's body.

The twelfth one comes from Janie B. Taylor, a biologist at the National Institute of Health (NIH), across the street from Bethesda Naval Hospital, and one of two African-American orderlies allegedly present during the autopsy. As Taylor told the ARRB:

James Rinnovatore & Allan Eaglesham, page 7), Edward Reed (Rinnovatore & Eaglesham, page 6) Captain John Stover (*Best Evidence* by David Lifton, page 630), John VanHoesen (*Inside the ARRB* by Douglas Horne, pages 989-992) and Dr. James Young (December of 2001 and January of 2002 during an interview with U.S. Navy Bureau of Medicine and Surgery historians) reported seeing a body bag.

56   Shipping casket: 11-13 witnesses and a document – Dennis David (*Best Evidence: The Research Video*; Rinnovatore & Eaglesham, page 5), Paul O'Connor (*Best Evidence: The Research Video*), Ed Reed (Rinnovatore & Eaglesham, page 6), Floyd Reibe (Rinnovatore & Eaglesham, page 6), Donald Rebentisch (*Best Evidence* by David Lifton, page 701), James Jenkins *(Inside the ARRB* by Douglas Horne, pages 989-992), Captain John Stover (*Inside the ARRB* by Douglas Horne, pages 989-992) and possibly Dr. Robert Karnei (*Inside the ARRB* by Douglas Horne, page 127). In addition, the Gawler's Funeral Home "First Call Sheet" references a "metal shipping casket": *Inside the ARRB* by Douglas Horne (2009), Volume One, Exhibit 69; Richard Muma and Paul Neigler (1/24/81 AP story *Fort Worth Star Telegram* and 1/25/81 UPI story *Miami Herald*); and an unnamed "Bethesda Nurse," an Ensign in the Navy working in the OB-GYN- March 1992 Network Publications article entitled "Bethesda Nurse" by Woody Woodland; Jerrol Custer told the ARRB that he saw two caskets (*Inside the ARRB* by Doug Horne, page 991), while Dr. James Young spoke about a different casket/ two caskets (December of 2001 and January of 2002 during an interview with U.S. Navy Bureau of Medicine and Surgery historians).

57   Black Cadillac hearse: 3 witnesses and the Air Force One tapes – Dennis David ((*Best Evidence: The Research Video*; Rinnovatore & Eaglesham, page 5), Jerrol Custer (Rinnovatore & Eaglesham, page 21), Donald Rebentisch (*Best Evidence* by David Lifton, page 701); Air Force One tapes- mention of a "black Cadillac": *Inside the ARRB* by Doug Horne (2009), page 1101.

58   Decoy ambulance: 9 witnesses – James Felder, Hubert Clark, Timothy Cheek, Richard Gaudreau, Richard Lipsey, J.S. Layton Ledbetter and George Barnum (*Best Evidence* by David Lifton (1981), pages 398-422); Richard Muma and Paul Neigler (1/24/81 AP story *Fort Worth Star Telegram* and 1/25/81 UPI story *Miami Herald*).

A man named Clarence Israel (deceased) of Rockville, MD told Taylor that his brother (deceased and no name given) was one of two African-American orderlies present in the autopsy room of the Medical Center the day of the autopsy. Israel said his brother had not mentioned the story to anyone including his wife & daughter who his brother outlived. His brother wanted to ensure that his story was known because he was verbally threatened by a guard at the time of the autopsy. Taylor said that African-Americans during that time period were often ignored and that non-African-American workers in many workplaces would assume that an African-American's presence did not count. She believed that activities were often done in their presence with the perception that the activities would never be reported. Israel told her the orderlies saw one doctor was in the autopsy room at the Medical Center who was waiting for some time prior to the arrival of the body and any other physicians. When the body arrived, many people were forced out of the room and the doctor performed some type of mutilation of three bullet punctures to the head area. The doctor was working at a very "hurried" pace and was done within a few minutes, at which point he left the autopsy room.[59]

Researcher Tyler Newcomb, the son of author Fred Newcomb, interviewed Janie Taylor. Newcomb discovered that the unnamed man was named Elbert Israel. Speaking to Mrs. Elbert Israel, he received confirmation that the Israel brothers were indeed on duty the night of 11/22/63 at Bethesda. Taylor told Newcomb that the criminal acts Clarence witnessed that night led him to start drinking.[60]

Corroboration for this account appears to come from Bethesda autopsy technician Paul O'Connor regarding a mysterious "Dr. Michael Miller":

> I was told by this so-called Dr. Michael Miller that "the body was altered at Walter Reed or at Bethesda and he thinks it was Bethesda, and put back in the coffin and taken around the corner and down back of the hospital to the morgue" … A "Dr. Morgan" or "Miller" in the Baltimore, D.C. area called Paul O'Connor late one night and said that someone – we'll call him X – took a ballpeen hammer to the head either at Walter Reed or Bethesda. O'Connor thinks he said it was Bethesda – "to disrupt the wound and the physical characteristics of the wound." Paul thought that X had something to do with it. X transferred out after the autopsy.[61]

---

59   11/24/95 ARRB interview of Taylor [see also *High Treason* by Harrison Livingstone and Robert Groden (1998 edition), pages 439, 492-493].
60   *Murder From Within* by Fred Newcomb and Perry Adams (2011 edition), pages xiv-xviii.
61   *High Treason 2* by Harrison Livingstone (1992), pages 271, 311 and 549 – Paul O'Connor

The thirteenth one comes from statements (mentioned earlier in this book) made to the FBI by Parkland Doctor Gene Akin. Akin came forward in 1984 and stated that "when he saw President Kennedy in the emergency room on 11/22/63, he thought he saw a bullet entrance wound on the President's forehead. The President was covered with blood in the head area and the back of his head was blown wide open. Akin feels that his observation as to the possible entrance wound on the President's forehead is significant and that he did not mention this item when he was interviewed in 1963-1964 because he did not want to be killed by any conspirators. Akin stated that if this entrance wound was not documented in the Presidential autopsy, then plastic surgery was probably conducted to cover this up."[62]

The fourteenth and final "smoking gun" comes from an 8/15/91 interview that author Harry Livingstone had with Joseph Hagan of Gawlers Funeral Home. Hagan told Livingstone that the face was undamaged except for a small laceration extending about a half inch into the forehead towards the right eyebrow, which can be seen in the right profile autopsy photograph.[63]

It is important to remember that, as no one contests from either side of the debate, officially speaking, *no surgery of any kind* was done to the head or spinal cord at Parkland Hospital.

Another interesting anomaly: none of the Parkland Hospital doctors questioned by the Warren Commission – nor any of the nurses – saw the small "entry" hole allegedly on the rear of the skull.[64] In addition, Secret Service agent Roy Kellerman also told the HSCA that there were "no small holes in the head" although, to be fair, this is contradicted by his drawing depicting both a large and a small hole on the rear of JFK's head.[65]

Regarding Secret Service agent Roy Kellerman, David Lifton and Doug Horne (and others) view him with some suspicion. While I am on the fence about the agent, based on the pro-conspiracy statements he made to both the Warren Commission and the HSCA, for those who feel he may have had something to do with elicit tampering and/or moving of the body, the following excerpt from the recently released unedited Air Force One tapes are grist for the mill:

(5/26/91 interview).
62   6/28/84 FBI Memorandum, SA Udo H. Specht to SAC, Dallas, re: interviews with Akin (RIF#124-10158-10449).
63   *Killing the Truth* by Harrison Livingstone (1993), page 680.
64   3 H 361 (Carrico); 3 H 372 and 6 H 16 (Perry); 6 H 25 (Clark); 6 H 35 (McClelland); 6 H 71 (Peters); 6 H 136 (Bowron); 6 H 141 (Henchcliffe).
65   8/24 and 8/25/77 interviews with the HSCA's Jim Kelly and Andy Purdy.

Airman: Stand by Duplex –

Gerry Behn: (code name Duplex) Hello Digest?

Roy Kellerman: (code name Digest) Ok. Jerry?

Behn: Hello Digest?"

Kellerman: [garbled] in here now, ah, we're at the airport, 26000, everybody aboard.

Behn: Okay go ahead Digest.

Kellerman: We're waiting for the swearing in.

Behn: That is for Volunteer [code name for LBJ], is that right?

Kellerman: Yes, we are having [garbled] before we take off, Jerry.

Behn: That's affirmative. Do you have any idea what, ah, Lace [code name for Jackie] wants to do and what Volunteer wants to do on their arrival here?

Kellerman: No, I will call you back. Suggest – we have a 2 hour 15 minute flight into Andrews. We have a full plane of at least 40."

Behn: Ok, go ahead Digest.

Kellerman: *I'll have to call you again after the, ah, body....* However, I'm sure the, ah, Volunteer boys [LBJ's agents] will go over his [JFK's] car and so forth. We will need [garbled] and several others.

Behn: All right, let me know what Volunteer wants to do when they, ah, land if they want to come into Crown [code name for the White House] by, ah, helicopter.

Kellerman: That's a Roger. I'll call you again.

Behn: OK." [emphasis added]

JFK's body was *already* on the plane. What did Kellerman mean by that cryptic comment that was not there before the unedited transcript became available?

In addition, fellow Secret Service agent Roger Warner mentioned in his report that, " … Mrs. Kennedy had requested no photographs or persons be allowed near the area where she would board Air Force One …"[66] This alleged "request" came approximately "ten minutes" before Jackie and the body of JFK arrived at the airport. Since it was the Secret Service who prevented the media from taking pictures of the bloody limousine just a short time before, it appears strongly that it was an agent (or agents) who

---

66   25 H 787.

actually made this request.[67] If this was really Jackie's request, why was official White House photographer Cecil Stoughton allowed to take numerous photos of this very area at that same time?[68] Stoughton probably made these photos on the sly, unknown to the agents. Warner even wrote that, "... no photographs were taken ... "[69] Evidently, the Secret Service did not want any compromising photos taken that day, such as the uncleaned limousine with a bullet hole in the windshield and dented chrome; or the identities of the agents carrying the coffin containing JFK's body. In fact, Agent Clint Hill revealed in his report dated 11/30/63: "[calling from Parkland Hospital] I requested that no press be admitted to the area in which Air Force One was to be placed."[70]

Finally, Secret Service agent Forrest Sorrels inexplicably told the FBI (agent Alfred D. Neeley, to be exact) the following:

> Mr. Forrest V. Sorrels ... advised that he was at the Parkland Memorial Hospital when President Kennedy was brought to the hospital and said that *he remained there until his body was taken to Love Field.* Mr. Sorrels stated that there were no photographs taken of President Kennedy at the Parkland Hospital. He stated there were no photographs taken of him as he was being taken into the Parkland Hospital on a stretcher. [Emphasis added][71]

Sorrels made this bizarre statement, yet there is seemingly no question that he went back to Dealey Plaza soon after arriving at Parkland Hospital.[72] Indeed, Sorrels also told the HSCA:

> He believed the President was dead before he arrived at the hospital. After arriving at Parkland Hospital, he decided that he could be of more help back at the scene of the shooting.[73]

I wrote "seemingly" previously because of the following photos: the older man in the middle (between Secret Service agent Rufus Young-

---

67   18 H 801-802. Newcomb interview with DPD Stavis Ellis, early 1970's.
68   See Stoughton photos in *Best Evidence* and Richard Trask's *That Day In Dallas.*
69   DPD Bobby Joe Dale told author Larry Sneed (*No More Silence*): " ... there was a DPS trooper taking pictures, and the Secret Service hollered at him to get his camera out of there [page 137]."Airman first class aircraft mechanic William E. Sale wrote: "One photographer took a picture as JFK's copper colored coffin was being carried up the rear steps. A Secret Service agent pointed at him and a group of Dallas police chased him along the warehouse roof." [Undated Sale letter, presumably from 1988, in the author's collection].
70   CD 3 Exhibits.
71   2/27/64 FBI interview (CD 735, page 12); see also *Murder From Within* by Fred Newcomb and Perry Adams (2011 edition), page 144.
72   7 H 332-360 and 13 H 55-83: testimony; 7 H 592: affidavit.
73   3/15/78 interview with the HSCA (RIF#180-10074-10392).

blood and LBJ) has been identified by several sources as Sorrels, while the below inset image (arrow) depicts a man in front of the Book Depository also identified by several sources as Sorrels (this was taken from a darker newsreel film stock). LBJ left Parkland Hospital at 1:26 PST,[74] while JFK's body left Parkland Hospital sometime around 2:04 PST: [75]

One wonders if this all relates in some shape or form to JFK's body being stowed elsewhere on the plane and/or manipulations? Was someone passing himself off as Sorrels back in Dealey Plaza? Witness Howard Brennan claimed he spoke to Sorrels within 3-5 minutes of the shooting.[76] There is the standard line most everyone accepts that states that Sorrels returned to Dealey Plaza about 25 minutes after the assassination, yet there is his FBI interview statement and the above photo with LBJ. I am not advocating a "two Sorrels" theory, but something does not add up.

A final note: several of the Bethesda witnesses – Paul O'Connor, James Jenkins, and Floyd Reibe – told author Harry Livingstone that some of the items depicted in the autopsy photos were not in the actual Bethesda autopsy room. O'Connor and Jenkins also told both Livingstone and author William Law that they did not recall the metal head rest (or stirrup) seen in the autopsy photos, stating that a block was used instead.[77] However, researcher Allan Eaglesham has claimed that these items were definitely in the autopsy room and that it is more a question of *when* the

74   https://retronewser.com/2013/11/22/vice-president-johnson-leaves-parkland-hospital-50-years-ago-this-hour-1963/.
75   http://educationforum.ipbhost.com/topic/23759-what-time-did-jfk-leave-parkland/.
76   *The Warren Omission* by Walt Brown (1996), page 265.
77   *High Treason 2* by Harry Livingstone (1992), pages 291-292; *In the Eye of History* by William Law (2005 edition), pages 57 and 91.

photos were taken, rather than *if* the photos were indeed taken at Bethesda.[78] Still, as Doug Horne has demonstrated, when these photos were taken is an important issue, especially if one is compelled to believe (as Horne does) that body manipulations and alterations were performed at Bethesda before the formal autopsy began.

ANOTHER CENTRAL ISSUE: SECOND OSWALDS

Regarding all the stories of "second Oswalds" popping up shortly before the assassination,[79] my number one suspect is Michael Paine, the estranged husband of Ruth Paine, the woman who took in Marina Oswald and her children and who got Oswald the job at the Book Depository. I first came to this conclusion in 1996 and presented my findings at the COPA conference in Washington, D.C. that same year. Paine experts Steven Jones, Barbara LaMonica and Carol Hewett, as well as the audience, were stunned at the resemblance (Paine on the left, Oswald on the right). Again, we have all that raw WFAA/ABC footage I came across in 1991 to thank for this – as many people told me, their only image of Paine was how he appeared 30 years later on the *Frontline* television program, not as he appeared back in 1963:

As I demonstrated in my last book,[80] a relatively new document was discovered showing that Secret Service agent Floyd Boring, the number two agent on Kennedy's White House Detail and the planner of the Texas trip from the agency's point of view (and who had also been on the Florida trip and countless other trips before that), claimed on 12/2/63 that the chauffeur to Agriculture Secretary Orville Freeman stated that he encountered Oswald in Washington, D.C. on 9/27/63! As researcher Deb Galentine wrote to me: "LHO supposedly arrived in Mexico City on 9/27/63. But this report has him in Washington DC on that date. Ruth Paine had recently

---

78   http://www.manuscriptservice.com/AutopsyRoom/.
79   *Harvey and Lee* by John Armstrong (2003); *The Assassinations: Probe Magazine on JFK, MLK, RFK and Malcolm X* by James DiEugenio and Lisa Pease, Editors (2003), pages 90-200.
80   *Who's Who in the Secret Service* by Vince Palamara (2018), Appendix 3.

returned to New Orleans shortly before this date from the Washington DC area. She had incorporated a visit to CIA headquarters while in the D.C. area in order to "see her sister." I have doubts about Ruth traveling alone on her road trip with two small children. I suspect she took her husband along. So it may be possible that Michael Paine stayed behind in the area. Someone in the D.C./PA/Baltimore area was impersonating LHO in several places during that time frame." Researcher Carolina Lynn also weighed in on the matter:

> This is intriguing on many levels. First, the witness is a chauffeur for Secretary of Agriculture Orville Freeman, a seemingly very credible witness. The driver spoke to a D.C. policeman about the demeanor of the "Oswald" look-alike he encountered. [Sadly, the report says the policeman did not interview or ID "Oswald"]. Second, the report throughout refers to the "suspect" as Harvey Lee Oswald," a switching of the name that author John Armstrong believes is government code to indicate the Russian-native doppelganger of the New Orleans-born Lee Harvey Oswald... "Lee Harvey Oswald" had by the date of this report, Dec. 2, 1963, become the most notorious name in U.S. history, repeated over and over on TV and radio and in newspapers. So it is hard to believe the name reversal could be "accidental." Third, The Warren Omission Report is adamant that "Oswald" was in Mexico City on September 27, 1963, the verified date of the DC incident, so this person was not the same "Oswald" in Mexico!

Interestingly, in a 6/3/60 FBI memo to the Office of Security, Department of State, at a time when the real Oswald was in Russia, none other than FBI Director J. Edgar Hoover himself noted: "Since there is a possibility that an imposter is using Oswald's birth certificate, any current information the Department of State may have concerning subject will be appreciated."[81] In addition, while the real Oswald was in Russia, Oswald's name was curiously placed on 1/20/61 on the original bid form for Bolton Ford, Inc. The purchaser was listed as "Friends of Democratic Cuba," 402 St. Charles Street, New Orleans, Louisiana" which was incorporated on 1/9/61.[82] Former Chicago FBI Special Agent in Charge W. Guy Banister was on the articles of incorporation for the Friends of Democratic Cuba. As author Jim DiEugenio stated, "Its ostensible purpose was to raise funds for the anti-Castro cause."[83]

---

81   Numerous, such as *Not In Your Lifetime* by Anthony Summers (1998), pp. 294-295..

82   *Harvey and Lee* by John Armstrong (2003), pages 325-326; *JFK* movie (1991); .

83   *Destiny Betrayed* by James DiEugenio (2012), pages 109-110.

YET ANOTHER CENTRAL ISSUE: THREATS TO KENNEDY (ESPECIALLY IN NOVEMBER 1963)

As I explore in my first book,[84] I believe the attempts on Kennedy's life on 11/2/63 in Chicago (resulting, at least in part, in a cancelled motorcade and a potential patsy named Thomas Arthur Vallee) and the ones in both Miami and Tampa on 11/18/63 (involving a potential patsy in Gilbert Policarpo Lopez),[85] [86] a mere four days before Dallas, demonstrate a pattern. In short, the assassination of President Kennedy was a moving crime, not an isolated incident. As author Flip de Mey also established,[87] there were "patsies" in these other cities, ready to take the (sole) blame if an assassination was successful. Oswald was the designated fall guy for Dallas.

Earlier in the same year, on 3/23/63 in Chicago, to be exact, there were other threats to JFK. Col. George J. McNally, WH Signal Corps and former Secret Service agent: "But during the Chicago visit, the motorcade was slowed to the pace of a mounted Black Horse Troop, and the police got a warning of Puerto Rican snipers. Helicopters searched the roofs along the way, and no incidents occurred."[88] Also regarding 3/23/63,

> A postcard was received in the Saturday morning mail of the Chicago office threatening the life of the President during the motorcade from O'Hare Field to the Conrad Hilton Hotel.[89]

So, as one can see, Dallas did not exist in a vacuum. With regard to the Miami trip, as noted earlier in this book, White House Detail advance agent Lubert

> "Bert" de Freese admitted to the HSCA that "a threat did surface in connection with the Miami trip ... there was an active threat against the President which the Secret Service was aware in No-

---

84   *Survivor's Guilt* (2013), Chapter two. See also *The JFK Assassination* by James DiEugenio (2018), pages 271-278.
85   *Who Really Killed Kennedy?: 50 Years Later: Stunning New Revelations About the JFK Assassination* by Jerome Corsi (2016)- kindle edition; From the newly-released files: https://www.archives.gov/files/research/jfk/releases/104-10419-10352.pdf.
86   From the newly-released files: https://www.archives.gov/files/research/jfk/releases/104-10506-10025.pdf.
87   *The Lee Harvey Oswald Files* (2016).
88   *A Million Miles of Presidents* by Colonel George McNally, p. 204.
89   RIF #154-10003-10012: Chicago, IL trip 3/23/63 Secret Service survey report. 6 motorcycles surrounding limo, Lawton riding on (JFK's side of) rear of limo, Mayor's follow-up car with four detectives in addition to SS follow-up car, police facing crowd (not JFK) on the route, no-one permitted on overpasses except four policemen guarding them, press/photographers close to JFK, Hatcher with Kilduff. PRS: one threat (the postcard).

vember 1963 in the period immediately prior to JFK's trip to Miami made by a group of people."[90]

In addition to this threat information, and separate from the 11/9 Milteer threat, a CO2 PRS file, released to the HSCA on 5/3/78 and available only recently, reveals yet another threat subject: John Warrington.[91] Kinney told the author, "we had a scare" down there, an unspecified "organized crime" threat related to this same trip. In fact, there were six pages of threat subjects and information, including the subjects Orlando Bosch, Pedro Diaz Lanz, Enrique Llaca, Jr., and others.[92]

In addition, I found quite a few newspaper articles when looking thru old newspaper archives reporting threats on Kennedy's life in various cities around the country between 1960-1963. Again, we must view the assassination of President Kennedy on 11/22/63 as the one attempt that succeeded, not a mere lightning bolt from the sky as if a quirk of fate or a fluke event.

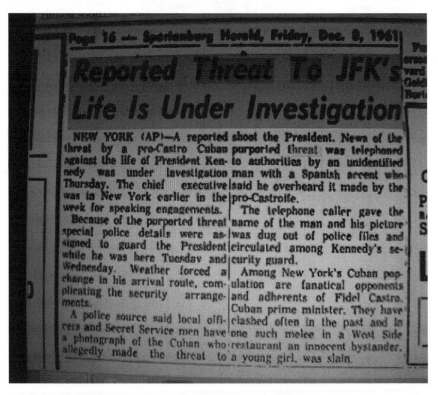

Page 16 — Spartanburg Herald, Friday, Dec. 8, 1961

Reported Threat To JFK's Life Is Under Investigation

NEW YORK (AP)—A reported threat by a pro-Castro Cuban against the life of President Kennedy was under investigation Thursday. The chief executive was in New York earlier in the week for speaking engagements.

Because of the purported threat special police details were assigned to guard the President while he was here Tuesday and Wednesday. Weather forced a change in his arrival route, complicating the security arrangements.

A police source said local officers and Secret Service men have a photograph of the Cuban who allegedly made the threat to a young girl.

shoot the President. News of the threat by a pro-Castro Cuban purported threat was telephoned to authorities by an unidentified man with a Spanish accent who said he overheard it made by the pro-Castroite.

The telephone caller gave the name of the man and his picture was dug out of police files and circulated among Kennedy's security guard.

Among New York's Cuban population are fanatical opponents and adherents of Fidel Castro, Cuban prime minister. They have clashed often in the past and in one such melee in a West Side restaurant an innocent bystander, was slain.

---

90   HSCA interview with de Freese 1978.
91   RIF#'s 180-10118-10041 and 10033. See also Gerald Blaine's *The Kennedy Detail*.
92   Secret Service Final Survey Report for Miami, FL 11/18/63: RIF#154-10002-10422.

THE TAMPA TRIBUNE

★ ★ ★
Threats On Kennedy Made Here

Tampa police and Secret Service agents scanned crowds for a man who had vowed to assassinate the President here last Monday, Chief of Police J. P. Mullins said yesterday.

In issuing notice to all participating security police prior to the President's motorcade tour in Tampa, Mullins had said: "I would like to advise all officers that threats against the President have been made from this area in the last few days."

A memo from the White House Secret Service dated Nov. 8 reported:

"Subject made statement of a plan to assassinate the President in October 1963. Subject stated he will use a gun, and if he couldn't get closer he would find another way. Subject is described as: White, male, 20, slender build," etc.

Mullins said Secret Service had been advised of three persons in the area who reportedly had made threats on the President's life. One of the three was—and still is—in jail here under heavy bond.

Mullins said he did not know if the other two may have followed the Presidential caravan to Dallas.

Sarasota County Sheriff Ross E. Boyer also said yesterday that officers who protected Kennedy in Tampa Monday were warned about "a young man" who had threatened to kill the President during that trip.

Sat. Nov. 16th

The Cuban Commandoes have the BOMBS ready for killing JFK and Mayor KING HIGH either at the AIRPORT at the Convention Hall.

A Catholic PADRE is going to give instructions at the Cuban Womens Broadcast at 8:45 tonight by "RELOJ RADIO" and then all are invited to Dance at Bayfront Park Auditorium and take along a BOTTLE of wine, Wiskey,Etc.,to decide who will throw the bombs. At King High because he did sign the Ord.about taxir druibers being only American Citizens and sending refugees away,Etc. Mary

MIAMI BEACH, FLA.
8 30 PM
16 NOV
1963

THIS SIDE OF CARD IS FOR ADDRESS

U.S.POSTAGE
4¢

The Chief of Police
Miami, Florida.

Lawrence Journal-World - Oct 12, 196 he Sunday Sun - Apr 5, 1961 Browse this newspaper x Brow

JFK DEATH THREAT BRINGS ALERT

NEW YORK (AP) — A telephoned death threat against President Kennedy today led to a special police alert at the Manhattan end of the Lincoln Tunnel under the Hudson River. The chief executive used that route in returning from New Jersey.

Secret Service agents said the anonymous caller named that area and said "the President will be blasted" there. Police headquarters was informed and officers on duty near the tunnel were ordered to increase their vigilance during the President's passage.

Threat Doubles Kennedy Guard

President Attends Easter Service Surrounded by Secret Service Men

PALM BEACH, Fla. (CP) — The security guard was doubled when U.S. President John Kennedy and his wife attended Easter church services.

The president refused to comment on alleged kidnapping-assassination plots against his family.

The vacationing president, who arrived last Thursday, will return to Washington Tuesday.

Pro-Castro Cubans allegedly

Upset Car Tears Open Trailer

REFER TO FILE NO. 1-16-602.111

TREASURY DEPARTMENT
UNITED STATES SECRET SERVICE
FIELD FORCE

OFFICE   White House Detail
ADDRESS P. O. LOCK BOX NO.

Washington, D. C.

March 29, 1963

Supplemental Survey Report

Re: President's Visit to Chicago, Ill.,
        to Attend Dedication of Chicago
        O'Hare International Airport, and
        Luncheon Celebrating the Dedication
        at the Conrad Hilton Hotel, Chicago,
        Ill., on Saturday, March 23, 1963.

Mr. James J. Rowley
Chief, U. S. Secret Service
Washington, D. C.

Sir:

Supplementing my Protective Survey Report dated March 22, 1963, the following changes and/or additions occurred:

12:30 p.m.   The President was met by Mr. McNamara and Mr. Parrish, manager and executive manager of the Conrad Hilton Hotel.

2:50 p.m.   The President was introduced by Mayor Daley and addressed the 1400 luncheon guests.

3:10 p.m.   The President, accompanied by Mayor Daley and Senator Douglas, departed the Conrad Hilton Hotel.

3:50 p.m.   The President and party arrived at Chicago O'Hare International Airport, Commercial Side, Terminal No. 2, Gate F-1.

4:00 p.m.   The Presidential aircraft departed for Washington, D. C.

Protective Research

A postcard was received in the Saturday morning mail of the Chicago office threatening the life of the President during the motorcade from O'Hare

000002

- 2 -   3-29-63

Field to the Conrad Hilton Hotel.

All special agents of this Service involved in the movement and senior
supervisory officers of the Chicago Police Department were apprised
of this development.

As a precautionary move two additional motorcycles were employed in
the motorcade flanking the President's limousine at the right and left
rear fenders. This resulted in a shielding effect with six motorcycles
surrounding the vehicle. In addition, the SS follow-up car rode the
right rear fender and the Mayor's follow-up car, with four detectives,
and SA Lawton, rode the left rear fender.

The threat did not materialize; special agents of the Chicago field
office will conduct the usual investigation in an effort to determine the
author of the postcard.

The Chicago Police Department was requested to keep the information
concerning the threat confidential.

                                        Very truly yours,

                                        David B. Grant
                                        David B. Grant
                                        Special Agent

Approved:

Gerald A. Behn
Gerald A. Behn
Special Agent in Charge

DBG:ebd

cc: Chicago

                              5744 Gaston Avenue
                              Dallas, 14, Texas
                              October 28, 1963

Mr. Pierre Salinger
Press Secretary
The White House
Washington, D. C.

Dear Mr. Salinger:

Although I do not consider myself an 'alarmist', I do
fervently hope that President Kennedy can be dissuaded
from appearing in public in the City of Dallas, Texas,
as much as I would appreciate and enjoy hearing and
seeing him.

This "hoodlum mob" here in Dallas is frenzied and in-
furiated because their attack upon Ambassador Adlai
Stevenson on the 24th, backfired on them. I have heard
that some of them have said that they "have just
started".

No number of policemen, plainclothes men nor militia
can control the "air", Mr. Salinger--- it is a dread-
ful thought, but all remember the fate of President
McKinley.

These people are crazy, or crazed, and I am sure that
we must realize that their actions in the future are
unpredictable.

                                   Sincerely yours,

                                   Nelle M. Doyle
                                   Mrs. Nelle M. Doyle

NMD:s

168

Bulletin 6/3/20/76

Plan to Kill Kennedy in '62 Is Disclosed

Oakland, Calif. — (AP) — A Cuban carrying a gun and apparently planning to kill President John F. Kennedy was arrested in Mexico City during Kennedy's state visit there in 1962, the Oakland Tribune says.

The unidentified man was taken into custody by Mexican authorities, who had been alerted by American officials, but he apparently never was prosecuted, the newspaper said in a copyright story quoting a former U.S. ambassador to Mexico, Thomas C. Mann.

The Tribune said it learned from other sources that the CIA had uncovered the purported plot before Kennedy's June 29-July 1 trip. That was about 17 months before Kennedy was assassinated in Dallas.

"We did pick up information when (Kennedy) went out one Sunday to (the Basilica of the Virgin of Guadalupe) that there was a Cuban with a tic in his eye and a gun in his pocket," Mann was quoted as saying.

"The Mexican government sent some people out there, and I believe it was their people — and not our security people who were closer to the President — who found such a person in a huge crowd, around maybe 300,000 people.

CHAPTER SIX

LOOSE ENDS (AND EVEN MORE EVIDENCE OF CONSPIRACY)

There remains a smattering of topics with regard to the study of the Kennedy assassination that I feel need to be addressed. Some of my views on these issues may be controversial or differ from yours, but these are my learned opinions based on many years of reading and research. As with the prior chapters, I believe you will find these views of interest.

DID OSWALD KNOW RUBY?

While there is a tantalizing frame or two of newsreel film on 11/24/63 that seems to show Oswald and Ruby meeting eyes before Ruby lunges forward to shoot Oswald, and while there are intriguing allegations of a connection between the two (albeit often by a combination of credible, somewhat credible, dubious or unconfirmed sources like Carroll Jarnagin, Wally Weston, Kathy Kay, Shari Angel, and so on[1]), I would say it is definitely possible but not proven.[2] Honestly, at this very late date, it may never be proven, either. That said, I will have a little more to say about this in the next chapter. In the meantime, I would assess this possibility at a somewhat unsatisfying 50-75 percent probability of being true. In any event, I agree with the HSCA: "Neither Oswald or Ruby turned out to be 'loners'" as the Warren Commission falsely stated.[3]

IS THE JIM GARRISON CASE VALID?

Yes. Garrison made mistakes and definitely shot from the hip at times, and Lord knows anti-conspiracy authors Fred Litwin and John McAdams work hard to debunk Garrison,[4] but, warts and all, the Garrison case, including the evidence against David Ferrie, Guy Banister and Clay Shaw, stands (Regarding David Ferrie, many people don't realize that

1   *Rendezvous With Death* by H.R. Underwood (2013), pages 208-213; *The Girl on the Stairs* by Barry Ernest (2013), pages 80-81, 91, 114-117, 142.
2   https://www.archives.gov/files/research/jfk/releases/2018/docid-32177778.pdf.
3   HSCA Report, page 180.
4   *On The Trail of Delusion: Jim Garrison, The Great Accuser* by Fred Litwin (2020); https://mcadams.posc.mu.edu/garrison.htm.

he is mentioned during testimony contained in Warren Commission volume 8: during the testimony of Edward Voebel, a teenage acquaintance of Oswald,[5] and Frederick O'Sullivan, a childhood friend of Oswald).[6] The work of author Jim DiEugenio and the ARRB file releases goes a long way toward strengthening and rehabilitating Garrison's case. There was a time when any mention of Clay Shaw had me rolling my eyes, as I did not believe he truly had anything to do with the case, despite his portrayal in the *JFK* movie and so forth. I highly recommend DiEugenio's *Destiny Betrayed: JFK, Cuba and the Garrison Case* (the second edition from 2012, not the dated, slimmer version from 1992) and *The JFK Assassination* (the 2018 updated paperback version of his 2013 book *Reclaiming Parkland*). Joan Mellen's 2005 book *A Farewell to Justice* and especially Lisa Pease's *Real History* website[7] are also very worthwhile Garrison resources.

Writer Albert L. Rossi[8] (when discussing DiEugenio's book *Destiny Betrayed*, second edition) identified 15 items of achievement and post-trial clarification (one might even say vindication) with regard to Garrison's case for conspiracy. I have summarized them as follows:

> 1. In 1993, a photo of Oswald and David Ferrie from the Civil Air Patrol was shown on *Frontline*, thus confirming a relationship between the two that some disputed as not being factual.

> 2. One of Garrison's most important findings was Oswald's presence at Guy Banister's office at 544 Camp/531 Lafayette Street.

> 3. Davy's and DiEugenio's legwork has also reinforced Fruge's and Dischler's original discoveries about Shaw, Ferrie and Oswald in Clinton-Jackson.

> 4. Donald Deneselya's recollection of a CIA debriefing of Oswald in New York was reported on *Frontline* in 1993. John Newman then found a CIA memo wherein the chief of the Soviet Russia division wrote of such a debriefing as motivated by an "operational interest in the Harvey [Oswald] Story."

> 5. DiEugenio builds a strong case for Warren DeBrueys as Oswald's FBI handler in New Orleans. The FBI destroyed the files on Orestes Pena, a witness to one of their meetings, just prior to the creation of the HSCA. It was DeBrueys that Oswald asked to see after his arrest following the leafleting incident. William Walter found an informant file on Oswald with DeBrueys' name on it. De-

5   8 H 14.
6   8 H 29-31.
7   http://www.realhistoryarchives.com/collections/assassinations/jfk/garrison.htm.
8   https://kennedysandking.com/john-f-kennedy-reviews/651.

Brueys most certainly knew of Oswald's association with Banister before the assassination. FBI agent James Hosty later told Church Committee witness Carver Gayton that Oswald indeed was an informant. The FBI, which had its own anti-Fair Play for Cuba Committee (FPCC) program, was probably told not to interfere with a parallel CIA-run operation in which Oswald appeared to be a key player. The existence of such a CIA discreditation program, run by David Phillips and James McCord, was revealed by the ARRB. This explains why the CIA ordered 45 copies of the first printing of Corliss Lamont's pamphlet, "The Crime Against Cuba," in June of 1961; it was either Guy Banister who then requested these from CIA, or someone, perhaps Phillips again, provided them as part of the program he was running with McCord.

6. In connection with this CIA-directed anti-FPCC charade, there is evidence that Oswald's Marine acquaintance and Oswald look-a-like Kerry Thornley frequented Oswald and Marina in New Orleans and partnered with him in the leafleting activity.

7. DiEugenio makes evident not only the more than casual acquaintance between the de Mohrenschildts and the Paines, but also the numerous links of both Michael's and Ruth's families to the CIA and Dulles. Both Michael and Ruth were themselves involved in undercover work. One document released by the ARRB reveals that Michael Paine engaged in infiltration activities at SMU in Dallas similar to those of Oswald.

8. The link (revealed by declassified ARRB documents) between Robert Maheu, who ran a cover company in D.C. for the recruitment of assassins to kill Castro, and Guy Banister, via Carmine Bellino.

9. A declassified memo from 1964, written by Leon Hubert and Burt Griffin, stated that "underworld figures, anti-Castro Cubans and extreme right-wing" elements were the most promising leads with respect to a Dallas-based gun-smuggling ring. The memo also suggests that Oswald's Cuban connections in Dallas were never explored. We now know that a group of Cubans met at a safe house at 3128 Harlendale for months up until about a week before the assassination, when they vacated it; Oswald was also seen there.

10. A declassified HSCA document, a 1977 memo from Garrison to L.J. Delsa and Bob Buras, recounts the story of Clara Gay, a client of Attorney G. Wray Gill whose office David Ferrie shared. She happened to call Gill right after Ferrie was interviewed by Garrison and the FBI and overheard the secretary deny Gill's knowledge of

Ferrie's activities. Clara then went to the office, and noticed on Ferrie's desk a diagram of Dealey Plaza with "Elm Street" on it, which she unsuccessfully tried to snatch in order to turn over to the FBI.

11. DiEugenio calls the "most ignored piece of key evidence" a package addressed to Oswald, but bearing a sticker with a non-existent address, which lay around the dead letter section of the Dallas post office unnoticed for twelve days.[9] Inside was a sheet of brown wrapping paper resembling the one recovered at the Book Depository, inside which Oswald supposedly smuggled the rifle into the building. There were absolutely no latent fingerprints on it. What is of further interest is the fact that the police found a postage-due notice at the Irving post office for a package sent on November 20 to a Lee Oswald at the Paine's address, 2515 W. Fifth Street.

12. Bernardo DeTorres, who was the first of the Garrison infiltrators was suspected by Gaeton Fonzi, Ed Lopez and Al Gonzalez of being a conspirator. DeTorres also admitted to having been enlisted by the Secret Service to guard Kennedy on his November 1963 Miami trip. He claimed to an informant of the HSCA that he possessed pictures taken during the assassination.

13. One of the "smoking guns" in this case is Mexico City. Two extremely important documents were declassified by the ARRB in this area: the Slawson-Coleman report and the Lopez-Hardway report. Some doubt Oswald was even there; but if he was, the appearances at the Cuban Consulate and Russian Embassy were very likely by impostors. There are, remarkably, no photos of him, despite routine daily takes from CIA surveillance cameras, and the man who spoke with Sylvia Duran does not fit Oswald's physical description; moreover, this person was reportedly fluent in Spanish, which there is no evidence Oswald knew, and apparently struggled with Russian, of which Oswald had a good command. Oswald's undisturbed return to Dallas was guaranteed by the fact that the FBI's FLASH warning on him was cancelled on October 9, just hours before the cable from the Mexico City station concerning his visit arrived in Washington.

14. Since a phone call made by Duran to the Russian Embassy did not clearly mention Oswald's name, a fake call had to be made. Using a tape of this call was risky because Oswald had been exposed in the media that summer in New Orleans. For some reason, Anne Goodpasture, Phillips's trusted associate at the Mexico City station, sent the tape to FBI agent Eldon Rudd on the evening of the 22nd. After Hoover was told that the voice on it was not Oswald's, Goodpasture

9   *Accessories After the Fact* by Sylvia Meagher (1967), pages 63-64.

and Rudd invented a cover story that the tape actually had been routinely erased, a story belied by other sources. LBJ either did not draw the obvious conclusions from Hoover's revelations, or decided not to act on them, but instead played along by using this phony evidence of a foreign plot to keep the lid on the investigation. In a memo discovered by DiEugenio, Garrison wrote that he 1) Doubts the existence of any photo of Oswald, because it would have certainly appeared in the Report; 2) Asks why consulate employees did not recognize photos of the real Oswald; 3) Notices that Duran's name is printed in Oswald's notebook; 4) Wonders why there is no bus manifest for Oswald's trip; 5) Notes there are no fingerprints on Oswald's tourist card. As DiEugenio asserts, Garrison was the only investigator at that stage to recognize the proof of the plot in this Mexican episode.

15. Ramsey Clark's 1967 slip-up to the press about the FBI investigating Shaw in 1963 was based in fact. For the FBI had indeed run a check on Shaw then; it is uncertain whether they ever communicated this to the Commission. Gaeton Fonzi rediscovered the connection, first uncovered by Garrison, between Shaw, Ferrie and Banister through Freeport Sulphur, Moa Bay and Nicaro Nickel. Shaw's longtime links to CIA: William Davy discovered from a declassified CIA note that one of the files on him had been destroyed. In 1994 Peter Vea also uncovered a document in the National Archives dating from 1967 (during the period Garrison was investigating him) giving Shaw covert security approval in the project QKENCHANT. We also now possess further confirmation of Shaw's involvement with Permindex, which had ties to the Schroeder Banking Corporation and thereby with Heinrich Himmler's onetime network, and which supported the French renegade military outfit, the OAS.

Were There Truly Mysterious Deaths Associated with the Kennedy assassination?

A huge "yes" to that, although the numbers and statistical probabilities and improbabilities have been greatly exaggerated.[10] Hands down, the best book on this specific subject is the Richard Belzer and David Wayne book called *Hit List* from 2013. The authors did a masterful job compiling the most notable and believable mysterious and untimely deaths and they avoid all the silly and extremely unlikely subjects that

10   With all due respect, I find the logic unconvincing in the pro-conspiracy book *Reclaiming Science: The JFK Conspiracy* by Richard Charnin (2014), due in no small measure to selection bias, poorly applied logic, math and an appalling lack of peer review and sourcing. I know the author had his heart in the right place, but his work was used to better effect in the infinitely superior book *Hit List* by Richard Belzer and David Wayne (2013).

are regularly added to these lists (examples: Roy Kellerman, who died in 1984; Bill Greer, who died in 1985).

I would add Secret Service agent Thomas Shipman to the list (see earlier discussion, as well as my previous books). On the one hand, it is hard to believe there was a true "hit squad" out there attempting to permanently silence witnesses. On the other hand, the evidence amassed by the authors of *Hit List* is hard to ignore and dismiss as mere coincidences or the byproducts of attrition, especially concerning the circumstances of some (Rose Cherami, Gary Underhill,[11] Mary Pinchot Meyer, etc.) and the timing of others (the Mafia figures around the time of the Church Committee hearings; the six FBI agents who died in a 6 month period around the time of the HSCA hearings, etc.). We are talking here about a period from 1963 to 1977 + one in 1978, a few of whom died on the same day (Charles Nicoletti and George de Mohrenschildt; Hugh Ward and Deslesseps Morrison; David Ferrie and Eladio del Valle) or one day apart (Dorothy Kilgallen and Florence Pritchett Smith)!

This one is particularly spooky – Captain Michael D. Groves, MDW Honor Guard, who died 12/3/63. As authors Craig Roberts and John Armstrong write: "Captain Groves, who commanded the JFK Honor Guard for Kennedy's funeral, died under mysterious circumstances seven days after the funeral. While eating dinner, he took a bite of food, paused briefly as a pained look came over his face, then passed out and fell face down into his plate. He died instantly. On December 12th, his possessions and mementos – which had been sent home to Birmingham, Michigan – were destroyed in a fire of mysterious origin. The Honor Guard, for some mysterious reason, had been practicing for a presidential funeral for three days before the assassination. Captain Groves was 27 years old at the time of this death. Cause of death: Unknown. Possibly poison."[12]

From Internet SSN Death listing: Name: MICHAEL GROVES Born: 19 Aug 1936 Died: Dec 1963.

WAS THE ZAPRUDER FILM ALTERED?

On the one hand, I do not believe the Zapruder film was altered, as the chain of possession of the original film seems to disprove this notion.[13] On the other hand, I am persuaded and compelled to think that

11   *Destiny Betrayed* by James DiEugenio (2012), pages 77, 98-100.
12   *JFK: The Dead Witnesses* by Craig Roberts and John Armstrong (1995), p. 3; *Killing the Truth* by Harrison Livingstone (1993), page 742 – "[Donald] Rebentisch remembers the color guard captain, and said he died a week later from the strain."; *The Death of a President* by William Manchester (1967), page 638.
13   *The Zapruder Film: Reframing JFK's Assassination* by David Wrone, 2003; *The JFK Assassi-*

individual frames may have been removed in order to hide evidence of the limousine slowing down. In addition, the back of Kennedy's head does appear a little too dark for comfort. The problem is that some people take this idea to extremes, believing the extant film is a cartoon, a wholesale fake and so forth.[14] I cannot go that far. This idea was a real hot topic from around 1995 to 2004, but it has cooled considerably since. The one notable exception is the ARRB's Doug Horne, who wrote extensively about what he deemed to be Zapruder film alteration in 2009.[15]

With all this in mind, my answer is an unsatisfying "maybe." If it was altered in any fashion (frames removed, etc.), the Secret Service had custody of the original film.[16]

All that being taken into consideration, I am most compelled by what Robert Groden has stated passionately for decades, having worked with the original film and so forth: the Zapruder film was not altered. So, I may waffle on one key component of possible tampering (frame removal), but I am more persuaded by Robert Groden's beliefs on the matter.

Now, having said all that (and further demonstrating that hardly anything is black and white in this case), there are two Secret Service-related tidbits of information about the Zapruder film that causes one to wonder. Former Secret Service agent Bill Carter, who briefly protected JFK, wrote in his book about "the raw footage of the film shot by Abraham Zapruder" and that when the film was shown years later, "the portion that was so graphic had been cut out."[17]

The second tidbit comes from former Secret Service agent Marty Venker's book: "They [the Secret Service] showed you the gruesome version [of the Zapruder film during training] that the public usually didn't see, where parts of President Kennedy's brain sprayed all over Jackie."[18]

Did the Limousine Stop During the Assassination?

No. However, I strongly believe that the presidential limousine slowed down. In fact, to some, this deceleration seemed like a stop, even though it was not an actual complete stop. In a study I began back in 1991 (and which was part of my first presentation at Jerry Rose's Third Decade conference along with author's Harry Livingstone, George Michael Evica,

nation Debates: Lone Gunman versus Conspiracy by Michael L. Kurtz (2006), pages 103-106.
14   The Hoax of the Century: Decoding the Forgery of the Zapruder Film by Harrison Livingstone, 2004; The Great Zapruder Film Hoax by Prof. James Fetzer, 2003.
15   Inside The ARRB by Doug Horne (2009), pages 1185-1378.
16   Killing Kennedy by Harrison Livingstone, 1995..
17   Get Carter by Bill Carter (2005), page 54.
18   Confessions of an Ex-Secret Service Agent by George Rush (1988), pages 24-25.

Robert Cutler, and many others), I have now documented over 70 witnesses who stated that the limousine either slowed down or stopped.[19] This is evidence of Secret Service negligence or worse, as well as tying into the whole notion of Zapruder film tampering.

At the end of the day, I am in agreement with Robert Groden on this issue: the car slowed down but did not stop.

WAS THE LIMOUSINE TRULY CLEANED UP AT PARKLAND HOSPITAL?

Yes. The weight of the evidence demonstrates that at least some *attempt* was made to clean some of the blood, bone and brain debris from the limousine, although the attempt was only marginally successful, at best, as the photos of the backseat of the limousine back at the White House Garage on the night of 11/22/63 depict a fairly bloody scene still remained (unless the middle and front areas received a more concentrated level of cleaning). That said, the stainless steel bucket shown in several photos and films may or may not be related to the actual clean up attempt, as Secret Service agent Sam Kinney (whom I interviewed three times) was putting the bubble top back on to the limousine (with the assistance of fellow agent George Hickey and a Dallas police officer)[20] and the bucket may have contained water or lubrication for the screws of the top.

Secret Service agent Gerald O'Rourke told the *Rocky Mountain News* on 11/20/03 "that on the day of the assassination, one agent was ordered to clean out the cars used in the motorcade, getting rid of blood and other evidence. The agent told O'Rourke that he found a piece of skull, asked the White House doctor what to do with it, and was told to destroy it."

NBC reporter Robert MacNeil later wrote: "The president's car was there [Parkland Hospital], still at the point where it had pulled up, and they had taken the president out into that emergency entrance...I remember that the Secret Service men were then starting to mop up the back seat of the big Lincoln the president was put in, and a few minutes later they started putting the fabric top on it. And when I went over to look at it a little closer, one of the agents waved me aside and said, 'You can't look.' Later, of course, it seemed ironic that this wall of protection went up when

---

19   *Murder in Dealey Plaza* edited by Professor James Fetzer (2000), pages 119-128; see my first book *Survivor's Guilt*, chapter 8, as well as chapter 10 of this current book.

20   18 H 731-732 – SS Agent Sam Kinney; 18 H 763-764 – SS Agent George Hickey: The two agents who put on the bubbletop – with the assistance of a DPD motorcycle officer – at Parkland: they are pictured in the infamous photos/films of the bucket beside the limousine: *JFK Assassination File* by DPD Chief Jesse Curry (1969), page 36 (see also page 34: same photo, different angle in UPI's *Four Days*, p. 25); Texas News newsreel (*Kennedy In Texas* video); WFAA/ ABC video 11/22/63; Cooper/ Sturges film; *Reasonable Doubt* by Henry Hurt (1985), page 84.

it of course could do no good..."[21] Parkland Hospital Orderly Joe L. Richards was asked to get a bucket of water; he complied.[22]

However, nurse Shirley Randall was asked if she "would get someone to come and wash the blood out of the car." She said that she would but was so nervous and excited she forgot about it.[23] Author William Manchester wrote: "An inaccurate story reported that they washed out the back seat with a bucket of water. Actually, this was contemplated."[24] Dallas Police motorcycle officer Bobby Joe Dale said: "...nobody messed with anything inside the car in any manner, shape, or form. Nobody said, "Clean this up!" We then put the top up and secured it."[25] Agent Sam Kinney told the HSCA on 2/26/78: "someone wanted to wash the (Presidential) car [at Parkland]. I said no one touch."

That said, reporter Hugh Sidey stated: "A guard was set up around the Lincoln as Secret Service men got a pail of water and tried to wash the blood from the car."[26] ABC reporter Don Gardner reported on television to an international audience of many millions of people: "Outside the hospital, blood had to be wiped from the limousine." Reporter Tom Wicker stated: "...the police were guarding the Presidential car closely. A bucket of water stood by the car, suggesting that the back seat had been scrubbed out."[27] Author Jim Bishop reported: "...the Secret Service detail was sorry that hospital orderlies had sponged it [the limousine] out."[28] Author Richard Trask interviewed White House photographer Cecil Stoughton. Trask wrote: "[Cecil] Stoughton recalls that a man was washing the seat "with a cloth, and he had a bucket. There was blood all over the seat, and flower petals and stuff on the floor." On page 37 there is a Stoughton photo with the caption "A bucket at his feet, an agent [Kinney] is seen leaning into the back seat of the Lincoln cleaning up some of the gore."[29] Likewise, photographer Thomas Craven told Trask: "The Secret Service cleaning the blood out of the car – the flowers still lying in the back seat – and just chaos until the police figured out what was happening, and then they started to push us off."[30]

21   *The Way We Were-1963: The Year Kennedy Was Shot* by Robert MacNeil (1988), page 197.
22   21 H 226.
23   21 H 217.
24   *The Death of a President* by William Manchester, p. 180n [1988 edition].
25   *No More Silence* by Larry Sneed (1998), pp. 135-136.
26   *Time*, 11/29/63, p. 24.
27   *New York Times*, 11/23/63, p. 2.
28   *The Day Kennedy Was Shot* by Jim Bishop, p. 352 [1992 edition].
29   *That Day In Dallas* by Richard Trask (1998), page 35 [based off a 7/10/85 interview with Stoughton; same as page 42 of Trask's *Pictures of the Pain*].
30   *Pictures of The Pain* by Richard Trask (1994), pages 377 and 383 [based off a 5/23/85 interview with Thomas Craven, Jr.].

Reporter Henry Burroughs stated in a 10/14/98 letter to the author: "The limousines that had carried the Presidential party and the Vice-Presidential party were askew. An agent with a stainless steel hospital bucket was cleaning up the rear seat of the President's limousine. Flowers were strewn over rear seats of both limos."

While Kinney and Dale dissent, MacNeil, Sidey, Gardner, Wicker, Burroughs, Bishop, Stoughton and Craven confirm that the limousine was cleaned (the statements of Richards, Randall and Manchester are, in my opinion, inconclusive).

WAS THE BACK SEAT OF THE LIMOUSINE PHOTOGRAPHED AT PARKLAND HOSPITAL AND DO THOSE PHOTOS SURVIVE?

Yes and No. Yes, a film was taken by a young boy and no, nothing has survived. Hurchel Jacks, the Texas Highway Patrolman assigned to drive LBJ's car in Dallas motorcade, wrote: " We were assigned by the [Secret Service] to prevent any pictures of any kind to be taken of the President's car or the inside."[31] Mrs. H.D. (Bobbie) Jacks, the widow of Hurchel Jacks (Jacks passed away 12/19/95), wrote the author on 8/31/98 the following: "...he guarded Kennedy's car to make sure that no photos were taken."[32] Milton Wright, Texas Highway Patrolman assigned to drive Mayor Cabell's car in the Dallas motorcade, stated: "we were instructed to keep the news media away from the car."[33] Both Dallas Police officers James W. Courson and Stavis Ellis told author Larry Sneed about an incident whereupon a Secret Service agent destroyed the film of a young boy who took pictures of the limousine at Parkland.[34]

In addition, no films or photos have ever come forward depicting the rear of the limousine while at Parkland Hospital. There is a still photo and a film of Vice President Johnson's car that is quite often mistaken as being the rear of the limousine, but the vehicle is quite obviously not Kennedy's car.

ARE JFK'S BRAIN AND THE TISSUE SLIDES STILL MISSING?

Yes. Dr. Cyril Wecht first made this discovery back in 1972. The HSCA also confirmed these materials are indeed missing.[35]

31   18 H 801.
32   See also *Encyclopedia of the JFK Assassination* by Michael Benson (2002), page 121.
33   CD3 Exhibits.
34   *No More Silence* by Larry Sneed (1998), pages 130 and 148.
35   HSCA Volume 7, page 177.

Was a 7.65 German Mauser found on the Sixth Floor of the Texas School Book Depository (in Addition to or Instead of the 6.5 mm Mannlicher-Carcano Rifle Tied to Oswald)?

This is an issue I am torn about. It is very hard to believe that Deputy Sheriff Roger Craig was making this up.[36] Craig, a Korean War veteran who was also a POW, was a police officer of tremendous integrity, as a recent book further confirms.[37] Deputy Sheriff Eugene Boone and Deputy Constable Seymour Weitzman stated that the rifle found was a Mauser in reports they filed after the assassination and in their Warren Commission testimony. Furthermore, Boone testified to the Warren Commission that Captain Will Fritz and Lt. J.C. Day both stated on 11/22/63 that the weapon found was indeed a Mauser. Dallas District Attorney Henry Wade also called the found rifle a Mauser.[38] Police Captain Patrick Gannaway said "a Mauser rifle was found on a fifth floor landing of the building."[39] In addition, the major networks, as well as several major newspapers, called the rifle found on the sixth floor a Mauser.[40] Finally, a CIA report dated 11/25/63 also identified a Mauser as a weapon found on the sixth floor.[41]

I lean toward a possibility that there was indeed a Mauser found, in addition to the Carcano, which was unquestionably found, filmed and photographed that day. My heart says "yes" while my mind says "no" (some sort of honest mistake). Again, at this very late juncture, this is as far as we can go with this.

Or is it?

Dr. David Mantik and James DiEugenio both reported, during the ARRB era, author Noel Twyman found a receipt for a 7.65 Mauser shell recovered from Dealey Plaza.[42]

36   *The Deputy Interviews: The True Story of J.F.K. Assassination Witness, and Former Dallas Deputy Sheriff, Roger Dean Craig* by Steve Cameron, 2019; *JFK: Absolute Proof* by Robert Groden (2013), page 278.
37   *The Deputy Interviews: The True Story of J.F.K. Assassination Witness, and Former Dallas Deputy Sheriff, Roger Dean Craig* by Steve Cameron, 2019, pages 15-16.
38   Many sources, an example of which is *Oswald Talked* by Mary La Fontaine (1996), pages 372-374; *The Deputy Interviews: The True Story of J.F.K. Assassination Witness, and Former Dallas Deputy Sheriff, Roger Dean Craig* by Steve Cameron, 2019, pages 117-122.
39   November 23, 1963 issue of the *New York Herald Tribune*.
40   A Texas School Book Depository employee, Warren Caster, brought a couple rifles into the building two days before the assassination, including a Mauser. It seems that this was an innocent situation not connected to the assassination- *No Case To Answer* by Ian Griggs (2005), pages 19-21.
41   CIA Document No. 1367, declassified spring 1976- *The Deep State in the Heart of Texas* by Richard Bartholomew (2018), pages 58 and 86. See also the 1976 video *Two Men in Dallas* and *The Deputy Interviews: The True Story of J.F.K. Assassination Witness, and Former Dallas Deputy Sheriff, Roger Dean Craig* by Steve Cameron, 2019, page 122.
42   https://kennedysandking.com/john-f-kennedy-articles/874   ;   http://themantikview.

Is the Acoustical Evidence Genuine (Were the Shots During the Assassination Recorded On the Dallas Police Radio Dictabelt As Alleged)?

It is quite possible after all.
Let me explain.

I originally believed this evidence to be true- evidence of more than three shots, evidence of conspiracy. Then I was starting to think that the shots were *not* recorded during the assassination after all. With all due respect to the HSCA (Bolt, Beranek and Newman; Drs. Mark Weiss and Ernest Aschkenasy), as well as any authors and researchers who still believed this evidence is valid, I started to believe this was junk science mixed with a healthy dose of wishful thinking, coupled with a misidentification of the actual officer who recorded onto the dictabelt at the relevant time. Officer H.B. McClain denied he was the officer who had the stuck open microphone.

The National Academy of Science seemingly debunked this evidence in 1982. Researcher Steve Barber seemed to prove that the recording could not have been made during the exact time of the assassination in Dealey Plaza.[43] I will concede that the work of Don Thomas to resurrect the acoustics evidence is compelling,[44] but I remained not entirely convinced, especially because author Larry Sabato conducted an exhaustive new study with regard to the acoustics evidence and reported in his 2013 book that they are not valid.[45] I was confused.

That said, I never used the acoustics findings to "prove" crossfire and conspiracy in the JFK case. Ironically and importantly, Louis Stokes of the HSCA made the point on *Face The Nation* in early 1979 (when the HSCA report was released) that the acoustical findings merely confirmed other evidence of conspiracy. As also mentioned earlier, HSCA Chief Counsel G. Robert Blakey told author Anthony Summers: "I think our conclusion [of a probable conspiracy] was correct. On balance, I say there were two shooters in the Plaza, and not just because of the acoustics ... (but because of) all the other evidence and testimony ... I find on balance that the earwitness and eyewitness testimony is credible."[46] So, as one can see,

com/pdf/Wagner_Review_II.pdf.

43   Many sources, an example of which is PBS Nova Program *Who Shot President Kennedy?* (1988), *Killing the Truth* by Harrison Livingstone (1993), etc.

44   Articles by Thomas include: *Echo Correlation Analysis and the Acoustic Evidence in the Kennedy Assassination* (2001), *Hear No Evil: The Acoustical Evidence in the Kennedy Assassination* (2001), *Crosstalk: Synchronization of Putative Gunshots with Events in Dealey Plaza* (2002), and *Impulsive Behavior: The CourtTV - Sensimetrics Acoustical Evidence Study* (2003); http://www.whokilledjfk. net/hear_no_evil.htm.

45   *The Kennedy Half-Century* by Larry Sabato (2013), pages 240-247.

46   *Not In Your Lifetime* by Anthony Summers (2013), pages 29-30.

the acoustic evidence was not the only reason that the HSCA found a probable conspiracy, as many still falsely claim.

Then it happened.

At the eleventh hour, so to speak, legendary author and investigative reporter Josiah Thompson comes out with the book *Last Second in Dallas* in 2020: "Detailed analysis of Zapruder film frames matched by the *newly validated acoustic evidence* show a second shot struck the president's head from behind less than a second later. Result: two killing shots to the head from opposite directions in the final second of the shooting."

So I am back in the I-believe-the-acoustics-evidence category. You wanted honesty, you got it. I have gone back and forth on my belief in this evidence, but the work of Josiah Thompson (and Don Thomas) tipped the scales back in the pro-conspiracy/authentic category. Ultimately, as with the HSCA, my firm belief in conspiracy does not rise or fall with this evidence.

Is the Neutron Activation Analysis (NAA) Performed By Dr. Vincent Guinn For the HSCA, Which Allegedly "Proved" That the Bullet Fragments Came From CE399 (The Magic Bullet) and Oswald's Rifle Valid?

Point blank: no. This is junk science that has been thoroughly debunked.[47] As author Sherry Fiester has demonstrated, the ballistics do *not* prove that there was only one shooter.[48]

Are the Backyard Photos Depicting Oswald Holding What Appears To Be the Pistol and Rifle He Owned (And Used in the Attacks On 11/22/63) Genuine?

Painfully for me, I must begrudgingly concede that they probably are. Keeping in mind the anomalies in the photos that seem to show, at first glance, alterations in the photos,[49] Marina Oswald has admitted taking the photos. There are compelling online arguments from conspiracy researchers, but several different poses (not just one) of the backyard photos exist, so all of them would have to have been faked and retouched. As anyone who has seen the *JFK* movie is much aware of, Oswald himself said to Captain Fritz that the photo was fake – his head superimposed onto someone else's body.

---

47   *Cold Case Kennedy* by Flip de Mey (2013), pages 148-149. *The JFK Assassination* by Jim DiEugenio (2018), pages 95-100; *Not In Your Lifetime* by Anthony Summers (2013), page 54; *Enemy of the Truth* by Sherry Fiester (2012), pages 138-167.

48   *Enemy of the Truth* by Sherry Fiester (2012), pages 166-167.

49   See, for example, the work of the late Jack White in his 1990 video *Fake: The Forged Photo That Framed Oswald*; https://kennedysandking.com/john-f-kennedy-articles/674.

Since I have no problem whatsoever conceding that the Mannlicher-Carcano rifle found on the sixth floor on 11/22/63 was indeed Oswald's rifle, it is no problem or contradiction at all to concede that the photos (may) also depict this very same rifle in the photos (likewise, since I concede the possibility that Oswald did indeed shoot Tippit, the pistol shown could very well be his. Remember, Oswald himself did admit to carrying his pistol into the Texas Theater). I believe it is more a question of *why* the photos were taken rather than *if* they are genuine or fakes used to frame Oswald. It could very well be that Oswald was building a covert resume as a Castro sympathizer and warrior and these photos were for that purpose (keep in mind that he started a one-man chapter of the Fair Play for Cuba Committee in New Orleans and was writing to the real founder of the committee, V.T. Lee[50]). Then, after the assassination, these photos were used as evidence of his culpability *as a shooter* in the murder of JFK (and the killing of Officer Tippit).

Now, if you want Oswald photos that do make me lean towards photo forgery/composites, get a load of these-they look like two different men put together as one:

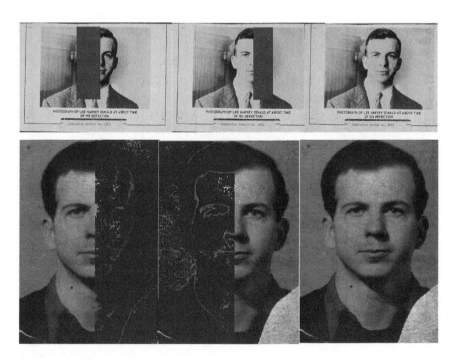

Did Oswald Fire at General Edwin Walker in April 1963?

Possibly, but doubtful. Keeping in mind the witnesses who saw an automobile leaving the scene (Oswald did not own a car and some say he didn't drive) and two different people at the scene, as well, even if Oswald was involved (which I do doubt, as the ballistics do not add up, as even Walker himself said), this does not prove that he killed Kennedy.[51] Just as the killing of Tippit is NOT "the rosetta stone" of the assassination, the attempted assassination of Walker is not probative of Oswald's guilt in the assassination. Was he somehow involved in the Walker attempt without being a shooter or acting alone? Possibly. If he was, he missed an easy stationary target. Still, this could have been used by conspirators as a stepping stone to 11/22/63: Oswald could have been malleable enough, like a pawn on a chessboard, to follow orders and do what he was told (even if it meant "just" bringing his rifle for *someone else* to use in the assassination or someone brought Oswald's rifle to the depository *without his knowledge*. Or, naively, he was assured that his weapon would be taken from the depository [like the weapons used in the frontal assault] and, thus, could not be traced back to him, as the bullets would have no ballistic match to an *unfound* weapon. It could even be that Oswald was manipulated to believe that this was going to be a fake attack on Kennedy in order to blame the assassination on Castro's Cuba or that he penetrated the conspiracy and was trying to prevent it but was double crossed).

Author Gerald McKnight sums up the Walker shooting case quite well[52]:

1. The Dallas Police never considered him as a suspect in over seven months.

2. The evidence indicated more than one man was involved.

3. The ammunition was steel-jacketed, not copper-jacketed as in the Kennedy case.

4. Walker was a rightwing extremist who Kennedy had removed from his command for distribution of Birchite propaganda. So the political calculus behind the shootings was confused.

5. The conspirators had access to a car which, officially, Oswald did not.

51   *The JFK Assassination* by Jim DiEugenio (2018), pages 100-112; *Not In Your Lifetime* by Anthony Summers (2013), page 530.
52   *Breach of Trust* by Gerald McKnight (2005), pages 48-50.

6. The police deduced the weapon was a high-powered rifle, which the Mannlicher-Carcano was not.

7. Walker and his private investigators suspected a former employee, William M. Duff, as the sniper.

But as McKnight shows, the capper in this regard is CE 573, the mutilated remainder of the bullet recovered from Walker's home. In 1978, Walker was watching a televised hearing of the House Select Committee on Assassinations. Chief Counsel Robert Blakey held up CE 573 for the camera while discussing the firearms evidence in the JFK case. As McKnight notes: "Walker, a thirty-year career army officer with extensive combat experience in World War II, and with more than a passing familiarity with military weaponry, was stunned. According to Walker, what Blakey represented as the bullet fired into his home bore no resemblance to the piece of lead the police had recovered, which he had held in his own hand and closely examined." [53]

DID EYEWITNESS HOWARD BRENNAN SEE OSWALD IN THE SIXTH FLOOR WINDOW OF THE TEXAS SCHOOL BOOK DEPOSITORY CARRYING OUT THE ASSASSINATION?

No, no, no-definitely not. Many authors before me have run down a laundry list of problems with his accounts (plural) in both his Warren Commission testimony and in his book, among other sources.[54] Brennan even told the FBI that he "could not positively identify Oswald as the person he saw fire the rifle" and this was after Brennan had seen Oswald on television![55] Furthermore, author Jim Marrs noted that "it was determined that Brennan had poor eyesight and, in fact, a close examination of the Zapruder film shows that Brennan was not looking up at the time of the shooting." Brennan testified that he did not see the rifle discharge, nor did he see the recoil or the flash.[56] In fact, despite receiving Brennan's alleged identification of Oswald the previous day, Dallas Police Chief Jesse Curry denied that they had a witness who saw someone shoot the president![57] Brennan denied to the Warren Commission that he told NBC's George Murray that he "saw smoke and paper wadding come out of the boxes on a slope below the railroad trestle at the time of the as-

53   *Breach of Trust* by Gerald McKnight (2005), page 52..
54   *Not In Your Lifetime* by Anthony Summers (2013), pages 94-95
55   *Breach of Trust* by Gerald McKnight (2005), page 398; 3 H 143-147; *Gemberling Report*, 11/30/63.
56   3 H 154.
57   24 H 781.

sassination." Brennan lamely asked: "Is there another Howard Brennan?" Brennan then said: "I would like to ask a question off the record." This was how his testimony officially ended. Strange.

Brennan's job foreman, Sandy Speaker, told Marrs: "They took [Brennan] off for three weeks. I don't know if they were Secret Service or FBI, but they were federal people. He came back a nervous wreck and within a year his hair had turned snow white. He wouldn't talk about [the assassination] after that. He was scared to death. They made him say what they wanted him to say."[58] Brennan forfeited what was left of his credibility in his silly 1987 book called *Eyewitness to History* when he claimed that his FBI bodyguard was the exact double of the late president in every detail: "The agent told us some of his experiences doubling for the President. They were fascinating." Alrighty, then. But it gets worse: Brennan claims that Chief Justice Earl Warren invited him to meet Mrs. Kennedy on 3/24/64, months before she was even able to testify because her grief was so unbearable![59] I can imagine the conversation now: "Hello, Jackie-here is the fellow who saw the man who blew Jack's brains out. He wanted to say hello."

Brennan also claimed he spoke to Secret Service agent Forrest Sorrels within 3-5 minutes of the shooting, yet, officially speaking, Sorrels did not even return to the scene until a good 25 minutes afterward via automobile.[60] Oops.

Brennan never identified Oswald in a police lineup, either.[61] In fact, due to the fine work of British police inspector Ian Griggs, there is a real question as to whether or not Brennan was ever at any lineup. In his book, *No Case To Answer*, Griggs performed what is probably the most complete and thorough inquiry into the Dallas Police lineups in the literature.[62] He details each and every lineup, the people who were there, and when each one took place. None of the police records include Brennan's name.[63] None of the Warren Commission records on the subject include his name.[64] Griggs then tracked down the listed witnesses who were supposed to be at each lineup. No one recalled Brennan being there.[65] Cap-

---

58   *Crossfire* by Jim Marrs (1989), pages 25-26.

59   *The Warren Omission* by Walt Brown (1996), pages 139-140.

60   *The Warren Omission* by Walt Brown (1996), page 265.

61   *The Warren Omission* by Walt Brown (1996), pages 202-203; *Who Really Killed Kennedy?: 50 Years Later: Stunning New Revelations About the JFK Assassination* by Jerome Corsi (2016)- kindle edition.

62   *No Case To Answer* by Ian Griggs (2005), pages 77-106.

63   *No Case To Answer* by Ian Griggs (2005), pages 85-90.

64   *No Case To Answer* by Ian Griggs (2005), page 93.

65   *No Case To Answer* by Ian Griggs (2005), page 94.

tain Will Fritz was at each lineup and described them for the Commission. In his testimony he volunteered nothing about Brennan being at any
of them.[66] When asked how many people were in each lineup, Brennan
said seven, "more or less one" in each.[67] As Griggs notes, there were only
six spots in the lineup platform, and there appear to have never been any
more than four people in any lineup.[68] When asked if all the other men
in the lineup were caucasians, or if there were any blacks in the lineups,
Brennan replied with a startling answer. He said he did not remember.[69]
The reader should recall that this was Texas in 1963 when all public facil-
ities are still segregated. Because of all these problems, and more, Griggs
concludes one of two things happened. Either Brennan was so unreliable
that the police dared not show him a lineup. Or, Brennan performed so
poorly at a lineup that the record of it was expunged.

That is the bottom line for this so-called "star witness" of the Warren
Commission: he had no credibility whatsoever. I agree with author Gerald McKnight: Brennan was a "self-promoting" bystander driven by a
need to be associated with some great tragedy, who pretends knowledge
after the fact of events over which he truly had no vital information.[70] I
mean, sure: a few other pro-conspiracy witnesses were guilty of later-day
exaggerations, but their basic main story from day one was solid, no matter what embellishments they may have added for dramatic effect in a
book. Brennan, from day one, was full of baloney.

But there's even more: when HSCA staff contacted him, it was with the
idea of talking quietly with him at his home in Texas. But, according to an
outside contact report dated March 13, 1978, Brennan "stated that the
only way he will talk to anyone from this Committee, is if he is subpoenaed." A month later the Committee asked him to reconsider and, when
he refused, informed him that he would be subpoenaed to testify before
the committee on May 2. Brennan wasted no time in informing the Committee staff that he "would not come to Washington and that he would
fight any subpoena. And, in fact, Brennan was belligerent about not testifying. He stated that he would avoid any subpoena by getting his doctor to
state that it would be bad for his health to testify about the assassination.
He further told me that even if he was forced to come to Washington he

66   *No Case To Answer* by Ian Griggs (2005), page 93.
67   3 H 147.
68   *No Case To Answer* by Ian Griggs (2005), pages 85-90; CD 1083.
69   3 H 147.
70   As noted in *Who Really Killed Kennedy?: 50 Years Later: Stunning New Revelations About the JFK Assassination* by Jerome Corsi (2016)- kindle edition.

would simply not testify if he didn't want to."[71] Between May 15 and May 19, 1978, 11 attempts were made to present Brennan with previous statements he had made which were finally left with him on May 19. But when Committee staff returned a few days later to collect the form asserting that his previous statements were correct, a very odd lacuna appeared in the record. It was discovered that Brennan had refused to sign the form! The HSCA even went as far as granting Brennan immunity from prosecution, but he would not budge. Oswald was dead almost fifteen years at that point, Howard – what did you have to hide? Are these the actions of a truthful man? Brennan was a fraud and he knew it. Knowing that the HSCA might actually subject him to a real cross examination, he did not want anything like that to surface. Whether this was the fact that he was pressured into identifying Oswald, or that *he pretended to have knowledge he never really possessed to begin with in order to gain attention*, we will likely never know. In the end, what matters is that he failed to identify Oswald on November 22, 1963, and he admitted that seeing Oswald's picture on television shortly after the assassination had clouded and influenced his own recollections.[72]

But he got his "revenge": that silly 1987 book called *Eyewitness to History*.

A bizarre postscript: Secret Service agent Mike Howard and his brother Pat tried to plant a false allegation that a janitor saw Oswald pull the trigger![73] The second "Brennan," so to speak? Perhaps Mike Howard was trying to be a "Brennan" of his own: he ridiculously claimed in 2016 that he found a little green address book belonging to Oswald and "on its 17th page under the heading "I WILL KILL" Oswald listed four men: an FBI agent named James Hosty; a right-wing general, Edwin Walker; and Vice President Richard Nixon. At the top of the list was the governor of Texas, John Connally. Through Connally's name, Oswald had allegedly drawn a dagger, with blood drops dripping downward."[74] Conveniently, no one has ever seen this page but Howard and it disappeared. Alrighty, then.

Are the Autopsy X-rays Fake?

Based on the pioneering work of Dr. David Mantik,[75] I believe the x-ray of the head was altered via the use of a patch to obscure the rear head

---

71   HSCA contact report, 4/20/78, Record No. 180-10068-10381.
72   My thanks to researcher Martin Hay for his insights on this matter.
73   25 H 721-722, 725, 844-850.
74   https://www.latimes.com/opinion/op-ed/la-oe-reston-jfk-assassination-target-20161122-story.html.
75   *A Coup in Camelot* DVD/Blu Ray (2016); *The Men Who Killed Kennedy* (2003); *Murder in Dealey Plaza* edited by Prof. James Fetzer (2000); *John F. Kennedy's Head Wounds: A Final Synthesis – and a New Analysis of the Harper Fragment* by Dr. Mantik, 2015; Inside The ARRB by Doug Horne (2009).

wound. The other x-rays are genuine; it is just a matter of interpretation.[76] That said, what is truly bizarre are the mysterious pencil lines on the right lateral skull x-ray of Kennedy, at least as it involves Dr. John Ebersole's HSCA testimony about the matter. Ebersole first testified:

> "There is a second line at the angle to that first one [pencil line] which I also made. The attempt here was to get a line from the high point of the forehead back to the occipital."[77]

This is definitely open to interpretation, to put it mildly, especially when one considers that Ebersole originally said that the right rear of the head was missing. But it gets worse.

Ebersole testified further:

> "...*sometime within a month of the assassination* I received a call from the White House medical staff – a member of the White House medical staff, a [Navy] Captain James Young [the same one we encountered in chapter two regarding a skull fragment and a bullet being found in the rear of either the presidential limousine or the follow-up car]. *Dr. Young asked me if I could review the skull x-rays for the purpose of getting some measurements for a sculpture.* I said, yes, I thought that was feasible. I was driven to the White House Annex where I did see the skull films and took certain measurements and in taking those measurements may well have drawn lines on the film. It was then necessary for me to go back to Bethesda and determine some magnification or subtraction factors. I understand in the use of the portable x-ray equipment the structures depicted are not necessarily related to actual size and life. Now if one duplicates the conditions with the skull, you can establish a magnification factor or a subtraction factor. So after seeing the films at the White House Annex, going back to Bethesda and using a human skull to determine magnification factors, actually they were substantive factors. The image on the film was larger than in life one would expect from the physical setup. *I then phoned Dr. Young on an open telephone using the expression like, something to the effect that "Aunt Margaret's skirts needed the following change,"* and gave him the numbers to multiple the numbers I had previously provided from examining the x-rays at the White House Annex (emphasis added)."[78]

76   See also *The JFK Assassination Debates: Lone Gunman versus Conspiracy* by Michael L. Kurtz (2006), pages 126-130.
77   *Inside the ARRB* by Doug Horne (2009), page 554.
78   *Inside the ARRB* by Doug Horne (2009), page 556.

As Dr. David Mantik wrote:

> The strange episode about "Aunt Margaret's skirts" suggests that Ebersole was being tested on his reaction to the altered films. (The official excuse of needing his help for a Kennedy bust makes no sense. If x-ray films were really useful for this purpose, then those taken during life would have been much more appropriate than the badly fragmented skull seen at the autopsy.) Ebersole, however, is either very tongue-in-cheek about all of this or else astonishingly naïve.

As Doug Horne added, only engineers and architects need exact measurements down to the precise centimeter, not artists, who are only concerned about exact proportions which can be obtained from photographs. Horne added that no one has even seen this so-called sculpture, either.[79]

It appears, then, that the pencil lines were bullet trajectories and the whole ridiculous "bust of Kennedy" story was a ruse regarding the alteration of the x-rays to obscure the right rear exit wound (and to test Ebersole's reactions to the x-rays). A medical cover-up was in full flight.

Dallas Times Herald — 3-9-78

Doctor says bullets fired behind JFK

LANCASTER, Pa. (AP) — The radiologist who performed the autopsy X-rays on the body of President John F. Kennedy broke a 15-year silence on the presidential assassination Wednesday, claiming the fatal bullets could not have come from the front as some persons have claimed.

Dr. John H. Ebersole, now chief of radiation therapy at Lan-

Dallas restaurateur subpoenaed in JFK probe, Page 1D.
---

caster General Hospital, said his conclusions parallel those of the federal Warren Commission, which said the bullets were fired from somewhere behind the Kennedy motorcade in Dallas on Nov. 22, 1963.

Warren Commission critics have claimed bullets may have been fired from a position in front of the motorcade.

Ebersole, formerly assistant chief of radiology at Bethesda, Md., Naval Hospital where the autopsy was performed, said he was speaking out on the issue because he has been summoned to meet with investigators from the House Select Committee on Assassinations Saturday at the National Archives where the X-rays are stored.

"I would say unequivocally the bullet came from the side or back," Ebersole said. "The front of the body, except for a very slight bruise above the right eye on the forehead, was absolutely intact. It was the back of the head that was blown off.

"There is no way that I can see on the basis of the X-rays that the bullet came from anywhere in the 180 degree angle to the front, assuming Kennedy was facing forward. It looked to me like an almost right to left shot from the rear."

Ebersole said he has not been told the reason for being called to meet with congressional investigators, but said he believes some X-ray pencil marks may be puzzling them. Ebersole said he marked some of the Kennedy X-rays to assist a sculptor at the request of the White House.

The sculptor was making a Kennedy bust, he said.

---

79   *Inside the ARRB* by Doug Horne (2009), page 558.

Although Ebersole claimed the shots must have come from the rear, he stated (once again in this news article) that the back of JFK's head was gone, as well as mentioning the suspicious "bust of Kennedy" incident:

Dr. Mantik's detailed studies[80] have demonstrated that the left lateral x-ray is a copy film and not an original, a crucial discovery he has stated was the most important piece of evidence to emerge from his nine visits to the National Archives.[81] Via the ARRB's grilling of autopsy doctors James Humes, J. Thornton Boswell, and Pierre Finck, we learned that none of these three men remembered seeing the strange 6.5 millimeter object depicted on the back of the x-rays, yet they vividly remember retrieving the two much smaller bullet fragments. Humes testified: "Truthfully, I don't remember anything that size when I looked at these films." For his part, Boswell testified: "No. We did not find one [bullet fragment] that large. I'm sure of that."[82] Finck testified: "I don't [know what the object is]. It's a radio-opaque object, opaque to x-rays ... I don't [remember one that size]."[83] Mantik strongly believes that this 6.5 millimeter object is fake and added to implicate Oswald.

For his part, Dr. Joseph Riley, an expert in neuroanatomy who often disagrees with Dr. Mantik, believes the x-rays are authentic but are misinterpreted:

> The autopsy evidence demonstrates conclusively that John Kennedy was struck in the head by two bullets, one from the rear and one from the right front.[84]

Randy Robertson MD, a radiologist based in Tennessee, was also authorized by Senator Paul Kirk, acting for the Kennedy family, to visit the National Archives at College Park to view the original autopsy photos and x-rays (the late Burke Marshall, then representing the Kennedy family, initially granted Robertson access to NARA's then-existing materials by virtue of his status as a board certified diagnostic radiologist with a historical interest in the assassination. Robertson viewed them several times during the early and mid-1990's, as well). Robertson also believes the x-rays (and photos) are authentic but, like Riley, states that they are misinterpreted.[85]

Robertson argues that the Clark Panel indeed found a bullet wound in the top of the head, but it was not the bullet wound found low in the back of the head at autopsy, and therefore a *second* head wound. Robertson

80   https://kennedysandking.com/images/pdf/david-mantik-houston-2017.pdf.
81   *Inside The ARRB* by Doug Horne (2009), page 562.
82   *Inside The ARRB* by Doug Horne (2009), pages 564 and 573.
83   *Inside The ARRB* by Doug Horne (2009), pages 579-580.
84   *Not In Your Lifetime* by Anthony Summers (2013), page 54.
85   http://www.manuscriptservice.com/DPQ/robert~1.htm.

goes on to say that the autopsy doctors were quite aware of the presence of *both head wounds* on the night of the autopsy, but to testify to both would have changed the course of history. Robertson is also on record as stating that "the autopsy doctors committed perjury before the Warren Commission" and "intentionally misidentified" autopsy photo #44 all in an effort to hide a frontal shot.[86]

Michael Chesser, M.D., is board certified in neurology and clinical neurophysiology. He has over 25 years of experience in clinical practice and is a former associate professor of neurology at the University of Arkansas for Medical Sciences. Chesser was also granted permission by Sen. Paul Kirk, the Kennedy family representative for the Deed of Gift, to view the JFK autopsy cranial x-rays and autopsy photographs. His conclusions:

- The autopsy x-rays do not support the conclusions of the Warren Commission or of the House Select Committee on Assassinations, that a bullet fired from the TSBD 6th floor caused the head wound(s).

- The x-rays show evidence of a right frontal entry wound and of a right lower occipital entry. The fragment trail appears to widen from front to back, and this points toward a frontal entry.

- There is evidence of alteration of the autopsy skull x-rays.[87]

ARE THE AUTOPSY PHOTOS FAKE?

I believe it is largely a combination of misinterpretation (the actual rear head wound exists in at least one photo),[88] while the other photos were manipulated via scalp being pulled over the rear skull wound to hide it from the camera. That said, the head wound as shown in the one autopsy photo of the back wound with the ruler looks suspect.[89] In this regard, I highly recommend the 2009 five-volume series *Inside The Assassination Records Review Board (ARRB)* by Douglas Horne.

Although the classic books *High Treason* and *High Treason 2* (and, to a lesser extent, *Killing the Truth* and *Killing Kennedy*) by Harrison Livingstone are quite valuable, as well, Horne's books are essential when studying this aspect of the medical evidence. Horne's books are a valuable repository of the medical evidence (from the Warren Commission,

86   "The Late Arriving Fragment: Reality Bites" by Dr. Randy Robertson (*The Fourth Decade*, Vol. 2, Number 5).

87   https://kennedysandking.com/images/pdf/michael-chesser-houston-2017.pdf.

88   *John F. Kennedy's Head Wounds: A Final Synthesis – and a New Analysis of the Harper Fragment* by Dr. David Mantik (2015).

89   See also *The JFK Assassination Debates: Lone Gunman versus Conspiracy* by Michael L. Kurtz (2006), pages 126-130.

Clark Panel and HSCA eras), in general, and all of the ARRB's impressive contributions to this area (1994-1998), in particular. The ARRB interviewed the following vital medical evidence witnesses, often under oath and in person: Dr. J. Thornton Boswell (including new wound sketches, as well as new skull model markings); Dr. James J. Humes (including new wound sketch); Dr. Pierre Finck; Dr. Robert Karnei; X-ray technician Jerrol Custer (including new wound sketch); X-ray technician Ed Reed; autopsy photographer John Stringer; assistant autopsy photographer Floyd Reibe; Mortician Tom Robinson (including both HSCA and new wound sketches); Mortician John VanHoesen; Mortician Joseph Hagan; Navy Petty Officer Dennis David; Roger Boyajian; FBI agent James Sibert (including both HSCA and new wound sketches); FBI agent Francis O'Neill (including HSCA wound sketch); Navy photographer Saundra Spencer (including new wound sketch); Navy photographer Vincent Madonia; Gloria Knudsen and her adult children (regarding Navy/White House photographer Robert Knudsen); Dr. Charles Crenshaw (including new wound sketch); Nurse Audrey Bell (including new wound sketch); Dr. Robert Grossman (including new wound sketch); Dr. Robert McClelland; Dr. Paul Peters; Dr. Charles Baxter; Dr. Ronald Coy Jones; Dr. Malcolm Perry; government photographer Joe O'Donnell; photographer Earl McDonald; Department of Justice official Carl Belcher; Janie B. Taylor; Leonard D. Saslaw; Velma Reumann (nee Vogler); Nancy Denlea, daughter of Dr. George Burkley; Ken Vrtacnik, AFIP; Dr. Richard L. Davis, AFIP; Secret Service agent James Mastrovito; Secret Service agent Floyd Boring; and Secret Service agent Robert Bouck.

Dr. Boswell demonstrated that much of the bone on the right rear of JFK's head was missing. Humes refused to draw the exit wound (!), yet drew the entrance wound very low on the skull, in direct conflict with the high entrance wound as noted by both the Clark Panel and the HSCA. Dr. Crenshaw drew an exit wound in the right rear location, noting that he could also see cerebellum. Nurse Bell also drew a rear exit wound, while also noting identical damage to the cerebellum. Dr. Grossman also drew damage to the right rear area, albeit smaller and one he deemed to be of entrance, yet he also noted cerebellum damage. Both Tom Robinson's HSCA and ARRB drawings depicted a wound on the right rear side of Kennedy's skull. Likewise, James Sibert's HSCA and ARRB drawings depict a wound in the right rear of the head, which was in sync with Francis O'Neill's HSCA drawing (Sibert's HSCA drawing also depicts a wound on Kennedy's back, not the back of the neck, as does O'Neill's drawing and, for that matter, Roy Kellerman's drawing, as well). Saundra Spencer's drawing follows suit and demonstrates a right rear head wound that looks like a typical exit wound.

Although, as I am much aware from interviewing him twice myself, Jerrol Custer was once a firm missing-back-of-the-head witness, he drew a sketch of the head wound that was still rearward, albeit in the parietal bone. Drs. McClelland and Peters once again stated that the right rear of President Kennedy's head was missing.

As far as the autopsy photos of the back of the head are concerned, FBI agent James Sibert stated:

> I don't have a recollection of it being that intact ... I don't remember seeing anything that was like this photo ... the hair looks like it has been straightened out and cleaned up more than what it was when we left the autopsy ... it looks like it could have been reconstructed or something."[90]

For his part, Frank O'Neill stated:

> This looks like it has been doctored in some way. Let me rephrase that, when I say "doctored." Like the stuff has been pushed back in, and it looks like more towards the end than the beginning [of the autopsy]. All you have to do was put the flap back over here, and the rest of the stuff is all covered on up ... quite frankly, I thought that there was a larger opening in the back ... opening in the back of the head.[91]

White House photographer Robert Knudsen, who testified before the HSCA, told his family that some of the JFK autopsy photos were badly altered to conceal a hole in the right rear of Kennedy's head.[92] Photographer Joe O'Donnell claimed that Knudsen showed him photos with the right rear of Kennedy's head missing (first viewing of photos) and without the right rear of Kennedy's head missing (second viewing of photos), as well as one with a probe emerging from JFK's stomach or right side.[93]

Stringer, Reibe and Custer are on record in pre-ARRB days stating that the right rear of JFK's head was gone, with both Reibe and Custer stating that the photos were fake.[94] They changed their tunes, to a certain extent,

---

90   *Inside the ARRB* by Doug Horne (2009), pages 30-31.

91   *Inside the ARRB* by Doug Horne (2009), pages 31-32.

92   *Inside the ARRB* by Doug Horne (2009), pages 247-254.

93   *Inside the ARRB* by Doug Horne (2009), page 285.

94   *JFK: The Case for Conspiracy* DVD; *High Treason 2* by Harrison Livingstone (1992); *Best Evidence* by David Lifton (1981).

before the ARRB, although Stringer – who said the cerebellum was disrupted – did not think the brain photos in existence were the ones he took, while Custer still believed that Kennedy was shot from the front (albeit a parietal rearward wound) and Reibe believed the head wound was (still) an occipital/right rear wound.[95] Dr. Karnei repeated what he told Harry Livingstone with regard to the right rear of JFK's head being missing.[96] Karnei was also very certain (as was Robert Knudsen to the HSCA and O'Donnell to the ARRB) that photographs were taken of probes in JFK's body that do not now exist.[97]

These are merely some of the highlights of just the medical evidence investigation undertaken by Doug Horne and Jeremy Gunn of the ARRB.

Parkland doctor Kenneth Salyer told Robert Groden, in reference to one of the autopsy photos:

> You know, there's something wrong with it. I'll leave it at that. I mean – this thing has been-something, you know, happened to this.… This is not right. No. See, this has been doctored here. This is lying open. See, the way you have him here – the way they've got him here is – skin flaps have been cut or altered or pushed up or changed, and this isn't the way he looked. This was – he looked – this was wide open with brain here. This is scalp pushed back and it's all distorted.[98]

Salyer also told Dr. Gary Aguilar that this autopsy photo appeared to have been tampered with.

Speaking of Dr. Gary Aguilar, he has given brilliant presentations at the COPA conferences in the 1990's and on *The Men Who Killed Kennedy* in 2003. His lengthy article in the 2001 book *Trauma Room One* (pages 170-264), written with the assistance of Dr. Cyril Wecht, is nothing short of outstanding. Of particular note is his reporting of what the ARRB's Doug Horne wrote in an ARRB memo: "When shown the Ida Dox drawing of the back of the head autopsy image found on page 104 of HSCA Volume 7 (Figure 1A), Dr. [Robert] Grossman immediately opined, 'that's completely incorrect.' Dr. Grossman then drew on a diagram of a human skull a moderately large defect square in the occiput that coincided with his clear recollection of the size and location of a defect in JFK's skull."[99] Dr. Aguilar also duly notes all the instances of missing autopsy photos, as well.

---

95   *Inside the ARRB* by Doug Horne (2009), page 238, 810-811
96   8/26/91 and 8/27/91 interview with Livingstone for *High Treason 2* (see Chapter 7)
97   *Inside the ARRB* by Doug Horne (2009), page 129
98   *JFK: The Case for Conspiracy* DVD
99   *Trauma Room One* by Charles Crenshaw (2001), page 213

Dr. David Mantik states that there are 15 indicators that argue for a large occipital (right rear) defect in JFK's head[100]:

1. The many witnesses (Dealey Plaza, Parkland, Bethesda) to a large posterior defect;

2. The three Dallas pathologists from Methodist Hospital that identified the Harper Fragment as occipital (Drs. Jack Harper, A.B. Cairns, and Gerard Noteboom);

3. Bethesda autopsy doctor J. Thornton Boswell's sketches at the autopsy and for the ARRB;

4. Bethesda autopsy doctor James J. Humes selected entry site while testifying to the ARRB;

5. The intrinsic features of the Harper Fragment itself;

6. The original catalog description from the 11/1/66 military review (performed by Humes, Boswell, Ebersole and Stringer) of Fox autopsy photo 8 as a posterior view (this was later corroborated by autopsy technician Paul O'Connor);

7. The ill-matched appositional bone borders for metallic exit debris on two different bones;

8. Small, visible dark areas on the AP X-ray (confirmed by Mantik's Optical Densitometry [OD] data);

9. The missing medial lambdoid sutures on the AP X-ray;

10. An abrupt change in OD at the back of the skull on the lateral X-ray (consistent with the Harper Fragment defect);

11. The dubious fit of the Harper Fragment into the parietal defect;

12. Dr. A.B. Cairns suspicion of an entry near the metallic smear and also his description of vascular grooves near the "base of the skull";

13. The location of the metallic smear on the outside of the Harper Fragment;

14. The presence of fat pads (from the Y-incision) in the upper left corner of Fox autopsy photo number 8;

15. The visibility of cerebellum via the posterior skull defect by Parkland doctors Jenkins, Baxter, Carrico, McClelland, Peters, Crenshaw, Perry, Clark, Williams and Grossman.

Needless to say, I agree with his assessment.

---

100   *John F. Kennedy's Head Wounds: A Final Synthesis – and a New Analysis of the Harper Fragment* by Dr. David Mantik (2015)- section 6

Michael Chesser, M.D., who we already heard from above regarding the x-rays and their alteration, stated that there is also evidence of alteration of some of the autopsy photographs.[101]

WHERE THERE REALLY TWO BRAIN EXAMINATIONS?

The case for two brain exams? I know it sounds preposterous on its face-perhaps even the title of a bad science fiction movie to the uninitiated. That said, based on the extremely detailed work of Doug Horne (as exhaustively chronicled in Volume 3 of his 5-volume series *Inside The ARRB*), I do indeed believe there were two brain examinations: one of a brain that really was JFK's and a later examination on a brain that was not Kennedy's.[102] As Horne himself summarized:

> The brain photographs in the National Archives that are purported to be photographs of President Kennedy's brain are not what they are represented to be; they are not pictures of his brain, but rather are photographs of someone else's brain. Normally, in cases of death due to injury to the brain, the brain is examined one or two weeks following the autopsy on the body, and photographs are taken of the pattern of damage. Following President Kennedy's autopsy, there were two subsequent brain examinations, not one: the first examination was of the President's brain, and those photographs were never introduced into the official record; the second examination was of a fraudulent specimen, whose photographs were subsequently introduced into the official record. The pattern of damage displayed in these 'official' brain photographs has nothing whatsoever to do with the assassination in Dallas, and in fact was undoubtedly used to shore up the official conclusion that President Kennedy was killed by a shot from above and behind.

Horne further writes:

> My most remarkable finding while on the Review Board staff, and a totally unexpected one, was that instead of one supplemental brain examination being conducted following the conclusion of President Kennedy's autopsy, as was expected, two different examinations were conducted, about a week apart from each other. A thorough timeline analysis of available documents, and of the testimony of autopsy witnesses taken by the ARRB, revealed that the remains of President Kennedy's badly damaged brain were examined on Monday morning, November 25, 1963 prior to the

---

101   https://kennedysandking.com/images/pdf/michael-chesser-houston-2017.pdf.
102   https://www.washingtonpost.com/wp-srv/national/longterm/jfk/jfk1110.htm.

state funeral, and that shortly thereafter the brain was turned over to RADM Burkley, Military Physician to the President; a second brain examination, of a fraudulent specimen, was conducted sometime between November 29th and December 2nd, 1963 – and it is the photographs from this second examination that are in the National Archives today.

Pertinent Facts Regarding the Two Examinations are as follows:

First Brain Exam, Monday, November 25th, 1963

Attendees: Dr. Humes, Dr. Boswell, and Navy civilian photographer John Stringer.

Events: John Stringer testified to the ARRB that he used both Ektachrome E3 color positive transparency film, and B & W Portrait Pan negative film; both were 4 by 5 inch format films exposed using duplex film holders; he only shot superior views of the intact specimen – no inferior views; the pathologists sectioned the brain, as is normal for death by gunshot wound, with transverse or "coronal" incisions – sometimes called "bread loaf" incisions – in order to trace the track of the bullet or bullets; and after each section of tissue was cut from the brain, Stringer photographed that section on a light box to show the damage.

Second Brain Exam, Between November 29th and December 2nd, 1963

Attendees: Dr. Humes, Dr. Boswell, Dr. Finck, and an unknown Navy photographer.

Events: Per the testimony of all 3 pathologists, the brain was not sectioned, as should have been normal procedure for any gunshot wound to the head – that is, transverse or coronal sections were not made. The brain looked different than it did at the autopsy on November 22nd, and Dr. Finck wrote about this in a report to his military superior on February 1, 1965. The color slides of the brain specimen in the National Archives were exposed on "Ansco" film, not Ektachrome E3 film; and the B & W negatives are also on "Ansco" film, and originated in a film pack (or magazine), not duplex holders. The brain photos in the Archives show both superior and inferior views, contrary to what John Stringer remembers shooting, and there are no photographs of sections among the Archives brain photographs, which is inconsistent with Stringer's sworn testimony about what he photographed.

Further indications that the brain photographs in the Archives are not President Kennedy's brain are as follows:

Two ARRB medical witnesses, former FBI agent Frank O'Neill and Gawler's funeral home mortician Tom Robinson, both recalled vividly that the major area of tissue missing from President

Kennedy's brain was in the rear of the brain. The brain photos in the Archives do not show any tissue missing in the rear of the brain, only in the top.

When former FBI agent Frank O'Neill viewed the Archives brain photographs during his deposition, he said that the photos he was viewing could not be President Kennedy's brain because when he viewed the removed brain at the autopsy, the damage was so great that more than half of it was gone – missing. He described the brain photos in the Archives as depicting a "virtually intact" brain.

Finally, the weight of the brain recorded in the supplemental autopsy report was 1500 grams, which exceeds the average weight of a normal, undamaged male brain. This is entirely inconsistent with a brain which was over half missing when observed at autopsy.

Conclusions

The conduct of a second brain examination on a fraudulent specimen, and the introduction of photographs of that specimen into the official record, was designed to do two things:

1. eliminate evidence of a fatal shot from the front, which was evident on the brain removed at autopsy and examined on Monday, November 25th, 1963; and

2. place into the record photographs of a brain with damage generally consistent with having been shot from above and behind.

Until I discovered that the photographs in the Archives could not be of President Kennedy's brain, the brain photos had been used by 3 separate investigative bodies – the Clark Panel, the Rockefeller Commission, and the House Select Committee on Assassinations – to support the Warren Commission's findings that President Kennedy was shot from above and behind, and to discount the expert observations from Parkland hospital in Dallas that President Kennedy had an exit wound in the back of his head.

In my opinion, the brain photographs in the National Archives, along with Dr. Mantik's Optical Densitometry analysis of the head x-rays, are two irrefutable examples of fraud in this case, and call into question the official conclusions of all prior investigations."

Again, I concur with these landmark findings. In fact, so did Dr. Robert B. Livingston, chief of the U.S. Neurobiological Laboratory and Scientific Director of both the National Institute for Mental Health and the National Institute for Neurological Diseases and Blindness in both the Eisenhower and Kennedy administrations. Livingston "concluded that diagrams of the brain in the National Archives must be of some brain other than that of John F. Kennedy,"[103] adding that "The Supplemental Autopsy Report stated that the brain weighed 1,500 grams, much too heavy and more than an average adult male brain, let alone one that had lost much of its mass. The fixative formalin solution could not add any significant amount to the brain weight."[104]

Dr. Boswell said he thought Dr. Richard L. Davis was present at the supplemental examination of the brain, yet Davis himself said "I never saw President Kennedy's brain."[105]

Michael Chesser, M.D., who was granted permission by Sen. Paul Kirk, the Kennedy family representative for the Deed of Gift, to view the JFK autopsy cranial x-rays and autopsy photographs, is already on record stating that some of the autopsy x-rays and photos are altered. Chesser also states that the brain photographs at the National Archives are not of President Kennedy's brain. The brain appeared small and deformed, and it appeared most like a brain which had been sitting in a jar for a long period of time (these photographs were purported to have been taken at the supplemental brain exam a few days after the autopsy).[106]

WAS THERE A DELIBERATE COVER-UP OF THE MEDICAL EVIDENCE?

To speak in the vernacular, "ya think?" Huge yes to this. One need look no further than this revolting statement found in HSCA Volume 7, page 37:

> In disagreement with the observations of the Parkland doctors are the 26 people present at the autopsy. *All of those interviewed who attended the autopsy corroborated the general location of the wounds as depicted in the photographs; none had differing accounts.* [emphasis added]

If not for the Oliver Stone movie *JFK* and the furor over the hidden files, the JFK Records act and the ARRB, the records allegedly backing up this bold statement would have been buried until 2029. However, when the autopsy witness HSCA interview reports (and drawings) were released in 1993, it became obvious why the records were buried: the above statement by the HSCA was a bold-face lie! Autopsy witnesses Chester Boyers, Jan Rudnicki, James Metzler, Gregory Cross, Floyd Riebe, Ed-

---

103   *Assassination Science* by Prof. James Fetzer (1997/1998), numerous, especially pages 161-175 and 366.
104   1/20/94 interview with Harry Livingstone in *Killing Kennedy* (1995), pages 266-267.
105   February 1996 ARRB interview of J. Thornton Boswell; 2/27/97 ARRB interview [see also *High Treason* by Harrison Livingstone and Robert Groden (1998 edition), pages 440-441.
106   https://kennedysandking.com/images/pdf/michael-chesser-houston-2017.pdf.

ward Reed, Paul O'Connor, James Jenkins, John Ebersole, Tom Robinson, Frank O'Neill, James Sibert, and Roy Kellerman all stated that JFK had a wound in the rear of his head (O'Connor, Jenkins, Robinson, O'Neill, Sibert and Kellerman also made drawings reflecting these statements).[107]

I was at the COPA conference in Washington, D.C. in October 1995 (also a video) when the HSCA's Andy Purdy admitted that this bold HSCA statement was false and it disturbed him greatly that this was allowed to happen (the lie and the burying of these records). Purdy was interviewed by the ARRB in January 1996 and said the very same things.[108]

In addition, Humes admitted he destroyed his autopsy notes and his first draft. Finck's notes were stolen, as well.[109]

WHY DIDN'T THE SHOOTER (OSWALD OR WHOMEVER) SHOOT KENNEDY AS HE WAS HEADING SLOWLY DOWN HOUSTON STREET TOWARD THE BOOK DEPOSITORY OR AT THE CORNER OF ELM AND HOUSTON?

I think the number one reason was because the Secret Service agents in the follow-up car (and, to a lesser extent, the two in the limousine with JFK and the policemen lining the street and riding in motorcycles) could have spotted him and returned fire before the assault was over or even before it truly began. In addition, the limousine could have taken evasive action by swerving or speeding up, as there would be much less doubt and confusion as to where the shots originated from if it was coming from an area staring spectators and law enforcement directly in their faces, so to speak. Escape for the gunman would be a near impossibility, as well.

I believe the second reason to wait until after the slow turn from Houston onto Elm was to get Kennedy into a crossfire from which there was no escape and to provide cover and confusion concerning eyewitnesses and gun-toting officers.

DOES THE CHARLES MENTESANA FILM DEPICT POLICE OFFICERS LOOKING AT A RIFLE ALLEGEDLY FOUND ON THE ROOF OF THE TEXAS SCHOOL BOOK DEPOSITORY?

Doubtful.[110] I believe it is merely an officer holding his own shotgun at a slight angle/parade rest. As conspiracy researcher Anthony Marsh wrote in 1995: "That is not a rifle; it is a shotgun. The barrel and the bore

107   *Inside the ARRB* by Douglas Horne (2009), pages 886-887.
108   *Inside the ARRB* by Douglas Horne (2009), page 888.
109   *Inside the ARRB* by Douglas Horne (2009), numerous.
110   *Rendezvous With Death* by H.R. Underwood (2013), pages 267-270.

are too big in diameter for a rifle. Some shotguns have distinctive profiles and magazine caps by which we can identify them at a glance. The shotgun the policeman was holding was his Remington 870.... Also, one of the cops in the tramp photos carried a Remington 870. There were at least three different makes and models of shotguns used by the DPD and the Remington 870 is one of the most popular police shotguns."

Does the Door Being Opened on the Vice Presidential Secret Service Follow-Up Car (In The Altgen's Photo) in Dallas on Elm Street During the Relative Start of the Shooting Mean Anything?

No. The door partially opened earlier in the motorcade, as films and photos reveal.[111] The vehicle had those so-called "suicide doors" that opened the opposite way, so the agents had the door partially opened to compensate for this mechanical handicap. Nothing to see here.

Is the McCone-Rowley Document Genuine?

No. Unfortunately esteemed author Robert Groden fell for this.[112] That said, it is a very good fake; even I believed it at first, as I am sure many others have, as well. Conspiracy researcher Anthony Marsh and others demonstrate that it is indeed a fake.[113]

What About the Three Tramps?

Back in the late 1980's to right after the Stone film came out, I was one of many who was convinced that the three tramps arrested after the assassination were not really tramps and were possible conspirators of some kind. Well, that was then and this is now. Since 1992, it has been pretty well established that the three tramps ... were just merely three tramps: Gus W. Abrams, Harold Doyle, and John F. Gedney, to be exact.[114] Next.

What About the Badgeman, the Umbrella Man, the Dark Complected Man, and the Black Dog Man: Are They Valid Images and/or Evidence of Conspiracy?

Pardon the pun, but I am truly on the fence about these issues. The Badgeman image, enhanced from the Moorman photo, is compelling as presented on *The Men Who Killed Kennedy*, but I go back and forth

111   And as noted in Robert Groden's 1993 book *The Killing of a President*
112   *JFK: Absolute Proof* by Robert Groden (2013), pages 5-8; https://kennedysandking.com/john-f-kennedy-reviews/groden-robert-absolute-proof.
113   http://mccone-rowley.blogspot.com/.
114   https://en.wikipedia.org/wiki/Three_tramps.

on whether it is truly valid or not. Same with the Umbrella Man and the Black Dog Man. While they were definitely there (of course), I am skeptical about Louie Steven Witt's claim that he was the Umbrella Man, but I cannot definitively debunk his claim, either.[115] In conjunction with the unidentified Dark Complected Man, I am tempted to believe they were signals (not assassins) of some sort but, again, I cannot state this with certainty. Finally, while the Black Dog Man was definitely there, he or she may have been a mere innocent spectator. If you find all of this unsatisfying, sorry: I promised you honest answers in the title of the book.

IS THE MAN IN THE DOORWAY AS DEPICTED IN THE ALTGENS PHOTO LEE HARVEY OSWALD?

Once and for all: no. The man has conclusively and exhaustively been proven to be Billy Lovelady, a fellow employee who bore a resemblance to Oswald.[116] I never fell for this one.

IS THE PERSON IN THE ENTRANCE WAY (THE SO-CALLED "PRAYER MAN") OSWALD?

No. The figure is that of Sarah Stanton, a Depository employee.[117] I admit I really fell for this one at first- the figure does sort of look like Oswald ... sort of.

DID SECRET SERVICE AGENT BILL GREER SHOOT JFK?

No. This is a ridiculous theory that will not die. Clear copies of the Zapruder film conclusively demonstrate that Greer did not fire a gun.

DID SECRET SERVICE AGENT GEORGE HICKEY SHOOT JFK (BY ACCIDENT)?

No. This theory is not as ridiculous for one reason: the ballistic work of the theory's chief proponent, Howard Donahue, demonstrates that

---

115   https://en.wikipedia.org/wiki/John_F._Kennedy_assassination_conspiracy_theories.

116   *JFK: Absolute Proof* by Robert Groden (2013), pages 269-270.

117   Sarah Stanton: 11-23-63 interview with FBI agent Nat Pinkston recounted in an 11-29-63 memo found in the Dallas FBI files at the Weisberg Archives; 11-23-63 interview recounted in 12-10-63 FBI report, CD7 p.20; 3-18-64 statement to the FBI, 22H675; Proof that the figure is Stanton-Buell Wesley Frazier statements: 3-11-64 testimony before the Warren Commission, 2H210-245; 2-13-69 testimony in the trial of Clay Shaw; 3-27-13 appearance at the Irving Central Library; 7-13-13 appearance at the Sixth Floor Museum, as shown on C-Span) (When asked how many shots he heard; 9-27-14 appearance at the AARC Conference in Bethesda, Maryland, video found on vimeo; Pauline Sanders corroborates Frazier and Stanton: 11-24-63 FBI report, 22H844; 3-19-64 statement to the FBI, 22H672; Billy Lovelady re: Stanton: 3-19-64 statement to the FBI, 22H662; 4-7-64 testimony before the Warren Commission, 6H336-341-When asked who was with him on the front steps when the shots were fired) "Bill Shelley and Sarah Stanton."

the fatal shot could not have come from the sixth floor window.[118] Dona-hue, a man who believed his government, sought a benign answer for why the shot could not have come from Oswald's rifle: a Secret Service "acci-dent." That said, the Bronson film demonstrates that Hickey did not have the AR-15 in his hands and pointed at JFK at the time of the head shot.

WHAT ABOUT THE RUSSIANS, CASTRO, NIXON, THE FEDERAL RESERVE, THE ISRAELI GOVERNMENT, ROSCOE WHITE, GEN-ERAL WALKER, SAUL, ROBERT EASTERLING[119] OR THE RIGHT WING AS POSSIBLE CONSPIRATORS?

No. These are all strawmen. After decades of reading and researching this case, I have come across no evidence whatsoever that any of these entities or persons were involved.[120] I never believed any of these en-tities were suspects, although I did think it odd that Nixon – in Dallas on 11/22/63 – did not remember where he was on the day Kennedy was shot.

IS THERE REALLY A CIA CONNECTION TO THE TEXAS SCHOOL BOOK DEPOSITORY?

Incredibly, the answer is yes. The former executive director of the Cen-tral Intelligence Agency, Charles Briggs, spent one year working on re-search for The Sixth Floor project in the Washington, D.C., offices of ex-hibition designers Bob Staples and Barbara Charles.[121] (Mr. Briggs passed away on November 4, 2015).[122] Author Jim DiEugenio wrote the follow-ing to the author:

> Is it not amazing how a guy can live in the shadows his whole life, and then suddenly, due to an obituary, we find out who he is. Briggs helped set up the sixth floor for CIA, he apparently oversaw

---

118   *Mortal Error* by Bonar Meninger (1992); *JFK: The Smoking Gun* by Colin McLaren (2013).

119   *Reasonable Doubt* by Henry Hurt (1985).

120   How about this silliness? *Who Shot JFK?: A Guide to the Major Conspiracy Theories* (1993) by Bob Callahan and Mark Zingarelli explores some of the more obscure theories regarding JFK's murder, such as "The Coca-Cola Theory." According to this theory, suggested by the editor of an organic gardening magazine, Oswald killed JFK due to mental impairment stemming from an ad-diction to refined sugar, as evidenced by his need for his favorite beverage immediately after the assassination. Or, in the "covering-all-your-bases" category, Normal Mailer, author of *Oswald's Tale: An American Mystery* (1995), concludes that Oswald was guilty, but holds that the evidence may point to a second gunman on the grassy knoll, who, purely by coincidence, was attempting to kill JFK at the same time as Oswald. "If there was indeed another shot, it was not necessarily fired by a conspirator of Oswald's. Such a gun could have belonged to another lone killer or to a conspirator working for some other group altogether." Alrighty, then.

121   https://jfkfacts.org/charles-briggs-retired-cia-officer-who-assisted-jfk-museum-was-ac-cused-of-deception-by-a-federal-judge/.

122   https://wikispooks.com/wiki/Charles_A._Briggs.

CIA interests in declassification for ARRB, and now we know he went through Angleton's files after he was removed by Colby. This guy was a player in the JFK case and no one knew it."

Researcher Chris Newton wrote the following to the author:

I inadvertently stumbled on this connection, here in this forum while investigating other issues, and Gary Mack and I had a "private" conversation about Charles' status. Charles Briggs had more knowledge of more secrets in the CIA than probably anyone other than Angleton (and it appears he was the keeper of Angleton's files as well, moving about 15% of the 400 yards of files into the main CIA database and overseeing the destruction of the rest).

WAS GEORGE H.W. BUSH, FORMER CIA DIRECTOR AND PRESIDENT, IN DEALEY PLAZA?

No. Photo analysis demonstrates that the man some people think is Bush is clearly not him. In addition, he wasn't even in Dallas during the assassination.[123] That said, Bush did know George de Mohrenschildt, Oswald's friend and handler:

28 September 1976

Mr. G. de Mohrenschildt
2737 Kings Road
Apartment 142
Dallas, Texas 75219

Dear George:

Please forgive the delay in my reply to your September 5th letter. It took time to explore thoroughly the matters you raised.

Let me say first that I know it must have been difficult for you to seek my help in the situation outlined in your letter. I believe I can appreciate your state of mind in view of your daughter's tragic death a few years ago and the current poor state of your wife's health. I was extremely sorry to hear of these circumstances.

In your situation, I can well imagine how the attentions you described in your letter affect both you and your wife. However, my staff has been unable to find any indication of interest in your activities on the part of Federal authorities in recent years. The flurry of interest that attended your testimony before the Warren Commission has long since subsided. I can only speculate that you may have become "newsworthy" again in view of the renewed interest in the Kennedy assassination and, thus, may be attracting the attention of people in the media.

I hope this letter has been of some comfort to you, George, although I realize I am unable to answer your question completely. Thank you for your good wishes on my new job. As you can imagine, I'm finding it interesting and challenging.

Very truly yours,

George Bush
Director

Why Do Lone-Nut Authors and Researchers Still Follow the Case For Years, If Not Decades, If Oswald Did It and It Is An Open-and-Shut Case?

Because it is *not* an open-and-shut case and they (secretly) know it. First of all, you can never prove a negative. In addition, even if one wants to posit that Oswald was the sole assassin, so what? How does that, in and of itself, disprove conspiracy? One need look no further than the Lincoln assassination to see both a lone gunman and a conspiracy. In addition, the attempt on President Truman's life was a conspiracy by two shooters.

I asked this question on a forum and received mostly crickets, except one response from lone-nut advocate David Von Pein to the effect that "because it is fun and there is still a .0001 chance I am wrong and there was indeed a conspiracy." So let me get this straight: you adamantly believe Oswald acted alone, yet you hang around for decades in case there is the slimmest of chances you are wrong? If everyone led their lives by this credo, nothing would be accomplished. We would be dead from paralysis by analysis in a never-ending quest to prove there is no chance we were wrong about not only historical events, but things that occur in every-day life.

The real reason they still "hang around" is the very same reason that we, so-called conspiracists, hang around: there is no 100 percent legal and historical proof of conspiracy. Nor is there 100 percent legal and historical proof of no conspiracy, either. However, because there are so many problems with the evidence (witnesses who state shots came from two directions, not just one; witnesses who state that the wounds indicated JFK was shot from two directions, not just from the rear; two government verdicts- the Warren Commission's "no conspiracy" and the HSCA's "probable conspiracy"; the Garrison case resulted in a not guilty verdict for Clay Shaw, yet members of the jury were persuaded that there was a conspiracy and much information has come forward in the intervening 50-plus years since the trial; the Zapruder film depicts Kennedy flying violently backward to the rear, not to the front; virtually every item of evidence and virtually every witness is questioned; virtually every piece of evidence has real issues regarding chain of possession and so forth; Oswald adamantly denied the deed, rather than what true assassins usually do – even John Wilkes Booth, Lincoln's assassin, as well as the Puerto Rican Nationalists who tried to kill Truman, never denied their evil intentions; and so on), the case endures.

Having said that, the reason I wrote this book is because I do believe there is proof of conspiracy: what you have been reading so far. However, one could argue that these points I have been making throughout these pages are compelling but do not constitute legal proof; so be it. Still, as I said early on, I know the game: there will be lone-nut researchers (and maybe even pro-conspiracy researchers with a pet theory I harmed) who will take issue with some or even many of the notions I espouse herein. Such is life when one is an author writing a book on this controversial case. That said, like I also mentioned earlier, I see both sides of the case, as I briefly flirted with the dark side. I am very open-minded and my Secret Service research does not stand or fall on the notion that there had to have been a conspiracy.

Nevertheless, the main point is a strong one: when you see Fred Litwin, David Von Pein, and others of their ilk still shadowing, stalking and creeping into pro-conspiracy venues online, there is a real reason for this: deep down in their heart of hearts, even they know something is rotten in Denmark. Think about it: if one is sure that Sandy Hook really happened, McKinley was killed by a lone nut acting alone, Garfield was killed by a lone nut acting alone, the Moon landing was genuine, that 9/11 wasn't committed by our government, and the earth is round, among many other topics, one would not even waste their time for one nano second visiting those forums to attempt to convince someone that what they believe is somehow wrong. I know I do not. This is because it is a true waste of time. Sometimes a cigar truly is a cigar.

Then why do the lone-nutters still venture into pro-conspiracy territory to try to "change our minds"?

Because, deep down inside, they are trying to change their own minds... back to their core beliefs. That is why.

Case in point:

"First off, I don't think Lee Harvey Oswald pulled the trigger ... as far as saying that he was guilty ... I find that extremely hard to believe. And I think I'll show enough evidence to indicate, or that I think I could circumstantially beyond a reasonable doubt, so to speak, prove to anybody else, that he was not the man behind the trigger ... it's extremely unlikely that Oswald could have been the gunman, based upon that. There are some photographs that were taken that indicate the gunman lingered in the window ... it deals with the boxes in the window... I think I will be able to show, beyond a reasonable doubt, that Oswald was not the killer of J.D. Tippit. That Tippit's murder was connected to the assassination of the President. And that the reason Oswald was arrested was because the FBI had advance knowledge of his activities."

Who said this?

None other than current lone-nut advocate Dale Myers back in 1982![124]

124   https://kennedysandking.com/john-f-kennedy-articles/i-don-t-think-lee-harvey-os-wald-pulled-the-trigger-an-interview-with-dale-myers

CHAPTER SEVEN

WHO DIDN'T DO IT AND WHY NOT

*We don't have any proof that Oswald fired the rifle, and never did. No-
body's yet been able to put him in that building with a gun in his hand.*
– Dallas Police Chief Jesse Curry[1]

*"The evidence that we have at the present time is not very, very strong… The
case, as it stands now, isn't strong enough to be able to get a conviction…. Oswald has still denied everything. He doesn't know anything about anything."*
– FBI Director J. Edgar Hoover to President Johnson 11/23/63

Whatever his role in this whole affair was (patsy or accomplice),
Lee Harvey Oswald was not an assassin of Kennedy. He was
not even on the sixth floor when the shots were fired, as Texas School Book Depository employees Victoria Adams, Sandra Styles, and
Dorothy Garner did not see or hear Oswald come down the noisy wooden
stairs from the sixth floor.[2] In addition, Oswald's boss, Roy Truly, and Dallas
Police motorcycle officer Marion Baker encountered Oswald (less than) 90
seconds after the shots were fired and he was calmly sipping a Coke he had

1   *Dallas Morning News*, 11/6/69: interview with Curry.
2   *The Girl on the Stairs* by Barry Ernest (2013); *The Lee Harvey Oswald Files* by Flip De Mey (2016).
Regarding Ernest's fine book, Sandra Styles (Butler) herself reached out to me in October of 2018, saying that she takes issue with Vickie Adams' timing, stating that it was not immediate that they headed
down the stairs. Barry Ernest wrote back to me on 3/11/20: "Here's the story re: Sandra Styles. During my
research and in an interview with Sandra on 2/13/02, she said her recollection was that she and Vicki first
went to the passenger elevator located outside the Scott Foresman office on the fourth floor, east side
of the TSBD. (You may want to view a diagram of that floor for a perspective.) She said only after waiting
unsuccessfully for that elevator did they then move to the back stairway, basically opposite on that floor
from where they were then standing. Sandra was not questioned by the WC. Nor did she mention any of
this in her brief FBI interviews. So I could find no record of any official comment made by her in this regard.
    When I asked Vicki about this the next day, she replied in a 2/14/02 email: "This is really surprising.
We did not go out that way. I think she has this really off." The Stroud document corroborates Vicki and
when I interviewed Dorothy Garner, she clearly remembered following both Vicki and Sandra out the rear
door of their office as they moved to the back stairway. Hence the reason why she was able to see Roy
Truly and Officer Marion Baker emerge onto that floor on their way up shortly after the assassination and
after Vicki and Sandra had gone down the stairs.. I brought all this to Sandra's attention, again on 2/14/02
after I had heard from Vicki, mentioning what Garner had said to me and even emailing her a copy of the
Stroud document, which she of course had never seen. Her response back to me later that same day was:
"Vicki was more observant than me, more detailed. I must be thinking of something else, some other time."
You'd have to know Vicki to realize she was a perfectionist when it came to details like this, confident with
what she knew to be true. And when she wasn't sure of something, she would not hesitate to admit that.
Regarding this specific point, she was emphatic about both women going directly to the back stairs. Both
the Stroud document and Dorothy Garner confirm this. I feel Sandra simply made an innocent mistake."

just purchased from a vending machine on the second floor lunchroom. Oswald was not out of breath or startled in the least.[3] In Captain Will Fritz's notes that were released only in the mid-1990's, Oswald's alibi is revealed: "claims 2nd floor Coke when off[icer] came in; to first floor had lunch; out with Bill Shelley in front."[4] Oswald knew Bill Shelley was standing in front of the building. And that is before the shooting, not after! Shelley had departed almost immediately after the shooting from the Texas School Book Depository (TSBD) steps. The undated draft of Will Fritz's report states: ""I asked him what part of the building he was in when the president was shot, and he said that he was having his lunch about that time on the first floor. Mr. Truly had told me that one of the police officers had stopped this man immediately after the shooting near the back stairway, so I asked Oswald where he was when the police officer stopped him. He said he was on the second floor drinking a coca cola when the officer came in."[5]

In the 11/23/63 joint report from FBI agent's Hosty and Bookhout it is written: "OSWALD stated that he went to lunch at approximately noon and he claimed he ate his lunch on the first floor in the lunchroom; however he went to the second floor where the Coca-Cola machine was located and ob-

---

3   Carolyn Arnold (Johnson) saw Oswald between 12:15 to 12:25, very shortly before the motorcade was scheduled to go by the Texas School Book Depository. She said that "she saw Oswald on the second floor as she was on her way out of the depository at about 12:25 p.m. to watch the motorcade…I do not recall that he (Oswald) was doing anything,' Mrs. Johnson said. 'I just recall that he was sitting there…in one of the booth seats on the right hand side as you go in. He was alone as usual and appeared to be having lunch. I did not speak to him but recognized him clearly.'" 11-26-63 FBI report, CD5 p41; 11-19-78 article in the *Dallas Morning News*; 11-26-78 article in the *Dallas Morning News* referencing the 11-19-78 article written the week before; November 1978 interview with Anthony Summers published in *Conspiracy*, 1980; *Not In Your Lifetime* by Anthony Summers (2013), pages 494-495.

Thanks to the amazing work of researcher extraordinaire Brian Doyle, we have possible further proof that Oswald's alibi was true. As Brian himself revealed to me on Facebook on 2/11/20: "In June 2018 I interviewed [Book Depository employee] Sarah Stanton's granddaughter Wanda. She spoke to me about what is probably the most important evidence discovery in years. Wanda told me that Sarah kept repeating the story of seeing Oswald on the second floor staircase landing outside the second floor lunchroom when she went out to watch the motorcade. Stanton saw Oswald out there holding a soda and thought he was a loner so she went out and asked him if he was going to go down and watch the motorcade. Oswald answered "No, I am going back into the break room." That "break room" was the second floor lunchroom where Carolyn Arnold would see Oswald shortly before 12:25. This is proof that Oswald was in the second floor lunchroom during the shots as he told Captain Fritz. Oswald was obviously waiting for Mrs. Reid and the other lady employees to leave before going back in to the "break room" when Stanton saw him hiding on the staircase landing." However, Mrs. Stanton told the FBI (report in WC, CD7): "She knows LEE HARVEY OSWALD by sight, being employed by the same concern, but is not personally acquainted with him and did not see OSWALD on November 22, 1963, and she never seen him with a gun." and in another FBI statement (3/18/1964): "I did not see Lee Harvey Oswald at that time or at any time during that day." However, a few witnesses claimed that their FBI reports did not accurately reflect what they told the interviewing agents, so there is always the possibility that these reports are not the final word on Stanton. Still, the FBI reports successfully muddy the waters and give lone-nut advocates a way to debunk this claim.

4   https://kennedysandking.com/john-f-kennedy-articles/785.

5   http://www.prayer-man.com/wp-content/uploads/2015/07/0412-002.jpg.

tained a bottle of Coca-Cola for his lunch. OSWALD claimed to be on the first floor when President JOHN F. KENNEDY passed by his building."[6]

In the 11/24/63 solo report from FBI agent James Bookhout, the agent reported: "Oswald stated that on November 22 1963, at the time of the search of the Texas School Book Depository building by Dallas police officers, he was on the second floor of said building, having just purchased a Coca-Cola from the soft-drink machine, at which time a police officer came into the room with pistol drawn and asked him if he worked there.

Mr. Truly was present and verified that he was an employee and the police officer thereafter left the room and continued through the building. Oswald stated that he took this Coke down to the first floor and stood around and had lunch in the employee's lunch room. He thereafter went outside and stood around for five or ten minutes with foreman Bill Shelley."[7]

Oswald even stood outside with Bill Shelley for 5 to 10 minutes after having had his lunch!

FBI agent James Hosty wrote in his book *Assignment Oswald* about an exchange he had with Oswald during his questioning while in police custody:

> "Where were you when the president went by the book depository?
> I was eating my lunch in the first floor lunchroom.
> What time was that?
> About noon.
> Were you ever on the second floor around the time the president was shot?
> Well, yeah. I went up there to get a bottle of Coca-Cola from the machine for my lunch.
> But where were you when the president actually passed your building?
> On the first floor in the lunchroom."

In Secret Service Inspector Thomas Kelley's first interview with Oswald,[8] the agent wrote:

> *I asked him if he viewed the parade and he said he had not.* I then asked him if he had shot the President and he said he had not. I asked him if he has shot governor Connally and he said he had not [emphasis added]." Oswald admitted, besides his innocence, that he did not view the parade.

6   http://www.prayer-man.com/wp-content/uploads/2015/12/Bookhout-Nov-23-2.jpg.
7   http://www.prayer-man.com/wp-content/uploads/2015/12/Bookhout-solo-report-Nov-24.jpg.
8   http://www.prayer-man.com/wp-content/uploads/2016/01/First-Interview-of-Lee-Harvey-Oswald-2-copy.jpg.

What's more, Depository Vice President Ochus V. Campbell told the *Dallas Times-Herald* on 11/22/1963:

> ... shortly after the shooting, we raced back into the building ... we saw him (Oswald) in a small storage room on the ground floor."[9] Mrs. Robert Reid, another Depository employee, testified to the Warren Commission that, right after the shooting: "I went up the stairs ... the front stairs ... I went into the office.... Well, I kept walking and I looked up and Oswald was coming in the back door of the office. I met him by the time I passed my desk several feet and I told him, I said, "Oh, the President has been shot, but maybe they didn't hit him." He mumbled something to me, I kept walking, he did, too. I didn't pay any attention to what he said because I had no thoughts of anything of him having any connection with it at all because he was very calm. He had gotten a coke and was holding it in his hands and I guess the reason it impressed me seeing him in there I thought it was a little strange that one of the warehouse boys would be up in the office at the time, not that he had done anything wrong. The only time I had seen him in the office was to come and get change and he already had his coke in his hand so he didn't come for change and I dismissed him. I didn't think anything else.[10]

According to the two FBI agents present at his interrogation, Oswald said

> ... he had eaten lunch in the lunchroom alone, but recalled possibly two Negro employees walking through the room during this period. He stated possibly one of these employees was called "Junior" and the other was a short individual whose name he could not recall but whom he would be able to recognize.[11]

Captain Will Fritz, in his notes not discovered until decades later, wrote: "two negr. came in, one Jr.- + short negro-."[12] Fritz mentioned "Junior" and the "short fellow" to the Warren Commission,[13] yet critically and falsely added that Oswald claimed that he ate *with* the men, yet Oswald actually said he ate alone. Predictably, the two employees in question, Junior Jarman and Harold Norman, denied that they ate lunch with Oswald, and therefore the Warren Commission stated that Oswald's alibi was a lie.[14]

In fact, during their Warren Commission testimony, Junior Jarman and Harold Norman separately confirmed that they had indeed "walked through"

---

9   See also the November 23, 1963 issue of the *New York Herald Tribune*.
10   3 H 274.
11   WR622.
12   Fritz Notes, p. 1.
13   4 H 213, 224.
14   WR180, 195.

the first floor lounge, known as the domino room, to retrieve their sandwiches, thus independently corroborating Oswald's account. Significantly, Harold Norman testified that usually some of the employees, including himself, would play dominos in this room during the lunch hour, but on this particular day, because of the pending passage of the Presidential motorcade, no one was playing dominos.[15] When asked if anyone else was in the domino room, Norman, who did eat his sandwich in the lounge before joining his friends to watch the motorcade, responded that in fact somebody else was present, but he could not remember who it was.[16] Hence Oswald had somehow correctly guessed not only the people who had been in the lunchroom that day (out of dozens and dozens of employees in the building), but their actions, even though they were different from the usual. Thus, the statements by the black employees actually corroborated Oswald's alibi.

To place this incident in proper perspective it is necessary to understand that there were actually two lunchrooms in the Book Depository. Texas was a part of the deep south and even the Mayor of Dallas acknowledged that the city had a reputation as the "Hate capitol of Dixie."[17] The building superintendent, Roy Truly, told writer William Manchester:

> Except for my niggers the boys are conservative, like me – like most Texans.[18]

Truly further stated that he disliked John F. Kennedy because he was a "race-mixer."[19] The main lunchroom on the second floor had soft drink and snack machines. The first floor lunchroom was used by the minority employees: blacks, Mexican-Americans, a mentally handicapped man, and the depository's one lone Marxist, Lee Harvey Oswald. Because he ate there regularly and because there were only a handful of minority employees in the Book Depository, it would have been easy for Oswald to guess who had eaten lunch there. But on the other hand, it would also have been easy for the Warren Commission to determine who actually had or had not eaten their lunch in the Domino room that day and by the process of elimination test Oswald's alibi. But the Warren Commission knew that such a test was problematic for the official version. That is because another black employee, Charles L. Givens, had seen Oswald eating his lunch there. In a statement given to the FBI a few hours after

---

15   3 H 189.
16   3 H 189.
17   WR41.
18   *The Death of a President* by William Manchester (1967), pages 132-133.
19   *The Death of a President* by William Manchester (1967), pages 49, 132-133.

the assassination, Givens recounted that he had seen Oswald eating his lunch by himself, reading a newspaper, in the first floor lunchroom.[20]

As researcher Bart Kamp stated:

> Lee Oswald did not lie when he claimed he was on the first floor when the president passed by the TSBD. Not only did [Harry] Holmes relay this; so did [Police Captain Will] Fritz in his interrogation notes, as did [FBI agent James] Bookhout and [FBI agent James] Hosty in their joint report. James "Junior" Jarman told the HSCA that Billy Lovelady told him that he had personally witnessed Oswald being allowed out of the front entrance by a policeman shortly after the assassination, and that Truly had said he was alright.[21]

A truck driver with Central Motor Freight in Dallas, Ken DuVall frequently picked up shipments of textbook boxes at the loading dock of the Texas School Book Depository. On November 22, 1963, he stated that he saw Lee Harvey Oswald in the second floor lunch room approximately thirty minutes before the assassination, establishing that Oswald was there for a while.[22] In addition to Givens, fellow Book Depository employees William Shelley, Eddie Piper, Carolyn Arnold and the aforementioned O.V. Campbell saw Oswald on the first floor between 11:50 am and 12:25 pm.[23] Fellow employee Bonnie Ray Williams was eating his lunch near the so-called "sniper's nest" on the sixth floor as late as 12:20 pm (the assassination occurred at 12:30 pm and the motorcade was running five minutes late), yet said he saw or heard no one.[24]

Speaking of William Shelley, in what is certainly a bizarre and alarming turn of events (if one can label this "situation" in this fashion), it turns out that Mr. Shelley was a CIA agent![25] [26]As researcher William Weston stated in his landmark April 2020 article "The CIA and the Texas School Book Depository"[27]:

---

20   CD 5, page 329.
21   https://kennedysandking.com/john-f-kennedy-articles/785.
22   5/6/2009 Sixth Floor Museum oral history. DuVall passed away 8/19/18.
23   https://miketgriffith.com/files/wherewasoswald.htm.
24   *The Girl on the Stairs* by Barry Ernest (2013), page 106.
25   https://kennedysandking.com/john-f-kennedy-articles/the-cia-and-the-texas-school-book-depository.
26   http://harveyandlee.net/TSBD_Elevator/TSBD_elevator.html.
27   See also Letter to the House Select Committee on Assassinations (HSCA Doc. 004079). Glaze misdated the letter "12/12/74," for the postmark on the envelope dated the year 1977. The true date should have been 12/12/77; Blakey's reply to Elzie Glaze dated January 19, 1978 (HSCA Doc. 004741); Letter by Elzie Dean Glaze to Doug Kellner and Frank Morrow of The Alternative Information Network, dated June 2, 1989; Larry Harris letter to William Weston, dated December 15, 1992 (Harris died 10/5/96); Weston contacted William Shelley on March 20, 1995 and asked him if he would be willing to answer a few questions. His response was an abrupt no. He then added,

There is evidence that Oswald worked with another CIA agent in Dallas [other than himself; more on that later on]. That would be William Shelley, who Oswald worked under for six weeks as an order filler for the Texas School Book Depository (TSBD). With perhaps two CIA agents on the same premises, a careful scrutiny of the company they worked for is needed to understand what happened the day President Kennedy was killed.... Roy Truly was, up to the time of his death in 1985, continuously frightened by "federal authorities." His wife Mildred refused to talk about the assassination even with members of her own family.[28] Carolyn Arnold, a secretary for Vice-president Ochus Campbell, told a friend in 1994 that she had been, and still was, terrified. She said that "there is a whole lot more to tell about the TSBD than what has been published – that the whole building should be suspected as more or less of a 'safe base' to operate from that day in November 1963."[29]

Weston continues, reading from a letter from journalist Elzie Dean Glaze:

In late 1977, while working as a reporter for the *Avalanche-Journal* newspaper in Lubbock, Texas, I submitted written testimony to the United States House of Representatives' newly-formed Select Committee on Assassinations. Enclosed is a copy of the response from G. Robert Blakey, Chief Counsel and Director of the Select Committee on Assassinations. Copies of my written testimony have disappeared from my personal files. My testimony included numerous meetings with a man named Bill Shelley ... Mr. Shelley claims to have been an intelligence officer during World War II and thereafter joined the CIA. Bill Shelley claims he was arrested by the Dallas Police and formally charged with the assassination of President Kennedy. He claims the charges were dropped, but he stated that he turned away several newspapers and magazines offering huge amounts of money for his personal account of the assassination. He refused to let me quote him or use his name in print. One of the aforementioned employees (whose name I cannot recall) stated that when she went to work for Bill Shelley at the school book depository in the early 1970's she was interviewed for the job by some type of "government agents" who asked if she had been recruited by the F.B.I. or C.I.A. As you can well imagine, she was quite confused because the job was low-paying and involved minor duties.

"Everything that I have to say on that subject is in the public record. You'll have to go with that.";
7/14/99 letter from Glaze to Weston; Elzie Dean Glaze obituary (he passed away 11/15/19): https://www.legacy.com/obituaries/name/elzie-glaze-obituary?pid=194723057.
28 *Crossfire* by Jim Marrs (198), page 319.
29 Carolyn Arnold statement in "Byrd/TSBD Concerns" posted by Martin Barkley on May 24, 2000 on the JFK Today website.

Both the HSCA (in 1977-1978) and renowned author Larry Ray Harris (in 1992) were involved in this fascinating inquiry, but nothing came of it, unfortunately. As Harris told Weston:

> If it is true that Shelley was affiliated in some way with CIA or U.S. intelligence, that would be a disturbing and potentially significant development.

We will return to Bill Shelley momentarily.

In addition to the witnesses who saw two men on the sixth floor (see chapter one), Carolyn Walther, Arnold Rowland, Ronald Fischer, Robert Edwards, James Crawford, and even Howard Brennan stated one of the men – presumably the shooter – wore light or even white-colored clothing, yet Dallas Police officer Marion Baker, who encountered Oswald in the lunch room 90 seconds or less after the assassination, initially confirmed that Oswald was wearing the same brown/burgundy-plaid shirt he was arrested in: "Yes, sir; I believe that is the shirt that he had on when he came (sic)," although he also said right afterward that "I wouldn't be sure of that. It seemed to me like that other shirt was a little bit darker than that whenever I saw him in the homicide office there."[30] Baker did later testify: "he looked like he didn't have the same thing on."[31] That said, a bus ticket in the pocket dated that afternoon provided further evidence that he had not changed his shirt.[32]

Book Depository employee Geneva Hine testified to the Warren Commission:

> I was alone until the lights all went out and the phones became dead because the motorcade was coming near us and no one was calling so I got up and thought I could see it from the east window in our office.[33]

As author John Armstrong wrote:

> It appears the electricity in the TSBD was turned off as the escort car turned from Main St. onto Houston St., less than one minute before shots were fired at the President. The electrical panels were located on the back side of the building on the first floor, close to the domino room and close to Bill Shelley's office.[34]

Bill Shelley, once again.

30   3 H 257.
31   3 H 262.
32   Walther: 24 H 522; Rowland: 2 H 171; Fischer: 6 H 194; Edwards: 6 H 203; Crawford: WR68; Brennan: CD 5, page 13; https://harveyandlee.net/Leaving/Leaving_the_TSBD.html.
33   6 H 395.
34   http://harveyandlee.net/TSBD_Elevator/TSBD_elevator.html.

For those in the minority who still think Oswald planned the shooting alone, there are a few items of information he must have had in order to pull it off, the most important being the knowledge that the motorcade and President Kennedy's limo would pass within shooting distance of the building. Where would he get such information? It had to have been, in that pre-Internet world where even radio and television never revealed such micro details in advance, the newspapers ... but which one?

1. Warren Commission Exhibit (CE) 1361 – *Dallas Morning News* 11/16/63: Mentions Main street only.

2. CE 1362 – *Dallas Times-Herald* 11/19/63: Selected route, no map.

3. CE 1363 – *Dallas Morning News* 11/19/63: Selected route, no map.

4. CE 1364 – *Dallas Morning News* 11/20/63: Main street only.

5. *Dallas Times-Herald* Final Edition 11/21/63: selected route with map (mentioned nowhere in Warren Commission Volumes – only microfilm records exist).

6. *Dallas Times-Herald* 11/22/63: Industrial Boulevard to the Trade Mart (Alternate route of Main to Industrial to Trade Mart.)

7. CE 1365 – *Dallas Morning News* 11/22/63: Main Street only: Map without Elm Street turn (The Warren Commission deleted the map when they published this in their work!)

So, out of 7 possibilities, 4 of the 7 do not mention the Houston-to-Elm dogleg turn right in front of his building. Main Street was farther away and, presumably, the vehicles would have been traveling at a faster rate of speed, to boot. Two of the three that do mention the Houston-to-Elm dogleg turn are dated Tuesday, 11/19/63.

Is there any evidence from anyone in the building or anyone close to Oswald that he knew about the motorcade route that day?[35] According to Marina Oswald, on the night before the assassination, she asked him about Kennedy's upcoming visit the next day and Lee seemed totally in the dark about when or where the motorcade would pass.[36] Junior Jarman told the Warren Commission that he did not learn about the motorcade passing in front of the Depository until the morning of 11/22/63 at about 9 A.M. About an hour later, Oswald was standing near a window looking

35   Thanks to researcher David Josephs for his insights on this matter.
36   18 H 638.

out at the gathering crowd. He asked Jarman what the people were there for. After Jarman told him, *he asked which way the motorcade was coming.* Which reveals, unlike the Commission assumption, that Oswald did not read the November 19th *Dallas Times-Herald.*

Between the evening of Tuesday Nov 19th and Thursday Nov 21st, Oswald allegedly decides to go to the home of Ruth and Michael Paine to get his rifle out of the garage and bring it to work on Friday so he can do the deed. Does he make sure to ask Texas School Book Depository colleague Buell Wesley Frazier for a ride home that day? For if he does not go home by Thursday night how can he get the rifle to work Friday?

Buell Wesley Frazier testified to the Warren Commission: "Well, I say, we were standing like I said at the four-headed table about half as large as this, not, quite half as large, but anyway I was standing there getting the orders in and he said, "Could I ride home with you this afternoon?"

And I said, "Sure. You know, like I told you, you can go home with me any time you want to, like I say anytime you want to go see your wife that is all right with me."[37]

Good thing Mr. Frazier was so accommodating. Asking Thursday for a ride home, a ride that would make or break his plan to kill JFK Friday seems cutting it a bit close. *What happens if, for whatever reason (vacation, other plans, real or phony sick call off, etc.), Frazier turns him down?* And he'd have to bring that paper bag he made to hold and hide the rifle with him, yet the man who sits by the paper dispenser, Troy West, never leaves his desk, eats his lunch at his desk and testifies to not being away from that area.[38] Despite this, somehow Oswald allegedly accomplishes this construction project with no one seeing him do it.

In addition, Ruth Paine never sees Oswald in the garage, never hears him and even goes on to tell reporters: "I said I did not see how he could have taken the gun from the garage without my knowing it."[39]

As respected researcher Carol Hewett pointed out, evidently Ruth did not know that Marina said Lee was with her that night in her room and fell asleep. Yet somehow, he allegedly got into the garage, into the blanket, disassembled the rifle, placed it in the paper bag and made it ready for his leaving the following morning.

Ruth Paine testified to the Warren Commission that she did not see Oswald go into the garage (where the rifle was).[40]

37   2 H 222.
38   6 H 360.
39   https://kennedysandking.com/john-f-kennedy-articles/660.
40   3 H 67.

Marina Oswald testified to the Warren Commission:

> He then stopped talking and sat down and watched television and then went to bed. I went to bed later. It was about 9 o'clock when he went to sleep. I went to sleep about 11:30. But it seemed to me that he was not really asleep. But I didn't talk to him. In the morning he got up, said goodbye, and left, and that I shouldn't get up – as always, I did not get up to prepare breakfast. This was quite usual.[41]

So the entire household was awake at 9 pm when Oswald goes to sleep (or pretends to go to sleep in anticipation of going to the garage). Oswald was taking a real chance at being discovered if he somehow went to the garage at this time to get his rifle ready. Nothing adds up.

According to the official story, for the two months leading up the assassination, Oswald's rifle was wrapped in a blanket in Ruth Paine's garage. If he did not retrieve it on the morning of the assassination then he never did so because at no other time was he seen taking a package from the Paine home, at no time was any rifle seen at his rooming house, and at no other time did he take a package into the Book Depository. November 22 was his one and only opportunity. Which means that if the package he carried that morning did not contain the rifle – and the preponderance of evidence tells us it did not – then someone else placed it on the sixth floor of the depository building, and Oswald was exactly what he said he was: A patsy.[42]

In any event, Oswald vehemently denied shooting the president, saying:

> "I am just a patsy"; "I don't know what dispatches you people have been given but I emphatically deny these charges"; "I have committed no acts of violence"; "I didn't shoot anybody, no sir"; "they're taking me in because of the fact I lived in the Soviet Union"; "don't believe the so-called evidence"; etc.[43]

The CIA's George O'Toole examined the tapes of Oswald's denials using Psychological Stress Evaluators and indicated that Oswald was telling the truth.[44] As FBI Director J. Edgar Hoover said to LBJ the day after the assassination: "this man Oswald has still denied everything. He doesn't

---

41   1 H 66.
42   Thanks to brilliant writer/researcher Martin Hay for this insight.
43   ABC/NBC/CBS television footage available on several programs including *The Men Who Killed Kennedy.* Oswald, Robert L. with Myrick and Barbara Land. *Lee: A Portrait of Lee Harvey Oswald by His Brother.* New York: Coward-McCann, 1967; *They Killed Our President: 63 Reasons to Believe There Was A Conspiracy to Assassinate JFK* by Jesse Ventura (2013), pages 89-97; *Not In Your Lifetime* by Anthony Summers (2013), page115.
44   *The Assassination Tapes* by George O'Toole (1975), pages 120-129.

know anything about anything."[45] Larry Huff was a Marine who was involved in an investigation of Oswald conducted in Atsugi, Japan. He said
the result of the investigation was that Oswald could not have committed
the assassination.[46]

Besides the uniqueness of a rifle being used in the assassination (as
opposed to a pistol), Oswald is the first alleged political assassin to deny
his accused deed. A case can be made that he indeed shot Officer J.D.
Tippit,[47] yet an equally powerful case can be espoused that he did not.[48] If
Oswald did indeed shoot Tippit, it could very well have been self defense,
as Tippit may have been "the first Jack Ruby," so to speak: in on the conspiracy to kill Oswald, JFK, or both. The HSCA's Andy Purdy believed
that Tippit may have been in on a conspiracy to kill Oswald.[49]

Apart from the "standard" issues of the poor quality of Oswald's rifle, the lack of results on his cheek from the paraffin test, the evidence
of shots from the front, and so forth,[50] I do indeed believe Oswald's rifle
was fired from the sixth floor[51] ... but *Oswald* did not fire it. The rifle was
fired to point people towards Oswald's place of employment, in general,
and the window from the floor he worked on, to be specific. The conspirators wanted to frame Oswald, so of course the ballistics would match
up with his rifle. That is the "good news" for lone nut theorists. But, once
again: the bad news for them is that Oswald wasn't the perpetrator. The
real Book Depository sniper could have hidden on the roof on Thursday
night, 11/21/63, into the next day. He subsequently could have left the

---

45   *They Killed Our President: 63 Reasons to Believe There Was A Conspiracy to Assassinate JFK*
by Jesse Ventura (2013), page 164.
46   5/8/78 interview with the HSCA: https://www.archives.gov/files/research/jfk/releas-
es/2018/docid-32248464.pdf.
47   *With Malice: Lee Harvey Oswald and The Murder of Officer J.D. Tippit* by Dale Myers (2013
edition); see also *The JFK Assassination Debates: Lone Gunman versus Conspiracy* by Michael L. Kurtz
(2006), pages 122-126.
48   *Into the Nightmare* by Joseph McBride (2013); *They Killed Our President: 63 Reasons to
Believe There Was A Conspiracy to Assassinate JFK* by Jesse Ventura (2013), pages 129-135; *The Girl on
the Stairs* by Barry Ernest (2013), pages 83-87; http://harveyandlee.net/Tippit/Tippit.html.
49   KRON 1988: *JFK: An Unsolved Murder-* https://www.youtube.com/watch?v=bw7YPK-
3wSQA.
50   The rifle was ordered under the name "A. Hidell," yet when Oswald opened PO Box 2915
in October 1963, he listed "Lee H. Oswald" as the only person authorized to receive mail: 17 H 679.
U.S. Postal regulation no. 355.111 clearly states that "Mail addressed to a person at a PO Box who is
not authorized to receive mail shall be endorsed 'addressee unknown' and returned to sender." How
then could Oswald have received a rifle ordered in the name of A. Hidell? Incidentally, it will come
as no surprise to many to learn that, although the Post Office should have retained the signature
of the person picking up the rifle for four years, it was "missing" by the time the FBI began it's work.
Living in Texas, it would have been easy to obtain a firearm over the counter without leaving an
extensive paper trail. My thanks to researcher Martin Hay for this insight.
51   Although I concede there are cogent questions about the rifle: *The JFK Assassination* by
James DiEugenio (2018), pages 81-87.

building after the shooting either dressed as a policeman, wearing a suit and coming across like a Secret Service or FBI agent (or businessman or reporter), or even dressed like a regular employee. Keep in mind, the building was not even completely secured until 1:35 p.m., a little more than an hour after the assassination![52] At a time when police and reporters, and Lord knows who else, were swarming the building, even an amateur, let alone a professional assassin, would have had no trouble at all leaving the scene of the shooting.

Furthermore, the rifle was extremely difficult if not impossible to put together in its alleged broken down (by individual parts) condition in the allotted time (or any other time) Oswald had, either with a dime or a screwdriver, neither of which Oswald was shown to have on him.[53] In addition, according to Dr. Roger McCarthy of Failure Analysis (the company upon whose work lone-assassin author Gerald Posner's work is based), testifying in a mock trial of Oswald in 1992, testified that the Carcano could not be assembled with a dime, which was too thick to fit the necessary slots; he added that the Carcano is "a difficult assembly."[54]

More importantly, the weapon could not be fired if it was assembled from being in a broken down state from a bag because it had to be sighted in first![55] The weapon literally would not work if it was merely put together somehow, then used in the assassination. It had to already be in fully-assembled and sighted fashion, but this poses problems with official history: besides no one seeing Oswald carry a package that could have contained even a broken down rifle into the building, let alone one holding a complete rifle, there is no way the bag could have contained his rifle for the previously-stated reason regarding functionality. Despite Buell Wesley Frazier's sole and (now) disputed claim that Oswald said the package on the back seat of Frazier's car contained curtain rods (and which was, presumably, really Oswald's disassembled rifle),[56] again, there

---

52   22 H 470; 26 H 805; 7 H 348; 4 H 204-205; *Enemy of the Truth* by Sherry Fiester (2012), pages 6-8.

53   *No Case To Answer* by Ian Griggs (2005), pages 165-172 + 199-200; *Cold Case Kennedy* by Flip de Mey (2013), page 370.

54   "Trial of the Century," American Bar Association annual convention, August 10,1992.

55   *The Lee Harvey Oswald Files* by Flip De Mey (2016), pages 66-69, 76, 116.

56   There is a very recent movement on foot to dispute one of the "sacred cows" of the case: that Frazier can be believed about the whole curtain rods story. This was discussed by several authors/researchers at a 2019 JFK assassination conference. Also in this regard, Frazier is coming out with a book written with the help of lone-nut theorists Dave Perry and Gus Russo, certainly cause for alarm. Interestingly, former CIA agent and author George O'Toole wrote: "Could Frazier have been a conspirator, given the job of implicating Oswald in the assassination?" (*The Assassination Tapes* by George O'Toole, page 204; see also *High Treason* by Harrison Livingstone and Robert Groden, 1998 edition, page 250). Ruth Paine got Oswald a job at the Book Depository after a suggestion from Linnie Randle, Frazier's sister. Frazier's lifelong friend was John M. Crawford, a

is literally no way, apart from the issues of the length of the bag, that the package could have contained any rifle, disassembled or otherwise.[57]

This means Oswald's rifle was already in the book depository in fully assembled and sighted in fashion. This also means that Oswald didn't bring it that morning; someone else did. Or, if he did, the rifle was brought in another time and someone else fired the rifle. What was in the bag? Either his lunch, as he stated, or something else altogether. As stated earlier, it is also possible that the Oswald rifle bullets were actually fired with a technically better weapon through the use of sabots,[58] while the Carcano rifle itself lay stuffed between boxes to be later discovered by the police as intended by the framers of Oswald.

Think about it logically, too. Pretend you are Oswald: "I think I will go to the place I work, of all places (not a hidden area or a building unconnected to me) and use my own rifle, not an untraceable one, to kill the president. Even though my job location and rifle will help identify me as the perpetrator, I am going to escape, rather than give myself up and announce the politics (or other reasons) behind what I did. Then I am going to adamantly deny shooting him so no political reason or motive of any kind will ever be known or achieved." Fellow Book Depository employee James Jarman told the HSCA, when asked if a stranger could have walked into the depository building and made it to the sixth floor without being noticed:

> Very easily ... that day the dock door was up and the side door was open ... (A stranger could) "just walk inside the building, step on the elevator, pull the gate down and go on upstairs (emphasis added).[59]

Personally speaking, I know that, with the exception of very small companies that I have worked for in the past, every medium to large company I have ever been involved with have scores of people coming and going that I am unfamiliar with or, if I did see them, I would merely *assume* that they were an employee of some sort (temporary or permanent), were going on an interview, making a delivery, etc. In other words, I would *assume* they had some sort of legitimate reason to be there. I very

close friend of Jack Ruby: *High Treason* by Harrison Livingstone and Robert Groden, 1998 edition, page 250. Regarding the curtain rod story, former British detective Ian Griggs believed that "Lee Harvey Oswald did not utter the words "curtain rods" in any conversation he had with Frazier": The Paper Bag that Never Was!, Mary Ferrell Archives- https://drive.google.com/file/d/1vHTMl9G3DjtF-3CmyLqNz3C6UjRgOS8le/view.

57   *Ibid.*

58   A sabot is a metal shell that fits around a bullet so it can be fired by a different caliber rifle. *Cold Case Kennedy* by Flip de Mey (2013), pages 146-147, 365; *The Lee Harvey Oswald Files* by Flip de Mey (2016), page 74.

59   9-25-77 interview with HSCA investigators Al Maxwell and William Brown.

rarely, if ever, question the presence of fellow human beings at a place of business, naturally assuming they have a legitimate *reason* to be there (and this is largely in the post-9/11 world we live in today that I make this observation, coupled with my natural curiosity, let alone comparing today's heightened sense of alert with the tranquil pre-assassination days of the late 1950's-early 1960's when people's radars weren't up about anything in particular. Heck, people left their doors unlocked and picked up strangers to give them rides back then). When one also realizes that the Texas School Book Depository building had no security guards or night watchmen, one can see just how easy it would be to breach a building like that from a conspirator's point of view.

My point is this: all those floors of the book depository contained different companies and scores of employees who were concerned about their own job and their own concerns. If someone was not acting suspiciously, I doubt most people would give a so-called stranger (in this case, the real assassin and perhaps a comrade) – assuming someone truly perceived an individual as a *true stranger*, per se – even a second thought, especially on a distracting day like that involving *an often once-in-a-lifetime presidential parade coming right by their own company* (example: a potential stranger could be viewed as perhaps the friend of a worker there to watch the motorcade, especially if they were "dressed down" like a warehouse fellow, so to speak. If they wore a business suit, they could even be viewed as an office supervisor, a police detective or even a security person, as some who saw strangers that day from street level, like Arnold Rowland, or from another building, like John Powell, believed and assumed[60]). Furthermore, if one were to factor in Oswald as conspirator or even an unwitting aide to the eventual murderous conspiracy about to unfold, perhaps Oswald himself aided and abetted the real assassin in the building (and perhaps a comrade with the shooter, as well) with building logistics, where to go, where to hide, etc.

As for the so-called "sniper's nest," I believe this was put together by a combination of (surprise, surprise) Oswald himself, his fellow co-workers, and perhaps even the real assassin with a comrade, to boot, perhaps not even all at the same time (I will address the issue of Oswald's fingerprints coming up). There was a floor-laying crew of fellow employees working full time on the sixth floor the week of the assassination.[61] As even lone-nut author Jim Moore conceded: "...many of the boxes the as-

60   *Not In Your Lifetime* by Anthony Summers (2013), page 61.
61   *Accessories After the Fact* by Sylvia Meagher (1967), page 43.

sassin stacked for his shield might well have been in place or nearly placed, and thus required little or no effort on the part of the gunman."[62] In fact, Commission Exhibit 723, a police photograph of the area of the sixth floor window, demonstrated that the boxes were also stacked along the east wall, as well.[63]

I believe what was merely just an ordinary stack of cardboard book boxes morphed into a place to smoke, to eat, hide out from the bosses... and, yes, ultimately, to fire the Oswald rifle. I know I worked in a warehouse once where some of the workers constructed an informal hiding place of boxes so customers who came in didn't see them first, but would call on someone else that they saw right away instead (the perfect place for lazy, shy and re-luctant workers to hide from the public). Now, imagine if someone fired a gun from that location later on. It would forever after get labeled as a "snip-er's nest" by the media, when it actually wasn't one originally.

Oswald was not known to have practiced with the rifle, to have prac-ticed disassembling and re-assembling it (and sighting it in), or to have purchased bullets (and no extra bullets were ever found... so Oswald allegedly fired three with one unfired round left behind and that was it?). The palm print found on the rifle (assuming it wasn't placed there after-the-fact via Oswald's *dead* hand[64]) is meaningless: it was *his* rifle. Re-searchers and authors have spent decades in denial going on and on about claims that the rifle wasn't Oswald's, it was a lousy weapon, etc. Again, the rifle *had* to be his and had to have been fired from the window to frame him. When one accepts this, one can get over the mental block of what appears, at first glance, to be strong lone-nut theorist evidence (said in your best David Belin or Gerald Posner or Vince Bugliosi voice: "it was Oswald's rifle to the exclusion of all other weapons"; "the bullets are bal-listically proven to have come from Oswald's rifle to the exclusion of all other weapons"; "the palmprint is Oswald's"; and so forth).

Despite the rifle being his, if Oswald was where he said he was at the time of the assassination (the second floor lunchroom), I don't care if dozens of his fingerprints, DNA, individual hair fibers, and so forth are on or near the rifle: he didn't do it. That said, Oswald was no angel and his ostensible disinterest in viewing the presidential motorcade is alarming, for Oswald was a political

---

62   *Conspiracy of One* by Jim Moore (1990), pages 43-44.
63   *The Killing of a President* by Robert Groden (1993), page 64.
64   *Crossfire* DVD (2013) and *The Men Who Killed Kennedy* (1991): funeral director Paul Groody states that the FBI fingerprinted Oswald's dead hand and left ink on his hands that he had to clean off. The police and the feds already had plenty of Oswald's prints form that weekend and from Oswald's prior arrest in New Orleans- why on earth would they need yet another set from his dead hands?.

animal and even supposedly (and quite ironically) an actual admirer of JFK. Why wouldn't he want to view the motorcade, even out of curiosity? It was free to view and literally a few precious feet away during lunch time. Everyone else was-why wasn't he? Was he waiting for a call from his handler(s)? Was he aware that his rifle was going to be used, albeit by someone else, like someone letting a murderer use his car as a getaway vehicle or even the use of his own pistol (a possibility no one has ever contemplated)? It just doesn't wash that Oswald, of all people, decided to not watch the motorcade...but this does not make him an assassin, of course. There is a third alternative; nothing is black and white, especially when one sees other points of view.[65] (Interestingly, there are two little-known comments in the literature that are food for thought in this regard. On a footnote buried in the 1968 intelligence-connected book *Farewell America*, page 339, it is written that Oswald

...realize[d] that this was no simulated assassination but the real thing...

In addition, from Michael Benson's *Encyclopedia of the JFK Assassination*, page 231, based on the work of Hugh C. McDonald,[66] former chief of detectives, Los Angeles County Sheriff's Department, FBI academy graduate, military intelligence veteran, and Hughes Aircraft employee, it is written that

...Oswald had been told that he was to stage a fake assassination attempt to alert the government of the necessity for beefed-up Secret Service security.

Finally, the police paraffin test on Oswald's hands demonstrated that Oswald handled a gun (probably his pistol he had on him at the Texas Theater), but, importantly, did not test positive for his right cheek, demonstrating that he did not fire a rifle.[67] While the paraffin test is not

---

65   As researcher Pat Speer so eloquently put it: "If Oswald was clever enough to steal a large piece of paper from his work without being noticed, bring it home on his person without being noticed, wrap his rifle in this paper without being noticed, hide this package in the building without being noticed, sneak it up to the sixth floor without being noticed, put his rifle back together without being noticed, hit at least two shots on a moving target without any practice, and race back down to the second floor without being noticed, only to appear innocent and calm when confronted by a police officer, it makes little sense he'd be so un-clever as to use a rifle sent to his own PO box, under a fictitious name easily traceable to himself, and have an ID in this name on his person when captured. Something just doesn't add up. While the simplest answer is that Oswald acted alone and was a devious and unpredictable lunatic, simple answers are often fed to simpletons to stop them from asking not-so-simple questions." http://www.patspeer.com/chapter4e%3Acastsofcontention.

66   *Appointment In Dallas* by Hugh C. McDonald (Zebra Books, 1975). McDonald is also the author of *LBJ and the JFK Conspiracy* (Condor, 1978), as well as three instructional books about police work which are still standard texts in many police academies..

67   *Rendezvous With Death* by H.R. Underwood (2013), page 119.

full proof, it is a guarantee that, if his right cheek would have tested positive, the police and Warren Commission would have trumpeted this finding to the world. What's more, former FBI agent William Turner reported that he'd spoken to Dr. Vincent Guinn about tests performed by Guinn, and that Guinn had found nitrates in abundance on casts of the cheeks of men who'd fired rifles like the one owned by Oswald.[68] If that weren't enough, Guinn called the FBI in 1964 suggesting they conduct neutron activation tests. From the testimony of the FBI's John Gallagher – the last testimony taken by the Warren Commission – the FBI had indeed conducted neutron activation analysis on the paraffin cast of Oswald's cheek.[69] Author Harold Weisberg, through a Freedom of Information Act lawsuit, received the controls for this test and found that gunshot residue was always present on the cheeks of those firing a rifle like Oswald's.[70]

(As a very interesting aside, Luke Mooney was one of the first of several Deputies who bravely ran to the grassy knoll picket fence and jumped over it, literally seconds after the JFK limo sped away. After only "a few minutes" of searching in vain for snipers behind the picket fence, Deputy Mooney decided to go to the Texas School Book Depository, which was next door to the grassy knoll. Mooney says it was only "a few minutes" and then he entered the TSBD, and he saw "two Deputies coming down." The Warren Commission attorneys asked who they were, and Mooney replied that he didn't know. But they were in uniform, so they must have had business up there. Right? But nobody knows what.

This is food for thought for those who think evidence was planted or the real shooter or shooters were helped … or were these the shooters themselves?[71] In addition, we can discard the myth that Oswald was allegedly the "only" employee missing after the assassination: there was no building-wide roll call, as there were several companies within the building with multiple employees of their own, many of whom did not return to work due to the assassination, including Charles Givens, Danny Arce and Bonnie Ray Williams.[72]). Not long after Oswald departed from the scene, Shelley told Truly that Oswald was missing and was also one of the building employees who identified Oswald for the police when he was brought into the station.[73] Yes- Bill Shelley once again.

68   *Reclaiming History* by Vincent Bugliosi (2007), CD-ROM endnotes, page 79.
69   Gerald McKnight, *Breach of Trust* (2005), page 211.
70   Harold Weisberg, *Post Mortem* (1975), page 437.
71   3 H 283-284.
72   *Hidden History* by Donald Jeffries (2014), page 353; 3H 183; Jim Marrs, *Crossfire*, page 314, citing reporter Kent Biffle.
73   Shelley affidavit, 24H226; *The Third Decade* journal May 1986.

Oswald's escape was leisurely and done in front of witnesses, a few of whom knew (of) him; certainly not the frantic actions of a highly nervous and pumped up presidential killer. According to one of the FBI reports of the first interrogation of Oswald in the Dallas homicide office:

> "OSWALD stated that he took this Coke down to the first floor and stood around and had lunch in the employees' lunch room. He thereafter went outside and stood around for five or ten minutes with foreman BILL SHELLEY, and thereafter went home. He stated that he left work because, in his opinion, based upon remarks of BILL SHELLEY, he did not believe that there was going to be any more work that day due to the confusion in the building."[74]

Oswald calmly sauntered slowly out the front, not the back, of his building, even letting a newsman, whom he thought was *a Secret Service agent*, know where a payphone could be located. He then boards a bus, then a taxi, offering to give up his seat and, thus, his turn for an elderly woman. Precious escape time, even just on foot, was wasted (in fact, Oswald probably would have been better off briskly walking away from the building, let alone jogging or running, if he was truly making an escape, per se). Keeping all this into focus, Roger Craig, Helen Forrest and James Pennington saw a man who looked remarkably like Oswald (possibly the *real* sixth floor assassin?) "suddenly run from the rear of the Depository building, down the incline (by the grassy knoll), and then enter a Rambler station wagon."[75]

As Helen Forrest said, "If it wasn't Oswald, it was his identical twin," while Roger Craig was adamant: "It *was* Oswald."[76] The three witnesses story of the Rambler grassy knoll pick-up was supported by passing drivers Marvin C. Robinson and Roy Cooper.[77] The Rambler sped off in the direction of the Oak Cliff section of Dallas[78] where officer J.D. Tippit was to meet his fate, allegedly at the hands of Oswald, assuming it was the real Oswald or the lookalike in question (or someone else entirely).

On the other hand, the real and official Oswald had the taxi driver drive past his rooming house, not directly in front of it, as if he was scoping out

---

74   FBI report of Oswald at the police station, Warren Report, page 619.
75   http://harveyandlee.net/Leaving/Leaving_the_TSBD.html.
76   *JFK and the Unspeakable* by James Douglass (2010), page 277-278 + 288-289; *The Girl on the Stairs* by Barry Ernest (2013), page 125; 23 H 817:11/22/63 FBI report – interview of Roger Craig; 24 H 23: 11/25/63 FBI report – second interview of Roger Craig; 24 H 765: transcript of Chief Curry's comments on WFAA/ ABC for 11/23/63 re: Craig's 'negro in a car'.
77   *The Deputy Interviews: The True Story of J.F.K. Assassination Witness, and Former Dallas Deputy Sheriff, Roger Dean Craig* by Steve Cameron, 2019, pages 195-199.
78   *JFK and the Unspeakable* by James Douglass (2010), page 277-278 + 288-289.

the place to see if the authorities were on to him; not the actions of an innocent man but, again, not necessarily a presidential murderer, either… perhaps a patsy, as he said he was. Interestingly, during the brief time Oswald was back at his rooming house, according to Oswald's landlady Earlene Roberts, a police officer stopped his car out front and honked the horn a couple times, then drove off, as if this was a signal.[79]

The murder of police officer J.D. Tippit is definitely a case of "there is more than meets the eye": I agree with the HSCA's Andy Purdy that it could very well be that Tippit was in on a conspiracy to silence Oswald ("the first Jack Ruby," so to speak) and Oswald, out of fear, a sense of betrayal, anger and panic killed Tippit "with malice aforethought" in that moment, so to speak (he was angered that his friend and comrade in arms was going to kill him). At that point, if Oswald was murdered without any evidence of his denials and so forth, the lone nut case would truly have been wrapped up in a super convenient, hard to deny bow.

Oswald's action going to and moving inside the theater appear to be ones of both panic and/or even seeking out a contact, as Oswald was sitting beside seemingly random people, as opposed to making himself as inconspicuous as possible, especially under the circumstances. On the one hand, he allegedly tried to fire his pistol and shouted "this is it," yet he also said "I am not resisting arrest" and a cop shouted "kill the president, will you" at a time the officers should not have suspected he was anything more than "just" a cop killer.

Once in custody, Oswald has *one wallet too many* with identifications for both himself and Alex Hidell, conveniently the fake name used to order the rifle and pistol.[80]

> We have up here the tape and the photograph of the man who was at the Soviet embassy, using Oswald's name. That picture and the tape do not correspond to this man's voice, or to his appearance. In other words, it appears that there is a second person who was at the Soviet embassy down there.
> – FBI Director J. Edgar Hoover to President Johnson 11/23/63

So who *was* Oswald? While he certainly was no James Bond or CIA official, I believe he was a low-level intelligence agent or informant of some sort,[81]

79   *The Girl on the Stairs* by Barry Ernest (2013), pages 76-77; 25 H 171: Earlene Roberts re: police car blowing horn.
80   *The Lee Harvey Oswald Files* by Flip De Mey (2016), pages 161-167; *The Deputy Interviews: The True Story of J.F.K. Assassination Witness, and Former Dallas Deputy Sheriff, Roger Dean Craig* by Steve Cameron, 2019, pages 168-170.
81   CIA finance officer James Wilcott testified to the HSCA on 3/22/78 that Oswald served

[82] used as a pawn or patsy, first in ways to make Castro's Cuba look bad (and, to a lesser extent, Russia), then as a tool in the assassination conspiracy.[83] It could very well be that Oswald got wind of an impending assassination and infiltrated this group (and even attempted to stop it), only to find himself left holding the bag, so to speak[84]. He certainly had the overt appearance of a political "nut": he was a former Marine who defected to Russia,[85] thus earning an Undesirable Discharge. He was poor to lower middle class with a Russian wife. He was part of a Fair Play for Cuba organization and demonstrated on their behalf. He went on New Orleans radio and television espousing himself to be a Marxist but not a Communist, a distinction that was too subtle for the average person to decipher or care about; a "red" was a "red."

Other items to consider regarding Oswald[86]:

- Oswald owned a Minox camera which was used almost exclusively for spy work;

- Oswald referred to "microdots" in his notes, a spy term not commonly known to people at the time. In fact, the NSA looked into this matter, as the newly-released files confirm[87];

- the extreme ease and speed with which Oswald left the US and entered Russia, then came back later with a Russian bride (that the FBI suspected was a KGB honey trap[88]) and baby;

---

the CIA specifically as a double agent in the Soviet Union who afterward came under suspicion by the agency. *Oakland Tribune*, 9/18/78; *JFK and the Unspeakable* by James Douglass (2010), page 146; *Not In Your Lifetime* by Anthony Summers (2013), page 509; from the newly-released files: https://www.archives.gov/files/research/jfk/releases/2018/104-10067-10372.pdf.

82   From the newly-released files- funny business going on around 1976 with Oswald's CIA files: https://www.archives.gov/files/research/jfk/releases/2018/104-10132-10293.pdf.

83   From the newly-released files- Oswald asked Carlos Bringuier if he was Cosa Notra (Mafia): https://www.archives.gov/files/research/jfk/releases/2018/docid-32261439.pdf.

84   Footnote buried in the 1968 book, *Farewell America*, page 339: Oswald " ... realize[d] that this was no simulated assassination but the real thing ... " Also, from *Encyclopedia of the JFK Assassination*, page 231: Based on the work of Hugh C. McDonald, former chief of detectives, Los Angeles County Sheriff's Department, FBI academy graduate, military intelligence veteran, and Hughes Aircraft employee: " ... Oswald had been told that he was to stage a fake assassination attempt to alert the government of the necessity for beefed-up Secret Service security." *Appointment In Dallas* by Hugh C. McDonald (Zebra Books, 1975). McDonald is also the author of *LBJ and the JFK Conspiracy* (Condor, 1978), as well as three instructional books about police work which are still standard texts in many police academies.

85   In early 1962, an agent from the U.S. Department of Immigration and Naturalization called on Oswald's brother Robert. Robert said that the agent "advised me he assumed that Lee was employed by the Government in some capacity in Russia." 1 H 429.

86   *Bloody Treason* by Noel Twyman (1997), pages 328-329, 340-341; *Not In Your Lifetime* by Anthony Summers (2013), numerous.

87   https://www.archives.gov/files/research/jfk/releases/2018/144-10001-10057_docid_6606009_binary_sealed.pdf.

88   *SMOKING GUNS IN THE NEW JFK ASSASSINATION FILES - Volumes I and II: UPDATED! There Are Over 306 Major Smoking Guns In The JFK Assassination Files That Prove Conspiracy* by Ralph Thomas (2018)

• the ease with which Oswald obtained a passport to Mexico City and the CIA-connected person, William Gaudet, who was on the list (#824084) right before Oswald (#824085) and who was also Mexico bound, knew about Oswald in New Orleans and knew about Guy Banister and David Ferrie and their interactions with Oswald. Gaudet also said that Sergio Arcacha Smith was a person of interest[89];

• Oswald's one-man "Fair Play For Cuba Committee" headquarters in New Orleans was located at the decidedly anti-communist housing of former ONI and FBI Agent Guy Banister's operations at 544 Camp Street. This building stood in the heart of the intelligence community – the ONI, the FBI, the CIA, and the Secret Service[90];

• Oswald's relationship to the intelligence-connected George de Mohrenschildt (who was also friends with the CIA's J. Walter Moore[91]) and the Paines;

• despite Oswald's knowledge of the U-2 spy plane flights over Russia and his defection to the Soviet Union (probably as part of a false defector program[92]), the CIA denies that Oswald was debriefed, which we now know was a lie.[93] As CIA Mexico City Station Chief Winston Scott stated: "we kept a special watch on [Oswald] ... he was of great interest to us."[94];

• Oswald's proficiency with the very difficult Russian language;

• Oswald receiving Communist literature and espousing the virtues of Russia and Cuba during his stint in the Marines, at the height of the cold war and the immediate post-McCarthy era, even earning the dubious nickname of "Oswaldskovitch," when anyone else would have been beaten to a pulp, investigated, or worse;

• Oswald's employment at Jaggers-Chiles-Stovall, Inc, in Dallas, a private contractor that did top-secret photographic work for the U.S. government. A fellow employee of Oswald at this firm, Dennis Ofstein, believed Oswald worked for the U.S. government[95];

• Oswald's employment at the Reilly Coffee Company, a center of right-wing anti-Castro activities with connections to intelligence

---

89   *Not In Your Lifetime* by Anthony Summers (2013), pages 307-310; 5/13/75 interview report with Bernard Fensterwald: https://www.archives.gov/files/research/jfk/releases/180-10112-10390.pdf.
90   Numerous sources including *Not In Your Lifetime, Crossfire*, and even the film *JFK*.
91   9 H 235.
92   From the newly-released files- false defector program code named US Defector Machine Program: https://www.archives.gov/files/research/jfk/releases/2018/104-10009-10026.pdf.
93   *Oswald and the CIA* by John Newman (1995); *Frontline: Who Was Lee Harvey Oswald* (1993); *Not In Your Lifetime* by Anthony Summers (2013), pages 177-178.
94   *Not In Your Lifetime* by Anthony Summers (2013), page 341.
95   *J. Edgar Hoover: The Father of the Cold War* by R. Andrew Kiel (2000), pages 150-151.

agencies. An inordinate amount of people who left the company at that time wound up at NASA and government defense contractors[96];

• Oswald was seen frequenting the Crescent City Garage, an establishment well known to the Secret Service: their official cars were stored there. Adrian Alba, owner of the garage, was also known to the agency. Both Alba and Oswald spent a great deal of time perusing Alba's gun magazines. The rifle traced to Oswald came from one of the coupons Oswald allegedly cut out from one of Alba's gun magazines, as "discovered" by the Secret Service, who confiscated the original magazine from Alba's garage, beating the FBI to the punch.[97]

Alba told the House Assassinations Committee that Oswald made contact with an "agent from Washington" within a short distance from his Crescent City Garage.[98] The agent in question had previously obtained a green Studebaker automobile from Alba. The record shows that the Studebaker was signed out by a Secret Service agent.[99] Oswald met this agent at least twice, according to Alba, one time even receiving a "good-sized envelope" which Oswald hid in his shirt on his way back to work[100];

• The anti-Castro group Oswald had been in contact with during the Summer of 1963 in New Orleans, the DRE, had been funded by the CIA and their code name was AMSPELL[101];

• Oswald's meeting in September 1963 with CIA officer David Atlee Phillips, aka Maurice Bishop, as confirmed by Alpha 66 leader Antonio Veciana, who was also involved with Bishop in assassination plots against Castro[102];

• Ruth Paine stated that Oswald went to Houston to see an unidentified friend on September 26, 1963, the same day that the White House officially announced JFK's trip to Dallas for the fall.[103];

• The ARRB's Doug Horne noted in a memo dated 4/16/96: "It is interesting to note that three events – Oswald's departure from New

96	https://aarclibrary.org/the-jfk-case-the-twelve-who-built-the-oswald-legend-part-9-oswald-takes-center-stage-as-an-intelligence-asset/.
97	26 H 764; 10 H 220; 23 H 728.
98	As reported in *Crossfire* by Jim Marrs (1989), page 229.
99	*Crossfire* by Jim Marrs (1989), page 230.
100	*Crossfire* by Jim Marrs (1989), page 229.
101	From the newly-released files: https://www.archives.gov/files/research/jfk/releases/2018/104-10181-10113.pdf.
102	From the newly-released files: https://www.archives.gov/files/research/jfk/releases/2018/180-10144-10292.pdf.
103	23 H 409; 3 H 10; WR 651; *Time*, 12/6/63; p. 33A *Dallas Morning News* dated September 26, 1963 states (reporting from Jackson Hole, Wyoming): "White House sources told the *Dallas Morning News* exclusively Wednesday night that President Kennedy will visit Texas Nov. 21 and 22 … The final White House decision to make the trip to Texas came late Tuesday night, these sources said … it was considered likely that the President will visit Dallas, Houston, San Antonio, and Fort Worth."

Orleans on or about 24/25 September (September 23 is the last full day he can be firmly placed there by eyewitnesses, but there are some indications he may not have left until September 24 or 25), the "Leon Oswald"-Angel-Leopoldo visit to Sylvia Odio in Dallas on 26 or 27 September, and the Oswald visits to the Cuban Embassy in Mexico City on September 27 – all occur immediately after unnamed White House sources report to the press that on September 24, 1963 a final decision was made to visit Texas on a 2-day trip scheduled for Nov. 21-22, 1963 ... the Secret Service Protective Survey Reports ... which were destroyed in 1995 commence with trip files starting on this same date: September 24, 1963.";

• *New/ignored evidence*: Speaking of that same date once again, 9/27/63, Oswald was seen in Washington, D.C. on 9/27/63, as reported by none other than – get this – the number two man on Kennedy's White House Detail, Floyd Boring, one of my three suspects from the Secret Service and the planner of the Texas trip from the agency's point of view![104] Here is the three-page document:

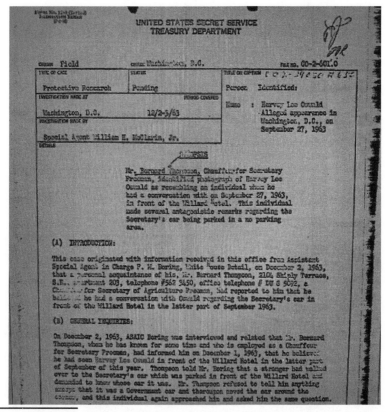

104   Commission Document (CD) 320 – Secret Service Rowley Memorandum of 1/24/64. See also *Who's Who in the Secret Service* by Vince Palamara (2018), pages 276-280

234

CO-2-601.0
Page 2

Mr. Boring said that Mr. Thompson was quite concerned about this matter at the time because he did not believe this individual was acting in a usual manner and that this matter had been preying on his mind for some time; that when the pictures of Oswald appeared in the paper after the President's assassination, Mr. Thompson thought that he recognized Oswald as being this same individual. Mr. Boring stated that Mr. Thompson is not a crank and that he has a sincere desire to give information which he believes to be of value in our investigation.

On December 3, 1963, a photograph of Harvey Lee Oswald was obtained from the Protective Research Section. The following known aliases of Harvey Lee Oswald were also obtained at that time: O. H. Lee, A. J. Hidell, Alek J. Hidell, Alex James Hidell, A. Haidell.

On December 3, 1963, Mr. Thompson was interviewed in the Washington field office. He stated that in the latter part of September, around the 25th of the month, at about 3:10 P.M., he arrived at the north entrance of the Willard Hotel which would be the corner of 14th & F Streets; that he parked in the no parking zone in front of the hotel entrance, as he was expecting Mrs. Freeman to come out of the hotel where she was attending a function; that an individual whom he did not know came out of the hotel entrance, walked directly to his car and demanded to know "Whose car is this." Mr. Thompson said that he replied that it was a Government car. Mr. Thompson said that this individual then said to him, "This must be some big official's car. This is a no parking zone. You have no right to park here." Mr. Thompson said that this man did not say this in a conversational type of tone, or a friendly tone in any sense, but that he appeared to be highly antagonistic and Mr. Thompson classified him as the "rabel rouser type." Mr. Thompson then said that rather than to get in an argument with this man, he drove slowly around the block again returning to the F Street side, but rather than parking directly in front of the hotel entrance, he parked nearer to 15th Street. The same individual who had accosted him before spotted the car, walked down the sidewalk from in front of the hotel entrance and stood opposite the car, staring at Mr. Thompson; that Mr. Thompson became concerned as he did not think this was normal behavior. He noticed that a White House car was parked directly in front of him and he thereupon spoke with the driver whose first name he recalls as George, and told him of the actions of this individual. He requested the White House driver to take a good look at this man and keep his eye on him while he, Mr. Thompson, went over and spoke with the policeman at the 14th Street inter-

CO-2-601.0
Page 3

section about this man. Mr. Thompson said that he spoke with this officer and advised what this individual had done and also requested permission from the officer to park in the entrance of the hotel while waiting for Mrs. Freeman. He said that the officer told him it was alright to park there while waiting for Mrs. Freeman and also that the officer walked with him down the sidewalk and took a good look at the man, however, the police officer did not stop and question the individual, but merely walked on down the sidewalk.

Mr. Thompson said that he was concerned about this incident and when he returned to the Agriculture Department, he informed his supervisor about it and also Mr. Thomas Hughes, the Secretary's Executive Officer.

At this point, Mr. Thompson examined a spread of photographs containing one of Oswald. After examining each photograph, he picked the photograph of Oswald as most resembling the individual involved in the incident described above. Mr. Thompson described the individual whom he saw as a white American male, early 20's, 5'7" tall, 130-135 lbs., slender build, dark hair, combed straight back with a slight wave, wearing a sport shirt and light colored trousers with narrow cuffs.

Mr. Thompson said that the only picture he really has looked at since the President's assassination, was a picture in the newspaper taken at the time Oswald was shot by Ruby in the Dallas Police Station, and that he felt that Oswald very closely resembled the individual described in the incident above.

On the same date, while Mr. Thompson was in the office, he telephonically contacted Mr. Thomas Hughes, Executive Officer to Secretary Freeman, in an effort to establish the date on which the foregoing incident occurred. Mr. Hughes checked Mrs. Freeman's social calendar and determined that the date was September 27, 1963.

On this same date, I spoke with Inspector Thacker in the Protective Research Section, in an effort to determine whether or not Oswald's movements and whereabouts on September 27 were known. Inspector Thacker informed me that Oswald's movements between September 23 and October 4, 1963, were still not definitely established. He advised me that new information on his whereabouts during this period was arriving, and that perhaps he would shortly be able to furnish information as to Oswald's whereabouts on September 27, 1963.

As researcher Deb Galentine wrote to the author:

> Oswald supposedly arrived in Mexico City on 9/27/63. But this report has him in Washington DC on that date. Ruth Paine had recently returned to New Orleans shortly before this date from the Washington DC area. She had incorporated a visit to CIA head-quarters while in the D.C. area in order to "see her sister." I have doubts about Ruth traveling alone on her road trip with two small children. I suspect she took her husband along. So it may be possible that Michael Paine stayed behind in the area. Someone in the D.C./PA/Baltimore area was impersonating Oswald in several places during that time frame."

Researcher Carolina Lynn also weighed in on the matter:

> This is intriguing on many levels. First, the witness is a chauffeur for Secretary of Agriculture Orville Freeman, a seemingly very credible witness. The driver spoke to a D.C. policeman about the demeanor of the "Oswald" look-alike he encountered. [Sadly, the report says the policeman did not interview or ID "Oswald"]. Second, the report throughout refers to the "suspect" as Harvey Lee Oswald," a switching of the name that author John Armstrong believes is government code to indicate the Russian-native doppelganger of the New Orleans-born Lee Harvey Oswald … "Lee Harvey Oswald" had by the date of this report, Dec. 2, 1963, become the most notorious name in U.S. history, repeated over and over on TV and radio and in newspapers. So it is hard to believe the name reversal could be "accidental." Third, *The Warren Omission Report* is adamant that "Oswald" was in Mexico City on September 27, 1963, the verified date of the DC incident, so this person was not the same "Oswald" in Mexico!

• Names of military intelligence personnel in Oswald's notebook, as well as FBI agent James Hosty[105];

• The ammunition used in Oswald's rifle from Western Cartridge Company may have a CIA connection[106];

• Oswald's name not being on the FBI index of dangerous persons or in the Secret Service's Protective Research Section (PRS) files;

• The Warren Commission's J. Lee Rankin to Treasury Secretary C. Douglas Dillon: "Have you made any inquiry into the Secret Service to

---

105   Kennedys And King - Oswald's Intelligence Connections: How Richard Schweiker clash-es with Fake History.
106   From the newly-released files: https://www.archives.gov/files/research/jfk/releas-es/2018/104-10147-10329.pdf.

determine whether or not Lee Harvey Oswald was ever an agent of that Service?" Dillon: "Yes. I heard rumors of this type of thing very early, and I asked the direct question of Chief Rowley and was informed that he never had any connection with the Secret Service."[107]

Dillon "heard rumors"?

From the new file releases (KUBARK=CIA):

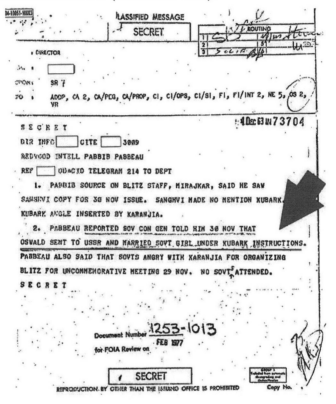

Oswald was certainly in the intelligence-connected David Ferrie/Guy Banister/Clay Shaw nexus.[108] [109] That said, there had to be more than

107   5 H 585. Interestingly, on 11/24/63, right after Ruby shot Oswald in the basement of the Dallas Police station, CBS newsman Robert Huffaker made a bizarre comment: "Everyone thought [Ruby] was a Secret Service agent."
108   See the books *Destiny Betrayed and The JFK Assassination* by James DiEugenio. See also *Not In Your Lifetime* by Anthony Summers (2013), pages 267-294. For the famous photo of Ferrie and Oswald together at a Civil Air Patrol gathering in New Orleans in 1955, see, for example, Robert Groden's 2013 book *JFK: Absolute Proof*, page 2, or *Not In Your Lifetime* by Anthony Summers (2013), page 460. A document from the newly-released files links Oswald, Ferrie and Shaw via a Civil Air Patrol address at the International Trade Mart: *JFK Beyond A Question Of Conspiracy: An Investigation And Revision Of History - Including New 2018 Material*. By Ralph Thomas (2018); Clay Shaw had a CIA 201 file, according to the newly-released files: https://www.archives.gov/files/research/jfk/releases/2018/104-10181-10110.pdf.
109   From the newly-released files-a CIA document in relation to Clay Shaw shows his association to an investigation of PERMINDEX: https://www.archives.gov/files/research/jfk/releases/2018/104-10181-10116.pdf.

"just" those local operators on the ground. I believe, as I stated in Chapter Five, that Allen Dulles, former CIA Director fired by Kennedy over the Bay of Pigs fiasco (and later part of the Warren Commission, so active some said it should have been called the Dulles Commission[110]); Charles Cabell (Deputy Director of the CIA also fired by JFK and whose brother was the equally CIA-connected[111] Mayor of Dallas); David Atlee Phillips (whom Antonio Veciana has confirmed was Maurice Bishop and who visited Oswald in Dallas in September 1963[112]); Cord Meyer (CIA)[113]; William Harvey (CIA)[114]; David Morales (CIA)[115]; James Angleton (CIA and whose office much of the intense scrutiny and coverage of Oswald emanated from[116]); and E. Howard Hunt (also CIA, later of Watergate infamy) probably played a role.[117] Oswald's direct (other) handlers in Dallas were probably Ruth Paine (whom Oswald's brother Robert did not like and suspected of being involved in the assassination),[118] Michael Paine, and George de Mohrenschildt,[119] all CIA/intelligence connected. In fact, Ruth, who had an incredible connection to Dulles and his mistress Mary Bancroft,[120] got Oswald the job at the book depository, Michael could have passed for an Oswald double, and George, who himself had an amazing connection to both George H.W.

---

110   *The Warren Omission* by Walt Brown (1996).

111   In a recent discovery, it turns out Dallas Mayor Earle Cabell was a CIA asset! Best-selling author David Talbot wrote: "What a cozy setup the CIA had in Dallas in 1963. Mayor Earle Cabell was not only the brother of Charles Cabell, the former CIA deputy chief who, along with his boss Allen Dulles, was fired by JFK. Now we learn that the Dallas mayor was also a CIA asset! This is part of a pattern: the Texas School Book Depository where Oswald supposedly fired from his sniper's nest was owned by right-wing oilman D.H. Byrd, who also had deep national security connections; the press corps covering the Kennedy motorcade was riddled with CIA assets." https://whowhatwhy. org/2017/08/02/dallas-mayor-jfk-assassination-cia-asset/.

112   *Trained to Kill by Antonio Veciana* (2017), pages 187-192; *Bond of Secrecy* by Saint John Hunt (2012), page 119-122, 143.

113   *The Devil's Chessboard* by David Talbot (2015), pages 504-505; *Bond of Secrecy* by Saint John Hunt (2012), pages 115-118, 131, 133, 140.

114   *The Devil's Chessboard* by David Talbot (2015), pages 468-478, 500-505, 507-509; *Bond of Secrecy* by Saint John Hunt (2012), page xxii.

115   *The Devil's Chessboard* by David Talbot (2015), pages 500-501, 503-504, 509; *Bond of Secrecy* by Saint John Hunt (2012), pages 131, 133-136, 140.

116   *The Devil's Chessboard* by David Talbot (2015), pages 542-543; *Oswald and the CIA* by John Newman (1995); https://kennedysandking.com/john-f-kennedy-articles/375 ; https://kennedysandking.com/john-f-kennedy-articles/361.

117   *The Devil's Chessboard* by David Talbot (2015); *Bond of Secrecy* by Saint John Hunt (2012); *Mary's Mosaic* by Peter Janney (2016); *The Lee Harvey Oswald Files* by Flip de Mey (2016); *They Killed Our President: 63 Reasons to Believe There Was A Conspiracy to Assassinate JFK* by Jesse Ventura (2013), page 288; *Brothers* by David Talbot (2007), pages 402-406.

118   1 H 346, 420.

119   *The Devil's Chessboard* by David Talbot (2015), pages 520-535, 543; *Not In Your Lifetime* by Anthony Summers (2013), pages 178-198.

120   *The Devil's Chessboard* by David Talbot (2015), pages 536-539, 543-545.

Bush and Jackie Kennedy,[121] was obviously "sheep dipping" Oswald.[122] As CIA agent David Morales said:

Well, we took care of that son-of-a-bitch, didn't we?[123]

An Army Intelligence investigation report dated 8/7/70, using Roy Hargraves and Gerald Patrick Hemming as sources, revealed that Lorenzo Hall and Lawrence Howard met with Oswald en route to Florida before the assassination and that the murder of JFK had been a plot involving elements of the CIA.[124] I spoke to Hemming in 1992 and I found him to be a credible source.

CIA agent Gary Underhill stated on 11/23/63 that

Oswald was a patsy. They set him up. It's too much. The bastards have done something outrageous. They've killed the President! I've been listening and hearing things. I couldn't believe they'd get away with it, but they did.[125]

As author John Armstrong expertly summarizes:

James B. Wilcott was a CIA accountant who disbursed CIA station funds in Tokyo, Japan. His duties routinely brought him in contact with all station people, and in particular with operational agents. On many occasions he had conversations with CIA personnel concerning Lee Harvey Oswald's employment as a CIA agent. Wilcott swore in a secret session of the House Select Committee on Assassinations that money he himself had disbursed was for "Oswald" or for the "Oswald project." He knew several other CIA employees who knew about the "Oswald project" and knew that Lee Harvey Oswald was paid by the CIA. Wilcott told the HSCA on 3/22/78 that Oswald was recruited by the CIA for the express purpose of a double agent assignment in the USSR. Wilcott said there was "very heavy talk" from November 22 through January, 1964 about Oswald's connection to the CIA. He also told a Garrison investigator that it was from these conversations that he learned that the "project" (assassination of JFK) may have been under the direction of Allen Dulles and Richard Bissell. It was done, he said, in

---

121   *The Devil's Chessboard* by David Talbot (2015), pages 530, 532-533.
122   *The JFK Assassination* by James DiEugenio (2018); *The Devil's Chessboard* by David Talbot (2015), pages 520-535.
123   *They Killed Our President: 63 Reasons to Believe There Was A Conspiracy to Assassinate JFK* by Jesse Ventura (2013), page 262.
124   http://documents.theblackvault.com/documents/jfk/NARA-Oct2017/2018/104-10518-10322.pdf.
125   *Destiny Betrayed* by James DiEugenio (2012), page 99.

retaliation for Kennedy reneging on a secret agreement with Dulles to support the invasion of Cuba. Elaborate preparations had been made to firmly put the blame on Castro, and an immediate attack on Cuba would follow the assassination. After Oswald (HARVEY) was killed by Jack Ruby, Wilcott discussed this with a close circle of friends. They had no doubt that Oswald had been a "patsy" and that former gun-runner and "cut-out" Jack Ruby was instructed by the CIA to kill Oswald."[126]

Explosive excerpts from James Wilcott's affidavit and interrogation by the HSCA, declassified by the ARRB:

THE ASSASSINATION SCENARIO

CIA people killed Kennedy. Either it was an outright project of Headquarters with the approval of McCone or it was done outside, perhaps under the direction of Dulles and Bissell. It was done in retaliation to Kennedy's renegging on a secret agreement with Dulles to support the invasion of Cuba. The other political factors previously mentioned were also issues, but the breaking of the secret agreement was the principal point. It was believed that unless Cuba was seized by military force all of Latin America would eventually go communist and the US would fall to the communists soon after. Elaborate preparations had been made to firmly put the blame on Castro, and an immediate attack on Cuba would follow. But something had gone wrong. The attack was called off at the last moment.

THE KENNEDY ASSASSINATION

000008

The Kennedy assassination came as no great shock to most of the people at Tokyo Station in Japan, a class A Station of the CIA. It seemed a logical culmination of the steadily building anguish and discontent over the Bay of Pigs fiasco and Commie sell out of the Kennedy Administration; that was the prevailing sentiment. This was particularly true of the higher echelon operational people. The branch chiefs and deputy chiefs, project intelligence officers and operational specialists viewed Kennedy as a threat to the clandestine services. The loss of special privileges, allowances, status and early retirement that come with the CIA cloak and dagger job were becoming a possibility, even a probability. The prestigeous positions of the bureaucratic dominions, ambitiously sought, might be no more. Adjustment to a less glamorous job in a common profession could be the result.

---

126   http://harveyandlee.net/Wilcott/Wilcott.htm.

CIA Agent Donald Norton said,

> Oswald was with the CIA, and if he did it then you better believe the whole CIA was involved,[127]

While former CIA agent Joseph Newbrough said,

> Oswald was an agent for the CIA and acting under orders.

CIA employee Donald Deneslya read reports of a CIA agent who had worked at a radio factory in Minsk and returned to the US with a Russian wife and child – that agent could only have been Oswald.[128]

To summarize: *local Dallas handlers of Oswald-* Ruth Paine, Michael Paine,[129] and George de Mohrenschildt; *local New Orleans handlers of Oswald-* David Ferrie, Guy Banister, and Clay Shaw; *actual plotters* (or men with foreknowledge before the fact or knowledge after the fact), all ex or then-current CIA, who also held power over the local Dallas and New Orleans handlers: Allen Dulles, Charles Cabell, Cord Meyer, David Atlee Phillips, David Sanchez Morales, James Angleton, William Harvey, and E. Howard Hunt.

Regarding Clay Shaw, at the 2013 Wecht Symposium, author Joan Mellen presented a newly discovered internal CIA document which states in black and white that

> Clay Shaw was a highly paid CIA contract source until 1956.

His relationship with the Agency clearly extended for quite some time past 1956, however, as other documents show that he retained a covert security clearance until at least March 16, 1967.

As Oswald's former landlady, Jesse Garner, told the HSCA, David Ferrie turned up at her house the evening of 11/22/63 asking about Oswald's library card. Apparently, Jack Martin had circulated the story that Ferrie's card had been found amongst Oswald's possessions after his arrest and Ferrie was worried that it might be true. When Garner refused to talk to him, Ferrie visited her neighbour, Doris Eames, asking if she "had any information regarding Oswald's library card."[130]

The FBI knew about Ferrie and his association with Lee Harvey Oswald through the Civil Air Patrol (CAP) on 11/22/63- document discovered by British researchers Malcolm Blunt and Bart Kamp in 2019:

---

127   See also http://harveyandlee.net/Norton/Norton.html.
128   http://harveyandlee.net/Wilcott/Wilcott.htm.
129   https://kennedysandking.com/john-f-kennedy-articles/330.
130   10HSCA113-114.

UNITED STATES GOVERNMENT

Memorandum

TO : SAC, NEW ORLEANS (89-69)

FROM : ASAC J. T. SYLVESTER, JR.

DATE: 11/25/63

SUBJECT: ASSASSINATION OF PRESIDENT
JOHN F. KENNEDY, 11/22/63,
DALLAS, TEXAS

Re: DAVID WILLIAM FERRIE

P. J. TROSCLAIR, Intelligence Unit, at 8:32 p.m., 11/22/63 telephonically contacted ASAC J. T. SYLVESTER at home. He inquired as to whether or not the gun had been identified and whether this office had any information concerning the gun that was used to shoot the President. He stated the reason he was asking was because they had received no request from the Dallas police or anyone; that the only information he had was via the radio and T. V. concerning this gun. He advised there were a lot of outlets in New Orleans that could be checked as LEE HARVEY OSWALD had lived here. He was advised that I had no definite information concerning this and that all of our leads would be coming out of Dallas if they desired any check.

He referred to DAVID WILLIAM FERRIE, advising he was tied in with a Cuban movement; was an ex-pilot of Eastern Airlines; had flown planes into Central America and was currently employed by G. WRAY GILL, an attorney. He stated he understood but he had to back it up that OSWALD was possibly friendly with FERRIE in view of his Cuban activities. I advised Mr. TROSCLAIR that we were interested in any information he might have which would indicate that OSWALD was friendly with FERRIE.

BILL REED of WWL T. V. on 11/24/63 at 12:25 p.m. stated they were running a check on DAVID FERRIE of 3303 Louisiana Ave. Pkwy., formerly connected with the Civil Air Patrol and Eastern Airlines, who allegedly a few years ago was a friend of LEE HARVEY OSWALD and that OSWALD might be connected with the Civil Air Patrol. He stated they were looking to interview FERRIE who is employed by G. WRAY GILL but were unsuccessful and FERRIE had an unlisted telephone.

5 - New Orleans
JTS:lil

SEARCHED_____ INDEXED_____
SERIALIZED_____ FILED_____
NOV 25 1963
FBI—NEW ORLEANS

Interestingly, Col. Cord Meyer, Sr. was Northeast Regional Director of the Civil Air Patrol (CAP), an organization both Oswald and Ferrie were members of, from January 1, 1952 to May 27, 1955 at which time his title changed to Regional Commander. He retired from the CAP on May 21, 1956.[131] Meyer was born in New York City, owned a business in New York City, had his CAP headquarters in New York City, was Commander of American Legion Air Service Post 501 in New York City, headed a draft board in New York City and as of 1954 was living at 116 East 66th St.[132] If

---

131   *Lee Harvey Oswald's Cold War: Why the Kennedy Assassination Should Be Reinvestigated* (2015) by Greg Parker; Northeast Region CAP website, history page; https://www.geni.com/people/Cord-Meyer-Sr/6000000012750644984.

132   earlyaviators.com, Cord Meyer, Sr. page; https://ner.cap.gov/index.php/dept-staff/historian

that weren't enough, (David) Harold "D.H." Byrd, the owner of the Texas School Book Depository, was Commander of the Texas Wing of the Civil Air Patrol from December 1, 1941 through May 25, 1948. He had been among a small group who had established the CAP in Washington.[133]

During the HSCA interview with former CAP member Robert Boylston on October 17, 1978, Boylston told Bob Buras and L.J. Delsa that Ferrie had paid $1,000 in tuition fees for him (Boylston) to study at the University of Loyola and had never asked for repayment. In addition, Ferrie was always hinting about "secret" orders of a military or intelligence nature. Two examples were given, one relating to the 1958 Lebanon Crisis and the other relating to Cuba circa 1961 (most likely a reference to the Bay of Pigs). Ferrie talked a great deal about a group who knew what was going on in this country and was going to take care of it. What's more, Ferrie knew people in Dallas once hopped a lift on an Air Force C-47 and that Boylston felt back then and still did, that some of the people around Ferrie, as well as Ferrie himself were not playing around when they talked of "taking care" of something.[134] Boylston's friend Van Burns added to the concerns during a May 21st 2001 interview with author Joan Mellen. Burns told Mellen that in September of 1959, he had seen Lee Oswald with Ferrie. This was just prior to Oswald leaving for Europe. Burns also stated that he had been interested in the CAP in those days and had learned that some cadets were studying the Russian language.[135]

The week before Kennedy's murder, Allen Dulles had been in Boston and New York on his book tour for *The Craft of Intelligence* (Howard Hunt had been a major ghostwriter.) On the day JFK was killed, Dulles landed in Washington in the morning, made a speech at the Brookings Institute, and after getting the word of JFK's murder, he went to Camp Peary.[136] This was a CIA location sometimes called The Farm. This was an alternative Agency headquarters, in which Dulles had built an office from where he could direct covert operations. He was there from Friday in the early evening until Sunday. What could he have been doing there? Of course,

---

133 Ever since the assassination, there has been an effort by some supporters of the Warren Commission to try and limit Byrd's historical involvement with the CAP to that of founding the Texas Air Wing. Byrd's autobiography along with other sources, puts the lie to that. Byrd was indeed a co-founder of the organization in Washington and was so heavily involved from day one that he earned the nickname of "Mr. CAP"; *Lee Harvey Oswald's Cold War: Why the Kennedy Assassination Should Be Reinvestigated* (2015) by Greg Parker
134 *Lee Harvey Oswald's Cold War: Why the Kennedy Assassination Should Be Reinvestigated* (2015) by Greg Parker
135 *Lee Harvey Oswald's Cold War: Why the Kennedy Assassination Should Be Reinvestigated* (2015) by Greg Parker
136 *The Devil's Chessboard* by David Talbot (2015), page 546

one thing he could have been doing was coordinating with Phillips, Hunt, Harvey and Angleton.

As far as who specifically was behind the assassination (and my suspects), none of this can be proven beyond a reasonable doubt and to a moral certainty, of course. Too much time has passed and too many are dead; it is what it is. Still, these are the most likely conspirators. Not the Mafia, the Mossad, the Russians, Castro, James Files, etc. Elements of the CIA wanted Kennedy dead and a desire to blame Castro's Cuba in order to invoke an invasion. The Bay of Pigs and the Cuban Missile Crisis failed. Kennedy pledged to never invade Cuba and he closed down all the anti-Castro camps and acts of sabotage that he could. Something had to be done.

After the assassination, Dulles began a lobbying campaign to get named to the Commission.[137] Dulles quickly became the most active member of the Commission. As Earl Warren later said, "I don't think Allen Dulles ever missed a meeting."[138] Dulles worked with Angleton, and others, to make sure that any tie by the CIA to Oswald was kept secret.[139] Moreover, Dulles himself leaked stories that Oswald may have been a KGB agent.[140] Dulles insisted that most of the report be consumed by a biography of Oswald, rather than the facts of the case. With his longtime friend John McCloy, and up and coming insider Jerry Ford, this trio controlled the Warren Commission pretty much completely.

Richard Sprague, chief counsel to the HSCA, said:

> If he had it to do over again, he would begin his investigation of the Kennedy assassination by probing "Oswald's ties to the Central Intelligence Agency."

Sen. Richard Schweiker said,

> We do know Oswald had intelligence connections. Everywhere you look with him, there are fingerprints of intelligence.

Victor Marchetti was the former Executive Assistant to the Deputy Director of the CIA. Marchetti said,

> The more I have learned, the more concerned I have become that the government was involved in the assassination of President John F. Kennedy.

---

137   *The Devil's Chessboard* by David Talbot (2015), pages 573-574.
138   *The Devil's Chessboard* by David Talbot (2015), page 575.
139   *The Devil's Chessboard* by David Talbot (2015), page 578.
140   *The Devil's Chessboard* by David Talbot (2015), page 583.

Marvin Watson, an adviser to President Lyndon Johnson, said that LBJ had told him that he was convinced that there was a plot in connection with the assassination. Watson said the President felt the CIA had something to do with this plot.[141]

Vietnam was not the motive; Cuba was. The assassination wouldn't be blamed on Vietnam, LBJ's ground war wouldn't begin until 1965 and the patsy had zero connection to this country. No, Cuba was the big prize and hopes of an invasion and more would have sprung immediately after if all would have gone according to hopes and plans. Even though this phase of the operation did not ultimately succeed, that is almost beside the point. Kennedy was dead and an alleged Cuban/Russian Castro-loving "red" did it. Mission accomplished, even if the spoils of war, so to speak, did not come to fruition.

As an aside, I seriously don't get the Oswald-was-a-loser talking point. By only the age of 24, at a time when many of today's millennials are living in their parent's basements or don't have much in their background of note (or both), Oswald had served in the U.S. Marines[142] as a U-2 spy plane radar operator in Japan; he learned an impossibly difficult foreign language (Russian); he lived in the Soviet Union at the height of the Cold War; he brought home an attractive Russian wife and had affairs with other Russian girls before that in his very nice apartment in Minsk; he was already a father of two children; and whether he was a Marxist who was passionate about Cuban policy or a low level Naval Intelligence operative who interacted with spooks and mobsters, you can't say he didn't have interesting hobbies and political passions. Oswald's favorite television show was *I Led Three Lives*. Indeed, Oswald did so. He lived a life many never achieve, even by old age.

That said, I agree with what Canadian researcher Ulric Shannon wrote back in 1996:

> When you're a researcher and you start seeing assassins in your soup, it's only natural that, at some point, the pendulum starts to swing the other way. I'm not psychic, but I had a feeling three or four years ago that a book like *Case Closed* was imminent. I knew

---

141   http://harveyandlee.net/Wilcott/Wilcott.htm.

142   HSCA Document #124-10010-10011 is a letter Director Hoover wrote to the Office of Security at the State Department dated June 3, 1960 asking for any current information the Department of State may have on Oswald. It was enclosed by the Board for reference with these five documents. Hoover believed that someone may be using Oswald's Birth Certificate to impersonate him. Of note is Hoover's description that though Oswald was released from active duty in the Marine Corps, "he has obligated service until 12/8/62." Does this mean that Lee was still under contract until December 8, 1962?

it when I heard Jim Garrison declare, in *The Men Who Killed Kennedy*, that the real Lee Harvey Oswald was not only innocent, but "was in all probability a hero." This is what I mean by a flaky construct. Let's keep in mind here that, whatever his role in the assassination, Oswald has been shown at the very least to have been a pathological liar and a chronic wifebeater; in addition, his actions in the immediate aftermath of the shooting are those of a man with guilty knowledge of something. Let's not be throwing Oswald any banquets, please."[143]

A Chicago connection: two different area newspapers chime in on the same date (11/26/63):

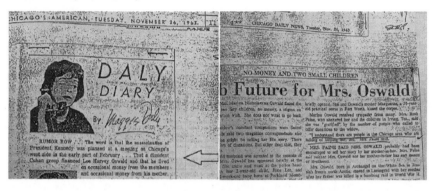

Chicago's American, 11/26/63: "The word is that the assassination of President Kennedy was planned at a meeting on Chicago's west side in the early part of February. That a dissident Cuban group financed Lee Harvey Oswald and that he lived on occasional money from the members and on occasional money from his mother."

Chicago Daily News, 11/26/63: "I understand there are people in the Chicago area who are talking of helping her [Marina Oswald], too," Mrs. [Ruth] Paine said."

Oswald's "fingerprints" ... oh, really?

Despite my conviction that Oswald's rifle[144] (not fired by Oswald) was used as one of the two or more weapons used in the assassination in order to frame him, researcher extraordinaire Pat Speer has written quite a lengthy piece on the so-called science of fingerprints, in general, and a closer look at the actual prints that were found on the boxes in the so-called "sniper's nest" that allegedly belonged to Oswald, to be exact.[145] (even lone-nut authors like H.R. Underwood concede that there

---

143   https://mcadams.posc.mu.edu/shannon.htm.
144   See also https://kennedysandking.com/john-f-kennedy-articles/1092.
145   http://www.patspeer.com/chapter-4d-boxing-day.

are problems with the alleged paper bag, so we won't go into any detail on that[146]). In 1995 Collaborative Testing Services tested 156 U.S. fingerprint examiners in collaboration with the International Association for Identification.. Here is the alarming results of the detailed study:

1. Some fingerprints are so similar that an expert can be fooled.

2. Misidentifications are commonplace.

Only 44% of the examiners identified all 7 latent prints correctly. 34 (22%) made one or more misidentifications. 4% failed to properly identify any of the 7 latent prints. Although 82% of the latent prints were identified, 48 (6%) of these identifications were misidentifications. In sum, then, 78% of the latent prints were properly identified.

3. Fingerprint examiners are subject to confirmation bias.

4. The identification of fingerprints is, in practice, highly subjective.

Besides the fact that Oswald *worked in the building* and was specifically *assigned to the sixth floor*, finding his fingerprints there is nowhere near as damning as it might appear at first glance. Having said that, one could view his prints on a couple of the boxes in the so-called "sniper's nest" as a little more problematic, so to speak. That said, Speer discovered that FBI fingerprint expert Sebastian Latona's exhibits of the actual fingerprints are quite dark and murky, which is indeed what I see when looking at them. When photocopies of these prints are displayed on both his website and the Mary Ferrell Archives site, the prints are much easier to read, but there is now a big problem: as Speer notes, and I fully agree, they do not look like a match!

Furthermore, Speer writes:

I have read dozens of articles on fingerprinting, and fingerprint fabrication. These revealed that virtually every documented or

---

146   *Rendezvous With Death* by H.R. Underwood (2013), pages 107-109; see also *The Girl on the Stairs* by Barry Ernest (2013), pages 127, 156-157. For example, Police Sergeant Gerald Hill told the Commission that the only paper bag he had seen was a "small lunch sack" and remarked of the larger bag, "...if it was found up there on the sixth floor, if it was there, I didn't see it." (7H65) As Griggs points out in his essay, Deputy Sheriffs Luke Mooney and Roger Craig and Police Detective Elmer Boyd all said much the same thing. (See, Griggs, No Case To Answer, pgs. 173-214) One fact overlooked by Griggs was that on the evening of November 22, 1963, Buell Frazier was given a polygraph examination by Dallas Police Detective R.D. Lewis and, while it was in progress, Lewis showed Frazier the long paper bag supposedly found in the "sniper's nest." Frazier told him that "he did not think that it resembled...the crinkly brown paper sack that Oswald had when he rode to work with him that morning..." (FBI 105-82555 Oswald HQ File, Section 17, p. 100) If Frazier, who got the best look at the package Oswald carried that morning, could not identify the bag produced by Dallas Police, it is difficult to imagine that it could ever have been introduced as evidence in court.; see also: https://drive.google.com/file/d/1vHTMl9G3DjtF3CmyLqNz3C6UjRgOS8le/view.

suspected case of fingerprint fabrication has been performed by an over-zealous policeman or crime scene investigator. One such policemen was so brazen even as to submit photocopies of fingerprints taken from fingerprint cards and claim they were prints he'd discovered at crime scenes. Other policeman were a bit smarter than that, and had suspects put their hands on the hoods or roofs of their police cars while conducting a search. They then lifted the prints off their cars, and then claimed they were lifted from a crime scene.

Speer then quotes from Pat Wertheim, the author of a number of articles on fingerprint fabrication and an expert witness who's testified at a number of high-profile trials involving fingerprint fabrication:

> Many hundreds or even thousands of cases of fabrication of fingerprint evidence have come to light in the century since fingerprints were first used by police as a means of identification. One can only guess how many fabrications have been committed in which defendants have been convicted or pled guilty. These cases of fabrication of latent fingerprint evidence will never be discovered…. In certain cases it may be very difficult to distinguish between authentic and fabricated prints and laboratory techniques such as a scanning electron microscope may be necessary to verify an authentic print."[147]

Speer further quotes from another Wertheim article:

> There are three common methods used by dishonest police to fabricate latent print evidence: 1) a lift from an inked print. 2) a mislabeled lift, 3) a staged photograph. One thing these fabricated latents frequently have in common is that they are "perfect" prints. In other words, a fabricator usually prepares a print so clear nobody could fail to see the identification. In addition to that, each of the three methods leaves tell-tale clues, to a greater or lesser degree. Consider the lift from an inked print. Clues to this fabrication are numerous. Ink is a different shade of black than fingerprint powder. Lifted inked prints are usually the fully rolled prints, a phenomenon virtually impossible in real latent print work. Lifts from inked prints usually include fibers and microscopic fiber marks.
>
> Next, consider mislabeled lifts. These are often the hardest of the fabrications to detect. The most reliable method of detection is by a close inspection of background noise. Each type of surface leaves a

---

147   See Brunelle, *Science and Practice Committee Report* (1976) II Fingerprint Fabrication, *Identification News*, Aug. 1976, p.7; *Scientific Evidence in Criminal Cases*, 1986, The Foundation Press, Inc, p. 461.

trademark background noise, and frequently, fabricators fail to take this into account. A mislabeled latent may also reflect an orientation inconsistent with normal handling. However, a clever fabricator may be able to make a mislabeled latent match expectations of genuineness to such a high degree that it would be virtually undetectable. The staged photograph is the third type of fabrication. These photographs are usually taken slightly out of focus in an attempt to hide details which would disclose the fabrication. Or, such a photograph may be over or under-exposed. Strange lines or shadows may be present. The photographs may also contain stray images not expected on the surface from which the latent purportedly came, or background noise may not be consistent with the surface claimed."[148]

Next, Speer presents images that truly tax verbal descriptions, so I am showing them, as well:

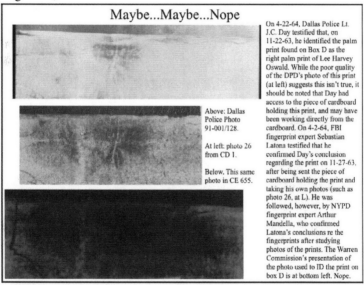

Maybe...Maybe...Nope

Above: Dallas Police Photo 91-001/128.

At left: photo 26 from CD 1.

Below. This same photo in CE 655.

On 4-22-64, Dallas Police Lt. J.C. Day testified that, on 11-22-63, he identified the palm print found on Box D as the right palm print of Lee Harvey Oswald. While the poor quality of the DPD's photo of this print (at left) suggests this isn't true, it should be noted that Day had access to the piece of cardboard holding this print, and may have been working directly from the cardboard. On 4-2-64, FBI fingerprint expert Sebastian Latona testified that he confirmed Day's conclusion regarding the print on 11-27-63, after being sent the piece of cardboard holding the print and taking his own photos (such as photo 26, at L). He was followed, however, by NYPD fingerprint expert Arthur Mandella, who confirmed Latona's conclusions re the fingerprints after studying photos of the prints. The Warren Commission's presentation of the photo used to ID the print on box D is at bottom left. Nope.

Pat Speer's work on this subject is magnificent and groundbreaking. It is also quite lengthy. What I have presented here is almost just the tip of the iceberg, but you get the central point. Then, when one is made aware of the many cases in which Dallas D.A. Henry Wade framed innocent individuals that were only exonerated years later,[149] one is compelled to believe Oswald when he told his brother Robert "do not believe the so-called evidence."

---

148   *Latent Fingerprint Fabrication* by Pat Wertheim, as found on the Iowa Division of the International Association of Identification website
149   *The JFK Assassination* by James DiEugenio (2018), pages 195-199; http://www.nbcnews.com/id/25917791/ns/us_news-crime_and_courts/t/after-dallas-das-death-convictions-undone/

A postscript on the fingerprint issue: while I do not necessarily have a problem with the palm print, allegedly Oswald's, that was found on the rifle (as I state above, it was his rifle and framing him was imperative to the mission), there is a major discrepancy with regard to it. As author Henry Hurt revealed in his excellent 1985 book *Reasonable Doubt* (page 109):

> In 1984, the author interviewed both [Dallas Police] Lieutenant [J.C.] Day and [FBI] Agent [Vincent] Drain about the mysterious print. Day remains adamant that the Oswald print was on the rifle when he first examined it a few hours after the shooting. Moreover, Day stated that when he gave the rifle to Agent Drain, he pointed out to the FBI man both the area where the print could be seen and the fingerprint dust used to bring it out. Lieutenant Day states that he cautioned Drain to be sure the area was not disturbed while the rifle was in transit to the FBI laboratory. Drain flatly disputes this, claiming Day never showed him such a print. "I just don't believe there was ever a print," said Drain. He noted that there was increasing pressure on the Dallas police to build evidence in the case. Asked to explain what might have happened, Agent Drain stated, "All I can figure is that it (Oswald's print) was some sort of cushion, because they were getting a lot of heat by Sunday night. You could take the print off Oswald's card and put it on the rifle. Something like that happened."

A Warren Commission memo dated August 28, 1964 states:

> [Warren Commission General Counsel J. Lee] Rankin advised because of the circumstances that now exist there was a serious concern in the minds of the commission as to whether or not the palm impression that has been obtained from the Dallas Police Department is a legitimate latent palm impression removed from the rifle barrel or whether it was obtained from some other source, and that for this reason this matter needs to be resolved.

Portion of FBI report from Hoover to Curry, mentioning how the rifle and revolver did not have Oswald's fingerprints on them. This is Warren Commission Exhibit 2003, from Volume 24, page 264. It is dated Saturday November 23rd, 1963; the day after the assassination:

No latent prints of value were developed on Oswald's revolver, the cartridge cases, the unfired cartridge, the clip in the rifle or the inner parts of the rifle.

Wow. But there's more.

Author Gary Savage, in his 1993 book *First Day Evidence*, chatted with his Dallas police uncle Rusty Livingston, who happened to work under none other than J.C. Day. The claim was made that a photo of the trigger guard depicted Oswald's prints. If true, this 30-year-old claim would nonetheless be explosive evidence that Oswald was a triggerman, not just a patsy with a guilty rifle, so to speak. On page 72 of the book (Quoting Rusty):

> I am sure that Lieutenant Day, who was in charge of the Crime Lab, dusted the rifle that was found on the sixth floor of the School Book Depository, and lifted a partial palm print off the underside of the barrel after the rifle was taken apart. They had an actual print there in the office that night. I compared it myself with Oswald's print, and it looked to me like there was enough to say yes, it was Oswald's print. I think all the other people on the day shift had already looked at the palm print before I arrived that night, but I went ahead and looked at the palm print myself and was satisfied that it was Oswald's.

As researcher Pat Speer states:

> Wow! That's a whopper, right? In 1964, Day says he showed the barrel lift to no one and then 29 years later Livingston comes out of the shadows to say he not only looked at it, but analyzed it, and concluded the print was Oswald's print. But there's a problem, besides the obvious. Livingston says he thought the day shift had all looked at this print. It's beyond belief that 1) he would have access to this print when no one else did, and 2) he would never realize the significance of his having studied this print prior to telling his nephew about it almost 30 years later. The thought occurs then that Rusty studied the palm print on the cardboard taken from Box D – which may very well have been studied by the day shift – and not the palm print purported to have been lifted from the rifle.... Day claimed he lifted a print from the rifle, that he told the FBI about this print but they failed to hear him, and that he failed to study this print prior to his being asked to do so by the Warren Commission.
>
> And here comes Rusty to his rescue, almost 30 years later. Not only did Rusty hear Day tell the FBI about this print, he studied Day's lift of this print on the night of the shooting and identified it as Oswald's print. And not only that, he performed the tests on the boxes that Day should have performed in the days after the shooting, and ID'ed Oswald's prints on these boxes as well. Dut-da-da-duh! Super Rusty to the rescue! The DPD Crime Lab's reputation is saved! Except ... it's not. It's further tarnished. No silver nitrate

was added to the boxes in Dallas. This was a procedure performed by the FBI in Washington. Nice try, Rusty. Except ... not."

But this is not all.

From the transcript of the 1993 PBS *Frontline* program "Who Was Lee Harvey Oswald":

> Sebastian Latona, the head of the FBI fingerprint division in 1963, told *Frontline* that the FBI examined only the rifle itself in making its determination that the trigger guard prints were of no value. [Latona carefully inspected the entire rifle just a few hours later after J.C. Day and he found "no latent prints of value" anywhere on it.[150]] Latona said the FBI never looked at the Dallas Police photographs of the trigger guard fingerprints. Although the record is not precise on this point, it appears that only one or two of the Dallas Police photographs of the trigger guard prints were forwarded to the Warren Commission, where they were examined by Arthur Mandella, a consultant to the commission. Mandella came to the same conclusion as the FBI, that the trigger guard prints were of no value.

From the same transcript:

> In 1978, Vincent Scalice had examined all the prints in the Kennedy case for the House Select Committee on Assassinations. At that time, he concluded that the trigger guard prints were "of no value for identification purposes."

Indeed, Day told the Commission

> ....from what I had I could not make a positive identification...[151]

Sebastian Latona judged them to be "of no value"[152] and a second FBI expert, Ronald Wittmus, agreed.[153] That makes three witnesses within 24 hours.

Strike one, two, three and ejection from the game regarding the trigger guard prints, right? Read on.

Continuing from the transcript:

> When Livingston began working with his nephew, Gary Savage, on a book about the assassination called *JFK: First Day Evidence*, they decided to have the fingerprints reexamined. They turned to Captain Jerry Powdrill of the West Monroe, Louisiana, Police Depart-

---

150   4 H 23.
151   4 H 262.
152   4 H 21.
153   7 H 590.

ment, a qualified fingerprint examiner. Powdrill found three points of identity between the trigger guard prints and Oswald's known prints and three possible points of identity. Six to ten points of identity are normally required in the U.S. to make a positive identification. Powdrill told *Frontline*, "I cannot say that sufficient evidence exists to conclude that the latent print [in the photograph] is in fact that of Lee Harvey Oswald; however, there are enough similarities to suggest that it is possible they are one in the same."

So much for that. But, wait:

Frontline asked George Bonebrake, a former supervisor of the FBI latent fingerprint division to examine copies of the fingerprint photographs. Bonebrake told *Frontline* the prints were not clear enough to make an identification of anyone. "They lack enough characteristic ridge detail to be of value for identification purposes," said Bonebrake."

Five "strikes" – Game over? Nope-one of the batters is back to try again:

Frontline also asked Vincent Scalice, former head of the New York City Police latent fingerprint unit, to examine the trigger guard prints.

Fifteen years later, Scalise changes his tune.
Continuing with the *Frontline* transcript:

"He [Scalice] apparently only had the one or two Dallas police photographs that were part of the Warren Commission files for study back then. "I have to assume," says Scalice, "that my original examination and comparison was carried out in all probability on one photograph. And that photograph was apparently a poor-quality photograph, and the latent prints did not contain a sufficient amount of detail in order to affect an identification. I know for a fact that I did not see all these four photographs in 1978, because if I had, I would have been able to make an identification at that point in time. So where these photographs were, I don't know. But after this reexamination, I definitely conclude these are Oswald's prints."

However, as Pat Speer notes,

The FBI not only studied the Dallas Police Department's photographs of the trigger guard, they sought out and studied the original negatives ... all 3 of them ... The Warren Commission's fingerprint expert, and the HSCA's fingerprint expert, appeared on the same TV program, and they both blew smoke. They both made out that they'd never studied photographs of the trigger guard, when the record suggests they had."

If that wasn't enough, Speer discovered shocking details about Scalise's background and so-called "neutrality":

Scalice's latter-day C.V. boasted that he'd "worked closely with the Federal Bureau of Investigation concerning the deaths of President John F. Kennedy and the Reverend Doctor Martin Luther King." Well, this is a bit of a shock seeing as he was supposed to be coming to an independent conclusion regarding the fingerprint evidence for these cases. Or was Scalice merely out for attention? It seems a bit of a coincidence that, but 18 months after his appearance on *Frontline*, in which he presented himself as a fingerprint expert, Scalise appeared at a press conference funded by right-wingers opposed to Bill and Hillary Clinton, and presented himself as a handwriting expert, and not just any handwriting expert, mind you, but as a handwriting expert claiming Vince Foster's suicide note had been forged. And that wasn't the last we heard of Scalice. On March 22, 1996, Scalice appeared once again on national TV, this time on the program *Unsolved Mysteries*. Well, did he add any details regarding his matching the trigger guard prints to Oswald's prints? Nope, no such luck. His appearance was devoted to his latest project – he doubled-down on his claim the Foster note was forged... Lt. Day, working with the actual trigger guard prints and not just photos of the trigger guard prints, told FBI agent Bookhout there were but 4 points on these prints that he was going to try to match to Oswald's prints ... it sure seems as though Scalice was trying to make a name for himself, and that he grossly oversold the similarity between the trigger guard prints and Oswald's prints."[154]

There is another alternative to the fingerprints tying Oswald to various items: I would not be the least bit surprised if the origins of the prints occurred whilst Oswald was in police custody and he was asked or coerced into touching the items ... or wasn't even made aware that what he was touching were items of special interest (for example-wrapping paper looks innocent enough: "was this the material your lunch sack was made of?"). Also, out of necessity, Oswald had to have touched the tables and possibly the chairs he sat in, as well as other items (examples: a glass of water, food utensils, the bars on his cell, the bed, the sink, etc.). Presto-more prints to

154   http://www.patspeer.com/chapter4c%3Athefingerprintsofmyth.

add to the props on the sixth floor. Keeping in mind what FBI agent Drain (not a "conspiracy buff") said above, since we know D.A. Wade was super corrupt and people were wrongly convicted and framed, I definitely view this planting of Oswald's prints as a distinct possibility.

A few years later, Dallas Police Chief Jesse Curry writes a book and comes clean:

'Not Sure' on Oswald, Author Curry Indicates

By TOM JOHNSON

Former Dallas Police Chief Jesse Curry said Wednesday he is "not sure" to this day whether Lee Harvey Oswald was the assassin of President John F. Kennedy.

"I'm not going to express my opinion," Curry said at a press conference. "I'm not sure about it. No one has ever been able to put him (Oswald) in the Texas School Book Depository with a rifle in his hand."

Curry, now chief of security for the Texas Bank, was police chief on Nov. 22, 1963, when Kennedy was slain and then-Gov. John Connally seriously wounded by gunfire as the presidential motorcade approached the Triple Underpass on Elm Street.

HE SUMMONED the press conference to announce the release of a book he put together which is said to contain his "personal file" of the assassination.

The book contains a wealth of photographs related to the tragedy but puts forth little new of significance as far as physical evidence in concerned.

Curry's feelings during the period from when the President was shot till the time when Jack Ruby in turn shot Oswald two days later is perhaps the most revealing facet of the work.

Curry complains, for example, that federal and state law enforcement officers insisted on being present at Oswald's interrogation sessions after his apprehension.

"Any experienced investigator will admit that the proper way to interrogate a prisoner is to be alone with the prisoner without distraction," Curry writes. "Because of the constant pressure from other investigative agencies. (Dallas police homicide Capt. Will) Fritz was never allowed to carry out an orderly private interview with Lee Harvey Oswald.

"THE DALLAS homicide bureau was caught in a politically motivated crossfire from the press and other law enforcement agencies . . . The interrogation was a 3-ring circus," Curry said.

Oswald indignantly denied any knowledge of the assassination or of the subsequent slaying of police officer J. D. Tippit, the former chief added.

"Oswald played the role of the indignant and belligerent prisoner who had no knowledge of anything. He had an arrogance that made it impossible to communicate even simple questions," Curry said.

"I have always wondered whether or not Capt. Fritz could have obtained crucial information from Oswald if he had been allowed to spend two or three hours alone with him under normal interrogative conditions."

CURRY TOLD REPORTERS he is not trying to present a new theory about the assassination nor is he attempting to support or validate the findings of the Warren Commission, which concluded that Oswald was the lone killer of both Kennedy and Tippit.

"I'm trying to present the reader with all the available parts to the assassination puzzle as they would be presented to a jury had it come to trial," Curry said. "The readers will be able to weigh these facts and form their own conclusions."

Curry told reporters he takes Connally's word for it that he (the governor) was hit by a different bullet than one which possibly pierced the President's throat.

One of the Warren Commission's conclusions is that one bullet hit both men, another hit neither and a third struck Kennedy in the head.

Curry, who led the motorcade to Parkland Hospital after the shooting, poignantly writes of Mrs. Kennedy's actions while waiting for attendants to remove the President to the hospital:

"SHE SAT IMMOBILIZED, unable to move. She just sat there holding the President's head in her lap — somehow hoping to heal it, like a little girl holds a doll . . . Little sounds like restrained whimpers were her only reaction at first."

Looking back on Ruby's slaying of Oswald in the police station basement Nov. 4, Curry said Wednesday he should not have let the throng of newsmen congregate there, as Ruby apparently slipped in during the confusion.

"There had been rumors that officers were beating Oswald up," he told reporters. "We decided to show the world that we were not.

"If I had thrown the press out," Curry said. "I would have been crucified. As it was, I got crucified anyway."

JACK RUBY (AND OFFICER J.D. TIPPIT)

They're going to find out about Cuba. They're going to find out about the guns, find out about New Orleans, find out about everything.[155]

– Jack Ruby while in jail

As for Jack Ruby, the man who killed Oswald, he throws a monkey wrench into the case. While I do not believe the Mafia was involved in the assassination to any great degree, Ruby was, at the very least, a low-level Mafia go-fer of some sort.[156] I agree with the HSCA's assessment: Ruby had police help in getting into the Dallas Police basement and he did not come down the ramp, thus debunking the Warren Commission. In fact, according to Dallas attorney Travis Kirk, Captain Will Fritz was a "close friend" of Ruby and it was "entirely possible and probable" that Fritz deliberately arranged for Ruby to shoot Oswald.[157] His killing of Oswald was not a spur-of-the-moment thing, but one that was pre-meditated and planned. Even lone-nut author Gerald Posner conceded that Ruby was probably stalking Oswald.[158] His motive for murder had nothing to do with any silly notions that Ruby was sad about JFK's death or wanted to spare Jackie the pain of a trial (Beverly Oliver, a Colony Club entertainer who often hung out at the Carousel Club, and considered Ruby a friend, reports "Ruby despised JFK.")[159] It could also be that the police let Ruby rub out Oswald because he was (allegedly) a cop killer. If this is the case, then the killing of Oswald by Ruby was a conspiracy but one on a very simple scale detached from the conspiracy to kill Kennedy: it was vengeance; an eye for an eye. The police couldn't kill Oswald so they let a police "groupie" – Ruby – silence him.

Secret Service agent Lane Bertram reported Jack Ruby's presence in Houston on 11/21/63 (when JFK was also present), as Ruby was stalking the President. Ruby had been seen by five witnesses on the 400 block of Milam Street

---

155   *Deep Politics and the Death of JFK* by Peter Dale Scott (1993), page 179.
156   Ruby apparently visited Mobster Santos Trafficante in a Cuban prison: *JFK Beyond A Question Of Conspiracy: An Investigation And Revision Of History - Including New 2018 Material!* By Ralph Thomas (2018).
157   *The Deputy Interviews: The True Story of J.F.K. Assassination Witness, and Former Dallas Deputy Sheriff, Roger Dean Craig* by Steve Cameron, 2019, page 27.
158   *Case Closed* by Gerald Posner (1993), pages 385-386.
159   1993 Sudbury Ontario conference; asked later to elaborate, she said Ruby didn't like Joe Sr., JFK or RFK, but thought Jackie was "classy"; she said she and Jack argued about the Kennedys. Bill Beal, photographer for the *Dallas Times-Herald*, snapped a couple photos of the Colony Club on the evening of 11/22/63. Pictured is none other than Beverly Oliver herself: https://emuseum.jfk.org/search/beverlyu%20oliver/null/images?page=2.

in Houston for "several hours," while Ruby was also spotted one block from JFK's "entrance route to and from the Rice Hotel where [JFK] stayed."[160]

Although a somewhat radical view, I also do not rule out that both Ruby and Tippit were not only involved in a plot to kill Oswald, but also involved in a conspiracy to kill President Kennedy.[161] One or both could have possibly even been one of the shooters in Dealey Plaza![162] Some may dismiss this notion, but I am compelled to believe there is merit to this idea. Respected KBOX reporter Sam Pate, who famously uttered the line "It appears as though something has happened in the motorcade route," claimed to have seen Ruby, Tippit and Oswald eating at a restaurant.[163] Another witness, Mary Dowling, stated that she saw Oswald and Tippit at the Dobbs House restaurant on 11/20/63 (and she heard from a colleague that Ruby was a night customer of the restaurant).[164] Ruby stripper Pixie Lynn claimed that Ruby and Oswald attended homosexual parties together.[165] Secret Service agent Roger Warner interviewed a Ruby employee, stripper Karen Carlin, on 11/24/63. His report reads in part:

> She stated to me that she was under the impression that Lee Harvey Oswald, Jack Ruby, and other individuals unknown to her were involved in a plot to assassinate President Kennedy and that she would be killed if she gave any information to the authorities.

Karen Carlin came out of hiding in October of 1992, after living under an assumed name. She confirmed the contents of her Secret Service interview with Warner and added that Ruby was definitely in on a conspiracy to silence Oswald.[166] Legendary author Penn Jones told author Barry Ernest back in March 1968:

> I certainly think Tippit was involved. I certainly think he was as big a patsy as Oswald.[167]

---

160   25 H 378 – 381; See also 23 H 169 report of SAIC of Houston Office Lane Bertram re: Joe Bonds, former business partner of Ruby's.

161   From the newly-released files-notes obtained from CIA files from Charles Berk to RFK and Allen Dulles (12/1/63) state that Jack Ruby was a fringe player in the assassination, Oswald had been set up and was supposed to meet his contact in the Texas Theater: https://www.archives.gov/files/research/jfk/releases/2018/180-10144-10227.pdf.

162   See Joseph McBride's *Into The Nightmare* (2013).

163   6/22/2005 Sixth Floor oral history; 1970 interview with Al Chapman: https://www.youtube.com/watch?v=ESXT-E2w9C4.

164   12/7/63 FBI interview of Dowling: https://drive.google.com/file/d/1k7sBiviQGi_MPi5O-wnxnakSmKDkDeaSo/view.

165   26 H 184-185.

166   26 H 509; *Kennedy Contract* by John Davis (1993), page 107.

167   *The Girl on the Stairs* by Barry Ernest (2013), page 76.

Interestingly, Ruby told his tax lawyer on 11/19/63 that he expected to be receiving money soon to cover his significant debts and his first use of a safe was in November 1963.[168] One of the newly-released files includes an allegation by a witness that Ruby invited him on the morning of 11/22/63 to watch the motorcade and asked him to come "watch the fireworks."[169] A memo from Dallas Police Lieutenant W.F. Dyson to Dallas Police Chief Jesse Curry dated 11/25/63 states that Ruby was in the Dallas Assistant District Attorney's office on 11/21/63 and said "You probably don't know me now, but you will."[170]

In addition, one must not dismiss Julia Ann Mercer's statements about seeing a man who looked like Ruby driving a pickup truck about an hour and a half before the assassination in Dealey Plaza, the sight of the eventual murder. What's more, a man walked around to the back of the pick-up truck and pulled out a rifle case wrapped in paper, then carried it up the slope of the grassy knoll. "The Secret Service is not very secret," she said.[171] When author Henry Hurt interviewed her for his 1985 book *Reasonable Doubt*, Mercer claimed the man with the rifle case was none other than Lee Harvey Oswald himself![172] Dallas Secret Service Special Agent in Charge Forrest Sorrels told the Warren Commission about finding a witness who saw both a stalled truck on Elm Street and a man who appeared to have a gun case shortly before the shooting.[173] Interestingly, as mentioned earlier, three witnesses – Seth Kantor, Roy Stamps and Wilma Tice – saw none other than Jack Ruby at Parkland Hospital. Researchers suspect Ruby of planting the bullet, CE399, at the hospital.[174] Even lone-assassin author Gerald Posner concedes that the Warren Commission's dismissal of Kantor's identification of Ruby at Parkland does not wash, yet he believes Ruby's presence there is innocent.[175]

A year after his conviction, in March 1965, Ruby conducted a brief televised news conference in which he stated:

> Everything pertaining to what's happening has never come to the
> surface. The world will never know the true facts of what occurred,

---

168   *The Plot to Kill the President* by Robert Blakey and Dick Billings (1981), page 308, citing reporter Seth Kantor; *Conspiracy* by Anthony Summers (1980), page 450; *Killing the Truth* by Harrison Livingstone (1993), page 91.

169   https://www.archives.gov/files/research/jfk/releases/docid-32167992.pdf.

170   *The Innocence of Oswald – 50+ Years of Lies, Deception & Deceit in the Murders of President John F. Kennedy & Officer J.D. Tippit* by Gary Fanin (2015).

171   *JFK and the Unspeakable* by James Douglass (2010), pages 255-258; the *JFK* movie (1991).

172   *Reasonable Doubt* by Henry Hurt (1985), pages 114-116. The HSCA was unable to find her but Hurt was able to locate and interview Mercer in 1983, provided that he did not reveal her current name or location.

173   7 H 351-352.

174   *Rendezvous With Death* by H.R. Underwood (2013), pages 365-366.

175   *Case Closed* by Gerald Posner (1993), page 374.

my motives. The people who had so much to gain, and had such an ulterior motive for putting me in the position I'm in, will never let the true facts come above board to the world.

When asked by a reporter,

Are these people in very high positions, Jack?.

He responded:

Yes.[176]

From the new file releases:

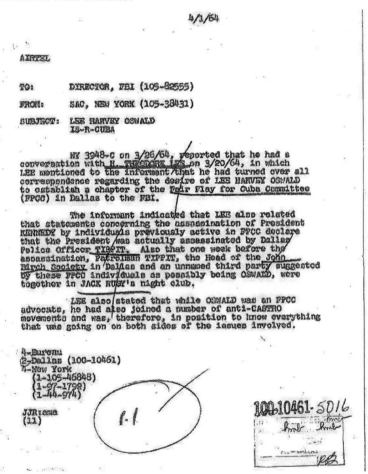

THE MAFIA

The Mafia (a.k.a. The Mob and La Cosa Nostra) was a suspect we all believed was involved in the assassination back when we didn't know

176   Film clip shown in several documentaries, including the 1978 Anthony Summers production *The Assassination of President Kennedy: What Do We Know Now That We Didn't Know Then.*

a whole lot about the case. In the pre-Internet, pre-Oliver Stone movie and pre-ARRB days of the 1970's and 1980's, there wasn't a whole lot to go on. Those were the days of typewriters, print journals, secondary sources (books), and guessing/theorizing. The 25th anniversary in 1988 was a real boon for the Mob-did-it field, as David Scheim, Dan Moldea, G. Robert Blakey and John Davis (later, Frank Ragano in the early 1990's) made a big splash on television espousing their narrow view. Mafia bosses Carlos Marcello, Sam Giancana, Santos Trafficante and others (like Jimmy Hoffa) were usually fingered as the prime suspects. Weaned on movies like *The Godfather (I, II and III)* and *Good Fellas*, it seemed it was an easy notion to envision the Mafia wanting to take out JFK. After all, they hated his brother, Attorney General Robert F. Kennedy (RFK) with a passion, as he was "eating mobsters for breakfast," to quote Dan Moldea's frequent talking point line on television back then. There is no doubt that Bobby Kennedy was prosecuting the Mafia boys with a vengeance, despite alleged Mob help in the 1960 election and Joseph P. Kennedy's connections to the Mob dating back to the alleged bootlegging days of The Prohibition.

This alleged statement by Carlos Marcello is highly tantalizing, but this was said at a time when Marcello was said to have the onset of dementia:

FEDERAL BUREAU OF INVESTIGATION

Date of transcription___3/7/86___

On March 4, 1986, JACK RONALD VANLANINGHAM, Inmate, SEAGOVILLE FEDERAL CORRECTIONAL INSTITUTE, was interviewed and provided the following information:

A confidential source who has provided reliable information in the past furnished the following:

On December 15, 1985, he was in the company of CARLOS MARCELLO and another inmate at the FEDERAL CORRECTIONAL INSTITUTE (FCI), Texarkana, Texas, in the court yard engaged in conversation. CARLOS MARCELLO discussed his intense dislike of former President JOHN KENNEDY as he often did. Unlike other such tirades against KENNEDY, however, on this occasion CARLOS MARCELLO said, referring to President KENNEDY, "Yeah, I had the son of a bitch killed. I'm glad I did. I'm sorry I couldn't have done it myself."

Keeping all of this into focus, there was one suspicious, mob-connected person arrested in Dealey Plaza on 11/22/63: Jim Braden.[177] Braden met with Ruby the day before. There were 700,000 people living in Dallas

---

177   *High Treason* by Harrison Livingstone and Robert Groden (1998 edition), pages 104, 160, 162, 262, 274, 275 and photo section.

at the time and these two individuals were at the same place during the same time on 11/21/63, then Braden is arrested the next day at the site of the assassination. What's more, Braden was also present at the assassination of RFK on 6/4/68: despite a distance of 1400 miles between Dallas and Los Angeles and a four and a half year time span, Braden was the only person on the planet who, amazingly, was present for both Kennedy brothers assassinations![178] And, if that wasn't enough, Braden was working in the very same building in New Orleans, the Pere Marquette building, and on the very same floor, as David Ferrie and G. Wray Gill, Carlos Marcello's attorney, all mere doors apart from each other.[179]

Even the HSCA, which found a "probable conspiracy" when their report was released in early 1979, seemed to point the finger at the Mob being the one group with the strongest "means, motive and opportunity" to kill President Kennedy. Chief Counsel G. Robert Blakey, author of *The Plot to Kill The President* (1981; later *Fatal Hour* in 1992), was a leading advocate of this point of view. Although Anthony Summers seminal book *Conspiracy* (1980) and even Henry Hurt's *Reasonable Doubt* (1985) led one, to a certain extent, in that direction, the fingers of intelligence started to creep into most thinking people's views by then. This was further induced via books by David Lifton (*Best Evidence* in 1981) and Livingstone and Groden's *High Treason* (in 1989). Again, although the possibility of the Mafia being involved was certainly not ruled out,[180] the evidence these other authors presented started to demonstrate that there was no way that the Mafia, by themselves, could have engineered the assassination. The failed autopsy, Kennedy's betrayal of the CIA during both the Bay of Pigs and Cuban Missile Crisis episodes, as well as other factors, made the Mafia a weak sister by comparison to the intelligence community. As Kevin Costner (as Jim Garrison) said in the movie *JFK* "the Mob wouldn't have the guts for a plan of this magnitude." However, another favorite target of suspicion was then unleashed: "This was a coup d'état with Lyndon Johnson waiting in the wings."

LBJ-Cui Bono?

Which brings us to the LBJ-did-it theory. While Ruby's killing of Oswald on 11/24/63 started many people thinking the Mob may have

---

178   *Cold Case Kennedy* by Flip de Mey (2013), pages 98-100.
179   *Cold Case Kennedy* by Flip de Mey (2013), page 100.
180   From the newly-released files- on 11/25/63, Mobster Jimmy Blue Eyes said they should have gotten the whole family including RFK: https://www.archives.gov/files/research/jfk/releases/2018/docid-32198798.pdf

had something to do with all of this (Ruby wearing a classic Mob Fedora hat, of all things), one can argue that people started to suspect Vice President Lyndon Johnson two days previously on 11/22/63. After all, LBJ was being investigated with regard to the Bobby Baker scandal and he did have connections to Billie Sol Estes and others that bore investigation. Johnson was uber-ambitious and hated RFK, although their relationship did improve after the assassination, as there are many photos of the two smiling together and even campaigning together in 1964 when Bobby was reaching for the New York Senate seat. Still, LBJ had his hands all over the Warren Commission, was from Texas, and was now in charge of the reins of power.

Books by Craig Zirbel (*The Texas Connection* in 1991 and the tabloid media coverage he received), Harrison Livingstone (*Killing the Truth* in 1993 and *The Radical Right* in 2004), Barr McClellan (*Blood, Money and Power* in 2003, plus his controversial appearance on *The Men Who Killed Kennedy*), Fred Newcomb and Perry Adams' *Murder From Within: Lyndon Johnson's Plot Against President Kennedy* (the 1974 book republished in 2011), Phillip Nelson (*LBJ: The Mastermind of the JFK Assassination* in 2011 and *LBJ: From Mastermind to "The Colossus"* in 2014), James Tague (*LBJ and the Kennedy Killing* in 2013) and Roger Stone (*The Man Who Killed Kennedy* in 2013 and the media coverage he received), among others, not to mention the *JFK* movie, went a long way toward stoking the flames of suspicion even further. If one looks at the JFK assassination case in the "who benefited the most" category, LBJ takes the prize with hardly a second choice close by. His burning ambition, angry looks, and the war in Vietnam he waged with a fury seemed to stoke the flames even brighter.

However, in my opinion, the theory was dealt a mortal blow by Joan Mellen in 2016 in her masterful book *Faustian Bargains: Lyndon Johnson and Mac Wallace in the Robber Baron Culture of Texas*. Simply put, LBJ's alleged "assassin," Mac Wallace, *was not even in Texas when the assassination occurred* and the mystery fingerprints on the sixth floor are definitely not his. Thanks to Mellen's meticulous research, we know these things to be fact now. She obtained clear fingerprints of Wallace and there is no match at all and, again, he wasn't even in the state when the shooting happened.

What's more, LBJ did not duck down during the motorcade, as unbiased photo analysis proves,[181] while the tales of LBJ's mistress Madeleine Brown and the "party at Clint Murchison's the night before" have been shown to be dubious, to put it mildly.[182] In addition, I have noticed a sea change with

---

181   *JFK: Absolute Proof* by Robert Groden (2013), page 272; *The Reckoning* by Marshal Evans (2018), pages 61-66
182   *The JFK Assassination* by James DiEugenio (2018), page 372

several friends and researchers when it comes to LBJ as of late. It appears that Robert Caro's masterful volumes on Johnson's life in politics has people reassessing him in the fair light of reason and history. There is no doubt that Johnson did much to burnish the memory of JFK and his legacy in a positive light via the passage of much New Frontier legislation that Kennedy did not live (or have the ability with Congress) to see through, such as the Civil Rights Act, to name a large one. In addition, the traditional notion that JFK would have withdrawn from Vietnam has been dealt a body blow via the previously revealed research of Deb Galentine and Larry Hancock, not to mention RFK's JFK Library oral history. When one also factors in Ted Kennedy's deep friendship with President Johnson and LBJ's cordial relationship with RFK (albeit strained when Bobby announced his candidacy in early 1968), it is hard to view LBJ as the devil we all once did. LBJ was undoubtedly crude and vulgar. He also escalated the Vietnam War as a ground war that is very hard to believe JFK would have also become entangled with. Image is everything; perception is reality for many. And, other than perhaps Lady Bird Johnson and Madeleine Brown, it is hard to imagine anyone believing Johnson's looks and manner even approached Kennedy's movie idol image and charisma. Still, none of this is evidence whatsoever that LBJ "did it."

What was very telling (and disappointing) to me was the reaction from both Roger Stone and Barr McClellan, as well as the crowd, at a JFK assassination conference I attended and presented at in the fall of 2016. Rather than deal with Mellen's evidence, Stone and company dismissed her out of hand without any counter evidence whatsoever. It was as if she rained on all their parades and they were left yelling without an umbrella. It was an eye opening and discouraging sight to behold. One even came away with the impression that many in the crowd did not even bother to actually read Mellen's book.

Marty Underwood shaking President Johnson's hand (Clint Hill, far right)

HONEST ANSWERS ABOUT THE MURDER OF PRESIDENT JOHN F. KENNEDY

LBJ believed there was a conspiracy and made no bones about it. He was also painfully aware of the suspicion others had towards his shocking rise to the presidency. Democratic National Committee (DNC) advance man Martin E. "Marty" Underwood, who had worked on the planning of JFK's Texas tour (specifically, his stop at Houston and his proposed stop at Austin), told me on 10/9/92 that he was dispatched to Mexico by President Johnson to learn more about the assassination. As Underwood tells it,

> Johnson said, "Marty, there are two cancers killing my presidency. One is Vietnam. The other is, invariably, every six months or so, one of the newspapers would come out and say 'Johnson was behind the assassination.'" Johnson said, "I wonder if your friends south of the border would help clear this up."

Once in Mexico, Underwood said,

> I was met by a little Mexican, tapped me on the shoulder, and got me in a CIA safe house, probably, ya know, totally insulated, and that's probably where I learned more about the assassination.

Underwood stated that the CIA, the FBI, and the mafia "knew (JFK) was going to be hit" on 11/22/63. This information came from his direct contacts with CIA officer Win Scott, the Mexico City Station Chief during Oswald's visit to that region. Underwood said,

> His [JFK's] number was on the board. I found out later, if they missed him in Dallas, they were thinking of getting him at the [LBJ] ranch.

However, Marty said that he also asked Scott if LBJ was involved in the assassination. Scott told him "not in any way, none whatsoever."

With all this in mind, I have just about ruled out LBJ as a conspirator, although his role in the cover-up is undisputed. What's more, as Colonel Fletcher Prouty has said, LBJ asked FBI Director Hoover if any of the shots were aimed at him (in a phone call soon after the assassination[183]). Why would Johnson say this if he was part of the plot? In addition, in an internal FBI memorandum from Cartha "Deke" DeLoach to Clyde Tolson, DeLoach writes: "the President [LBJ] felt that CIA had something to do with this plot." Plot![184]

A postscript: in the interests of full disclosure, I gave flattering blurbs to both of Phillip Nelson's books. This is not the only time my endorse-

---

183   *Bloody Treason* by Noel Twyman (1997), page 94.
184   *High Treason* by Harrison Livingstone and Robert Groden (1998 edition), page 59.

ment of a book would come back to haunt me somewhat; such is life (to be fair, I do still think there are many nuggets of good work in his books, apart from the central thesis). I would just say that, as with the mafia as a main suspect, my thoughts and feelings have evolved over time. It is very easy to "feel" or believe that LBJ was involved due to his character and blind ambition. However, the evidence is just not there. I wouldn't totally rule it out,[185] but I wouldn't rule it in, either. I know esteemed researcher Ed Tatro is working on a long-awaited book that has an LBJ-did-it thesis attached to it. Stay tuned.

It could very well be that Dallas was picked as an exceptional place to kill Kennedy because it was in Texas, LBJ's home state, so it would suitably muddy the waters in trying to determine who was behind the assassination (by making LBJ a "patsy" of sorts for taking blame in certain circles). But why specifically Dallas and Dealey Plaza? Besides the excellent opportunity for crossfire, right wing Dallas oilman David Harold "D.H." Byrd owned the Texas School Book Depository, founded the Civil Air Patrol (Oswald and Ferrie were members) and was a crony of LBJ.[186] In November, 1963, Byrd left Texas to go on a two-month safari in Africa. While he was away President John F. Kennedy was assassinated. Byrd was a member of the Dallas Petroleum Club. It has been argued that it was here that he met George de Mohrenschildt, David Atlee Phillips and George H. W. Bush. Richard Bartholomew has suggested that Byrd knew David Ferrie via the Civil Air Patrol.[187]

J. EDGAR HOOVER AND THE FBI

As for FBI Director J. Edgar Hoover, like LBJ, I believe he was involved in the cover-up[188] and may even have gotten wind of a plot or plots in the working and let it happen without proper warning to either President Kennedy or the Secret Service.[189]Still, I do not believe he was an active conspirator. Hoover lived in the nether world of blackmail, covert slander, coercion and so forth. Having an active role in a bloody murder was just not either his history or his style. He left the dirty work to others and reveled in the rewards. He despised the Kennedys but, like LBJ (at

---

185   *Bond of Secrecy* by Saint John Hunt (2012)- Hunt says that LBJ was involved.

186   *The Devil's Chessboard* by David Talbot (2015), pages 512, 524, 539-540.

187   *Assassination of John F. Kennedy Encyclopedia* by John Simkin (2012).

188   From the newly-released files: an FBI memo dated 11/22/63 in which Hoover does not wish to follow up on another lead in the case, hand writing on the report "not necessary to cover as true suspect located JH": *JFK Beyond A Question Of Conspiracy: An Investigation And Revision Of History - Including New 2018 Material!* By Ralph Thomas (2018).

189   This is also a view espoused by author Mark North in *Act of Treason* (1991).

least while he was Vice President), held a special animus toward Bobby. In Hoover's case, it was because Bobby was nominally his boss as Attorney General. Also, Hoover hated the fact that RFK was the president's brother and not even born when he began as Director of the FBI. With all this in mind, there is no evidence that Hoover was behind JFK's murder. Like LBJ, there is just an understandable "suspicion," as both men faced uncertain futures under a second term for JFK. Again, one must also remember what Hoover told Billy Byars, Jr. in 1964, as mentioned earlier in this book: "If I told you what I really know, it would be very dangerous to this country. Our whole political system could be disrupted."[190]

SCHOLARSHIP (OR THE LACK THEREOF) IN THE JFK ASSASSINATION CASE AND THE (DIS) INFORMATION SUPERHIGHWAY

I write the following reluctantly, as I respect any author tackling this subject if they do so in a scholarly and responsible fashion. But therein lies the problem: many of the books on the assassination are, sadly, not scholarly or responsible. To be fair (and I am on record saying this many times), the books from the last 5-10 years or so include some of the very best works on the subject to date. In addition to the benefits of hindsight and the ability to see fallacies in old arguments told at a time when information and access was limited, there is a real move these days within the research community – when it comes to authors, at least – to be more scholarly and document their arguments with primary sources and a wealth of sources from the past.

But there is a lot of crap out there, too. Books espousing Greer shooting JFK on purpose, Hickey shooting Kennedy by mistake, Mac Wallace as a sixth-floor shooter, and others of this ilk set the research community back many years. In addition, many works are repetitive, hard to read, and are essentially a rehash of other books, endlessly relitigating the so-called case for conspiracy by going back over every aspect of the case, thus repeating what many other authors have written before. The effect is to dull the senses as to the merits of the arguments. A fair amount of books are too short, while some are hopelessly too broad in length with too much unnecessary padding touching on tangential waters that merely cloud, confuse and frustrate the reader. So much has been written on the case, much of it in a pro-conspiracy slant, that the public (still "on our side" in

190   *Official and Confidential* by Anthony Summers (1993), page 383.

public opinion polls) may believe there was a conspiracy but they do not know it. In short, they are confused and do not know who or what to believe. Some authors go too far with their evidence and are a little too sure of their conclusions. I have a very open mind and (like researchers Pat Speer and Deb Galentine, among others) I have even strayed to the dark side (albeit briefly in 2007), believing that, while there were undoubtedly conspiracies to kill Kennedy, Oswald beat them all to the punch. I came to my senses soon after, but that is almost beside the point. Even Kevin Costner/Jim Garrison in the *JFK* movie says at one point: "Maybe Oswald is who everyone says he is and I am just being dumb about it." Self doubt can actually be a healthy thing at times.

Case in point with regard to my own books: while my Secret Service research certainly leads toward suspicion, I leave open the notion that the agent's negligence on that day was just that: sheer awful incompetence and not one done with a deadly desire to see the president dead. Now, other people go perhaps too far with my research, believing this or that agent was "dirty," had to have been a conspirator, and so forth. Although I have three agents I am suspicious of and am on record (in my books) as naming (for the record, they are Floyd Boring, Bill Greer, and Emory Roberts), I do not believe the Secret Service, as an institution, had anything to do with the assassination and many of these men were honorable agents merely following orders.

The best thing about the Internet is that anyone can post their thoughts, start a blog espousing their views, and even self-publish a book. The worst thing about the Internet is that anyone can post their thoughts, start a blog espousing their views, and even self-publish a book. Back in the "old days" (pre-kindle 2007, and especially pre-1998 or so, before Amazon and other online cites truly kicked in), if you didn't have a book published by a real publisher such as (the now defunct) Carroll & Graf or a similar publishing house and stocked in physical bookstores, you didn't "exist," so to speak, beyond maybe an article or two in limited circulation print journals and so forth. And, even then, if you were not able to garner any publicity for your book, your work died on the shelf, dead on arrival other than perhaps to your family and friends. It was "neat" that you were published, but it's like that old saying: if a tree falls in the woods and no one hears it, does it matter that you were even published to begin with (or something like that)?

The turn of the millennium saw self-publishing sites like Trafford, Author House, and the most successful and current of the three, CreateSpace, rear their heads. The only downfall with these alternatives to mainstream publishing is their reach: you won't find their titles in physical bookstores and Trafford and Author House came before the kindle/nook option, so that, in and of itself, limited your audience. Also, with all due respect to any authors who went these routes, I never had a real desire to resort to these alternatives, as they are "pay to play"; in other words, literally the only reason you are published is because you paid for it. I desired to receive an offer for publication from a regular publishing house – small, medium or large size – because it just feels more "legitimate" to me. I feel an inherent criticism from naysayers would be "oh, you're not really an author- you paid to get your book published!" Trolls who leave one-star reviews (without buying or reading your book) are bad enough without facing that handicap to begin with.

While recent books are trending upward (scholarly, documented, available to the masses via the Internet/ Amazon and in multiple forms like Kindle and so forth), the Internet itself is rapidly trending downward, as scores of amateurs (many well-meaning and some with ill intent) espouse silly and debunked notions about the case, some bordering on the obscene: Jackie shot Kennedy (!); Jackie didn't shoot Kennedy but she did want him dead because of his philandering; Connally shot Kennedy between the jump seats in the limo (just saw that one the other day); Greer shot Kennedy (the stupid theory that will not die); Hickey shot Kennedy (the new stupid theory that won't die); LBJ ducked down so he knew what was coming; the man-in-the-doorway was not Billy Lovelady, although it was; the Zapruder film was altered and is a mere cartoon; a shooter in the trunk shot JFK; the Mossad had Kennedy killed; the Jews did Kennedy in; and so on, along with an unhealthy dose of very dubious photo "interpretations" of "gunmen" on the knoll. For those seeking a quick solution to the crime and confirmation bias, the Internet was tailor made to please. Many Facebook forums exist, even for those who believe Oswald acted all by himself, and much name-calling and character assassination bubbles to the surface during "debates." About the only good forums I have come across (while certainly not perfect) are *JFK: Nothing But The Truth* by researcher extraordinaire Matt Douthit, *JFK: The Continuing Inquiry* and *The Education Forum*, especially now that a couple argumentative "lone nut" people were blocked.

Sadly, the Alex Jones and James Fetzer-induced "false flag" nonsense has permeated the research community online, with a fair share of people making silly and unjustified connections to current events, current politics and political leaders, etc. While the so-called "old days" of the case had their limitations and fair share of nonsense (such as the bizarre Michael Eddowes idea that Oswald was not buried in his grave), there was an innocence to those times in the research community. Also, your only real avenue for publicity (unless you were very lucky to have an actual book published) were the print journals such as *The Continuing Inquiry* and *The Third Decade* (later called *The Fourth Decade*) and, even then, they were monitored for content and publication refusal was commonplace. Now, with the click of a mouse and access to the Internet, you can instantly become an "expert" and espouse wild and unfounded ideas and get away with it with no other repercussion save ridicule.

THE STATE OF THE CASE

It seems that the case "peaked" in 2013, the fiftieth anniversary of the assassination, and now the media wants the case closed and Oswald firmly named the only assassin. I vividly remember the halcyon days of the late 1980's to early-mid 1990's when conspiracy books were commonplace in bookstores (complete with actual "JFK assassination" specialty shelves and areas of their own); television, albeit mostly of the tabloid variety (*Geraldo, Montel Williams, A Current Affair, Hard Copy*, etc.), regularly carried pro-conspiracy programming; *The Men Who Killed Kennedy* episodes (1-6) regularly aired on both the A&E Network and The History Channel; and the 1991 Oliver Stone movie *JFK* was seen by millions well into 1992 (and beyond via VHS and cable television).

Then came the one-two-three punch of the *Journal of the American Medical Association* (JAMA) (1992-1993, allegedly debunking the pro-conspiracy medical evidence), Gerald Posner (*Case Closed* in 1993) and Norman Mailer (*Oswald's Tale: An American Mystery* in 1995) to grind things to a virtual halt. The mainstream media lapped up these works, especially Posner, who thereafter became the chief spokesman for the Oswald-did-it-alone-get-a-life crowd. Still, the advent of the Internet and the rise of conferences held by ASK, COPA and JFK Lancer definitely softened the blow, as many angry pro-conspiracy authors and researchers united to rail against this new mainstream media movement of containment. The deaths of John Connally (1993), Jackie Kennedy (1994) and (in 1999) JFK Jr. made the case seem that much more remote and in the past.

The Assassination Records Review Board (1994-1998), formed via the JFK Records Act in the wake of the *JFK* movie, released millions of pages of documents that established a new level of scholarship in the case.

Many thought the start of a new century and (especially) 9/11 would dampen enthusiasm for the greatest murder mystery of the twentieth century but, if anything (thanks to both the ARRB and the Internet), the case still flourished. 2003 brought both the 40th anniversary and the massive ratings success of the three new episodes of *The Men Who Killed Kennedy* on The History Channel (the sales of the VHS and DVD versions were extremely profitable to the network, as well. I was on part seven, but I digress). However, there was a backlash, especially to the LBJ-did-it episode (number 9), with members of the Johnson family, along with former Presidents Ford and Carter, coming out against the program. The results were still surprising: the network buried the last three (new) episodes and even stopped airing parts 1-6 (although the DVDs of those first six episodes were still available online). As a side note, Newsmax TV has recently begun airing episodes 7-8 again in 2019 and 2020.

Then came Vincent Bugliosi in 2007 with his massive tome *Reclaiming History*. While the book was a disappointment in the sales category (no doubt largely due to its excessive length), Bugliosi was the toast of the town with the mainstream media and book reviewers. He became the new Posner, so to speak, lending his lone-nut views to any network that would have him: MSNBC, Fox, CNN, etc. The research community united in their revulsion to his book, though, and many scholarly reviews picked apart and debunked large parts of his book.[191] In fact, Jim DiEugenio countered with excellent online reviews soon after, then with *Reclaiming Parkland* in 2013, arguably the best book ever written on the case (later expanded and retitled *The JFK Assassination* in 2018).

Gerald Blaine and Clint Hill came out with their books in 2010 and 2012,[192] respectively (Hill with two more in 2013 and 2016), all with the goals of both reinforcing the Bugliosi view and shutting down any notion that there was any reason to be suspicious of the Secret Service in the death of JFK. As readers of my books are well aware, I am responsible for both of these former Kennedy agents coming out of the woodwork to write their books.

Then came 2013, the fiftieth anniversary, and it has been an uphill battle ever since. Luckily, there are two major publishers of conspiracy books still going strong (Trine Day and Skyhorse; there was really only one major player, the now defunct Carroll & Graf, in the 1990's) and, for better or for worse, the Internet is exploding with information and interest. Public

---

191   https://www.reclaiminghistory.org/.
192   Blaine's *The Kennedy Detail* and Hill's *Mrs. Kennedy and Me*.

opinion polls are still in our favor, albeit at a lower majority than times past. There are two major conferences held every year now, replacing COPA and Lancer: the Judyth Baker/Trine Day and CAPA conferences, both held in Dallas. Crowds still flock to Dealey Plaza in Dallas, the site of the JFK assassination, and millions make their yearly pilgrimage to the Sixth Floor Museum in Dallas, the old Texas School Book Depository.

2016 saw the Ted-Cruz's-dad-knew-Oswald story that was blown up by the media and Donald Trump. 2017 saw many more document releases and much media coverage of the same. Tabloid magazines espousing a conspiracy of some sort regularly appear in supermarket check-out lines to this day. So, hope springs eternal, although time has not been a friend: witnesses are passing away at an alarming rate, as the average person who was alive and aware when the assassination occurred has to be at least in their late 50's (assuming some 2-3 year olds remember that day), with the true average age of witnesses currently being between the ages of their late 70's to their 90's. Fortunately, JFK is still our last assassinated president and was "only" ten presidents ago. Coupled with the fact that many millions of people around the world still vividly remember him and countless audio/visuals of Kennedy keep him alive for those too young to have remembered him (or not even born when he was assassinated), interest in the assassination is alive and moderately well.

I say "moderately" because, while there is still a fervent interest in Kennedy's life, interest in his death has waned somewhat with the passage of time. There will never be justice for JFK; it is what it is. He won't be coming back; Jackie and many others are long dead, as well. We will never know to a legal and absolute certainty who killed him, who was behind it, or why. As journalist Peter Hamill once said: "If there was a conspiracy, they got away with it. Kennedy is still dead, as is Oswald and Ruby."

That said, another reason to have hope: many other historical topics (The Civil War, WWI, WWII, etc.) are now "old news," yet there will always be books and some level of interest (movies/television programs) in them. Witness the fevered excitement which greeted the 2012 epic movie *Lincoln*. I personally witnessed two packed movie houses filled with young people riveted to their seats about a president roughly 150 years prior to their time, knowing that every single human being from that time, as well as quite a few from generations afterward, are long dead and gone. In addition, books and television programs about Lincoln's life and death flourished in the immediate aftermath of the blockbuster Daniel Day-Lewis epic. Sometimes all it takes is a Hollywood movie to light a spark in people.

THE OFFICIAL "INVESTIGATIONS"

Looking back on the history of this case, all the major and minor investigations have been tainted, at least to a certain extent, either by individuals within the investigation itself, self-imposed handicaps on what could be looked at, time restraints, or all of the above. The Warren Commission (1963-1964) was hampered by the foxes guarding the chicken house, so to speak. Allen Dulles, the former CIA Director fired by President Kennedy over the Bay of Pigs debacle was a major member of the Commission. In fact, Walt Brown said this commission should have been called the Dulles Commission, as Allen was the most active of all the commissioners.[193] Best-selling author David Talbot wrote:

> What a cozy setup the CIA had in Dallas in 1963. Mayor Earle Cabell was not only the brother of Charles Cabell, the former CIA deputy chief who, along with his boss Allen Dulles, was fired by JFK. Now we learn that the Dallas mayor was also a CIA asset! This is part of a pattern: the Texas School Book Depository where Oswald supposedly fired from his sniper's nest was owned by right-wing oilman D.H. Byrd, who also had deep national security connections; the press corps covering the Kennedy motorcade was riddled with CIA assets.[194]

The Ramsey Clark Panel (named after LBJ's Attorney General) was convened in 1968 to whitewash and debunk the work of the early critics of the case such as Mark Lane, Josiah Thompson, Edward Epstein, Harold Weisberg, and others. The Clark Panel determined that President Kennedy was struck by two bullets fired from above and behind him, one of which traversed the base of the neck on the right side without striking bone and the other of which entered the skull from behind and destroyed its upper right side. The report also indicates that the skull shot entered well above the external occipital protuberance, which was at odds with the Warren Commission's findings. The Clark Panel was also used to blunt and distract from the Garrison case and any revelations of a pro-conspiracy nature that came out of the trial. While Clay Shaw was acquitted, members of the jury believed that Garrison demonstrated that there had been a conspiracy. In summary, the Clark Panel moved the head wound up a whopping 4 inches, mentioned particles they saw in the neck area, and they saw something that the pathologists and everyone else had not seen: a 6.5 mm fragment in the cowlick area at the rear of the skull. Still,

193 *The Warren Omission* by Walt Brown (1996).
194 https://whowhatwhy.org/2017/08/02/dallas-mayor-jfk-assassination-cia-asset/.

subtleties are lost on the public, no matter how important. All the public knew was that this panel endorsed the Commission's findings and Shaw was found not guilty. There was a temporary lull in the case as the 1960's gave way to the 1970's.

In light of the Watergate Hearings and all the cloak and dagger activities that were revealed to the American public, both the Rockefeller Commission and the Church Committee came into being in 1975 ostensibly to investigate the domestic abuses of both the FBI and CIA and, to a lesser extent, the performance of those agencies with regard to the Kennedy assassination. The Rockefeller Commission also dealt with the Kennedy assassination itself, specifically the head snap as seen in the Zapruder film (first shown to the general public also earlier in 1975), and the possible presence of E. Howard Hunt and Frank Sturgis in Dallas. Predictably, they came to the conclusion that neither man was in Dallas and that the Zapruder film's depiction of Kennedy's head moving violently backward and to the left could be chalked up to a neuromuscular reaction (the so-called "jet effect"). In other words, "who are you going to believe- me or your lying eyes?" Still, the effects of showing the Zapruder film to the general public at large in March 1975 would resonate despite any attempts to explain it all away.

The Rockefeller Commission was doomed from the start as it was convened by a former Warren Commissioner (President Gerald Ford) and included a prominent Commission lawyer (David Belin). The Church Committee (with its Schweiker-Hart subcommittee) faired a little better, as Senator Richard Schweiker believed that the Warren Commission was lied to by both the FBI and CIA (as it turns out, he was correct). Their report concluded that the investigation of the assassination by both the FBI and CIA was fundamentally deficient and that facts that may have greatly affected the investigation had not been forwarded to the Warren Commission by these agencies. The report hinted that there was a possibility that senior officials in both agencies made conscious decisions not to disclose potentially important information. Ultimately, the post-Watergate era created a public consensus for another actual investigation of the assassination. The public's wish was granted.

The House Select Committee on Assassinations (HSCA), which convened from 1976-1979, focused on the assassinations of JFK and Martin Luther King, Jr. (the initial proposal to also investigate the assassination of RFK was dropped). While this Congressional body came to the conclusion that Oswald fired all the deadly shots, they believed a shot did indeed come from the grassy knoll by an unknown assailant and that this shot missed. They thus came to the conclusion that there was a "probable conspiracy" in the death of JFK. As mentioned before, many people automatically assume that this conspiracy finding was solely based on the acoustics findings, but HSCA Chairman Louis Stokes debunked this notion on *Face The Nation* in January 1979, right when the report was issued, stating that other evidence (eye and ear witness testimony, etc.) buttressed this conclusion. That said, the HSCA (we have now learned) was greatly compromised by CIA employees George Joannides and Regis Blahut.[195]

In 1978 the CIA summoned Joannides out of retirement to serve as the agency's liaison to the HSCA. *Washington Post* reporter Jefferson Morley wrote: "the spy withheld information about his own actions in 1963 from the congressional investigators he was supposed to be assisting. It wasn't until 2001, 38 years after Kennedy's death, that Joannides' support for the Cuban exiles, who clashed with Oswald and monitored him, came to light."[196] HSCA Chief Counsel G. Robert Blakey later said Joannides role as CIA liaison to the committee was "criminal."[197] For his part, Blahut rifled the HSCA' files and illegally handled the autopsy photos, leading to suspicions of tampering.[198]

Former prosecutor, and Deputy Chief Counsel for the House Select Committee on Assassinations (HSCA), Robert Tanenbaum stated during a lecture in 2013,

> I can tell you from my experiences having tried several hundred cases to verdict, and being responsible for thousands of cases as head of the criminal courts, and running the homicide bureau, that I don't believe there's any courtroom in America where Oswald would have been convicted on the evidence that was presented before the Warren Commission.[199]

Still, despite the "probable conspiracy" verdict of the HSCA, the case went into somewhat of a lull for over 10 years, notable exceptions being Anthony Summers masterful book *Conspiracy*, David Lifton's controversial book *Best Evidence*, Henry Hurt's fine book *Reasonable Doubt*, Harrison Livingstone and Robert Groden's classic *High Treason*, and Jim

---

195   https://spartacus-educational.com/JFKjoannides.htm;   *Washington Post*,   6/28/79;
https://merdist.com/wp/2018/03/21/the-regis-blahut-case-revisited/.
196   *Salon* 12/17/2003.
197   *Not In Your Lifetime* by Anthony Summer (2013), page xix.
198   *High Treason* by Harrison Livingstone and Robert Groden (1998 edition), pages 92, 107, 332-333, and 341; *Not In Your Lifetime* by Anthony Summers (2013), page 479; from the newly-released files: https://www.archives.gov/files/research/jfk/releases/2018/docid-32269709.pdf.
199   https://kennedysandking.com/john-f-kennedy-articles/615.

Marrs nice compendium *Crossfire*. Not until the very end of the decade did things truly start to perk up, especially on television (right around the time of the 25th anniversary, the Lloyd Bentsen classic line in the debates about Jack Kennedy, and when the Reagan era officially gave way to the Bush 41 era). This late-decade groundswell planted the seeds that led to the 1991 movie *JFK* which, simply put, changed the game forever.

The Assassination Records Review Board (ARRB), which came into fruition via the JFK Records Act (which ultimately came into being via the fanfare over the blockbuster movie *JFK*), was convened from 1994-1998 and, although they were not an investigative body and, thus, would not come to any conclusions, pro or con, on the assassination (conspiracy versus no conspiracy), they did a lot of excellent work. Millions of pages of heretofore unknown or redacted documents were released in full, thus marking another era in the case. As ARRB member and author Doug Horne revealed, they also conducted an unofficial, off-the-record reinvestigation of the medical evidence, deposing the autopsy doctors and sundry other principal medical witnesses from both Parkland and Bethesda.[200]

The Secret Service greatly hampered the work of the ARRB by illegally destroying records that were requested of them. As the ARRB's Final Report duly notes:

> Congress passed the JFK Act in 1992. One month later, the Secret Service began its compliance efforts. However, in January 1995, the Secret Service destroyed Presidential protection survey reports for some of President Kennedy's trips in the fall of 1963. The Review Board learned of the destruction approximately one week after the Secret Service destroyed them, when the Board was drafting its request for additional information. The Board believed that the Secret Service files on the President's travel in the weeks preceding this murder would be relevant.

And, as it turned out, the Secret Service also withheld and destroyed documents during the life of both the Warren Commission and HSCA, as well.[201]

General Counsel for the Assassination Records Review Board (ARRB), Jeremy Gunn, said recently, "If we actually ask the question was Oswald guilty beyond a reasonable doubt ... I am convinced that Oswald would have been found not guilty beyond a reasonable doubt. To me there is just

---

200   *Inside the ARRB* by Doug Horne (2009), volumes 1-5.
201   From the newly-released files: https://www.archives.gov/files/research/jfk/releases/2018/180-10128-10002.pdf.

no question he is not guilty beyond a reasonable doubt."[202] After the brief fanfare of the release of the ARRB Final Report died down, the case largely caught fire on the Internet. In fact, if it wasn't for the Internet, one wonders if the case would have largely died with the turn of the 21st century and 9/11. If anything, the Internet became the major worldwide platform for all views on the case, rivaling and (one can argue) even surpassing the power of books and newspaper articles.

2003 was the 40th anniversary and the huge ratings success of the aforementioned *The Men Who Killed Kennedy* series. The Internet and the occasional book release saw the case thru until the 50th anniversary in 2013. After this media sensation, the case went on the backburner. Many wondered "where do we go from here? *Is* there anywhere *to* go?"

Then it happened: the 2016 presidential campaign and the aftermath.

A Twitter tweet from Donald Trump:

> **Donald J. Trump** ✔
> @realDonaldTrump
>
> Subject to the receipt of further information, I will be allowing, as President, the long blocked and classified JFK FILES to be opened.
>
> 8:35 AM · Oct 21, 2017
>
> 💬 10,430   🔁 15,995   ♡ 42,511

In 2017 and 2018,[203] we saw the much-publicized file releases that many (in an exaggeration) credited to President Trump (although, to be fair, the press releases for each installment would certainly lead one to that conclusion:

> President Donald J. Trump ordered all remaining records governed by section 5 of the JFK Act be released to the public. The President also directed agencies to complete another review of their proposed redactions and only redact information in the rarest of circumstances. The release by the National Archives today represents the first in a series of rolling releases pursuant to the President's memorandum based on prior reviews done by agencies. The records included in this public release have not been reviewed by NARA … On October 26, 2017, President Donald J. Trump directed agencies to re-review

202   https://kennedysandking.com/john-f-kennedy-articles/615.
203   The documents were released on 7/24/17, 10/26/17, 11/3/17, 11/9/17, 11/17/17, 12/15/17, and 4/26/18: https://www.archives.gov/research/jfk/release?page=7&sort=asc&order=Record%20Num.

each and every one of their redactions over the next 180 days....The versions released today were processed by agencies and, in accordance with the President's guidance, are being posted expeditiously in order to make the documents available to the public, even before the 2018 deadline established by the President on October 26, 2017.... In accordance with President Trump's direction on October 26, 2017, the National Archives today [4/26/18] posted 19,045 documents subject to the President John F. Kennedy Records Assassination Records Collection Act of 1992").

Still, as with the revelations from the ARRB releases roughly 20 years before, there were certainly some nuggets of value in these document dumps (another document dump is scheduled for 2021). The JFK assassination was in the news again, just as it was in 2016 during the silly Trump-initiated story that Ted Cruz's father knew Lee Harvey Oswald.

Also in 2018, author Christopher Fulton released his controversial best-seller *The Inheritance*. No less an authority than renowned author Dick Russell, who wrote the introduction, stated: "JFK's watch was the single most compelling piece of evidence that Lee Harvey Oswald did not act alone, that someone else fired the fatal shot from the front, that a conspiracy existed."[204] Sound amazing? Read the book – it is much too difficult to summarize.

Although poorly written and organized, prolific author Ralph Thomas is to be heartily commended for his numerous Kindle books highlighting these new document releases. Joe Backes has been a stalwart file release researcher since the 1990's and has made valuable contributions in this regard, as well, both at conferences and online.

Then, just when it looked like the JFK assassination was going to once again fade away, the subject came roaring back on March 26, 2020 when music legend Bob Dylan made worldwide headlines with a song about the Kennedy killing called *Murder Most Foul* that was filled with conspiratorial overtones.[205] These short excerpts are quite telling, to say the least:

> *"Thousands were watching, no one saw a thing*
> *It happened so quickly, so quick, by surprise*
> *Right there in front of everyone's eyes*
> *Greatest magic trick ever under the sun*
> *Perfectly executed, skillfully done"*

> *"They mutilated his body and they took out his brain ... magic bullet... I'm just a patsy... Never shot anyone from in front or behind."*

204   *The Inheritance* by Christopher Fulton (2018), page v.
205   https://en.wikipedia.org/wiki/Murder_Most_Foul_(song).

HOPE SPRINGS ETERNAL

I don't think interest will ever truly die with regard to the JFK assassination.

There have always been periods of inactivity (lulls) in the case, along with ambivalence or worse.

I remember being excited, during the lead up to Oliver Stone's film *JFK*, to attend my very first conference (as a speaker, too): the June 1991 *Third Decade* conference with Jerry Rose. Yet, only 60 people attended. In addition, there was a local newspaper story that stated: "Roughly 60 interested persons showed up for Prof. Jerry Rose's JFK assassination conference at SUNY Fredonia College, knowing full well that few in the outside world really cared."

Ouch.

Then the Stone film came out – things could not be better or so it seemed. And yet, there was still another side of the coin: equally long lines for the children's movie *Hook* competing with *JFK* and people giving what I thought were somewhat derisive looks at our line. Then came the avalanche of negative media commentary on the film (actually, this began before the film even came out!). I also remember a humbling experience for me: I was on a business trip in early 1992. In the midst of a dinner break, I was regaling my group with conspiracy details on the case. Then some guy burst my bubble: he said "You know who I think killed Kennedy? Bullwinkle killed Kennedy!" The rest of them all laughed and changed the subject.

Ouch.

Probably the biggest reality check was the attention – or lack thereof – given to the 1992 film *Ruby* (starring the recently departed Danny Aiello as Ruby). After seeing *JFK* three times in the theater and experiencing standing-room-only attendance and rapt attention to the film (never before or since have I felt such an "electric" feeling from a film), *Ruby* was quite humbling, to put it mildly: I was one of three people in attendance at the premiere (and one guy was certifiably goofy). Everyone was packing the adjoining theater to see *Basic Instinct*! The bloom was definitely off the rose a little by then, just a very short period of time later. One is reminded of a then-current witty statement: "Damn, that *JFK* movie was something else, wasn't it? Now, who is playing against the Cowboys tomorrow and what is the point spread?" The moral to the story being this: the public at large was/is fascinated by the case, to a certain extent, but they aren't obsessed like us, researching it and writing books. They have bills to pay, families to feed, and current events on their minds a heck of a lot more.

I think the reason we always have hope is the fact that we know that a certain best-selling book or (especially) a hot television special or movie can ignite interest in the case, albeit briefly. I also vividly remember attending a Borders Books Mark Lane mini-seminar in February 1992 for his hit book *Plausible Denial* that had 500-plus people in attendance. The fact that many of these people held competing-theory books in their hands for purchase and that they all seemed to "melt away" soon after was troubling for my obsessed-with-the-case mind: why aren't these people still "into it" like I am?

Also, while the *JFK* movie spawned many tabloid television show programs on the subject (*Geraldo, A Current Affair* with Maury Povich, *Jenny Jones*, etc.) and several actual pro-conspiracy specials (with James Earl Jones stumbling and fumbling his narration; Robert Conrad hosting a mafia-did-it show, etc.), there was a for-dramatic-entertainment-only feel to these shows. In addition, while there were whole "JFK assassination" shelves at Walden Books, Borders, and Barnes and Noble, there were a lot of new and reissued books with many competing and confusing (to John Q Citizen) theories – an agent accidentally shot JFK (*Mortal Error*), "Saul" shot JFK (Hugh McDonald's *Appointment in Dallas* reissued), the Weisberg books (brilliant research, poor writing), etc.

No wonder that it felt like a lot of people were confused, threw up their hands, and seemed to move on. I also believe the massive media saga of the O.J. Simpson murder case (1994-1997, including the civil trial), as well as the drama of the Clinton/Lewinsky scandal/impeachment mess soon afterward, "replaced" the case in the minds of the public looking at something to be further interested in, but I digress.

Then again...

The Stone film created the ARRB – millions of files were released that we are still going through, definitely a tremendous achievement.

Finally (keeping in mind the 60 researchers who attended the 1991 pre-Stone movie conference and the somewhat negative article that greeted it), roughly 150 researchers attended the last Judyth Baker/Trine Day conference in Dallas, while about that many attended the CAPA conference, also in Dallas at the same time; Dealey Plaza was heavy with people, researchers and regular folk alike from 11/22-11/23/2019 and a Japanese film crew was there filming a documentary for a major Japan television network.

I guess the moral to the story is: time marches on and cynicism can sometimes overtake us, but I believe interest will never die for this case. Part of the (major) appeal to the case is the still-huge interest in the Kennedys, in general, and JFK, in particular.

We can prove conspiracy and we have a good idea of who did it, but we can't prove it, just as we will never prove who the other shooter or shooters were.

Whatever his role or motives, Lee Harvey Oswald was not a shooter. His rifle was a guilty participant but he was not.

Cuba, not Vietnam, was the patsy, along with Oswald, in the assassination.

Without the death of President Kennedy, no LBJ, no Nixon, no Ford, no Carter, and maybe not even Reagan or the Bushes (Clinton, Obama and Trump are unknowns in this chain). No Vietnam War as an escalated ground war – more of a cold war than a hot one; no Watergate; the list goes on.

We lost a lot when we lost JFK. We must never forget that.

I doubt most of us ever will.

CHAPTER EIGHT

THE JOURNEY

Although I am as passionate and interested in the JFK case as I was when I was younger, there is something about those early days that really resonates with me. Some people call becoming interested in this subject "the sickness," others call it "the obsession." All I know is that no other historical topic has come close to matching the levels of excitement, curiosity and interest. Even when the nation was consumed with the O.J. Simpson case, it pales in comparison to this. Some naturally thought the turn of the new century and 9/11 would place the Kennedy assassination on the backburner, but it did not: the 40th anniversary in 2003 was huge and the ratings for *The Men Who Killed Kennedy* (and subsequent DVD sales) were through the roof.

But let me backtrack for a second.

Although John Davis' *Mafia Kingfish* was technically my first JFK assassination book that I purchased and owned (as opposed to a book I borrowed from a friend or the library), I found it long-winded and somewhat tangential to the case. No, it was Robert Groden and Harrison Livingstone's *High Treason* purchased in 1989 that really got my blood going. Who would have thought that, in a matter of a couple short years, I would meet both Davis and Livingstone at Jerry Rose's Third Decade conference in Fredonia, New York (June 1991, to be exact)? To be a 25-year-old "newbie" on the case and present my first paper next to these legendary figures (as well as authors George Michael Evica, Bob Cutler, and others) was truly an honor and one I think of often. It was also an honor to be mentioned in both the 1998 and 2006 editions of *High Treason*, but I digress.

In Livingstone's case, I would go on to work with him for a fair amount of time, off and on, after that conference. Harry, as I liked to call him, was a very sincere and passionate person. He was also a troubled soul. Required reading on this subject is Harry's 2012 personal memoir *Journey into the Whirlwind: A Personal Memoir and Story of Psychic Murder – The Dictatorship and Mind-Control of Writing and Publishing – The True Story of What One Publisher Did to An Author*. Although a daunting title, the work really taps into why Harry was the way he was. Let me explain.

Although Harry was definitely one of the most successful writers in the case ever (*High Treason* was a best-seller twice; *High Treason 2* was also a best-seller, as well, while Harry also published over a dozen other titles, several of which sold fairly well in their own right), even appearing on network television a few times, his personality really rubbed people the wrong way and, quite frankly, turned off a legion of people in the research community itself, as well as the public, to the point where Harry was never invited to speak at any major conferences after appearing at one more Third Decade conference (although he attended and "crashed" a few). The three major venues – A.S.K., COPA and Lancer – didn't want him. Harry's third book on the assassination, *Killing the Truth*, was the major catalyst, as he tore into sacred cows on the case like the legendary Harold Weisberg (whom he once put on a pedestal), Mary Ferrell, Mark Lane, and others.

Having worked with Harry on *High Treason 2* (including filming Bethesda autopsy x-ray technician Jerrol Custer on 11/22/91), *Killing the Truth* (including driving Harry to Shelby, Ohio for a lengthy interview with Steve Barber in 1992), and, to a lesser extent, his books *Killing Kennedy* and *The Radical Right*, supplying videos, articles, and insights, I saw two sides to Harry: "Uncle Harry" (as he sometimes called himself), a very nice and compassionate person never shy about spreading the wealth1 and giving credit when you helped him, and "Brusque Harry" (as I now think of him sometimes), a rude curmudgeon who became nasty with waiters, the public, his interview subjects and even his helpers like me.

I remember the drive to Shelby, Ohio in the Spring of 1992. Making small talk, I mentioned how well Harry's last two books did, sales-wise. Harry became angry and slammed his fist against the inside passenger car door, exclaiming loudly "I am an artist!" In other words, money and fame meant nothing to him; it was about the art, his other writings, and the truth. I believed him … but his "dark side," so to speak, could rise up out of nowhere and take you by surprise.

Harry turned on his former partner Robert Groden, as the two fought in courts of law and in the court of public opinion. Still, Harry could be surprising even with his so-called enemies: he showed up unannounced at the 1996 COPA conference and was politely silent as Groden won a touching award from the conference organizers. We all thought Harry was going to "crash" Robert's party, but he did not. I believe George Michael Evica (another author who "got into it" with Harry) was correct when he

---

1   Harry, in one of our phone conversations in 1992, told me that he received a royalty check for 200,000 dollars for *High Treason 2*. Soon after, without any prompting whatsoever, I received a check in the mail for 500 dollars from him!

said "Harry just needs a hug." In fact, Evica and Harry sat side by side at another Jerry Rose conference a few short years after their verbal fighting at the 1991 event and were cordial and, dare I say, friendly.

I am going on about Livingstone because he made a big impact on my research. As I said in the introduction, his advice ("unless you have something original to offer, don't bother – you'll just run yourself into the ground") was well taken, as was the example he set with performing primary research: actually contacting principal witnesses in the case. Along with a phone call from Dr. Cyril Wecht in 1991, it was Harry's example that set me on my course to contacting as many former Secret Service agents – and medical witnesses – as possible. Harry also taught me what not to do: burn your bridges. While I also, by and large, work alone like Harry, I try to conduct myself with respect and courtesy towards others. Still, Harry's passing in 2015 was a sad event for me. I will never forget you, Harry.

However, there were many other touchstones along the way. A letter I received from Harold Weisberg in 1992 was inspiring. Also in 1992, seeing Mark Lane in person when I was still basically an unknown amateur on the case (one conference presentation and one article to my credit then) was also inspirational. Lane visited my local Borders Books on his *Plausible Denial* book tour (over 500 people were there for his best-selling book and talk – those were the days). I remember getting his autograph and trying to talk to him about Marty Underwood's revelations, but I was greeted with a perfunctory "oh, really" as other people were shouting questions and vying for his attention. Ironically, it was Mark who called on me out of the blue in 2011 about wanting to include my work in what would be his next (and final) JFK book *Last Word*.

It was still 1992 when David Lifton started calling me unexpectedly for my insights and to feel out where I was going with both my research (he loved my then-unpublished first book title *Survivor's Guilt*) and my association with an enemy of his, Harry Livingstone, who harshly criticized Lifton, to put it mildly. Off and on, Lifton would continue to seek out my help and advice through the years (this time via e-mail) as he continues to labor on the much anticipated and way overdue follow-up to his seminal best-seller *Best Evidence* entitled *Final Charade*. Having met George Michael Evica at the 1991 Third Decade conference, it was an honor to present with him at the American Popular Culture conference in Louisville, Kentucky in March 1992. It was Evica that taught me the concepts of both a third alternative to mere innocence or guilt and the notion of security stripping. I would meet Evica again at COPA 1995 (when he added a lengthy coda to my presentation) and Lancer 1997 (when he both introduced my presentation and emceed the Q & A session afterwards). Evica's passing in 2007 was felt by many. He is missed.

Although we no longer communicate (based largely on Walt's disappointment in my brief turn to the dark side in 2007),[2] I am indebted to author Walt Brown for his early friendship, his impressive works on the case, and being associated with his old journal *JFK-Deep Politics Quarterly*, along with Jan Stevens. From roughly 1993 to 2002 or so, Walt was a source of wit and inspiration to me. In fact, his 1996 book *The Warren Omission* is still one of my very favorite books on the case. I wish him well just the same.

Likewise, the man who caused all my (brief) troubles, the late Vincent Bugliosi, is still a hero to me (well, for some of his non-JFK works). Although I now see the deep flaws in his massive 2007 tome *Reclaiming History*, I am still a huge fan of his O.J. Simpson case book *Outrage*, as well as his legendary prosecution of Charles Manson and his harsh feelings towards the Bush administration and the Iraq War. Speaking to Bugliosi on the phone was a joy. Vince was a very witty, funny and brilliant person (who was also passionate about Spanish music – he was kind enough to send me a free cd that contained his liner notes). His passing in 2015 was noted the world over. No matter what one thought of Bugliosi, he was one hell of a prosecutor and writer.

Two writers who brought me back to my senses, Jim Douglass (whom I spoke to a couple times before my brief sojourn to the other side) and Doug Horne (who also witnessed my 1995 and 1996 COPA presentations), are deeply appreciated. Douglass book *JFK and the Unspeakable* is a classic, while Horne's 5-volume series *Inside the ARRB* has gone a long way towards refining and expanding both the medical evidence case, in general, and David Lifton's work, specifically.

I am deeply indebted to author Judyth Baker for even being published to begin with. She graciously contacted me out of the blue in 2012 and suggested that I send my then-unpublished first book manuscript to Kris Millegan of Trine Day. Five books and three conference appearances later, the rest is history. Ironically, Judyth was on *The Men Who Killed Kennedy* in 2003 (part 8), as I was, as well (part 7). Both episodes are now airing once again (2019-2020) on Newsmax TV, but I digress. I know (as she

---

2   The only other author or researcher I know of who still holds it against me for my brief 2007-era turn to the dark side is Charles Drago, a novelist and good friend of the late George Michael Evica whom I had the pleasure of meeting at Fredonia in 1991 and Dallas in 1997. Although he seemed satisfied when I convinced him that I was "all better now" and my 2013 book *Survivor's Guilt* would be a pro-conspiracy volume, he became cold towards me soon after. Such is life. Still, I also wish him well. He is a brilliant writer and thinker (and quite a jazz enthusiast).

does) that Judyth can be a polarizing figure in the case, but the good she has done for the case (her brilliant conferences and getting other authors published, to name but two contributions) is tremendous. She is also a very nice lady.

It was quite an honor to be included in the Final Report of the Assassination Records Review Board (ARRB) in 1998. To know that President Clinton personally received a copy is a thrill (knowing that Trent Lott and Newt Gingrich also received copies is not such a thrill). Finally, knowing I wasn't even born when the Warren Commission was around and that I began my embryonic journey at age 12 in 1978 during the HSCA, it is that much more amazing to have been included in the third major investigation of the assassination (perhaps the third major "look" at the case is technically more accurate, yet the ARRB did quite a bit of investigating, albeit unofficially).

It is truly a blessing to be a published author these days (5 books in both kindle and paperback since 2013). As I have said before, back in the pre-kindle days, and certainly in the pre-Amazon/Internet days, your book faced an uphill battle to receive any kind of meaningful sales and recognition (not that today's era does not have obstacles, as well). Back in the "old days," if your book did not have any kind of mainstream press, preferably aided by a major anniversary of the assassination (and a major film like JFK garnering headlines, to boot), your book literally died on the shelves, dead on arrival. You had the thrill of being an actual published author, perhaps even on a decent publishing house, but no one bought it … no one cared. Now, with the advent of Amazon and kindle, the playing field has been greatly leveled in everyone's favor: people merely search for the latest titles (example: via a "JFK assassination" search). This is a great aid when one considers how much the mainstream media has shut down dissent on this case. Finally, the kindle option opens doors previously closed to those authors in the paper-only days.

Ironically, I have to thank former Secret Service agents Gerald Blaine and Clint Hill for rejuvenating my interest in the case! Back in 2008-2009, I was basically burnt out on the case and semi-retired (leaning toward actual retirement), never thinking I would be published. Then, someone contacted me and said an obscure former agent (Blaine) would be coming out with a book, which appeared to be a self-published affair at the time (before Blaine landed a book contract with Simon & Schuster). Then, Blaine's attorney contacted me about one of my blogs, Hill and Blaine mentioned me on C-SPAN in 2010 (and, again, in 2012) and the rest is history.

Relatively friendly agent authors I spoke to and/or corresponded with include Jerry Parr, Bill Carter, Darwin Horn, Mike Maddaloni, Rufus Youngblood and Gary Byrne. Although famous best-selling author William Manchester was a bit of a curmudgeon when I spoke to him back in 1993, his lovely daughter Julie is infinitely more approachable these days on social media. For all the many former Secret Service agents, family members and medical evidence witnesses I interviewed and corresponded with, please see my previous four books.

It was a pleasure meeting in person witnesses and other important people like Jim Gochenaur, Hugh Clark (also an author), Madeleine Brown (also an author), Beverly Oliver (also an author), Buell Wesley Frazier (author of an upcoming book with Dave Perry and Gus Russo), Shari Angel, Aubrey Rike (also an author), Mary Ann Moorman, Oliver Stone (also an author), Palmer McBride, Ed Hoffman (also an author), Tom Wilson and Jerrol Custer.

Former Secret Service agents Abraham Bolden, Dan Emmett and Robert DeProspero are in the "good" former agent category and my association with them has been very inspiring, to say the least. I reached out to Abe in 1993 and we have spoken and corresponded many times since, including on social media. Abe would go on to publish a terrific book entitled *The Echo from Dealey Plaza* in 2008. Dan Emmett reached out to me in 2011 regarding his excellent and yet-unpublished book *Within Arm's Length*. It was a thrill to be mentioned on the cover of the original edition of his book.

Also in 2011, my idol, Bob DeProspero, contacted me out of the blue, as well (it pays to have a heavy online presence). A few short years later, I would end up Associate Producer for the documentary on his life story, the DVD *The Man Behind The Suit*. Bob's passing in 2019 touched me deeply, as he was someone I looked up to. I also regret not being able to take him up on his offer to join him for Thanksgiving at his daughter's home in Virginia in 2016. Now, the chance to meet him in person is gone forever. Still, I cherish our correspondence and phone conversations.

Author John Armstrong (2003's *Harvey and Lee*) was a source of inspiration when he presented right before me at COPA 1996 and again at Lancer 1997. I got to spend a little time with John as I rode in his car around Dallas with Palmer McBride. John is a towering researcher in this case.[3] [4]

Author David Wayne has been very generous towards me these last few years, as I am mentioned positively in several of his best-selling books, in-

3   http://harveyandlee.net/
4   https://digitalcollections-baylor.quartexcollections.com/poage-collections/john-armstrong-collection

cluding *Hit List*. David's enthusiasm is contagious. It is an honor to know him. Likewise, it was an honor to be mentioned on 16 pages of another David Wayne co-authored book, the 2012 Jesse Ventura tome *They Killed Our President: 63 Reasons To Believe There Was A Conspiracy to Assassinate JFK*. It was also nice of Jesse to favorably mention me on his Facebook page in 2013.

Although he went off the rails after 9/11 and especially after Sandy Hook, I am indebted to Professor James Fetzer in those early days before he saw everything as a false flag and conspiracies of epic proportions were literally everywhere (I saw Fetzer again in 2016 at a conference and we exchanged pleasantries but that was about it). I had two prominent chapters in Fetzer's 2000 book *Murder in Dealey Plaza*, for which I am most grateful. At that time, it was the closest I thought I would ever get to being published (it was especially nice to be mentioned favorably in the *Publishers Weekly* review of the book, which seemed to be everywhere in over-the-counter bookstores at that time). Ironically, exactly one month before 9/11 (8/11/2001, to be exact), Professor Fetzer came unannounced to my apartment to advise me that he spoke to Nigel Turner about having me on the new installment(s) of *The Men Who Killed Kennedy* (slated for 2003). The next year, Nigel Turner himself would likewise pay an unannounced visit to my apartment and we then proceeded to my sister's house a couple blocks away in order to film me for 16 hours over two days (I only received a few minutes of air time, but I am grateful nonetheless).

Another person I am somewhat indebted to who fell from grace as of late is author Roger Stone. Having spoken to him a few times briefly on the phone and having also communicated on social media (all back in 2012-2013), I was grateful for Roger's help in getting my work noted in two lengthy Florida-based news sites, as well as a favorable mention on his *The Stone Zone* (as well as on a You Tube radio show with Tyler Nixon). I was also mentioned for some of my work in the paperback edition of his massive best-seller *The Man Who Killed Kennedy: The Case Against LBJ* in 2014. My wife and I met him in 2016 at the same JFK conference where Fetzer was presenting at. It was here that the bloom was really off the rose, as Stone's presentation was more about Hillary Clinton (just defeated by Donald Trump in the 2016 election) than it was about LBJ (or JFK). Then I started to view his work with a jaundiced eye, as it seemed his goal was more to paint all the Democrats in a bad light (example: LBJ as the plotter against JFK) and his pro-Trump commentaries on television became a major turn-off. Then, like Fetzer, he got into trouble and the rest is history.

Although I am no longer a big fan of their books, I appreciate the support by authors Lamar Waldron and Thom Hartmann. Their book *Ultimate Sacrifice* was the big book I was into in 2005-2006 right before *Reclaiming History* by Vince Bugliosi cast its spell on me, albeit briefly. I now look back on my passion for Waldron's book(s) with a little bit of embarrassment, truth be told, as authors such as Jim DiEugenio have thoroughly gutted the basic premise of their work.

Speaking of DiEugenio, I am a big fan of his seminal works *Destiny Betrayed* (soon to be an Oliver Stone documentary of the same name[5]) and *The JFK Assassination* (formerly known as *Reclaiming Parkland*). It was great seeing him with Oliver Stone, albeit briefly, at the 2019 JFK assassination conference in Dallas. Jim got a kick out of the fact that it seemed I wanted his photo more than I wanted one of Oliver! Likewise, I am also deeply appreciative of author Flip de Mey and his amazing books *Cold Case Kennedy* and *The Lee Harvey Oswald Files*. In addition, author Barry Ernest is to be commended for his classic book *The Girl on the Stairs*.

Author William Matson Law and I go way back: all the way to Lancer 1997, where we met several key witnesses, some of which I filmed with my old camcorder. The meeting was so inspirational that we would get together the next year to film Bethesda autopsy x-ray technician Jerrol Custer (yes, the same one from *High Treason 2* days; he remembered me a little). The results of this work would appear in Law's epic medical evidence volume *In The Eye of History* in 2005 (expanded and updated in 2015 by Trine Day. Yes, we share the same publisher, as well).

When I first met Robert Groden in person at *COPA* 1996, he was understandably weary of me, as I was a big fan of his estranged writing partner Harry Livingstone. Still, once we got past that, he was most kind and generous. Although I met Robert again briefly in Dallas in both 1997 and 2016, it was during 2018-2019 that we seemed to bond. First, he was a fan of my anti-Trump memes and so forth on social media and indicated as such, even phoning me once to tell me of his appreciation in that regard. Then, soon after, we met at the 2019 JFK assassination conference, where he and his lovely new bride Janet were the toast of the town. Both were very nice and it was super talking to them both. Robert is a legend in the

---

5   I was invited by Jim to be in this documentary but I was unable to secure the time from work under such short notice to do it. I regret this now. This is not the first time I was disappointed: History Channel producers invited me to be involved in a production called *The President's Book of Secrets* but I had the same problem- limited time and funds to go to Washington. Although I was filmed for the documentary *King Kill '63*, it was only shown once – at the Texas Theater in 2014 – and my part was not included. The documentary has yet to surface, although it is credited on Imdb : The Internet Movie Database.

research community but he comes across as very down to earth, which is refreshing, to put it mildly.

Speaking of *COPA* 1996, it was quite a thrill to have the one and only Josiah "Tink" Thompson come up to me immediately after my presentation and tell me "great job!" Speaking to him afterwards, one came away with the impression that Tink was truly a nice man. Tink phoned me out of the blue around 2004 to discuss some of my research. Again, it was a nice surprise. Also at that same *COPA* 1996 conference was Professor Phil Melanson. Although we exchanged pleasantries, it wasn't until 2003-2005 when he started to contact me via the Internet regarding what was to become his book on the Secret Service entitled *The Secret Service: The Hidden History of an Enigmatic Agency* (unbeknownst to me at the time, I was mentioned several times in that work and he was in the process of updating it). Phil's untimely passing in 2006 was a real shock and quite a loss, as well: his book *Spy Saga* was an early inspiration, as well.

Speaking of losses, it is sobering to think of all the people who have passed away or disappeared (lack of interest/no longer seeking to get published, etc.) from that June 1991 Fredonia, New York *Third Decade* conference. Researchers Jerry Rose, Kathlee Fitzgerald (2019) and Ray Carroll (2014), along with authors Harry Livingstone (2015), Robert Cutler, and George Michael Evica (2007), to name just the ones I know of. Then-seventeen year old Ulric Shannon quit the case a few years later to become a diplomat: Ambassador of Canada to Iraq! I still remember his disappointment when fellow Pittsburgher Kathlee and I could not make the journey to Fredonia for a mini-conference in January 1992 due to a horrific winter storm. I also cherish our conversations. Ulric wrote a few seminal articles on the case, including a review of my then-unpublished and much slimmer first book. I also remember phoning him and receiving his answering machine message, all in French-Canadian, which I did not understand. His insights on Posner, Weisberg, Livingstone, John Davis, Robert D. Morrow and others were fascinating.[6]

My, have times changed. The clock ticks on.

I can certainly see how someone can become frustrated and appear to quit the case. If you have nothing original to offer, no publisher interested in your manuscript, or both, it would be very understandable to feel like all hope was lost and it was the end of the road. You may watch the occasional documentary on the case and talk amongst your friends about

---

6   The reader is encouraged to check out this excellent article by Ulric Shannon from 1996: https://jfkassassination.net/shannon.htm

it, but that would be it. I know the feeling well: I was once a passionate guitarist and musician but I could not keep a band together as I grew older and, with no record label interested (despite a close call and some accolades), it was time to move on.

Back to dedications: the works of Dr. David Mantik and Brad Parker (both authors of seminal kindle-only books on the medical evidence) are very important to the study of this case. It was nice seeing Brad at Lancer 1997 (and filming him with Aubrey Rike), in addition to reconnecting with him again on social media a few years ago. Likewise, after having met Dr. Mantik at COPA 1995 and 1996, as well as seeing him at the 2003 Duquesne University conference, it was an honor appearing with him on both *The Men Who Killed Kennedy* and *A Coup in Camelot* (and seeing him in Dallas on 11/22/19). His daughter Meredith filmed me for a documentary in the works during parts of 2018 and 2019, as well.

It was a thrill to be contacted by legendary author Anthony Summers back in 1994 for his upcoming *Vanity Fair* article on the case (I had previously corresponded with Summers in 1991). My research on Roy and June Kellerman was included in his seminal article, written with the help of his wife and partner Robbyn Swan (Summers). In fact, I vividly remember phoning Anthony back once only to hear from a sleepy Robbyn on the other line telling me that the time zone difference in Ireland made it in the dead of night there! Anthony also contacted me for his 2005 book on Frank Sinatra entitled *Sinatra: The Life.*

It was also quite an honor to have been contacted by author David Talbot in 2006 for his then-forthcoming best-seller *Brothers* (I am mentioned on a few pages). Talbot's magnum opus on Allen Dulles, *The Devil's Chessboard: Allen Dulles, the CIA, and the Rise of America's Secret Government,* is a truly remarkable work, indeed. David had a health scare recently and I pray he is on the mend now.

Other authors I am indebted to include Paul Blake Smith, Gary Fannin (a pleasure working the book table with you at the conference in 2016 and seeing you again, albeit briefly, at the 2019 conference), Ed Souza, Noel Twyman (a pleasure meeting you in Dallas on 11/22/1997), Connie Kritzberg, Barry Krusch, Donna Mabry, Joseph McBride, Larry Sabato, Colin McLaren, Howard Donahue (essentially the author of *Mortal Error*), Phil Nelson, John Onesti, Robin Ramsay, James Rinnovatore, Dan Robertson, Tony Zappone, James Sawa, William Scott, John Simkin, J. Randy Toraborelli, Blaine Taylor, Richard Trask, Todd Wayne Vaughan, Mal Hyman, Keith Badman, Richard Charnin, Max Allen Collins, Marshal Evans (great seeing you in Dallas on 11/22/19), Sherry Fiester (RIP), Anthony Frewin, Ian Griggs (RIP), Charles Hurlburt, Gayle Nix Jackson, Don Jeffries, Gary Byrne, R. Andrew Kiel (a pleasure meeting you in Dallas on 11/22/2019), Lance Moore, and Larry Hancock. A special note of thanks goes out to researcher and friend Matt Douthit, a true young wunderkind whose writings and thinking on the case are truly amazing to behold. I look forward to his future works, as I do another young researcher with a promising future, author Willy O'Halloran, a.k.a. Yoda and Freddie Mercury II. Likewise, fellow friend Ben Papp, although mainly just interested in Kennedy's life (nothing wrong with that), has been a tremendous help to me in Dallas a few times. Ben also does a great Kennedy impersonation, along with a couple other presidents.

In the "missing in action" category, I have fond memories of corresponding and collaborating with researchers Bill Adams, Deanie Richards, Anna-Marie Kuhns-Walko and Russ Shearer in the late 1990's. They were always generous with sharing documents. I also enjoyed subscribing to researcher Gary Rowell's print journal *The Investigator* in the early to mid 1990's, as well as Paul Hoch's newsletter. In regard to documents, the late Ed Sherry ("Tree frog") and the late Doug Weldon were simply amazing with their document shares. I also liked corresponding with Milicent Cranor (who is back in action now!), Bill Drenas, Gordon Winslow, Carol Hewett, Steven Jones, Barbara LaMonica, David Starks and Frank De-Benedictis. While some people have passed away, I suspect several people basically retired from the case (like Kathleen Cunningham, an expert on the medical evidence). I suppose, as I stated above, without a book and the end of print journals (where everyone now is an "expert" with the advent of the net with its social media, blogging, and so forth), a fair amount of people felt that they had taken what they learned and shared as far as it could go. Then again, I never thought I would have one book published, let alone five; I am lucky.

When the Internet really "kicked in" in the late 1990's to the very early 2000's (after a sort of embryonic start with computer bulletin boards and early websites, newsgroups, and so forth), the sharing of data and views was simply overwhelming. That said, there was a lot of fighting, often amongst ourselves, with silliness pervading every nook and cranny of the so-called information superhighway a.k.a. the worldwide web. When blogging became popular around 2006 or so, I took the plunge full throttle and made huge gains in my online presence far from my humble My Space days. I obtained my You Tube channel in 2007 and it has grown exponentially since. When social media (Facebook, Twitter, and Instagram) took off around 2010-2012 or so, my online presence grew even further. Still, I prefer to work alone.

My heartfelt thanks go out to my family and especially the love of my life, my wife Amanda. I deeply appreciate all your love and support. Your presence with me in Dallas for the conferences has been so great.

This is my story and I am sticking to it.

CHAPTER NINE

MASTER LIST OF WITNESSES WHO INDICATED THAT JFK WAS SHOT FROM THE FRONT PLUS THE WOUNDS TO JFK

People ran toward the grassy knoll. No one seemed to look up at the Book Depository.

– Jim Willmon[1]

No credible evidence suggests that the shots were fired from the railroad bridge over the Triple Underpass, the nearby railroad yards or any place other than the Texas School Book Depository.

– Warren Report, page 61

This is the greatest compilation of eyewitness testimony and sworn statements about both the shooting in Dealey Plaza and the wounds to JFK ever published in book form. This may be a bold statement, but it is the truth. I believe the reader will have a very hard time believing that the only shots fired on the presidential limousine came only from behind.

1. J.C. Price: 11-24-63 FBI memo by Calvin Rice and Alfred Neeley to SAC Shanklin, found in the Weisberg Archives; 11-25-63 FBI report based on its 11-24-63 interview of Price, CD5, p62; Interview with Mark Lane in *Rush to Judgment*, filmed 3-27-66: "From behind the overpass over there, triple overpass, that's where I thought the shots were coming from."

2. Patsy Paschall: November 1995 KDFW television interview: "There was smoke coming from the knoll ... the smoke came from that knoll"; she thinks there was more to it than Oswald;

3. Robert West: 2-13-69 testimony in the trial of Clay Shaw: "The sound came from the northwest quadrant of Dealey Plaza.... This entire area north and west of Elm Street."; heard four shots;

4. W.W. Mabra: July-August 1988 interview recounted in *American History Illustrated*, November 1988: "People ran toward the knoll. Some said they saw smoke there. I thought at first the shot may have come from there."; *No More Silence* p. 518-529, published 1998: "As we were crossing Houston running in the direction of the grassy knoll, I could see what looked like a swirl of smoke.... By the time I got there, the smoke had disappeared";

5. Eugene L. Boone: 11-22-63 report, 19H508: "I heard three shots coming from the vicinity of where the president's car was .... Some of the bystanders said the shots came from the overpass. I ran across the street (Elm) and up the embankment over the retaining wall and into the freight yard."; 3-25-64 testimony before the Warren Commission, 3H291-295: "one of the bystanders over there seemed to think the shots came from up over the railroad in the freight yards, from over the triple underpass.";

6. A.D. McCurley: 11-22-63 report, 19H514: "I rushed towards the park and saw people running towards the railroad yards beyond Elm Street and I ran over and jumped a fence and a railroad worker stated to me that he believed the smoke from the bullets came from the vicinity of a stockade fence which surrounds the park area.";

7. L.C. Smith: 11-22-63 report, 19H516: I ran as fast as I could to Elm Street just west of Houston and I heard a woman unknown to me say the President was shot, in the head, and the shots came from the fence on the north side of Elm. I went at once behind the fence and searched also in the parking area.;

8. Buddy Walthers: 11-22-63 report, 19H518: "I immediately started running west across Houston Street and ran across Elm Street and up into the railroad yards.... Upon reaching the railroad yard and seeing other officers coming, I immediately went to the triple underpass on Elm Street in an effort to locate possible marks left by stray bullets. While I was looking for possible marks, some unknown person [James Tague] stated to me that something had hit his face while he was parked on Main Street, the next lane south from Elm, as the traffic had been stopped for the parade. Upon examining the curb and pavement in this vicinity I found where a bullet had splattered on the top edge of the curb on Main Street, which would place the direction of firing, high and behind the position the President's car was in when he was shot. Due to the fact that the projectile struck so near the underpass, it was, in my opinion, probably the last shot that was fired and had apparently went high and above the President's car."; *Red Roses from Texas*, by Nerin Gun, published

February 1964: "Buddy Walthers, the policeman from the Sheriff's office, states for his part that the shots – or at least one shot – came from the balustrade of the motorway bridge."; 7-23-64 testimony before the Warren Commission, 7H544-552: "I ran across here (indicating) and there is a wall along in here and I hopped over it. People were laying down on this grass – women and men were laying on top of their children on the grass...and then someone, I don't know, I say someone – a lot of people was sitting there – but it must have been behind that fence – there's a fence right along here.... And at that time I heard the shots as well as everybody else, but as we got over this fence, and a lot of officers and people were just rummaging through the train yards back in this parking area.";

9. Harry Weatherford: 11-23-63 report, 19H502: "I heard a loud report which I thought was a railroad torpedo, as it sounded as if it came from the railroad yard ... then I heard a second report which had more of an echo report and thought to myself, that this was a rifle and I started towards the corner when I heard the third report. By this time I was running toward the railroad yards where the sounds seemed to come from.";

10. Luke Mooney: 11-23-63 report, 19H528: "I immediately started running towards the front of the motorcade and within seconds heard a second and a third shot. I started running across Houston Street and down across the lawn to the triple underpass and up the terrace to the railroad yards. I searched along with many other officers, this area."; 3-25-64 testimony before the Warren Commission, 3H281-290: "Jumped over the fence and went into the railroad yards. And, of course, there was other officers over there. Who they were, I don't recall at this time. But Ralph Walters and I were running together. And we jumped into the railroad yards and began to look around there.... And, of course, we didn't see anything there. Of course the other officers had checked into the car there, and didn't find anything, I don't believe, but a Negro porter. Of course there were quite a few spectators milling around behind us.";

11. J.L. Oxford: 11-23-63 report, 19H530: "Officer McCurley and myself ran across Houston Street on across Elm and down to the underpass. When we got there, everyone was looking toward the railroad yards. We jumped the picket fence which runs along Elm Street and on over into the railroad yards. When we got over there, there was a man who told us that he had seen smoke up in the corner of the fence. We went to the corner of the fence to see what we could find, and searched the area thoroughly. ";

12. Allan Sweatt: 11-23-63 report, 19H531: "…we were told the shots had come from the fence. Deputy Wiseman and a City Officer went to the front door of the building and I continued towards the railroad yards with Deputy Harry Weatherford.";

13. Roger Craig: 1-23-63 FBI report based on an 11-22-63 interview, 23H817: "He … went through the parking area…"; 11-23-63 report, 19H524: "I started running around the corner and Officer Buddy Walthers and I ran across Houston Street and on up the terrace on Elm Street and into the railroad yards. We made a round through the railroad yards…"; 4-1-64 testimony before the Warren Commission, 6H260-273: "I ran up to the railroad yard and – uh – started to look around when the people began to all travel over that way. So, I began moving people back out of the railroad yard … as I reached the railroad yard, I talked to a girl getting her car that – uh – thought they came from the park area on the north side of Elm Street … she was standing there and it sounded real loud at that particular point…. And she thought that's where they came from.";

14. Seymour Weitzman: 11-23-63 Affidavit to Dallas County, 24H228: "I ran in a northwest direction and scaled a fence towards where we thought the shots came from."; 11-23-63 FBI report, CD5 p. 124: "He believed these sounds to have come from a northwesterly direction from where he was standing."; 11-25-63 FBI report based upon an 11-24-63 interview, CD5 p.126: "he heard three shots ring out and immediately ran to the point where Elm Street turns to go under the underpass."; 4-1-64 testimony before the Warren Commission, 7H105-109: "…somebody said the shots or the firecrackers, whatever it was at that time, we still didn't know the President was shot, came from the wall. I immediately scaled that wall…. We noticed numerous kinds of footprints that did not make sense because they were going different directions.";

15. Harold Elkins: 11-26-63 report, 19H540: "I immediately ran to the area from which it sounded like the shots had been fired. This is an area between the railroads and the Texas School Book Depository which is east of the railroads. There were several other officers in this area and we secured it from the public. After searching this area for about ten minutes and not finding any evidence, I went to a tower that overlooks the railroad yards and also has a vantage point over the area around the school book building. I talked to an employee there and he gave me the description of two automobiles that he had seen in the area just a few minutes earlier.":

16. Jack Faulkner: 11-22-63 report, 19H511: "I asked a woman if they had hit the President and she told me that he was dead, that he had been shot thru the head. I asked her where the shorts (note: he means shots) came from and she pointed toward the concrete arcade on the east (note: he means north) side of Elm Street, just west of Houston Street. There were many officers going toward the railroad yard by this time and I joined them in search of the assassin.";

17. I.C. Todd: 11-27-63 Dallas County Sheriff's report, 19H543: "I ran across the street and went behind the railroad tracks";

18. Arnold Rowland: testimony before the Warren Commission , 2 H 169-181: "it sounded like it came from the railroad yards. That is where I looked, that is where all the policemen, everyone, converged on the railroads ... it sounded like it came from this area 'C' [the knoll] and that all the officers, enforcement officers were converging on that area and I just didn't pay any attention to it [the depository] at that time."

19. Barbara Rowland: 4-7-64 testimony before the Warren Commission, 6H177-191: "the people generally ran towards the railroad tracks behind the school book depository building, and so I naturally assumed they came from there.";

20. Orville Nix: Interview with Mark Lane in *Rush to Judgment*, filmed 3-27-66: "I thought it came from the fence between the book depository and the railroad tracks.";

21. Richard Randolph Carr: 2-3-64 statement furnished the FBI, CD 385 p.25: "I looked toward the triple underpass just west of Houston and Elm streets. It seemed to me that the noise I had heard came from this direction. As I looked I saw several individuals falling to the ground. I do not recall that I looked toward the Texas School Book Depository Building after hearing the three reports. I immediately proceeded down the stairway of the building with the intention of going over to the triple underpass to see what happened."; 2-19-69 testimony in the trial of Clay Shaw: "They came from the – from where I was standing at the new courthouse, they came from in this direction here, behind this picket fence, and one knocked a bunch of grass up along in this area here (indicating). This area here is flat, looking at it from here, but the actual way it is, it is on a slope up this way and you could tell from the way it knocked it up that the bullet came from this direction (indicating). (When then asked to describe this location more precisely) "There was a picket fence along in this area here, it does not show it in here, and it seems the shots came from this direction, and underneath that

slope there were people.... The shots came from this direction, from behind this picket fence that I do not see here, and there is a slope here, there is a grassy slope down here and there were a lot of people, spectators down here, below on this grassy slope, but when those shots were fired the motorcycle policemen, the Secret Service and what-have-you, all came in this direction, the way the shots came from, some of the people that were sitting there or standing fell to the ground as if the shots were coming off of those.... At the end towards the overpass, right here.";

22. B.J. Martin: 8-7-68 interview of Martin, as reported by Tom Bethel and Al Oser, investigators working on behalf New Orleans District Attorney Jim Garrison: "... it's logical, he said, that the shots could have come from the right, and possibly from the front in view of the fact that he had been splattered with blood.";

23. Bobby Hargis: Undated typescript of interview with Hargis found within the *Dallas Times-Herald*'s photograph collection, as reported by Richard Trask in *Pictures of the Pain*, 1994. This is almost certainly the basis for the 11/22/63 *Dallas Times-Herald* article: "I didn't know for sure if the shots had come from the Book Depository. I thought they might have come from the trestle."; 4-3-64 testimony before the Warren Commission, 6H293-296: "Well, at the time it sounded like the shots were right next to me. There wasn't any way in the world I could tell where they were coming from, but at the time there was something in my head that said that they probably could have been coming from the railroad overpass, because I thought since I had got splattered, with blood – I was Just a little back and left of – just a little bit back and left of Mrs. Kennedy, but I didn't know. I had a feeling that it might have been from the Texas Book Depository, and these two places was the primary place that could have been shot from."; Interview by HSCA investigator Jack Moriarty dated 8-8-78, notes transcribed 8-23-78, JFK document #014362, RIF 180-10113-10272: "He ran to the grassy knoll and continued until he had reached the top section of the underpass."; 6-26-95 video-taped interview with Mark Oakes and Ian Griggs-On the explosion of Kennedy's head: "it didn't only hit me.... It showered everything in the car behind it.";

24. James Chaney: 11-22-63 interview with KLIF radio: "... the second shot struck him in the face."; 11-22-63 interview with Bill Lord on WFAA television: "Then, the, uh, second shot came, well, then I looked back just in time to see the President struck in the face by the second bullet." Reporter Lord then stated that Chaney was so close

that his uniform was splattered with blood.; 11-24-63 article in the *Houston Chronicle*, posted online by Chris Davidson: "Chaney was an infantryman in Europe during World War II, with experience in sharpshooting.... A second or two after the first shot, the second shot hit him. 'It was like you hit him in the face with a tomato. Blood went all over the car.... A piece of his skull was lying on the floor of the car.";

25. Sam Kinney: HSCA summary of an interview conducted on 2/26/78: "SA Kinney immediately recognized the first sound as that of gunfire, realizing that it was a "shot from over our right shoulder" which hit the President in the throat. The President, his movement (in Kinney's opinion) affected by the brace he wore, fell toward "Jackie," who "after catching him, set him back up."; "While Jackie was setting him back up, Connally turns right, then left then pow, pow. The second shot" (hit Connally and) "left Connally's back open. The third shot hit the president." As the third shot landed, SA Kinney was able to see "hair coming up."; 3-5-94 and 4-15-94 interviews with Vince Palamara, as reported by Palamara in January 1996's *JFK Deep Politics Quarterly*) "However, it was during interviews conducted on 3/5/94 and 4/15/94 that Kinney totally amazed me with details concerning his first-hand observations of the President's wounds. Sam told me twice that he saw the back of JFK's head come off immediately when the fatal shot struck him. (Kinney was watching JFK's head and the rear bumper of the limo – as a normal part of his duty to maintain a 5' distance between the follow-up car and JFK's limo, something he had done many times). Sam told me, 'It was the right rear – I saw that part blow out.' He added that his windshield and left arm were hit with blood and brain matter immediately after the head shot. Once at Parkland Hospital, Kinney helped remove the President from the back seat of the car, with help from Clint Hill, Roy Kellerman, and Dave Powers. This gave him an extremely vivid, up-close look at JFK's head wound. 'His brain was blown out," Kinney said, '...there was nothing left!' I pressed further, learning, 'There was brain matter all over the place... he had no brains left in his head'... Kinney, who believes there was a conspiracy (although he believes Oswald was the only shooter), wanted his story told.... As for the shooting on Elm Street, Kinney was adamant, on 3 separate calls, that he 'saw all three shots hit' and that 'the second shot hit Connally and he agrees with me.'" (3-5-94 and 4-15-94 interviews with Palamara, as quoted in the Summer 1997 *Kennedy Assassination Chronicles*) (Kennedy) "Would have survived the first one, probably. The second shot hit Connally right

in the back ... I saw all three shots hit." (On the head wound) "He had no brain left. It was blown out ... there was nothing left ... the back of the head ... I saw it hit and I saw his hair come out...I had brain matter all over my windshield and left arm, that's how close we were to it. ... It was the right rear part of his head, because that's the part I saw blown out. I saw hair come out, the piece blow out, then the skin went back in – an explosion in and out.";

26. Clint Hill: 11-30-63 report, 18H740-745: "Mrs. Kennedy shouted, "They've shot his head off;" then turned and raised out of her seat as if she were reaching to her right rear toward the back of the car for something that had blown out ... I noticed a portion of the President's head on the right rear side was missing and he was bleeding profusely. Part of his brain was gone. I saw a part of his skull with hair on it lying in the seat. ... At approximately 2:45 A.M., November 23, I was requested by ASAIC Kellerman to come to the morgue to once again view the body... I observed a wound about six inches down from the neckline on the back just to the right of the spinal column. I observed another wound on the right rear por-tion of the skull."; 3-9-64 testimony before the Warren Commission, 2H132-144: "The right rear portion of his head was missing. It was lying in the rear seat of the car. His brain was exposed. There was blood and bits of brain all over the entire rear portion of the car. Mrs. Kennedy was completely covered with blood. There was so much blood you could not tell if there had been any other wound or not, except for the one large gaping wound in the right rear portion of the head ... I saw an opening in the back, about 6 inches below the neckline to the right-hand side of the spinal column.";

27. Ken O'Donnell: A 1968 conversation with Congressman Tip O'Neill, as recounted in O'Neill's autobiography *Man of the House*, 1987: "I was surprised to hear O'Donnell say that he was sure he had heard two shots that came from behind the fence. 'That's not what you told the Warren Commission,' I said. 'You're right,' he re-plied. "I told the FBI what I had heard, but they said it couldn't have happened that way and that I must have been imagining things. So I testified the way they wanted me to. I just didn't want to stir up any more pain and trouble for the family. ... The family – everybody wanted this thing behind them."; 6-15-75 article in the *Chicago Tri-bune*. This article reported that a source within the CIA had told the Church Committee that Kennedy aides Kenneth O'Donnell and David Powers had been pressured by the FBI into leaving their suspicions that shots came from the front out of their statements.; Interview with O'Donnell's son, Kenneth O'Donnell, Jr. by David

Talbot, as reported in *Brothers*, published in 2007- (On the source of the shots heard by his father) "He said there was fire from two different directions." (Quoting his father on his father's impressions of the Warren Commission) "I'll tell you this right now, they didn't want to know." ... (It was) "the most pointless investigation I've ever seen.";

28. Dave Powers: Notes on a 4-8-64 interview with William Manchester, as reported in the TV documentary *The Kennedy Assassination: 24 Hours After* 2009: "A fragment of the bullet had come out of his forehead."; 5-18-64 affidavit, 7H472-474: "My first impression was that the shots came from the right and overhead, but I also had a fleeting impression that the noise appeared to come from the front in the area of the triple overpass."; A 1968 conversation between Ken O'Donnell and Tip O'Neill recounted in O'Neill's memoir *Man of the House*, 1987: "Dave Powers was with us at dinner that night, and his recollection of the shots was the same as O'Donnell's. Kenny O'Donnell is no longer alive, but during the writing of this book I checked with Dave Powers. As they say in the news business, he stands by his story.";

A 1980 conversation with Gary Mack, as recounted in a series of emails from Mack to John McAdams, posted online by John McAdams, 4/9/03: "Powers told me he and O'Donnell both thought one of the shots might have come from the front. When they told the FBI, the agents didn't take them seriously. Dave was quite insistent on that." (In a follow-up email posted by McAdams at the same time, Mack clarified) "Powers may have told me one or two of the shots might have come from the front – my note to you was not taken from any notes I took at the time. This was a long conversation we had by phone around 1980. Powers told me they didn't know that shots came from the front, just that they thought one or two might have. He never said or hinted they were intimidated to change their story or to keep quiet. But they were disappointed that no one they told the story to seemed very interested in what they thought.";

6-5-91 interview with Lamar Waldron and Thom Hartmann, as recounted in *Ultimate Sacrifice*, 2005: "We were shocked when Dave Powers, head of the John F. Kennedy Presidential Library in Boston and a close aide to JFK, vividly described seeing the shots from the 'grassy knoll.' Powers said he and fellow JFK aide Kenneth O'Donnell clearly saw the shots, since they were in the limo right behind JFK. Powers said they felt they were 'riding into an ambush' – explaining for the first time why the driver of JFK's limo slowed after the first shot. Powers also described how he was pressured to change his story for the Warren Commission."; *JFK Assassination from the Oval Office to Dealey Plaza* by Brent Holland (2013), page 31: Powers told authors Lamar Waldron and Thom Hartman that the shots came from the grassy knoll; *Mary's Mosaic* by Peter Janney (2013/2016), pages 284-285): "They were shooting from the front, from behind that fence.";

29. Tim McIntyre: 11-23-03 article by Jerry Jonas in the *Bucks County Courier-Times*, purportedly relating what McIntyre told Jonas in December 1963: "...horrified to witness what he described as the back of the president's head exploding."; 11-17-13 article by Jerry Jonas in the *Burlington County Times*, in which he further relates what McIntyre purportedly told him in December 1963: repeats same statement;

30. Paul Landis: 18 H 758-759: report dated 11/27/63: "My reaction at this time was that the shot came from somewhere towards the front..."; 18 H 751-757: detailed report dated 11/30/63 – "I still was not certain from which direction the second shot came, but my reaction at this time was that the shot came from somewhere towards the front, right-hand side of the road."; HSCA Report, pp. 89, 606 (referencing Landis's interview, February 17, 1979 outside contact report, JFK Document 014571): Landis confirmed the veracity of his reports; 5-31-12 public appearance at the Cleveland Polka Association monthly meeting, video found on You Tube: (When asked if Kennedy's head's moving back and to the left had led him to believe the shots came from the front) "That was something that went through my mind.";

31. Thomas "Lem" Johns: 8-8-78 interview with HSCA investigator, file # 180-10074-10079: "The first two sounded like they were on the side of me towards the grassy knoll."; 2-21-99 article by Michael Dorman in *Newsday*, when discussing the possibility the fibers found on the bullet nose were fibers from JFK's tie: "'If you get the tie nicked by a different bullet, you've got a second gunman – simple as that,' Johns said. 'I've never thought that was out of the question.'"; In the 2013 DVD about his life entitled *Lem Johns: Secret Service Man,* Johns stated that a shot came from the grassy knoll. I spoke to Johns in 2004 and he said the same thing;

32. Thomas Atkins: As quoted in the tabloid *Midnight*, 3-1-77: "The shots came from below and off to the right side from where I was. I never thought the shots came from above. They did not sound like shots coming from anything higher than street level. They all sounded similar to me and did not seem to be coming from different points around the plaza.";

33. H.B. McClain: 1998 video-taped interview with Mark Oakes, Gregg Jaynes, and Steve Barber: "I question about him [Oswald] being the only one involved. Because I've done a little hunting of my own. And I've never shot anything that went away from me and then come back to me. Usually they hit the ground rolling if they're running. Or they just fall. But the films I've seen show his head going away from the school book depository and then coming right back. I feel like there's somebody over on that railroad track that shot him the second time.";

34. Forrest Sorrels: 11-28-63 statement, 21H548: "I looked towards the top of the terrace to my right as the sound of the shots seemed to come from that direction."; 5-7-64 testimony before the Warren Commission, 7H332-360: "... I just said "What's that?" And turned around to look up on this terrace part there, because the sound sounded like it came from the back and up in that direction."; *Rush to Judgment* film by Mark Lane 1966: According to eyewitness Orville Nix, Sorrels believed the shots came from the front;

35. S.M. Holland: 11-22-63 statement to Dallas County Sheriff's Department, 19H480, 24H212: "I looked over toward the arcade and trees and saw a puff of smoke come over from the trees and I heard three more shots after the first one but that was the only puff of smoke I saw.... After the first shot the President slumped over and Mrs. Kennedy jumped up and tried to get over in the back seat to him and then the second shot rang out."; 11-24-63 FBI report, CD5 p. 49-50: "Simultaneously with the first shot, he stated he heard either three or four more shots fired together.... The only unusual thing that Holland could recall was an approximate one and one-half to two foot diameter of what he believed was gray smoke which appeared to him to be coming from the trees which would have been on the right of the presidential car but observed no one there or in the vicinity."; 4-8-64 testimony before the Warren Commission, 6H239-248: "I heard a third report and I counted four shots and about the same time all this was happening and in this group of trees.... There was a shot, a report, I don't know whether it was a shot.... And a puff of smoke came out about 6 or 8 feet above the ground right out from under those trees...you could see that puff of smoke, like someone had thrown a firecracker, or something out.... It wasn't as loud as the previous reports or shots.";

Interview with Mark Lane in *Rush to Judgment*, filmed 3-21-66: "I looked over to where I thought the shot came from and I saw a puff of smoke still lingering underneath the trees in front of the wooden fence. The report sounded like it came from behind the wooden fence ... I know where that third shot came from ...

from behind the picket fence, close to the little plaza ... there's no doubt in my mind, there's no doubt whatsoever in my mind and the statements that I made in the Sheriff's Office immediately after the shooting, and the statement that I made to the Warren Commission, I made it very plainly there was no doubt in my mind what there was definitely a shot fired from behind that picket fence. I made it plain to the Warren Commission and I think I made the same statement in the Sheriff's Office. There was a fourth shot."; Additional segments in the transcript to the 3-21-66 interview with Mark Lane, as found in the Wisconsin Historical Society and posted online by John McAdams: "I looked over to where I thought the shot came from, and I saw a puff of smoke still laying underneath the trees. About like you would toss a firecracker out and it would go off and still leave a puff of smoke...The puff of smoke was about 30 or 40 feet from the fence, the picket fence, out under some green trees ... I saw the puff of smoke in front of the wooden fence. The report sounded like it came from behind the wooden fence.";

6-28-66 UPI article, found in the *Los Angeles Herald-Examiner*: Holland is certain that a separate shot came from beneath trees on a grassy knoll north and west of the depository building.... The third shot came from behind the picket fence to the north of Elm Street. There was a puff of smoke under the trees there like someone had thrown out a Chinese firecracker and a report of a gun entirely different from the one which fired from the book building. I don't know whether it hit anything.' Holland said the fourth shot from the depository struck the President in the head, blowing away a large portion of his skull."; 11-22-66 UPI article, found in the *Albuquerque Tribune*: "There definitely was a shot fired from behind that fence.... Four or five of us saw it, the smoke," Holland said. "One of my employees even saw the muzzle flash..."I was close enough to see it and hear it," Holland said. "And if you don't think you can see rifle smoke against a clump of trees, you're mistaken."

He added that he is certain there were at least four shots fired, and perhaps five. "Now, the ones that came from up the street (the depository area) were quite a bit louder than the one from the fence. That's how I could tell they were from different rifles."; 11-30-66 taped interview with Josiah Thompson, as recounted in *Six Seconds in Dallas*, 1967: "Right under these trees, right at that exact spot, about ten or fifteen feet from this corner, the corner of the fence here, right under this tree, particular tree. It's that exact spot, right there.... That's where it was...just like somebody had thrown a firecracker and left a little puff of smoke there; it was just laying there. It was a white smoke; it wasn't a black smoke or like a black powder. It was like a puff of a cigarette, but it was about nine feet off the ground. It would be just about in line with, or maybe just a little bit higher than that fence, but by the time it got out underneath the tree, well, it would be about eight or nine feet." (When asked about Clemon Johnson's suggestion the smoke seen by the railroad men came from a Dallas police motorcycle abandoned on the street after the shooting) "I saw the smoke before the motorcyclist left the street to go up there.";

Late 1966 interview with Lawrence Schiller recounted in *The Scavengers and the Critics of the Warren Report*, published 1967: "Third and fourth were so close together. The third shot came from the fence." (When asked where he was looking at the time of the third shot) "My attention on the third and fourth shots was to my left, behind the picket fence, or over to the picket fence, and where I saw that puff of smoke coming from and heard the report."; Schiller interview as presented on the Capitol Records release *The Controversy*, 1967: "The first loud report, well, he kinda slumped forward a little bit and his right hand went up to his neck. In a second or two, Governor Connally he slumped over just like dropping a sack of flour, and there was just a short pause in there. Until there was another report that wasn't as loud as the first two. It came from my left and behind a picket fence, and there was a puff of smoke that kinda lingered out under that green tree right out behind that picket fence about 8 or 9 feet off of the ground. The third shot came from the fence and it wasn't near as loud as the fourth shot, or the first and second shot.";

Interview with CBS broadcast 6-26-67: "there was a third report that wasn't nearly as loud as the two previous reports. It came from that picket fence, and then there was a fourth report. The third and the fourth reports was almost simultaneously. But, the third report wasn't nearly as loud as the two previous reports or the fourth report. And I glanced over underneath that green tree and you see a – a little puff of smoke. It looked like a puff of steam or cigarette smoke. And the smoke was about – oh, eight or ten feet off the ground, and about fifteen feet this side of that tree."; 3-25-68 interview with Barry Ernest recounted in *The Girl on the Stairs*, first published 2011: "As the motorcade approached in the middle lane of Elm, I heard four shots, the first two sounded like they were behind the president with that shot from the knoll being different from the rest.' When I asked what he meant by 'different,' he said it sounded 'I don't know, just different than the others, like it was a pistol, or a different type of rifle or something. The third and fourth shots were very close together, almost at exactly the same second.' Holland said his eyes were focused on Kennedy when 'the second, or possibly the third shot' caused the president's head to 'suddenly lurch backward.' At that moment, he said, his attention was immediately drawn to the left, straight at the far corner of the wooden fence on top of the knoll, where he felt that shot, the 'different' shot, had originated. 'And I saw a puff of smoke come out from that corner and it just didn't hang there but it slowly drifted out under the trees and over the grassy area toward the street below.' The smoke, he added, traveled out about 20 feet from the fence and was located slightly behind a large tree on the knoll.";

36. Austin Miller: 11-22-63 statement to the Dallas County Sheriff's Department, 19H485, 24H217: "One shot apparently hit the street past the car. I saw something which I thought was smoke or steam coming from a group of trees north of Elm off the railroad tracks."; 4-8-64 testimony before the Warren Commission, 6H223-227: (When asked from where he thought the shots came) "the way it sounded like, it came from the, I would say right there in the car."; 8-1-68 interview with Barry Ernest as recounted in *The Girl on the Stairs*, 2011: When asked about the smoke) "He said it definitely was smoke he saw 'around the trees in the corner of the picket fence on the grassy knoll.' (When asked if it could have been exhaust) 'No,' he firmly replied. Miller said he felt there had been three shots, that he saw the smoke just as he heard the third shot.";

37. Royce Skelton: 11-22-63 statement to the Dallas County Sheriff's Department, 16H496: "We saw the motorcade come around the corner and I heard something which I thought was fireworks. I saw something hit the pavement at the left rear of the car, then the car got in the right hand lane and I heard two more shots. I heard a woman say "Oh, no" or something and grab a man inside the car. I then heard another shot and saw the bullet hit the pavement. The concrete was knocked to the south away from the car. It hit the pavement in the left or middle lane."; 4-8-64 testimony before the Warren Commission, 6H236-238: "I thought I heard four – I mean – I couldn't be sure … after those two shots, and the car came on down closer to the triple underpass, well, there was another shot – two more shots I heard, but one of them – I saw a bullet, or I guess it was a bullet … hit in the left front of the President's car on the cement, and when it did, the smoke carried with it – away from the building.";

38. Frank Reilly: 12-19-63 FBI report, CD205 p.29: "He saw two cars turn on Elm toward the underpass and at this time heard three shots which he thought came from the trees west of the Texas School Book Depository."; 4-8-64 testimony before the Warren Commission, 6H227-231: "three shots…. It seemed to me like they come out of the trees … on the North side of Elm Street at the corner up there … it's at that park where all the shrubs is up there – it's to the north of Elm Street – up the slope.";

39. Clemon Johnson: 3-18-64 FBI report, 22H836: "Mr. Johnson stated that white smoke was observed near the pavilion, but he felt that this smoke came from a motorcycle abandoned near this spot by a Dallas policeman." [see S.M. Holland's denial that this was the source of the smoke, above]; *No More Silence*, p.79-83, published 1998: I didn't have any idea where the shots came from, not even a guess … I did see smoke, lots of puffs of smoke, but I was of the opinion that the smoke was coming out of those motorcycles. The smoke was coming up off the ground out where the motorcycles were, not on the grassy knoll." [in addition to Holland's denial of this excuse, above, Johnson's explanation for the smoke seen on the knoll also is not credible because Officer Haygood, who parked his bike on the street by the knoll, never reached the knoll until Kennedy's limousine was long gone].

40. Walter Winborn: 3-17-65 interview by Barbara Bridges, as noted in *Best Evidence*, published 1980: "there was a lot of smoke … from out of the trees, to the left." (5-5-66 interview with Stewart Galanor): "I just saw some smoke coming out in a – a motorcycle patrolman leaped off his machine and go up towards that smoke that come out from under the trees on the right hand side of the motorcade…. There was a wooden fence there." (When asked if he told the FBI about the smoke) "Oh yes. Oh yes.";

41. Richard Dodd: Interview with Mark Lane presented in the movie *Rush to Judgment*, filmed 3-24-66: "We all, three or four of us, seen about the same thing, the shot, the smoke came from behind the hedge on the north side of the Plaza. And a motorcycle policeman dropped his motorcycle in the street with a gun in his hand and run up the embankment to the hedge.";

42. Nolan Potter: 3-19-64 FBI report, 2H834: "when the President's car … had driven past the Texas School Book Depository Building, he heard three loud reports which sounded like firecrackers. He then saw President Kennedy slump over in his car …. Potter said he recalls seeing smoke in front of the Texas School Book Depository

rising above the trees." [From the railroad bridge looking up Elm, the knoll was just to the left of the book depository. A puff of smoke coming out from the knoll would rise up above the trees in front of the depository. Or was Potter saying the trees were *in front* of the book depository? Or did the FBI intentionally misreport this detail? Remember, Potter said the car had driven *past* the school book depository, as well];

43. James Leon Simmons: 3-19-64 FBI report, 22H833: "Simmons said he thought he saw exhaust fumes of smoke near the embankment in front of the Texas School Book Depository Building." [this is the same "mistake" that the FBI made in Potter's report about the smoke, above. Read on for further clarifications from Simmons]; Interview with Mark Lane in *Rush to Judgment*, filmed 3-28-66: "As the presidential limousine was rounding the curve on Elm Street, there was a loud explosion ... it sounded like a loud firecracker or a gunshot, and it sounded like it came from the left and in front of us toward the wooden fence. And there was a puff of smoke that came underneath the trees on the embankment. It was right directly in front of the wooden fence."; An additional segment in the 3-28-66 interview with Lane on the transcript of the interview made available by the Wisconsin Historical Society and posted online by John McAdams: "As the limousine rounded the curve on Elm Street there was a loud explosion – seemed to be from fireworks or gunshot – didn't know at the time. But it seemed like it came from the fence to the left and in front of us."; 2-15-69 testimony in the trial of Clay Shaw: "Well, after I heard the shots I looked to see if I could see where they were coming from and underneath the trees up on the grassy knoll by the fence I detected what appeared to be a puff of smoke or wisp of smoke.";

44. Thomas Murphy: 3-20-64 FBI report, 22H835: "Murphy said in his opinion that these shots came from just west of the Texas School Book Depository."; 5-6-66 interview with Stewart Galanor: (When asked how many shots he heard) "More than three." (When asked where the shots came from) "they come from a tree to the left, of my left, which is to the immediate right of the site of the assassination ... on the hill up there. There are two or three hackberry and elm trees. And I say it come from there." (When asked if he saw smoke) "Yeah, smoke ... in that tree.";

45. James Tague: 12-16-63 FBI report, CD205 p31: "He heard a loud noise, and at that time he looked around as he thought someone had shot a firecracker. He then heard two more loud noises in

quick succession.... During the time of the shooting he felt something hit him on the right cheek.... .He thought that possibly one of the bullets had hit the curb near his feet and possibly a piece of the curbing had hit him on the cheek ..."; 7-23-64 testimony before the Warren Commission, 7H552-558: "my first impression was that up by the, whatever you call the monument... somebody was throwing firecrackers up there."; Interview with Mark Lane in *Rush to Judgment*, filmed March, 1966: "My first impression was that they had come from the left of me ... somewhere towards the wooden fence.";

46. Mrs. Jack Franzen: 12-11-63 Airtel from Dallas FBI as a response to a Bureau Airtel of 12-6 – apparently they sought some clarification – FBI Headquarters File 102-82555, Sec 27, p41: "She recalled that after the President's car sped away, she observed police officers and plain-clothes men searching an area adjacent to the TSBD Building and assumed the shots came from that area.";

47. Malcolm Summers: [can be seen diving to the ground in Zapruder frame 345] 11-23-63 statement to Dallas Sheriff's Department, 19H500: "...all of the people started running up the terrace away from the President's car and I got up and started running also, not realizing what had happened. In just a few moments the president's car sped off."; July-August 1988 interview recounted in *American History Illustrated*, November 1988: "In a few seconds everybody was running toward the railroad tracks behind the knoll."; Interview in TV special *Who Murdered JFK?*, first broadcast 11-2-88: "I ran across the Elm Street to run up there toward that knoll, yessir, and we were stopped by a man in a suit and he had an overcoat over his arm. And he, I saw a gun under that overcoat. And his comment was 'Don't y'all come up here any further, you could get shot, or killed,' one of those words.... A few months later they told me they didn't have an FBI man in that area. If they didn't have anybody, it's a good question who that was."; PBS program *Who Shot President Kennedy?*, first broadcast 11-15-88: "I do think the first shot came from the school book depository up there. And when the second one came I did not know who all was shooting. I was thinking there was more than one person shooting. The first shot sounded just like a little pop. It sounded like a firecracker from a far away distance. The others sounded real close, real close."; 7-11-91 video-taped interview with Mark Oakes-When asked if the shots were too close together to have been fired by one gunman: "My doubt was always because they were so close together.... At the time I heard it it didn't seem to me like they were more than two or three seconds apart. It was just so simultaneously that it was unreal."; 11-16-91 AP article on an

assassination conference found in the Victoria Advocate: "Summers said the second and third shots were fired so close together that "I certainly thought more than one person was shooting."; *No More Silence* p.102-107, published 1998: "as to the spacing of the shots, there was much more time between the first one and the second two, the second and the third. They were real close.";

48. James Altgens: 11-22-63 eyewitness account, presented as an AP dispatch presumably around 1:30 PM. This more detailed account was also published in the 11-25-63 issue of *Stars and Stripes*: "At first I thought the shots came from the opposite side of the street. I ran over there to see if I could get some pictures."; 11-21-85 interview with Richard Trask in Dealey Plaza as quoted in *Pictures of the Pain*, 1994 – On the rush of witnesses to the grassy knoll: "Well, I thought they were onto something.";

49. Emmett Hudson: 11-22-63 statement to Dallas Sheriff's Department, 19H481: I definately [sic] heard 3 shots. The shots that I heard definately [sic] came from behind and above me. When I laid down on the ground I laid on my right side and my view was still toward the street where the President's car had passed. I did look around but I did not see any firearms at all. This shot sounded to me like a high powered rifle."; 11-26-63 FBI report, CD5 p.30-31: "He said he was looking directly at President Kennedy and saw his head slump to one side simultaneously with the loud report made by the first shot fired by the assassin. He said he then heard two more reports which sounded like shots, such reports coming in rapid succession after the first shot. He volunteered the shots were fired 'just about as fast as you could expect a man to operate a bolt action rifle' or words to that effect."; 8-2-68 interview with Barry Ernest recounted in *The Girl on the Stairs*, published 2011: "'Well, there were definitely three that I heard,' he explained, 'But one of them was a bit unusual.' (When asked what he meant by unusual) 'Well, it sounded different from the others. It was louder, sharper, cleaner than the others. And two of them was close together, like bang......bang, bang.' (When asked if the shots could have come from the picket fence) 'I don't know,' Hudson said, after a pause. 'I really don't. There was so much excitement and it all happened so fast, I'm just not sure.'";

50. Wilfred Daetz: 12-7-66 letter from Dallas Police Chief Charles Batchelor to Dallas FBI agent-in-charge J. Gordon Shanklin: he subject stated that on November 22, 1963, at the time of the assassination of President Kennedy, he was standing on the grass on the north side of Elm Street – on the slope approaching the triple underpass.

He recalls only one shot and that immediately after the shot he ran up the slope toward the railroad tracks and was stopped by an unknown police officer who pointed a pistol at him and shouted "Where are you going?" He then returned down the slope. The subject stated that he could hear very little out of his left ear and that he heard the shot with his right ear and in his opinion the shot came from his right which was in the direction of the railroad tracks. He also stated he saw a puff of smoke come from behind the fence near the railroad tracks. He stated that he was so excited he doesn't recall any additional shots. He further stated that at the time of the incident, he did not reveal himself and had talked to no one regarding this until the recent publicity. He states that then he revealed himself and made a statement to the Federal Bureau of Investigation in New York City.";

51. Lee Bowers: 4-2-64 testimony before the Warren Commission, 6H 284-289: Directly in line, towards the mouth of the underpass, there were two men. One man, middle-aged, or slightly older, fairly heavy-set, in a white shirt, fairly dark trousers. Another younger man, about mid-twenties, in either a plaid shirt or plaid coat or jacket...They were standing within 10 or 15 feet of each other, and gave no appearance of being together, as far as I knew.... They were facing and looking up towards Main and Houston, and following the caravan as it came down." (When asked if he could see the corner of Houston and Elm from his location) "after they passed the corner of Elm and Houston the car came in sight again ... I heard three shots. One, then a slight pause, then two very close together. Also reverberation from the shots...The sounds came either from up against the School Depository Building or near the mouth of the triple underpass...At the moment I heard the sound, I was looking directly towards the area – at the moment of the first shot, as close as my recollection serves, the car was out of sight behind this decorative masonry wall in the area.... It came in sight immediately following the last shot.... At the time of the shooting there seemed to be some commotion ... I just am unable to describe it rather than it was something out of the ordinary, a sort of milling around, but something occurred in this particular spot which was out of the ordinary, which attracted my eye for some reason, which I could not identify."; 6-28-66 UPI article, found in the *Los Angeles Herald-Examiner*: "He observed two men in the area between the fence and the colonnade before the shooting but did not notice them later. Had an automobile been wedged in that area, he could not have missed it. Bowers says he saw a 'flash' or 'some kind of disturbance' under the trees atop the knoll at the time of the shooting. He saw

no individual firing or anyone rushing from the scene but he thinks there is 'at least a 50-50 chance that something happened there' and it could have been a second gunman."; Interview with Mark Lane in *Rush to Judgment*, 1966: "At the time of the shooting, in the vicinity of where the two men I described were, there was a flash of light or – there was something which occurred that caught my eye. What this was I couldn't say at the time and at this time I couldn't identify it, other than that there was some unusual occurrence, a flash of light or smoke or something, which caused me to feel that something out of the ordinary had occurred there. … There were three shots. These were spaced with one shot, then a pause, and then two shots in very close order, such as perhaps (He raps on table with his hand "rap … rap rap"). Almost on top of each other, while there was some pause between the first and second shots." (When asked if he told this to the FBI) "When I stated that I felt like the second and third shots could not have been fired from the same rifle, they reminded me that I wasn't an expert, and I had to agree.";

52. Abraham Zapruder: 9:55 PM 11-22-63, memo of SS Agent Max Phillips accompanying a copy of the Zapruder film: "According to Mr. Zapruder, the position of the assassin was behind Mr. Zapruder."; March-May 1964 memo written for the *Dallas Morning News* by newsman Harry McCormick, in which McCormick's recollections of 11-22-63 were recorded for posterity, as published *in JFK Assassination: The Reporters' Notes*, 2013: "There were three shots. Two hit the president and the other Gov. Connally."; 7-22-64 testimony before the Warren Commission, 7H569-576-When asked where the shots came from: "I also thought it came from back of me … I assumed that they came from there, because as the police started running back of me, it looked like it came from back of me.";

53. Marilyn Sitzman: 11-22-63 notes on an interview of Sitzman by a *Dallas Times-Herald* reporter, presumably Darwin Payne, as presented in *The Zapruder Film* by David Wrone, 2003: "Shot hit pres. Right in the temple."; Article by Hal Verb in the 9-30-94 *JFK Resource Group* Newsletter: "…I recalled an interview I had with Marilyn Sitzman, an eyewitness to the JFK assassination who was standing with Abraham Zapruder (in fact, holding him so that he wouldn't fall as he was filming the motorcade). She and I were standing right near the pedestal whew both she and Zapruder stood upon. It was the last day of the Dallas "ASK" conference (Oct. 25, 1992). Sitzman told me she knew a lot about guns and weapons having grown up with them. She told me the shot that killed the President came from behind and that the gunman must've used a silencer. She said that

if it were not a silencer the shot would have knocked down both of them because of where they were so precariously standing. She then told me of the great "reverberation" that was felt. I showed her a map of the Dealey Plaza area (she signed it) and she pointed to the area when she thought the shot was fired from. Curiously enough, it was not from the alleged and traditionally targeted picket fence area but from a location in the direction of the north pergola. This would be to the left of and behind where Charles Hester was standing.";

54. William Newman: 11-22-63 interview on WFAA, prior to the announcement of the President's death, at approximately 12:45: "We were halfway in between the triple underpass. We were at the curb when this incident happened. But the President's car was some fifty feet in front of us still yet in front of us coming toward us when we heard the first shot and the President. I don't know who was hit first but the President jumped up in his seat, and I thought it scared him, I thought it was a firecracker, cause he looked, you know, fear. And then as the car got directly in front of us well a gunshot apparently from behind us hit the President in the side of the temple." (As he says this last line he points to his left temple) (When asked if he thought the first shot came from the same location) "I think it came from the same location apparently back up on the mall, whatcha-callit." (When asked if he thought the shot came from the viaduct) "Yes, sir, no, no, not on the viaduct itself but up on top of the hill, on the mound, of ground, in the garden.";

11-22-63 second interview on WFAA, prior to the announce-ment of Kennedy's death, at approximately 1:00 PM – When asked if he felt the shots came from different directions: "No sir, actual-ly I feel that they both come from directly behind where we were standing. The President, it looked like he was looking in that direc-tion. I don't know whether he was hit first. Apparently he wasn't. It looked like he jumped up in his seat, and when he jumped up he was shot directly in his head. I don't know whatchacallit – the mall behind us – but apparently (interviewer Jay Watson finishing his thought) "that's where he [the assassin] was."; Pierce Allman 11-22-63 eyewitness report on WFAA, between 1:45 and 2:00 PM CST: "I notice Mr. Newman says he felt the shots were fired from a knoll."; 11/22/63 Sheriff Department Affidavit, 19 H 490: "I thought the shots had come from the garden directly behind me"; 11-29-66 taped interview with Josiah Thompson, as recounted in *Six Seconds in Dallas*, 1967-When asked if he thought shots came from in back of him: "That's right. Well, of course, the President's being shot in the side of the head by the third shot – I thought the shot was fired from directly behind where we were standing. And that's what scared us, because I thought we were right in the direct path of gunfire." (When asked again if his impression was that the bullet entered the side of the head) "Right. Right. My thoughts were that the shot entered there and apparently the thoughts of the Warren Commission were that the shot came out that side." (When asked again if his impression was that the shots came from behind where he was standing) "Right. Well I think everybody thought the shots were from where I'm saying – behind us – because everybody went in that direction. Must have… The thought never entered my mind that it was coming from the rear.";

2-17-69 testimony in the trial of Clay Shaw: "From the sound of the shots, the report of the rifle or whatever it was, it sounded like they were coming directly behind from where I was standing… I thought the shots were coming from back here, and apparently everybody else did because they all ran in that direction."; 7-23-86 testimony in televised mock trial, *On Trial: Lee Harvey Oswald*: Sir, I thought the shots were coming from directly behind. (When asked to mark on the map where he thought the shots came from) It would be somewhere back in this general area. (He then makes a large mark across the southern side of the Elm Street extension back behind the eastern half of the arcade, to the West of the School Book Depository); Interview in *The Men Who Killed Kennedy*, broadcast 1988: "When the third shot was fired I thought it came from directly behind, towards the grassy knoll behind me. I base that primarily on the third shot, from what I saw, the sight of the President's head coming off, and from the sound of the rifle, the report of the rifle";

Interview with Jim Marrs published in *Crossfire*, 1989: "He [JFK] was knocked violently back against the seat, almost as if he had been hit by a baseball bat. At that time, I was looking right at the President and I thought the shots were coming from directly behind us."; 7-10-91 video-taped interview with Mark Oakes: "It appeared yes right in this area here (as he motions to his right temple) on the side of his head"; As quoted in *JFK: Breaking the Silence*, by Bill Sloan, 1993: "It seemed to me that the shooting was coming from directly behind me and I thought we must be right in the line of fire." (Sloan then writes: "Bill makes it clear – as he has all along – that when he says 'directly behind me' he means a point on the grassy knoll near the concrete pergola, which along with the wooden picket fence, forms the northern boundary of Dealey Plaza)."; 11-20-97 interview published in *No Case To Answer* by Ian Griggs, 2005: "From my view it was just "behind" and it was a visual impact it had on me of seeing the head wound and seeing President Kennedy go across the seat. That gave me the impression of the shot being fired from behind..."; *No More Silence* p. 94-101, published 1998: "I thought the shot came from directly behind us in the grassy knoll area. The only basis I had for that was what I visually saw: the President going across the car and seeing the side of his head come off. The sound played little factor. I believe it was a visual thing at that time.";

Oral History interview for the Sixth Floor Museum, 7-10-03: "It was the visual impact that it had on me more so than the noise – seeing the side of the President's head blow off, seeing the President go across the car seat into Mrs. Kennedy's lap, in her direction. It gave me the impression that the shots were coming from directly behind where I was standing."; 11-19-08 AP article by Dylan Lovan: "I do tend to want to lean in the direction that it was a conspiracy, meaning more than one person was involved. But so far, no one's ever come forward with concrete evidence."; Tru TV program *Conspiracy Theory*, first broadcast 11-19-10: "I thought the shot had come from directly behind (as he says this he points to the arcade at the top of the knoll). (At this point interviewer Jesse Ventura interjects "Directly behind?" Newman then confirms) "Directly behind." (A quick shot of the picket fence – which is 30 feet or more to the west of where Newman was pointing – is then shown.); Living History presentation at The Sixth Floor Museum, 11-9-13: "The first two shots I didn't recognize as gunfire. But the third shot I recognized as gunfire most certainly and I thought the shot was coming from behind." (When asked if he thought more than Oswald was involved) "The idea of a conspiracy will probably never in my lifetime be totally removed from my mind.";

History Channel program *The JFK Assassination: the Definitive Guide*, first broadcast 11-22-13: I thought that shot had come from over the top of our heads straight behind us up on the grassy knoll."; 11-18-16 interview with Stephen Fagin at the JFK Lancer Conference in Dallas: "I still believe it's very possible the shot did come from behind ... I was thinking somewhere between the school book depository and the structure that's there, towards those bushes. (When asked what he believed regarding a conspiracy) "I can very easily defend either position..."; 10-29-18 guest appearance at Sixth Floor Museum. Note: this was during a debate between Howard Willens and Robert Blakey: "What I saw was the reaction in the car, that made me think the shot came from behind."; 1-21-18 appearance on the Travel Channel program *Mysteries at the Mu-*

seum: "Based on what I saw, I thought the shots came from behind. (He points to the white pergola behind him.)";

55. Gayle Newman: Oral History for the Sixth Floor Museum, 7-10-03-When later asked if she shared her husband's impression the shots came from behind: "Yes, mine is just visual. Y'know, the impact at the side of his head, and the way he fell over. Just visual."; 2-7-11 Living History interview with the Sixth Floor Museum: "From the noise that we heard we thought the shots were coming directly behind us and we were afraid that we were fixing to be shot." (Her personal opinion as to conspiracy) "I just feel like someone else had to be helping."; Fox News Reporting: 50 Years of Questions, 11-9-13: "We thought the shots had come from over our heads behind the grassy knoll, towards the concrete embankment."; 11-18-16 interview with Stephen Fagin at the JFK Lancer Conference in Dallas: "I assumed that the shots had come from behind us because the way he fell.";

56. Mary Moorman: 5-24-11 interview conducted live on iantique. com: "I believe there's a whole lot more to the story than what's been told. I don't know about how many shooters or don't really care other than to know for sure what's happened."; 11-18-13 article on Moorman in the *Richmond Times-Dispatch*: When the Warren Commission concluded that Lee Harvey Oswald was the lone gunman, Moorman wasn't convinced. 'I really don't know what exactly happened, but I do know there is bound to be a lot more to the story that hasn't been told,' she said. 'I was hoping it would come out in my lifetime, but who knows. So much has been hidden by the government; anything can take place and it can be hidden. Oswald probably wasn't a lone person, he probably had backers. I really do think it was a conspiracy,' she said.";

57. Jean Hill: 11-22-63 WBAP radio interview, first played around 1:10 PM, and then repeated around 1:21. This was also played on WBAP TV, apparently around 1:19.) "the shots came directly across the street from us, and just as the President's car became directly even with us ... he and Jackie were looking at a dog that was in the middle of the seat, and about that time two shots rang out just as he looked up – just as the President looked up and these two shots rang out and he grabbed his chest, looked like he was in pain, and he fell over in his seat. And Jackie fell over on him and said "My God, he's been shot!" After that more shots rang out and the car sped away... the shots came from the hill ... it was just east of the underpass... (when asked if she saw anyone) I thought I saw this man running but I looked at the President and, y'know, for awhile, and I looked

up there and I thought I saw a man running and so right after that – I guess I didn't have any better sense – I started running up there, too."; 3:30 PM 11-22-63 KRLD radio interview: "...some of the motorcycles pulled away. And some of them pulled over to the side and started running up the bank. There's a hill on the other side... And the shots came from there..."; 3-17-64 FBI report on a 3-13-64 interview, CD 897, p43-44: Mrs. Hill stated she heard from four to six shots in all and believes they came from a spot just west of the Texas School Book Depository. She thought there was slight interval between the first three shots and the remaining shots."; 3-24-64 testimony before the Warren Commission, 6H205-223: "I have always said there were some four to six shots. There were three shots, one right after the other, and a distinct pause, or just a moment's pause, and then I heard more."; saw a man running from just west of the TSBDB toward the railroad tracks. "I just thought at the time – that's the man who did it ... at that time I didn't realize that the shots were coming from the building. I frankly thought they were coming from the knoll";

8-8-68 report of Tom Bethel and Al Oser, investigators working on behalf New Orleans District Attorney Jim Garrison: "One of the few things that Mrs. Hill did concede was that she had heard from four to six shots and we showed her a part of the testimony about the direction of the shots in which she told Spector that the shots sounded like they had come from the knoll, and she read that and said that that was correct.... Going over what she said about the shots again she said that there were definitely no less than four shots and may have been as many as six."; Interview presented as part of radio show *Thou Shalt Not Kill*, on Canadian radio station CTFR, broadcast 5-10-76: "Four to six. I know that I heard four or more.... There was a time lapse. I know two seemingly came together. I know I heard one, and then I heard two more, and I feel pretty sure I heard two other disconnected shots. But they didn't sound as though they were coming from the same gun, from the same location, or the same kind of gun." ; 1978 interview with Anthony Summers, as recounted in *Conspiracy*, 1980: "I heard four to six shots, and I'm pretty used to guns. They weren't echoes or anything like that. They were different guns that were being fired.... The President was killed and then, of course, pandemonium reigned and I looked up, and at the time I looked up across the street I saw smoke like from a gun coming from the parapet, that built-up part on the knoll."; Spring, 1987 conversation with Cyril Wecht, as recounted in Wecht's book *Cause of Death*, 1993: "I was staring directly at the grassy knoll area when the shots went off,' Jean told me ... 'As soon as I heard the shots, I focused completely over that way because that's where I thought the shots came from,' Jean said. 'I saw two men holding guns. One was behind the picket fence. As soon as the shots were fired, the men began fleeing, and instinctively, I started following them." ; July-August 1988 interview recounted in *American History Illustrated*, November 1988: "There was a flash of light from that grassy knoll. I thought it was the good guys and the bad guys. Shots from the back. Then, shooting from the front. I believe I heard four to six shots in all. Mary tried to pull me to the ground. I stood there. I wanted to find out what was happening. People seemed frozen at first. Then I noticed one man, though, moving from the front of the Depository building, hurrying towards that parking lot behind the grassy knoll."; 11-22-88 televised interview with Geraldo Rivera: "As the series of shots rang out, I thought I saw someone firing from the grassy knoll, from the fence behind there ... there was a rifle blast from behind the fence on the grassy knoll."; Interview with Jim Marrs recounted in *Crossfire*, published 1989: "I saw a man fire from behind the wooden fence. I saw a puff of smoke and some sort of movement on the grassy knoll where he was.";

11-21-91 *Dallas Morning News* article on a showing of Oliver Stone's *JFK*: She was one of numerous witnesses who said they saw shots from a grassy knoll west of the depository building. "I'm the one who named it "the grassy knoll,' too,' she said."; December, 1991 appearance on the *Maury Povich Show*: "There was a series of shots, and I saw the flash of light and a puff of smoke from the knoll in front of us.... Oh, I saw it ... Oh, I did ... I know someone was shooting from there...I just saw the smoke and the light from the knoll where I knew someone had shot. And at that instant, his head was blown off. And the blood and the brains and all that, this made a red cloud around Mr. Kennedy's head. And the blood and everything splattered my boyfriend's [B.J. Martin's] motorcycle. And it was just horrible. It was something you never forget. I just saw this look in his eyes that, and his head was gone."; December, 1991 appearance on the *Today Show*: "I saw someone shooting from the knoll, from back behind the fence ... a flash of light and a puff of smoke."; 1-22-92 appearance on *The Oprah Winfrey Show*: "I did see the flash of light, the puff of smoke, at the moment the President's head was ripped off."; Interview with James Earl Jones in the television production *The JFK Conspiracy*, Spring, 1992: "I saw smoke, a puff of smoke, and a flash of light from the knoll, where someone was shooting from behind the fence."; *JFK: The Last Dissenting Witness*, 1992, co-written with Bill Sloan: "On the other side of the street, at the top of the little green mound universally known today as the 'grassy knoll,' Jean had seen an incredible sight.... A muzzle flash, a puff of smoke, and the shadowy figure of a man holding a rifle, barely visible above the wooden fence at the top of the knoll, still in the very act of murdering the president of the United States.";

Interview in documentary *Beyond JFK: The Question of Conspiracy*, 1992: It was right up there. The man was shooting from right, just this side of that tree, that large tree. And that's where I saw the shots come from.... The Warren Commission says that it happened from the school book depository, right up there in that corner window. But I don't know about that. I don't know anything about those shots up there. All I know is what I saw on the knoll. And I definitely saw the man shooting from the knoll."; Interview broadcast in CBS program *Who Killed JFK: the Final Chapter?*, 11-19-93: "The shots started ringing out. I looked up across the street behind the picket fence up there by the tree. Right there in the bushes this man was shooting with a rifle and I saw a puff of smoke and a flash of light at the very instant that Kennedy's head exploded."; 11-19-93 article in *USA Today*: "'At the very instant that Kennedy's head exploded, I saw a rifle flash and a puff of smoke on the grassy knoll behind the picket fence.' She says she saw 'the outline' of the shooter, although no one reported spotting a second gunman at the time of the killing."; Interview on Black Op Radio, 6-15-00: "a puff of smoke, a flash of light from the rifle. I caught a glimpse of someone up there.";

58. Cheryl McKinnon: From an 11-22-83 article in the *San Diego Star News*: "On Nov. 22, 1963, I stood, along with hundreds of others, on the grassy knoll in Dealey Plaza waiting for just one thing – a chance to see, even for just a moment, that magical person, the president, John F. Kennedy.... As we stood watching the motorcade turn onto Elm Street, I tried to grasp every detail.... Suddenly three shots in rapid succession rang out. Myself and dozens of others standing nearby turned in horror toward the back of the Grassy Knoll where it seemed the sounds had originated. Puffs of white smoke still hung in the air in patches. But no one was visible. Turning back to the street, now suddenly frightened, I suddenly realized the President was no longer sitting up in the seat waving to the crowd. He was slumped over to his wife whose facial expression left no doubt as to what had occurred ... the only thing I am absolutely sure of today is that at least two of the shots fired that day in Dealey Plaza came from behind where I stood on the knoll, not from the book depository.";

59. Charles Brehm: 11-22-63 notes on an interview of Brehm by *Dallas Times-Herald* reporter Darwin Payne immediately after the shooting, as presented in *The Zapruder Film* by David Wrone, 2003: "The shots came from in front of or beside of the President."; 11-22-63 article in the *Dallas Times-Herald*: "Brehm seemed to think the shots came from in front of or beside the President."; 3-28-66 interview with Mark Lane as quoted in *Rush To Judgment*, 1966: "I very definitely saw the effect of the second bullet that struck the President.... That which appeared to be a portion of the President's skull went flying slightly to the rear of the President's car and directly to its left. It did fly over toward the curb and to the left and to the rear.";

3-28-66 interview with Mark Lane, transcript found at the Wisconsin Historical Society: "Odd as it may seem, I had thought that the shots had come from the County jail house there...But it did not seem likely so I had assumed they came from the Book Depository...The first two hit and the third did not hit anything."; 3-30-68 interview with Barry Ernest as recounted in *The Girl on the Stairs*, 2011: "...a second shot rang out, he said. This was the one that struck the president in the head and caused 'a piece of Kennedy's skull to fly back toward me.'"; 1988 interview recounted in *No More Silence*, published 1998, p.60-69: "The people were running helter-skelter here and there. They were running up to the top of that hill it seemed to me in an almost sheep-like fashion following somebody running up those steps. There was a policeman who ran up those steps also. Apparently people thought he was chasing something, which he certainly wasn't.";

60. Alan Smith: 11-22-63 datelined article found in the 11-23-63 *Chicago Tribune*: "The car was about 10 feet from me when a bullet hit the President in his forehead.... The car went about five feet and stopped.";

61. John Chism: 11-22-63 statement to Dallas Sheriff's Department, 19H471: "we were directly in front of the Stemmons Freeway sign..."; 12-18-63 FBI report, 24H525: "[he] was of the opinion the shots came from behind him."; 8-8-68 report of Tom Bethel and Al Oser, investigators working on behalf New Orleans District Attorney Jim Garrison: "An important aspect of Mr. Chism's testimony is his statement as to the direction of the sound which he described as being over his right shoulder. This would put it in the direction of the concrete pagoda on the grassy knoll. Then together with so many people, he ran up the knoll and into the pagoda area."; 11-20-13 appearance by Ricky Chism at the Sixth Floor Museum, in which he presented his parent's recollections: "When the first shot came

and it hit the ground, well, the next two shots he thought came from over by the grassy knoll where the train tracks were. So he started running towards the train tracks.";

62. Marvin Faye Chism: 11-22-63 statement to the Dallas Sheriff's Department, 19H472: "It came from what I thought was behind us and I looked but I couldn't see anything."; 11-20-13 appearance by Ricky Chism at the Sixth Floor Museum, in which he presented his mom's recollections – On why his mom believed there had been a ricochet: "She seen the spark hit the ground."; 11-22-13 article in the Plano Star Courier on an appearance by Mrs. Chism's son Ricky at The Sixth Floor Museum: "She'd seen the spark hit the ground," Chism said of the first shot.";

63. Ernest Brandt: November 1995 discussion with researcher Hal Verb as related in Verb's summer 2001 article in the *Kennedy Assassination Chronicles*: "I thought the shots came from behind me – the pergola – where else could it have come from?" (to be fair, though, this statement is anomalous, as Brandt seems to embrace the single assassin theory in his other statements);

64. John Templin: 7-28-95 Oral History interview for the Sixth Floor Museum: "Well, the first shot definitely came from the School Book, but the second shot sounded somewhat different to me in that it sounded like it might have come from back behind here where the boxcar ... you remember, TP had a switching track at that time back here, and there was always a hundred or a hundred and fifty boxcars back here. And I thought, "Hey, maybe somebody's on the ground shooting. I really couldn't tell." But then, the third shot came from back up, I'm sure, back up at the School Book Depository, but I rationalized for years that maybe the sound of the shot reverberated off of an open boxcar door and echoed out and made it sound like it was coming from down lower. That's the only explanation I could have for it maybe sounding different.";

65. Mary Woodward: 11-23-63 newspaper article "Witness From the News Describes Assassination" written by Woodward for the *Dallas Morning News*: "We decided to cross Elm Street and wait there on the grassy slope just east of the Triple Underpass ... suddenly there was a horrible, ear-splitting noise coming from behind us and a little to the right."; 12-7-63 FBI report, 24H520: "She stated that her first reaction was that the shots had been fired from above her head and from possibly behind her. Her next reaction was that the shots might have come from the overpass which was to her right."; 12-23-63 FBI report, recounting a 12-5-63 discussion be-

tween U.S. Attorney Barefoot Sanders and an FBI agent, CD205, p39: "According to this reporter, these women, names unknown, stated that the shots, according to their opinion, came from a direction other than from the Texas School Book Depository Building."; 3-24-64 testimony of Mark Lane before the Warren Commission, 2H32-61: "Here we have a statement, then, by an employee of the *Dallas Morning News*, evidently speaking – she indicated to me that she was speaking on behalf of all four employees, all of whom stated that the shots came from the direction of the overpass, which was to their fight, and not at all from the Book Depository Building, which was to their left.";

Interview in *The Men Who Killed Kennedy*, broadcast 1988: "One thing I am totally positive about in my own mind is how many shots there were. And there were three shots. The second two shots were immediate. It was almost as if one were an echo of the other. They came so quickly the sound of one did not cease until the second shot. With the second and third shot I did see the president being hit. I literally saw his head explode. So, I felt that the shots had come, as I wrote in my article, from behind me and to my right, which would have been the direction of the grassy knoll, and the railroad overpass."; 11-22-92 interview with Walt Brown as presented in *Treachery in Dallas*, 1995: "The cadence she gave for the shot sequence put the last two almost simultaneous. I then asked her the obvious remaining (and immediately leading) question: The knoll! She nodded in the affirmative, with a very persuasive intensity in her eyes."; 11-21-93 Reporters Remember conference on C-Span: (We) stationed ourselves just down from the School Book Depository building and waited for the parade to come by.) And we were chatting, and as we were talking, I looked up at the grassy knoll. And I said to my friends, 'That's a very dangerous-looking spot to me, it must be, there must be a lot of security up there, because it looks like a perfect spot, if somebody wanted to do something'... in reality, I do believe they did come from the School Book Depository Building. So I get a little bit upset when I get put into the other column...": now changing her tune after 30 years.;

66. Aurelia Alonzo: Woodward's companions on November 22, 1963. (12-7-63 FBI report, CD7 p.19) "Ann Donaldson ... Margaret Brown ... and Miss Aurelio Alonzo ... were interviewed December 6, 1963.... All furnished the same information as that previously furnished by Mary Elizabeth Woodward.";

67. Margaret Brown: Woodward's companions on November 22, 1963. (12-7-63 FBI report, CD7 p.19) "Ann Donaldson ... Marga-

ret Brown ... and Miss Aurelio Alonzo ... were interviewed December 6, 1963. ... All furnished the same information as that previously furnished by Mary Elizabeth Woodward.";

68. Ann Donaldson: Woodward's companions on November 22, 1963. (12-7-63 FBI report, CD7 p.19) "Ann Donaldson ... Margaret Brown ... and Miss Aurelio Alonzo ... were interviewed December 6, 1963. ... All furnished the same information as that previously furnished by Mary Elizabeth Woodward.";

69. A.J. Millican: 11-22-63 handwritten statement to Sheriff Bill Decker, 19H486: "I was standing on the North side of Elm Street, about halfway between Houston and the Underpass. ... Just after the President's car passed, I heard three shots come from up toward Houston and Elm right by the Book Depository Building, and then I immediately heard two more shots come from the Arcade between the Book Store and the Underpass, and then three more shots came from the same direction only sounded further back. ... Then everybody started running up the hill. A man standing on the South side of Elm Street was either hit in the foot or the ankle and fell down.";

70. Peggy Hawkins: 3-26-64 FBI report, CD897 p.35-36: "She said she immediately recognized them as firearm shots and not as fireworks and had the impression that they came from the direction of the railroad yards adjacent to the TSBD building.";

71. Rosemary Willis (Roach) : 11-8-78 HSCA staff interview, summarized in HSCA Report, vol. 12, p.7: "her father became upset when the policeman in the area appeared to run away from where he thought the shots came from; that is, they were running away from the grassy knoll."; 6-5-79 UPI article found in the *Reading Eagle*: "I heard three shots and they all came from across the street from the direction of the book depository. ... Oswald was up there as clear as can be. I think he was up there on purpose to make people think he was the one. The sounds I heard came from the book depository but they weren't necessarily the shots that killed him. Someone with a gun with a silencer could have been in the gutter where they later found shells, or on the railroad trestle or behind the wall."; 11-19-93 article in *USA Today*: "She says she saw the gun smoke of a second gunman – evidence of a conspiracy. ... For her part, Roach is sure there was a conspiracy. She says she heard four shots – not three, as was concluded by the Warren Commission. She believes she saw a man in a storm sewer near the site, a man who some theorists say was a conspirator. She insists at least one shot came from the grassy knoll, a hillock from which many believe a second gunman was fir-

ing. At the moment of the fatal head shot, she says, she spotted a puff of smoke atop the knoll. 'It was definitely gun smoke,' Roach says.";
Interview with Texas Monthly, published November, 1998: "... My ears heard four shots.... I really think that there were six, but I heard four and I'll tell you why ... the first shot rang out. It was to the front of me, and to the right of me, up high. The second shot that I heard came across my right shoulder. By that time, the limousine had already moved further down. And that shot came across my shoulder. And the next one, right after that, still came from the right but not from as far back, it was up some. Still behind me, but not as far back as the other one. And the next one that came was from the grassy knoll and I saw the smoke coming through the trees, into the air. ... Fragments of his head ascended into the air, and from my vision, focal point, the smoke and fragments, you know, everything met.";

72. Phil Willis: Warren Commission testimony: the police officers he saw were running towards the knoll, "evidently thinking it came from that direction" (7 H 496-497); 6-5-79 UPI article found in the *Reading Eagle*: "There's no doubt in our mind the final shot that blew his head off did not come from the depository (located to the rear of the motorcade). His head blew up like a halo. The brains and matter went to the left and rear."; 11-22-85 Trask interview, p.171, *Pictures of the Pain*: "I don't care what any experts say. They're full of baloney. I've shot too many deer ... no one will ever convince us that the last shot did not come from the right front, from the knoll area." ; Interview in *The Men Who Killed Kennedy*, in episode 5, first shown 1988: "At least one shot – including the one that took the President's skull off – had to come from the right front." Same interview, but broadcast in a different episode: "No one will ever convince me – I know damn well the shot that blew his head off, came from the right front."; Interview with Jim Marrs in *Crossfire*, published 1989: "I always thought there had to be another shot from somewhere. I have always gone against the one-gunman theory. I always thought there had to have been some help. I saw blood going to the rear and left. That doesn't happen if that bullet came from the Depository."; *JFK: The Case for Conspiracy* DVD: he reiterates his previous comments;

73. Linda Willis: 1978 Interview with Jim Marrs, published in *Crossfire*, 1989: "I very much agree that shots came from somewhere other than the Depository. And, where we were standing, we had a good view."; 11-7-78 HSCA staff interview, summarized in HSCA Report, Vol. 12 p.8: "The only information she provided relevant to the shots was that she had a distinct impression that the head wound to President Kennedy was the result of a front-to-rear shot. She also

heard three shots and saw the President's head "blow-up."; *The Men Who Killed Kennedy*, broadcast 1988: "The particular head shot must have come from another direction besides behind him because the back of his head blew off. ... The back of his head blew off.";

74. Marilyn Willis: *The Men Who Killed Kennedy*, broadcast 1988: "The head shot seemed to come from the right front. It seemed to strike him here and all the brain matter went out the back of his head. It was like a red halo, a red circle with bright matter in the middle of it." (When asked her clearest memory) "The head shot – seeing his head blow up – I can see it just as plain – it's red, it's cone-shaped, going back."; Interview with Robert Groden for his video, *JFK: The Case for Conspiracy*, 1993: "His head was back this way (she leans her head back) It looked like a red halo – just matter coming out of his head." (When asked from where she thought the shots derived) "Well, the results of what I saw, his head exploded, absolutely exploded. I would think that the shots came from behind the picket fence, which borders the top of the grassy knoll." (When asked where the wound was) "This side" (She grabs her head above her right ear, exactly where the large wound is on the Zapruder film) like this, and it goes to the back. (She leans her head back) His head was like this, see.";

75. Hank Farmer: 11-22-63 FBI memo from Joe Pearce to Dallas Special Agent-in-Charge J. Gordon Shanklin. This memo was never forwarded to FBI headquarters, but was discovered by researcher Harold Weisberg in the Dallas FBI office's files, which he'd gained access to as a result of a FOIA lawsuit: "He stated he saw KENNEDY hit by the bullet and felt that bullet entered KENNEDY's face. He stated he then saw Governor CONNALLY shot and this shot entered CONNALLY's back. FARMER stated therefore, it is his opinion that the two shots were fired by two individuals from opposite directions.";

76. Mrs. Dolores Kounas: 11-25-63 FBI report based upon an 11-24-63 interview, 22H846: "sounded as though these shots were coming from the triple underpass."; 3-23-64 statement to the FBI, 22H659: "I had thought the shots came from a westerly direction in the vicinity of the viaduct.";

77. Roberta Parker: 12-16-63 FBI report, CD205 p.504: "The shot sounded to her as thought it had come from a cement memorial building to the north of the Texas School Book Depository on Elm Street.";

78. Hugh Betzner: 11-22-63 statement to Dallas Sheriff's Department, 19H467: "Police and a lot of spectators started running up the hill on the opposite side of the street from me to a fence of wood.

I assumed that was where the shot was fired from at that time. I kept watching the crowd."; 11-23-63 article by Betzner for UPI: "I went around to the other side of the monument, and it looked like the police thought the shots came from a wooden fence on top of the hill. So I went up there, because I figured that if he got shot from the fence, I might have a picture of the man who did the shooting. My last picture was taken looking that way.";

79. Amos Euins: 10-21-77 interview with HSCA investigators Al Maxwell and Clarence Day – When asked from where he thought the shots were fired: "Well, it's hard to say – it's really hard to say. But, I mean to my opinion – now, you know, even after so many years, I still wouldn't say – even if the guy who was up there – I don't believe they all came from there. It was just too fast. I mean it was just like somebody had a – you've heard an automatic (At this point he makes the sound pow pow pow pow) It was just like that. It wasn't no pow ... pow. It was right quick. It was fast ..." (When asked if he thought any shots were fired from the building) "It's a possibility. It's a possibility ... that a shot could have came from there. But it still was others." When asked if he thought there was more than one gun firing) "Right. It had to be. It had to be ... It was just pow-pow-pow [no spacing between].";

80. Ronald Fischer: 4-1-64 testimony before the Warren Commission, 6H191-200: "At first I thought there were four, but as I think about it more, there must have been just three.... The – uh – first shot fooled me, I think, because of the sound bouncing off the buildings. But the second shot was too much like the first and it was too loud – both shots were too loud to be a firecracker.... They appeared to be coming from just west of the School Book Depository ... there were some railroad cars back in there."; 11-19-78 article in the *Dallas Morning News*: "Fisher recently told the news that David W. Belin, an assistant counsel of the Warren Commission, tried to 'intimidate' him into testifying the one man he was able to see didn't have the light-colored hair he insisted he did have. 'He (Belin) and I had a fight almost in the interview room over the color of the man's hair,' Fisher said. 'He wanted me to tell him the man was dark-headed and I wouldn't do it.' Oswald's hair 'doesn't appear to me in the photographs to be as light as the man that I saw,' Fisher said, 'and that's what Belin was upset about.'"; 7-9-98 video-taped interview with Mark Oakes: "I originally said in my deposition in the Sheriff's office that there were four shots. And there were a number of people who had claimed that they heard four shots.... I still think that there were probably four shots but I couldn't swear to it.";

81. Edgar Leon Smith: 7-24-64 testimony before the Warren Commission, 7H565-569: "I thought when it came to my mind that there were shots, and I was pretty sure there were when I saw his car because they were leaving in such a hurry, I thought they were coming from this area here, and I ran over there and checked back of it and, of course, there wasn't anything there. (When asked to verify that he thought the shot came from a little concrete structure in back of the arcade) "Yes, sir." (When Liebeler points out that this was "Toward the railroad tracks there?") "That's true. (And north?) "Yes. ... I ran down here.... And I ran up to here and I couldn't get over so I went back around then." (Liebeler then clarifies "You went farther down Elm Street and right behind this concrete structure here; is that correct?") "And on back into there." (Liebeler adds "And into the parking area behind the concrete structure there") "Yes, and there's where I stayed for an hour or so and after I got around there, they started checking everybody that was going in and out of the – well, I don't know who they was checking because there was so much milling around, because there was a bunch of county officers back there plus the policemen."; *No More Silence*, p.197-203, published 1998: "I couldn't really tell where the shots came from, but they sounded like they all came from the same direction. Certainly it didn't seem to me that they came from the sixth floor.... At the time of the shooting, I was looking more toward the grassy knoll ... I reacted by running across the street from the south side of Elm toward the underpass.";

82. Joe Marshall Smith: 12-9-63 FBI report, as summarized in CD205 p39: "He stated he did smell what he thought was gunpowder but stated this smell was in the parking lot by the TSBD Building and not by the underpass. He advised he never at any time went to the underpass and could not advise if there was the smell of gunpowder in the underpass."; 12-13-63 article in the Texas Observer, as reported in *Six Seconds in Dallas*, 1967: "Patrolman Smith had earlier told Ronnie Dugger of the the *Texas Observer* that he had 'caught the smell of gunpowder' behind the fence. 'I could tell it was in the air.'"; 7-16-64 Statement to the Dallas Police Department, 22H600: "I heard the shots and thought they were coming from bushes of the overpass."; 7-23-64 testimony before the Warren Commission, 7H531-539: "This woman came up to me and she was just in hysterics. She told me, 'They are shooting the President from the bushes.' So I immediately proceeded up here. (Liebeler asks: "You proceeded up to an area immediately behind the concrete structure here that is described by Elm Street and the street

that runs immediately in front of the Texas School Book Depository, is that right?") "I was checking all the bushes and I checked all the cars in the parking lot ... I checked all the cars. I looked into all the cars and checked around the bushes. Of course, I wasn't alone. There was some deputy sheriff with me, and I believe one Secret Service man when I got there. I got to make this statement, too. I felt awfully silly, but after the shot and this woman, I pulled my pistol from my holster, and I thought, this is silly, I don't know who I am looking for, and I put it back. Just as I did, he showed me that he was a Secret Service agent ... he saw me coming with my pistol and right away he showed me who he was." (When asked if he remembered the identity of this agent) "No, sir; I don't – because then we started checking the cars. In fact, I was checking the bushes, and I went through the cars, and I started over here in this particular section." (Liebeler asks "Down toward the railroad tracks where they go over the triple underpass?") "Yes." (Liebeler then asks "Did you have any basis for believing where the shots came from, or where to look for somebody, other than what the lady told you?") "No, sir; except that maybe it was a power of suggestion. But it sounded to me like they may have came from this vicinity here.";

83. James Crawford: 1-10-64 FBI report, CD329 p.22: "Mr. Crawford heard sounds which at first were believed by Crawford to be the backfiring of an automobile. Mr. Crawford believed these sounds came from one of the cars in the front of the Presidential motorcade which was approaching the Triple Underpass...";

84. Danny Arce: 3-18-64 statement to the FBI, 22H634: "To the best of my knowledge there were three shots and they came from the direction of the railroad tracks."; 4-7-64 testimony before the Warren Commission, 6H365-367: "I thought they came from the railroad tracks to the west of the Texas School Book Depository... From the tracks on the west deal." (When asked if he looked back at the building) "No, I didn't think they came from there. I just looked directly to the railroad tracks and all the people started running up there and I just ran along with them."; 8-8-68 report on a phone call with Tom Bethel and Al Oser, investigators working on behalf New Orleans District Attorney Jim Garrison: "Arce stated...that he heard three shots and they all sounded the same, and they sounded as though they had come from the railroad tracks to the west of the Book Depository."; July-August 1988 interview recounted in *American History Illustrated*, November 1988: "I was right on the front steps of the Texas School Book Depository when the motorcade came along. Just after the President's car passed, I heard a shot. Then

two more shots. It seemed to me the shots came from the grassy knoll. I went over there. A lot of people ran there, I wanted to know who was doing the shooting. When Oswald was arrested, I didn't see how he could be the right man. I thought the police made a mistake. Oswald could have been a perfect guy to hang this on.";

85. Mrs. Donald Baker (Virgie Rackley): 11-25-63 FBI report based upon an 11-24-63 interview, CD5 p.66-67: "It sounded as though these sounds were coming from the direction of the Triple Underpass and looking in that direction after the first shot she saw something bounce from the roadway in front of the Presidential automobile and now presumes it was a bullet bouncing off the pavement."; 7-22-64 testimony before the Warren Commission, 7H507-515: "it sounded like it was coming from – there was a railroad track ... so I guess it would be by the underpass.";

86. Cleola Shields: 11/12/77 interview with HSCA: "she heard what sounded like a firecracker coming from the direction of the railroad crossing ... we all ran to the railroad trestle and looked in the box cars.";

87. Ochus V. Campbell: 11-24-63 FBI report, 22H845: "believed the noise came away from his building."; 11-26-63 FBI report, CD5 p336: "Mr. Campbell advised he had viewed the Presidential Motorcade and subsequently heard the shots being fired from a point which he thought was near the railroad tracks located over the viaduct on Elm Street."; 2-17-64 statement to the Dallas Police Department, box 3 folder 19 file 4 of the Dallas JFK Archive: "We then walked across Elm Street and stood on the curb near the parade as it turned from Houston Street down under the underpass. I heard the shots, it sounded like they came from the knoll near the railroad tracks. I thought it was firecrackers."; 3-19-64 statement to the FBI, 22H638: "I heard shots being fired from a point which I thought was near the railroad tracks located over the viaduct on Elm Street"; 1-24-63 FBI report, 22H844: "he insisted the shots came from the embankment."; Mrs. Robert Reid was standing beside him and Superintendent Roy Truly as the motorcade passed right by them and the shots rang out. "And I turned to Mr. Campbell," she testified in Washington, "and I said, 'Oh, my goodness, I am afraid those came from our building.' But Mr. Campbell, he said, "Oh, Mrs. Reid, no, it came from the grassy area down this way.'" (3 H 273-274)

88. Roy Truly: 11-23-63 FBI report based upon the 11-22-63 interview with Pinkston, CD5 p322: "He was unable to place exactly the source of these shots but believed they came from the area of

the railroad yards adjoining the depository building."; 11-23-63 FBI report based upon an 11-23-63 interview with Kenneth Jackson, CD5 p324: "He moved toward the building and thought at first the shots the shots came from behind the building."; 3-24-64 testimony before the Warren Commission, 3H212-241: "I heard an explosion, which I thought was a toy cannon or a loud firecracker from west of the building.";

89. Irma Jean Vanzan: 9-25-77 HSCA audio-taped interview: "The Secret Service man ran towards the track.... And I thought that's where the sound was coming from because it had an echo to the shot";

90. Lupe Whitaker (a.k.a. Lucy Whitaker): 2-18-64 report of the Dallas Police Department, box 3 folder 19 file 19 of the Dallas JFK Archive: "She stated the shots sounded like they came from the west of the building but they did sound as if they came from above.";

91. Madie Reese: 11-24-63 FBI report based upon an 11-23-63 interview, CD5 p.59: "At first she thought the shots came from the alcove near the benches.";

92. Mrs. Avery Davis: 2-18-64 report of the Dallas Police Department, box 3, folder 19, file 6 of Dallas JFK Archive: "From her location she heard the three shots but thought they came from the railroad to the west."; 3-20-64 statement to the FBI, 22H642: "I did not know from which direction the shots had come but thought they were from the direction of the viaduct which crosses Elm Street west from where I was standing.";

93. Judy McCully: 2-18-64 report of the Dallas Police Department, box 3 folder 19 file 13 of the Dallas JFK Archive: "The shots sounded like they came from the right side of the building in the arcade.";

94. Billy Lovelady: 11-22-63 sworn affidavit, 24H214: "When the President came by, Bill Shelley and I was standing on the steps in front of the building where I work ... I could not tell where the shots came from but sounded like they were across the street from us.... After it was over we went back into the building..."; 3-19-64 statement to the FBI, 22H662: "I heard several loud reports which I first thought to be firecrackers, and which appeared to me to be in the direction of the Elm Street viaduct just ahead of the motorcade. I did not at any time believe the shots had come from the Texas School Book Depository Building. I am acquainted with Lee Harvey Oswald as a fellow employee only and I recall that on the morning of November 22, 1963, I was on the sixth floor of the Texas School Book

Depository putting down a new wooden floor when Oswald came over to me and asked where a certain book was stored. I don't recall name of the book but told him that book was out of stock. That is the last time I saw Oswald prior to the assassination of President John F. Kennedy ... I recall that following the shooting, I ran toward the spot where President Kennedy's car had stopped."; 4-7-64 testimony before the Warren Commission, 6H336-341-When asked from where he thought the shots had been fired) "Right there around that concrete little deal on that knoll ... to my right. I was standing as you are going down the steps, I was standing on the right, sounded like it was in that area.... Between the underpass and the building right on that knoll."; 11-21-71 article in the *Dallas-Times Herald* built upon an interview with Lovelady: "I thought the shots came from my right, which would be near the railroad tracks, and everybody began running that way. All of a sudden I wondered what in the world we were doing running toward a gunman."; 7-5-78 interview with an HSCA investigator-When asked where he thought they came from) "To my right ... to my right, toward the railroad tracks.";

95. William Shelley: 4-7-64 testimony before the Warren Commission, 6H327-334: "Sounded like it came from the west ... officers started running down to the lumber yards and Billy and I walked down that way. We walked on down to the first railroad track there on the dead-end street and stood there and watched them searching cars down there in the parking lots for a little while.";

96. Otis Williams: 3-19-64 statement to the FBI, 22H683: "I thought these blasts or shots came from the direction of the viaduct which crosses Elm Street."; *No More Silence* p.116-120, published 1998: "I thought it came from the underpass.";

97. Buell Wesley Frazier: 12-5-63 sworn statement to the U.S. Secret Service, CD87 p796: "[I] thought they had come from somewhere around the triple underpass or railroad tracks."; 3-11-64 testimony before the Warren Commission, 2H210-245: "to be frank with you I thought it come from down there, where that underpass is."; 7-23-86 testimony in televised mock trial, *On Trial: Lee Harvey Oswald* – When asked if he thought the shots came from the railroad) "Yes, sir, from the knoll there." (When asked again about the direction of the shots) "I thought they came from the knoll here." (He is then asked to write the words "grassy knoll" on a map of Dealey Plaza and put an X where he thought the shots had come from. He writes the words on the map to the west of the arcade, and then puts an X by these words at the northernmost point of the picket fence, in the

railroad yards to the west of the arcade.); 7-13-13 appearance at the Sixth Floor Museum, as shown on C-Span-When asked if he had a sense where the shots were coming from) "The first one, when I was standing back on the top of the steps, sounded like it come to my right down where the motorcade was, But then the second and third sounded much closer...";

98. Steven Wilson: 3-25-64 statement to the FBI, 22H684: "At that time it seemed the shots came from the west end of the building or from the colonnade located on Elm Street across from the west end of our building."; 8-8-68 report on an interview performed by Tom Bethel or Al Oser, investigators working on behalf New Orleans District Attorney Jim Garrison: "the reports appeared to have come from his right which would have meant the end of the west portion of the Texas School Book Depository or the concrete pagoda area of the grassy knoll.";

99. Dorothy Ann Garner: 3-20-64 statement to the FBI, 22H648: "I thought at the time the shots or reports came from a point to the west of the building.";

100. Victoria Adams: 4-7-64 testimony before the Warren Commission, 6H386-393: "It seemed as if it came from the right below rather than from the left above.";

101. Jane Berry: CD5: "from west of where she was standing [Depository]"; Note: anti-conspiracy author John McAdams also includes her as a knoll witness;

102. Doris Burns: 6 H 399, 22 H 637: "Facing east and it sounded to me as if it came toward my back"; Note: anti-conspiracy author John McAdams also includes her as a knoll witness;

103. Police Chief Jesse Curry: *Retired Dallas Police Chief, Jesse Curry Reveals His Personal JFK Assassination File* by Jesse Curry, self-published: Dallas 1969; *The Dallas Morning News*, pp. 58-59: Curry heard the first gunshot and immediately shouted over the police radio: "Get a man on top of that triple underpass and see what happened up there!"; 1977 Canadian Broadcasting Company interview with Peter Dale Scott (on You Tube): admits that, judging by the direction of the blood and brain matter, that a shot would seem to have come from the front; 1978 BBC Anthony Summers interview (also on You Tube): said the same thing;

104. Joe Molina: Warren Commission testimony, 6 H 371: "came from the west"; Detective F.M. Turner's report, page 2: "shots came from west of their building.";

105. Jean Newman: Sheriff's Department Affidavit 11/22/63: 19 H 489: "The first impression I had was that the shots came from my right" (the knoll);

106. Garland Slack: FBI interview 12/2/63, 26 H 364: Thought the first shots came from the overpass;

107. S.R. Yates: 21 H 423: shots came from the overpass; Note: anti-conspiracy author John McAdams also includes him as a knoll witness;

108. Samuel Paternostro: FBI interview 1/20/64, 24 H 536: shots came from TSBD, Criminal Courts, or Triple Overpass;

109. Postal Inspector Harry D. Holmes: *No More Silence* by Larry Sneed (1998), p. 352: "... there was just a cone of blood and corruption that went up right in the back of his head and neck. I thought it was red paper on a firecracker. It looked like a firecracker lit up which looks like little bits of red paper as it goes up. But in reality it was his skull and brains and everything else that went up perhaps as much as six or eight feet. Just like that!";

110. Beverly Oliver: appears in captioned photographs and negatives by Bill Beal of the *Dallas Times-Herald* from 11/22/63- entrance of the Colony Club (available via The Sixth Floor Museum); *The Men Who Killed Kennedy* 1988/1991/1995 [see also *High Treason*, p. 461]: saw "the back of his [JFK's] head come off." Shots came from the knoll; *JFK: The Case for Conspiracy* 1993/2003 DVD: "The whole back of his head went flying out the back of the car [indicating]." Shots came from the knoll;

111. Ed Hoffman: *The Men Who Killed Kennedy* 1988/1991: saw two men behind picket fence atop the grassy knoll, one of which fired upon JFK;

112. Gordon Arnold: *San Francisco Chronicle* 8/28/78: shot came from knoll; *The Men Who Killed Kennedy* 1988/1991;

113. Elsie Dorman: 22 H 644, CD 5: *Not* from the front but from a different building: "She felt that these shots were coming from the area of the Records Building.";

114. KBOX reporter Sam Pate (famous for his line "It appears as though something has happened in the motorcade route."): believed a shot came from the front and saw a puff from the Elm Street storm drain- 1970 interview with researcher Al Chapman: https://www.youtube.com/watch?v=ESXT-E2w9C4; 6/22/2005 Sixth Floor Museum Oral History;

Thanks to legendary author Robert Groden for this image-top row, L-R: Dr. Ronald Jones, Dr. Charles Carrico, Dr. Richard Dulany, Dr. Paul Peters, Dr. Kenneth Salyer, Dr. Robert McClelland, Dr. Charles Crenshaw; bottom row, L-R: Nurse Audrey Bell, Theran Ward, Aubrey Rike, Paul O'Connor, Floyd Riebe, Jerrol Custer, Frank O'Neill:

115. Winston Lawson: Warren Commission testimony 4 H 352-353: Reports came from "the area between Elm St. and Main St., the grassy area between the two streets"; Note: anti-conspiracy author John McAdams also includes him as an "Infield" witness; Lawson stated that he "saw a huge hole in the back of the president's head," as reported in *The Virginian-Pilot* on June 17, 2010;

116. Hurchel Jacks: 18 H 801: 11/28/63 report re: 11/22/63: "Before the President's body was covered it appeared that the bullet had struck him above the right ear or near the temple;

117. Dr. Kemp Clark, Chief Neurosurgeon, Parkland Hospital: WR 516-518/ 17 H 1-3 / CE 392 [undated summary; see also 21 H 150-152: Clark's 11/23/63 report to Admiral Burkley with the verbatim summary. In addition, see *Assassination Science*, pp. 416-418: this is an FBI report dated 11/25/63 which includes the verbatim summary to Burkley from 11/23/63]: "...in the occipital region of the skull..."; "There was a large wound in the right occipito parietal region..."; "Both cerebral and cerebellar tissue were extruding from the wound."; WR 524-525/ 17 H 9-10 /CE 392: handwritten report 11/22/63 – "The President was bleeding profusely from the back of the head. There was a large (3 x 3 cm) remnant of cerebral tissue present ... there was a smaller amount of cerebellar tissue present also"; "There was a large wound beginning in the right occiput extending into the parietal region..."; Parkland Press conference, 11/22/63, 3:16 PM CST [*Assassination Science*, pp. 427]: "A missile had gone in or out of the back of his head ... the back of his head.... I was busy with his head wound.... The head wound could have been either the exit wound from the neck or it could have been a tangential wound, as it was simply a large, gaping loss of tissue.";

118.   Dr. Malcolm Perry, Parkland Hospital: WR 521-522/ 17 H 6-7/ CE392: report written 11/22/63 – "A large wound of the right posterior cranium..."; Parkland press conference, 11/22/63 [see *Assassination Science*, pp. 419-427] – "There was an entrance wound in the neck ... It appeared to be coming at him. ... The wound appeared to be an entrance wound in the front of the throat; yes, that is correct. The exit wound, I don't know. It could have been the head or there could have been a second wound of the head." (Apparently, based off this conference, the Associated Press dispatch on 11/22/63 stated that Dr. Perry "said the entrance wound was in the front of the head," while all the AP wires for this day stated that JFK had a large hole in the "back" of his head.); Filmed interview by Bob Welch, WBAP-TV/ NBC (Texas News), 11/23/63 [available on You Tube] – "He had a severe, lethal wound"; "There was a neck wound anteriorly and a large wound of his head in the right posterior area."; "passage of the bullet through the neck"; 6 H 9, 11, and 15 / testimony (3/25/64): "I noted there was a large wound of the right posterior parietal area in the head exposing lacerated brain...a large avulsive injury of the right occipitoparietal area in which both scalp and portions of skull were absent..."; the throat wound was "between 3 and 5 mm in size.";1-11-78, (audiotaped) interview with HSCA's Andrew Purdy (7 HSCA 292293; 302; 312 re: neck) – "Dr. Perry... believed the head wound was located on the 'occipital parietal' region of the skull and that the right posterior aspect of the skull was missing..."; "...the parietal occipital head wound was largely avulsive and there was visible brain tissue in the macard and some cerebellum seen..."; "I thought it [the neck wound] looked like an entrance wound because it was so small."

119.   Dr. Robert McClelland, Parkland Hospital: WR 526-527 / 17 H 11-12 / CE 392: report written 11/22/63 – "...a massive gunshot wound of the head with a fragment wound of the trachea... The cause of death was due to massive head and brain injury from a gunshot wound of the left temple."; *St. Louis Post-Dispatch*, 12/1/63 – "This [the neck wound] did appear to be an entrance wound."; Article by Richard Dudman in *The New Republic*, 12/21/63 [*Assassination Science*, p. 167]: "Dr. Robert McClelland... told me afterward that they still believed it [the neck wound] to be an entry wound."; 6 H 33-34, 35, 37: Warren Commission testimony: "...I could very closely examine the head wound, and I noted that the right posterior portion of the skull had been extremely blasted ... probably a third or so, at least, of the brain tissue, posterior cerebral tissue and some of the cerebellar tissue had been blasted out..."; "...there was

definitely a piece of cerebellum that extruded from the wound…";
"…the loss of cerebral and cerebellar tissues were so great … massive head injuries with loss of large amounts of cerebral and cerebellar tissues…"; "The initial impression that we had was that perhaps the wound in the neck, the anterior part of the neck, was an entrance wound and that it had perhaps taken a trajectory off the anterior vertebral body and again into the skull itself, exiting out the back, to produce the massive injury in the head.";

120. Dr. Marion Jenkins, Parkland Hospital: WR 529-530 / 17 H 14-15 / CE 392: report addressed to Administrator C.J. Price dated 11/22/63 (the verbatim, retyped report, this time addressed to Dean A.J. Gill, can be found at 20 H 252-253) – " a great laceration on the right side of the head (temporal and occipital), causing a great defect in the skull plate so that there was herniation and laceration of great areas of the brain, even to the extent that the cerebellum had protruded from the wound."[See also p. 35 of Jesse Curry's 1969 book entitled *JFK Assassination File*]; 6 H 48 and 51 / testimony – ""Part of the brain was herniated; I really think part of the cerebellum, as I recognized it, was herniated from the wound…"; "…the wound with the exploded area of the scalp, as I interpreted it being exploded, I would interpret it being a wound of exit…"; "…I thought there was a wound on the left temporal area, right in the hairline and right above the zygomatic process."; 11/10/77 HSCA interview conducted by Andrew Purdy (7 HSCA 285-7) – He (Dr. Jenkins) "…was positioned at the head of the table so he had one of the closest views of the head wound … believes he was '…the only one who knew the extent of the head wound.'… Regarding the head wound, Dr. Jenkins said that only one segment of bone was blown out – it was a segment of occipital or temporal bone. He noted that a portion of the cerebellum (lower rear brain) was hanging out from a hole in the right-rear of the head."; 11/24/78 *American Medical News* – JFK "…had part of his head blown away and part of his cerebellum was hanging out";

121. Dr. Charles Carrico, Parkland Hospital: WR 519-520 / 17 H 4-5 / CE 392: handwritten report dated 11/22/63 – "[the skull] wound had avulsed the calvarium and shredded brain tissue present with profuse oozing … attempts to control slow oozing from cerebral and cerebellar tissue via packs instituted…."; "small penetrating wound of ent. neck"; 6 H 3 and 6/ testimony (3/25/64) – "There seemed to be a 4-5 cm. area of avulsion of the scalp and the skull was fragmented and bleeding cerebral and cerebellar tissue…. The [skull] wound that I saw was a large gaping wound, located in the

right occipitoparietal area. I would estimate to be about 5 to 7 cm. in size, more or less circular, with avulsions of the calvarium and scalp tissue. As I stated before, I believe there was shredded macerated cerebral and cerebellar tissues both in the wounds and on the fragments of the skull attached to the dura."; throat wound: "probably a 4 to 7 mm wound" and had "no jagged edges or stellate lacerations"; 7 HSCA 266-280 [see esp. pages 268 and 278]: 1/11/78 (audio-taped) interview – "The head wound was a much larger wound than the neck wound. It is 5 by 7 cm., two and a half by three inches, ragged, had blood and hair all around it, located in the part of the parietal-occipital region ... a fairly large wound in the right side of the head, in the parietal, occipital area. One could see blood and brains, both cerebellum and cerebrum fragments in that wound.";

122. Dr. Ronald Jones, Parkland Hospital: 20 H 333: handwritten report dated 11/23/63 – "... severe skull and brain injury was noted as well as a small hole in anterior midline of neck thought to be a bullet entrance wound ... air was bubbling through the neck wound."; 6 H 53-54, 56 / testimony (3/24/64) – "... he had a large wound in the right posterior side of the head ... There was large defect in the back side of the head as the President lay on the cart with what appeared to be some brain hanging out of this wound with multiple pieces of skull noted with the brain ..."; "what appeared to be an exit wound in the posterior portion of the skull ... the only speculation that I could have as far as to how this could occur with a single wound would be that it would enter the anterior neck and possibly strike a vertebral body and then change its course and exit in the region of the posterior portion of the head."; "The hole [in the throat] was very small and relatively clean cut, as you would see in a bullet that is entering rather than exiting from a patient."; Jan. 1983 interview with Lifton (*Best Evidence*, p. 705) – "If you brought him in here today, I'd still say he was shot from the front.";

123. Dr. Gene Akin, Parkland Hospital: 6 H 65 and 67/testimony – "The back of the right occipital-parietal portion of his head was shattered, with brain substance extruding."; "I assume the right occipital-parietal region was the exit, so to speak, that he had probably been hit on the other side of the head, or at least tangentially in the back of the head ..."; "this [the neck wound] must have been an entrance wound ..."; 6/28/84 FBI Memorandum, SA Udo H. Specht to SAC, Dallas, re: interviews with Akin (RIF#124-10158-10449): "when he saw President Kennedy in the emergency room on 11/22/63, he thought he saw a bullet entrance wound on the President's forehead. The President was covered with blood in the

head area and the back of his head was blown wide open. Akin feels that his observation as to the possible entrance wound on the President's forehead is significant and that he did not mention this item when he was interviewed in 1963-1964 because he did not want to be killed by any conspirators. Akin stated that if this entrance wound was not documented in the Presidential autopsy, then plastic surgery was probably conducted to cover this up.";

124. Dr. Paul Peters, Parkland Hospital: 6 H 70-71 / testimony – "It was pointed out that an examination of the brain had been done… we saw the wound of entry in the throat and noted the large occipital wound…";"…I noticed that there was a large defect in the occiput…. It seemed to me that in the right occipital-parietal area that there was a large defect."; 11/12/66 interview with Lifton (*Best Evidence*, pages 317 and 324) – " a hole in the occiput … exited through the back of the head…"; "I'd be willing to swear that the wound was in the occiput, you know. I could see the occipital lobes clearly, and so I know it was that far back, on the skull. I could look inside the skull, and I thought it looked like cerebellum was injured, or missing, because the occipital lobes seemed to rest almost on the foramen magnum … the cerebellum and brainstem, might have been injured, or missing.";

125. Dr. Charles Crenshaw, Parkland Hospital: WC references to his presence on 11/22/63: 6 H 40 (Baxter), 6 H 31-32 (McClelland), 6 H 80-81 (Salyer), 6 H 141 (Henchcliffe), 6 H 60 (Curtis) + 15 H 761: index; WC reference to his presence on 11/24/63: 21 H 265 (report by Parkland Administrator Charles Price); January 1964 *Texas State Journal of Medicine* article entitled Three Patients at Parkland, p. 72 – "Dr. Jenkins recalls that the following physicians were members of the resuscitation team: Drs. Jenkins and Akin … Drs. Gerry Gustafson, Dale Coln, and Charles Crenshaw, all residents in surgery, who were prepared to introduce cannulae into the veins via cutdowns or percutaneous puncture … three members of the staff were performing venous cutdowns, one in each lower extremity and one in the left forearm. These were performed by Drs. Coln, Crenshaw, and Gustafson." ; *High Treason 2*, pp. 110-115 and 549 (interviews of 7/12/80 [90?] and 9/21/91) – "…it was in the parietal-occipital area"; thinks the body was tampered with at Bethesda; *Conspiracy of Silence* (1992), p. 86 (and throughout; later renamed *Trauma Room One* (2001) and *JFK Has Been Shot* (2013)]: "His entire right cerebral hemisphere appeared to be gone. It looked like a crater – an empty cavity… From the damage I saw, there was no doubt in my mind that the bullet had entered his head through the

front, and as it surgically passed through his cranium, the missile obliterated part of the temporal and all the parietal and occipital lobes before it lacerated the cerebellum."; [p. 79] "I also identified a small opening about the diameter of a pencil at the midline of his throat to be an entry bullet hole. There was no doubt in my mind about that wound.";

126. Dr. Charles Baxter, Parkland Hospital: WR 523 / 17 H 8 / CE392 – handwritten report dated 11/22/63: "...the right temporal and occipital bones were missing and the brain was lying on the table, with [extensive?] maceration and contusion..."; 6 H 40, 41, 42 (re: neck) and 44 / testimony (3/24/64) – "There was a large gaping wound in the skull ... literally the right side of his head had been blown off. With this and the observation that the cerebellum was present..."; throat wound: "4 to 5 mm in widest diameter ... it was a very small wound. And, it was directly in the midline ... this would more resemble a wound of entry ... [but] ... I think that the wound could well represent either exit or entry wound.";

127. Dr. Robert Grossman[2], Parkland Hospital: 6 H 81 (Salyer) – confirms Grossman's presence in Trauma Room One; *High Treason*, pages 30, 36, 51, 53, 459 (*Boston Globe*, June 21, 1981-notes placed in JFK Library [see also *Killing Kennedy* by Livingstone, pp. 303-304; *Between the Signal and the Noise* by Roger Bruce Feinman (1993) and Groden's *The Killing of a President*, p. 181; *JFK: Absolute Proof* by Robert Groden (2013), page 153: saw two separate head wounds: a large defect in the parietal area above the right ear, as well as "a large [albeit smaller than the first wound described], separate wound, located squarely in the occiput."; "...described a large hole squarely in the occiput, far too large for a bullet entry wound..."; Grossman: "It was clear to me...that the right parietal bone had been lifted up by a bullet which had exited."; noticed the skin flap near the right temple; Dr. Clark picked up the back of the head to demonstrate the wound; ARRB interview 3/21/97: Dr. Grossman also drew damage to the right rear area, albeit smaller and one he deemed to be of entrance; also noted cerebellum damage;

128. Dr. Richard Dulany, Parkland Hospital: 6 H 114 /testimony (3/25/64) – "...he had a large head wound – that was the first thing I noticed." Arlen Specter did not have him elaborate on any details.; *High Treason*, pages 43, 46, 460, and 489 (*Boston Globe*, 6/21/81 [see also *Killing Kennedy* by Livingstone, page 303]): "The copy of the autopsy photo was shown to him by the *Globe* and he stated that

it was not accurate. When shown the official picture, he said that there was a "definite conflict" and "that's not the way I remember it."; "Somebody lifted up his head and showed me the back of his head. We couldn't see much until they picked up his head. I was standing beside him. The wound was on the back of his head. On the back side ... the whole back-side was gone ... it was a big gaping wound.";

129. Dr. Adolph Giesecke, Parkland Hospital: 6 H 74 / testimony – "...I noticed that he had a very large cranial wound, with loss of brain substance, and it seemed most of the bleeding was coming from the cranial wound ... from the vertex to the left ear, and from the brow line to the occiput on the left-hand side of the head the cranium was entirely missing."; *High Treason*, pages 30, 46-49, 231 (*The Continuing Inquiry*, 10/80; Livingstone's 1979 interview tape-JFK Library; *Boston Globe*, 6/21/81; letter to Livingstone, 4/1/81 [see also *Killing Kennedy* by Livingstone, p. 304]): "...we shined a light in the cranial vault there, and noticed a large amount of brain missing."; Livingstone: "Was this [the back of the head depicted in the official picture] blown out?" Giesecke: "Yes. It was missing."; "From what I saw, I think that's [the McClelland drawing] a reasonable representation."; confirmed to the Globe that the back of the head was missing ; "in doing so (pulling down the flap), the underlying bony defect is obscured.";

130. Dr. Fouad Bashour, Parkland Hospital: WR 528 / 17 H 13 / CE392: handwritten report dated 11/22/63 – very brief report that doesn't mention the wounds; 6 H 61-62 /testimony – "...the head wound was massive...": no details were elicited during Bashour's brief testimony; *High Treason*, p. 45 (*The Continuing Inquiry*, 10/80; see also *Conspiracy*, p. 481) – "He was most insistent that the official picture was not representative of the wounds, and he continually laid his hand both on the back of Livinsgtone's head and his own to show where the large hole was. "Why do they cover it up?" he repeated numerous times. "This is not the way it was!" he kept repeating, shaking his head no.";

131. Dr. Kenneth Salyer, Parkland Hospital: 6 H 81 /testimony – "...he did have some sucking wound of some type on his neck...";"... (JFK) had a wound of his right temporal region ... I came in on the left side of him and noticed that his major wound seemed to be in his right temporal area, at least from the point of view that I could see him, and other than that – nothing other than he did have a gaping scalp wound – cranial wound."; *JFK: The Case for Conspiracy* video (see also Groden's *The Killing of a President*, p. 87): "This wound

extended into the parietal area."; thought one of the autopsy photos was tampered with [the one on page 82 of Groden's *The Killing of a President*]: "You know, there's something wrong with it. I'll leave it at that. I mean – -this thing has been-something, you know, happened to this.... This is not right. No. See, this has been doctored here. This is lying open. See, the way you have him here – the way they've got him here is – skin flaps have been cut or altered or pushed up or changed, and this isn't the way he looked. This was – he looked – this was wide open with brain here. This is scalp pushed back and it's all distorted."; sees two "rounded, beveled" wounds, right next to each other, in the autopsy photo that shows the cranium empty; Interview with Dr. Gary Aguilar: "Salyer reported... that the wound was right sided but extended both posterior to and anterior to the ear. He repeated a claim made to Robert Groden that the photograph appeared to have been tampered with."; Sixth Floor Museum oral histories 4/11/2008 and 11/18/2008: the description for his oral histories states: "His personal memories of the president's head wound do not correspond with subsequently published autopsy photographs.";

132. Dr. William Midgett, Parkland Hospital: 6 H 135-136 (Bowron), 21 H 213 (Lozano) – confirm Midgett's presence and duties; 4/16/92 interview with Gerald Posner for *Case Closed*, 287, 310-311:"... it was more parietal than occipital – that much I could see."; 2/8/93 interview with Wallace Milam [transcript provided to author] – "Midgett saw one wound – in the head. He called it "right parietal area" and said it was behind the ear. He estimated it as being 6 cm in diameter. A piece of skull was missing and there was an absence of brain (Midgett called it "a hole" where the brain had been). Midgett said, "The brain was all over the car.";

133. Dr. Donald Teel Curtis, Parkland Hospital: WC references : WR 53, 66; 3 H 359-360 (Carrico); 6 H 2,4 (Carrico again); 6 H 11(Perry);6 H 40 (Baxter); 6 H 53 (Jones); 20 H 5 (Giesecke's report re: Connally); 6 H 60 / testimony – "...I went around to the right side of [JFK] and saw the head wound...fragments of bone and a gross injury to the cranial contents, with copious amounts of hemorrhage.": no specific details on orientation and the like where elicited from Curtis; 10/25/94 letter from Curtis to Brad Parker: "The drawing by Dr. Robert McClelland is essentially my recollection of the wound suffered by John F. Kennedy."; 9/30/98 letter to Vince Palamara: "1. The wound involving the right posterior lateral surface of the skull appeared to me to be an exit wound or a tangential entrance wound. 2. I am unaware as to the details of the "official story" therefore I am unable to comment on my interpretation.";

134. Dr. Philip Williams, Parkland Hospital: 21 H 215 (Nurse Bertha Lozano's report): documents his presence; *High Treason 2*, photo section + pp. 287, 294, 301-302, 308-312 (interviewed 4/6/91 and 5/10/92) – "Certainly the President's cerebellum was severely damaged and "swinging in the breeze," as it was described by Dr. Philip Williams"; "The bone in the back of President Kennedy's head was missing"; disputes the x-rays;

135. Dr. Jackie Hunt, Parkland Hospital: 6 H 76-79 / testimony – was blocked from seeing the wounds; other WC references: WR 53, 517, 529; 3 H 371; 6 H 40,46,64,73; 17 H 2, 14; 20 H 5-6; 21 H 151; January 1964 *Texas State Journal of Medicine* article "Three Patients at Parkland," pages 63 and 70 – present for JFK's treatment, as well as Connally's; *High Treason*, p. 52 (*The Continuing Inquiry*, 10/80; author's tape-JFK Library): "... Livingstone showed her the [official autopsy] picture in 1979 and she instantly denounced it. She did not see the back of the head because she was standing directly over the President, but she insisted that the back part of the head was blown out and rejected the official picture. "That's the way it was described to me," she said, saying that the back of the head was gone. Had the large defect been anywhere else, she would have seen it and described it. Dr. Akin said that if you looked directly down on Kennedy, you could not see the large hole. Therefore, Dr. Hunt's testimony is significant. Dr. Hunt responded to Livingstone's question: "so, the exit wound would be in the occipital-parietal area?" "Yeah, uh-huh. It would be somewhere on the right posterior part of it..." She pointed to the sketch from *Six Seconds in Dallas*: "That's the way it was described to me. I went around this way and got the equipment connected and started – but I saw the man's face like so, and I never – the exit wound was on the other side – and what was back there, I don't know. That is the way it was described to me, "she said, pointing to the sketch showing the large hole in the back of the head. "I did not see that. I did not see this part of his head. That would have been here," she said, and put the palm of her hand on the back of Livingstone's head. She did this before Livingstone showed her the sketch from Thompson.";

136. Dr. Donald Seldin, Parkland Hospital: WC references by others present: WR 528; 3 H 371; 6 H 11,32,60-61,64; 17 H 13; 20 H 5; 21 H 184-185, 258, 263; Mentioned by Dr. Perry on 11/23/63 on WBAP/NBC Texas News film; January 1964 *Texas State Journal of Medicine* article "Three Patients at Parkland," p. 63 – "[Bashour] and Dr. Donald Seldin, professor and chairman of the Department of Internal Medicine, went to the emergency room. Upon examination, they found that the President had no pulsations, no heart

beats, no blood pressure."; 8/27/98 letter to Vince Palamara: "The bullet struck the President in the forehead and literally exploded in his skull, so that the entire frontal, parietal and temporal bones were shattered. ... I believe that the official story is accurate in all details.";

137. Dr. William Zedlitz, Parkland Hospital: WC reference: 6 H 83; 11/4/98 letter to Vince Palamara: "obviously had a massive head injury to the right occipito-parietal area (right posterior-lateral) of his cranium. This area was a mass of bloody tissue with multiple skin, hair, and bony fragments matted together with blood and brain tissue and covered an area approximately ten by twelve centimeters in diameter. His left eye also seemed to be bulging from his eye socket. At this point, Dr. Carrico indicated that he was unable to effectively ventilate the patient via the endotracheal tube. Dr. Baxter and Perry immediately began to perform a tracheostomy. Prior to making the incision, it was noted that a small (5mm to 7mm) hole in the front of the neck below the thyroid cartilage was present. This was in the exact location where the tracheostomy was to be performed. Dr. Baxter and Perry decided to do the procedure by extending the transverse incision on either side of this hole so that the tracheostomy tube ended up being inserted in the site of the former hole."

138. Dr. David Stewart, Parkland Hospital: *New Lebanon, Tennessee, Democrat,* 3/30/67 , 4/10/67 *The Joe Dolan Show,* KNEW radio, Oakland, CA and *Post Mortem* by Harold Weisberg, pp. 60-61: Dolan said he was particularly concerned with the "statement about the shot" that killed JFK "coming from the front." Dr. Stewart said, "Yes, sir. This was the finding of all the physicians who were in attendance. There was a small wound in the left front of the President's head and there was a quite massive wound of exit at the right backside of the head and it was felt by all of the physicians at the time to be a wound of entry which went in the front."; 12/11/81 letter to Livingstone (*High Treason,* pp. 51-52 , *High Treason 2,* p. 107, and *Killing the Truth,* p. 652) – "there was never any controversy concerning the wounds between the doctors in attendance. I was with them either separately or in groups on many occasions over a long period of time. ... Concerning [the official photo of the back of the head], there is no way the wound described to me by Dr. Perry and others could be the wound shown in the picture. The massive destructive wound could not remotely be pulled together well enough to give a normal contour to the head that is present in this picture.";

139. Dr. Joe D. Goldstrich, Parkland Hospital: *JFK: Breaking the Silence* (1993) by Bill Sloan, Chapter 4: pp. 84-97: "The first thing I

saw was JFK lying on his back on an operating table... I didn't have a clear view of the back of his head, but I have a vague recollection of seeing a portion of his brain exposed.... It [the neck wound] was a small, almost perfectly round – somewhere between the size of a nickel and a quarter [?] – and it was right in the middle of the front of his neck, just below the Adam's apple... the wound was exactly the right size and exactly the right spot to accommodate a tracheos-tomy tube."; disturbed by the photos of JFK's neck at autopsy: "The whole front of his neck was wide open... It had simply been fileted."; "... I realized how impossible it would have been for the neck wound I saw to have been an exit wound...";

140. Dr. Lito Porto, Parkland Hospital: *High Treason*, p. 460 – "The first doctor to see what he said was a bullet entry wound near the left temple was Dr. Leto (sic) Porto."; 9/8/98 call from Dr. Boris Porto to Vince Palamara (relaying info. from his father) – His father said that "he needs to keep his mouth quiet" but referred me to Drs. Charlie Baxter and Jim Carrico; Boris: "he was there ... he was the neurosurgery chief resident, the first one to come out of that pro-gram" – Kemp Clark was "overseeing my father";

141. Dr. William Kenneth Horsley: Courtesy researcher Matt Douthit: "I was convinced by the wound that I saw that the fatal shot had come from in front of the president."

142. Dr. Robert E. Schorlemer, Parkland Hospital: *JFK Absolute Proof* by Robert Groden (2013), page 153: "half of the calivarium of the skull had been blown away with the underlying brain exposed and the flap produced lying behind his head.";

143. Dr. Robert Shaw, Parkland Hospital (Connally's chief surgeon): 11/22/63 WFAA/ABC video- Press Conference 7:00 CST: Regard-ing Connally, "The bullet is in the leg ... it hasn't been removed ... it will be removed before he goes to the recovery room"- what about CE399 (the stretcher bullet) that entered the record around five hours earlier?; Regarding JFK-11/27/63 *New York Herald-Tribune*: article by Martin Steadman: a bullet had entered the front of JFK's throat and "coursed downward into his lung [and] was removed in the Bethesda Naval Hospital where the autopsy was performed."; 11/29/63 *Houston Post*: "The assassin was behind him [JFK], yet the bullet entered at the front of his neck. Mr. Kennedy must have turned to his left to talk to Mrs. Kennedy or to wave to someone.";

144. Dr. James "Red" Duke, Parkland Hospital (operated on Con-nally): WR 531; 4 H 103; 6 H 78, 84, 110, 117; 17 H 16; 20 H 6; 21 H 170, 199, 208; January 1964 *Texas State Journal of Medicine*

article "Three Patients at Parkland," p. 70 re: treatment of Connally; HSCA references: 7 HSCA 325; *JFK Absolute Proof* by Robert Groden (2013), page 153- Dr. Duke is pictured with this statement: "Although Dr. Duke has never made a public statement about the head wounds, he has told several friends and others about the "Massive exit wound in the rear of the President's head."

145. Dr. Donald Jackson, Parkland Hospital (operated on Oswald): 21 H 171, 205, 215; 9/8/98 letter to Vince Palamara: "I am encouraged that historians such as yourself are continuing an investigation into this important event. I continue to be dissatisfied with the explanation of the Warren Commission. The reason for my skepticism is linked to discrepancies in descriptions of the Kennedy wounds between the Parkland Emergency Room and the autopsy findings. Drs. McClelland, Perry, and Jenkins gave accurate descriptions of the wounds as they saw them in the Emergency Room. The descriptions in Washington were radically different. In addition, Dr. McClelland and several other colleagues went to Washington and reviewed the findings with the medical authorities. It seemed at that time, that they then reversed themselves on the findings that they had described in Dallas. I do not question their veracity but I am confused by this discrepancy. It is possible that there is a simple explanation that I am not aware of.";

146. Dr. William Risk, Parkland Hospital (worked on Oswald): "As far as a conspiracy or not, I only know what most Americans know, and that is what we have been told of the facts. However, as a physician, I have the feeling there was more than one "shooter" and more than one bullet involved because of the nature of the wounds. I would suggest that, if you have not already done so, you get a copy of an article from the *Journal of the Texas Medical Association*, January 1964, entitled "Three Patients at Parkland." This article is a *medical* version of those days. The wounds described there, to me, suggest entrance and exit wounds which differ from the "one bullet theory.";

147. Nurse Patricia Hutton, Parkland Hospital: 21 H 216: report of activities on 11/22/63 – "Mr. Kennedy was bleeding profusely from a wound in the back of his head. ... A doctor asked me to place a pressure dressing on the head wound. This was no use, however, because of the massive opening on the back of the head."; 1/8/83 interview by David Lifton (*Best Evidence*, p. 706) – "The large throat wound shown in the photographs was not the tracheotomy incision that she saw in the emergency room on November 22,1963 ("It doesn't look like any that I've taken part in, let me put it that way.")

and the head wound was at the back, not as shown in the pictures. "I was standing behind him when I was putting pressure on the head," she said, "and it was right in front of me. It wasn't around the side and up on top." Shown the large hole on the forward right hand side depicted in the x-rays, she exclaimed: "No way!"; *High Treason*, p.43 and 459-460 (*Boston Globe*, 6/21/81 [see also *Killing the Truth*, pages 652 and 702]): "She was asked to put a pressure bandage on the head wound. "I tried to do so but there was really nothing to put a pressure bandage on. It was too massive. So he told me just to leave it be. "She said the large wound was at "the back of the head." "Definitely in the back?" she was asked. "Yes." She strongly rejects the official picture. "; "She said the wound was low on the head, and about the size of a fist.";

148. Nurse Doris Nelson, Parkland Hospital: 21 H 155: 11/25/63 affidavit re: Record of Death; 20 H 640-643 /21 H 241-244: report of activities; 6 H 145 /testimony – "…I could look and see [JFK] and tell that it was him … mainly his head [part she saw]": Specter did not ask nor did she volunteer info. regarding the head wound; 12/82 interview with David Lifton (*Best Evidence*, p. 704): "Doris Nelson told me the tracheotomy was not the one she remembered: "Looks a little large to me … [it] shouldn't be that big.… It wasn't any 7-8 cm. [It was] just wide enough to get the trach tube in."; "She looked at [the official autopsy photos of the back of the head] and shook her head from side to side … she remembered a large wound there."; *High Treason*, pp. 43-44, 454 (*Boston Globe*, 6/21/81 [see also *Killing the Truth*, p. 702]): "Nurse Nelson drew a picture of the head wound, mostly in the parietal area, but well towards the rear of the head. Her drawing conflicts strongly with the official autopsy photograph. When she saw that picture she said immediately, "It's not true.… There wasn't even hair back there. It was blown away. All that area (on the back of the head) was blown out."; *High Treason 2*, pp. 103-105 – "All I saw was missing skull and brains on the back of his head … it was right there, in the right rear. In the right rear!";

149. Nurse Audrey Bell, Parkland Hospital: 6 H 52 (Jones); other WC references: WR 536; 17 H 21, 841; 20 H 333; 21 H 172, 187, 246, 248; 24 H 260; January 1964 *Texas State Journal of Medicine* article Three Patients at Parkland, p. 74 – Oswald's treatment: "The bullet which was palpable in the right posterior axillary line was removed and sent out by the operating room supervisor, Miss Audrey Bell, to be turned over to the legal authorities."; 12/82 interview by David Lifton (*Best Evidence*, p. 704) – "The wound she saw was so localized at the rear that, from her position on the right

hand side, with Kennedy lying face up, she couldn't see any damage ... Perry pointed to the back of the President's head." Re: trach photo: "Looks like somebody has enlarged it.... You don't make trachs that big. Not if you've got as much experience as Perry has."; *Nova* program *Who Shot President Kennedy?*, 11/15/88 – described the throat wound as one of entrance; said that there was no surgery done on the President at Parkland; *JFK: An Unsolved Murder*, KRON, 11/18/88 (repeated in *JFK: The Case for Conspiracy* along with a 1993 interview): "There was a massive wound at the back of his head"; throat wound was an entrance wound; from the 1993 segment: -denounces official photo; wound at the right rear of head: "back of the head.... Oh, yes, there was a big hole there."

150. Nurse Diana Bowron, Parkland Hospital: 19 H 167-170: 11/23/63 newspaper articles: "There was a gaping wound in the back of his head."; 21 H 203-204: Bowron's report to Elizabeth Wright: nothing specific about the nature of the wounds; 6 H 136 / testimony (3/24/64): "... I saw the condition of his head.... The back of his head.... Well, it was very bad – you know... I just saw one large hole."; *Killing the Truth*, Chapter 6 and photo section (drawings/ notations): "Well, to me it was an exit hole ... I assumed and I still do that that was an exit wound.... There was very little brain left"; denounced the photos; saw a hole well down on JFK's back (interviewed by Livingstone 1/8/93, 3/15/93, 5/2/93. Corresponded with Livingstone 4/25/93 and 5/11/93); [p. 718] "... the entry wound in his throat ... looked like an entry wound.";

151. Nurse Donna Willie, Parkland Hospital: *High Treason*, p.456 (based off article by Nicole Levicoff of the *Jenkintown [PA] Times Chronicle*) – "the President had a wound in his throat that the Commission said was an exit wound or was made from a tracheotomy... the entry wound is always small, and the exit wound is much larger. I saw the entry wound in the front of the President's neck. I know he was shot from the front, and I couldn't understand why that wasn't released.";

152. Nurse Margaret M. Hinchliffe (Hood), Parkland Hospital: 21 H 239-240: report of activities for 11/22/63; 6 H 141 and 143 / testimony: "... his head was very bloody..."; "... a little hole in the middle of his neck.... About as big as the end of my little finger... An entrance bullet hole – it looked to me like ... I have never seen an exit bullet hole – I don't remember seeing one that looked like that."; "... it was just a small wound and wasn't jagged like most of the exit bullet wounds that I have seen."; *High Treason*, pages 45, 68-

69,454 (*Boston Globe*, 6/21/81 [see also *Killing the Truth*, p. 702]): "Interviewed by reporters in 1981, she drew a picture of the large wound on a model of a skull. She sketched a gaping hole in the occipital region, which extended only slightly into the parietal area, thereby rejecting out of hand the official picture. She also insisted the President had an "entry" wound in his throat."; 6/25/93 interview with Wallace Milam [transcript provided to the author]: "After Kennedy died and doctors left, she and Diana Bowron washed the body.... Face was cleaned by wiping [no wounds seen]. Piece of plastic was put over head wound in back of head. Did not cover face and front part of head. Purpose was to keep head from bleeding on casket interior...Hinchliffe remembers a plastic sheet [not necessarily a mattress liner], no body bag.... Hinchliffe and Bowron washed off the back also.... Hinchliffe says she did not see any back wound, but could not rule out that there may have been one."; "Throat wound – Definitely an entrance wound. Resented Arlen Specter trying to get her to say it might be an exit wound. Tracheotomy incision – Didn't know if it was made through or below the bullet wound. Described incision as "just a normal trach incision." Head wound – In very back of head. She put her hand back there. Everything was missing – bone, scalp, hair. She made the size of the wound about the circumference of a tea glass... Autopsy photos – She said that Crenshaw had sent her a copy of his book with the autopsy photos in it. She thought he was sending them to her to get her to verify them. She said the autopsy photos were nothing like what she saw. She referred particularly to the back of the head being intact, when she saw it to have been blown out.";

153. Nurse Phyllis Hall, Parkland Hospital: *Mirror UK* 11/10/13: "I could see a bullet lodged between his ear and his shoulder. It was pointed at its tip and showed no signs of damage. I remember looking at it – there was no blunting of the bullet or scarring around the shell from where it had been fired. I'd had a great deal of experience working with gunshot wounds but I had never seen anything like this before. It was about one-and-a-half inches long – nothing like the bullets that were later produced. It was taken away but never have I seen it presented in evidence or heard what happened to it. It remains a mystery ... I truly believe no man could have carried out the attack without some sort of help, and after seeing the mystery bullet in Mr. Kennedy's head I feel there is something far deeper to his death than we the public know."

154. Nurse Sharon Calloway, Parkland Hospital: 1/27/2002 Sixth Floor Museum oral history: An X-Ray Technology School intern at

Parkland Memorial Hospital in 1963, Calloway saw the back of President Kennedy's head before he was moved into Trauma Room One. She later worked closely with the Dallas County medical examiner, Dr. Earl F. Rose, and recalled his feelings about the handling of the president's remains. Ms. Calloway passed away on December 15, 2014. Although she said that "the top of his head was gone" (as opposed to the rear), Ms. Calloway's recollections of President Kennedy differ significantly from those of medical personnel, law enforcement officials, and others at Parkland Memorial Hospital that day in another major way, casting doubts on her credibility (I never heard of her except for this oral history). In this oral history, Calloway recalled that the president was dead on arrival and remained on a stretcher in an Emergency Room hallway "for probably about half an hour after he got to the hospital" before his body was taken into Trauma Room One! All other eyewitness accounts have the president being taken immediately into Trauma One for resuscitation efforts. I would therefore, take her account as a statistical anomaly to ignore;

155. Nurse Sharon Tuohy, Parkland Hospital: HSCA interview 12/1 and 12/4/76: The base of the back of his head had a large cavity, big enough for 2 fists to go into ... not directly in the center. More to the right, his right."; [Any damag e to the top of the head?] "not at all."; [the neck wound was] "small. Between the size of a nickel and a dime. Bloody."; https://www.youtube.com/watch?v=OcAr-jV84TkI

156. Father Oscar Huber (delivered Last Rites at Parkland Hospital): WR 55, 7 H 489, 21 H 159, 160, 195, 233: WC references for Huber. Huber was interviewed 11/24/63 on WFAA and 11/25/63 on WBAP/Texas News (see *Kennedy in Texas* video 1984). The 11/24/63 *Philadelphia Sunday Bulletin* reported that Father Huber said that JFK had a terrible wound over his left eye [see *Best Evidence*, p. 46, and *Who's Who in the JFK Assassination*, p. 202]; 8/26/64 and 9/20/64 interviews with William Manchester (*The Death of a President*, numerous, including p. 216): performed the sign of the cross on JFK's forehead, evidently still intact; interviewed by Jim Bishop (*The Day Kennedy Was Shot*, p. 684); *The (Denver) Register*, 12/8/63: article by Huber entitled "President Kennedy's Final Hours"; JFK Library Oral History 1964; photo of Huber: p. 23 of *JFK: For a New Generation* by Conover Hunt; *Four Days In November* (1964, David Wolper): including part of his WFAA interview;

157. Aubrey Rike: Interview (with Dennis McGuire) on WFAA/ABC on 11/22/63: the Secret Service took the hearse away and

"they left us just standing there."; 21 H 242 (Nurse Doris Nelson's report) – 'After Mr. O'Neal, and some of the boys who work with him (only one of whose name I knew-Audrey Riker [sic]) placed the President in the casket, and closed it."; CD 1245/ FBI report of 5/28/64 interview with Rike: tells of the epileptic seizure incident; "Rike stated he was advised by a Secret Service Agent at Parkland Hospital that his ambulance was not to be moved because they might need it to move the President to another location. Rike stated he cleared the hospital at 3:00 p.m. and returned to Oneal Incorporated, Funeral Directors."; *Best Evidence: The Research Video* ([Oct.] 1980/ 1990 [clips repeated in *The Fifth Estate-Who Killed JFK?* 1983, *Nova, Who Shot President Kennedy?* 11/15/88, *Dispatches: The Day The Dream Died* 11/16/88 London, and *A Current Affair* 9/4/90] – "[JFK] still dripping quite a bit of blood from the wound in the back of his head [motioning]";

A.S.K. conference, Dallas, Texas, 11/14/91: felt a jagged wound edge at the back of the head, as well as brain matter; said that some of the autopsy photos show what he saw but others do not; 4/6/91 [unreleased film], 6/10/91, and 8/15/91 interviews with Livingstone (*High Treason 2*, photo section + pages 80, 81, 89, 112, 114-119, 130-131, 238, 271, 275, 297, 305-308, 312, and 527 [re: *JFK* movie]) – "I saw the back of the head was gone'"; The Killing of a President by Robert Groden, page 88: "You could feel the sharp edges of the bone at the edge of the hole in the back of his head."; 11/22/97 video interview by Vince Palamara (on You Tube): placed his hand three times to the right rear of his head to show where the wound was located at: "I could feel the brain and the jagged edge...yeah, it [the back of the head] was gone...almost in the middle of the back of the head; on the side a little bit. "Regarding the autopsy photos, Rike believes they "pulled [the] hair back over" the wound; "didn't notice the bullet wound in the shoulder"; throat wound: "thought it was an exit wound"; witnessed the episode where the FBI agent was knocked to the floor with a punch while trying to enter Trauma Room One; said that, regarding the ambulance false alarms ("bogus calls ... in that vicinity") being tied into the assassination, "that was the FBI's theory"!;

158. Reporter Seth Kantor: 20 H 353: Kantor's notepad for 11/22/63 – "intered [sic] right temple"; 15 H 71-96 / testimony – saw "a great deposit of blood" on the ground to the right of JFK's limo;

159. Milton T. Wright, Jr., Texas Highway Patrolman (driver of Mayor Cabell's car): 18 H 802: report dated 11/28/63 – "At the

hospital we unloaded the Governor first and then the President. Then we were instructed to keep the news media away from the car." – nothing specific about the wounds; 8/28/98 letter to Vince Palamara."I do recall helping to move the President from the car to the stretcher. As I recall about a 1/4 [quarter] of his head was missing, mostly to the left of the back of the head."; 9/3/98 e-mail to Vince Palamara: "the wound was left ear to back of head, generally.";

160. DPD James W. ("J.W.") Courson, one of two mid motorcade motorcycle officers: *No More Silence* by Larry Sneed (1998), pp. 127-131: "The driver immediately got out into the center lane with me on his left rear and another officer on the right. Mrs. Kennedy had, by that time, go... back down in the seat and was holding the President's head in ... lap. I was able to see that his head was horribly mangled. Skull, b... seat.... Flowers were scattered and blood material was all along the cers and I helped take the Pres... around the car.... Two other off... the stretcher. From what I was a... out of the car and p... seemed to be in the right rear of h... see of the wound... cause there was so much blood. The... but it was ha... be laying over the forehead. I didn't ac...part of the sk... I saw only the back part of his head."; see an exit...

161. Fort Worth Newsman Roy Stamps: ... wounds], 366-367; *JFK: Conspiracy of Silence...* *Lee Harvey Oswald* by Walt Brown, pp. 505-506 ... cle "The Head Shot From The Front" (1996) by ... [re: wounds]: like Seth Kantor (and Wilma Tice)... Parkland. Also, regarding JFK's head wound, he... and saw Kennedy lying in the car on his side. His f... over the side of the car. The back of his head was gone.

162. Dr. Jack C. Harper, Methodist Hospital: 8/17/... of Harper and Cairns with the HSCA (see also pp. 26...) ing Kennedy by Livingstone]: "Dr. Harper said the cons... doctors who viewed the skull fragment was that it wa... occipital region."; 9/15/98 letter from William A. Harper... Palamara – "Your letter to my uncle Dr. Jack C. Harper has bee... forwarded to me for response. My uncle told me that the fragment I found was from the occipital area of the skull. I have seen drawings in various publications that would indicate that it belonged to this region. With regard to the question of the existence [of] photographs, it is my understanding that my uncle gave his pictures to an assassination investigative agency.";

351

163. Dr. A.B. Cairns, Methodist Hospital: 8/17/77 interviews of Harper and Cairns with the HSCA (see also pp. 261-262 of *Killing Kennedy* by Livingstone]: Dr. A.B. Cairns ... said the piece of skull fragment came from an area approximately two and a half to three inches above the spine area. He said it had the markings of a piece of skull fragment from the lower occipital area, specifically: suture and inner markings where blood vessels run around the base of the skull."; CD 1395, p. 50/ FBI interview of Cairns + pages 46 and 44: "Dr. Cairns stated the bone specimen looked like it came from the occipital region of the skull."; The doctors made 12 photographs of it at Methodist Hospital; a woman wrote RFK in June 1964 and told him that in Dallas she had snapshots, taken at a hospital, of JFK's head!; RFK forwarded s letter to the WC and J. Lee Rankin's assistant, Howard Willens immediately requested the FBI to investigate the matter.;

dist Hospital: *Best Evidence*, p. ard Noteboom, M P. Smith [7/20/72 letter from terview with R bone and held the same opinion on]): "also s5/98 letter to Vince Palamara – "Re: d Cairns]est estimate of the fragment was that it , JFK. n transparency slides, which were turned ool

, CIA: 18 H 795: Secret Service agent Andy n "unidentified CIA agent" who had credentials."; th Bill Sloan for *JFK: Breaking the Silence* (1993), Chapter 9, pp. 175-189: "I distinctly saw an entry wound in the left temple. To my knowledge, only two other people beside myself have admitted to seeing this wound. It was assumed to be a blood clot by the doctors at Parkland, but it was an entry wound, and it could not have been fired from the rear. The bullet from this wound exited the right side of the president's head, blowing out a section of skull and obscuring the entry wound of a second bullet that struck him from the right front almost simultaneously. There were two large, separate holes in the upper right side of the head, separated by about three-quarters of an inch of bone matter and skin tissue. The wound in the throat, although greatly enlarged by a tracheostomy, was also an entry wound. All the wounds had a puffy, torn appearance as though they had been probed prior to the autopsy. There was also an entry wound high in the back, between the neck and the shoulder. It had penetrated approximately the depth of one finger joint – I actually put my small finger into the hole – then made a forty-five degree turn to the left. To my knowledge, this bullet never left the body.";

166. Jacqueline Kennedy: 4/11/72 declassified Warren Commission testimony excerpts (as reproduced in *Post Mortem* by Harold Weisberg, pp. 380-381: "I was trying to hold his hair on. But from the front there was nothing. I suppose there must have been. But from the back you could see, you know, you were trying to hold his hair on, and his skull on."; *Killing Kennedy* by Harrison Livingstone, pages 22 and 30 [see also *Killing the Truth*, p. 652] – claims that, regarding the autopsy photos of the back of JFK's head, "my information that the photograph is fraudulent came from Jacqueline Kennedy through her staff in 1979 and from representatives of the Kennedy family"; "'This isn't the way it was!' This is what Jacqueline Kennedy Onassis told me through her staff..." [?!];

167. Justice of the Peace Theran Ward: signed and unsig certificates- [signed] depicted in Crenshaw's *JFK: Consp lence* (1992), [unsigned] Groden's *The Killing of a Presic* and [both] *Assassination Science*, pp. 428-429: both stat quest, November 22, 1963," one is signed by W checked "yes" in both! [both] Cause of Dea wounds of the head and neck."; [unsigned] tice: "Two gunshot wounds (1) Near the cen just above the right shoulder. (2) One inch to the right center o back of the head."; [unsigned] "Shot by an unknown assassin high powered rifle"; 10/28/91 interview with Livingstone (*l Treason 2*, p. 83): "it's not safe" to talk about the case; authorized removal of the body on 11/22/63; *The Killing of a President* (199 p. 88 – photo [from video outtakes?] of Ward pointing toward rear of the head to show where the skull wound was: "[It was] f back here.";

168. Doctor/Admiral George Gregory Burkley, Physician to President: 11/22/63 Press Conference by Asst. WH Press sec, Kilduff- *Best Evidence*, pp. 330-331: "Dr. Burkley told me, it is ple matter, Tom, of a bullet right through the head": he the to his right temple! Question: "can you say where the bul his head, Mac?" "It is my understanding that it entered i ple, the right temple."; "They [the shots] came from the This information was repeated by Chet Huntley on NBC "President Kennedy, we are now informed, was shot in the right temple. 'It was a simple matter of a bullet right through the head,' said Dr. George Burkley, the White House medical officer."; 22 H 93-97: 11/27/63 report of his activities surrounding the assassination of JFK: "his appearance in the casket gave no evidence of the injury he had received."; interview with author Michael Kurtz (*The*

JFK Assassination Debates: Lone Gunman Versus Conspiracy, pages 39-40): "admitted that Kennedy had a large wound that had "all the appearances of an exit wound" in the back of his head.... Burkley stated that he always believed in a conspiracy.";

169. Bill Greer: 2 H 124 and 127/ testimony (3/9/64): "His head was all shot, this whole part was all a matter of blood like he had been hit." Specter: "Indicating the top and right rear side of the head?" Greer: "Yes, sir; it looked like that was all blown off."; "... they [the autopsy doctors]saw this hole in the right shoulder or back of the head, and in the back ... this wound was in the back...they took a lot of X-rays, we looked at them and couldn't find any trace of any bullet anywhere in the X-rays at all, nothing showed on the ...re this bullet or lead could have gone ... in the soft part ...der ... I believe the doctors probed to see if they could ...ere was a bullet there ... I questioned one of the doc- ...about that, and when we found out that they had found ...questioned the doctor about it and he said if ...ssure on the chest that it could very well have ...ack out, where it went in at, that is what they said at ...e...I hadn't heard anything like that, any traces of it going ...rough"; 2/28/78 HSCA interview: "He was puzzled about the ...e bullet (399) theory. He could not see how one bullet could ...e caused both Kennedy and Connally such extensive wounds."; ...eer recalls Kellerman going to a telephone and talking to some- one about a bullet found in Dallas. The doctors turned Kennedy over and found the bullet hole in his shoulder. He indicated a point on his right shoulder, which approximated the spot. He said one of the doctors inserted a metal probe in Kennedy's back, which only went in a short way. Greer says he asked the doctor if the bullet in [the] back could have worked itself out during heart message. The doctors continued to take x-rays, looking for lead, but they couldn't find where the bullet went.";

170. Roy Kellerman: FBI Report (Sibert & O'Neill) 11/27/63: Kellerman advised he did not notice the extent of the injury to the President although he noticed a wound in the back of his head."; 18 H 724-727: Kellerman's report dated 11/29/63: "I accompanied the President to the emergency room. His eyes were closed but I could see no visible damage to his face."; 2 H 73-74, 78-82, 85, 90-91, 93/ testimony: "I did not see any wounds in that man's face."; "He had a large wound this size" Specter: "Indicating a circle with your finger of the diameter of 5 inches; would that be approximately correct?" "Yes, circular; yes, on this part of the head." Specter: "Indicating the

rear portion of the head." "Yes." Specter: "More to the right side of the head?" "Right. This was removed." ; "...I saw nothing in his face to indicate an injury, whether the shot had come through or not. He was clear."; "When this car was checked over that night for its return to Washington, I was informed the following day of the pieces of these missiles that were found in the front seat, and I believe aside from the skull, that was in the rear seat, I couldn't conceive even from elevation how this shot hit President Kennedy like it did. I wanted to view this vehicle, whether this was a slant blow off the car, whether it hit the car first and then hit him, or what other marks are on this vehicle, and that is what prompted me to go around and check it over myself.";

(2 H 90) re: ASAIC Boring and the bullet fragments found in the limo; (2 H 91) "There was in the early – this was on the day [11/22/63] in Parkland Memorial Hospital, and this information comes from Dr. George Burkley ... I asked him the condition of Governor Connally, and have they removed the bullet from him ... Dr. Burkley said that to his knowledge he still has the bullet in him.... This was after we got into the hospital after the shooting, sir, between then and 2 o'clock."; "Gentlemen, I think if you would view the films [of the assassination] yourself you may come up with a little different answer."; "A Colonel Finck – during the examination of the President, from the hole that was in the shoulder, and with a probe, and we were standing right alongside of him, he is probing inside the shoulder with his instrument and I said, "Colonel, where did it go?" He said, "There are no lanes for an outlet of this entry in this man's shoulder"..."I said, "Colonel, would it have been possible that while he was on the stretcher in Dallas that it works itself out?" And he said, "Yes.""; 8/24 and 8/25/77 interviews with the HSCA's Jim Kelly and Andy Purdy: at Parkland- face unmarked; "One large hole in the head and no small holes in the head" – contradicted by his own drawing showing a large and a small hole on the back of the head!; 1970's contact with one of Kellerman's daughters by Harold Weisberg (letter to author from Weisberg 3/92: "she hopes the day would come when these men (Kellerman and Greer) could say in public what they told their families."; 3/2/92 and 9/27/92 interviews with Roy's widow June Kellerman (see also the Dec. 1994 issue of *Vanity Fair* magazine-article by Anthony and Robbyn Summers, p. 88: info. provided to authors): Roy accepted that there was a conspiracy;

171. JFK's Air Force Aid, Major General Godfrey "God" T. McHugh (rode in the VIP car with Major General Ted Clifton): 11/19/67 and

4/30/78 interviews with David Lifton (*Best Evidence*, pp. 399-401, 413-414, 420-421, 430-432) – "McHugh believed the Warren Report was correct…"; "…McHugh volunteered that he had assisted in the photographing of Kennedy's body…'I was holding his body several times when they were turning it over and photographing it."; Lifton: "And you saw the wounds in the head then too?" "Oh, yes; but they started fixing it up very well. You see, again, people keep saying that his face was demolished and all; he was in absolute perfect shape, except the back of the head, top back of the head, had an explosive bullet in it and was badly damaged … and that had blown apart part of his forehead, which was recuperated and put intact, back in place … so his face was exactly as if he had been alive. There was nothing wrong with his face."; "The back of the head was all smashed in…. His face was not hurt." Lifton: "Where did they get the bone to put the bone back?" "It was brought back. They found it in the car."; "Ninety-nine percent the back, the top back of the head … that's the portion that had been badly damaged by the bullet…. The portion that is in the back of the head, when you're lying down in the bathtub, you hit the back of the head."; CFTR radio interview 1976: "back of his head blown off"; back wound was lower than neck wound.;

172. Autopsy photographer John Thomas Stringer, Jr.: 8/25/72 and 8/26/72 interviews with David Lifton (*Best Evidence*, pp. 515516, 517-518): Lifton: "When you lifted him out, was the main damage to the skull on the top or in the back?" "In the back…. In the occipital, in the neck there, up above the neck … in the back part … some of it was blown off – yes, I mean, toward, out of the top in the back, yes." Lifton: "Top in the back. But the top in the front was pretty intact?" "Yes, sure…. Right."; 4/29/90 and 5/11/90 interviews with Harry Livingstone (*Killing the Truth*, page 690): "back of the head was gone.";

173. FBI Agent James W. Sibert: HSCA interview with James Kelly and Andy Purdy, 8/25/77 (see *Killing Kennedy* by Harrison Livingstone, pp. 343-344, and *Bloody Treason*, page 100 by Noel Twyman, for drawings]: "Regarding the head wound, Sibert said it was in the "…Upper back of the head."; "The head wound was in the upper back of the head … a large head wound in the upper back of the head with a section of the scull [sic] bone missing…"; his drawings depict a large wound squarely on the back of the head, as well as a small wound well down on the back, very much like the one in the autopsy face sheet; Humes and Finck agreed, after probing, that there was no exit wound of the bullet in the back: "concluded it only went so

far and they couldn't find it."; "Sibert recalls that much of the piece of the missing bone section came in somewhat later"; 'Sibert said he was present when the bone piece was brought in which had been found in the limousine."; "Sibert said the doctors were discussing the amount of fragmentation of the bullet and the fact that they couldn't find a large piece. They were wondering if it was a kind of bullet, which "fragmentizes" completely.";

174. FBI Agent Francis X. O'Neill, Jr.: HSCA interview with Andy Purdy and Mark Flanagan, 1/10/78: [see *Killing Kennedy* by Harrison Livingstone, pp. 348-349 for drawings] – while stating that the autopsy doctors believed that "the bullet that entered the head struck the center, low portion of the head and exited from the top, right side, towards the front," his drawings depict an "entry" at the low rear central portion of Kennedy's skull, as well as an "exit" on the right rear quadrant of the head no more anterior than the posterior portion of the ear!; said that Admiral Galloway ordered a complete autopsy; "He does remember the doctors measuring the piece of skull that was found in the limousine and brought to Bethesda during the autopsy. O'Neill stated that in his opinion JFK could have had an open casket."; "O'Neill ended the interview by stating that he is "positive" that the bullet that entered the back came out of the back."; Also-Affidavit dated 11/8/78: "I do not see how the bullet that entered below the shoulder in the back could have come out the front of the throat. ... It was and is my opinion that the bullet entered the back came out the back. There was also no real sense either way that the wounds were caused by the same kind of bullet." Discussed the possibility of a "plastic" or "ice" bullet – one that dissolves after contact.;

175. Mortician Thomas Evan Robinson: HSCA taped interview conducted by Andy Purdy and Jim Conzelman 1/12/77: Purdy: "Approximately where was this wound located?" "Directly behind the back of his head." Purdy: "Approximately between the ears or higher up?" "No, I would say pretty much between them.": Robinson's drawing depicts a defect directly in the central, lower rear portion of the skull. Purdy: "Could you tell how large the opening had been caused by the bullets?" "A good bit of the bone had been blown away. There was nothing there to piece together, so I would say probably about [the size of] a small orange." Purdy: "Could you give us an estimate of inches and the nature of the shape?" "Three." Purdy: "And the shape?" "Circular." Purdy: "Was it fairly smooth or fairly ragged?" "Ragged."; He also said there was a little wound, described as a hole of about a quarter-inch in diameter, on the right

side of the forehead up near the hairline. Robinson said that he "... probably put a little wax in it.";

176. Pathologist Dr. Robert Frederick Karnei, Jr.: 8/23/77 interview with the HSCA (conducted by Andy Purdy and Jim Conzelman) – Karnei assisted with the autopsy and normally would have performed the autopsy; said that there was "extensive damage" to the brain; he recalled the autopsy doctors putting the probe in and taking pictures. He said they felt the hole that was in the back was a wound of entrance and the doctors were "trying to figure out where the bullet came out."; Dr. Finck was "working with a probe and arranging photographs."; 8/26/91 and 8/27/91 interview with Livingstone for *High Treason 2* (see Chapter 7): Livingstone: "The large defect was in the very back of the head?" "Right, yeah.... Most of the brain that was missing was in the back part of the head ... Most of the bone that was missing was destroyed in the back of the head."[p. 182] ;

177. Joseph E. Hagan, Chief Asst. to Joseph H. Gawler, undertaker: 8/15/91 and 8/28/91 interviews with Livingstone for *High Treason 2* (see pages 137, 196, and 581; see also *Killing the Truth*, pages 653, 680, 681, and 728): "I couldn't remember any bone missing in the face or from the frontal bone. That was pretty well intact to the best of my memory."; there were a lot of pictures taken from the gallery; "There was extensive damage to the President's head, most of it back up in here (indicating with his hand the rearward right side and the back) ... We had to replace just all of that area with plaster of paris due to the extent of the wounds that were there ... If it hadn't of been that big, we wouldn't have had to use plaster of paris, see ... Quite a bit of bone was lacking ... we had no problems in here (indicating the area of the coronal suture).... Back up in here (again gestures back of head), his head would have been down in the pillow and, if I remember correctly, we had taken a little out of the pillow where his head would fit down in the pillow."; The face was undamaged except for a small laceration extending about a half inch into the forehead towards the right eyebrow, which can be seen in the right profile photograph;

178. Paul Kelly O'Connor, Bethesda laboratory technologist: 8/25/79 interview with David Lifton (*Best Evidence*, photo 37+pp. 598-606): "... he didn't have any brains left.... The wound in his head was terrific ... eight by four inches.... The wound was in the occipital-parietal area ... clear up around the frontal area of the brain ... the cranium was empty..."; the wound in the throat was "a great big hole in his larynx ... the esophagus was laid open";

179. James Curtis Jenkins, Bethesda laboratory technologist: 8/24/77 HSCA interview with Jim Kelly and Andy Purdy: Jenkins stated that when the body was unwrapped he saw a head wound in the "middle temporal region back to the occipital." His drawing clearly conflicts with official history. ; the back wound was "just below the collar to the right of the midline" and it was "very shallow... it didn't enter the peritoneal (chest) cavity."; he didn't believe that the doctor found that the probe "penetrated into the chest" and the doctors "couldn't prove the bullet came into the cavity."; Jenkins said "...with the Warren Commission findings, you can understand why I'm skeptical." He was "surprised at the conclusions the doctors reached" with regard to the head wound. Jenkins does not recall a small hole in the head as depicted on the autopsy descriptive sheet – he said that the big hole in the head would have covered the area where the little hole was drawn on this sheet. Jenkins said that the wound to the head entered the top rear quadrant from the front side.; Jenkins recalled that the doctors extensively attempted to probe the back wound. He said the probe they used was a metal one, approximately eight inches long. He said that "...most of the probe went in ... between the skin ..." and not into the chest cavity. He said Humes could probe the bottom of the wound with his little finger and said that the metal probe went in 2 - 4 inches. He said it was quite a "...fact of controversy..." that the doctors "...couldn't prove the bullet came into the cavity.";

180. Edward F. Reed, Jr., Bethesda X-ray technician: Interview with the HSCA (RIF#180-10105-10399 [see also *Cover-Up* by Stewart Galanor, p. 33]): the head wound "was very large and located in the right hemisphere in the occipital region."; 11/25/79 interview with David Lifton (*Best Evidence*, photo 40+p. 619 and 696) – Believed JFK had been shot from the front because the skull wound he saw was "more posterior than anterior." ; did not see a small entry wound on the rear of the head; "It wasn't like a tracheotomy, a normal tracheotomy. It was a lot larger."; felt that the head shot came from the front;

181. Jerrol F. Custer, Bethesda X-ray technician: 9/30/79 and 10/7/79 interviews with David Lifton (*Best Evidence*, pp. 619621+696): "Custer told me the President's head wound was enormous – "I could have put both of my hands in the wound. Okay?" – and that he believed he had been shot from the front."; "... when a bullet goes into the body, it goes in small and comes out big. Okay? Well, that is exactly how the skull looked. Okay? ... from the front, to the back."; did not see an entry wound at the rear of JFK's

head; Custer said that he exposed, and returned to the morgue, X-rays showing that the rear of the President's head was blown off.; "Custer felt the head shot came from the front."; *JFK: An Unsolved Murder*, KRON, 11/18/88 [clips repeated in *JFK: The Case for Conspiracy* 1993 video]: When asked if the official X-ray is the one he took, Custer said "No. This area here was gone [demonstrates the back of the head]. There was no scalp there…from the top of the head to the base of the skull. That part was gone.";

182. Jan Gail "Nick" Rudnicki, Dr. Boswell's lab assistant: 5/8/78 interview with the HSCA's Mark Flanagan [RIF#180-10105-10397] – "the back-right quadrant of the head was missing."; saw the bullet wound "in the shoulder blade region of the back"; said that there was a discussion by the autopsy doctors about "the possibility that two bullets struck the head in the same general area, causing a massive defect.";

183. James E. Metzler, Bethesda Hospital corpsman: Interview with the HSCA (RIF#180-10105-10401 [see also *Cover-Up* by Stewart Galanor, p. 33]): Helped carry JFK's body from the coffin to the autopsy table; recalled the head wound in the "right side of the head behind the right ear extending down to the center of the back of the skull.";

184. Dr. John H. "Jack" Ebersole, Assistant Chief of radiology: 3/9/78 interview with Gil Delaney of the *Lancaster (PA) Intelligencer-Journal* [see also *Best Evidence*, p. 543]: "When the body was removed from the casket, there was a very obvious horrible gaping wound to the back of the head…The front of the body, except for a very slight bruise above the right eye on the forehead, was absolutely intact. It was the back of the head that was blown off.… Later on in the evening, between midnight and one A.M., a large portion of the skull was sent up from Dallas … that represented the back portion of the skull.";

185. Richard A. Lipsey, aide to General Wehle: 1/18/78 (audio-taped) interview with the HSCA's Andy Purdy and Mark Flanagan: "Lipsey says he feels he knows "for a fact" that someone shot JFK three times and that these bullets came from behind."; said that the autopsists "were 'absolutely, unequivocally' convinced that he (JFK) had been shot three times … there were three separate wounds and three separate bullets."; "identified the entrance in the lower head as being just inside the hairline," but also made the claim that there was "no real entrance in the rear of the head … one bullet blasted away an entire portion (entrance and exit) … one bullet entered the back of the head and exited resulting in part of the face and head being blown away.";

186. Maj. Gen. Philip C. Wehle, Commanding Officer of the Military District of Washington, D.C.: 8/19/77 interview with the HS-

CA's Andy Purdy: "(Wehle) noticed a slight bruise over the right temple of the President but did not see any significant damage to any other part of the head. He noted that the wound was in the back of the head so he would not see it because the President was lying face up; he also said he did not see any damage to the top of the head, but said the President had a lot of hair which could have hidden that … there could have been an open casket";

187. Captain John H. "Smokey" Stover, Jr., Commanding Officer of the National Naval Medical School: 5/11/78 interview with the HSCA's Mark Flanagan (RIF#180-10102-10407 [see also 7 HSCA 25]) – "Stover observed … a wound on the top of the head, second, a wound in the upper back";

188. Chester Herschel Boyers, Jr., Chief Petty Officer in charge of Pathology Department: 4/25/78 interview with the HSCA's Mark Flanagan: "In regard to the wounds Boyers recalls an entrance wound in the rear of the head to the right of the external occipital protuberance which exited along the top, right side of the head towards the rear and just above the right eyebrow. He also saw an entrance wound in the right shoulder blade, specifically just under the scapula and next to it. Boyers also noted a tracheotomy incision in the neck." Boyers stated that the path of the bullet that entered JFK's upper back seemed to indicate that the bullet exited through the tracheotomy.; "…only fragments were recovered. Boyers never saw a fully intact missile."; "Concerning the wounds of President Kennedy, Mr. Boyers stated that there was a large wound to the right side and towards the rear of the head…He estimated the massive wound in the head measured 3 inches by 3 inches.";

189. Floyd Albert Riebe, a medical photographer at Bethesda: *JFK: An Unsolved Murder*, KRON, 11/18/88 (repeated in *JFK: The Case for Conspiracy* video 1993): "a big gaping hole in the back of the head. It was like somebody put a piece of dynamite in a tin can and lit it off. There was nothing there."; Strongly disagreed with the autopsy photos: "The two pictures you showed me are not what I saw that night." Interviewer: "What did it look like?" "It had a big hole in it. This whole area was gone.… It's being phonied someplace. It's make-believe."; ARRB deposition 5/7/97: still said "the occipital" area was the "big gaping hole" and demonstrated with putting his hand on the back of his head;

190. Lt. Cmdr. Gregory H. Cross, resident in surgery: 4/24/78 Outside contact report by the HSCA's Mark Flanagan (RIF#18010105-

10396, Agency File Number 014460) – "The only wound Cross saw was situated in the posterior aspect of the head.";

191. Edwin Stroble, Gawler's Funeral Home: *The (Illinois) Herald & Review*, 11/25/13. In a 1964 letter to a friend, Stroble said that JFK was hit "about the seventh vertebrae in his back.";

192. John Van Hoesen, Gawler's Funeral Home: 9/26/96 interview with the ARRB's Doug Horne – described the hole in JFK's head as being the size of an orange in "…the centerline of the back of the head, and its location was in the upper posterior of the skull … at or just below the cowlick area.";

193. Captain/ Dr. Robert Owen "Jiggs" Canada, Jr., USN, Director/ Commanding Officer, Bethesda Naval Hospital: 6-6-68 interview by Michael Kurtz (*The JFK Assassination Debates*, 2006): "Canada said he'd observed a "very large, 3 to 5 cm wound in the right rear of the president's head, in the lower right occipital region, 2.5 cm below the external occipital protuberance and 3.5 cm to the right of the midline of the skull."; "When informed that the official autopsy protocol mentioned only a small entrance wound in the rear of the head, Dr. Canada responded that that document had to have been rewritten to conform to the lone assassin theory." According to Kurtz, Canada then named names, and revealed that Capt. John Stover, the commanding officer of the medical school within the hospital, while "undoubtedly acting on orders from his superiors," had "demanded that the autopsy protocol be re-written to conform to the lone assassin thesis." According to Kurtz, Canada further "stated that he heard through the grapevine" that Stover had also "ordered all naval personnel present at the autopsy to maintain silence on penalty of court-martial." ; Canada also told him Kennedy's back wound was at the level of the third thoracic vertebra and that the bullet "lodged in the chest near the stomach, and did not exit." ; Canada told him the autopsy doctors knew on the night of the autopsy that Kennedy's tracheotomy incision had concealed an entrance wound, but that they "could not write that in the official protocol because it would have proven the existence of a gunman firing from the front."; "Dr. Canada insisted that the contents of this interview be kept secret until at least a quarter century after his death. Because that time period has elapsed, I present its essential points for the first time.";

194. Comdr. James Joseph ("Jim") Humes: WR 538-543 / 16 H 978-983 / CE 387 [see also *Assassination Science*, pp. 430435]: the autopsy report – "There is a large irregular defect of the scalp and skull on the right involving chiefly the parietal bone but extending

somewhat into the temporal and *occipital regions. In this region there is an actual absence of scalp and bone producing a defect which measures approximately 13 cm in greatest diameter..."* (emphasis added);

195. Comdr. J. Thornton ("Jay") Boswell: WR 538-543 / 16 H 978-983 / CE 387 [see also *Assassination Science*, pp. 430435]: the autopsy report – "There is a large irregular defect of the scalp and skull on the right involving chiefly the parietal bone but extending somewhat into the temporal and occipital regions. In this region there is an actual absence of scalp and bone producing a defect which measures approximately 13 cm in greatest diameter..."(emphasis added);

196. Lt. Col. Pierre A. Finck, AFIP: WR 538-543 / 16 H 978-983 / CE 387 [see also *Assassination Science*, pp. 430435]: the autopsy report – "There is a large irregular defect of the scalp and skull on the right involving chiefly the parietal bone but extending somewhat into the temporal and occipital regions. In this region there is an actual absence of scalp and bone producing a defect which measures approximately 13 cm in greatest diameter..."(emphasis added);

197. White House Photographer (Chief Petty Officer) Robert L. Knudsen, USN: 8/11/78 interview with the HSCA's Andy Purdy (RIF# 180-10105-10333) [see also *High Treason* (1998 edition), pp. 428-432]: "I am certain...there were the probes showing the point of entry and exit...It seems to me that the entry point was a little bit lower in the back – well, the point in the back was a little bit lower than the point in the front. So the probe was going diagonally from top to bottom, front to back.... Right about where the neck-tie is."; 7/31/98 Associated Press story by Deb Riechman: "His son Bob said that his father told him that 'hair had been drawn in' on one photo to conceal a missing portion of the top-back of President Kennedy's head," according to a [ARRB] review board memo about a meeting with Knudsen's family."; Gloria Knudsen and children Bob and Terri: 5/10/96 conversation with the ARRB's Douglas Horne [see also *High Treason* (1998 edition), pp. 494-497] – "All three family members recounted that Mr. Knudsen had told them he photographed the autopsy of President Kennedy, and was the only one to do so... He [Knudsen] witnessed and photographed probes inserted in the President's body which left no doubt of the number and direction of bullet trajectories; son Bob thought that his father had described 3 probes in the body (2 in the thorax/ neck, and one in the head)... after he appeared before the HSCA in 1978, he told his family (at different times) that 4 or 5 of the pictures he was shown by the HSCA did not represent what he saw or took that night, and that one of the

photographs he viewed had been altered. His son Bob said that his father told him that "hair had been drawn in" on one photo to conceal a missing portion of the top-back of President Kennedy's head…Mrs. Gloria Knudsen said that her husband Robert had told her that the whole top of the President's head was gone, and that the President's brain(s) were largely missing (blown out)."; His family said he "appeared before an official government body…sometime in 1988, about 6 months before he died … on Capital Hill … may have been a Congressional inquiry of some kind … Mr. Knudsen came away from this experience very disturbed, saying that 4 photographs were "missing" and that one was "badly altered"…the wounds he saw in the photos shown him in 1988 did not represent what he saw or took. He also told them that some of the details in the room in the background of the photos were "wrong."; Mr. Knudsen expressed skepticism with his daughter Terri over the years about the conclusions of the Warren Report in regard to the President's wounds and the manner in which he was shot, because of the observations he had made the night of the autopsy.";

198. Saundra Kay "Sandy" Spencer, a lab technician at the Naval Photographic Center: 12/13/96 interview with the ARRB [see also *High Treason* (1998 edition), pp. 416-418]: she remembers a wound in the back of the President's head which she described as a 'blown out chunk' about 2 to 2.5 inches wide located in about the center of the back of the President's head, about 3 or 4 inches above the hairline at the back of his head… she remembered no damage to the right side of the President's head.";

199. Joe O'Donnell, a government photographer employed by USIA in 1963: 1/29/97 interview with the ARRB's Jeremy Gunn and Douglas Horne [see also *High Treason* (1998 edition), pp. 418-420] – "frequently detailed to the White House"; Within the week after JFK's murder, O'Donnell said Knudsen showed him an autopsy photograph revealing "a hole in the forehead above the right eye which was a round wound about 3/8" in diameter which he interpreted as a gunshot wound," and "a hole in the back of the head, about 2" above the hairline, about the size of a grapefruit; the hole clearly penetrated the skull and was very deep." A few days later, Knudsen showed him another photo which showed the back of the head intact: "he remembers seeing neatly combed hair which looked slightly wet, or damp in appearance." He also saw photos of JFK with probes in him;

200. Lawrence F. "Larry" O'Brien, Special Assistant to the President: His book entitled *No Final Victories: A Life in Politics from John*

F. Kennedy to Watergate (1974) [see also *Reflections on JFK's Assassination* by John B. Jovich (1988), pages 35 and 37]: At Parkland Hospital: "It was chaotic, doctors, nurses running in and out. Medical equipment being wheeled into the room. At one point Jackie and I stepped into the adjoining room where the President's body lay. All I recall is I thought he looked as he always had." – Perhaps because the wound was in the *back* of the head?;

201. Vincent E. Drain, FBI Special Agent: *No More Silence* by Larry Sneed (1998), p. 246: "When I arrived in the trauma room, the doctors were working with President Kennedy... The head was badly damaged from the lower right base across the top extending across the top of the ear. It appeared to me as though the bullet traveled upward and had taken off the right portion of his skull. It may have been the security officer or one of the other officers who gave me a portion of the skull, which was about the size of a teacup, much larger than a silver dollar. Apparently the explosion had jerked it because the hair was still on it. I carried that back to Washington later that night and turned it over to the FBI laboratory.";

202. Dr. James Young, White House physician: December of 2001 and January of 2002 interview with U.S. Navy Bureau of Medicine and Surgery historians: "Doctor Burkley immediately evaluated the situation as hopeless as soon as he saw the gaping, bloody macerated huge wound and defect in the right posterior occipital area. "; "When seeing him, I walked to the head of the table and looked at the gaping defect in the right posterior and middle cerebral areas, which had no obvious skull covering lying anywhere in sight. "

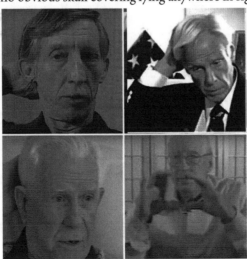

Clockwise-Dennis David, Tom Robinson, Joe O'Donnell, and James Sibert:

CHAPTER TEN

MASTER LIST OF WITNESSES WHO STATED THAT THE LIMOUSINE SLOWED OR STOPPED – A DEADLY DELAY ON ELM STREET

The following is a complete listing, the largest one ever compiled, of every single witness I could find – over 70 in all – who stated that the limousine either slowed down or stopped. This deadly delay on Elm Street was Secret Service agent Bill Greer's fault, pure and simple; he was the limousine driver. As even lone-nut authors agree, Greer's inept driving of the limo during the shooting allowed the assassination to be a tragic success.

- UPI's *Four Days*, 1964, p. 17 – "In the right hand picture [a frame from the Muchmore film], the driver slams on the brakes and the police escort pulls up."

- *Newsweek*, 12/2/63, p. 2 – "For a chaotic moment, the motorcade ground to an uncertain halt."

- *Time*, 11/29/63, p. 23 – "There was a shocking momentary stillness, a frozen tableau."

- *Case Closed* by Gerald Posner, 1993, p. 234 – "Incredibly, Greer, sensing that something was wrong in the back of the car, slowed the vehicle to almost a standstill."

- Gerald Posner, with Dan Rather, on CBS' *Who Killed JFK: The Final Chapter?* 11/19/93 – By turning around the second time and looking at JFK as the car slows down, Posner says that, "What he [Greer] has done is inadvertently given Oswald the easiest of the three shots." [As side notes, two other lone-nut authors chimed in – author Vincent Bugliosi wrote the author on 7/14/07: "I want you to know that I am very impressed with your research abilities and the enormous amount of work you put into your investigation of the Secret Service regarding the assassination. You are, unquestionably, the main authority on the Secret Service with regard to the assassination. I agree with you that they did not do a good job protecting the president (e.g. see p. 1443 of my book).")). Former Warren Commission lawyer and author Howard Willens wrote the author on 7/23/13: "I definitely agree that the Secret Service could and should have done more to protect the President."]

1. *Houston Chronicle* Reporter Bo Byers (rode in White House Press Bus) – twice stated that the Presidential Limousine "almost came to a stop, a dead stop"; in fact, he has had nightmares about this. [C-SPAN, 11/20/93, "Journalists Remember The Kennedy Assassination"; see also the 1/94 *Fourth Decade* article by Sheldon Inkol]

2. ABC Reporter Bob Clark (rode in the National Press Pool Car) – Reported on the air that the limousine stopped on Elm Street during the shooting [WFAA/ ABC, 11/22/63]

3. UPI White House Reporter Merriman Smith (rode in the same car as Clark, above) – "The President's car, possibly as much as 150 or 200 yards ahead, seemed to falter briefly..." [UPI story, 11/23/63, as reported in *Four Days*, UPI, p. 32]

4. DPD motorcycle officer James W. Courson (one of two mid-motorcade motorcycles) – "The limousine came to a stop and Mrs. Kennedy was on the back. I noticed that as I came around the corner at Elm. Then the Secret Service agent [Clint Hill] helped push her back into the car, and the motorcade took off at a high rate of speed." [*No More Silence* by Larry Sneed (1998), p. 129]

5. DPD motorcycle officer Bobby Joe Dale (one of two rear mid-motorcade motorcycles) – "After the shots were fired, the whole motorcade came to a stop. I stood and looked through the plaza, noticed there was commotion, and saw people running around his [JFK's] car. It started to move, then it slowed again; that's when I saw Mrs. Kennedy coming back on the trunk and another guy [Clint Hill] pushing her back into the car." [*No More Silence* by Larry Sneed (1998), p. 134]

6. Clemon Earl Johnson – "You could see it [the limo] speed up and then stop, then speed up, and you could see it stop while they [sic; Clint Hill] threw Mrs. Kennedy back up in the car. Then they just left out of there like a bat of the eye and were just gone." [*No More Silence* by Larry Sneed (1998), p. 80]

7. Malcolm Summers – "Then there was some hesitation in the caravan itself, a momentary halt, to give the Secret Service man

[Clint Hill] a chance to catch up with the car and jump on. It seems to me that it started back up by the time he got to the car." [*No More Silence* by Larry Sneed (1998), p. 104]

8. NBC reporter Robert MacNeil (rode in White House Press Bus) –"The President's driver slammed on the brakes – after the third shot." [*The Way We Were, 1963: The Year Kennedy Was Shot* by Robert MacNeil (1988), p. 193]

9. AP photographer Henry Burroughs (rode in Camera Car #2) – "We heard the shots and the motorcade stopped." [letter, Burroughs to Palamara, dated 10/14/98]

10. DPD Earle Brown – "…The first I noticed the [JFK's] car was when it stopped … after it made the turn and when the shots were fired, it stopped." [6 H 233]

11. DPD motorcycle officer Bobby Hargis (one of the four Presidential motorcycle officers) – "At that time [immediately before the head shot] the Presidential car slowed down. I heard somebody say 'Get going.' I felt blood hit me in the face and the Presidential car stopped almost immediately after that." [6 H 294; Murder From Within by Fred Newcomb& Perry Adams (1974), p. 71. 6/26/95 videotaped interview with Mark Oakes and Ian Griggs: "That guy (Greer) slowed down, maybe his orders was to slow down … slowed down almost to a stop." Like Posner, Hargis feels Greer gave Oswald the chance to kill Kennedy.]

12. DPD D.V. Harkness – "I saw the first shot and the President's car slow[ed] down to almost a stop. I heard the first shot and saw the President's car almost come to a stop and some of the agents [were] piling on the car." [6 H 309]

13. DPD James Chaney (one of the four Presidential motorcycle officers) – stated that the Presidential limousine stopped momentarily after the first shot (according to the testimony of Mark Lane; corroborated by the testimony of fellow DPD motorcycle officer Marion Baker: Chaney told him that "at the time, after the shooting, from the time the first shot rang out, the car stopped completely, pulled to the left and stopped. Now I have heard several of them say that, Mr. Truly was standing out there, he said it stopped. Several officers said it stopped completely." [2 H 44-45 (Lane) – referring to Chaney's statement as reported in the *Houston Chronicle* dated 11/24/63; 3 H 266 (Baker)]

14. DPD motorcycle officer B.J. Martin (one of the four Presidential motorcyclists) – saw JFK's car stop "just for a moment." [*Murder From Within* by Fred Newcomb & Perry Adams (1974), p. 71]

15. DPD motorcycle officer Douglas L. Jackson (one of the four Presidential motorcyclists) – stated "that the car just all but stopped ... just a moment." [*Murder From Within* by Fred Newcomb & Perry Adams (1974), p. 71]

16. 16) Texas Highway Patrolman Joe Henry Rich (drove LBJ's car) – stated that "the motorcade came to a stop momentarily." [*Murder From Within* by Fred Newcomb & Perry Adams (1974), p. 71]

17. DPD J.W. Foster – stated that "immediately after President Kennedy was struck the car in which he was riding pulled to the curb." [CD 897, pp. 20, 21; *Murder From Within* by Fred Newcomb & Perry Adams (1974), p. 97]

18. Secret Service Agent Sam Kinney (driver of the follow-up car behind JFK's limo) – indicates, via his report to Chief Rowley, that Greer hit the gas after the fatal head shot to JFK and after the President's slump to the left toward Jackie. [18 H 731-732]. From the HSCA's 2/26/78 interview of Kinney: "He also remarked that 'when Greer (the driver of the Presidential limousine) looked back, his foot must have come off the accelerator.' Kinney observed that at the time of the first shot, the speed of the motorcade was '3 to 5 miles an hour.'" [RIF#180-10078-10493; author's interviews with Kinney, 1992-1994]

19. Secret Service Agent Clint Hill (follow-up car, rear of limo) – "I jumped from the follow-up car and ran toward the Presidential automobile. I heard a second firecracker-type noise. SA Greer had, as I jumped onto the Presidential automobile, accelerated the Presidential automobile forward." [18 H 742; Nix film; *The Secret Service* and *Inside The Secret Service* videos from 1995] 5-9-12 interview on MyFOXNY: "And if you watch the Zapruder film real close you'll see that the brake lights come on. He tapped the brake to see if he could get any response from the tires because he thought he'd blown a tire. So he did slow down slightly at that time, but he never stopped, and he kept on going. And then he started to accelerate just before I got there."

20. Secret Service Agent John Ready (follow-up car) – "I heard what sounded like firecrackers going off from my post on the right front running board. The President's car slowed." [18 H 750]

21. Secret Service Agent Glen Bennett (follow-up car) – after the fatal head shot "the President's car immediately kicked into high gear." [18 H 760; 24 H 541-542]. During his 1/30/78 HSCA interview, Bennett said the follow-up car was moving at "10-12 m.p.h.," an indication of the pace of the motorcade on Elm Street [RIF#180-10082-10452]

22. Secret Service Agent "Lem" Johns (V.P. follow-up car) – "I felt that if there was danger [it was] due to the slow speed of the automobile." [18 H 774]. During his 8/8/78 HSCA interview, Johns said that "Our car was moving very slowly," a further indication of the pace of the motorcade on Elm Street [RIF# 180-10074-10079; Altgens photo]

23. Secret Service Agent Winston Lawson (rode in the lead car) – "I think it [the lead car on Elm Street] was a little further ahead [of JFK's limo] than it had been in the motorcade, because when I looked back we were further ahead." [4 H 352], an indication of the lag in the limo during the assassination.

24. Secret Service Agent William "Tim" McIntyre (follow-up car) – "He stated that Greer, driver of the Presidential limousine, accelerated after the third shot." [RIF#180-10082-10454: 1/31/78 HSCA interview]

25. Mrs. Earle "Dearie" Cabell (rode in the Mayor's car) – the motorcade "stopped dead still when the noise of the shot was heard." [7 H 487; *Accessories After the Fact* by Sylvia Meagher (1967), p. 4; *Murder From Within* by Fred Newcomb & Perry Adams (1974), p. 71]

26. Phil Willis – "The [Presidential] party had come to a temporary halt before proceeding on to the underpass." [7 H 497; *Crossfire* by Jim Marrs (1989), p. 24]

27. Mrs. Phil Willis – Marilyn – after the fatal head shot, "she stated the Presidential limousine paused momentarily and then sped away under the Triple Underpass." [FBI report dated 6/19/64; *Photographic Whitewash* by Harold Weisberg (1967), p. 179]

28. Mrs. John Connally – Nellie (rode in JFK's limo) – JFK's car did not accelerate until after the fatal head shot. [4 H 147; WR 50; *Best Evidence* by David Lifton (1988), p. 122]

29. Texas Governor John Connally (rode in JFK's limo and himself a victim of the assassination) – "After the third shot, I heard Roy Kellerman tell the driver, 'Bill, get out of line.' And then I saw him move, and I assumed he was moving a button or something on the panel of the automobile, and he said 'Get us to a hospital quick.' At about this time, we began to pull out of the cavalcade, out of line." [4 H 133; WR50; *Crossfire* by Jim Marrs (1989), p. 13];

30. *Dallas Morning News* reporter Robert Baskin (rode in the National Press Pool Car) – stated that "the motorcade ground to a halt." [*Dallas Morning News*, 11/23/63, p. 2; *Murder From Within* by Fred Newcomb & Perry Adams (1974), p. 71]

31. *Dallas Morning News* reporter Mary Woodward (Pillsworth) – "Instead of speeding up the car, the car came to a halt."; she saw the President's car come to a halt after the first shot. Then, after hearing two more shots, close together, the car sped up. [2 H 43 (Lane); *Dallas Morning News*, 11/23/63; 24 H 520; *The Men Who Killed Kennedy*, 1988]. She spoke forcefully about the car almost coming to a stop and the lack of proper reaction by the Secret Service in 1993. [C-SPAN, 11/20/93, "Journalists Remember The Kennedy Assassination"; see also the 1/94 *Fourth Decade* article by Sheldon Inkol]

32. AP photographer James Altgens – "He said the President's car was proceeding at about ten miles per hour at the time [of the shooting]. Altgens stated the driver of the Presidential limousine apparently realized what had happened and speeded up toward the Stemmons Expressway." [FBI report dated 6/5/64; *Photographic Whitewash* by Harold Weisberg (1967), p. 203] "The car's driver realized what had happened and almost if by reflex speeded up toward the Stemmons Expressway." [AP dispatch, 11/22/63; *Cover-Up* by Stewart Galanor (1998), Document 28] Interview presented as part of radio show *Thou Shalt Not Kill*, on Canadian radio station CTFR broadcast 5-10-76: "The caravan never did stop, but if it ever came close to stopping it was right at that point. And as I turned and made the picture of the Secret Service man going up to help Jackie back into the limousine, I heard someone on the radio say, "We've been hit. Get us to the nearest hospital quick." And that's when they threw into high gear and took off."

33. Alan Smith – "the car was ten feet from me when a bullet hit the President in the forehead…the car went about five feet and stopped." [*Chicago Tribune*, 11/23/63, p. 9; *Murder From Within* by Fred Newcomb& Perry Adams (1974), p. 71]

34. Mrs. Ruth M. Smith – confirmed that the Presidential limousine had come to a stop. [CD 206, p. 9; *Murder From Within* by Fred Newcomb & Perry Adams (1974), p. 97]

35. TSBD Supervisor Roy Truly – after the first shot "I saw the President's car swerve to the left and stop somewhere down in the area … [it stopped] for a second or two or something like that. I just saw it stop." [3 H 221, 266]

36. L.P. Terry – "The parade stopped right in front of the building [TSBD]." [*Crossfire* by Jim Marrs (1989), p. 26]

37. Ochus V. Campbell – after hearing shots, "he then observed the car bearing President Kennedy to slow down, a near stop, and

a motorcycle policeman rushed up. Immediately following this, he observed the car rush away from the scene." [22 H 845]

38. Peggy Joyce Hawkins – she was on the front steps of the TSBD and "estimated that the President's car was less than 50 feet away from her when he was shot, that the car slowed down almost coming to a full stop." [3-26-64 FBI report, CD897 p.35-36; *Murder From Within* by Fred Newcomb & Perry Adams (1974), p. 97]

39. Billy Lovelady – "I recall that following the shooting, I ran toward the spot where President Kennedy's car had stopped." [22 H 662];

40. An unnamed witness – from his vantage point in the courthouse building, stated that, "The cavalcade stopped there and there was bedlam." [*Dallas Times-Herald*, 11/24/63; *Murder From Within* by Fred Newcomb & Perry Adams (1974), p. 97]

41. Postal Inspector Harry Holmes (from the Post Office Annex, while viewing through binoculars) – "The car almost came to a stop, and Mrs. Kennedy pulled loose of him and crawled out over the turtleback of this Presidential car." [7 H 291]. He noticed the car pull to a halt, and Holmes thought: "They are dodging something being thrown." [*The Day Kennedy Was Shot* by Jim Bishop (1967), p. 176]

42. Peggy Burney – she stated that JFK's car had come to a stop. [*Dallas Times-Herald*, 11/24/63; *Murder From Within* by Fred Newcomb & Perry Adams (1974), p. 97. Interestingly, during the 11/20/93 C-SPAN "Journalists Remember" conference, Vivian Castleberry of the *Dallas Times-Herald* made the claim that her first cousin, Peggy Burney, was Abraham Zapruder's assistant "and was next to him when he shot his famous film. She called and said, 'Vivian, today I saw the President die.'"! See Sheldon Inkol's article on this conference in the January 1994 *Fourth Decade*]

43. David Broeder – "The President's car paused momentarily, then on orders from a Secret Service agent, spurted ahead." [*Washington Evening Star*, 11/23/63, p. 8]

44. Sam Holland – stated that the Presidential limousine slowed down on Elm Street. [taped interview with Holland conducted in April, 1965]

45. Maurice Orr – noted that the motorcade stopped. [Arch Kimbrough, Mary Ferrell, and Sue Fitch, *Chronology*, unpublished manuscript; see also *Conspiracy* by Anthony Summers, pages 20 & 23]

46. Mrs. Herman (Billy P.) Clay – "When I heard the second and third shots I knew someone was shooting at the President. I did

not know if the President had been hit, but I knew something was wrong. At this point the car President Kennedy was in slowed and I, along with others, moved toward the President's car. As we neared the car it sped off." [22 H 641]

47. Mrs. Rose Clark – "She noted that the President's automobile came almost to a halt following the three shots, before it picked up speed and drove away." [24 H 533]

48. Hugh Betzner – "I looked down the street and I could see the President's car and another one and they looked like the cars were stopped … then the President's car sped on under the underpass… I walked down toward where the President's car had stopped."" [19 H 467]

49. John Chism – after the shots he saw "the motorcade beginning to speed up." [*Crossfire* by Jim Marrs (1989), p. 29]

50. Bill Newman – after the fatal head shot "the car momentarily stopped and the driver seemed to have a radio or phone up to his ear and he seemed to be waiting on some word. Some Secret Service men reached into their car and came out with some sort of machine gun. Then the cars roared off"; "I've maintained that they stopped. I still say they did. It was only a momentary stop." [*Crossfire* by Jim Marrs (1989), p. 70; *Murder From Within* by Fred Newcomb & Perry Adams (1974), p. 96] "I believe Kennedy's car came to a full stop after the final shot." [*JFK: Breaking the Silence* by Bill Sloan (1993), p. 169] "I believe it was the passenger in the front seat [Roy Kellerman] – there were two men in the front seat – had a telephone or something to his ear and the car momentarily stopped. Now everywhere that you read about it, you don't read anything about the car stopping. And when I say "stopped" I mean very momentarily, like they hit the brakes and just a few seconds passed and then they floorboarded [sic] and accelerated on." [11/20/97 videotaped interview with Bill Law, Mark Row, & Ian Griggs, as transcribed in *November Patriots* by Connie Kritzberg and Larry Hancock (1998), p. 362] "One of the two men in the front seat of the car had a telephone in his hand, and as I was looking back at the car covering my son, I can remember seeing the tail lights of the car, and just for a moment they hesitated and stopped, and then they floorboarded [sic] the car and shot off." [*No More Silence* by Larry Sneed (1998), p. 96]

51. Charles Brehm – "Brehm expressed his opinion that between the first and third shots, the President's car only seemed to move some 10 or 12 feet. It seemed to him that the automobile almost came to a halt after the first shot. After the third shot, the car in

which the President was riding increased its speed and went under the freeway overpass and out of sight." [22 H 837-838]

52. Mary Moorman – "She recalls that the President's automobile was moving at the time she took the second picture, and when she heard the shots, and has the impression that the car either stopped momentarily or hesitated and then drove off in a hurry." [22 H 838-839]

53. Jean Hill – "The motorcade came to almost a halt at the time the shots rang out and I would say it [JFK's limo] was just approximately, if not – it couldn't have been in the same position, I'm sure it wasn't, but just a very, very short distance from where it had been. It [JFK's limo] was just almost stunned." [6 H 208-209; Hill's testimony on this matter was dramatized in the Oliver Stone movie JFK (1991): "The driver had stopped – I don't know what was wrong with that driver." See also JFK: The Book of the Film (1992), p. 122. Therein is referenced a March 1991 conversation with Jean Hill.]

54. James Leon Simmons – "The car stopped or almost stopped." [2/15/69 Clay Shaw trial testimony; Forgive My Grief Vol. III by Penn Jones, p. 53; High Treason by Robert Groden and Harrison Livingstone (1990 Berkley Edition), p. 22]

55. Norman Similas – "The Presidential limousine had passed me and slowed down slightly." [Liberty Magazine, 7/15/64, p. 13; Photographic Whitewash by Harold Weisberg (1967), p. 233];

56. Presidential Aide Ken O'Donnell (rode in the follow-up car) – "If the Secret Service men in the front had reacted quicker to the first two shots at the President's car, if the driver had stepped on the gas before instead of after the fatal third shot was fired, would President Kennedy be alive today? [as quoted in Marrs Crossfire, p. 248, based off a passage from O'Donnell and Powers' book Johnny, We Hardly Knew Ye]. On page 40 of O'Donnell's book Johnny, We Hardly Knew Ye, the aide reports that "Greer had been remorseful all day, feeling that he could have saved President Kennedy's life by swerving the car or speeding suddenly after the first shots." Indeed, William E. Sale, an airman first class aircraft mechanic assigned to Carswell AFB and who was stationed at Love Field before, during, and after the assassination, stated that "when the agent who was driving JFK's car came back to Air Force One he was as white as a ghost and had to be helped back to the plane *[undated Sale letter, 1988]

57. Presidential aide Dave Powers (rode in the follow-up car) – "At that time we were traveling very slowly. At about the time of the third shot, the President's car accelerated sharply." [7 H 473-475].

On 11/22/88, Powers was interviewed by CBS' Charles Kuralt. Powers remarked about the remorse Greer felt about not speeding up in time to save JFK's life and agreed with Kuralt that, if Greer had sped up before the fatal head shot instead of afterwards, JFK might still be alive today [CBS, 11/22/88 – this is a very dramatic and compelling short interview]. If that weren't enough, the ARRB's Tom Samoluk told me that, during the course of an interview he conducted in 1996 in which the Board was in the process of obtaining Powers' film, Powers said that he agreed with my take on the Secret Service!

58. Texas Senator Ralph Yarborough (rode in LBJ's car) – "When the noise of the shot was heard, the motorcade slowed to what seemed to me a complete stop (though it could have been a near stop) After the third shot was fired, but only after the third shot was fired, the cavalcade speeded up, gained speed rapidly, and roared away to the Parkland Hospital."; "The cars all stopped. I put in there [his affidavit], 'I don't want to hurt anyone's feelings but for the protection of future Presidents, they [the Secret Service] should be trained to take off when a shot is fired." [7 H 439-440; *Crossfire* by Jim Marrs (1989), p. 482; see also *The Men Who Killed Kennedy*, 1988: "The Secret Service in the car in front of us kind of casually looked around and were rather slow to react."]

59. First Lady Jacqueline Kennedy (rode in the Presidential limousine) – "We could see a tunnel in front of us. Everything was really slow then… [immediately after shooting] And just being down in the car with his head in my lap. And it just seemed an eternity. And finally I remember a voice behind me, or something, and then I remember the people in the front seat, or somebody, finally knew something was wrong, and a voice yelling, which must have been Mr. Hill, "Get to the hospital," or maybe it was Mr. Kellerman, in the front seat. We were really slowing turning the corner [Houston and Elm]. I remember a sensation of enormous speed, which must have been when we took off…those poor men in the front" [5 H 179-181] Mary Gallagher reported in her book: "She mentioned one Secret Service man who had not acted during the crucial moment, and said bitterly to me, 'He might just as well have been Miss Shaw!'" [*My Life With Jacqueline Kennedy* by Mary Barelli Gallagher (1969), p. 342 – Secret Service Agent Marty Venker and Jackie biographer C. David Heymann confirm that this unnamed agent was indeed Greer (*Confessions of an Ex-Secret Service Agent*, p. 25; *A Woman Called Jackie*, p. 401)] Jackie also told Gallagher that "You should

get yourself a good driver so that nothing ever happens to you" [*My Life With Jacqueline Kennedy*, p. 351]

60. Congressman Henry Gonzalez: 11-23-63 UPI article found in the *San Antonio Light*: "The motorcade moved down an incline and went under an overpass. It had slowed to a halt at this point"; 8-25-75 UPI article found in the *Fort Pierce Florida News Tribune*: "I have never mentioned this to anyone before. But when the first shot sounded, the cars were already at a complete halt or just crawling. Odd that we should have come to a virtual stop even before the first shot, at the exact spot."

61. DPD motorcycle officer Stavis Ellis: 4-21-71 interview of Elliis by Whitney, someone working for researcher Fred Newcomb, as presented by Larry Rivera and Jim Fetzer on the *Veterans Today* website, 4-3-14: "Well no it didn't stop, it almost stopped. If you've ever ridden a motor, you know if you go so slow, your motor will want to lean to one side, you have to put your foot down and balance it, but we were going so slow, that's what was happening we were having to kick our foot down, a very slow pace, this was, after the first shot was fired, we were – we cut the speed, the Secret Service cut the speed, on the convoy." (When asked how long) "Well, it was just momentarily, it never did stop, it almost stopped, it got so slow, we were just barely moving – and then they hollered Go Go Go! Lets go. Get him to the hospital as quick as you can!"; *The Kennedy Assassination Tapes*, 1979: "It also seemed like the limousine stopped or almost stopped, and agents from the following car started running toward the President's limousine."

62. Jack Bell: 11-22-64 AP article found in the *Ada Oklahoma Evening News*: "The President's car had stopped."

63. Dave Wiegman: *Pictures of the Pain*, p.371-372, Trask interview 3-18-89: "I'd done this before in other motorcades because a lot of times the President will stop and do something.... The motorcade has stopped, plus you heard a report."

64. Julian Reed: 11-22-13 interview with *Wall Street Journal* posted on You Tube: "The limousine almost stopped for a moment and then rushed under the underpass."

65. Charles Bronson: Letter to his sister, 11-24-63, as quoted in the *Dallas Morning News* in 1978 and *Pictures of the Pain*, p.283: "Then I looked and saw a few people lay flat on the ground just as the presidential car stopped for a split second and then take off."

66. James Tague: *The Day Kennedy Died*, on the Smithsonian Channel, 11-17-13– Alternative take presented on the website for the

program: "I remember it slowing down, then somebody throws a firecracker. And then all of a sudden crack crack, two rifle shots, and something stings me in the face."

67. Jack Franzen: Family interview recorded 6-18-97 available online: "The limousine driver and the guy in the front seat almost – momentarily – stopped the car and he turned his head and everything was alright, so he turned back and proceeded to come on down toward us."

68. Jeff Franzen: Article by Franzen published on Slate.com, 11-20-13: "the car slowed down"

69. Toni Foster: 2000 article in the *Kennedy Assassination Chronicles*: "For some reason the car stopped. It did stop for seconds. I don't even know why it stopped and all of a sudden it sped up and they went under the underpass. I could never figure out why the car stopped."

70. Louie Steven Witt: Handwritten notes by HSCA investigator Jack Moriarty on an 8-12-78 interview with Witt, found on the Baylor University website, in the John Armstrong collection: "The President's car stopped."

71. John Templin: 7-28-95 Oral History interview for the Sixth Floor Museum – When asked if he kind of saw the limo come to a stop: "Yes, sir ... I think when President Kennedy was shot fatally in the head, the second shot, the limo was almost, if not completely, stopped. I think a natural reaction of anyone, I don't care how well trained he is, if he hears a shot or something, his natural reaction is to hit the brakes. Wouldn't you agree with that? ... It's just human nature to hit for that brake, and the brake lights definitely came on.

72. *Dallas Morning News* reporter Ann Donaldson: 11-22-63 first person account published in the *Washington Evening Star*, Second Extra Edition: "Mrs. Jacqueline Kennedy threw herself over his body as the President's car speeded up as soon as the driver realized what had happened... The car did not stop"; 11-10-03 Oral History interview with The Sixth Floor Museum: "There was a pause in the presidential car and then it just sped up and went on the other side."

73. Sandra Styles: Appearance in the Travel Channel program *America Declassified: JFK Exclusive Access*, 11-3-13: "The presidential car stopped."

74. Cleola Shields: 11/12/77 interview with HSCA: "the car made a little pause then took off."

William Manchester, who interviewed Greer, tells us what the driver told Jackie on 11/22/63 at Parkland Hospital: "Oh, Mrs. Kennedy, oh my God, oh my God. I didn't mean to do it [?!?!], I didn't hear [who, Kellerman?], I should have swerved the car [how about hitting the gas?], I couldn't help it[!]. Oh, Mrs. Kennedy, as soon as I saw it[?] I swerved. If only I'd seen it in time! Oh!" (*The Death of a President*, p.290). All these witnesses and the Zapruder film document Secret Service agent William R. Greer's deceleration of the presidential limousine, as well as his two separate looks back at JFK during the assassination (Greer denied all of this to the Warren Commission). By decelerating from an already slow 11.2 mph, Greer greatly endangered the President's life, and, as even Gerald Posner admitted, Greer contributed greatly to the success of the assassination. When we consider that Greer disobeyed a direct order from his superior, Roy Kellerman, to get out of line before the fatal shot struck the President's head, it is hard to give Agent Greer the benefit of the doubt. As ASAIC Roy H. Kellerman said: "Greer then looked in the back of the car. Maybe he didn't believe me"(*The Death of a President* by William Manchester, p.160). Clearly, Greer was responsible, at fault, and felt remorse. In short, Greer had survivor's guilt.

But, then, stories and feelings changed.

Agent Greer to the FBI 11/22/63: "Greer stated that he first heard what he thought was possibly a motorcycle backfire and glanced around and noticed that the President had evidently been hit [notice that, early on, Greer admits seeing JFK, which the Zapruder proves he did two times before the fatal head shot occurred]. He thereafter got on the radio and communicated with the other vehicles, stating that they desired to get the President to the hospital immediately [in reality, Greer did not talk on the radio, and Greer went on to deny ever saying this during his WC testimony]. Greer stated that they (the Secret Service) have always been instructed to keep the motorcade moving at a considerable speed in as much as a moving car offers a much more difficult target than a vehicle traveling at a very slow speed. He pointed out that on numerous occasions he has attempted to keep the car moving at a rather fast rate, but in view of the President's popularity and desire to maintain close liaison with the people, he has, on occasion, been instructed by the President to "slow down." Greer stated that he has been asking himself if there was anything he could have done to have avoided this incident, but stated that things happened so fast that he could not account for full developments in this matter(!) [the "JFK-as-scapegoat" theme – and so much for Greer's remorse from earlier the same day]."(Sibert & O'Neill Report, 11/22/63)

Agent Greer to the FBI 11/27/63: "He heard a noise which sounded like a motorcycle backfire. On hearing this noise he glanced to his right toward Kellerman and out of the corner of his eye noticed that the Governor appeared to be falling toward his wife [notice that Greer now mentions nothing about seeing JFK hit – he does the same thing in his undated report in the WC volumes (18 H 723)] He thereafter recalls hearing some type of outcry after which Kellerman said, "Let's get out of here." He further related that at the time of hearing the sound he was starting down an incline which passes beneath a railroad crossing and after passing under this viaduct, he closed in on the lead car and yelled to the occupants and a nearby police motorcyclist, "Hospital, Hospital! [nothing about using the radio this time out]" Thereafter follows a complete physical description of Greer, as if the FBI agents considered him a suspect, including age, height, and color of eyes! (Sibert & O'Neill Report, 11/29/63)

Critical excerpts from Greer's 3/9/64 Warren Commission testimony before Arlen Specter:

> **Mr. Specter:** Were you able to see anything of President Kennedy as you glanced to the rear?
>
> **Mr. Greer:** No, sir; I didn't see anything of the President, I didn't look, I wasn't far enough around to see the President.
>
> **Mr. Specter:** When you started that glance, are you able to recollect whether you started to glance before, exactly simultaneously with or after that second shot?
>
> **Mr. Greer:** It was almost simultaneously that he had – something had hit, you know, when I had seen him. It seemed like in the same second almost that something had hit, you know, whenever I turned around. I saw him start to fall.
>
> **Mr. Specter:** Did you step on the accelerator before, simultaneously or after Mr. Kellerman instructed you to accelerate?
>
> **Mr. Greer:** It was about simultaneously.
>
> **Mr. Specter:** So that it was your reaction to accelerate prior to the time –
>
> **Mr. Greer:** Yes, sir.
>
> **Mr. Specter:** You had gotten that instruction?
>
> **Mr. Greer:** Yes, sir; it was my reaction that caused me to accelerate.
>
> **Mr. Specter:** Do you recollect whether you accelerated before or at the same time or after the third shot?

Mr. Greer: I couldn't really say. Just as soon as I turned my head back from the second shot, right away I accelerated right then. It was a matter of my reflexes to the accelerator.

Mr. Specter: Was it at about that time that you heard the third shot?

Mr. Greer: Yes, sir; just as soon as I turned my head

[...]

Mr. Specter: To the best of your current recollection, did you notice that the President had been hit?

Mr. Greer: No, sir; I didn't know how badly he was injured or anything other than that. I didn't know.

Mr. Specter: Did you know at all, from the glance which you have described that he had been hit or injured in any way?

Mr. Greer: I knew he was injured in some way, but I didn't know how bad or what.

Mr. Specter: How did you know that?

Mr. Greer: If I remember now, I just don't remember how I knew, but I knew we were in trouble. I knew that he was injured, but I can't remember, recollect, just how I knew there were injuries in there. I didn't know who all was hurt, even.

Mr. Specter: Are you able to recollect whether you saw the President after the shots as you were proceeding toward Parkland Hospital?

Mr. Greer: No; I don't remember ever seeing him anymore until I got to the hospital, and he was lying across the seat, you know, and that is the first I had seen of him.

Mr. Specter: Your best recollection is, then, that you had the impression he was injured but you couldn't ascertain the source of that information?

Mr. Greer: Right. I couldn't ascertain the source.

Warren Commission finding: "The driver, Special Agent William R. Greer, has testified that he accelerated the car after what was probably the second shot.... The Presidential car did not stop or almost come to a complete halt after the firing of the first shot or any other shots." (WC Report, page 641)

11/19/64 interview with *Death of a President* author William Manchester [RIF#180-10116-10119] – "After the second shot I glanced back.

I saw blood on the Governor's white shirt, and I knew we were in trouble. The blood was coming out of his right breast. When I heard the first shot, I had thought it was a backfire. I was tramping on the accelerator and at the same time Roy was saying, let's get out of here fast."

But remember what Roy Kellerman said: "Greer then looked in the back of the car. Maybe he didn't believe me"(*The Death of a President* by William Manchester, p.160).

2/28/78 HSCA interview [RIF#180-10099-10491] – "The first shot sounded to him like a backfire. He did not react to it. After the second shot he turned to his right and saw blood on Governor Connally's shirt. At the same moment he heard Kellerman say "We're hit. Let's get out of here," or words to that effect. He said he immediately accelerated and followed the pilot car to Parkland Hospital [However, DNC Advance man Jack Puterbaugh, who rode in the pilot car, said they "pulled over and let the motorcade pass" (HSCA interview 4/14/78). The *Washington Post* from 2/28/85 reported Greer as saying that "I just looked straight ahead at the car in which the police chief was leading our way to the hospital" – this is the lead car. Nevertheless, the Daniel film and still photos depict the limousine ahead of the lead car, as it appears it was the lead motorcyclists who guided Greer to Parkland.

Bill Greer passed away from cancer on 2/23/85.

From a 9/17/91 interview with Bill's son Richard:

When asked, "What did your father think of JFK," Richard did not respond the first time. When this author asked him a second time, he responded: "Well, we're Methodists ... and JFK was Catholic..." (Bill Greer was born and raised in County Tyrone, Ireland; 2 H 112 - 113)

"My father certainly didn't blame himself; it's not one of those things – if only I was driving one mile per hour faster

"My father had absolutely no survivor's guilt ... he figured that events were kind out of their control...it was pretty common knowledge that a person riding in an open car was subject to a bullet at any time..."

In any event, although the presidential limousine did not actually come to a full and complete stop during the assassination[1], it did slow down long enough to greatly help in the success of the assassination.

CHAPTER ELEVEN

FINAL THOUGHTS AND SPECIAL THANKS

S o, where do we go from here? Frankly, there really is nowhere to go with the case (unless Caroline Kennedy or some relative in the distant future allows an exhumation and another forensic autopsy, a very remote possibility, to put it mildly, unless one gleans hope from the exhumation of former President Zachary Taylor[1]). Too much time has passed and too many have passed away. I am not trying to disappoint anyone with this statement, but that is the stark reality of the situation. We have been fortunate to have three major federal investigations of the case: the Warren Commission (yes, even their deeply flawed investigation reaped a lot of valuable raw data via the 26 volumes of hearings and exhibits, as well as Commission Documents), the House Select Committee on Assassinations (the 12 volumes of accompanying data and all the file releases are quite important) and the Assassination Records Review Board (I consider them another investigation because of their detailed off-the-record medical evidence review). Although we had further files releases in 2017-2018, with another one scheduled for 2021 (President Biden: please release them), there will not be a fourth investigation.

As I said, the vast majority of players in the case, major and minor, are gone; often, long gone. Time marches on without any rest or consideration. Attrition is a normal function in the world we live in.

Who is left?

As of this writing (obviously subject to change or error: it is over 57 years later), Marina Oswald and her two daughters Rachel and June; Ruth Paine[2] and her children; Marie Tippit and her children.

From the main motorcade, only Secret Service agents Clint Hill and Paul Landis from the follow-up car; Milton Wright, the driver of Mayor Cabell's car; photographer Robert H. Jackson and Julian Read (Connal-

---

1   The remains of Taylor, who died in 1850, were exhumed on 6/17/91, due to persistent generations-old rumors that he had been assassinated via arsenic poisoning: https://en.wikipedia.org/wiki/Zachary_Taylor

2   Paine did oral histories for the Sixth Floor Museum on 9/22/19 and 11/19/19.

ly's press secretary); photographer Dave Wiegman; from the two White House press busses, NBC's Robert MacNeil and Keith Shelton; from the official party bus, Pamela Turnure, Jackie's press secretary, Mary Gallagher and Marie Fehmer Chiarodo, secretary to LBJ. That is it.

Other White House Detail/Washington Secret Service agents still living who were on some segment of the Texas trip: Gerald Blaine, Walt Coughlin, Ron Pontius, Ken Giannoules, Bill Duncan, Mike Howard, Frank Yeager, Michael Shannon, Robert Burke, Gerald O'Rourke, Paul Rundle, Gerald Bechtle and Jim Goodenough.

Other Secret Service agents who protected Kennedy who are still alive: Abraham Bolden, Ed Z. Tucker, Radford Jones, Dick Keiser, Toby Chandler, Lois Sims, Tom Wells, Bill Skiles, Donald Brett, Jim Johnson, Tom Fridley, Milt Wilhite, Jack Warner, Scott Trundle, Ken Wiesman and Eve Dempsher, the secretary. Field office agents still around: Charles "Chuck" Taylor, Gary Seale, Robert Snow. That's all, unless there are some field office agents still kicking.

From the JFK White House: Mimi Alford, Mary Barelli Gallagher, Eileen Carver, Janet Desrosiers (Fontaine), Lenore Donnelly, Barbara Coleman (Salinger's office; later worked for RFK), Helen Lempart (from Ken O'Donnell's office) and Jill Cowan might be the only ones left.

From the Dallas police, sheriff's department and detective bureau: Paul McCaghren, W.E. "Rusty" Robbins, and Elmer Boyd may be the only ones left.

From the eyewitnesses in the plaza and/or 11/22/63 figures connected in some form or fashion to Ruby and/or Oswald: the Newman family, Joe Brehm (who was 5 at the time), Beverly Oliver, Mary Ann Moorman, Linda Willis, Rosemary Willis, Marvin Chism, Rickey Chism, Tina Towner, Sandra Styles, Buell Wesley Frazier, Pierce Allman, Hugh Aynesworth, Johnny Calvin Brewer and Judyth Baker. That very well may be all that are left, not including spectators on Main Street and so forth.

From Parkland Hospital: Dr. Ronald Coy Jones, Dr. Kenneth Salyer, Dr. Robert Grossman, Dr. Richard Dulany, Dr. Philip Williams[3], Dr. Joe D. Goldstrich, Dr. Lito Porto, Dr. Robert Schorlemer, Dr. Harlan Pollock (worked on Oswald), Nurse Diana Bowron, Nurse Phyllis Hall and Nurse Pat Hutton (Gustafson); possibly Dr. Gene Akin and a couple others, as well.

From Bethesda: James Curtis Jenkins, Dr. Robert Karnei, Jan Rudnicki, Richard Lipsey, Gregory Cross; perhaps one or two others, as well.

3   21 H 215; Williams was interviewed for *High Treason 2* (1992); Williams did three oral histories for the Sixth Floor Museum: 5/22/2003, 7/8/2008, and 4/28/16

From the media: in addition to the aforementioned MacNeil, Aynesworth and Allman, Charles Murphy, Darwin Payne, Peggy Simpson, George Phenix, Jerry Richmond, Lawrence Schiller, Bob Schieffer, Bill Mercer[4] and ABC's Bill Lord are still alive; perhaps a couple others.

From the Warren Commission: staff attorneys Howard Willens, Melvin Eisenberg, W. David Slawson and Burt Griffin. Staff member Stuart Pollak and Lloyd Weinreb; maybe a few others. All the main Warren Commission members are long gone.

From the old guard researchers and authors, only Bob Groden (HSCA), Cyril Wecht (HSCA), Robert Tannenbaum (HSCA), G. Robert Blakey (HSCA), Gary Cornwell (HSCA), Larry Sturdivan (HSCA), David Lifton, Peter Dale Scott, Paul Hoch, Wallace Milam and Josiah Thompson are still around (from the HSCA, Andy Purdy, Mark Flanagan, and Eddie Lopez are still with us, as well).

From the Kennedys themselves: Caroline Kennedy is basically it (other than Bobby's kids and cousins). Jackie, Teddy, Bobby, and JFK Jr. are all gone.

I agree with author William Davy's assessment: "There is simply no excuse for not using a 3-pronged approach in JFK research:

> 1. *Interviews:* (Admittedly getting harder with the passage of time and key people dying off).
>
> 2. *The Paper Chase:* (Extremely important in light of the ARRB's work). And yes:
>
> 3. *Secondary sources:* books, magazines, newspapers, etc. (But they better be damned good ones by credible authors)."

I wrote this book as a hard labor of love. My goal was to document everything that points to conspiracy in the assassination of President John F. Kennedy. I had the tremendous advantage of hindsight over many years, as many authors and researchers came before me. I also was able to pull from my previous four books and the many primary subjects I interviewed and corresponded with: Secret Service agents, assassination eyewitnesses, Parkland doctors and nurses, Bethesda technicians, and others. I wanted my book to be the one work people could go to for referencing all notions of conspiracy in the death of JFK.

I feel I have achieved that goal. Ultimately, it us up to you, the reader, to decide.

4   An award-winning broadcast journalist, Mercer is a member of the Texas Radio Hall of Fame. As a broadcaster with KRLD Radio and TV, Mercer reported live from Dallas police headquarters on November 22, 1963. At a midnight press briefing, he was the one to initially inform suspect Lee Harvey Oswald that he had been charged with the president's murder. Mercer has done several Sixth Floor Museum oral histories between 1998 and 2019.

Postscript: The Fall of 2020 saw several recent major television programs rerun on a few cable channels, while there were also two successful virtual conferences held in Dallas (due to COVID-19). Hope always will spring eternal.

In no particular order, my special thanks: to Pat Speer – I really enjoy your website (http://www.patspeer.com/)and your insights on the case evidence; to Jim DiEugenio and Flip de Mey: my two favorite authors; to Harry Livingstone: yes, I am mentioning you again. Thank you for believing in me and requesting my assistance on several research-related items and the journeys that went with them. Being mentioned in *High Treason 2*, the first book that ever mentioned my name (other than the phone book, of course) was quite a thrill. Rest in Peace, Harry; to Robert Groden- you are a brilliant and passionate warrior for the truth; to Matt Douthit: the wunderkind! You are a savant and a genius on the medical evidence; to Willy O'Halloran: like Matt, your youth and interest in this case at this late date is an inspiration; to Judyth Baker – thank you so very much for requesting that I submit my first book manuscript to Trine Day and to inviting us to three conferences – much appreciated; to Kris Millegan: mere words will never express my gratitude – you're awesome; to Barry Ernest: your brilliant book *The Girl on the Stairs* is a game changer; to Jerry Rose – I will always be grateful for inviting me to be a speaker at the first Third Decade conference back when I just turned 25, as well as all the articles of mine that you published in your journal.

Rest in Peace; to George Michael Evica- your ideas about security stripping and a third alternative made me see my Secret Service research from a different perspective. Rest in Peace; to Dr. Cyril Wecht- you are from my hometown and you have been an inspiration. You, sir, are a genius and a brilliant speaker. Your sons are great, too; to John Judge- thank you for inviting me to be a speaker at COPA 1995 and 1996 (and 2013, which I was unable to attend). Rest in Peace; to Jan Stevens – sorry we fell out of touch. I appreciate your friendship and our talks about the case from roughly 1995-2001; to Walt Brown – I still admire you greatly. Your book The Warren Omission is one of my favorites. You are a brilliant, funny, and witty writer. It was an honor to be connected to your journal (with Jan Stevens) *JFK/Deep Politics Quarterly* from roughly 1995-2002. Sorry if you still hold a grudge about my brief 2007-era switch to the dark side. I understand. I wish you all the best; to Deb Conway – thank you so much for all you did for me at JFK Lancer 1997 (inviting me as a speaker, etc.). It was nice seeing you in the plaza in 2016 and again in 2019; to Abraham

Bolden- it is an honor to know you, sir. You are a national treasure and a hero to many; to Robert DeProspero- my favorite Secret Service agent of all time. It was quite a thrill to hear from you out of the blue in 2011 and to occasionally correspond, speak to you, and be a part of the documentary on your life entitled *The Man Behind The Suit*.

Rest in peace; to Mark Lane- you also came out of the blue in 2011, asking for my assistance for your book *Last Word*. It was an honor to be a part of it. Rest in Peace; to former Secret Service agent Dan Emmett: 2011 was a banner year, as you also came out of nowhere to request that I review your book. Thanks for your friendship, insights, and placing my blurb on the original edition of *Within Arm's Length*; to Nigel Turner: it was a pleasure to be a part of *The Men Who Killed Kennedy* (number 7) in 2003 that still airs on Newsmax TV 2019-2020; to Art Van Kampen and Stephen Goetsch, the men behind the *A Coup in Camelot* documentary- what a thrill it is to be a major part of this important film; to Meredith and David Mantik – Meredith, thanks for making me a part of your upcoming documentary. David – it was great seeing you in Dallas in 2019. I greatly respect your writing and thinking on the medical evidence; to William Matson Law: buddy, it was so great meeting you at JFK Lancer 1997 and filming Jerrol Custer, the autopsy x-ray technician from my hometown, in 1998. Your book *In The Eye of History* is brilliant. Thanks for all you (still) do; to David Lifton: it has been an honor corresponding with you via e-mail, off and on, for the past 8 years or so (and I enjoyed our lengthy phone conversations back in 1992); to authors James Douglass and Doug Horne: thank you for your brilliant books and for setting me back on the right track; to Barry Keane: your early Facebook messages and comments back in 2011-2012 kept me going; to Joseph McBride: thanks for the great book; to Jessica Shores and Linda Giovanna Zambanini: two great ladies doing tremendous research! Thanks for all your help; and, last but certainly not least, to you, the reader: I am nothing without you! Thank you so much for your interest and your support.

BIBLIOGRAPHY

(THE MOTHER OF ALL JFK ASSASSINATION BOOK BIBLIOGRAPHIES – 1963-2021)

S imply put, this is the greatest Kennedy assassination book bibliography ever compiled. Enjoy!

Aaronovitch, David. *Voodoo Histories: The Role of the Conspiracy Theory in Shaping Modern History*. Riverhead Books, 2010.

Abrahamsen, David. *A Study of Lee Harvey Oswald: Psychological Capability of Murder*. New York Academy of Medicine, 1967.

Abrams, Dan and David Fisher. *Kennedy's Avenger: Assassination, Conspiracy, and the Forgotten Trial of Jack Ruby*. Hanover Square Press, 2021.

Adams, Chris with Mary Ward. *Dallas: Lone Assassin or Pawn*. iUniverse, 2013.

Adamson, Bruce Campbell. *Oswald's Closest Friend: The George de Mohrenschildt Story*. Santa Cruz, CA: Self-published, 2001.

Adamson, Bruce Campbell. *The JFK Assassination Timeline Chart - 290 pages Large Print (The George de Mohrenschildt 11 volume series)*. Santa Cruz, CA: Self-published, 2012.

Adamson, Bruce Campbell. *Oswald's Closest Friend; The de Mohrenschildt Story - George H.W. Bush ties to Oswald (The George de Mohrenschildt Story Book 1)*. Santa Cruz, CA: Self-published, 2012.

Adamson, Bruce Campbell. *Oswald's Closest Friend; The de Mohrenschildt Story - George H.W. Bush on the Grassy Knoll pt 2 (Oswald's Closest Friend; The George de Mohrenschildt Story part two Book 1)*. Santa Cruz, CA: Self-published, 2012.

Adamson, Bruce Campbell. *Oswald's Closest Friend; The de Mohrenschildt Story - De Mohrenschildt Clears Conscience pt 3 (Oswald's Closest Friend; The George de Mohrenschildt Story Book 1)*. Santa Cruz, CA: Self-published, 2012.

Adamson, Bruce Campbell. *The Very First Cold Warrior: Professor Dimitri Von Mohrenschildt (Oswald's Closest Friend; The George de Mohrenschildt Story Book 4)*. Santa Cruz, CA: Self-published, 2012.

Adamson, Bruce Campbell. *By George: His Haitian Bay was not for Papa Doc Duvalier (Oswald's Closest Friend; The George de Mohrenschildt Story Book 5)*. Santa Cruz, CA: Self-published, 2012.

Adamson, Bruce Campbell. *The Paine Dullles Felt, Must be Let Luce (Oswald's Closest Friend; The George de Mohrenschildt Story Book 6)*. Santa Cruz, CA: Self-published, 2012.

Adamson, Bruce Campbell. *Right Men Going in Wrong Direction (Oswald's Closest Friend; The George de Mohrenschildt Story Book 7)*. Santa Cruz, CA: Self-published, 2012.

Adamson, Bruce Campbell. *Wolfen Communism Without Trotsky and John F. Kennedy (Oswald's Closest Friend; The George de Mohrenschildt Story Book 8)*. Santa Cruz, CA: Self-published, 2012.

Adamson, Bruce Campbell. *Diana, The Queen of Hearts & the CIA/MI6, Prince of Darkness Book 9*. Self-published, 2012.

Adamson, Bruce Campbell. *Adamson Report; Zapruder, Bush & CIA's Dallas Council on World Affairs - vol. X - Part I (Oswald's Closest Friend; The George de Mohrenschildt Story Book 10)*. Santa Cruz, CA: Self-published, 2012.

Adamson, Bruce Campbell. *I Can Not Tell A Lie! George De Mohrenschildt (Nor The Truth) (Oswald's Closest Friend; The George de Mohrenschildt Story Book 11)*. Santa Cruz, CA: Self-published, 2012.

Adamson, Bruce Campbell. *In Camera 50th JFK Assassination Investigation (Oswald's Closest Friend; The George de Mohrenschildt Story Book 12)*. Santa Cruz, CA: Self-published, 2012.

Adamson, Bruce Campbell. *In-Camera Investigation of CIA's Republic National Bank Building ties to Oswald (Oswald's Closest Friend; The George de Mohrenschildt Story Vol.-2-Part-1 Book 2)*. Santa Cruz, CA: Self-published, 2012.

Adamson, Bruce Campbell. *Spanish Fly is Radioactive; In 1966 US dropped 4 H-Bombs on Palomares, Spain (Oswald's Closest Friend; The George de Mohrenschildt Story Book 14)*. Santa Cruz, CA: Self-published, 2012.

Adamson, Bruce Campbell. *Larry Flynt Kills JFK Assassination Article After Offering 1,000,000 Reward (Oswald's Closest Friend; The George de Mohrenschildt Story)*. Santa Cruz, CA: Self-published, 2012.

Adamson, Bruce Campbell. *JFK Assassination Ketch-in Up to H.L. Hunt (A Patsy ?) (vol. 3 Oswald's Closest Friend; The George de Mohrenschildt Story*. Santa Cruz, CA: Self-published, 2012.

Adams, Don. *From an Office Building with a High-Powered Rifle: One FBI Agent's View of the JFK Assassination*. Trine Day, 2012.

Addabbo, Nunzio and Elizabeth. *Target *JFK*: Final Chapter in the Assassination*. Sci-Fi Arizona, Incorporated, 2002.

Adelson, Alan. *The Ruby Oswald Affair*. Seattle: Romar Books, 1988.

Airheart, Steven S. *Searching the Shadows: A Layman's Investigation into the Assassination of John F. Kennedy*. Texas: Shadow Publications, 1993.

Albarelli, H.B. *A Secret Order: Investigating the High Strangeness and Synchronicity in the JFK Assassination*. Trine Day, 2013.

Albarelli, H.B. *Coup in Dallas: Who Killed JFK and Why.* Skyhorse, 2020.

Allen, Graeme J. *JFK and Castro: A Review of the 2017* Release Assassination Files. Amazon, 2017.

Amoroso, Alexandra. *Camelot ... What It Was and How It Ended: The Assassination of John F. Kennedy and Tragedy that Followed.* Independently published, 2019.

Amrine, Michael. *This Awesome Challenge: The Hundred Days of Lyndon Johnson.* New York: Popular Library, 1964.

Andersen, Christopher. *Jackie After Jack: Portrait of the Lady.* Warner Books, 1999.

Anderson, G.L. *What IS the Secret of JFK Assassination? Myths, Theories and Lies of the JFK Assassination.* Amazon, 2013.

Anderson, Lois E. *John F. Kennedy.* CT: Longmeadow Press, 1992.

Angel, Shari with Coke Buchanan. *Runway to Heaven.* Starburst Press, 1996.

Ankeny, Brian C. *Z-Rifle: A Synopsis of the Kennedy Assassination.* B.C. Ankeny, 1985.

Anonymous. *The Man on the Grassy Knoll.* Grey Knight Books, 2011.

Anonymous. *The Press Corps and the Kennedy Assassination.* Association for Education in Journalism, 1970.

Anson, Robert Sam. "They've Killed the President!" *The Search for the Murders of John F. Kennedy.* New York: Bantam Books, 1975.

Anthony, Carl Sferrazza. *The Kennedy White House.* New York: Touchstone, 2001.

Armstrong, John. *Harvey and Lee: How The CIA Framed Oswald.* Quasar, 2003.

Assassination Records Review Board. *The Final Report of the Assassination Records Review Board* (aka ARRB). ARRB, September, 1998.

Association of Former Agents of the United States Secret Service. *Looking Back and Seeing The Future: The United States Secret Service 1865-1990.* Dallas: Taylor Publishing Company, 1991.

Associated Press. *The Torch is Passed.* New York: Associated Press, 1963.

Astucia, Salvador. *Opium Lords : Israel, the Golden Triangle, the Kennedy Assassination.* Amazon, 2015.

Aubrey, Edmund. *Sherlock Holmes in Dallas.* Dodd, Mead & Company, 1980.

Aubrey, Edmund. *The Case of the Murdered President.* Congdon and Weed, 1983.

Ayers, Bradley Earl. *The Zenith Secret: A CIA Insider Exposes the Secret War Against Cuba and the Plots that Killed the Kennedy Brothers.* Drench Kiss Media Corp, 2007.

Aynesworth, Hugh. *JFK: Breaking The News.* Richardson, TX: IFP, 2003.

Aynesworth, Hugh. *November 22, 1963: Witness to History.* Brown Books, 2013.

Ayton, Mel and David Von Pein. *Beyond Reasonable Doubt.* Strategic Media Books, 2014.

Ayton, Mel. *The JFK Assassination: Dispelling The Myths.* UK: Woodfield Publishing, 2002.

Back, Kurt W. *From Bright Ideas To Social Research: The Studies Of The Kennedy Assassination*. PN, 1965.

BACM Research. *John F. Kennedy - Jacqueline Onassis Kennedy White House - Secret Service - CIA - NSA and other Historical Documents*. Amazon, 2018.

Baden, Michael. *Unnatural Death: Confessions of a Medical Examiner*. NY: Ivy Books, 1989.

Badman, Keith. *Marilyn Monroe: The Final Years*. Thomas Dunne Books, 2012.

Baird, Adam. *Volume One: A Happy Alternative to the Kennedy Assassination*. Amazon, 2016.

Baker, Judyth. *David Ferrie*. Trine Day, 2014.

Baker, Judyth. *Kennedy & Oswald: The Big Picture*. Trine Day, 2017.

Baker, Judyth. *Lee Harvey Oswald: The True Story of the Accused Assassin of President John F. Kennedy, by His Lover* (2 Volumes). Trafford, 2006.

Baker, Judyth. *Me & Lee*. Trine Day, 2010.

Baker, Lafayette. *The United States Secret Service in the Late War*. University Press of the Pacific, 2001.

Balverde, Manual. *l'Enquete: OAS. Dans Le Mettre de JFK ?* Independently published, 2019.

Bara, Mike. *Ancient Aliens & JFK: The Race to the Moon and the Kennedy Assassination*. Adventures Unlimited Press, 2018.

Barber, Stephan N. *Double Decker*. Self-published, 1989.

Barbour, John. *Your Mother's Not a Virgin!: The Bumpy Life and Times of the Canadian Dropout who changed the Face of American TV!* Trine Day, 2019.

Barker, Eddie. *Eddie Barker's Notebook*. John M. Hardy Publishing Co., 2006.

Barletta, John R. with Rochelle Schweizer. *Riding With Reagan*. New York: Citadel Presss, 2005.

Bartholomew, Richard. *The Deep State in the Heart of Texas: The Texas Connections to the Kennedy Assassination*. Say Something Real Press, 2018.

Bash, King. *Oswald Missed!!: (and other crackpot Kennedy assassination theories)*. King Bash Company, 2013.

Bauer, Edward. *The Final Truth: Solving the Mystery of the JFK Assassination*. CreateSpace, 2012.

Baughman, U.E. *Secret Service Chief*. New York: Harper & Row, Popular Library edition, January 1963.

Bealle, Morris A. *Guns of the Regressive Right Or How to Kill a President: the Only Reconstruction of the Kennedy Assassination That Makes Sense*. Columbia Publishing Company, 1964.

Becker, Donald. *The JFK Assassination: A Researcher's Guide*. Authorhouse, 2010.

Beckley, Timothy Green. Secret Exploits of Admiral Richard E. Byrd: The Hollow Earth, Nazi Occultism, Secret Societies And The JFK Assassination. Inner Light- Global Communications, 2017.

Beddow, David T. A Ferrie Tale. Archway, 2019.

Belin, David. *Final Disclosure: The Full Truth About the Assassination of President Kennedy*. Scribner, 1988.

Belin, David. *November 22, 1963: You Are The Jury*. Quadrangle/ The New York Times Book Company, 1973.

Belli, Melvin with Maurice Carroll. *Dallas Justice*. New York: David McKay, 1964.

Belsky, R.G. *The Kennedy Connection: A Gil Malloy Novel*. Atria Books, 2014.

Belzer, Richard and David Wayne. *Corporate Conspiracies: How Wall Street Took Over Washington*. Skyhorse, 2017.

Belzer, Richard and David Wayne. *Dead Wrong*. Skyhorse, 2012.

Belzer, Richard and David Wayne. *Dead Wrong 2: Diana, Princess of Wales*. Vigliano, 2013.

Belzer, Richard and David Wayne. *Hit List*. Skyhorse, 2013.

Belzer, Richard. *UFO's, JFK and Elvis: Conspiracies You Don't Have to Be Crazy to Believe*. New York: Ballantine Books, 1999.

Bennett, Arnold. *Jackie, Bobby and Manchester*. Bee-Line Books, 1967.

Benoit, Peter. *The Assassination of John F. Kennedy*. Cornerstones of Freedom, 2013.

Benson, Michael. *Who's Who in the JFK Assassination*. New York: Citadel Press, 1993.

Benson, Michael. *Encyclopedia of the JFK Assassination*. New York: Checkmark Books, 2002.

Berger, Leon. *The Kennedy Trilogy: The Kennedy Imperative, The Kennedy Momentum, and The Kennedy Revelation*. Open Road Media, 2014.

Berney, Lou. *Destination Dallas*. HarperCollins, 2019.

Berney, Lou. *November Road: A Novel*. William Morrow, 2018.

Berry, Wendell. *November Twenty Six Nineteen Hundred Sixty Three*. George Braziller, 1964.

Beschloss, Michael R. *The Crisis Years: Kennedy and Khrushchev, 1960-1963*. HarperCollins, 1991.

Beschloss, Michael R. *Taking Charge: The Johnson White House Tapes, 1963-1964*. New York: Simon & Schuster, 1997.

Beschloss, Michael R. *Reaching For Glory: Lyndon Johnson's Secret White House Tapes, 1964-1965*. New York: Simon & Schuster, 2002.

Beschloss, Steven. *The Gunman and His Mother: Lee Harvey Oswald, Marguerite Oswald, and the Making of an Assassin*. Independently published, 2013.

Bevilaqua, John. *JFK - The Final Solution: Red Scares, White Power and Blue Death: Dawn Phase Fascism*. CreateSpace, 2013.

Beyer, Mark. *High Interest Books: Secret Service. Children's Press*, a Division of Scholastic Incorporated, 2003.

Biel, Joe. *The CIA Makes Sci Fi Unexciting: The Life of Lee Harvey Oswald*. Microcosm Publishing, 2011.

Biles, Joe G. *In History's Shadow: Lee Harvey Oswald, Kerry Thornley & the Garrison Investigation.* iUniverse, 2002.

Biographiq. *Lee Harvey Oswald - Portrait of a Presidential Assassin.* Biographiq, 2008.

Bishop, Jim. *The Day Kennedy Was Shot.* New York: Harper Perennial edition, 1992.

Blaine, Gerald and Lisa McCubbin. *The Kennedy Detail.* New York: Simon & Schuster, 2010

Blakey, G. Robert. *Fatal Hour.* Berkeley, 1992.

Blakey, G. Robert. *The Plot to Kill the President.* Times Books, 1981.

Blare, Erik. *The Oswald Book.* Xlibris, 2008.

Blevins, Leroy. *Evidence of a Conspiracy.* CreateSpace, 2016.

Blevins, Leroy. *JFK Assassins.* CreateSpace, 2018.

Blevins, Leroy. *JFK Assassination Evidence of Other Gunmen.* CreateSpace, 2014.

Blevins, Leroy. *The JFK Assassination Report: 13 Shots.* CreateSpace, 2014.

Blevins, Leroy. *JFK Assassination Colorized Images.* CreateSpace, 2014.

Blevins, Leroy. *Who Murdered JFK?* CreateSpace, 2014.

Blevins, Leroy. *Dallas TX Nov 22,1963 & 12:30 PM.* CreateSpace, 2015.

Blevins, Leroy. *Evidence Files: Case Closed.* CreateSpace, 2015.

Blight, James and Janet M. Lang, David A. Welch, editors. *Virtual JFK: Vietnam if Kennedy had Lived.* Lanham, MD: Bowman and Litchfield Publishers, 2009.

Bloomgarden, Henry S. *The Gun: A "Biography" of the Gun That Killed John F. Kennedy.* New York: Grossman Publishers, 1975.

Blumenthal, Sid and Harvey Yazijian, Editors. *Government by Gunplay: Assassination Conspiracy Theories from Dallas to Today.* New York: Signet, 976.

Bockris, Victor. *Keith Richards: The Biography.* Da Capo Press, 1998.

Bojczuk, Jeremy. *22 November 1963: A Brief Guide to the JFK Assassination.* Boxgrove Publishing, 2014.

Bolden, Abraham. *The Echo From Dealey Plaza.* Crown, 2008.

Bolden, Abraham. *Nothing But A Nig*er: The resurrection of judicial injustices committed against Dred Scott.* Independently published, 2018.

Bond, Brandon David. *Eternal November: The Assassination of John F. Kennedy.* CreateSpace, 2016.

Bonner, Judy. *Investigation of a Homicide: The Murder of John F. Kennedy.* Anderson, S.C. Droke House (distributed by Grosset and Dunlap), 1969.

Bookrags. *Summary & Study Guide Case Closed: Lee Harvey Oswald and the Assassination of JFK by Gerald Posner.* Amazon, 2011.

Bowen, Walter S. & Harry E. Neal. *The United States Secret Service.* Philadelphia: Chilton Company and Book Division Publishers, 1960.

Bowles, J.C. *The Kennedy Assassination Tapes.* Dallas, TX: self-published, 1979..

Bowman, David. *The JFK Assassination: The Darkest Agenda.* Vaga Books, 2014.

Boyd, John W. *Parkland Hospital.* Arcadia Publishing, 2015.

Brady, Derek. *Conspiracy Theories: A Stunning Look At The Worlds Conspiracy Theories: Area 51, 9/11, The JFK Assassination, Aliens, Cover Ups, Corrupt Governments And More* (Volume 1). CreateSpace, 2016.

Brandt, Charles. *I Heard You Paint Houses: Frank The Irishman Sheeran and the Inside Story of the Mafia, the Teamsters, and the Final Ride of Jimmy Hoffa.* Steerforth, 2004.

Braver, Adam. *November 22, 1963: A Novel.* Tin House Books, 2008.

Braxton, C. Fenway. *Foibles and Follies: My Year Stumbling Through the Undergrowth that is the Quagmire called the JFK Research Community.* Martian Publishing, 2015.

Braxton, C. Fenway. *The Plot to Kill Lee Harvey Oswald.* CreateSpace, 2014.

Brener, Milton E. *The Garrison Case: A Study in the Abuse of Power.* New York: Clarkson N. Potter, 1969.

Brennan, Howard L. with J. Edward Cherryholmes. *Eyewitness to History: The Kennedy Assassination as Seen by Howard L. Brennan.* Waco, TX: Texian Press, 1987.

Brenner, Randy. *Swan Song for El Caballo.* Press Club Publishing, 2013.

Bridger, Mark and Barry Keane. *JFK: Echoes from Elm Street.* Liverpool Academic Press, 2013.

Bringuier, Carlos. *Red Friday: November 22nd 1963.* Chicago, Illinois: Charles Hallberg & Co., 1969.

Bringuier, Carlos. *Crime Without Punishment: How Castro Assassinated President Kennedy and Got Away with It.* Authorhouse, 2013.

Brinkley, Howard. *The Next 30 Days: How a Nation Rebuilt in the 30 Days Following the Death of JFK.* CreateSpace, 2013.

Brode, Douglas: *Patsy: The Life and Times of Lee Harvey Oswald.* Sunbury Press, 2013.

Brooks, Stewart M. *Our Assassinated Presidents: The True Medical Stories.* Random House, 1986.

Brottman, Mikita. *Car Crash Culture.* New York: Palgrave, 2001.

Brown, Madeleine. *Texas in the Morning: The Love Story of Madeleine Brown and President Lyndon Johnson.* Baltimore: Conservatory Press, 1997.

Brown, Pamela. *Inside 'Inside the Target Car': Behind the scenes of the development of the 2008 Discovery Channel program with its limo expert.* Amazon, 2019.

Brown, Pamela. *Midnight Blue to Black: the vanishing act of the JFK Presidential Assassination Limousine SS100X in broad daylight.* Amazon, 2018.

Brown, Ray "Tex" and Don Lasseter. *Broken Silence: The Truth About Lee Harvey Oswald, LBJ and the Assassination of JFK.* New York: Pinnacle Books, 1996.

Brown, Walt. *Judyth Vary Baker- in Her Own Words.* Campania Partners, LLC, 2019.

Brown, Walt. *Master Chronology of JFK Assassination: Read Me.* Vigiliano Books, 2013.

Brown, Walt. *Master Chronology of JFK Assassination Book I: Dynasty.* Vigiliano Books, 2013.

Brown, Walt. *Master Chronology of JFK Assassination Book II: Death.* Vigiliano Books, 2013.

Brown, Walt. *Master Chronology of JFK Assassination Book III: Disappointment.* Vigiliano Books, 2013.

Brown, Walt. *Master Chronology of JFK Assassination Book IV: Discovery.* Vigiliano Books, 2013.

Brown, Walt. *Master Chronology of JFK Assassination Appendix I: JFK's Speeches.* Vigiliano Books, 2013.

Brown, Walt. *Master Chronology of JFK Assassination Appendix II: Marina Oswald* (Annotated). Vigiliano Books, 2013.

Brown, Walt. *Master Chronology of JFK Assassination Appendix III: Characterizations.* Vigiliano Books, 2013.

Brown, Walt. *Master Chronology of JFK Assassination Appendix IV: Odyssey.* Vigiliano Books, 2013.

Brown, Walt. Master *Chronology of JFK Assassination Appendix V: The Assassination Parables.* Vigiliano Books, 2013.

Brown, Walt. *Master Chronology of JFK Assassination Appendix VI: The Medical, In Their Own Words.* Vigiliano Books, 2013.

Brown, Walt. *Master Chronology of JFK Assassination Appendix VII: Cuba* (Annotated). Vigiliano Books, 2013.

Brown, Walt. *Master Chronology of JFK Assassination Appendix VIII: The Investigators* (Annotated). Vigiliano Books, 2013.

Brown, Walt. *Master Chronology of JFK Assassination Appendix IX: Organized Crime* (Annotated). Vigiliano Books, 2013.

Brown, Walt. *Master Chronology of JFK Assassination Appendix X: "Facts."* Vigiliano Books, 2013.

Brown, Walt. *Master Chronology of JFK Assassination Appendix XI: Motorcade Participants* (Annotated). Vigiliano Books, 2013.

Brown, Walt. *Master Chronology of JFK Assassination Appendix XII: Secret Service Perceptions* (Annotated). Vigiliano Books, 2013.

Brown, Walt. *Master Chronology of JFK Assassination Appendix XIII: Jack Ruby.* Vigiliano Books, 2013.

Brown, Walt. *Master Chronology of JFK Assassination Appendix XIV: The U-2.* Vigiliano Books, 2013.

Brown, Walt. *Master Chronology of JFK Assassination Appendix XV: Dealey Plaza Eyewitnesses* (Annotated). Vigiliano Books, 2013.

Brown, Walt. *The JFK Assassination Quiz Book.* Santa Barbara, CA: Open Archive Press, 1995.

Brown, Walt. *Treachery in Dallas.* New York: Carroll & Graf, 1995.

Brown, Walt. *Referenced Index Guide To The Warren Commission.* Delaware: Delmax, 1995.

Brown, Walt. *The Warren Omission.* Delaware: Delmax, 1996.

Brown, Walt. *The Global Index to the Assassination of JFK.* 1998; CD-ROM.

Brown, Walt. *The Guns Of Texas Are Upon You.* PA: Last Hurrah Press, 2005.

Brown, Walt. *The People V. Lee Harvey Oswald.* Carroll and Graf, 1992.

Bruno, Jerry & Jeff Greenfield. *The Advance Man.* New York: Bantam Books, 1971.

Brussell, Mae. *A Mae Brussell Reader.* Santa Barbara, CA: Prevailing Winds Research, 1991.

Brussell, Mae, compiler. *The Last Words of Lee Harvey Oswald.* On pages 47-52 in Wallechinsky, David and Irving Wallace. *The People's Almanac #2.* New York: Bantam Books, 1978.

Buchanan, Thomas. *Who Killed Kennedy?* New York: G.P. Putnam, 1964.

Bugge, Brian. *The Mystique of Conspiracy: Oswald, Castro, and the CIA.* Provocative Ideas, 2007.

Bugliosi, Vincent. *Four Days in November.* W. W. Norton & Company, 2008.

Bugliosi, Vincent. *Parkland.* W. W. Norton & Company, 2013.

Bugliosi, Vincent. *Reclaiming History: The Assassination of President John F. Kennedy.* W. W. Norton & Company, 2007.

Burgess, J.A. *The Shot: A Photographer's Story.* Archway Publishing, 2016.

Burleigh, Nina. *A Very Private Woman: The Life and Unsolved Murder of Presidential Mistress Mary Meyer.* New York: Bantam Books, 1998.

Burnside, Robert Schramm. *JFK and the World Oligarchy: When "Enough is Never Enough."* CreateSpace, 2012.

Businessnews Publishing. *Summary: The Kennedy Assassination - 24 Hours After: Review and Analysis of Steven M. Gillon's Book.* Political Book Summaries, 2017.

Butler, Maurice. *Out From The Shadow: The Story of Charles L. Gittens Who Broke the Color Barrier in the United States Secret Service.* Xlibris, 2012.

Buyer, Richard. *Why the JFK Assassination* Still Matters. Wheatmark, 2009.

Byrne, Gary. *Secrets of the Secret Service.* Center Street, 2018.

Cabell, Craig. *From Assassination to Extermination Craig Cabell: The John F Kennedy and Doctor Who Book Launch Speech.* Bellack Productions, 2014.

Cabell, Craig. *Killing Kennedy.* John Blake, 2013.

Cabell, Craig. *The Last Shot in Dealey Plaza.* Independently published, 2017.

Cabell, Craig. *Operation 40 and the Big Event.* Independently published, 2017.

Calder, Michael. *JFK vs. CIA: Central Intelligence Agency's Assassination of the President.* Los Angeles, California: West LA Publishers, 1998.

Callahan, Bob. *Who Shot JFK? A Guide to the Major Conspiracy Theories.* New York: Simon & Schuster, 1993.

Cameron, Steve. *The Deputy Interviews: The True Story of J.F.K. Assassination Witness, and Former Dallas Deputy Sheriff, Roger Dean Craig.* Self-published, 2019.

Canal, John. *Silencing the Lone Assassin: The Murders of JFK and Lee Harvey Oswald*. St. Paul, MN: Paragon House, 2000.

Carey, Charles W. *Interpreting Primary Documents – The Kennedy Assassination*. Greenhaven Press, 2004.

Carley, Steven G. *The Case of Jack Ruby*. SGC Production, 2013.

Carlier, Francois. *Elm Street: Oswald A Tue Kennedy!* Publibook, 2008.

Caro, Robert A. *The Path to Power: The Years of Lyndon Johnson I*. Knopf, 1982

Caro, Robert A. *Means of Ascent: The Years of Lyndon Johnson II*. Knopf, 1990.

Caro, Robert A. *Master of the Senate: The Years of Lyndon Johnson III*. Knopf, 2002.

Caro, Robert A. *The Passage of Power: The Years of Lyndon Johnson IV*. Knopf, 2012.

Carpenter, Donald H. *Man of a Million Fragments: The True Story of Clay Shaw*. Donald H. Carpenter LLC, 2014.

Carr, Waggoner. *Texas Supplemental Report on the Assassination of President John F. Kennedy and the Serious Wounding of Governor John B. Connally 11/22/63*. Texas, 1964.

Carr, William H. *JFK: The Life and Death of a President*. New York: Lancer Books, 1964.

Carr, William H. *JFK: A Complete Biography 1917-1963*. Magnum Easy Eye Books, 1968.

Carter, Bill. *Get Carter: Backstage in History from JFK's Assassination to the Rolling Stones*. Fine's Creek Publishing, LLC, 2005.

Carter, Jacob. *Before History Dies*. WordCrafts Press, 2015.

Carter, Jacob. *The Table of Truth: An Autopsy of the JFK Research Community*. WordCrafts Press, 2018.

Carter, Jamie. *Lee*. Amazon, 2014.

Cassard, J. Philippe. *The JFK Assassination Facts They Don't Want You to Know*. Self-published, 2019.

Caufield, Jeffrey H. *General Walker and the Murder of President Kennedy: The Extensive New Evidence of a Radical-Right Conspiracy*. Moreland Press, 2015.

Cellura, Frank A. *The Last Nail in the Warren Commission Coffin: Startling Revelations in the Assassination of President Kennedy*. Outskirts Press, 2015.

Cellura, Frank A. *Perpetual Cover-Up: President John F. Kennedy's Assassination Mystery*. Outskirts Press, 2018.

Chaidez, Larry. *Bibliography of the Life and Assassination of President John F. Kennedy*. Self-published, 1985.

Chambers, P.G. *Head Shot: The Science Behind the JFK Assassination*. New York: Amherst, 2010.

Chandler, Chris. *Myths of the JFK Assassination*. The World & I, 2012.

Chapman, Gil and Ann. *Was Oswald Alone?* San Diego: Publishers Export Co, 1967

Charnin, Richard. *Reclaiming Science: The JFK Conspiracy*. CreateSpace, 2014.

Chase, Bridget. *American Orgasm: Variant Action Satire Cover*. Chase Entertainment, 2018.

Cheever, Susan. *Drinking In America: Our Secret History*. Twelve, 2015.

Chepesiuk, Ron. *The Trafficantes, Godfathers from Tampa, Florida: The Mafia, the CIA and the JFK Assassination*. Spurlock Photography, 2010.

Childs, Allen. *We Were There: Revelations from the Dallas Doctors Who Attended to JFK on November 22, 1963*. Skyhorse, 2013.

Christensen, R. A *Preliminary Analysis of Some of the Pictures of the Kennedy Assassination*. Self-published, 1967.

Cirignano, Douglas. *American Conspiracies and Cover-ups: JFK, 9/11, the Fed, Rigged Elections, Suppressed Cancer Cures, and the Greatest Conspiracies of Our Time*. Skyhorse, 2019.

Clarence, John. *The Gold House – The Discovery: Book One of the Gold House Trilogy*. Soledad Publishing, 2013.

Clark, Champ. *The Assassination: Death of the President*. Alexandria, VA: Time-Life Books, 1987.

Clark, Hugh and William Matson Law. *Betrayal: A JFK Honor Guard Speaks*. Trine Day, 2016.

Clarke, James W. *Americans Assassins: The Darker Side of Politics*. Princeton University Press, 1982.

Clarke, James W. *Defining Danger: American Assassins and the New Domestic Terrorists*. Transaction Publishers, 2006.

Cochran, Brian. *JFK Assassination: The story of the USA president who Lead the White House. The biography of John F. Kennedy and His History*. Independently published, 2020.

Colby, C.B. *Secret Service: History, Duties, and Equipment*. New York: Coward-McCann, Inc., 1966.

Coleman, Phil. *Inside Camelot: The True Story of the Assassination of JFK*. Independently published, 2017.

Collins, Mark. *Lee Harvey Oswald: A Biography*. CreateSpace, 2018.

Collins, Max Allan. *In The Line of Fire*. New York: Jove Books, 1993. (based on the screenplay written by Jeff Maguire).

Collins, Max Allan. *Target Lancer*. Forge Books, 2012.

Collins, MJ. *An Umbrella of Lies: The Discovery of a Covert Cameraman During the JFK Assassination*. Self-published, 2019.

Collins, Terry Lee and Li Yishan. *The Assassination of John F. Kennedy: November 22, 1963 (24-Hour History)*. Heinemann, 2014.

Conifer, Dave. *Man of Steel* (Cold Cases Book 1). CreateSpace, 2010.

Coniuratio, Max. *A Layperson Looks At The JFK Assassination*. Null, 2010.

Connally, John. *In History's Shadow: An American Odyssey*. Hyperion Press, 1999.

Connally, Nellie. *From Love Field: Our Final Hours with President John F. Kennedy*. New York: Rugged Land, 2003.

Connelly, Michael. *The President's Team: The 1963 Army-Navy Game and the Assassination of JFK*. MVP Books, 2009.

Connors, Nancy Evans. *Grassy Knoll*. Inspired Forever Books, 2018.

Cook, Monte. *The Skeptic's Guide to Conspiracies: From the Knights Templar to the JFK Assassination: Uncovering the [Real] Truth Behind the World's Most Controversial Conspiracy Theories*. Adams Media, 2009.

Cooper, Milton William. *Beyond a Pale Horse*. Sedona, AZ: Light Technology, 1991.

Coppens, Philip. *Killing Kennedy: Uncovering the Truth Behind the Kennedy Assassination*. Amazon, 2012.

Corbett, Frank. *John Kennedy Assassination Film Analysis*. Itek Corporation, 1976.

Corbett, Jacob. *The Kennedy Assassination Handbook: All New Revelations! 50 Years of Investigation!* CreateSpace, 2013.

Cornell, Bob. *Where Were You? The Assassination of JFK*. Amazon, 2015.

Cornwell, Gary. *Real Answers*. Spicewood, Texas: Paleface Press, 1998.

Corry, John. *The Manchester Affair*. G.P. Putnam's Sons, 1967.

Corsi, Jerome. *Who Really Killed Kennedy?: 50 Years Later: Stunning New Revelations About the JFK Assassination*. WND Books, 2013.

Counterfit, Johnny. *JFK – Averting the Assassination*. Self-published, 2016.

Cox, Alex. *The President and the Provocateur: The Parallel Lives of JFK and Lee Harvey Oswald*. Feral House, 2013.

Craig, John R. and Philip A. Rogers. *The Man on the Grassy Knoll*. New York: Avon Books, 1992.

Craig, John S.. *The Guns of Dealey Plaza – Weapons and the Kennedy Assassination*. Lulu, 2016.

Craig, Roger. *When They Kill A President*. Self-published, 1971; reissued 2020.

Crawford, Kempton, Packer, Lane, Nash, Buchanan. *Critical Reactions to the Warren Report*. Marzani & Munsell, 1964.

Crawley, John. *The Man on the Grassy Knoll*. Lulu, 2011.

Crenshaw, Charles A. with J. Gary Shaw, and Jens Hansen. *JFK: Conspiracy of Silence*. New York: Signet, 1992.

Crenshaw, Charles A. with J. Gary Shaw, and Jens Hansen. *JFK Has Been Shot*. Pinnacle, 2013.

Crenshaw, Charles A. with J. Gary Shaw, D. Bradley Kizzia, J.D., Gary Aguilar, M.D., and Cyril Wecht, M.D., J.D. *Trauma Room One*. New York: Paraview Press, 2001.

Cross, Richard. *Lee Harvey Oswald: A Rogue KGB Agent*. CreateSpace, 2015.

Cross, Richard. *The Overlooked Letters: The Kennedy Assassination*. Outskirts Press, 2013.

Culver, Andrew. A Crafty Madness: The Tragedies of Lee Harvey Oswald, Sirhan Sirhan, and Syed Farook. Independently published, 2019.

Culver, Andrew. *Oswald's Odyssey: Two Hours in Dallas*. Independently published, 2017.

Culver, Andrew. *The Grassy Knoll: A Novel*. Independently published, 2019.

Cunniff, Albert B. *JFK Assassination: Nothing But the Truth*. Books Unlimited, 1994.

Curington, John. *H.L. Hunt: Motive & Opportunity*. 23 House, 2018.

Curry, Jesse. *JFK Assassination File*. Dallas: American Poster & Publishing Co., 1969.

Cutler, Robert. *Goodnight Mr. Callabash*. GKG Partners, 1991.

Cutler, Robert. *The Umbrella Man*. Beverly Farms, MA: Self-published, 1975.

Dallas Morning News. *JFK Assassination: The Reporters' Notes*. Pediment Publishing, 2013.

Dallek, Robert. *JFK: An Unfinished Life*. Back Bay Books, 2003.

Dane, Stan. *Prayer Man*. Martian Publishing, 2015.

Dankbaar, Wim. *Files on JFK: Interviews with Confessed Assassin James E. Files, and More New Evidence of the Conspiracy that Killed JFK*. JFKMurderSolved, 2008.

D'Arc, Joan. *Conspiracy Reader: From the Deaths of JFK and John Lennon to Government-Sponsored Alien Cover-Ups*. Skyhorse, 2012.

Davenport, Ken. *The Two Gates*. CreateSpace, 2017.

David, Jay. *The Weight of The Evidence: The Warren Report & Its Critics*. Meredith, 1968.

Davies, Col. *Named! The Master Spy and Hitmen Who Shot JFK*. Melbourne, Australia: Bookman Press, 1993.

Davis, John. *Kennedy Contract*. Harper Mass Market Paperbacks, 1993.

Davis, John. *Mafia Kingfish: Carlos Marcello and the Assassination of John F. Kennedy*. McGraw-Hill, 1988.

Davis, John. *The Kennedys: Dynasty and Disaster*. New York: S.P.I. Books, 1984.

Davis, Mike. *The JFK Assassination Evidence Handbook: Issues, Evidence & Answers*. Independently Published, 2018.

Davis, Mike. *The JFK Assassination Witness Index*. Independently published, 2018.

Davis, Renee K. *Marina Oswald: Was the Heat On?* Unknown Binding, 1984.

Davis, Ronald J. *Murdered By The Invisible Hand: The Silent Conspiracy Of Death!* CreateSpace, 2016.

Davis, Steve B. *Near Miss: The Attempted Assassination of JFK*. Lulu, 2014.

Davison, Jean. *Oswald's Game*. New York: W.W. Norton & Co, 1983

Davy, William. *Let Justice Be Done: New light on the Jim Garrison Investigation*. Jordan Publishing, 1999.

Davy, William. *Through The Looking Glass: The Mysterious World of Clay Shaw*. Self-published, 1995.

Dean, Jeanie S. *The Whole World Stopped: An Elegy for John F. Kennedy and the American Dream*. Primativa Press, 2013.

Debrosse, Jim. *See No Evil: The JFK Assassination and the U.S. Media*. Trine Day, 2018.

DeCuir, Randy. *Cousin Lee: The roots of Lee Harvey Oswald*. CreateSpace, 2013.

Deeb, Michael J. and Robert Lockwood Mills. *The Kennedy Assassination: Was Oswald the Only Assassin?* CreateSpace, 2014.

Deeb, Michael J. and Robert Lockwood Mills. *The Kennedy Assassination : Vol II: Who Really Killed JFK* (Volume 2). CreateSpace, 2015.

Degrilla, Sean R. *Malcontent: Lee Harvey Oswald's Confession* by Conduct. Neely Street Press, 2019.

Deibel, Mike. *The 22nd of November*. CreateSpace, 2015.

DeLillo, Don. *Libra*. Viking, 1988.

DeLoria, Robin T. *Mirror of Doubt*. Pittsburgh, Pennsylvania: Dorrance Publishing, 1993.

De Mey, Flip. *Cold Case Kennedy*. Lannoo, 2013.

De Mey, Flip. *The Lee Harvey Oswald Files*. Lannoo, 2016.

De Mohrenschildt, George. *"I Am a Patsy!": My Contact With Lee Harvey Oswald, The Warren Commission, and The JFK Assassination Conspiracy*. CreateSpace, 1983.

De Mohrenschildt, George. *Lee Harvey Oswald as I Knew Him*. University Press of Kansas, 2014.

Dempsey, John Mark. *The Jack Ruby Trial Revisited: The Diary of Jury Foreman Max Causey*.Denton: University of North Texas Press, 2000.

Dempsey, William E. *Revenge at Dealey Plaza*. CreateSpace, 2016.

Denson, Robert B. *Destiny in Dallas*. Dallas: Denco Corporation, 1964.

De Oca, J. Saenz. *Michel Victor Mertz: El francés que asesinó a John Fitzgerald Kennedy*. Independently published, 2018.

Desantis, Gary. *The 6th Floor*. Lulu, 2013.

Desocio, Richard James. *Clash of Dynasties: Why Gov. Nelson Rockefeller Killed JFK, RFK, and Ordered the Watergate Break-In to End the Presidential Hopes of Ted Kennedy*. Authorhouse, 2017.

Desocio, Richard James. *Rockefellerocracy: Kennedy Assassinations, Watergate and Monopoly of the Philanthropic Foundations*. AuthorHouse, 2013.

De Varona, Frank. *Cuba, the Bay of Pigs, the Kennedy Assassination, the Vatican, and the New World Order*. Independently published, 2018.

Dexter, Sean. *Maggie's Drawers: The JFK Assassination*. Amazon, 2012.

Dherbier,Yann-Brice & Pierre-Henri Verlhac. *John Fitzgerald Kennedy: A Life In Pictures*. New York: Phaidon Press, 2003.

Dickason, Anita. *JFK Assassination Eyewitness: Rush to Conspiracy: The Real Facts of Lee Bowers' Death*. Archway Publishing, 2013.

DiEugenio, James. *Destiny Betrayed*. Sheridan Square Press, 1992; Skyhorse, 2012.

DiEugenio, James and Lisa Pease, editors. *The Assassinations: Probe Magazine on JFK, MLK, RFK, and Malcolm X*. Los Angeles, CA: Feral House, 2003.

DiEugenio, James. *Reclaiming Parkland*. Skyhorse, 2013.

DiEugenio, James. *The JFK Assassination*. Skyhorse, 2018.

Donnelly, Judy. *Who Shot the President? The Death of John F. Kennedy*. Random House, 1988.

Donovan, Robert J. *The Assassins*. New York: Popular Library, 1962.

Dorff, Robert. *22 Days Hath November*. Bob Dorff Books, 2007.

Dorman, Michael. *The Secret Service Story*. New York: Dell Publishing, 1967.

Douglas, Gregory. *Regicide: The Official Assassination of John F. Kennedy*. Monte Sano Media, 2002.

Douglass, James. *JFK and the Unspeakable*. Touchstone, 2010.

Downs, Lindsay. *A Conspiracy Uncovered*. Amazon, 2020.

Driskell, Chuck. *Fringe Theory: A Novel*. Independently published, 2018.

Duffy, Jack. *The Man From 2063*. Tate Publishing, 2012.

Duffy, James P. & Vincent L. Ricci. *A Complete Book of Facts*. New York: Thunder's Mouth Press, 1992.

Duffy, James R. *A Hit Waiting to Happen*. Full Court Press, 2013.

Duffy, James R. *Conspiracy: Who Killed Kennedy?* New York: S.P.I. Books, 1992.

Duffy, James R. *Lone Crazed Gunman?* The Full Court Press, 2004.

Dufour, Francois. *The Assassination of JFK*. KatouMalou, 2013.

Durr, Frank R. *In the Shadow of the Sphinx: A New Look into the Bay of Pigs and JFK Assassination*. Xlibris, 2007.

Eachus, Irving. *The Men from the Grassy Knoll*. CreateSpace, 2013.

Eaves, Richard Wayne. *The Girl Who Shot JFK*. Independently published, 2019.

Eddowes, Michael. *Khrushchev Killed Kennedy*. Dallas: Self-published, 1975.

Eddowes, Michael. *Lee Harvey Oswald: Report on the Activities of an Imposter who Assassinated President John F. Kennedy*. Self-published, 1978.

Eddowes, Michael. *November 22, How They Killed Kennedy*. London: Neville Spearman Ltd., 1976.

Eddowes, Michael. *The Oswald File*. New York: Clarkson N. Potter, 1977.

Edwards, Sue Bradford. *The Assassination of John F. Kennedy*. Essential Library, 2019.

Elliott, Todd C. *A Rose By Many Other Names: Rose Cherami and the JFK Assassination*. Trine Day, 2013.

Emmett, Dan. *I Am A Secret Service Agent: My Life Spent Protecting The President*. St. Martin's Press Griffin, 2017.

Emmett, Dan. *Within Arm's Length*. California: IUniverse, 2012; St. Martin's Press, 2014.

Endicott, Michael. *Walking With Presidents: Stories From Inside The Perimeter*. BookSurge Publishing, 2009.

Engdahl, Sylvia. *The John F. Kennedy Assassination* (Perspectives on Modern World History). Greenhaven Press, 2010.

Epstein, Edward Jay. *Counterplot.* New York: Viking Books, 1969.

Epstein, Edward Jay. *Inquest: The Warren Commission and the Establishment of Truth.* Viking, 1966.

Epstein, Edward Jay. *Jim Garrison's Game: An EJE Original.* EJE Publications, 2011.

Epstein, Edward Jay. *Legend: The Secret World of Lee Harvey Oswald.* McGraw-Hill, 1978.

Epstein, Edward Jay. *Sixty Versions of the Kennedy Assassination: A Primer on Conspiracy Theories.* CreateSpace, 2013.

Epstein, Edward Jay. *The Assassination Chronicles.* New York: Carroll & Graf, 1992.

Epstein, Edward Jay. *The JFK Assassination Diary: My Search For Answers to the Mystery of the Century.* CreateSpace, 2013.

Ernest, Barry. *The Girl on the Stairs.* Pelican, 2013.

Escalante, Fabian. *The Cuba Project: CIA Covert Operations 1959-1962.* Melbourne, Australia: Ocean Press, 2004.

Escalante, Fabian. *JFK: The Cuba Files: The Untold Story of the Plot to Kill Kennedy.* Ocean Press, 2006.

Evans, Marshal. *JFK: The Reckoning.* Self-published, 2018.

Evans, Monte. *The Rather Narrative : Is Dan Rather the JFK Conspiracy's San Andreas Fault?* Self-published, 1990.

Evans, Peter. *Nemesis: The True Story of Aristotle Onassis, Jackie O, and the Love Triangle That Brought Down the Kennedys.* William Morrow, 2004.

Evica, George Michael. *A Certain Arrogance: The Sacrificing of Lee Harvey Oswald and the Wartime Manipulation of Religious Groups by U.S. Intelligence.* Trine Day, 2011.

Evica, George Michael. *And We Are All Mortal: New Evidence and Analysis in the John F. Kennedy Assassination.* West Hartford, CT: University of Hartford, 1978.

Exner, Judith. *My Story (as told to Ovid Demaris).* New York: Grove, 1977.

Fagin, Stephen. *Assassination and Commemoration: JFK, Dallas, and The Sixth Floor Museum at Dealey Plaza.* University of Oklahoma Press, 2013.

Fairchild, Wayne. *Innocence of Oswald and the JFK Assassins.* Research Publications, 1998.

Fairchild, Wayne. *Suppressed Facts in the JFK Assassination.* Research Publications, LLC, 2017.

Fannin, Gary. *The Innocence of Oswald – 50+ Years of Lies, Deception & Deceit in the Murders of President John F. Kennedy & Officer J.D. Tippit.* Self-published, 2015.

Farrell, Joseph P. *LBJ and the Conspiracy to Kill Kennedy: A Coalescence of Interests.* Adventures Unlimited Press, 2011.

Feinman, Roger Bruce. *Between the Signal and the Noise.* Self-published, 1993.

Felder, James. *Dealey Plaza Visitors Guide. (Conspiracy: Fact or Fiction?)* Grassy Knoll Press, 2003.

Feldman, Harold. *Fifty-One Witnesses: The Grassy Knoll.* San Francisco: Idlewild Publishers, 1965.

Fenster, Mark. *Conspiracy Theories: Secrecy and Power in American Culture.* Minneapolis: University of Minnesota Press, 1999.

Fensterwald, Bernard Jr. *Coincidence or Conspiracy?* New York: Zebra Books, 1977.

Fetzer, James. *Assassination Science.* Chicago: Catfeet Press, 1998.

Fetzer, James. *Murder In Dealey Plaza.* Chicago: Catfeet Press, 2000.

Fetzer, James. *The Great Zapruder Film Hoax.* Chicago: Catfeet Press, 2003.

Fetzer, James. *JFK – Who, How, and Why: Solving the World's Greatest Murder Mystery.* Moon Rock Books, 2017.

Fiester, Sherry. *Enemy of the Truth: Myths, Forensics, and the Kennedy Assassination.* JFK Lancer, 2012.

Fischer, David. *Lee Harvey Oswald: What the Government Knew.* CreateSpace, 2014.

Fitton, Robert P. 1963 *Chapter 75: What Really Happened in Dealey Plaza.* Independently published, 2017.

Fitton, Robert P. *Return to Dallas.* Fitton Books, 2020.

Fitton, Robert P. *Spying on Lee Harvey Oswald and the Plot to Kill President Kennedy.* Fitton Books, 2016.

Fitzgerald, L.D.C. *I'm Just a Patsy! Lee Harvey Oswald In His Own Words.* Ursa Minor Publishing, 2012.

Fitzpatrick, Ellen. *Letters to Jackie: Condolences from a Grieving Nation.* Ecco, 2010.

Fitzpatrick, Jay. *The Patsy.* Hard Pressed, 2017.

Flammonde, Paris. *The Kennedy Conspiracy.* New York: Meredith Press, 1969; *later expanded and updated as Assassination of America. The Kennedy's Coup d'Etat. The End of an Era, and Examination of the Jim Garrison Investigations, and the Effects on the Growing Totalitarianism in the Expanding Hegemonic American Empire,* 2006.

Fleming, Glenn B. *S-172: Lee Harvey Oswald's Links to Intelligence Agencies.* Empire Publications, 2013.

Fleming, Glenn B. *The Two Faces of Lee Harvey Oswald: A Tale of Deception, Betrayal, and Murder.* UK: Empire Books, 2003.

Fleming, Tim. *JFK and the End of America: Inside the Allen Dulles/LBJ Plot That Killed Kennedy.* Strategic Book Publishing, 2018.

Fonzi, Gaeton. *The Last Investigation.* New York: Thunder's Mouth. 1993.

Ford, Dennis. *Things Don't Add Up: A Novel of Kennedy Assassination Research.* iUniverse, 2013.

Ford, Gerald R. and John R. Stiles. *Portrait of the Assassin.* New York: Simon & Schuster, 1965.

Fowler, Wade. *The Compass Island Incident: November 1963.* Milford House Press, 2017.

Fox, Sylvan. *The Unanswered Questions about President Kennedy's Assassination.* New York: Award Books, 1965.

Fraley, Craig. *Extraordinary Evidence: JFK Assassination Afterthoughts.* CreateSpace, 2015.

Freed, Donald and Mark Lane. *Executive Action.* New York: Dell, 1973.

Frewin, Anthony. *Lee Harvey Oswald Affaire Classee* (Serpent Noir). Serpent A Plume, 2001.

Frewin, Anthony. *Sixty-Three Closure.* New York: No Exit Press, 2000.

Frewin, Anthony. *The Assassination of John F. Kennedy: An Annotated Film, TV, and Videography, 1963-1992.* Westport, CT: Greenwood Press, 1993.

Frick, Robert A. *Six U.S. Political Assassins: Booth, Guiteau, Czolgosz, Oswald, Ray, Sirhan.* Independently published, 2019.

Friday, Stewart. *Kalediscope [sic]: A Formal Defense of Lee Harvey Oswald on Original Jurisdiction of the Supreme Court of the United States.* Greenville Associated Press, 2017.

Friday, Stewart. *Kennedy Revenged: A Google Video Reference Guide to the JFK Assassination, In Defense of Lee Oswald, and Our Findings of Fact.* Greenville Associates Press, 2018.

Friedly, Michael and David Gallen. *Martin Luther King, Jr.: the FBI File.* New York: Carroll & Graf, 1993.

Fritz, Will. *The Kennedy Mutiny.* Akron, OH: Self-published, 2002.

Fuhrman, Mark. *A Simple Act of Murder: November 22, 1963.* New York: William Morrow, 2006.

Furiati, Claudia. *ZR Rifle: The Plot to Kill Kennedy and Castro; Cuba Opens Secret Files.* Melbourne, Australia: Ocean Press, 1994.

Fulton, Christopher. *The Inheritance: Poisoned Fruit of JFK's Assassination.* Trine Day, 2018.

Gaines, Ann Graham. *The U.S. Secret Service.* Philadelphia: Chelsea House Publishers, 2001.

Galanor, Stewart. *Cover Up.* New York: Kestrel, 1998.

Gallagher, Jerry. *The Man on The Grassy Knoll: The Assassins.* CreateSpace, 2013.

Gallagher, Mary Barelli. *My Life With Jacqueline Kennedy.* New York: David McKay, 1969.

Galvin, Fred. *Nine Dreams to Dallas.* Independently published, 2019.

Gandy, Michael. *Two Kennedy Assassination Mysteries.* Amazon, 2012.

Ganis, Ralph. *The Skorzeny Papers: Evidence for the Plot to Kill JFK.* Hot Books, 2018.

Gardner, David. *Murder, Lies, and Cover-Ups: Who Killed Marilyn Monroe, JFK, Michael Jackson, Elvis Presley, and Princess Diana?* Skyhorse, 2018.

Garrison, Jim. *A Heritage of Stone.* New York: Putnam, 1970.

Garrison, Jim. *On The Trail of the Assassins.* Sheridan Square Press, 1988.

Gatewood, Jim. *Captain Will Fritz and the Dallas Mafia.* Mullaney Corp, 2004.

Gatewood, Jim. *Decker: A Biography of Sheriff Bill Decker, Dallas County, Texas, 1898-1970.* Mullaney Corp, 1999.

Gatewood, Jim. *John F. Kennedy Assassination a Mafia Conspiracy.* Mullaney Press, 2008.

Gatewood, Jim. *Report of the Citizens' Commision on the Assassination of President John F. Kennedy.* Mullaney Corporation, 2013.

Gedney, John Forrester. *The Making of a Bum: From Notoriety to Sobriety*. Melbourne, FL: Gami Publishing, 2001.

George, Alice. *The Assassination of John F. Kennedy: Political Trauma and American Memory* (Critical Moments in American History). Routledge, 2012.

Gertz, Elmer. *Moment of Madness: The Peoples vs. Jack Ruby*. Chicago, Illinois: The Follett Publishing Co., 1968.

Giancana, Antoinette. *JFK and Sam: The Connection Between the Giancana and Kennedy Assassinations*. Cumberland House Publishing, 2005.

Giancana, Sam and Chuck. *Double Cross: The Explosive, Inside Story of the Mobster Who Controlled America*. Warner Books, 1992.

Gibbons, Edward J. *Seven Days in November 1963: The Kennedy Assassination*. iUniverse, 2013.

Gibson, Donald. *Battling Wall Street: The Kennedy Presidency*. New York: Sheridan Square Press, 1994.

Gibson, Donald. *The Kennedy Assassination Cover-Up*. Progressive Publishers, 2014.

Gibson, Donald. *The Kennedy Assassination Cover-up Revisited*. Nova Science Pub, 2005.

Gilbride, Richard. *Matrix for Assassination*. Trafford, 2009.

Gillon, Steven M. *Lee Harvey Oswald: 48 Hours to Live: Oswald, Kennedy, and the Conspiracy that Will Not Die*. Sterling, 2013.

Gillon, Steven M. *The Kennedy Assassination – 24 Hours After: Lyndon B. Johnson's Pivotal First Day as President*. New York: Basic, 2009.

Giuliano, Geoffrey. *Lee Harvey Oswald - In His Own Words*. Author's Republic, 2019.

Gleaves, Richard. Under the Grassy Knoll: a JFK novella. Independently published, 2018.

Goebel, Greg. *The Rise & Fall of JFK Truth*. Amazon, 2015.

Gogerly, Liz. *The Kennedy Assassination (Days That Shook the World)*. Hodder Children's Book, 2002.

Gold, John C. *365 to DALLAS: An Assassin's Tale*. Goldness Publishing, 2018.

Goldberg, Robert Alan. *Enemies Within: The Culture of Conspiracy in Modern America*. New Haven: Yale University Press, 2001.

Golden, Jeff. *Unafraid: A Novel of the Possible*. iUniverse, 2008.

Goldstein, Margaret J. *What are Conspiracy Theories?* Lerner Publications, 2019.

Goldstein, Steve. **Kennedy Killed.** G & A Publishing, 2013.

Gollar, Joel Thomas. *More Than Meets the Eye: The Last Years of Lee Harvey Oswald*. Gollar, 2018.

Gonzalez, Servando. *Partners in Crime: The Rockefeller, CFR, CIA and Castro Connection to the Kennedy Assassination*. CreateSpace, 2017.

Goode, Mark R. *Frozen in Time: The Assassination of JFK*. CreateSpace, 2015.

Goode, Stephen. *Assassination! Kennedy, King*, Kennedy. Franklin Watts, 1979.

Goodman, Bob. *Triangle of Fire.* Laquerian Publishing, 1993.

Goranoff, Kyrill. *Why Did You Kill Your President?* Self-published, 1971.

Gorightly, Adam. *Caught in the Crossfire: Kerry Thornley, Oswald and the Garrison Investigation.* Feral House, 2014.

Gorightly, Adam. *The Prankster and the Conspiracy: The Story of Kerry Thornley and How He Met Oswald and Inspired the Counterculture.* Paraview Press, 2003.

Graff, Garrett M. *Angel is Airborne: JFK's Final Flight from Dallas.* Amazon, 2013.

Graham, Warren. *Touching History: My Journey with the JFK Assassination.* Independently published, 2018.

Granberry, Michael. *Oswald Slept Here: Lives Changed by a Flash of History.* The *Dallas Morning News*, 2011.

Grant, Steven. *Badlands.* Dark Horse Books, 2018.

Gratz, J. Timothy and Mark Howell. *The Extra Rifle in Dealey Plaza and Too Many Bullets: Fifty Years Later, the Florida Keys' Connections to the Warren Commission Report* (JFK Assassination Unraveled) (Volume 2). CreateSpace, 2015.

Gratz, J. Timothy and Mark Howell. *The Men At Sylvia's Door And The Agent With Dirty Fingernails: Fifty Years Later, the Florida Keys' Connections to the Warren Commission* (JFK Assassination Unraveled) (Volume 1). CreateSpace, 2014.

Greig, Charlotte. *Assassins: Cold-Blooded and Pre-Meditated Killings that Shook the World.* Arcturus, 2019.

Green, Joseph E. *Dissenting Views II: More Investigations into History, Philosophy, Cinema, & Conspiracy.* Dash Chandler, 2014.

Green, Steven. *The Actual Naming Of The JFK Assassins: Eisenhower Is Accused, 20 Assassins Are Named, Conspiracy Is Proven.* Independently published, 2017.

Green, Tim. *The Fourth Perimeter.* Warner Books, 2003.

Greenberg, Bradley S. and Edwin B. Parker. *The Kennedy Assassination and the American Public.* Stanford University Press, 1965.

Griffith, Darin. *Window with a View.* Darin Griffith, 2014.

Griffith, Michael T. *Compelling Evidence.* JFK Lancer, 1996.

Griggs, Ian. *No Case To Answer.* JFK Lancer Productions, 2005.

Groden, Robert & Harrison Edward Livingstone. *High Treason.* Baltimore: Conservatory Press, 1989 (updated in 1998 and 2006)

Groden, Robert. *JFK: Absolute Proof.* Self-published, 2013.

Groden, Robert. *The Killing of a President.* New York: Viking Studio Books, 1993.

Groden, Robert. *The Search For Lee Harvey Oswald.* New York: Penguin Studio Books, 1995.

Gross, Virginia T. *The President is Dead: A Story of the Kennedy Assassination.* Viking Books, 1993.

Gun, Nerin. *Red Roses From Texas.* London: Frederick Muller, 1964.

Gunderson, Jessica. *Assassins' America*. Capstone Young Readers, 2018.

Gurion, Wesley. *Who Shot JFK? The Truth At Last!* Amazon, 2013.

Guth, Delloyd J. and David R. Wrone. *The Assassination of John F. Kennedy: A Comprehensive Historical and Legal Bibliography, 1963-1979*. Greenwood, 1980.

Guthrie, Forrest G. *Special Agent in Charge*. Onlinebinding.com, 2014.

Hager, Steven. *Dirty Money, Secret Societies and Killing JFK*. CreateSpace, 2014.

Haines, Robin. *Probable Cause Re-Thinking The JFK Plot*. CreateSpace, 2017.

Haldeman, H.R. & Joseph Dimona. *The Ends of Power*. New York: Dell, 1978.

Hamer, John. *JFK – A Very British Coup: The Definitive Truth of the Assassination*. Self-published, 2019.

Hamilton, S.L. *John F. Kennedy (Days of Tragedy)*. ABDO & Daughters, 1989.

Hampton, Wilborn. *Kennedy Assassinated! The World Mourns: A Reporter's Story*. Candlewick, 2001.

Hancock, Larry. *Nexus*. JFK Lancer Production, 2011.

Hancock, Larry. *Someone Would Have Talked*. Texas: Lancer, 2003.

Hanson, William H. *The Shooting of John F. Kennedy: One Assassin, Three Shots, Three Hits – No Misses*. San Antonio, TX: Naylor, 1969.

Hardy, Freya. *JFK Assassination: 50 Years On in 60 Minutes*. RW Press, 2013.

Harkins, William H. *The Assassination of John F. Kennedy*. Mitchell Lane Publishers, 2007.

Harrington, William. *Columbo: The Grassy Knoll*. New York: Tom Doherty Associates, 1993.

Harris, Patrick. *The Seven Big Lies of the Medical Evidence and the Shot That Killed JFK*. Outskirts Press, 2015.

Harris, Steve. *America's Secret History: How the Deep State, the Fed, the JFK, MLK, and RFK Assassinations, and Much More Led to Donald Trump's Presidency*. Skyhorse, 2020.

Hartogs, Renatus and Lucy Freeman. *The Two Assassins*. New York: Thomas Y. Crowell, 1965; Zebra Books, 1976

Hartwright, Christian. *The JFK Assassination: Dissecting the Corpus With Occam And Cassius*. Cui Bono Books, 1999.

Haslam, Edward. *Dr. Mary's Monkey: How the Unsolved Murder of a Doctor, a Secret Laboratory in New Orleans and Cancer-Causing Monkey Viruses Are Linked to Lee Harvey Oswald, the JFK Assassination and Emerging Global Epidemics*. Trine Day, 2014.

Haslam, Edward. *Mary, Ferrie & the Monkey Virus: The Story of an Underground Medical Laboratory*. Wordsworth Communication Service, 1995.

Hastings, Michael. *Lee Harvey Oswald*. Penguin Books, 1966.

Hastings, Michael. Lee Harvey Oswald: A Far Mean Streak of Independence Brought on by Negleck [sic]. Oberon Books, 2013.

Hawkins, J.C. *Betrayal At Bethesda: The Intertwined Fates of James Forrestal, Joseph McCarthy, and John F. Kennedy.* CreateSpace, 2017.

Hayden, Daniel. *Rumors From the Grassy Knoll.* Amazon, 2013.

Hayman, LeRoy. *The Assassinations of John and Robert Kennedy.* Scholastic Book Services, 1976.

Hazelwood, Denise. *The JFK Cut-N-Paste Assassination: Putting It Back Together.* Self-published, 2015.

Hazelwood, Denise. *Micro-Studies of an Assassination: Investigations into Various Pieces of Evidence in the JFK Assassination.* CreateSpace, 2016.

Hazelwood, Denise. *Micro-Studies 2: More Investigations into the JFK Assassination Evidence.* Amazon, 2016.

Hazelwood, Denise. *Micro-Studies 3: Further Investigations into the JFK Assassination Evidence.* Amazon, 2018.

Hazelwood, Denise. *Micro-Studies 4: Additional Investigations into the JFK Assassination Evidence.* Independently published, 2020.

Heath, Sarah. *The Big Event.* Amazon, 2018.

Heiner, Kent. *Without Smoking Gun: Was the Death of Lt. Cmdr. William Pitzer Part of the JFK Assassination Cover-up Conspiracy?* Trine Day, 2004.

Held, E.B. *A Spy's Guide to the Kennedy Assassination.* CreateSpace, 2013.

Hemenway, Phillip. *Riding the Tiger's Back: A Footnote to the Assassination of JFK.* Heidelberg Graphics, 1992.

Henderson, Garry L. *The Assassinations.* CreateSpace, 2017.

Hepburn, James. *Farewell America.* Vaduz, Liechtensten, Canada, & Belgium: Frontiers Publishing Company, 1968.

Hepburn II, James. *Hogwash: An Idiot's Guide to the JFK Assassination: Chronicle of a Death Foretold.* Revelation, 2016.

Hersh, Burton. *Bobby and J. Edgar.* Basic, Books, 2007.

Hersh, Burton. *The Old Boys: The American Elite and the Origins of the CIA.* New York: Scribner's, 1992.

Hersh, Seymour. *The Dark Side of Camelot.* Boston: Little, Brown & Co., 1997.

Heymann, C. David. *A Woman Called Jackie.* New York: Lyle Stuart, 1989.

Hill, Alexander. *JFK 's Biography: Discover the History of USA President John F. Kennedy and the Story of His Assassination.* Amazon, 2020.

Hill, Clinton and Lisa McCubbin. *Five Days in November.* Gallery Books, 2013.

Hill, Clinton and Lisa McCubbin. *Five Presidents: My Extraordinary Journey with Eisenhower, Kennedy, Johnson, Nixon, and Ford.* Gallery Books, 2016.

Hill, Clinton and Lisa McCubbin. *Mrs Kennedy and Me.* New York: Simon and Schuster, 2012

Hill, Gary. T*he Other Oswald: A Wilderness of Mirrors.* Trine Day, 2020.

Hinckle, Warren and William Turner. *Deadly Secrets: The CIA-Mafia War Against Castro and the Assassination of JFK*. New York: Thunder's Mouth Press, 1993.

Hinckle, Warren. *If You Have A Lemon, Make Lemonade*. New York: Bantam Books, 1976.

Hinckle, Warren and William Turner. *The Fish Is Red: The Story of the Secret War Against Castro*. Harpercollins, 1981.

Hinrichs, Dave. *Patsy*. SynergEBooks, 2013.

Hlavach, Laura and Darwin Payne, Editors. *Reporting the Kennedy Assassination: Journalists Who Were There Recall Their Experiences*. Dallas, Texas: Three Forks Press, 1996.

Hoffman, Ed and Ron Friedrich. *Eyewitness. Texas:* JFK Lancer Publications, 1998.

Hofstadter, Richard. *The Paranoid Style in American Politics and Other Essays*. New York: Alfred A. Knopf, 1965.

Hogan, Michael J. *The Afterlife of John Fitzgerald Kennedy: A Biography*. Cambridge University Press, 2017.

Holden, Henry. *To Be A U.S. Secret Service Agent*. Zenith Press, 2006.

Holland, Brent. *JFK Assassination from the Oval Office to Dealey Plaza*. JFK Lancer Productions, 2013.

Holland, Max. *The Kennedy Assassination Tapes*. New York: Alfred A. Knopf, 2004.

Holland, Max. *The Presidential Recordings: Lyndon B. Johnson: The Kennedy Assassination and the Transfer of Power: November 1963-January 1964*. W.W. Norton & Company, 2005.

Hollar, Rickland. *The Dream Slayer: A Novel of the John F. Kennedy Assassination and Funeral*. CreateSpace, 2012.

Holloway, Diane. *Dallas and the Jack Ruby Trial: Memoir of Judge Joe B. Brown*, Sr. San Jose, CA: Author's Choice Press, 2001.

Holloway, Diane. *Autobiography of Lee Harvey Oswald: My Life in My Words*. iUniverse, 2008.

Holloway, Diane. *The Mind of Oswald*. Trafford, 2000.

Holloway, Jacob. *The JFK Assassination 11.22.63*. Self-published, 2016.

Holmes, Robert. *A Spy Like No Other: The Cuban Missile Crisis, The KGB and the Kennedy Assassination*. Biteback Publishing, 2013.

Hooke, Richard and Larry Rivera. *The Man with the Mona Lisa Smile*. Richard M. Hooke, 2016.

Hooke, Richard. *The Men That Don't Fit In - JFK Researcher's Expanded Edition*. Richard M. Hooke, 2017.

Hooke, Richard. *Twelve Shots that Shook the World*. Richard M. Hooke, 2016.

Holt, Chauncey. *Self-Portrait of a Scoundrel*. Trine Day, 2013.

Horn, Sr., Darwin David. *Dar's Story: Memoirs of a Secret Service Agent*. Santa Barbara, CA: Haagen Printing, 2002.

Hornberger, Jacob. *Regime Change: The JFK Assassination*. Amazon, 2016.

Hornberger, Jacob. *The Kennedy Autopsy. Future of Freedom Foundation*, 2015.

411

Hornberger, Jacob. *The Kennedy Autopsy 2: LBJ's Role In the Assassination.* The Future of Freedom Foundation, 2019.

Horne, Douglas. *Inside The ARRB, Volumes 1-5.* Self-published, 2009.

Horne, Douglas. *JFK's War with the National Security Establishment: Why Kennedy Was Assassinated.* The Future of Freedom Foundation, 2014.

Horton-Newton, Elizabeth. *View From the Sixth Floor: An Oswald Tale.* CreateSpace, 2014.

Hossell, Karen Price. *The Assassination of John F. Kennedy: Death of the New Frontier* (Point of Impact). Heinemann, 2002.

Hosty, James P., Jr., with Thomas Hosty. *Assignment: Oswald.* New York: Arcade Publishing, 1996.

Hourly History. *John F. Kennedy: A Life From Beginning to End.* Independently published, 2017.

Houts, Marshall. *Where Death Delights: The Story of Dr. Milton Hepburn and Forensic Medicine.* New York: Coward-McCann, 1967; Dell, 1968.

Hubbard-Burrell, Joan. *What Really Happened? JFK Five Hundred and One Questions and Answers.* Ponderosa Press, 1992.

Huber, Patrick. *He's Dead, All Right!: Father Oscar L. Huber, the Kennedy Assassination, and the News Leak Controversy.* CreateSpace, 2013.

Huettner, John A. *Deconstructing Oswald.* Independently published, 2018.

Huffaker, Bob. *When the News Went Live: Dallas 1963.* Taylor Trade Publishing, 2013.

Huffman, Mark. *JFK in '64: A Novel.* Independently published, 2018.

Hughes, J.W. *Square Peg for a Round Hole.* Self-published, 1993.

Hughes, Mark. *The Conspiracy Files: JFK.* Amazon, 2016.

Hughes-Wilson, Colonel John. *JFK: An American Coup D'etat: The Truth Behind the Kennedy Assassination.* John Blake, 2016.

Hunsicker, Harry. *Crosshairs: A Lee Henry Oswald Mystery.* Minotaur Books, 2007.

Hunsicker, Harry. *Still River* (Lee Henry Oswald Mystery Series #1). Minotaur Books, 2005.

Hunsicker, Harry. *The Next Time You Die* (Lee Henry Oswald Mystery Series #2). Minotaur Books, 2006.

Hunt, Conover. *JFK: For a New Generation.* Southern Methodist University Press, 1996.

Hunt, Conover. *The Sixth Floor: John F. Kennedy and the Memory of a Nation.* Dallas County Historical Foundation, 1989.

Hunt, Saint John. *Bond of Secrecy: My Life with CIA Spy and Watergate Conspirator E. Howard Hunt.* Trine Day, 2012.

Hunter, Diana with Alice Anderson. *Jack Ruby's Girls.* Atlanta: Hallux Inc., 1970.

Hunter, Stephen and John Bainbridge, Jr. *American Gunfight.* New York: Simon and Schuster, 2005.

Hunter, Stephen. *The Third Bullet.* Simon & Schuster, 2013.

Hurlburt, Charles E. *It's Time for the Truth! The JFK Cover-Up.* Pelican, 2014.

Hurt, Henry. *Reasonable Doubt.* New York: Henry Holt & Co., 1985.

Hyde, Wayne. *What Does A Secret Service Agent Do?* New York: Dodd, Mead, and Co., 1962.

Hyman, Mal. *Burying the Lead: The Media and the JFK Assassination.* Trine Day, 2019.

Hyo, Kim. *Daisy Note: World Events (9-11, Kennedy Assassination, Vietnam, and More).* Daisy Note, 2006.

Irwin, T.H. and Hazel Hale. *A Bibliography of Books Newspaper and Magazine Articles, published in English outside the United States of America related to the Assassination of John F. Kennedy.* Self-published, 1978.

Israel, Lee. *A Biography of Dorothy Kilgallen.* New York: Delacorte, 1979.

Ivry, Dov. *In Defense of Lee Harvey's Girl – London Prize Ring Rules Apply.* CreateSpace, 2015.

Ivry, Dov. *Oswald And The Doppelgangers.* Amazon, 2017.

Ivry, Dov. *Who Killed JFK? Cherchez La Femme.* CreateSpace, 2017.

Jackson III, G.M. *Lee Harvey Oswald's Speech at Spring Hill College: A Report.* Amazon, 2019.

Jackson, Gayle Nix. *Pieces of the Puzzle: An Anthology.* Semper Ad Meliora, 2017.

Jackson, Gayle Nix. *The Missing JFK Assassination Film.* Skyhorse, 2016.

Jacobsen, Seth Reuben. *JFK and the Unspeakable: The Graphic Adaptation - Chapter 1: The Assassination.* Jacobsen, Seth Reuben, 2013.

Jacobsen, Seth Reuben. *JFK and the Unspeakable: The Graphic Adaptation - Chapter 2: The Making of a President: Part One.* Jacobsen, Seth Reuben, 2014.

Jacobsen, Seth Reuben. *JFK and the Unspeakable: The Graphic Adaptation - Chapter 3: The Making of a President: Part Two.* Jacobsen, Seth Reuben, 2014.

Jacobsen, Seth Reuben. *JFK and the Unspeakable: The Graphic Adaptation - Chapter 4: The Making of a President: Part Three.* Jacobsen, Seth Reuben, 2014.

James, Richard. *Why President Kennedy & Brother Robert Died: An Assassination Theory.* 1st Books Library, 2002.

James, Rosemary and Jack Wardlaw. *Plot or Politics? The Garrison Case and its Cast.* New Orleans, Louisiana: Pelican, 1967.

Janney, Peter. *Mary's Mosaic: The CIA Conspiracy to Murder John F. Kennedy, Mary Pinchot Meyer, and Their Vision for World Peace.* Skyhorse, 2012.

Jarman, Jim. *Deadly Delusion.* Amazon, 2010.

Jeffries, Donald. *Hidden History: An Exposé of Modern Crimes, Conspiracies, and Cover-Ups in American Politics.* Skyhorse, 2014.

Jenkins, James C. with William Matson Law. *At The Cold Shoulder of History: The Chilling Story of a 21-year old Navy Hospital Corpsman Who Stood at the Shoulder of JFK during the Bethesda Autopsy.* Trine Day, 2018.

Jennings, D.A. *The Chasm of Conspiracy.* Independently published, 2018.

Jensen, J. Arthur. *The Kennedy Assassination*. Xlibris, 2001.

Joesten, Joachim. *How Kennedy Was Killed*. Tandem-Dawnay, 1968.

Joesten, Joachim. *Marina Oswald*. London: Peter Dawnay, 1967.

Joesten, Joachim. *The Dark Side of Lyndon Baines Johnson*. London: Peter Dawnay, 1968.

Joesten, Joachim. *The Garrison Inquiry: Truth & Consequences*. London: Peter Dawnay, 1967.

Joesten, Joachim. *Oswald: Assassin or Fall Guy?* New York: Marzani & Munsell, 1964.

Joesten, Joachim. *Oswald: The Truth*. London: Peter Dawnay, 1967.

Joesten, Joachim. *The Gap in the Warren Report*. Marzani & Munsell, 1965.

Johnson, Dennis. *The Shadows of November*. CreateSpace, 2013.

Johnson, Lady Bird. *White House Diary*. Funk & Wagnall's Publishing Co., 1970.

Johnson, Marion. *Inventory of the Records of the President's Commission on the Assassination of President Kennedy*. National Archives, 1973.

Johnson, Rob. *Did Beatniks Kill John F. Kennedy?: Bongo Joe's Requiem for the President*. Beatdom Books, 2017.

Johnson, Scott P. *The Faces of Lee Harvey Oswald: The Evolution of an Alleged Assassin*. Lexington Books, 2013.

Johnston, James H. *Murder, Inc.: The CIA Under John F. Kennedy*. Potomac Books, 2019.

Johnston, James P. and Jon Roe. *Flight From Dallas: New Evidence of CIA Involvement in the Murder of President John F. Kennedy*. Bloomington, IN: First Books, 2003.

Jones, Barry. *Treasonous Cabal: A Primer on the Violent Overthrow of John F. Kennedy and His Presidency*. CreateSpace, 2018.

Jones, Howard. *Death of a Generation: How the Assassinations of Diem and JFK Prolonged the Vietnam War*. Oxford University Press, 2003.

Jones, Penn. *Forgive My Grief Vol. I*. Midlothian, Texas: self-published, 1966.

Jones, Penn. *Forgive My Grief Vol. II*. Midlothian, Texas: self-published, 1967.

Jones, Penn. *Forgive My Grief Vol. III*. Midlothian, Texas: self-published, 1969 (revised 1976).

Jones, Penn. *Forgive My Grief Vol. IV*. Midlothian, Texas: self-published, 1974.

Jorgensen, Megan. *Betrayal of a Legend: JFK 1963-1985: A Conspiracy of Treason*. Self-published, 2020.

Josephson, Tajza. *Who Really Killed John F. Kennedy*. Amazon, 2017.

Jovich, John B. *Reflections on JFK's Assassination*. Woodbine House, 1988.

Judge, John Patrick. *Judge for Yourself: A Treasury of Writing by John Judge*. Say Something Real Press LLC, 2017.

Justice, Victor. *Misplaced Loyalties: The Assassinations of Marilyn Monroe & the Kennedy Brothers*. Trafford, 2006.

Kaiser, David. *The Road to Dallas: The Assassination of John F. Kennedy*. Belknap Press, 2008.

Kaiser, Scott. *Edwin Kaiser's Covert Life: And His Little Black Book Linking Cuba, Watergate & the JFK Assassination.* Trine Day, 2015.

Kalb, Marvin. *One Scandalous Story.* Free Press, 2001.

Kallen, Stuart A. *The John F. Kennedy Assassination* (Crime Scene Investigations). Lucent Books, 2009.

Kantor, Seth. *Who Was Jack Ruby?* New York: Everest House, 1978.

Kantor, Seth. *The Ruby Cover-up.* Kensington Mass Market, 1992.

Kaplan, John and Jon R. Waltz. *The Trial of Jack Ruby: A Classic Study of Courtroom Strategies.* New York: MacMillan, 1965.

Kaplan, Larry S. *When the Past Came Calling.* CreateSpace, 2014.

Keane, Gerald B. *JFK's Last Motorcade: Kennedy Assassination Revisited.* CreateSpace, 2015.

Keith, Jim. *The Gemstone File.* Avondale Estates, Georgia: Illumi Press, 1992.

Kelin, John. *Praise from a Future Generation: The Assassination of John F. Kennedy and the First Generation Critics of the Warren Report.* San Antonio: Wings, 2007.

Kelleher, Brian. *The Complete Unraveling of the JFK Assassination: A Lost Bullet's Deadly Trail.* Kelleher & Associates, 2014.

Kelleher, James. *He Was Expendable: National Security, Political and Bureaucratic Cover-Ups in the Murder of President John F. Kennedy.* Lulu, 2016.

Keller, David. *Occam's Razor and the Events of November 22, 1963.* CreateSpace, 2012.

Kelly, Patrick. *Who Killed JFK? Just a Patsy.* Patsy Publishing, 2005.

Kelly, Tracey. *A Day That Changed History: The Assassination of John F. Kennedy* (Turning Points in History). Smart Apple Media, 2013.

Kennedy, A. *John F. Kennedy: Up Close And Personal.* Amazon, 2015.

Kennedy, Caroline and Jacqueline. *Jacqueline Kennedy : Historic Conversations on Life with John F. Kennedy.* Hyperion, 2011.

Kennedy, Jim and John F. Matthews. *Four Dark Days In History: a Photo History of President Kennedy's Assassination.* Special Publications, Inc., 1963.

Kennedy Jr., Robert. *American Values: Lessons I Learned from My Family.* Harper, 2018.

Kent, Sherwood. *Most Dangerous.* Trine Day, 2013.

Kessler, Ronald. *The First Family Detail: Secret Service Agents Reveal the Hidden Lives of the Presidents.* Crown, 2014.

Kessler, Ronald. *In The President's Secret Service.* Crown Publishers, 2009.

Kesterson, Don. *Pawns: Magic Bullet.* Amber Publishers, 2018.

Kiel, R. Andrew. *J. Edgar Hoover: The Father of the Cold War.* UPA, 2000.

Kimball, Donald L. *Assassination: The Murder of John F. Kennedy.* Fayette: Trends and Events, 1988.

Kimball, Donald L. *Assassination II: The Kennedy Killing Conclusions of Conspiracy.* Fayette: Trends and Events, 1993.

Kimbrough, Arch, Mary Ferrell, and Sue Fitch. *Chronology.* Unpublished manuscript.

King, Dean. *Death in Dallas.The JFK Assassination: The Amazing Life and Tragic Death of President Kennedy* (Tragedies That Shaped America Book 3). Amazon, 2012.

King, Stephen. *11/22/63: A Novel.* Scribner, 2011.

Kinzer, Stephen. *The Brothers: John Foster Dulles, Allen Dulles, and Their Secret World War.* Times Books, 2013.

Kirkpatrick, Jr., Lyman B. *The Real CIA.* New York: The Macmillan Company, 1968.

Kirkwood, James. *American Grotesque: An Account of the Clay Shaw- Jim Garrison Affair in the City of New Orleans.* New York: Simon & Schuster, 1970; Harper, 1992.

Klein, Edward. *Just Jackie: Her Private Years.* Ballantine Books, 1999.

Klein, Edward. *The Kennedy Curse: Why Tragedy Has Haunted America's First Family for 150 Years.* New York: St. Martin's Press, 2003.

Knight, Peter. *Conspiracy Culture: From Kennedy to The X Files.* Routledge, 2001.

Knight, Peter. *Conspiracy Nation: The Politics of Paranoia in Postwar America.* NYU Press, 2002.

Knight, Peter. *Conspiracy Theories in American History: An Encyclopedia: Conspiracy Theories in American History.* ABC-CLIO, 2003.

Knight-Jadczyk. *JFK: The Assassination of America.* Red Pill Press, 2013.

Koepke, James. *Chasing Ghosts: The Remarkable Story of One Man's Investigation of the Assassination of President John F. Kennedy.* PublishAmerica, 2004.

Koerner, John. *Why The CIA Killed JFK and Malcolm X: The Secret Drug Trade in Laos.* Chronos Books, 2014.

Kornbluth, Jesse. *JFK and Mary Meyer: A Love Story.* Skyhorse, 2020.

Krause, K.R. *Blue Scare.* Kevin Krause, 2012.

Kritzberg, Constance and Larry Hancock. *November Patriots.* Colorado, Undercover Press, 1998.

Kritzberg, Constance. *JFK: Secrets from the Sixth Floor Window.* Consolidated Press International, 1995.

Kross, Peter. *JFK: The French Connection.* Adventures Unlimited Press, 2012.

Kross, Peter. *Oswald, The CIA and The Warren Commission.* Bridger House Publishers, Inc, 2011.

Kross, Peter. *The JFK Files.* Adventures Unlimited Press, 2019.

Kroth, Jerry. *Conspiracy in Camelot: A Complete History of the John Fitzgerald Kennedy Assassination.* Algora Publishing, 2003.

Kroth, Jerry. *Coup d'etat: The Assassination of President John F. Kennedy.* Genotype, 2013.

Kroth, Jerry. *The Kennedy Assassination: What Really Happened: A Deathbed Confession, New Discoveries, and Trump's 2017-18* Document Release Implicates LBJ in the Murder. Genotype, 2018.

Krusch, Barry. *Impossible: The Case Against Lee Harvey Oswald, Volume One.* ICI Press, 2012.

Krusch, Barry. *Impossible: The Case Against Lee Harvey Oswald, Volume Two.* ICI Press, 2012.

Krusch, Barry. *Impossible: The Case Against Lee Harvey Oswald, Volume Three.* ICI Press, 2012.

Kuhn, Ferdinand. *The Story of the Secret Service.* New York: Random House, 1957.

Kunhardt, Philip B. Jr. *Life in Camelot: The Kennedy Years.* Boston: Little, Brown, 1988.

Kurtz, Michael. *Crime of the Century: The Kennedy Assassination From A Historian's Perspective.* University of Tennessee Press, 1993 (second edition).

Kurtz, Michael. *The JFK Assassination Debates.* University Press of Kansas, 2006.

Ladds, Stephen. *JFK Assassination Final Revelations.* Dog Ear Publishing, 2017.

La Fontaine, Ray and Mary. *Oswald Talked.* Gretna, LA: Pelican Publishing, 1996.

Lamb, Richard M. *President Kennedy and Psychology of Character Assassination.* Richard M. Lamb, 2013.

Lambert, Patricia. *False Witness.* M. Evans and Company, 1998.

Landau, Elaine. *Assassins, Traitors, and Spies.* Lerner Classroom, 2013.

Lane, Mark. *Rush To Judgment.* Holt, Rinehart, and Winston, 1966.

Lane, Mark. *A Citizen's Dissent.* New York: Holt, Rhinehart & Winston, 1968.

Lane, Mark. *Plausible Denial.* New York: Thunder's Mouth Press, 1991.

Lane, Mark. *Last Word.* Skyhorse, 2011.

Lateer, James W. *The Three Barons: The Organizational Chart of the Kennedy Assassination.* Trine Day, 2017.

Latell, Brian. *Castro's Secrets: Cuban Intelligence, The CIA, and the Assassination of John F. Kennedy.* St. Martin's Press, 2012.

Lattimer, John K. *Kennedy and Lincoln: Medical and Ballistic Comparisons of Their Assassinations.* New York: Harcourt Brace Jovanovich, 1980.

Lattimer, John K. *Similarities in Fatal Woundings of John Wilkes Booth and Lee Harvey Oswald.* SN, 1966.

Laufenberg, Keith G. *The Anxious Assassins.* Royal Crown Royal Publishing, LLC, 2017.

Law, William. *In The Eye of History: Disclosures in the JFK Assassination Medical Evidence.* Trine Day, 2015.

Lawrence, Lincoln. *Mind Control, Oswald and JFK: Were We Controlled?* Kempton, IL: Adventures Unlimited Press, 1997.

Lawrence, Lincoln. *Were We Controlled?* New Hyde Park, New York: University Books, 1967.

Leaming, Barbara. *Mrs. Kennedy: The Missing History of the Kennedy Years.* Free Press, 2002.

Lee, Bill. *Oswald and Oswalt in Washington.* B. and L. Lee, 1990.

Leek, Sybil and Bert R. *Sugar. The Assassination Chain*. New York: Corwin Books, 1976.

Lehrer, James. *A Bus of My Own*. Putnam Publishing Group, 1992.

Lehrer, James. *Top Down: A Novel of the Kennedy Assassination*. Random House, 2013.

Leonard, Barry. *Kennedy Assassination: Surveillance of Civil Rights Activists*. Diane Pub Co., 1997.

Leonard, Jerry. *The Perfect Assassin: Lee Harvey Oswald, the CIA and Mind Control*. Authorhouse, 2002.

Leonnig, Carol. *Zero Fail: The Rise and Fall of the Secret Service*. Random House, 2021.

Leslie, Warren. *Dallas Public and Private*. New York: Avon Books, 1964.

Levatino, Christian Victor. *PROOF: The Big Event: From Dallas to DC*. Unknown Binding, 2013.

Lewis, Jon E. *The Mammoth Book of Cover-Ups: The 100 Most Terrifying Conspiracies of All Time*. Running Press Book Publishers, 2008.

Lewis, Kenneth. *JFK: Summary of the 19,045 assassination documents released April 26, 2018*. Amazon, 2018.

Lewis, Richard Warren and Lawrence Schiller. *The Scavengers and Critics of the Warren Report*. New York: Delacorte Press, 1967.

Lewis, Ron. *Flashback: The Untold Story of Lee Harvey Oswald*. Oregon: Lewcom Productions, 1993.

Library of Congress. *John Fitzgerald Kennedy, 1917-1963, A Chronological List Of References*. Library of Congress, 1964.

Life, The Editors of. *Life: The Day Kennedy Died*. TI Inc Books, 2014.

Lifton, David. *Best Evidence*. New York: Carroll & Graf edition, 1988.

Lifton, David. *Document Addendum to the Warren Report*. El Segundo, CA: Sightext Press, 1968.

List, J.A. *Before the JFK Assassination: 69 Things That Happened in America on November 21, 1963*. Inverted Pyramid Media, 2014.

Litwin, Fred. *I Was A Teenage JFK Conspiracy Freak*. Northern Blues Books, 2018.

Litwin, Fred. *On The Trail of Delusion: Jim Garrison, The Great Accuser*. Northern Blues Books, 2020.

Livermore, Lawrence. *Proper Assessment of the JFK Assassination Bullet Lead Evidence from Metallurgical and Statistical Perspectives*. CreateSpace, 2014.

Livingston, Alan. *Intersection with History: How My Family Crossed Paths with JFK and Oswald*. Three Nineteens Publishing, 2018.

Livingstone, Harrison Edward. *High Treason 2*. New York: Carroll & Graf, 1992.

Livingstone, Harrison Edward. *Killing the Truth*. New York: Carroll & Graf, 1993.

Livingstone, Harrison Edward. *Killing Kennedy*. New York: Carroll & Graf, 1995.

Livingstone, Harrison Edward and Robert Groden. *High Treason*. New York: Carroll & Graf, 1998 (with updated material).

Livingstone, Harrison Edward. *Stunning New Evidence*. Self-published online book, 2000.

Livingstone, Harrison Edward. *The Hoax of the Century: Decoding the Forgery of the Zapruder Film*. Trafford Publishing, 2004.

Livingstone, Harrison Edward. *The Radical Right and the Murder of John F. Kennedy*. Trafford, 2004.

Livingstone, Harrison Edward. *Journey into the Whirlwind: A Personal Memoir and Story of Psychic Murder- The dictatorship and mind-control of writing and publishing-The True Story Of What One Publisher Did To An Author*. CreateSpace, 2012.

Livingstone, Harrison Edward. *Kaleidoscope: A Review of Douglas Horne's Inside the Assassination Records Review Board*. CreateSpace, 2012.

Livingstone, Harrison Edward. *Panjandrum: Secrets of President John F. Kennedy's Skull X-Rays*. CreateSpace, 2013.

Livingstone, Harrison Edward. *"The Swamp" or The Lunatic Network: The Investigation of the Assassination of JFK*. Self-published, 1999.

Lloyd, H.N. *Murder Tales: The JFK Conspiracy*. Amazon, 2013.

Lobby, Liberty. *JFK: The Mystery Unraveled*. Self-published, 1986.

Lodin, Nils. *The Kennedy Assassinations: Who Murdered JFK and RFK?* Vulkan, 2016.

Loken, John. *Oswald's Trigger Films: The Manchurian Candidate, We Were Strangers, Suddenly?* Ann Arbor, MI: Falcon Books, 2000.

Lorenz, Marita with Ted Schwarz. *Marita: One Woman's Extraordinary Tale of Love and Espionage from Castro to Kennedy*. New York: Thunder's Mouth Press, 1993.

Lorenz, Marita. *Marita: The Spy Who Loved Castro*. Pegasus Books, 2017.

Lubin, David M. *Shooting Kennedy: JFK and the Culture of Images*. Berkeley: University of California Press, 2003.

Lucian. *Conspiracy: JFK's Second Shooter*. Lucian, 2014.

Mabry, Donna. *Deadly Ambition*. CreateSpace, 2011.

MacFarlane, Ian Colin. *The Assassination of John F. Kennedy: A New Review*. Paceprint, 1974.

MacFarlane, Ian Colin A. *Proof of Conspiracy in the Assassination of President Kennedy*. Melbourne, Australia: Book Distributors, 1975.

Machtig, Brett and Ashley Machtig. *The Secret Killer of President John F. Kennedy*. MGI Publications, 2020.

MacKenzie, Rod. *The Men That Don't Fit In: My Role in the Conspiracy to Assassinate President John F. Kennedy*. CreateSpace, 2012.

MacNeil, Robert. *The Right Place at the Right Time*. Little, Brown, & Co., 1982.

MacNeil, Robert. *The Way We Were, 1963: The Year Kennedy Was Shot*. New York: Carroll & Graf, 1988.

Maddaloni, Michael. *Not On The Level*. AuthorHouse, 2006.

Maddaloni, Michael. *Transitions: A Guide on Moving from Law Enforcement or the Military into a Second Career*. AuthorHouse, 2002.

Mader, Julius. *Who's Who in the CIA*. Berlin: Julius Mader, 1968.

Mahoney, Richard D. *Sons and Brothers: The Days of Jack and Bobby Kennedy*. Arcade Publishing, 1999.

Mahoney, Tim. *Jack's Boy*. Timothy Mahoney, 2017.

Maier, Thomas. *Mafia Spies: The Inside Story of the CIA, Gangsters, JFK, and Castro*. Skyhorse, 2019.

Mailer, Norman. *Oswald's Tale: An American Mystery*. Random House, 1995.

Majerus, Mike. *Phantom Shot: Eyewitnesses Solve the JFK Assassination*. CreateSpace, 2013.

Mallon, Thomas. *Mrs. Paine's Garage and the Murder of John F. Kennedy*. New York: Pantheon, 2002.

Manchester, William. *The Death of a President*. New York: Perennial Library edition, 1988.

Manchester, William. *One Brief Shining Moment*. Boston: Little, Brown & Co., 1983.

Manley, Patrick. *An Honest Man: A former CIA operative describes the events surrounding the death of President John F. Kennedy*. CreateSpace, 2002.

Mantik, David W. *John F. Kennedy's Head Wounds: A Final Synthesis – and a New Analysis of the Harper Fragment*. Self-published, 2015.

Mara, Wil. *Frame 232*. Tyndale House Publishers, 2013.

Mara, Wil. *The Assassination of President John F. Kennedy*. Children's Press, 2015.

Marcades, Michael. *Rose Cherami-Gathering Fallen Pedals*. JFK Lancer 2016; Peniel Unlimited 2020

Marchetti, Victor and John Marks. *The CIA and the Cult of Intelligence*. New York: Dell, 1974.

Marcin, Fred. *Friendly Fire in Dallas: Solving the Kennedy Assassination Fifty Years Later*. CreateSpace, 2013.

Marcus, Raymond. Addendum B: *Addendum to the HSCA, the Zapruder Film, and the Single Bullet Theory*. Self-published, 1995.

Marcus, Raymond. *Truth vs. Political Truth (essays for a work in progress)*. Self-published, 2001.

Marcus, Raymond. *The Bastard Bullet: A Search for Legitimacy for Commission Exhibit 399*. Los Angeles: Self-published, 1966.

Marcus, Raymond. *The HSCA, The Zapruder Film, and the Single Bullet Theory*. Self-published, 1992.

Margrove, Gary. *Bush Killed Kennedy*. Amazon, 2013.

420

Marks, Stanley. *Coup d'Etat!: November 22, 1963.* Los Angeles, California: Bureau of International Affairs, 1970.

Marks, Stanley. *Murder Most Foul! The Conspiracy that Murdered President Kennedy.* Los Angeles, California: Bureau of International Affairs, 1967.

Marks, Stanley. *Two Days of Infamy: November 22, 1963 and September 28, 1964.* Los Angeles, California: Bureau of International Affairs, 1969.

Marrs, Jim. *Crossfire.* New York: Carrol & Graf, 1989.

Marshesso, Pierre. *Double Life: The JFK Assassinations.* CreateSpace, 2013.

Martin, David C. *Wilderness of Mirrors.* Harper and Row, 1980.

Martin, Ralph. *A Hero For Our Time.* New York: Fawcett Crest, 1988.

Martin, Ralph. *Seeds of Destruction: Joe Kennedy and His Sons.* Putnam Publishing Group, 1995.

Mateos, Georg. *1963 Dallas The Man on the Grassy Knoll.* Lulu, 2006.

Mateos, Georg. *The Sniper's Song.* Lulu, 2007.

Mathis, Tegan. *Sins of the Vicar: How Alexander Haig Murdered John F. Kennedy.* CreateSpace, 2013.

Matthews, James P. *Four Dark Days in History.* Los Angeles: Special Publications, 1963.

Matusky, Gregory & John Hayes. *Know Your Government: The U.S. Secret Service.* New York: Chelsea House Publishers, 1988.

Maxwell, R.H. *J.F.K. Assassination Death By Committee: 50th Anniversary.* CreateSpace, 2013.

Mayer, Bob. *The Kennedy Endeavor: The President Series.* Cool Gus Publishing, 2013.

Mayo, John B. *Bulletin from Dallas: The President Is Dead.* New York: Exposition Press, 1967.

Mayo, Jonathan. *The Assassination of JFK: Minute by Minute.* Short Books Ltd, 2013.

McAdams, John. *JFK Assassination Logic: How to Think About Claims of Conspiracy.* Potomac Books, 2011

McAuliffe, Carolyn. *The Assassination of John F. Kennedy* (At Issue in History). Greenhaven Press, 2003.

McBirnie, William Stewart. *What Was Behind Lee Harvey Oswald?* Glendale, California: Acare Publications, 1980..

McBride, Joseph. *Into the Nightmare.* Hightower Press, 2013.

McCarry, Charles. *The Tears of Autumn.* Harry N. Abrams, 2005.

McCarthy, Dennis V.N. with Philip W. Smith. *Protecting the President.* New York: Dell Publishing Co, Inc., 1985.

McClellan, Barr. *Blood, Money, and Power.* New York: Hannover House, 2003.

McConnell, Brian. *The History of Assassination.* Nashville: Aurora Publishers, 1970.

McCullough, David. *Truman*. New York: Simon & Schuster, 1992.

McDonald, Hugh C. *Appointment In Dallas*. New York: Zebra Books, 1975.

McDonald, Hugh C. *LBJ and the JFK Conspiracy*. Condor, 1978.

McDonough, Sam Dennis. *Oswald Conspirators and John F. Kennedy: The Complete Fact-Filled Book About the Assassination of John F. Kennedy*. Sam Dennis McDonough, 2013.

McGaw, Barry. *The Conspiracy Theory Report Volume One: The Tachyonic Antitelephone The real reason for the Voyager Missions, including the JFK assassination and other influenced events*. Amazon, 2018.

McKay, David M. *A Diversion in Dealey Plaza: The JFK Assassination*. CreateSpace, 2016.

McKenna, Peter. *All His Bright Light Gone: The Death of John F. Kennedy and the Decline of America*. New Frontier Publishing, 2016.

McKnight, Gerald. *Breach of Trust: How the Warren Commission Failed the Nation And Why*. University Press of Kansas, 2005.

McLaren, Colin. *The Smoking Gun*. Hachette Australia, 2013.

McLaughlin, Joe. *Trail of Death: Alfredo Gomez and the Assassination of President Kennedy*. Authorhouse, 2006.

McLean, Paul A. *JFK, John Wilkes Booth and the Real Oswald: The Man from Watergate and the John F. Kennedy Assassination Files*. CreateSpace, 2013.

McManus, Richard. *Some Unpopular History of the United States: The JFK Years & the Assassination Cover-up*. Amazon, 2016.

McMillan, Priscilla Johnson. *Marina and Lee: The Tormented Love and Fatal Obsession Behind Lee Harvey Oswald's Assassination of John F. Kennedy*. HarperCollins, 1977; Steerforth, 2013.

McNally, George J. *A Million Miles of Presidents*. 1600 Communications Associations, Inc., 1982.

McWhorter, Jerry. *Conspiracy of Silence - Witness to an Assassination*. FriesenPress, 2014.

Meagher, Sylvia. *Accessories After the Fact*. New York: Bobbs-Merrill, 1967.

Meagher, Sylvia. *Subject Index to the Warren Report and Hearings and Exhibits*. New York: Scarecrow Press, 1966.

Meagher, Sylvia, in collaboration with Gary Owens. *Master Index to the J.F.K. Assassination Investigations*. The Scarecrow Press, 1980.

Meek, Jeffrey. *A Lone Gunman?* Independently published, 2011.

Melanson, Philip H. *Spy Saga: Lee Harvey Oswald and U.S. Intelligence*. Praeger, 1990.

Melanson, Philip H. *The Politics of Protection*. New York: Praeger Publishers, 1984.

Melanson, Philip H. with Peter F. Stevens. *The Secret Service: The Hidden History of an Enigmatic Agency*. New York: Carroll & Graf, 2003. Also: further updated version, 2005.

Mellen, Joan. *A Farewell to Justice: Jim Garrison, JFK's Assassination, and the Case That Should Have Changed History*. Potomac Books, 2005.

Mellen, Joan. *Faustian Bargains: Lyndon Johnson and Mac Wallace in the Robber Baron Culture of Texas.* Bloomsbury, 2016.

Mellen, Joan. *Jim Garrison: His Life and Times, The Early Years.* JFK Lancer, 2008.

Mellen, Joan. *Our Man in Haiti: George de Mohrenschildt and the CIA in the Nightmare Republic.* Trine Day, 2012.

Mellen, Joan. *The Great Game in Cuba: How the CIA Sabotaged Its Own Plot to Unseat Fidel Castro.* Skyhorse, 2013.

Meltzer, Brad. History *Decoded: The 10 Greatest Conspiracies of All Time.* Workman Publishing Company, 2013.

Menninger, Bonar. *Mortal Error.* New York: St. Martin's Press, 1992; CreateSpace 2013.

Meslay, Olivier and Scott Barker. *Hotel Texas: An Art Exhibition for the President and Mrs. John F. Kennedy.* Dallas Museum of Art, 2013.

Metta, Michele. *On the Trail of Clay Shaw: The Italian Undercover CIA and Mossad Station and the Assassination of JFK.* Independently published, 2019.

Metta, Michele. *CMC: The Italian Undercover Cia And Mossad Station And The Assassination Of JFK.* Independently published, 2018.

Michel, Don. *Getting to Know – the Officer Who Arrested Lee Harvey Oswald.* Amazon, 2017.

Milam, Wallace. *Blakey's "Linchpin": Dr. Guinn, Neutron Activation Analysis, and the Single Bullet Theory.* JFK Lancer, 1998.

Miller, Don. *The Questionmark Newsletter: John Fitzgerald Kennedy: The Assassination and Aftermath.* Self-published, 1994.

Miller, Jonathan and Michael Hastings. *Three Political Plays: The Emperor; For the West (Uganda); Lee Harvey Oswald.* Penguin, 1990.

Miller, Tom. *Jack Ruby's Kitchen Sink: Offbeat Travels Through America's Southwest.* Washington, D.C.: Adventure Press, 2001.

Miller, Tom. *The Assassination Please Almanac.* Chicago: Henry Regnery Co., 1977.

Minutaglio, Bill and Steven L. Davis. *Dallas '63.* Twelve, 2013.

Mishkin, Dan. *Warren Commission Report: A Graphic Investigation into the Kennedy Assassination.* Harry N. Abrams, 2014.

Mitchell, Richard. *The Shooter's Son: Return to the Grassy Knoll.* Independently published, 2019.

Moak, Kathy Kilmer. *November 22, 1963: Memories of East Dallas Students, 40 Years Later.* Self-published, 2003.

Model, Peter F. and Robert J. Groden. *JFK: The Case for Conspiracy.* New York: Manor Books, 1976.

Mogelever, Jacob. *Death To Traitors- The Story of General Lafayette C. Baker, Lincoln's Forgotten Secret Service Chief.* Doubleday, 1960.

Moldea, Dan E. *The Hoffa Wars: The Rise and Fall of Jimmy Hoffa.* New York: Shapolsky, 1993.

Monaldo, Alex. *Conspiracies: Conspiracy Theories – The Most Famous Conspiracies Including: The New World Order, False Flags, Government Cover-ups, CIA, & FBI.* CreateSpace, 2016.

Montague, Charlotte. *John F. Kennedy: The Life and Death of a US President.* Chartwell Books, 2017.

Moore, Jim. *Conspiracy of One: The Definitive Book on the Kennedy Assassination.* Fort Worth, TX: Summit Group, 1991.

Moore, Lance. *Killing JFK: 50 Years, 50 Lies.* CreateSpace, 2013.

Moore, Shannon Baker. *John F. Kennedys Assassination Rocks America* (Events That Changed America). Events That Changed America, 2018.

Morgan, David, Editor, & Sally M. Promey, Editor. *The Visual Culture of American Religions.* University of California Press, 2001.

Morin, Relman. Assassination: *The Death of President John F. Kennedy.* New American Library (Signet), 1968.

Morley, Jefferson. *CIA & JFK: The Secret Assassination Files.* The Future of Freedom Foundation, 2016.

Morley, Jefferson. *Our Man in Mexico: Winston Scott and the Hidden History of the CIA.* Lawrence, KS: University of Kansas Press, 2008.

Morris, W.R. *The Men Behind The Guns (Former Undercover Agent Reveals All The Facts About The Kennedy Assassination).* Angel Lea Books, 1975.

Morris, W.R. and R.B. Cutler. *Alias Oswald.* Manchester, MA: GKG Partners, 1985.

Morrisey, Michael David. *Correspondence with Vincent Salandria.* Lulu, 2007.

Morrow, Robert D. *Betrayal. Chicago,* IL: Henry Regrery Co., 1976.

Morrow, Robert D. *First Hand Knowledge: How I Participated in the CIA-Mafia Murder of President Kennedy.* New York: S.P.I. Books, 1992.

Moscovit, Andrei. *Did Castro Kill Kennedy?* Cuban American National Foundation, 1991.

Moss, Armand. *Disinformation, Misinformation, and the "Conspiracy" to Kill JFK Exposed.* Hamden, CT: Archon Books, 1987.

Mottez, Vincent. *Les Boucs émissaires de l'Histoire.* Interforum, 2019.

Motto, Carmine J. *Undercover.* Springfield, Illinois: Charles C. Thomas, Publisher, 1971.

Motto, Carmine J. *In Crime's Way: A Generation of Secret Service Adventures.* Boca Raton, FL: CRC Press, 1999.

Moulden, Stuart. *The Mob and the Kennedy Assassination: Jack Ruby. Testimony by Mobsters Lewis McWillie, Joseph Campisi and Irwin Weiner.* CreateSpace, 2012.

Mulvaney, Jay. *Dear Mrs. Kennedy: The World Shares Its Grief Letters November 1963.* St. Martin's, 2010.

Murdoch, Robert. *Ambush in Dealey Plaza: Killing President Kennedy and Officer Tippit.* LookBack Publications, 2014.

Murphy, Charles. *I Covered the Kennedy Assassination.* Amazon, 2013.

Murr, Gary. *The Murder of Police Officer J.D. Tippit.* Canada: Unpublished manuscript, 1971.

Murray, Norbert. Legacy of an Assassination. The Pro-People Press, 1964.

Myers, Dale. *With Malice: Lee Harvey Oswald and the Murder of Officer J.D. Tippit.* Oak Cliff Press, 1998; updated 2013.

Nagle, John M. *A Guide to the Sites of November 22, 1963: Facts, Questions, Pictures and History. Dallas:* Self-published, 2005.

Names, Larry. *The Oswald Reflection.* Laranmark Press, 2012.

Nash, H.C. *Citizen's Arrest: The Dissent of Penn Jones, Jr. in the Assassination of JFK.* Latitudes Press, 1977.

Nash, H.C. *Patsy of the Ages: Lee Harvey Oswald and His Nation Half a Century Later.* CreateSpace, 2015.

NBC News. *Seventy Two Hours and Thirty Minutes, as Broadcast on the NBC Television Network by NBC News.* New York: Random House, 1966.

Neal, Harry Edward. *The Story of the Secret Service.* New York: Grosset and Dunlap, 1971.

Neal, Harry Edward. *The Secret Service In Action.* New York: Elsevier/Nelson books, 1980.

Nechiporenko, Oleg. *Passport to Assassination: The Never-Before-Told Story of Lee Harvey Oswald by the KGB Colonel Who Knew Him.* New York: Carol Publishing, 1993.

Nelson, Phillip. *LBJ: The Mastermind of the JFK Assassination.* Skyhorse, 2011.

Nelson, Phillip. *LBJ: From Mastermind to "The Colossus."* Skyhorse, 2014.

Neroth, Pelle. *Murder on the Death Star: The assassination of Kennedy and its relevance to the Trump era.* Independently published, 2017.

Netzley, Patricia D. *The Assassination of President John F. Kennedy.* New York: New Discovery Books, 1994.

Newcomb, Fred & Perry Adams. *Murder From Within.* Self-published: Santa Barabara, CA, 1974; AuthorHouse, 2011.

Newman, Albert H. *The Assassination of John F. Kennedy: The Reasons Why.* New York: Clarkson N. Potter, 1970.

Newman, Craig. *The Assassination of JFK - Who Really Did It And Why.* Independently published, 2017.

Newman, John. *Countdown to Darkness: The Assassination of President Kennedy Volume II* (Volume 2). CreateSpace, 2017.

Newman, John. *Into the Storm: The Assassination of President Kennedy Volume 3.* CreateSpace, 2019.

Newman, John. *JFK and Vietnam.* Warner, 1992; CreateSpace, 2017.

Newman, John. *Oswald and the CIA.* New York: Carroll & Graf, 1995; Skyhorse, 2008.

Newman, John. *Where Angels Tread Lightly: The Assassination of President Kennedy Volume 1.* CreateSpace, 2015.

Newseum. *President Kennedy Has Been Shot.* Sourcebooks Media Fusion, 2003.

New York Times. *The Witnesses: The Highlights of Hearings Before the Warren Commission on the Assassination of President Kennedy.* McGraw Hill, 1965.

Nolan, David B. *Trial of Lee Harvey Oswald.* Authorhouse, 2015.

Nolan, Jonathan. *The Testimony of Roger Craig.* Flying Tiger Comics, 2013.

Nolan, Patrick. *CIA Rogues and the Killing of the Kennedys: How and Why US Agents Conspired to Assassinate JFK and RFK.* Skyhorse, 2013.

North, Mark. *Act of Treason.* New York: Carroll & Graf, 1991.

North, Mark. *Betrayal in Dallas: LBJ, the Pearl Street Mafia, and the Murder of President Kennedy.* Skyhorse, 2011.

Norvell, James D. *Treason, Treachery & Deceit: The Murderers of JFK, MLK & RFK.* Xlibris, 2014.

Noyes, Peter. *Legacy of Doubt.* New York: Pinnacle Books, 1973.

O'Brien, Dave. *Through The 'Oswald' Window: : Reveals Stunning Fresh Insights, Three Assassins, Conspiracy & Cover-Up in the JFK Assassination!* Dave O'Brien, 2017.

O'Brien, Lawrence. *No Final Victories: A Life in Politics from John F. Kennedy to Watergate.* Doubleday, 1974.

O'Donnell, Helen. *A Common Good: The Friendship of Robert F. Kennedy and Kenneth P. O'Donnell.* New York: William Morrow & Co., 1998.

O'Donnell, Kenneth P., David F. Powers, and Joseph McCarthy. *Johnny, We Hardly Knew Ye.* Boston: Little, Brown & Co., 1972. [Note: All references in this book are to the Pocket Books paperback edition from 1973]

Oglesby, Carl. *The JFK Assassination: The Facts and the Theories.* New York: Signet, 1992.

Oglesby, Carl. *The Yankee and Cowboy War: Conspiracies from Dallas to Watergate.* Sheed, Andrews and McMeel, 1976.

Oglesby, Carl. *Who Killed JFK?* Berkeley: Odonian Press, 1992.

O'Gorman, Ned. *The Iconoclastic Imagination: Image, Catastrophe, and Economy in America from the Kennedy Assassination to September 11.* University of Chicago Press, 2015.

O'Halloran, Willy. *Death of Democracy.* Self-published, 2020.

O'Leary, Brad and Edward Lee. *The Deaths of the Cold War Kings: The Assassinations of Diem & JFK.* Cemetery Dance Publications, 2000.

O'Leary, Brad & L.E. Seymour. *Triangle of Death.* Nashville, TN: WND Books, 2003.

Oliver, Beverly with Coke Buchanan. *Nightmare In Dallas.* Starburst Publishing, 1994.

Oliver, Revilo. *Dallas Marksmanship, Parts 1 and 2.* Freedom Views Committee, 1964.

Oliver, Willard and Nancy E. Marion. *Killing the President: Assassinations, Attempts, and Rumored Attempts on U.S. Commanders-in-Chief.* Praeger, 2010.

Oltmans, Willem. *Reportage Over de Moordenaars.* Utrecht, Holland: Bruba & Zoon, 1977.

Oltmans, Willem. *Reporting on the Kennedy Assassination.* University Press of Kansas, 2017.

O'Neill Jr., Francis X. *A Fox Among Wolves: The Autobiography of Francis X. O'Neill, Jr, Retired FBI Agent.* Codfish Press, 2011.

O'Neill, Tip. *Man of the House.* New York, Random House, 1987.

Onesti, John. *Assassination Point Blank.* JWO Publishing, 2014.

O'Reilly, Bill and Mark Dugard. *Killing Kennedy.* Henry Holt and Company, 2012.

O'Reilly, Bill. *Kennedy's Last Days: The Assassination That Defined a Generation.* Henry Holt and Company, 2013.

Oringer, Richard H. *Harvey Lee.* Orin Publishing, 2014.

O'Shea, Barbara and William Parks. *We Remember the Day of President Kennedy's Assassination:* November 22, 1963. William R. Parks, 2017.

Oswald, Marguerite C. *Aftermath of an Execution – The Burial and Final Rights of Lee Harvey Oswald as Told by His Mother.* Dallas, Texas: Self Published, 1964.

Oswald, Robert L. with Myrick and Barbara Land. *Lee: A Portrait of Lee Harvey Oswald by His Brother.* New York: Coward-McCann, 1967.

Otfinoski, Steven. *Tragedy in Dallas: The Story of the Assassination of John F. Kennedy.* Capstone Press, 2016.

O'Toole, George. *The Assassination Tapes.* New York: Penthouse Press, 1975.

Otto, Richard. *The Paradox of our National Security Complex: How Secrecy and Security Diminish Our Liberty and Threaten Our Democratic Republic.* Chronos Books, 2017.

Owen, Dean R. *November 22, 1963: Reflections on the Life, Assassination, and Legacy of John F. Kennedy.* Skyhorse, 2013.

Pacepa, Lon Mihai. *Programmed to Kill: Lee Harvey Oswald, the Soviet KGB, and the Kennedy Assassination.* Ivan R. Dee, 2007.

Paine, Lauran. *The Assassin's World.* Taplinger Publishing Company, 1975.

Palamara, Vincent. *Survivor's Guilt: The Secret Service and the Failure to Protect President Kennedy.* Trine Day, 2013.

Palamara, Vincent. *JFK: From Parkland to Bethesda.* Trine Day, 2015.

Palamara, Vincent. *The Not-So-Secret Service.* Trine Day, 2017.

Palamara, Vincent. *Who's Who in the Secret Service.* Trine Day, 2018.

Paper, Lew. *Deadly Risks.* Seven Locks Press, 2008.

Paris, James L. *JFK Assassination: Executive Order 11110 - Did The Fed Kill JFK?* Premier Financial Communications, 2013.

Parissien, Steven. *Assassins: Assassinations That Shook the World from Julius Caesar to JFK.* Quercus, 2009.

Parker, Brad. *First On the Scene: Interviews With Parkland Hospital Doctors on the Assassination of President John F. Kennedy.* JFK Lancer, 2014.

Parker, Greg. *Lee Harvey Oswald's Cold War: Why the Kennedy Assassination should be Reinvestigated - Volumes One & Two.* New Disease Press, 2014.

Parr, Jerry with Carolyn Parr. *In the Secret Service: The True Story of the Man Who Saved President Reagan's Life*. Tyndale House, 2013.

Patterson, James. *The House of Kennedy*. Little, Brown and Company, 2020.

Patterson, R.J. *The Warren Omissions*. CreateSpace, 2017.

Payne, R.E. Gus. *Falsely Accused: Jim Garrison's Investigation of JFK's Assassination and the United States of America Versus R.E. Payne*. Authorhouse, 2006.

Pearl, Jack. *The Dangerous Assassins*. Monarch Books, 1964.

Pell, Derek. *Assassination Rhapsody*. Brooklyn, NY: Autonomedia, 1989.

Peterson, Sara and K.W. Zachry. *The Lone Star Speaks: Untold Texas Stories About the JFK Assassination*. Bancroft Press, 2020.

Perret, Geoffrey. *Jack: A Life Like No Other*. New York: Random House, 2001.

Peteja, Ed Edwards. *My Life Researching the JFK Assassination*. Independently published, 2013.

Petro, Joseph with Jeffrey Robinson. *Standing Next To History: An Agent's Life Inside The Secret Service*. New York: Thomas Dunne Books, 2004.

Phelan, James. *Scandals, Scamps and Scoundrels: The Casebook of an Investigative Reporter*. New York: Random House, 1982.

Phillips, Donald. *A Deeper, Darker Truth*. DTP, 2009.

Piccard, George. *Liquid Conspiracy: JFK, LSD, the CIA, Area 51 & UFOs*. Adventures Unlimited Press, 1999.

Piereson, James. *Camelot and the Cultural Revolution: How the Assassination of John F. Kennedy Shattered American Liberalism*. Encounter Books, 2007.

Pietrusza, David. *Mysterious Deaths- John F. Kennedy*. Lucent Books, 1996.

Piper, Michael Collins. *False Flags: Template for Terror*. America First Books, 2019.

Piper, Michael Collins. *Final Judgement: The Missing Link in the JFK Assassination Conspiracy*. Washington, D.C.: The Wolfe Press, 1993.

Piper, Michael Collins. *Final Judgement: The Missing Link in the JFK Assassination Conspiracy- Volume 1*. American Free Press, 2017.

Piper, Michael Collins. *Final Judgement: The Missing Link in the JFK Assassination Conspiracy-Volume 2*. American Free Press, 2017.

Pizzimenti, Mark. *Dissidence: A Novel of Lee Harvey Oswald*. Acedia Press, 2006.

Polasek, Randolph. *Powers Behind JFK Assassination - Expanded Edition*. Lulu, 2011.

Poncy, George. *Something Has Happened in the Motorcade*. Grey Knight Books, 2012.

Popkin, Richard. *The Second Oswald*. New York: Avon, 1966.

Posner, Gerald. *Case Closed*. New York: Random House, 1993.

Pratt, David. *JFK, Oswald, Cuba, and the Mafia*. Bev Editions, 2013.

Price, R.K. *The Thunderbird Conspiracy: 50th Anniversary of JFK Murder*. Quiet Owl Books, 2012.

Prouty, L. Fletcher. *JFK: The CIA, Vietnam, and the Plot to Assassinate John F. Kennedy.* Skyhorse, 2011.

Prouty, L. Fletcher. *The Secret Team: The CIA and Its Allies in Control of the United States and the World.* Prentice-Hall, 1973; Skyhorse, 2011.

Pruitt, Keith. *Beyond Coverup: The Coup That Murdered a President.* Words of Wisdom, 2019.

Pruitt, Rebekka. *Lee Harvey Oswald On Trial: A Novel.* CreateSpace, 2015.

Publications International Ltd. *Great American Conspiracies.* Publications International, Ltd., 2018.

Quinlan, Casey J. and Brian K. Edwards. *Beyond the Fence Line: The Eyewitness Account of Ed Hoffman and the Murder of President John F. Kennedy.* JFK Lancer, 2008.

Ragano, Frank and Selwyn Raab. *Mob Lawyer.* New York: Scribner's, 1994.

Rajski, Capt. Raymond B. *Nation Grieved: Kennedy Assassination in Editorial Cartoons.* Charles E. Tuttle, 1967.

Ralston, Ross F. *History's Verdict: The Acquittal of Lee Harvey Oswald.* Self Published, 1975.

Ramparts Magazine, The Editors of. *In the Shadow of Dallas.* Ramparts Magazine, 1966.

Ramsay, Robin. *Who Shot JFK?* Pocket Essentials, 2014.

Rand, Michael with Howard Loxton and Len Deighton. *The Assassination of President Kennedy.* London: Jonathan Cape, 1967.

Randall, Sam. *Clear Thinking About the JFK Assassination.* Amazon, 2019.

Rappleye, Charles and Ed Becker. *All American Mafioso: The Johnny Rosselli Story.* New York: Doubleday, 1991.

Rasor, Rex. *I Killed JFK: or King of the Cap Guns.* CreateSpace, 2017.

Rawlinson, Stuart. *Lee Harvey Oswald: American Hero: How They Killed Kennedy.* Amazon, 2018.

Ray, Pamela with James Files. *Interview With History: The JFK Assassination.* Author-House, 2007.

Read, Julian. *JFK's Final Hours in Texas: An Eyewitness Remembers the Tragedy and Its Aftermath.* University of Texas, 2013.

Redfern, Nick. *Assassinations: The Plots, Politics, and Powers behind History-Changing Murders.* Visible Ink Press, 2020.

Redfield, Albert. *JFK: A History of the Beginning to the End.* Amazon, 2014.

Reed, Gary and Chris Jones. *The Red Diaries: The Kennedy Conspiracy.* Caliber Comics, 2016.

Reginald, Robert. *The Attempted Assassination of John F. Kennedy: A Political Fantasy.* Borgo Press, 2007.

Reilly, Michael. *Reilly of the White House.* New York: Simon & Schuster, 1946.

Reiman, Richard. *Oswald's Motives: The Last Mystery of the JFK Assassination.* Independently published, 2020.

Rem, Edward P. *J.F.K. Assassination "Rifle Shots Phenomenon Exploded": J.F.K. Assassination "The Smoking Gun."* T.B.I. Publishing Company, 2002.

Remington, Rodger A. *Falling Chips: A deconstruction of the single-bullet theory of the JFK assassination.* Xlibris, 2005.

Remington, Rodger A. *Biting the Elephant.* Trafford, 2009.

Remington, Rodger A. *The Warren Report: Evidence Vs. "Conclusions."* Xlibris, 2003.

Remington, Rodger A. *The People V. the Warren Report: Suggestions for Historians.* Xlibris, 2002.

Report of the Warren Commission on the Assassination of President Kennedy (and 26 volumes of hearings and exhibits). Washington, D.C. U.S. Government Printing Office, 1964.

Reston, Jr., James. *The Accidental Victim: JFK, Lee Harvey Oswald, and the Real Target in Dallas.* New York: Zola Books, 2013.

Reston, Jr., James. *The Lone Star-the Life of John Connally.* New York: Harper and Row, 1989.

Revell, Oliver "Buck." *A G-Man's Journal: A Legendary Career Inside the FBI- From The Kennedy Assassination to the Oklahoma City Bombing.* Atria, 1998.

Reynolds, Robert Grey. *Guy Banister: The FBI,* New Orleans and the JFK Assassination. Amazon, 2015.

Rike, Aubrey with Colin McSween. *At the Door of Memory- Aubrey Rike: A Witness to History and the assassination of President Kennedy.* JFK Lancer, 2008.

Ringgold, Gene and Roger La Manna. *Assassin: The Lee Harvey Oswald Biography.* Professional Services, 1964.

Ringgold, Gene. *The Bizarre and Intimate Life of an Assassin: The Lee Harvey Oswald Biography.* Associated Professional Services, 1964.

Rinnovatore, James and Allen Eaglesham. *Aftermath of the JFK Assassination: Parkland Hospital to the Bethesda Morgue.* ARJE, 2012.

Rinnovatore, James and Allen Eaglesham. *The JFK Assassination Revisited: A Synthesis.* AuthorHouse, 2014.

River, Charles. *Killing The President: The Assassinations of Abraham Lincoln and John F. Kennedy.* CreateSpace, 2013.

River, Charles. *Presidential Assassinations: The History of the Killing of Abraham Lincoln, James Garfield, William McKinley, and John F. Kennedy.* CreateSpace, 2016.

River, Charles. *The Life and Death of John F. Kennedy: The Remarkable Life and Shocking Assassination of America's Youngest President.* Independently published, 2020.

Rivera, Larry. *The JFK Horsemen: Framing Lee, Altering the Altgens6 and Resolving Other Mysteries.* Moon Rock Books, 2018.

Rivera, Sheila. *Assassination of John F. Kennedy.* Abdo Publishing, 2004.

Roberts, Charles. *The Truth About the Assassination.* Grossett & Dunlap, 1967.

Roberts, Craig. *Kill Zone: A Sniper Looks at Dealey Plaza.* Tulsa, OK: Consolidated Press International, 1997.

Roberts, Craig and John Armstrong. *JFK: The Dead Witnesses*. Consolidated Press International, 1995.

Robertson, Dan. *Definitive Proof: The Secret Service Murder of President John Fitzgerald Kennedy*. Lulu, 2007.

Robertson, David. *The Carousel Club: A Novel of the Kennedy Assassination*. Amazon, 2013.

Robertson, Jerry. *Documents and Photos from John Armstrong's Book Harvey and Lee*. Lafayette, IN: Self-published, 2004.

Robinson, Stephen. *JFK Assassination: Volume 1*. Amazon, 2017.

Robinson, Stephen. *JFK Assassination: The Complete Collection, Volume 2*. Amazon, 2018.

Robinson, Stephen. *JFK Assassination: Volume 3*. Amazon, 2017.

Robson, David. *The Kennedy Assassination* (Mysterious & Unknown). Referencepoint Press, 2008.

Rockefeller, J.D. *The Assassination of John F. Kennedy*. CreateSpace, 2016.

Rodriguez, Jose. *Grassy Knoll*. Xlibris, 2006.

Roffe, Daniel. *JFK Motorcade: The Accidental Shooting Death of President John F. Kennedy*. Harrowood Books, 2013.

Rogers, Doyle. *The JFK Assassination: Inside The Story*. Amazon, 2013.

Roffman, Howard. *Presumed Guilty*. London: Associated University Presses, 1975.

Roman, M.C. *Death by Holga: 11.22.63 (Photographs of the People, Places and Things Associated with the Kennedy Assassination Taken with a Holga Camera)*. Dallas Art Press, 2013.

Ross, Colin A. *Lee Harvey Oswald and Other Plays*. Manitou Communications, Inc, 2008.

Ross, Robert Gaylorn, Sr. *The Elite Serial Killers of Lincoln, JFK, RFK and MLK*. Spicewood, Texas: RIE, 2001.

Rothschild, Mike. *The World's Worst Conspiracies*. Arcturus, 2019.

Roy, Robert. *The Patsy: The Probable Story of Lee Harvey Oswald*. CreateSpace, 2017.

Ruppert, Michael. *Crossing The Rubicon*. New Society Publishers, 2004.

Rusconi, Jane and Bob Harris. *Encyclopedia of the JFK Assassination* (CD-ROM). Zane Publishing, 1994.

Rush, George. *Confessions of an Ex-Secret Service Agent*. New York: Pocket Books, a division of Simon & Schuster Inc., 1988.

Russell, Brian and Charles Sellier. *Conspiracy To Kill A President*. New York: Bantam, 1982.

Russell, Dick. *On the Trail of the JFK Assassins – A Revealing Look at America's Most Infamous Unsolved Crime*. New York: Skyhorse Publishing, 2008.

Russell, Dick. *The Man Who Knew Too Much*. New York: Carroll & Graf, 1992; updated 2003.

Russo, Gus. *Brothers in Arms*. New York: Bloomsbury, 2008.

Russo, Gus. *Live By The Sword*. Latham, MD: Bancroft Press, 1998.

Russo, Gus and Harry Moses. *Where Were You?: America Remembers The JFK Assassination*. Lyons Press, 2018.

Russo, William. *Booth & Oswald*. Long Time Ago Press, 2010.

Rutland, A.B. *Assassins In Grassy Knoll Man Who Killed Beloved President Deathbed Confession*. Bourne Brothers, 2013.

Ryan, Marc. *Three Shots were fired: JFK's Assassination and TV's First Global Story*. Marc Ryan, 2013.

Sabato, Larry. *The Kennedy Half-Century*. Bloomsbury, 2013.

Saffold, Kenneth. *The JFK Assassination, Do The Math*. Kenneth W Saffold, 2012.

Saffold, Kenneth. *JFK Assassination: The Warren Commission Fraud v2*. Kenneth W Saffold, 2015.

Sahl, Mort. *Heartland*. New York: Harcourt Brace Jovanovich, 1976.

Salandria, Vincent. *False Mystery: Essays on the Assassination of JFK*. Louisville, Colorado: Square Deal Press, 2004.

Saldan, Rick. *Kennedy Death Squads: Evidence Showing Sirhan and Oswald Did Not Mastermind the RFK & JFK Assassinations*. Amazon, 2018.

Salerian, Alen. *JFK: The Magnificent Journey*. CreateSpace, 2015.

Salinger, Pierre & William S. Butler. *John F. Kennedy, Commander in Chief*. New York: Penguin Studio, 1997.

Salla, Michael. *Kennedy's Last Stand: Eisenhower, UFOs, MJ-12 & JFK's Assassination*. Exopolitics Institute, 2013.

Sample, Glen and Mark Collum. *The Men on the Sixth Floor*. Garden Grove, CA: Sample Graphics, 2001.

Sanderson, Bill. *Bulletins from Dallas: Reporting the JFK Assassination*. Skyhorse, 2016.

Sauvage, Leo. *The Oswald Affair*. Cleveland: World Publishing, 1966.

Savage, Gary. *JFK: First Day Evidence*. Monroe, LA: Shoppe Press, 1993.

Savage, James. *Jim Garrison's Bourbon Street Brawl*. Lafayette, LA: University of Louisiana at Lafayette Press, 2010.

Savastano, Carmine. *Two Princes And A King: A Concise Review of Three Political Assassinations*. Neapolis Media Group, 2016.

Savodnik, Peter. *The Interloper: Lee Harvey Oswald Inside the Soviet Union*. Basic Books, 2013.

Sawa, James P. and Glenn A. Vasbinder. *A Compilation of the Books Relating to the Life and Assassination of President John Fitzgerald Kennedy*. Lancer: 1997.

Sawyer, Thomas E. *For Good of Country: The Plot to Kill an American President*. Thomas E. Sawyer, 2019.

Scally, Christopher. *So Near... And Yet So Far: The House Select Committee on Assassinations' Investigation into the Murder of President John F. Kennedy*. New York: Aries, 1980.

Scarbrough, Allen. *On the Assassination of JFK*. Amazon, 2013.

Schaefer, F.C. *All the Way with JFK: An Alternate History of 1964*. Independently published, 2017.

Scheim, David. *Contract on America*. Kensington Mass Market, 1991.

Scheim, David. *The Mafia Killed President Kennedy*. W.H. Allen, 1988.

Schotz, Martin. *History Will Not Absolve Us : Orwellian Control, Public Denial, & the Murder of President Kennedy*. Kurtz, Ulmer and Delucia, 1996.

Schulz, Jamie. *That Park Near The Underpass - A Primer on the Assassination of President John Kennedy*. Jamie Charles Schulz, 2012.

Schwimmer, George. *Doppelganger: The Legend of Lee Harvey Oswald*. CreateSpace, 2016.

Schwimmer, George. *O: The Legend of Lee Harvey Oswald - A Play*. Amazon, 2019.

Sckolnick, Lewis B. *Lee Harvey Oswald: CIA Pre-Assassination File*. Rector Pr Ltd Pub, 1992.

Scott, Peter Dale. *Crime and Cover-Up: The CIA, the Mafia, and the Dallas-Watergate Connection*. Santa Barbara: Open Archive Press, 1993.

Scott, Peter Dale. *Dallas '63: The First Deep State Revolt Against the White House*. Open Road Media, 2018.

Scott, Peter Dale. *Deep Politics and the Death of JFK*. University of California Press, 1996.

Scott, Peter Dale. *Deep Politics II: Essays on Oswald, Mexico, and Cuba*. Stokie, IL: Green Archive Publications, 1995.

Scott, Peter Dale. *Oswald, Mexico, and Deep Politics: Revelations from CIA Records on the Assassination*. Skyhorse, 2013.

Scott, Peter Dale. *The Dallas Conspiracy*. Unpublished manuscript.

Scott, Peter Dale. *War Conspiracy: JFK, 9/11, and the Deep Politics of War*. Skyhorse, 2013.

Scott, Peter Dale, Paul L. Hoch and Russell Stetler. *The Assassinations: Dallas and Beyond – A Guide to Cover-Ups and Assassinations*. New York: Random House, 1976.

Scott, William E. *November 22, 1963: A Reference Guide to the JFK Assassination*. University Press of America, 1999.

Seaton, Joel. *Presidential Witness: The Camelot Conspiracy*. Independently published, 2020.

Security Studies. *Conspiracy Interpretations of the Assassination of President Kennedy: International and Domestic*. Security Studies, 1968.

Seidman, David. *Extreme Careers-Secret Service Agents: Life Protecting the President*. New York: The Rosen Publishing Group, Inc., 2003.

Semple, Robert B, Jr. *Four Days in November: The Original Coverage of the John F. Kennedy Assassination by the Staff of the New York Times*. New York: St. Martin's Press, 2003.

Serritella, Alex P. *Johnson Did It: LBJ's Role in the JFK Assassination*. Bookstand Publishing, 2018.

Server, Lee. *Handsome Johnny: The Life and Death of Johnny Rosselli: Gentleman Gangster, Hollywood Producer, CIA Assassin*. St. Martin's Press, 2018.

Shanahan, Dan. *Camelot Eclipsed: Connecting The Dots*. Self-published, 2017.

Shannan, Pat. *The JFK Assassination and the Uncensored Story of the Two Oswalds.* Liberty Lifeline Foundation, 2013.

Shaw, J. Gary with Larry R. Harris. *Cover-Up: The Governmental Conspiracy to Conceal the Facts about the Public Execution of John Kennedy.* Cleburne, TX: Self-published, 1976.

Shaw, Mark. *Collateral Damage: The Mysterious Deaths of Marilyn Monroe and Dorothy Kilgallen, and the Ties that Bind Them to Robert Kennedy and the JFK Assassination.* Post Hill Press, 2021.

Shaw, Mark. *Denial of Justice: Dorothy Kilgallen, Abuse of Power, and the Most Compelling JFK Assassination Investigation in History.* Post Hill Press, 2018.

Shaw, Mark. *The Reporter Who Knew Too Much: The Mysterious Death of What's My Line TV Star and Media Icon Dorothy Kilgallen.* Post Hill Press, 2016.

Shaw, Mark. *The Poison Patriarch: How the Betrayals of Joseph P. Kennedy Caused the Assassination of JFK.* Skyhorse, 2013.

Shay, Kevin James. *Death of the Rising Sun: A Search for Truth in the John F. Kennedy Assassination.* Amazon, 2016.

Shenon, Philip. *A Cruel and Shocking Act: The Secret History of the Kennedy Assassination.* Henry Holt & Company, 2013.

Shipp, Bert N. *Details at 10: Behind the Headlines of Texas Television History.* History Press Library, 2011.

Shively, Charles. *JFK Assassination.* Greenwood Pub Group, 2002.

Shono, L.D. *He Died For Peace: The Assassination of John F. Kennedy.* CreateSpace, 2013.

Shows, Robert. *A Sentence of Death. Words that Killed a President.* Ecanus Publishing, 2012.

Shrake, Edwin. *Strange Peaches.* John M. Hardy Publishing Company, 2007.

Simkin, John. *Assassination of John F. Kennedy Encyclopedia.* Spartacus, 2012.

Simon, Art. *Dangerous Knowledge: The JFK Assassination in Art and Film.* Philadelphia, Pennsylvania: Temple University Press, 1996.

Sites, Paul. *Lee Harvey Oswald and the American Dream.* Pageant Press, 1967.

Sloan, Bill with Jean Hill. *JFK: The Last Dissenting Witness.* Gretna, Louisiana: Pelican, 1992.

Sloan, Bill. *JFK: Breaking the Silence.* Dallas: Taylor Publishing Co., 1993; retitled in 2012 as a kindle only release: *The Kennedy Conspiracy: 12 Startling Revelations About the JFK Assassination.*

Sloan, Bill. *The Other Assassin.* S.P.I. Books, 1992.

Sloate, Susan. *Forward to Camelot: 50th Anniversary Edition.* Drake Valley Press, 2013.

Smith, Brendan Powell. *Assassination!: The Brick Chronicle of Attempts on the Lives of Twelve US Presidents.* Skyhorse, 2013.

Smith, Jacob. *John F. Kennedy For Kids - Learn Fun Facts About The Life, Presidency & Assassination of JFK.* Amazon, 2014.

Smith, James Francis. *The Grassy Knoll Assassination: Sherlock Holmes Investigates President Kennedy's Murder*. Atlantic Publishing Group, 2019.

Smith, Jeffrey K. *The Presidential Assassins: John Wilkes Booth, Charles Julius Guiteau, Leon Frank Czolgosz, and Lee Harvey Oswald*. CreateSpace, 2013.

Smith, Jeffrey K. *Rendezvous In Dallas: The Assassination of John F. Kennedy*. Authorhouse, 2009.

Smith, Matthew. *Conspiracy: The Plot to Stop the Kennedys*. New York: Citadel Press Books, 2005.

Smith, Matthew: *JFK: Say Goodbye to America- The Sensational and Untold Story Behind the Assassination of John F. Kennedy*. Edinburgh: Mainstream Publishing, 2004.

Smith, Matthew. *JFK: The Second Plot*. Edinburgh: Mainstream Publishing, 1992.

Smith, Matthew. *Vendetta: The Kennedys*. Edinburgh: Mainstream Publishing, 1993.

Smith, Matthew. *Who Killed Kennedy?: The Definitive Account of Fifty Years of Conspiracy*. Mainstream Publishing, 2013.

Smith, Paul Blake. *3 Presidents – 2 Accidents*. W & B Publishers, 2016.

Smith, Paul Blake. *JFK and the Willard Hotel Plot: The Explosive New Theory of Oswald in D.C.* W & B Publishers, 2018.

Smith, R. Harris. *OSS: The Secret History of America's First Central Intelligence Agency*. Berkeley: University of California Press, 1972.

Smith, Timothy G. Merriman. *Smith's Book of Presidents; A White House Memoir*. Norton, 1972.

Sneed, Larry. *No More Silence*. Dallas: Three Forks Press, 1998.

Southwell, David. *The Kennedy Assassination: The Truth Behind the Conspiracy that Killed the President*. Carlton Books, 2012.

Souza, Ed. *Undeniable Truths: The Clear and Simple Facts Surrounding the Murder of President John F. Kennedy*. iUniverse, 2014.

Sparrow, John. *After the Assassination: A Positive Appraisal of the Warren Report*. New York: Chilmark Press, 1967.

Specter, Arlen. *Passion For Truth*. New York: William Morrow, 2000.

Spencer, Lauren. *The Assassination of John F. Kennedy*. Rosen Publishing Group, 2002.

Spignesi, Stephen. *On Target: Famous Assassinations and Attempts from Julius Caesar to John Lennon*. Bounty Books, 2006.

Sprague, Richard E. *The Taking of America 1-2-3*. Self-published, 1979.

Sprinkle, Brian. *The Armchair Detective: Your Guide Through the Maze of the JFK Assassination*. Rainbow Books, 1992.

Stafford, Jean. *A Mother in History: Marguerite Oswald, The Mother of the Man Who Killed Kennedy*. Farrar, Strauss, and Giroux, 1965.

Stang, Alan. *They Killed the President: Lee Harvey Oswald Wasn't Alone*. American Opinion, 1976.

Stanley, Joseph. *The John F. Kennedy Assassination: The Shooting That Shook America* (Crime Scene Investigations). Lucent Books, 2017.

Starling, Edmund W. and T. Sagrue. *Starling of the White House.* New York: Simon & Schuster, 1946.

Stegmann, Leonard. *November 22, 1963: A Quiz.* Amazon, 2014.

Stein, R. Conrad. *Story of the Assassination of John F. Kennedy.* Cornerstones of Freedom, 1985.

Steiner, Jack, and Bill Burrows. *Conspiracy Theories: Government Cover Ups, Aliens & Unsolved Mysteries: Global Warming, Trump, Area 51, FBI, JFK Assassination, World War 3, 1984.* Action Productions, 2017.

Stevens, Al. *The Shadow on the Grassy Knoll.* Mockingbird Songs & Stories, 2013.

Stewart, Shawn. *The Confession of Lee Harvey Oswald.* Amazon, 1999.

Stockland, Patricia M. *The Assassination of John F. Kennedy.* Essential Library, 2007.

Stokes, David R. *Camelot's Cousin: The Spy Who Betrayed Kennedy.* CreateSpace, 2013.

Stone, Jennifer. *Suspicious Minds Scorpion Fire: 50 years on John F. Kennedy assassination fits the Scorpion Rituals.* Aljen, 2014.

Stone, Oliver & Zachary Sklar. *JFK: The Book of the Film.* New York: Applause Books, 1992.

Stone, Roger. *The Man Who Killed Kennedy: The Case Against LBJ.* Skyhorse, 2013.

Story, George. *JFK, 55 Years, Conspiracy & Contradiction Coincidence & Confusion.* Cape Ann Unbound Publishing, 2018.

Stoughton, Cecil with Ted Clifton and Hugh Sidey. *The Memories, 1961-1963.* New York: W.W. Norton & Co., 1973.

Strausbaugh, John. *Alone With The President.* Blast Books, 1994.

Sturdivan, Larry. T*he JFK Myths: A Scientific Investigation of the Kennedy Assassination.* Paragon House, 2005.

Sullivan, Mike. *JFK's Assassination 50 Years On.* The Sun, 2013.

Summers, Alan J. *The Grassy Knoll Badgeman.* Authorhouse UK, 2008.

Summers, Anthony. *Conspiracy.* McGraw-Hill, 1980; revised paperback 1981; Paragon House, 1989.

Summers, Anthony. *Goddess: The Secret Lives of Marilyn Monroe.* MacMillan, 1985.

Summers, Anthony. *Not In Your Lifetime.* New York: Marlowe & Company, 1998; Open Road Integrated Media, 2013.

Summers, Anthony. *The Arrogance of Power.* Penguin USA, 2001.

Summers, Anthony. *Sinatra: The Life.* Knopf, 2005.

Summers, Anthony and Robbyn Swan. *The Eleventh Day: The Full Story of 9/11 and Osama Bin Laden.* Ballantine Books, 2011.

Sundborg, Pierre. *Tragic Truth: Oswald Shot Kennedy by Accident.* CreateSpace, 2016.

Suskind, Samuel. *Oswald: The Shocking Investigation.* CreateSpace, 2015.

Sutherland, Corine. *Lee Harvey Oswald's "Confederates"* Independently published, 2019.

Sutherland, Corine. *Lee Harvey Oswald, John F. Kennedy, and "Twelve Angry Men."* Independently published, 2018.

Sutherland, Corine. *Lee Harvey Oswald, the Warren Commission, Man of La Mancha, the Dealey Plaza Tree.* Independently published, 2019.

Sutherland, Corine. *John F. Kennedy Assassination, Hamlet, and the Twenty-fifth Amendment.* Independently published, 2018.

Swanson, James L. *End of Days: The Assassination of John F. Kennedy.* William Morrow, 2013.

Swanson, James L. *"The President Has Been Shot!": The Assassination of John F. Kennedy.* Scholastic Press, 2013.

Swanson, Michael. *The War State: The Cold War Origins Of The Military-Industrial Complex And The Power Elite, 1945-1963.* CreateSpace, 2013.

Swearingen, M. Wesley. *To Kill A President.* Self-published, 2008.

Swike, Jack. *The Missing Chapter: Lee Harvey Oswald In The Far East.* CreateSpace, 2008.

Tagg, Eric R. *Brush with History: A Day in the Life of Deputy E.R. Buddy Walthers.* Shot in the Light Publishing, 1998.

Tague, James. *LBJ and the Kennedy Killing.* Trine Day, 2013.

Tague, James. *Truth Withheld: A Survivor's Story - Why We Will Never Know the Truth about the JFK Assassination by James T. Tague.* Excel Digital Press, 2003.

Talbot, David. *Brothers.* Free Press, 2007.

Talbot, David. *The Devil's Chessboard: Allen Dulles, the CIA, and the Rise of America's Secret Government.* Harper, 2015.

Tanenbaum, Robert K. *Corruption of Blood.* Dutton, 1995.

Taraborrelli, J. Randy. *Jackie, Janet and Lee.* St. Martin's Press, 2018.

Tarnavsky, Alex. *Masters of Deceit: An Epic Novel of the Monstrous Plot Behind the Kenndy Assassination.* CreateSpace, 2014.

Taylor, Blaine. *Dallas 50 Years On: The Murder of John F. Kennedy.* Fonthill Media, 2013.

Taylor, Richard Keith. *Red Mist: Marilyn Monroe. JFK. Murder. Assassination.* One Witness. Ransom Greene Press, 2017.

Temple of Mysteries. *JFK Assassination.* Temple of Mysteries, 2011.

Tennessean, The. *JFK In Nashville.* The Tennessean, 2013.

terHorst, J.F. & Col. Raplh Albertazzie. *The Flying White House.* New York: Coward, McCann, and Geoghgan, Inc, 1979.

Terry, Marshall. *Dallas Stories.* Self-published, 1987.

The History Hour. *John F. Kennedy: Death of the President.* Independently published, 2018.

Thomas, David Byron and Jim Lesar. *Hear No Evil: Politics, Science, and the Forensic Evidence in the Kennedy Assassination.* Skyhorse, 2013.

Thomas, Kenn. *Inside The Gemstone File: Mind Control and Conspiracy Series.* Adventures Unlimited Press, 2015.

Thomas, Kenn. *NASA, Nazis & JFK: The Torbitt Document & the Kennedy Assassination.* Adventures Unlimited Press, 1996.

Thomas, Ralph D. *Missing Links in the JFK Assassination Conspiracy.* Austin, TX: Thomas Investigative Publications, 1992.

Thomas, Ralph D. *Photo Computer Image Processing and the Crime of the Century.* Austin TX: Thomas Investigative Publications, 1992.

Thomas, Ralph. *Wall Of Secrecy - Inside The JFK Assassination: - How James Angleton & William Harvey Set Up An Assassination Team Inside The CIA.* Amazon, 2018.

Thomas, Ralph. *Project Northwoods, Operation Mockingbird And The Assassination Of JFK – MLK And RFK: An Investigative Report.* Amazon, 2018.

Thomas, Ralph. *Silenced! Strange Deaths Of People Who Knew Too Much About The JFK Assassination: 92 Witnesses, Researchers, CIA Agents, Police Officers, Reporters, Girlfriends Who Just Knew Way Too Much!* Amazon, 2017.

Thomas, Ralph. *2018 Missing Links - Thomas Beckham, Anti-Castro Cubans, The Cia And The JFK Assassination: - A Package Delivery To Dallas Texas And How The Operation Was Set Up And Covered Up.* Amazon, 2018.

Thomas, Ralph. *JFK Assassination and the David Ferrie Files: - An Investigative Report With New And Related 2017/2018 JFK Document* Releases. Amazon, 2018.

Thomas, Ralph. *Confessions, Admissions And Prime Suspects In The JFK Assassination: An Investigative Report- Now Containing A New Prime Suspect Uncovered From the 2018 JFK Document Releases!* Amazon, 2017.

Thomas, Ralph. *JFK Assassination : The James B. Wilcott Files And The CIA Oswald Project: An Investigative Report.* Amazon, 2017.

Thomas, Ralph. *Deep State Hit List- Strange Deaths Of People Who Knew Too Much: JFK-MLK - RFK Assassinations And The Clinton Scandals.* Amazon, 2018.

Thomas, Ralph. *JFK Assassination Research, Records And Resources: An Online Goldmine Of Researcher's Information.* Amazon, 2018.

Thomas, Ralph. *JFK Files - The Roscoe White Story: -Grassy Knoll Assassin Or Hoax?* Amazon, 2018.

Thomas, Ralph. *JFK- MLK- RFK Conspiracy Assassinations Investigative Summary: The Summary Investigative Evidence Lists That Point To Conspiracy.* Amazon, 2018.

Thomas, Ralph. *Smoke And Mirrors - The JFK Autopsy: An Investigative Report.* Amazon, 2017.

Thomas, Ralph. *Lee Harvey Oswald -Portrait Of A Patsy And US Intelligence Agent: A/K/A: Leon Oswald, Lee Henry Oswald, O.H. Lee, Leon Henry, Alex Hidell, Harvey Lee.* Amazon, 2017.

Thomas, Ralph. *Covert Affairs! JFK And The Death Of Two Ladies: Marilyn Monroe Mary Pinchot Meyer And Smoking Guns!* Amazon, 2017.

Thomas, Ralph. *Smoking Guns In The New JFK Assassination Files - Volumes I And Ii: Updated! There Are Over 306 Major Smoking Guns In The JFK Assassination Files That Prove Conspiracy.* Amazon, 2017.

Thomas, Ralph. *Nixon Espionage And The JFK Assassination - The Missing Watergate Links: An Investigative Report.* Amazon, 2017.

Thomas, Ralph. *Altered! The Zapruder Film: An Investigative Report.* Amazon, 2017.

Thomas, Ralph. *JFK Beyond A Question Of Conspiracy: An Investigation And Revision Of History - Including New 2018 Material!* Amazon, 2018.

Thomas, Ralph. *Missing Links In The JFK Assassination 2018: Interpen, The CIA And Prime Suspects.* Amazon, 2018.

Thomas, Ralph. *Miami, Chicago, Tampa And Dallas Four Plots Of Conspiracy To Assassinate JFK: An Investigative Report From JFK Beyond A Question Of Conspiracy.* Amazon, 2018.

Thomas, Ralph. *JFK Conspiracy - Ruby, Oswald And A Grand Illusion -The Magic Trick Of The Century: Also Starring Phil, Roscoe And Patrick.* Amazon, 2018.

Thomas, Ralph. *General Edwin Walker, The Meetings In LA And The JFK Assassination: -An Investigative Report.* Amazon, 2018.

Thomas, Ralph. *The Defense Investigation Of Lee Harvey Oswald : - And The School Book Depository Building - An Investigative Report.* Amazon, 2018.

Thomas, Ralph. *JFK Assassination Witnesses: -Accounts And Locations Of Shots Fired An Investigative Report.* Amazon, 2017.

Thomas, Ralph. *Smoking Guns In The New JFK Files That Indicate A Conspiracy - Volume 1: -Smoking Gun #1 to #151.* Amazon, 2018.

Thomas, Ralph. *Smoking Guns In The New JFK Files That Prove A Conspiracy- Volume II: -#152 To #306 (Includes Information From The New 2018 JFK File Releases.* Amazon, 2018.

Thomas, Ralph. *Indisputable Facts Of The JFK Assassination Conspiracy: An Investigative Report.* Amazon, 2018.

Thomas, Ralph. *Renegade Elements Of Conspiracy In The JFK Assassination: Evidence Of Renegade Elements In The CIA And Anti-Castro Cubans.* Amazon, 2018.

Thomas, Ralph. *The Moment Of The JFK Assassination Conspiracy: An Investigative Report.* Amazon, 2018.

Thomas, Ralph. *Assassination Conspiracy- Three In Five Years - JFK - MLK And RFK: An Investigative Report.* Amazon, 2017.

Thomas, Ralph. *Deception Of The JFK Assassination In High Places: How The Federal Government Was Able To Put Out The OSWALD Cover Story.* Amazon, 2017.

Thomas, Ralph. *Foreknowledge! And Other Aborted Plots In The JFK Assassination: 30 People With Foreknowledge And 3 Other Aborted Plots To Assassinate JFK.* Amazon, 2017.

Thompson, Josiah. *Last Second in Dallas.* University Press of Kansas, 2020.

Thompson, Josiah. *Six Seconds in Dallas.* New York: Bernard Geis, 1967.

Thompson, Robert E. *The Trial of Lee Harvey Oswald.* New York: Ace Books, 1977.

Thompson, W.C. *Bibliography to Assassination of President John Kennedy*. W.C. Thompson, 1968.

Thomson, George C. *The Quest For Truth: Or How Kennedy Was Really Assassinated*. Glendale, California: G.C. Thomson Engineering Co., 1964.

Thor, Valiant. *Valiant Thor's JFK Assassination Reader: Featuring the Torbitt Document*. New Saucerian Press, 2019.

Thornbro, William. *An Uncertain Justice: Examination of the Eyewitness and Photographic Evidence in the Assassination of John F. Kennedy*. Xlibris, 2009.

Thornley, Kerry. *Oswald. Chicago*: New Classics House, 1965.

Thornley, Kerry. *The Idle Warriors*. Avondale Estates, GA: IllumiNet Press, 1991.

Time-Life Books, The Editors of. *Assassination: True Crime*. Richmond, VA: Time-Life Books, 1994.

Tipton, Denton J. *The X-Files: JFK Disclosure*. IDW Publishing, 2018.

Titovets, Ernst. *Oswald: Russian Episode*. Minsk: Mon Litera, 2010.

Torbitt, William. *Nomenclature of an Assassination Cabal*. Prevailing Winds Research, 1970.

Torbitt II, William. *Mistaken Identity: What the Warren Commission Did Not Want You to Know*. Infinity Publishing, 2016.

Torrance, Harold. *The JFK Assassination: Eye on History*. Instructional Fair, 2002.

Tougas, Joseph Jesse. *President Kennedy's Killer and the America He Left Behind: The Assassin, the Crime, and the End of a Hopeful Vision in Chaotic Times*. Compass Point Books, 2018.

Towner, Tina. *Tina Towner: My Story as the Youngest Photographer at the Kennedy Assassination*. Self-published, 2012.

Trask, Richard. *National Nightmare on Six feet of Film: Mr. Zapruder's Home Movie and the Murder of President Kennedy*. Danvers, MA: Yeoman Press, 2005.

Trask, Richard. *Photographic Memory: the Kennedy Assassination, 22 November 1963*. Dallas, TX: 6th Floor Museum, 1996.

Trask, Richard. *Pictures of the Pain*. Danvers, MA: Yeoman Press, 1994.

Trask, Richard. *That Day in Dallas*. Danvers, MA: Yeoman Press, 1998.

Treasury, U.S. *Report of the US. Secret Service on the Assassination of President Kennedy*. Amazon, 2015.

Tripathi, Shubham. *The Guns of November: A Research of the Firearms and the Ballistics of the JFK Assassination*. Independently published, 2020.

Truels, William. *Breach of Faith*. Oklahoma City, OK: Concorde Publishing Company, 1996.

Truels, William. *The Quatrains of Camelot: An Epic Narrative Poem of the JFK Assassination, with Additional Poems on RFK, FDR, the Kingfish, and Marilyn Monroe*. Concorde Publishing, 2007.

Tucker, Brian Lee. *Same Old Conspiracy Theory*. Amazon, 2017.

Twyman, Noel. *Bloody Treason*. Rancho Santa Fe, CA: Laurel Publishing, 1997.

Twyman, Noel. *Illusion and Denial in the John F. Kennedy Assassination.* Laurel Mystery Books, 2010.

Underwood, H.R. *Rendezvous with Death.* Trafford, 2013.

Unger, Irwin. *LBJ: A Life.* John Wiley & Sons, 1999.

United States Congress. *The Effectiveness of Public Law 102-526, the President John F. Kennedy Assassination Records Collection Act of 1992.* Palala Press, 2015.

UPI & American Heritage. *Four Days.* 1964.

U.S. Congress, House of Representatives. *Report of the Select Committee on Assassinations (and 12 volumes of Hearings and Exhibits- aka the HSCA).* Washington, D.C. U.S. Government Printing Office, 1979.

U.S. Government Printing Office. *The Investigation of the Assassination of President John F. Kennedy: Performance of the Intelligence Agencies.* CreateSpace, 2015.

Vaccara, Stefano. *Carlos Marcello: The Man Behind the JFK Assassination.* Enigma Books, 2003.

Vagnes, Oyvind. *Zaprudered: The Kennedy Assassination Film in Visual Culture.* University of Texas Press, 2011.

Valenti, Mark. *Lee Harvey Oswald: In His Own Words.* CreateSpace, 2014.

Van Buren, Abigail. *Where Were You When President Kennedy Was Shot?* Kansas City, MO: Andrews and McMeel, 1993.

Vance, John. *Echoes of November.* Moonshine Cove Publishing, LLC, 2016.

Van Gelder, Lawrence. *The Untold Story: Why the Kennedys Lost the Book Battles.* Award Books, 1967.

Vankin, Jonathan. *Conspiracies, Cover-Ups, and Crimes: Political Manipulation and Mind Control in America.* New York: Paragon House, 1991.

Vaughan, Todd Wayne. *Presidential Motorcade Schematic Listing.* Jackson, MI: self-published, 1993.

Veciana, Antonio. *Trained to Kill: The Inside Story of CIA Plots against Castro, Kennedy, and Che.* Skyhorse, 2017.

Ventura, Jesse with Dick Russell. *63 Documents the Government Doesn't Want You to Read.* Skyhorse, 2011.

Ventura, Jesse with Dick Russell. *American Conspiracies.* Skyhorse, 2015.

Ventura, Jesse with Dick Russell and David Wayne. *They Killed Our President: 63 Reasons to Believe There Was A Conspiracy to Assassinate JFK.* Skyhorse, 2012.

Vergith, Theodore S. *The Murderous Illusion.* Xlibris, 2000.

Vincent, E. Duke. *The Camelot Conspiracy: A Novel of the Kennedys, Castro and the CIA.* The Overlook Press, 2011.

Wagner, Robert A. *The Assassination of JFK: Perspectives Half A Century Later.* Dog Ear Publishing, 2016.

Waldron, Lamar with Thom Hartmann. *Legacy of Secrecy.* Counterpoint, 2008.

Waldron, Lamar. *The Hidden History of the JFK Assassination*. Counterpoint, 2013.

Waldron, Lamar with Thom Hartmann. *Ultimate Sacrifice*. New York: Carroll & Graf, 2005.

Waldron, Lamar. *Watergate: The Hidden History*. Counterpoint, 2013.

Warner, Dale G. *Who Killed the President?* The American Press, 1964.

Watts, Steven. *JFK and the Masculine Mystique: Sex and Power on the New Frontier*. Thomas Dunne Books, 2016.

Webb, Lucas and Robert Reginald. *The Attempted Assassination of John F. Kennedy: A Political Fantasy*. Borgo Press, 2007.

Weberman, Alan J. and Michael Canfield. *Coup d Etat in America: The CIA and the Assassination of John F. Kennedy*. San Francisco, CA: Quick American Archives, 1992.

Weberman, Alan, J. *The Oswald Code*. Independent Research Associates, 2014.

Webster, Sheldon Burton. *House of Deception: The CIA's Secret Opium War & Assassination of JFK*. Authorhouse, 2006.

Wecht, *Cyril H. Cause of Death*. New York: Penguin, 1994.

Wecht, Cyril. *Tales from the Morgue: Forensic Answers to Nine Famous Cases Including The Scott Peterson & Chandra Levy Cases*. Prometheus Books, 2005.

Weeber, Stanley C. *Lee Harvey Oswald: A Socio-Behavioral Reconstruction of His Career*. Edwin Mellen Pr, 2003.

Weisberg, Harold. *Case Open: The Unanswered JFK Assassination Questions*. Carroll and Graf, 1994.

Weisberg, Harold. *Hoax*. Unpublished manuscript available at the Harold Weisberg Archives online, 1994.

Weisberg, Harold. *Inside The Assassination Industry. Unpublished manuscript available at the Harold Weisberg Archives online, 1998/2004.*

Weisberg, Harold. *Never Again*. Carroll and Graf, 1995.

Weisberg, Harold. *Oswald in New Orleans: A Case for Conspiracy with the CIA*. Skyhorse, 2013.

Weisberg, Harold. *Post Mortem. MD*: self-published 1975; Skyhorse, 2013.

Weisberg, Harold. *Whitewash: The Report on the Warren Report*. Skyhorse, 2013.

Weisberg, Harold. *Whitewash II: The FBI-Secret Service Cover-Up*. Skyhorse, 2013.

Weisberg, Harold. *Whitewash III: The Photographic Whitewash of the JFK Assassination*. Skyhorse, 2013.

Weisberg, Harold. *Whitewash IV: The Top Secret Warren Commission Transcript of the JFK Assassination*. Skyhorse, 2013.

Welford, Nancy Wertz. *The Faux Baron: George de Mohrenschildt: An Aristocrat's Journey from the Russian Revolution to the Assassination of John F. Kennedy*. CreateSpace, 2014.

Wells, William. *Dealey Plaza: The End of Camelot*. CreateSpace, 2014.

Welsh, David and Penn Jones. *In the Shadow of Dallas: A Primer on the Assassination of President Kennedy*. Ramparts, 1967.

Whalen, Thomas J. *JFK and His Enemies*. Rowman & Littlefield Publishers, 2014.

White, Stephen. *Should We Now Believe the Warren Report?* New York: Macmillan, 1968.

Widing, Roy. *11-22-63: New Evidence*. Quality House, 2011.

Wikipedia. *Witnesses To The John F. Kennedy Assassination: Lee Harvey Oswald, Jacqueline Kennedy Onassis, Jack Valenti, Abraham Zapruder, John Connally*. Books LLC, 2011.

Wilber, Charles. *Medicolegal Investigation of the President John F. Kennedy Murder*. Springfield, Illinois: Charles C. Thomas Publisher, 1978.

Wilcox, Robert K. *Target JFK: The Spy Who Killed Kennedy?* Regnery History, 2016.

Wilds, Bernard and Ralph Cinque. *Oswald is Innocent: The Proof, The Whole Proof And Nothing But The Proof!* Amazon, 2019.

Wilkens, Tommy and Hilde. *Walking The Razor's Edge: The Dutchman and The Baron*. Amazon, 2019.

Wilkie, Don. *American Secret Service Agent*. Frederick A. Stokes Co., 1934.

Willens, Howard. *History Will Prove Us Right : Inside the Warren Commission Investigation into the Assassination of John F. Kennedy*. Harry N. Abrams, 2013.

Williams, Joe. *The Grassy Knoll Report*. Amazon, 2013.

Williams, John Delane. *Lee Harvey Oswald, Lyndon Johnson & the JFK Assassination*. Trine Day, 2019.

Williams, Robert. *Conspiracy and Cover-Up? The Kennedy Assassination and 9/11*. Amazon, 2012.

Willis, Garry and Ovid Demaris. *Jack Ruby: The Man Who Killed the Man Who Killed Kennedy*. New York: New American Library, 1968; De Capo Press, 1994.

Wilson, Frank J. and Beth Day. *Special Agent*. New York: Holt, Rinehart and Winston, 1965.

Wilson, Kirk. *Unsolved Crimes: The Top Ten Unsolved Murders of the 20th Century*. New York: Carroll & Graf, 2002.

Wilson, Robert Clifton. *GUILTY until proven INNOCENT: A novel about Lee Harvey and Marguerite Oswald*. CreateSpace, 2013.

Winks, Robin W. *Cloak and Gown*. Vintage/ Ebury, 1987.

Winters, Willis. *Dealey Plaza*. Arcadia Publishing, 2013.

Wise, Dan with Marietta Maxfield. *The Day Kennedy Died*. San Antonio: Naylor, 1964.

Wise, David and Thomas B. Ross. *The Invisible Government*. New York: Bantam Books, Inc., 1964.

Wolf, Marvin J. and Larry Mintz. *Saving Camelot*. Rambam Press, 2013.

Wood III, Ira David. *JFK Assassination Chronology*. Amazon, 2011.

Woodhouse, Horace Martin. *Anatomy of an Assassination: 101 Things You Didn't Know About the Killing of John F. Kennedy.* CreateSpace, 2013.

Woodson, Hue. *One Brief Shining Moment: A Novel of the JFK Assassination.* Independently published, 2017.

Woolley, Brian. *November 22.* Seaview Books, 1981.

Wrone, David R. *The Assassination of John Fitzgerald Kennedy An Annotated Bibliography.* State Historical Society, 1972.

Wrone, David R. *The Zapruder Film: Reframing JFK's Assassination.* Lawrence: University Press of Kansas, 2003.

Yardum, Harry. *The Grassy Knoll Witnesses: Who Shot JFK?* Authorhouse, 2009.

Yeagle, Gary. *Dreamer's Gospel: The Truth is Seldom Certain.* Independently published, 2019.

Young, Bryan. *A Children's Illustrated History of Presidential Assassination.* Silence in the Library, 2014.

Youngblood, Rufus. *20 Years in the Secret Service.* New York: Simon & Schuster, 1973; updated 2018.

Zabel, Bryce. *Surrounded by Enemies: A Breakpoint Novel.* Diversion Books, 2015.

Zachry, K.W. and Sara Peterson. *The Lone Star Speaks: Untold Texas Stories About the JFK Assassination.* Bancroft Press, 2020.

Zappone, Tony. *John F. Kennedy: An Amazing Day for a President and a Kid with His Camera.* Self-published, 2013.

Zapruder, Alexandra. *Twenty-Six Seconds: A Personal History of the Zapruder Film.* Twelve, 2016.

Zazzi, Richard Joseph. *Killer on the Grassy Knoll.* Amazon, 2014.

Zelizer, Barbie. *Covering the Body: The Kennedy Assassination, the Media, and the Shaping of Collective Memory.* Chicago: Chicago University Press, 1992.

Zimmerle, C.T. *Grassy Knoll.* CreateSpace, 2010.

Zirbel, Craig. *The Texas Connection: The Assassination of President John F. Kennedy.* Scottsdale, AZ: Texas Connection, 1991.

Zirbel, Craig. *JFK LBJ: The Final Chapter on the Assassination of John F. Kennedy.* The Final Chapter LLC, 2010.

Note: upcoming releases by witness Buell Wesley Frazier, Secret Service agent Paul Landis, renowned author David Lifton, and researcher extraordinaire Matt Douthit demonstrate that interest in this case continues and always will.

APPENDIX

CLINT HILL AND GERALD BLAINE DISCUSS MY WORK ON TELEVISION – (TWICE)

11/10/10 C-SPAN: Gerald Blaine, Clint Hill and Vince Palamara:

BRIAN LAMB, CEO of C-SPAN: Now, we got some video from YouTube – one of the things you say in your book that made you want to write this book was all the conspiracy theories and you talked about the movie from Oliver Stone. This is a man named Vince Palamara. Do you know him?

BLAINE: I am familiar with him, I don't know him.

LAMB: He says that – and I guess we'll talk about this, that he sent you a 22-page letter?

HILL: I recall receiving a letter which I sent back to him. I didn't bother with it.

LAMB: You didn't talk to him ever?

HILL: He called me and I said "Hello" but that was about it.

LAMB: And over the years, have you both been called about this assassination on many occasions.

HILL: I had been called numerous times.

LAMB: What has been your attitude, how have you approached the people…

HILL: For the most part, I just said I have no comment, I just have nothing to say.

LAMB: And why is that?

HILL: Well, most of it is from people who are writing conspiracy theory books that don't make any sense to me so if they are not going to deal in facts, then I don't want anything to do with it.

LAMB: And how about you?

BLAINE: I have never talked to any author of a book and that – I just felt we had it on our commission books: "worthy of trust of confidence" – and I felt those were issues that you should never talk to anybody on the outside about. And it was – I had to weigh and evaluate when I wrote this book because I felt I wasn't talking about the Secret Service, I wasn't talking about the Kennedy Family, but I was talking about the agents that I work with and the incidents that occurred and those were my friends. So that's when I decided to write.

LAMB: Did you have to get permission to do this from the secret service?

HILL: No.

LAMB: So this wasn't cleared by the Secret Service?

HILL: No.

BLAINE: No, but we had lunch today with the director of the Secret Service who thanked us very much for our contribution.

LAMB: Here is this video, it's not very long and this man's name is Vince Pala-mara, he is a citizen who has taken it on his own to become an expert. He is from Pennsylvania and I don't know him, I haven't talked to him and I have just seen it on the web and he is – I believe he is a graduate of Duquesne University so let us watch this and I'll get your reaction.

BLAINE: Ok. [START OF VIDEO].

VINCE PALAMARA: Hi, this is Vince Palamara, the self-described Secret Service expert that Jerry Blaine accuses me of without naming me, Ok? Back with my obsession about The Kennedy Detail. I have to read this, this is rich. Page 287 [of Blaine's book] is where Blaine is claiming what Rowley said. [Quoting from the book] "Rowley turned to Jerry Blaine. "And Jerry, since you were in the lead car, did you ever hear this over your radio as well?" "Yes, sir. I did. I heard exactly what Floyd just told you." The thing about this-this is the whole 'Ivy League charlatans' crap. Jerry Blaine told me that the 'Ivy League charlatans' thing "came from the guys. I can't remember – I can't remember who said it." (Said sarcastically) Boy, his memory got real good five years later because now, he is claiming he heard it over the radio from Floyd Boring. It's unbelievable, and it's just amazing to me – you know, there never would have been a book if I didn't send a 22 page letter to Clint Hill that pissed him off so much that his very good friend, Jerry Blaine, came out with his book as a counter. Ok? These are some good things in it. I recommend everyone to buy it, no censorship, it's my First Amendment rights, Ok? There are some nice pictures and there are even some good assassination related things in here, but it's very odd. Other people have picked up on this, that's why there are some really bad reviews on Amazon right now, mine is the best at three stars, too. It's very obvious that it's a thinly veiled attempt to rewrite history and blame President Kennedy – without trying to blame him – for his own assassination. [END OF VIDEO].

LAMB: First of all, his is not the best of the reviews, there are seven with five stars just for the record that I saw today when I looked on Amazon. What's your reaction, could you hear?

BLAINE: Well, he wrote an assessment of the book about the – first time about five weeks before it was released. The second time on Amazon.com, he and four of his friends or four of his aliases put a statement on assessing the book a one, a two, and a three (stars). My assessment of Mr. Palamara is that he called probably all of the agents, and what agent who answers a phone is going to answer a question "was President Kennedy easy to protect?" Well, probably he was too easy to protect because he was assassinated. But the fact is that the agents aren't going to tell him anything and he alludes to the fact that when I wrote the book, most of these people were dead. Well, I worked with these people, I knew them like brothers and I knew exactly what was going on and always respected Jim Rowley because he stood up to the issue and said "Look, we can't say the President invited himself to be killed so let's squash this." So that was the word throughout the Secret Service and he – Mr. Palamara is – there are a number of things that have happened (sic) that he has no credibility. He is a self-described expert in his area which I don't know what it is, he was born after the assassination and he keeps creating solutions to the assassination until they are proven wrong. So he is… (Cutting Blaine off)

LAMB: A lot about –

HILL: But he alleges that because he sent me a letter 22 pages in length apparently, and that I discussed that with Jerry. I forgot that I ever got a 22-page letter from this particular individual until I heard him say it on TV and I never discussed it with Jerry or anybody else because it wasn't important to me. And so far as him being an expert, I don't know where the expert part came from. I spent a long time in the Secret Service in protection and I'm not an expert, but apparently he became an expert somewhere up in Pennsylvania, I don't know where."

But Blaine wasn't finished with me just yet: "The Zapruder film, when the Zapruder film was run at normal speed, another theme that Palamara throws out is that Bill Greer stopped the car, when it's run at its normal speed, you will notice the car absolutely does not stop at all. This happened in less than six seconds after the President was hit in the throat and moving along."

Oh, so you agree with my "solutions" that JFK was shot in the neck from the front, do you, Mr. Blaine? And there were close to 60 witnesses to the limousine slowing or stopping, including 7 Secret Service agents and Jacqueline Kennedy – not my "theme" or theory, just the facts. In a bizarre postscript, Blaine participated in a video interview around the same time in which he states: "We were violating our fellow agents who have passed on."[1] I wholeheartedly agree.

5/27/12 C-SPAN: CLINT HILL ADDRESSES VINCE PALAMARA:

HILL: Well my wife and I are not together and haven't been for some time.

LAMB: She's still alive?

HILL: Yes.

LAMB: Did you – did you keep notes?

HILL:: I did, but I destroyed them a few years ago which really made it more difficult.

LAMB: Why did you destroy them?

HILL: I promised that I would never write a book. I vowed that I would never do so, never contribute to a book, never talk to anybody about it and so just to kind of make sure I would never get myself involved, I burned everything. There are a few mementos I kept, but for the most part, I burned all my notes. And now, when the opportunity presents itself and I decided to do it, I had to go back and talk to other agents who I worked with, who did have – still have some notes. And to check everything through newspaper archives for dates and times and places to make sure I was accurate and so it was very tedious to go through this and write the book.

LAMB: Do you remember the year you burned your notes? HILL: It is 2012 [now] – it was [long pause] maybe 2005, something like that [Note: 2005 was the year I contacted Hill for the first time with my 22-page letter referenced above, so, needless to say, I find the specific timing of his note burning suspicious, to put it mildly].

LAMB: As an aside by the way, the fellow we talked about in the last interview, Vince Palamara.

HILL: Yes.

LAMB: You've seen his letter about your book?

HILL: I have not read it, no.

LAMB: I'm sure you probably know that he said that "Mrs. Kennedy and Me" is highly recommended to everyone for its honesty and rich body of truth." He actually fully endorsed your book[2] even though he's been critical of (pause)... are you worried that he's not being ...? (Cutting Lamb off)

HILL: Maybe he has some secret agenda, I don't know. But I accept his praise, thank you."

Clint Hill, Gerald Blaine and Paul Landis with then-current Secret Service Director Joe Clancy (Obama/early Trump era) on different occasions.

---

2   Not a full endorsement, but I like much of it. It is much better than Blaine's propaganda, although I have issues with the assassination-related details.

Index